RECREATION
LAKES
of CALIFORNIA

BY: GREG DIRKSEN

Presented by The Dirksen Family
Jim, Diane, Greg, Trevor & Jake

Authors: Diane Dirksen & Jake Dirksen

Recreation Sales Publishing
P.O. Box 1028
Aptos, CA 95001
Ph: (800) 668-0076
email: reclakes@sbcglobal.net
Website: **www.rec-lakes.com**

ISBN 0-943798-21-3

14th Edition

This book is dedicated to the memory of
John D. McKinney
In his honor we have not published a 13th Edition

<u>*Integrity, Honor, Dedication & A Cherished Loved One...*</u>
<u>*...He is Missed*</u>

<u>*MAPS ARE NOT TO SCALE*</u>
AND SHOULD BE USED
IN CONJUNCTION WITH STANDARD ROAD MAPS.

INFORMATION IS PRESENTED AS IT APPEARS
WHEN LAKES ARE AT FULL CAPACITY.
WEATHER CONDITIONS MUST BE CONSIDERED.
ALL FEES AND INFORMATION ARE SUBJECT TO CHANGE.

INTRODUCTION

Each Lake is described according to location, elevation, size and facilities. The book is divided into three sections which are marked by black bleedoffs at the bottom of the page; the left is the North Section, the middle is Central and the right is the South Section of California. Campgrounds for tents and R.V.s, picnic areas, launch ramps, marinas and other facilities are located on each map. Also hiking, bicycle and equestrian trails are shown. While boating, fishing and camping are basic to most Lakes, we have also included swimming, hiking, backpacking and equestrian information. Waterslides, boat tours, golf courses, airports and other specific attractions are mentioned. The maps show major recreation areas near each Lake, such as State and National Parks, Wilderness Areas and the Pacific Crest Trail.

Information is as accurate and current as possible at the time of publication although area codes and fees are constantly changing. *RECREATION LAKES OF CALIFORNIA* will help you enjoy the many outdoor activities, spectacular scenery and unique environments this wonderful State has to offer.

The support of the US Forest Service, the Bureau of Land Management, Army Corps of Engineers, the California State Park System, the Department of Fish and Game is invaluable. Chambers of Commerce, Visitor's Bureaus and the many private owners and managers of facilities are equally supportive. We give our special appreciation to you, the reader. Your use of *RECREATION LAKES of CALIFORNIA* has made it a bestseller.

Thank you!

BY: GREG DIRKSEN. ©

TABLE OF CONTENTS

Lakes correspond to page numbers, divided into three sections: *North, Central* and *South*—areas of California. Each section begins with a Map illustrating that region, with an approximate location of each Lake in that area, referenced by a page number. Several maps include supplementary pages with information on campgrounds, resorts, marine facilities and other recreational opportunities. *See **Index** at back of book for a complete alphabetical listing of Lakes.*

North Section

Lakes . . . . .1 - 60

Central Section

Lakes . . . . .61 - 151

South Section

Lakes . . . . .152 - 199

Back of Book

Camping Gear Checklist . . . . A

Untreated Water - Giardiasis Disease and Pet Information . . . . B

Boating, Swimming and Waterskiing Hand Signals C

Wilderness Areas and Pacific Crest Trail Map . . . . D

National Forests and State Park Maps . . . . E

Federal Recreation Passport Program and
Campground Reservations . . . . F

California State Park System
and Department of Fish and Game Offices . . . . G

U.S. Forest Service Ranger Stations and Wilderness Permits . . . . H - L

Alphabetical Index of Lakes . . . . M - P

Numbers around highways represent lakes in numerical order in this book. *See Index for complete listing.*

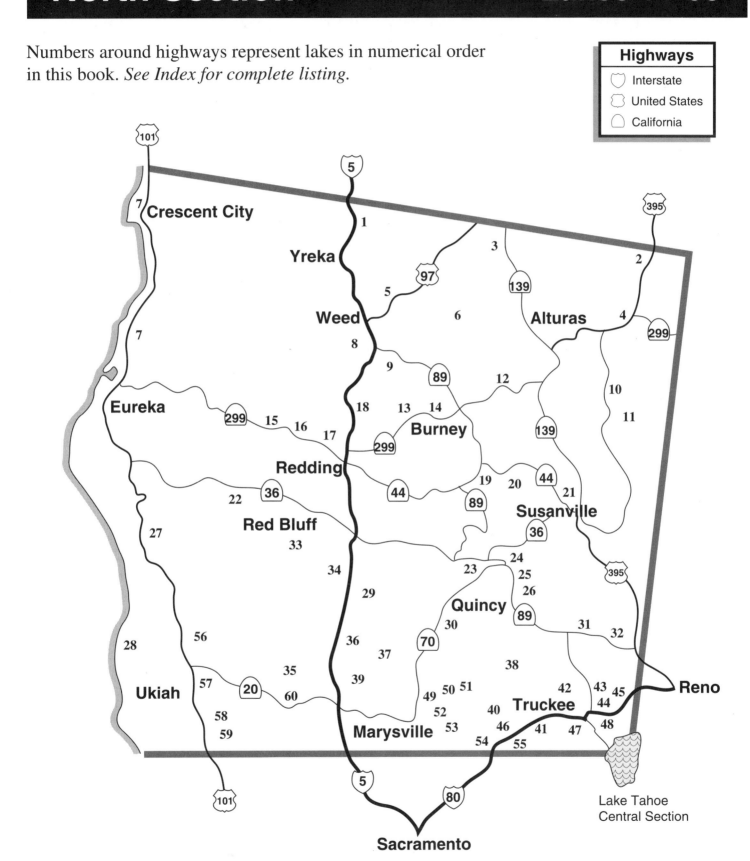

Lake Tahoe
Central Section

IRON GATE RESERVOIR and COPCO LAKE

Iron Gate Reservoir and Copco Lake are located east of Interstate 5 near the Oregon border. Iron Gate, elevation 2,343 feet, is almost 7 miles long and covers a surface area of 825 acres. Copco Lake, elevation 2,613 feet, has a surface area of 1,000 acres and is 5 miles long. The Wild Upper Klamath River above Copco Lake has native rainbow trout. Six fishing access areas with parking are available. From May through October, this is a popular part of the River for experienced whitewater rafters. You can put in at John Boyle Dam, go 17 miles and take out at Copco Lake. River guides are available from September through March. Campgrounds are available at both Lakes and managed jointly by Pacific Power and the Bureau of Land Management. There is an abundant yellow perch fishery as well as rainbow trout and largemouth bass. The Klamath River provides a good salmon and steelhead crop.

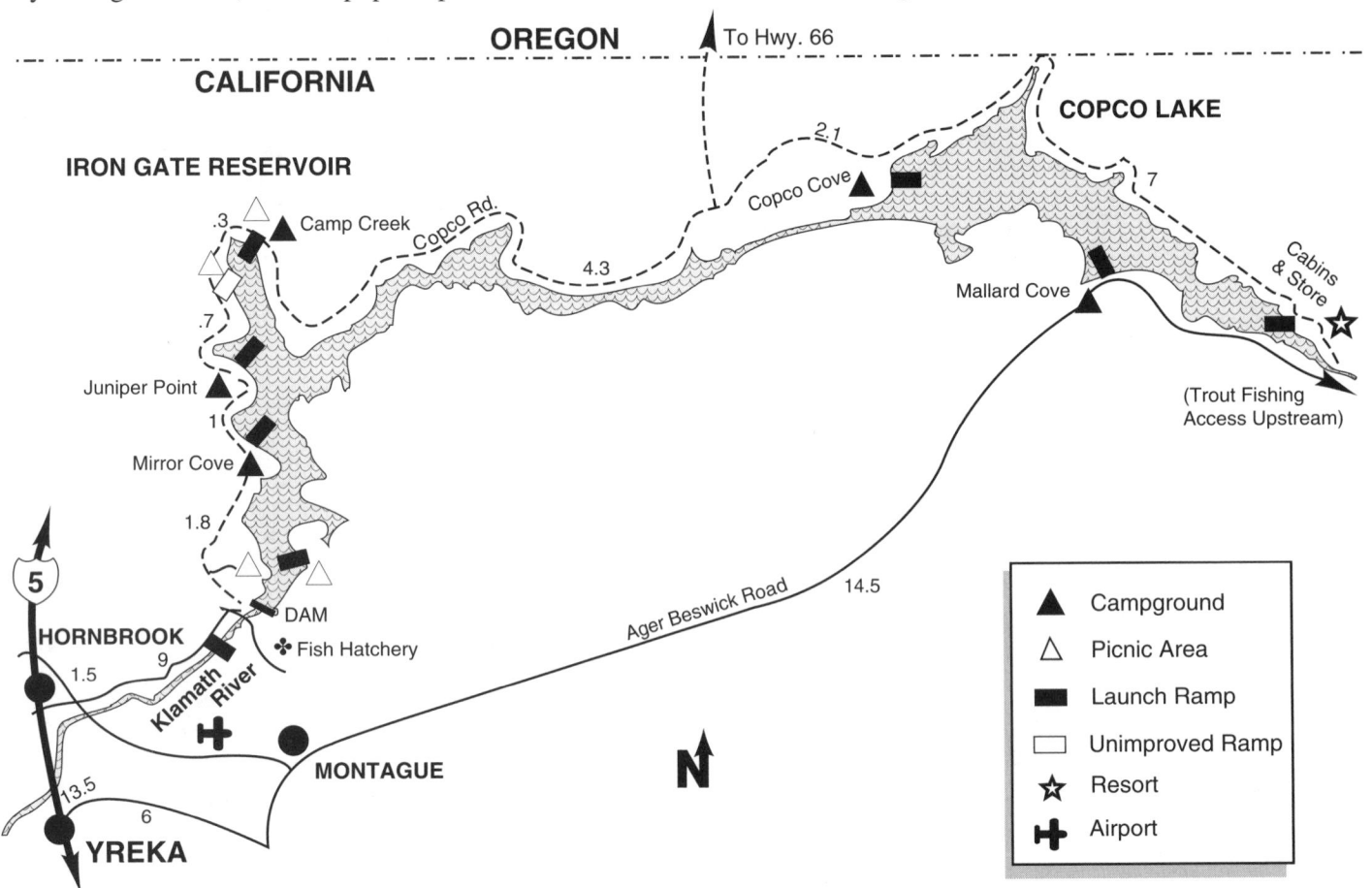

CAMPING	BOATING	RECREATION	OTHER

Iron Gate Reservoir:
  Camp Creek - 21 Sites
    for R.V.s Plus Large
    Overflow Area
  Juniper Point - 9 Sites,
    No Water
  Mirror Cove - 11 Sites,
    No Water
 	
Copco Lake:
  Free Campsites at
    Copco Cove &
    Mallard Cove
	Power, Row, Canoe, Sail
	  & Inflatable
	10 MPH Speed Limit in
	  Designated Areas
	Copco Lake - Upper 1/3
	  Set Aside for Fishing
	  (No Wake)
	Launch Ramps
	Rentals: Fishing Boats
	  with Motors - Copco
	  Lake Store Only
	Docks
		Fishing:
		  Trout, Catfish, Crappie,
		  Largemouth Bass,
		  Yellow Perch, Salmon
		  & Steelhead-Klamath
		  River
		Swimming
		Picnicking
		Hiking & Riding Trails
		Whitewater Rafting
		Hunting:
		  Deer, Quail, Dove,
		  Waterfowl, Wild Turkey
			Copco Lake Store
			  27734 Copco Rd.
			  Montague 96064
			  Ph: (530) 459-3655
			  Groceries, Bait & Tackle
			  Cabin Rentals
			    Ph: (530) 459-3051
			  Nearest Gas - 20 Miles
			
			Full Facilities at Hornbrook
			
			River Flow & Reservoir
			Levels: Ph: (800) 547-1501

INFORMATION: Pacific Power - Recreation Department—Ph: (503) 813-6666

GOOSE, CAVE and LILY LAKES and FEE RESERVOIR

Goose Lake rests on the California-Oregon border at an elevation of 4,800 feet. This shallow 108,800 surface acre Lake is used primarily for boating and wildlife viewing. Cave and Lily Lakes offer excellent fishing for brook and rainbow trout but boating is limited to small non-motorized boats, canoes and kayaks. These two small mountain Lakes are neighbors at 6,600 feet elevation in the Modoc National Forest. Poor access roads limit use of trailers. Fee Reservoir, at 4,000 feet, can produce large rainbow trout. This remote Reservoir is operated by the Bureau of Land Management. Any facilities are 30 miles away.

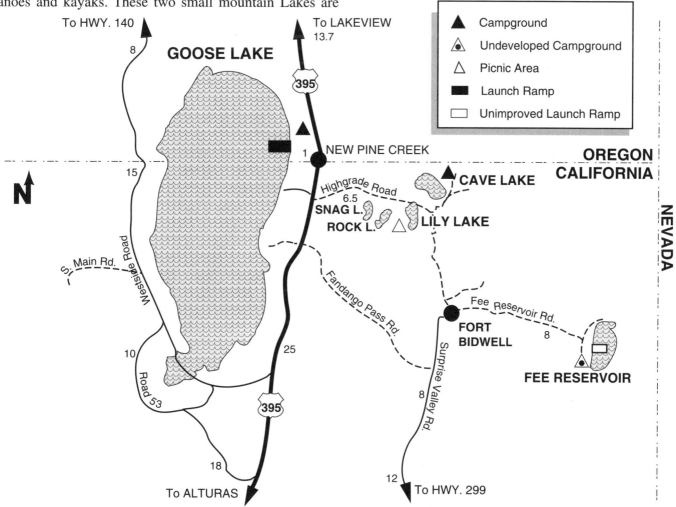

INFORMATION: Goose Lake State Recreation Area - Oregon State Parks—Ph: (541) 947-3111 or (800) 551-6949

CAMPING	BOATING	RECREATION	OTHER

Goose Lake - First Come:
  Oregon State Parks
  47 Tent/RV Sites to 50 ft.
  Electric Hookups: $12
  Disposal Station
  Plus Overflow Primitive
    Sites: $10
  Extra Vehicle: $5
Cave Lake:
  6 Tent/RV Sites - No Fee
Fee Reservoir:
  7 Undev. Tent/RV Sites
    to 24 ft. - No Water
	Goose Lake:
	  Open to all Boating
	  Paved Launch Ramp
	Lily & Cave Lakes:
	  No Motors
	  Hand Launch
	Fee Reservoir:
	  Unimproved Launch
	    Ramp
	  Shallow Draft Boats
	    Advised
		Fishing: Brook &
		  Rainbow Trout
		Picnicking - Lily Lake
		  6 Sites
		  Drinking Water
		Hiking & Riding Trails
		Backpacking
		Nature Study
		Swimming
		Hunting: Upland Game,
		  Waterfowl, Deer
		Birdwatching
			Warner Mountain
			  Ranger District
			  385 Wallace St.
			  Cedarville 96104
			  Ph: (530) 279-6116
			Bureau of Land Management
			  Surprise Field Office
			  602 Cressler St.
			  Cedarville 96104
			  Ph: (530) 279-6101
			
			Facilities Limited to Nearby
			  Towns

LOWER KLAMATH, TULE and CLEAR LAKES—KLAMATH BASIN NATIONAL WILDLIFE REFUGES

This is waterfowl country. These Lakes are within the Klamath Basin National Wildlife Refuges which has one of the greatest concentrations of migratory waterfowl in the world. Photography and wildlife observation are popular activities. Over 270 species of birds have been identified. The American bald eagle, golden eagle and peregrin falcon are among the birds that can be observed. Except for canoeing at Tulelake, boating is secondary to hunting. There is no fishing. This is a hunter's paradise. Since rules and boundaries are strictly enforced, it is essential you contact the Fish and Wildlife Service for information. Accommodations can be a problem, especially during hunting season. Plan ahead by contacting the facilities listed below or the *Chamber of Commerce, 800 Main St., Tulelake 96134, Ph: (530) 667-5312.*

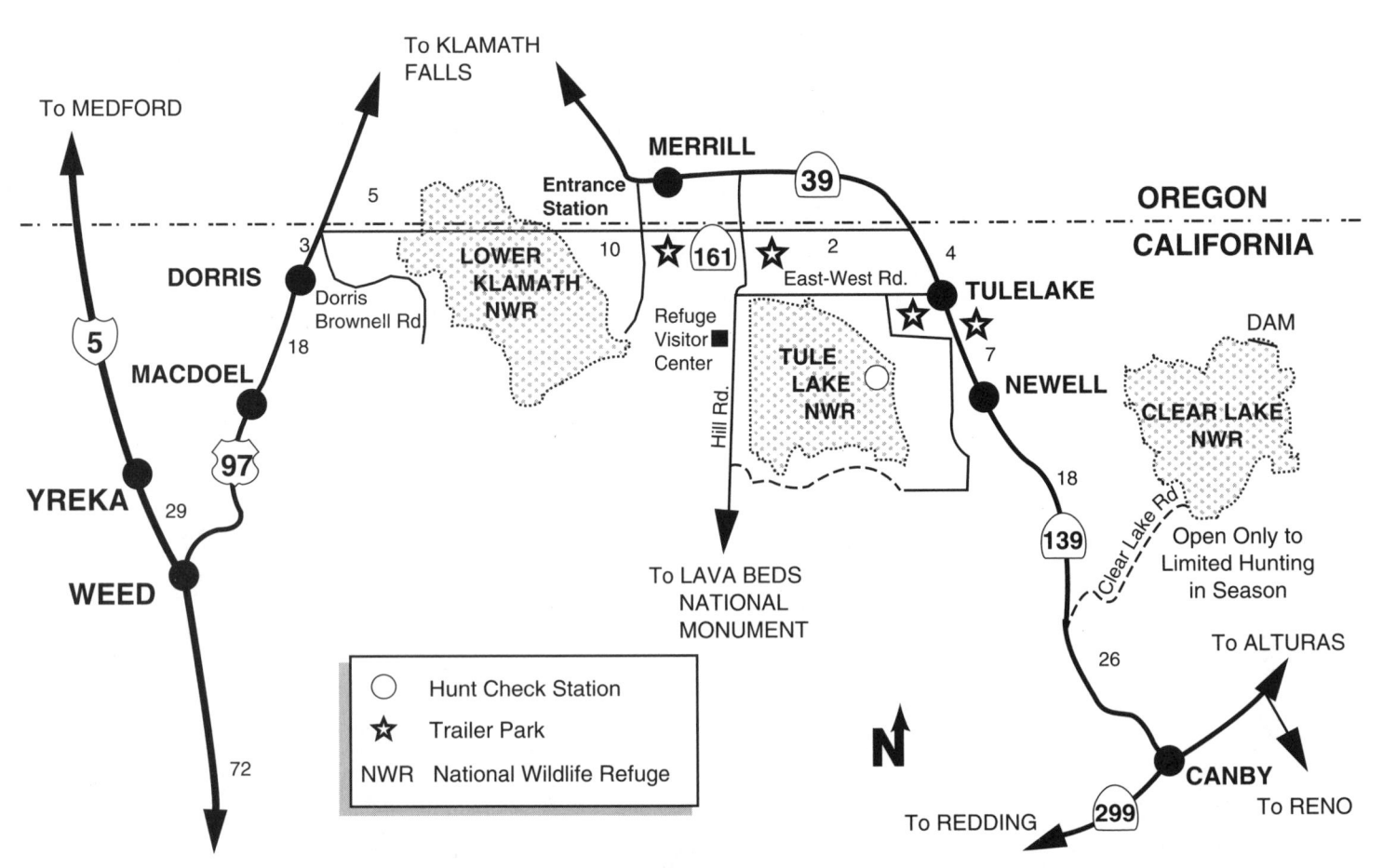

INFORMATION: Klamath Basin NWR, 4009 Hill Rd., Tulelake 96134—Ph: (530) 667-2231

CAMPING	BOATING	RECREATION	OTHER
Shady Lanes R.V. Park: 795 Modoc Ave. Tulelake 96134 Ph: (530) 667-2617 58 R.V. Sites Full Hookups	Boats are Allowed Only During Hunting Season Except for Canoe Area at Tulelake NWR - Open July through September Air Thrust & Water Thrust Boats are Prohibited	Hunting: Geese, Ducks, Coots, Snipe & Pheasants *Steel Shot is Required for Waterfowl Hunting* Birdwatching Nature Study Photography	Refuge Visitor Center: Open Monday-Friday 8:00 am - 4:30 pm Open Saturday & Sunday 10:00 am - 4:00 pm
Stateline R.V. Park: 30138 Lower Klamath Rd. Tulelake 96134 Ph: (530) 667-4849 60 Tent/R.V. Sites Full Hookups		Lower Klamath NWR: Marked Auto Tours for Wildlife Viewing Photoblinds	Lava Beds Nat. Monument: 40 Tent/R.V. Sites Fee: $10 First Come, First Served Plus 1 Group Site by Reservation Ph: (530) 667-2282

BIG SAGE, "C", "F", DUNCAN, GRAVEN, BAYLEY and DORRIS RESERVOIRS—DELTA LAKE

Although facilities are limited, there are recreational opportunities at these Lakes in the Modoc National Forest and Modoc County. Big Sage Reservoir rests at an elevation of 4,900 feet on a sage and juniper covered plateau. This 5,400 acre Reservoir is open to all boating and provides a warm water fishery. Nearby Reservoirs "C", and "F" and Duncan provide a good opportunity to catch the large Eagle Lake trout. Dorris Reservoir is in the Modoc National Wildlife Refuge. It is closed during waterfowl hunting season. The angler will find trout and a warm water fishery. Graven, Bayley and Delta are under the jurisdiction of Modoc County. They are shallow and muddy and primarily known for their good catfishing. Bayley also has excellent trout fishing. The roads into these Reservoirs are very rough.

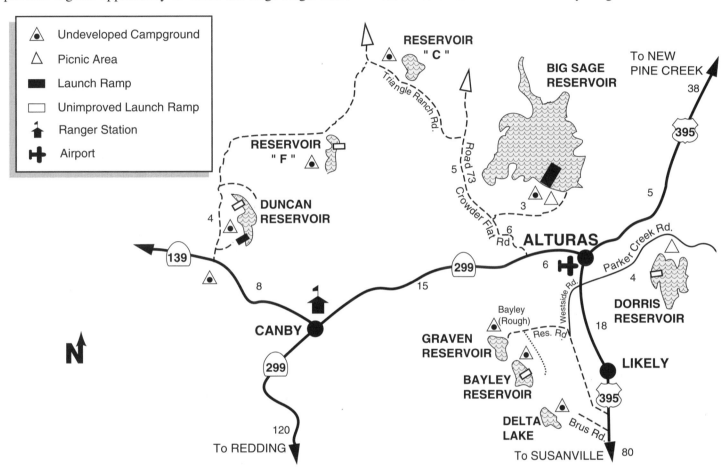

INFORMATION: Devil's Garden Ranger District, 800 West 12th St., Alturas 96101—Ph: (530) 233-5811

CAMPING	BOATING	RECREATION	OTHER

Undeveloped Campsites as Shown on Map
No Drinking Water
Limited Trailer Access
 	
Dorris Reservoir:
  Walk-In Public
    Access
  Mid-January to
    March 31 and
  Early October
  Before Waterfowl
    Season
	Big Sage: Open to All
	  Boating
	  Paved Launch Ramp
	Dorris:
	  Boating: Apr. 1-Sept. 30
	  Waterskiing: June 1 -
	    Sept. 30
	  Unimproved Ramp
	  Underwater Hazards
	
	Other Lakes Open to
	  Small Hand Launched
	  Boats
		Fishing: Trout, Bass,
		  Catfish & Panfish plus
		  Eagle Lake Trout at
		  Res. "C", Res."F" &
		  Duncan
		Hiking & Riding Trails
		Nature & Bird Study
		Hunting: Waterfowl,
		  Upland Game, Deer &
		  Antelope
		No Hunting at Dorris
			Dorris Reservoir:
			  Modoc National
			  Wildlife Refuge
			  P.O. Box 1610
			  Alturas 96101
			  Ph: (530) 233-3572
			
			Graven, Bayley & Delta:
			  Modoc County
			  202 W. 4th St.
			  Alturas 96101
			  Ph: (530) 233-3939

INDIAN TOM, MEISS, JUANITA, ORR and SHASTINA LAKES

These Lakes along Highway 97 from Weed to the Oregon Border provide a variety of recreational experiences. The alkaline waters in Indian Tom support a unique Cutthroat fishery. Meiss Lake is within the Butte Valley Wildlife Area. Waterfowl hunting and wildlife observation are the primary activities. Juanita is a mountain Lake resting at an elevation of 5,100 feet. There is a nice campground which provides

facilities for the physically disabled. The trout fishing is good. Orr is a USFS Lake open to the public for boating, fishing and wildlife viewing. Lake Shastina is a popular private facility providing good fishing and is open to all boating. Contact the Chamber of Commerce at P.O. Box 366, Weed 96094 or phone (530) 938-4624 for information.

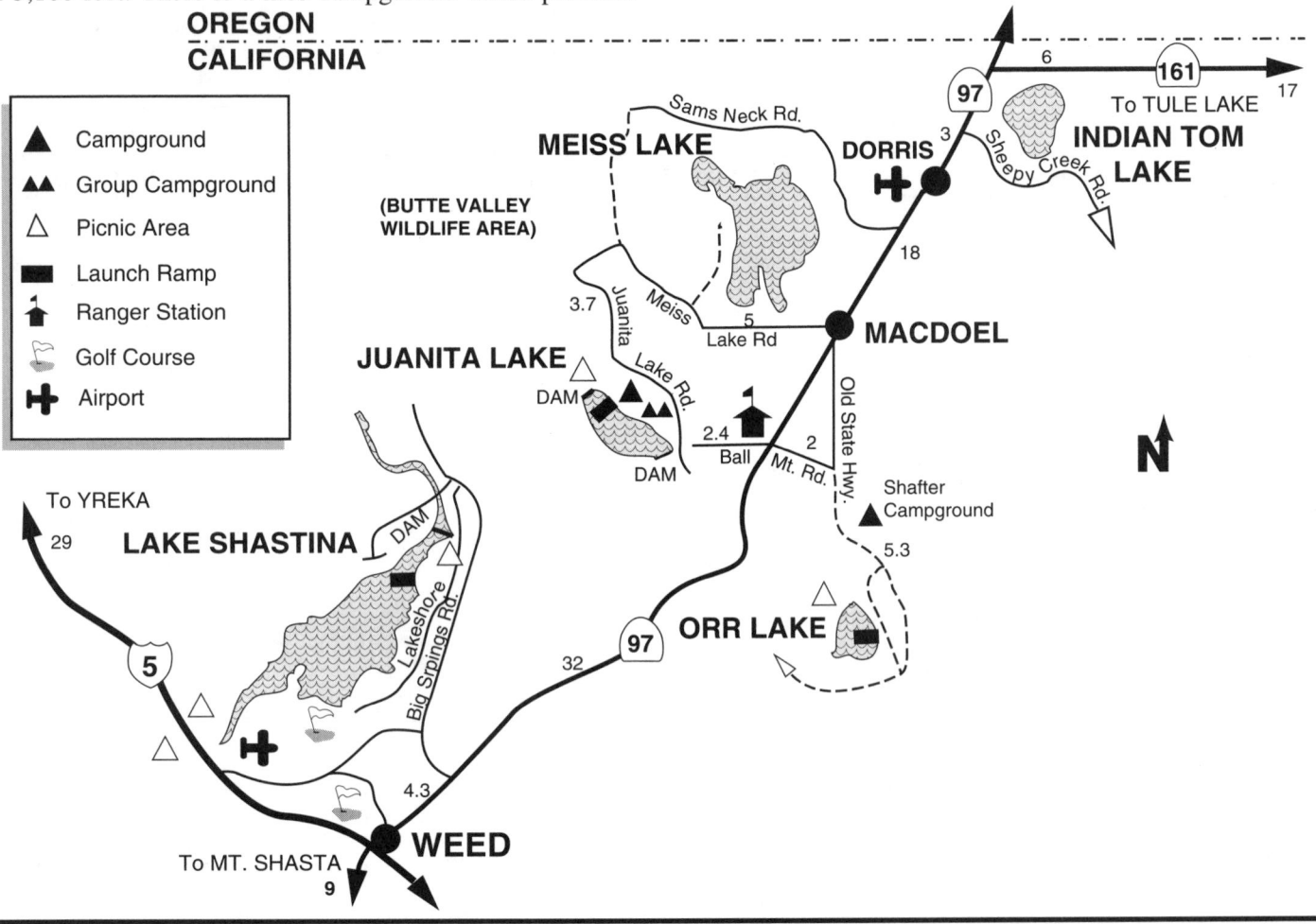

INFORMATION: Goosenest Ranger Station, 37805 Hwy. 97, Macdoel 96058—Ph: (530) 398-4391

CAMPING	BOATING	RECREATION	OTHER

Juanita Lake:
  22 Dev. Sites
  2 Handicap Sites
  Fee: $10
  1 Multiple Unit Site
  Fee: $15
Group Camp - 50 People
  Maximum Fee: $30
  Reservations Required
Shafter Campground:
  10 Sites - $6
	Juanita:
	  Open to All
	  Non-Powered Boating
	  Launch Ramp
	Shastina:
	  Open to All
	  Boating
	Orr & Indian Tom:
	  Small Hand Launch
	  Craft - Max. 10 HP
	Meiss (State Fish & Game):
	  Shallow Draft
	  Non-Powered Boating
		Fishing:
		Juanita: Brown &
		  Rainbow Trout,
		  Largemouth Bass &
		  Brown Bullhead Catfish
		Shastina: Trout, Silver
		  Salmon, Bass,
		  Catfish & Crappie
		Indian Tom: Cutthroat
		Hunting: Waterfowl, Deer,
		  Quail
		Swimming & Picnicking
		Hiking & Backpacking
			Full Facilities in Weed &
			  Tule Lake & Dorris
			Gas & Grocery Store at
			  Macdoel
			Butte Valley
			  Wildlife Area
			  P.O. Box 249
			  Macdoel 96058
			  Ph: (530) 398-4627
			Juanita Lake:
			  1-1/2 Mile Barrier Free
			  Trail Around Lake

MEDICINE LAKE

Medicine Lake is in the Modoc National Forest at an elevation of 6,700 feet. Once the center of a volcano, this 640 surface-acre Lake has no known outlets and is 150 feet deep in places. The lodgepole pine-covered campgrounds are maintained by the U.S. Forest Service. Points of interest include Lava Beds National Monument, Glass Mountain, Burnt Lava Flow, Medicine Lake Glass Flow and Undertakers Crater. Although remote, this is a popular Lake for boating, waterskiing and sailing. The fishing is good from shore or boat. The small 5 surface-acre Bullseye Lake has a rainbow and brook trout fishery.

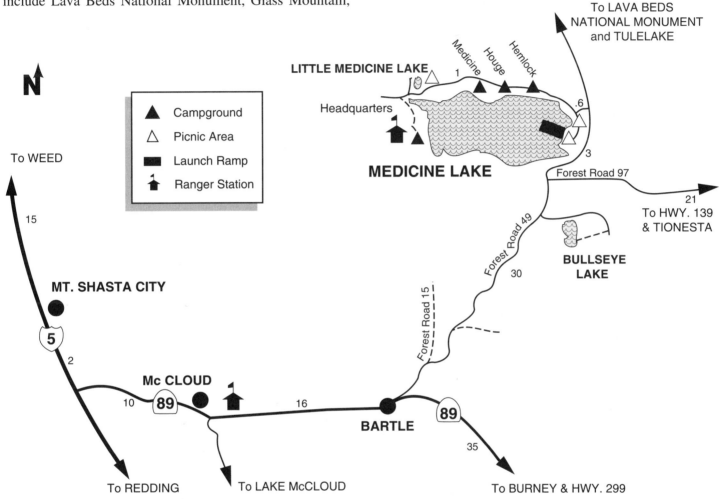

INFORMATION: Doublehead Ranger District, P.O. Box 369, Tulelake 96134—Ph: (530) 667-2246

CAMPING	BOATING	RECREATION	OTHER
73 Dev. Sites for Tents & R.V.s Fee: $7 per Vehicle per Night No Hookups No Reservations	Power, Row, Canoe, Sail, Inflatable, Waterski, Jets Launch Ramp - Paved Courtesy Dock Bullseye Lake: No Motors Hand Launch	Fishing: Rainbow & Brook Trout Swimming Picnicking Hiking Horseback Riding Hunting: Deer, Bear, Grouse Accessible Disabled Facilities	Other Facilities: 14 Miles at Lava Beds National Monument & 35 miles at Tulelake Full Facilities: 33 miles at Bartle & 25 miles at Tionesta

LAKE EARL, FISH LAKE, FRESHWATER LAGOON, STONE LAGOON and BIG LAGOON

Big Lagoon and its smaller neighbors, Stone and Freshwater Lagoons, are three of California's most unusual Lakes. Separated from the Pacific Ocean by a narrow strip of sand, these Lakes offer the angler a unique opportunity to fish for trout in fresh water and a few feet away, cast for surf perch in salt water. Lakes Earl and Talawa are part of the Lake Earl Wildlife Area. These shallow water Lakes offer a variety of game fish as well as an abundance of waterfowl and animal life. Fish Lake, at an elevation of 1,800 feet, is a popular freshwater fishing spot. No motors are allowed on this small 22-acre Lake. The Forest Service maintains a nice campground amid fir and huckleberries. There are a variety of trails leading to Red Mountain Lake and on to Blue Lake.

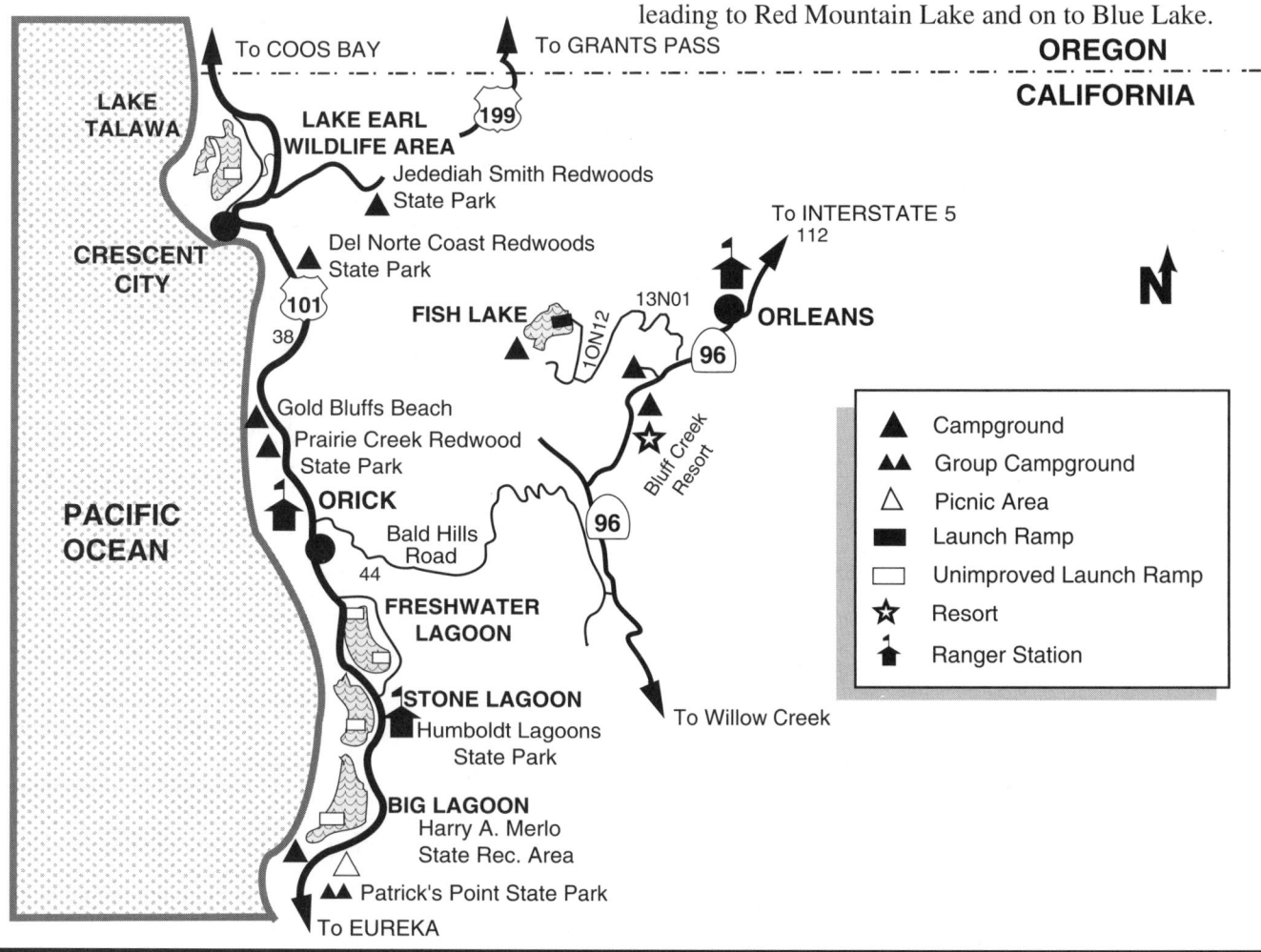

INFORMATION: Calif. State Parks, North Coast Redwoods, 3431 Fort Ave., Eureka 95501—Ph: (707) 445-6547

CAMPING	BOATING	RECREATION	OTHER

Redwood State Parks:
   Jedediah Smith
   Del Norte Coast
   Prairie Creek
   Gold Bluffs Beach
State Parks:
   Patrick's Point
Reserve:
   Ph: (800) 444-7275
	Lake Earl: Fishing Boats
	   Beach Launch
	Stone Lagoon: Canoes &
	   Fishing Boats
	   Check Speed Limit
	Big Lagoon: Fishing &
	   Small Sailboats
	Fish Lake: Non-Power
	   Boats Only
	   Launch Ramp
		Fishing: Rainbow, Brown
		   & Cutthroat Trout
		Stone Lagoon: Special
		   Fishing Regulations
		Picnicking
		Swimming at Lagoons
		Hiking & Nature Trails
		Beach Combing
		Tidal Pools
		Redwood Groves
		Birdwatching
		Hunting: Waterfowl
			Fish Lake:
			   Orleans Ranger Station
			   P. O. Drawer 410
			   Orleans 95556
			   Ph: (530) 627-3291
			
			R.V. Park at Bluff
			Creek Resort

LAKE SISKIYOU and CASTLE LAKE

Lake Siskiyou is a man-made Reservoir, at an elevation of 3,181 feet, located in the shadows of Mount Shasta. At the headwaters of the Sacramento River, the Lake has 437 surface acres with 5-1/4 shoreline miles surrounded by pine trees. There are 1,000 feet of sandy swimming beach, a complete marina and store. The Pacific Crest Trail is located nearby and the fishing is good. Crystal clear Castle Lake is located just south of Lake Siskiyou. Although primarily for fishing, swimming can be enjoyed at this small Lake. There is a picnic area near Castle Lake and 5 campsites for tents.

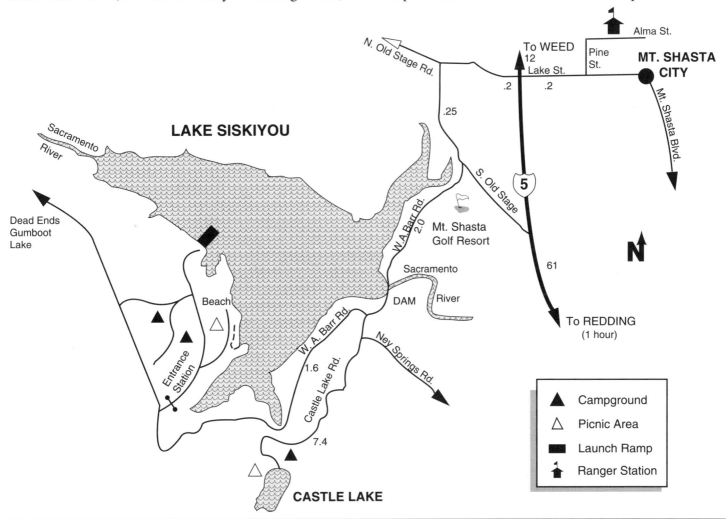

INFORMATION: Lake Siskiyou, P.O. Box 276, Mount Shasta 96067—Ph: (530) 926-2618

CAMPING	BOATING	RECREATION	OTHER

363 Dev. Sites for
   Tents & RVs
   Full Hookups with TV
   Fee: $18 - $25
   Group Campsites
   Disposal Station
   Day Use: $1 per person
 	
Castle Lake:
   Mount Shasta
   Ranger District:
      5 Tent Sites
	Power, Row, Canoe,
	   Windsurfing, Sail &
	   Inflatables
	   10 MPH Speed Limit
	Marina - Bait & Tackle Shop
	Launch Ramp - Free
	Rentals: Fishing, Canoe,
	   Pedalboats, Pontoons,
	   Kayaks and
	   Misc. Watertoys
	Berths, Docks, Moorings,
	Dry Storage
		Fishing: Rainbow,
		   Kamloop, Brown, &
		   Brook Trout
		   & Smallmouth Bass
		Fishing Dock & Cleaning
		   Station
		Swimming
		Picnicking & Hiking
		Backpacking [Parking]
		Playground
		Volleyball Court
		Free Family Movies
		Video Arcade, Horseshoes
			Rental R.V.s
			Lakeside Cabins
			Groceries, Deli, Gift Shop
			Laundromat
			Propane
			Community-Sized BBQ
			Handicap Fishing Dock
			2 Rec. Halls with Large
			   User Kitchens

LAKE MC CLOUD

Lake McCloud is at an elevation of 3,000 feet. The surface area of this 520-acre Lake belongs to P.G. & E., and the surrounding land belongs to the Hearst Corporation. The U.S. Forest Service was deeded a narrow strip of land between the road and high watermark from the boat ramp to Star City Creek. The shoreline is steep and pine trees tower above the rocky terrain. This is a popular Lake for fishing. Friday's RV Retreat and Fly Fishing Ranch is an ideal place with about 400 acres to explore. A Forest Service campground is located on the McCloud River at Ah-Di-Na. The Pacific Crest Trail passes through this area.

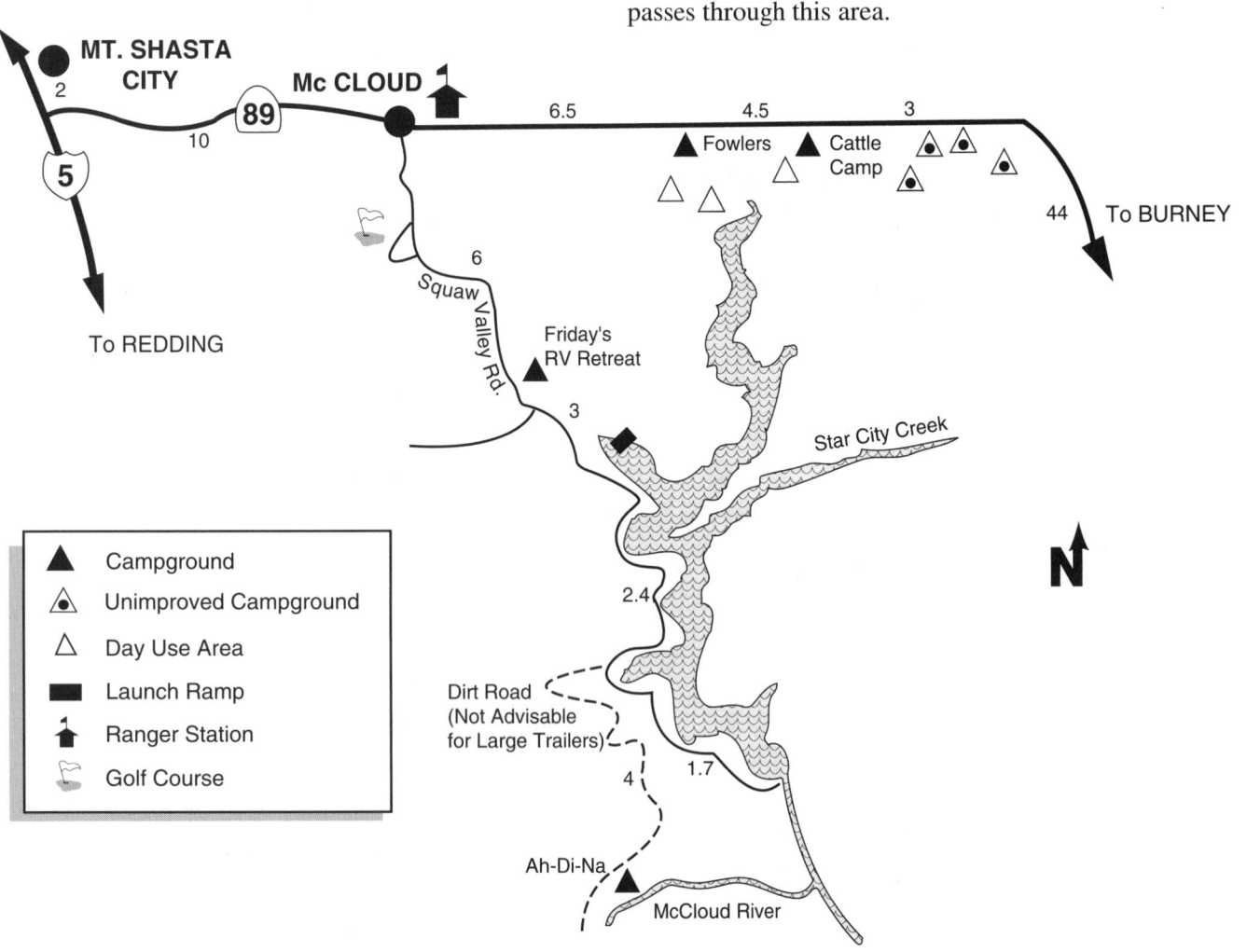

Legend:
- ▲ Campground
- ⚐ Unimproved Campground
- △ Day Use Area
- ■ Launch Ramp
- ☗ Ranger Station
- Golf Course

INFORMATION: McCloud Ranger District, P. O. Box 1620, McCloud 96057—Ph: (530) 964-2184

CAMPING	BOATING	RECREATION	OTHER

Ah-Di-Na:
   16 Camp Sites
   Narrow Dirt Road
 	
Along McCloud River:
   Fowlers:
      40 Dev. Sites
       R.V.s to 32 ft.
   Cattle Camp:
      25 Dev. Sites
   Other Undev. Sites
	Power, Row, Canoe
	Launch Ramp
		Fishing: Rainbow &
		   Brown Trout
		   (All Dolly Varden
		   Trout must be released)
		Fly Fishing School and
		   Ponds at Friday's
		   RV Retreat
		Picnicking
		Hiking Trails
		Nature Study
			Friday's RV Retreat
			P. O. Box 68
			McCloud 96057
			Ph: (530) 964-2878
			   Cabin Available
			   30 Sites for
			      Tents & R.V.s
			   Full Hookups
			      Fees: $15 - $22
			   Hot Showers,
			   Laundromat
			Open May 1 to Oct. 15
			Full Facilities in McCloud

WEST VALLEY RESERVOIR

West Valley Reservoir, with 970 surface acres, is located in the northeastern corner of California, off Highway 395 just east of Likely. Resting at an elevation of 4,770 feet, the 7 miles of shoreline is relatively sparse with only a few clusters of small trees. All types of boating are permitted including boat camping. Waterskiing is popular. Eagle Lake trout are the primary game fish and they are often good sized. There are also catfish and Sacramento perch. Support facilities are limited to a single-lane paved ramp and primitive campsites. This is a relatively remote Reservoir, but if you are a dedicated angler, give it a try. The Lake is usually frozen over from December to early March.

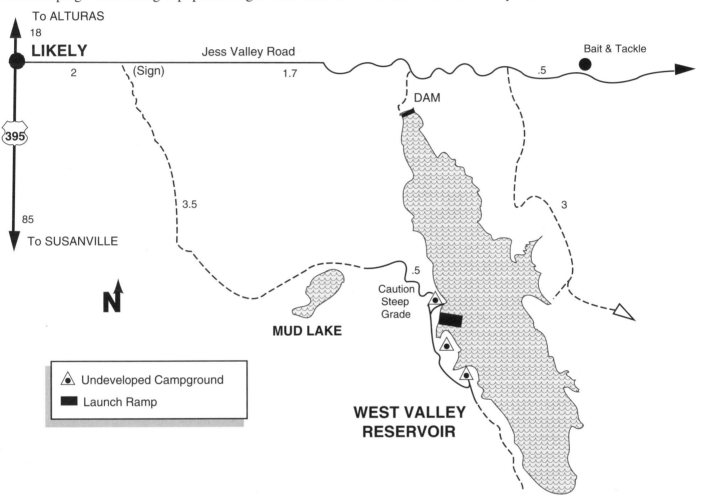

To ALTURAS
18
LIKELY
2   (Sign)   Jess Valley Road   1.7
395
85
To SUSANVILLE
3.5
DAM
Bait & Tackle
.5
3
.5
Caution
Steep
Grade
MUD LAKE

N

△ Undeveloped Campground
■ Launch Ramp

WEST VALLEY
RESERVOIR

INFORMATION: Modoc County, 202 W. 4th Street, Alturas 96101—Ph: (530) 233-3939

CAMPING	BOATING	RECREATION	OTHER

Primitive Camping
   Water & Toilets
	Power, Row, Canoe, Sail,
	   Waterski, Jets,
	   Windsurfing &
	   Inflatable
	
	Overnight Camping In
	   Boat Permitted
	   Anywhere
	
	*High Winds Can Be
	   Hazardous*
		Fishing:
		   Eagle Lake Trout,
		   Catfish, Sacramento
		   Perch
		Swimming
		Picnicking
		Hiking
		Backpacking [Parking]
		Hunting:
		   Deer & Rabbit
			Full Facilities - 6 miles at
			   Likely

BLUE LAKE

Blue Lake, located 28 miles southeast of Alturas, is in the Modoc National Forest. This mountain Lake of 160 surface acres is surrounded by Ponderosa Pines, White Firs and meadows at an elevation of 6,000 feet. This is a popular, well-used facility near the South Warner Wilderness area. The Lake fishing is good for rainbow and brown trout. There are no boating facilities other than a paved launch ramp, but most boating is permitted with a 15 mph speed limit. For the hiker, backpacker, horseback rider or energetic fisherman, the South Warner Wilderness offers good trails. You can fish from shore at Clear Lake.

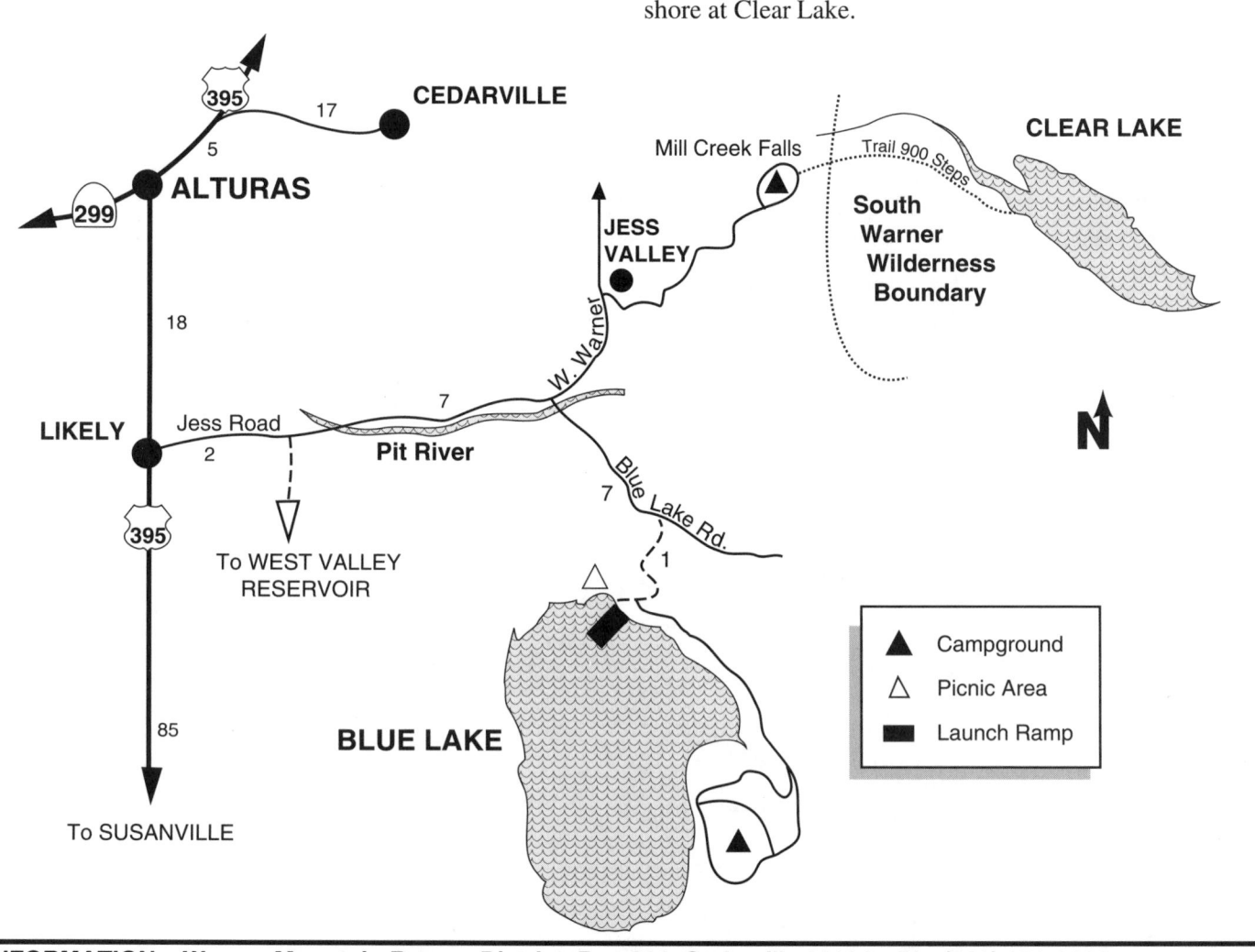

CEDARVILLE	Mill Creek Falls	CLEAR LAKE

(map)

▲	Campground
△	Picnic Area
◼	Launch Ramp

INFORMATION: Warner Mountain Ranger District, Box 220, Cedarville 96104—Ph: (530) 279-6116

CAMPING	BOATING	RECREATION	OTHER

Blue Lake Camp:
    48 Dev. Sites for
    Tents/RVs
    Under 22 Feet
    Fee: $7
 	
Mill Creek Falls:
    19 Dev. Sites for
    Tents/RVs
    Under 22 Feet
    Fee: $6
	Power, Row, Canoe, Sail,
	    & Inflatable
	15 MPH Speed Limit
	*No Waterskiing or
	    Jets*
	Paved Launch Ramp
	Handicap Accessible
	    Facilities at Blue Lake
		Fishing: Rainbow &
		    Brown Trout
		Handicap Accessible
		    Fishing Platform
		Picnicking
		Hiking
		Swimming
		Hunting: Deer in Vicinity
			Likely:
			    Grocery Store
			    Restaurant
			    Gas Station
			
			Full Facilities - 28 miles at
			    Alturas

EASTMAN, TULE, BIG, FALL RIVER, CRYSTAL and BAUM LAKES

The Fall River Valley is an angler's paradise. Nestled between the Sierra and Cascade mountain ranges, these Lakes are fed by Hat Creek, Pit and Fall Rivers. Baum has 89 surface acres and Crystal has 60 acres. Each of these Lakes are connected and support trophy sized brown trout as well as rainbow and eastern brook. The warm water fisheries of Big,

Tule, Eastman and Fall River Lakes are all contiguous. This area also has rainbow trout up to 4 pounds. The streams and rivers offer prime fishing. Hat Creek and Fall River are designated "Wild Trout" Streams which provide trophy sized trout. Artificial lures must be used and other special rules apply.

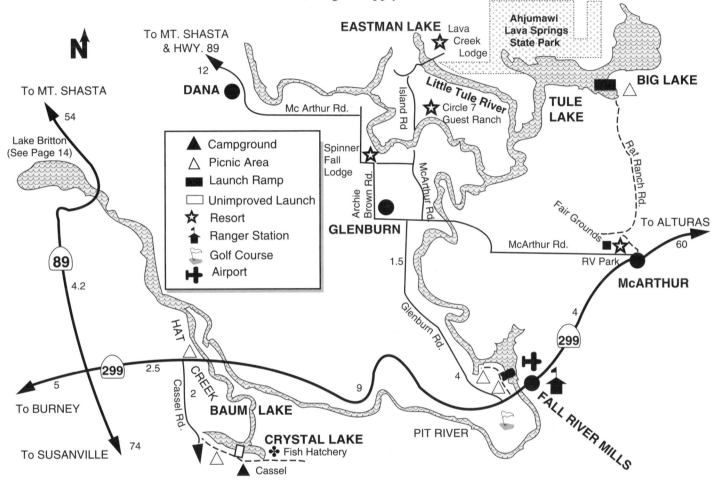

INFORMATION: Chamber of Commerce, P.O. Box 475, Fall River Mills, 96028—Ph: (530) 336-5840

CAMPING	BOATING	RECREATION	OTHER
See Lake Britton	Baum & Crystal:	Fishing: Largemouth	Lava Creek Lodge:
	No Power Boating	Bass, Catfish, Green	Glenburn Star Route
P.G. & E.:	Other Lakes:	Sunfish, Brown,	Island Road
Ph: (916) 386-5164	10 MPH	Rainbow & Eastern	Fall River Mills 96028
Cassel - 1 mile	Lava Creek Lodge:	Brook Trout	Ph: (530) 336-6288
South of Baum	Boat Rentals, Guides &	Hiking: Pacific Crest Trail	Rooms & Cabins
Lake - 27 Sites	Boat Launch	Hunting: Ducks, Geese,	Spinner Fall Lodge:
Fee: $10	Spinner Fall Lodge:	Quail, Dove, Pheasant	28076 Metzger Rd.
Ahjumawi State Park	Guest Boat Rentals	& Bear	Fall River Mills 96028
Ph: (530) 335-2777	Guides Available	Swimming: Fall River	Ph: (530) 336-5300
Above Big Lake		Lake & Big Lake	Lodging, Bar, Restaurant
9 Primitive Sites		Full Facilities at	Circle 7 Guest Ranch
Boat-in Only		Fall River Mills	Ph: (530) 336-5827

IRON CANYON RESERVOIR

Iron Canyon Reservoir is at an elevation of 2,700 feet in the Shasta-Trinity National Forest. This beautiful 500-surface acre Lake has 15 miles of shoreline. Larger boats with a deep draft are not recommended due to shallow Lake levels. The Lake level varies greatly during the year depending on weather and P.G. & E. power needs. There are some big trout and the fishing can be good. The Forest Service has a self-service campground providing a quiet atmosphere amid pine and fir trees. P.G. & E., in co-operation with the Forest Service, has a campground and paved launch ramp at Hawkins Landing. This Lake is perfect for those seeking solitude.

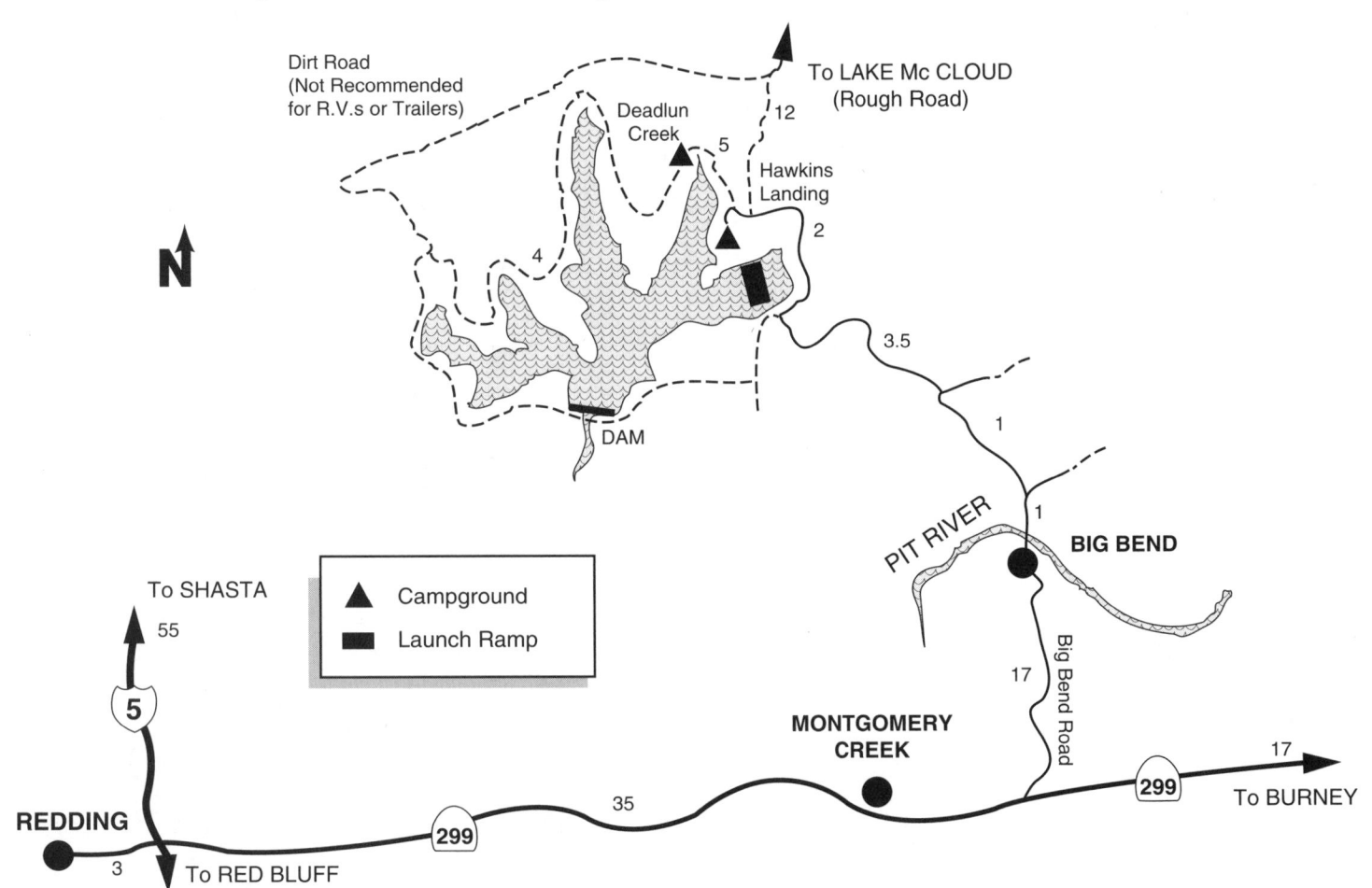

INFORMATION: Shasta Lake Ranger District, 14225 Holiday Drive, Redding 96003—Ph: (530) 275-1587

CAMPING	BOATING	RECREATION	OTHER

Deadlun Creek:
    25 Dev. Sites for
    Tents & RVs to 16 feet
    No Fee
Plus Undeveloped
    Camping Ares
    Campfire Permit Req'd.
P.G. & E.
    Ph: (916) 386-5164
Hawkins Landing:
    10 Dev. Sites for
    Tents/RVs
    Fee: $15
	Power, Row, Canoe, &
	    Inflatables
	Watch for Shallow Lake
	    Levels
	
	Launch Ramp at Hawkins
	    Landing Campground
		Fishing: Rainbow &
		    Brown Trout
		Swimming
		Picnicking
		Hiking
		    Pacific Crest Trail
		Off Road Driving Trails
		Bird Watching
		Hunting: Deer
			At Big Bend:
			    Grocery Store
			    Bait & Tackle
			    Gas Station
			    (Hours of Operation
			    are Limited)
			Guard Station
			    and Fire Station
			
			*Caution: Heavy Logging
			Truck Traffic at Times*

LAKE BRITTON

Lake Britton, located in the Shasta-Trinity National Forest, is at an elevation of 2,760 feet. This 1,600 surface acre Lake has 18 miles of shoreline and is nestled amid evergreen forests on the Pit River. The McArthur-Burney Falls Memorial State Park has 900 acres stretching from Burney Falls along Burney Creek to the shoreline of Lake Britton. Burney Creek is planted with trout weekly in season. This park, established in 1920, is not only one of the oldest in the State Park System, but one of the best facilities in Northern California. There are also U.S. Forest Service and P.G. & E. campgrounds in the area. Called by Teddy Roosevelt "the eighth wonder of the world," Burney Falls is the popular attraction in this area. This is a good boating Lake although *caution should be used as there can be floating debris and fluctuating water levels.*

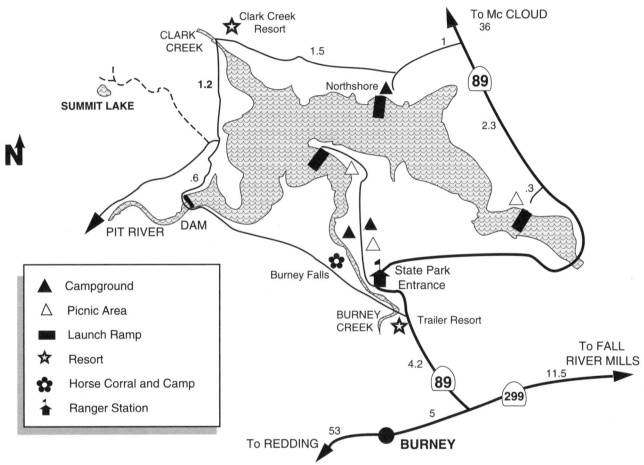

▲	Campground
△	Picnic Area
■	Launch Ramp
☆	Resort
❀	Horse Corral and Camp
♙	Ranger Station

INFORMATION: State Park, Route 1, Box 1260, Burney 96013—Ph: (530) 335-2777

CAMPING	BOATING	RECREATION	OTHER

State Park Camps:
    128 Dev. Sites for
    Tents/R.V.s to 35 Feet
Fee: $12
Reserve:
    Ph: (800) 444-7275
P.G.&E.:
Ph: (916) 386-5164
Northshore:
Dev. Sites for
    Tents/R.V.s
Fee: $15
Plus Group Sites
	Power, Row, Canoe, Sail,
	    Waterskiing, Jets,
	    Windsurf & Inflatables
	Launch Ramps - Fee
	Rentals: Fishing Boats &
	    Canoes
	Moorings
	Boat Storage
		Fishing: Trout, Crappie,
		    Bass
		Swimming
		Picnicking
		Backpacking
		Nature Trails
		Equestrian Trails &
		    Corral
		Bird Watching
		Campfire Program
			Snack Bar
			Grocery Store
			Bait & Tackle
			Gas Station
			
			Full Facilities - 11 miles at
			    Burney
			
			Clark Creek Resort:
			    Cabins
			    Restaurant

Trinity Lake rests at an elevation of 2,370 feet just below the rugged, granite peaks of the Trinity Alps Wilderness and is one of California's finest recreation spots. A part of the Whiskeytown-Shasta-Trinity National Recreation Area, this 16,400 surface acre Lake offers prime outdoor opportunities. Houseboaters find the 145 miles of pine, cedar and oak-covered shoreline ideal for "getting away from it all." There are hundreds of quiet coves for the angler to tie up and catch a meal or better yet, catch a world record smallmouth bass. Water levels may fluctuate in the late season which can create hazards but boaters will always find an expansive body of water for sailing or waterskiing.

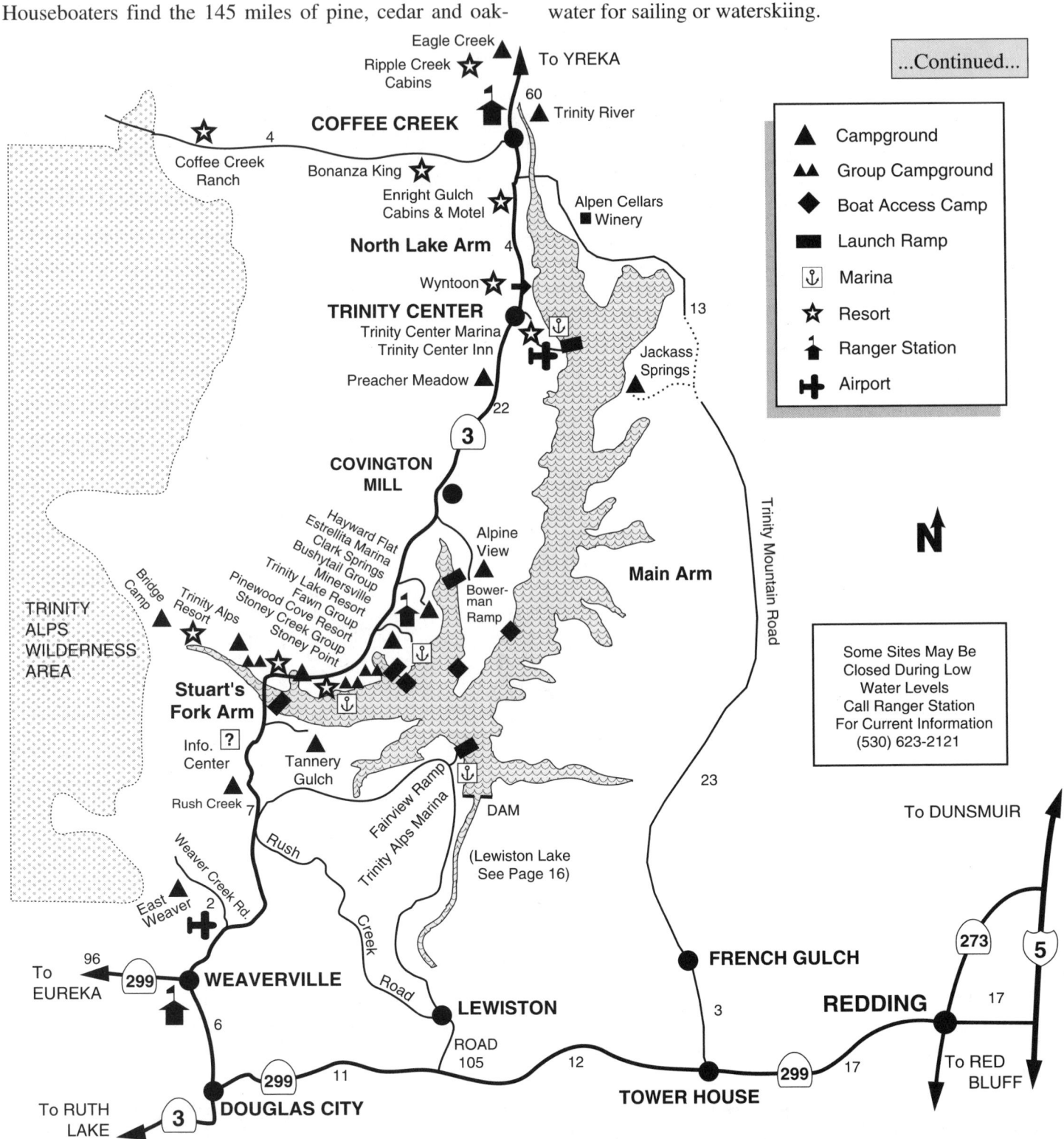

...Continued...

Legend	
▲	Campground
▲▲	Group Campground
◆	Boat Access Camp
▬	Launch Ramp
⚓	Marina
☆	Resort
🚩	Ranger Station
✈	Airport

Some Sites May Be
Closed During Low
Water Levels
Call Ranger Station
For Current Information
(530) 623-2121

U.S.F.S. CAMPGROUNDS
Fees Subject to Change

STUART FORK ARM and South Area:

HAYWARD FLAT - 98 Sites, R.V.s to 40 ft., Beach, Fee: $15 - Single Family Sites, $20-Multiple, $5 Extra Vehicle
TANNERY GULCH - 87 Sites, R.V.s to 40 ft., Launch Ramp for Campers Only, Beach, Amphitheater,
Fee: $15 - Single Family Sites, $20 - Multiple Family Sites, $5 Extra Vehicle
The Two Above Campgrounds: Reservations Ph: (877) 444-6777
CLARK SPRINGS - 21 Sites, R.V.s to 20 ft., Fee: $10 (Next to Clark Springs Day Area)
MINERSVILLE - 21 Sites, R.V.s to 18 ft., Fee: $12 to $20
STONEY POINT - 22 Walk-In Sites, Tents Only, Fee: $11
BRIDGE CAMP - 10 Sites, R.V.s to 12 ft., Fee: $10
EAST WEAVER - 15 Sites, R.V.s to 16 ft., Fee: $9
RUSH CREEK - 10 Sites, R.V.s to 16 ft., No Water, Fee: $6

MAIN ARM:

JACKASS SPRINGS - 21 Sites, R.V.s to 32 ft., Dirt Access and Interior Road, No Water, No Fee
PREACHER MEADOW - 45 Sites, R.V.s to 32 ft., Fee: $10
ALPINE VIEW - 66 Sites, R.V.s to 32 ft., Fee: $15 to $20, $5 Extra Vehicle, Wheel Chair Access

NORTH SHORE:

TRINITY RIVER - 7 Sites, R.V.s to 32 ft., Fee: $9
EAGLE CREEK - 17 Sites, R.V.s to 27 ft., Fee: $9

BOAT ACCESS ONLY SITES: Vault Toilets, No Water, No Fee
CAPTAIN'S POINT - 3 Boat-In Sites
RIDGEVILLE - 21 Boat-In Sites
RIDGEVILLE ISLAND - 3 Boat-In Sites
MARINER'S ROOST - 7 Boat-In Sites

GROUP CAMPGROUNDS - **Reserve: Ph: (877) 444-6777**
BUSHYTAIL - 30 Sites, R.V.s to 20 ft. - Fee: $80
FAWN - RV/Tent Sites - 3 Loops, 100 People Per Loop, Fee: $80 Per Loop
STONEY CREEK - Tent Sites - 50 People Maximum, Fee: $65

(Additional Primitive Campsites around Trinity Lake) | ...Continued.... |

INFORMATION: Weaverville Ranger Station, Box 1190, Weaverville 96093—Ph: (530) 623-2121

CAMPING	BOATING	RECREATION	OTHER

U.S.F.S.
    Dev. Tent/RV Sites
    No Hookups
    Boat-In Sites
    3 Group Campgrounds
 	
See Following Pages for
    Private Facilities
	Open to All Boating
	    4 Full Service Marinas
	    7 Public Launch Ramps
	    Launch Fee: $5
	Rentals:
	    Houseboats, Fishing,
	    Pontoon & Ski Boats
	
	Annual General Passes:
	    $40 - $60 a year
	    for Day Use Areas
	    and All Boat Ramps
		Fishing: Large &
		    Smallmouth Bass,
		    Bluegill, Catfish,
		    Kokanee, Brown &
		    Rainbow Trout
		Swim Beaches
		Picnic Areas
		Hiking & Equestrian Trails
		Backpacking
		Hunting: Deer, Bear
			Complete Destination
			    Facilities at Some
			    Resorts and at Trinity
			
			Center
			
			Airports - Trinity Center,
			    Weaverville

TRINITY LAKE.............Continued

PRIVATE MARINAS

TRINITY ALPS MARINA - Trinity Center 96091 - (530) 286-2282 - Launch Ramp, Mooring, Fuel Dock, OMC Dealership, Houseboats, Ski Boats, Fishing Boats, Jets, Ski Equipment, Tubes & Canoe Rentals, Grocery & Souvenir Store.

ESTRELLITA MARINA - 49160 State Hwy. 3, Trinity Center 96091 - (530) 286-2215 or (800) 747-2215 - Houseboat Rentals, Day Boats, Personal Watercraft, Fishing Boats, Ski Boats, Grocery Store, Fuel Dock, Propane, Mooring, OMC Service Dealer.

TRINITY LAKE RESORTS & MARINAS - 45810 State Hwy. 3, Trinity Center 96091 - (530) 286-2225 - Restaurant & Lounge, Cabins, Full Service Marina, Paved Launch Ramp, OMC Dealershp, Repairs, Fuel Dock, Propane, Mooring, Dry Storage, Houseboats, Deck, Ski and Fishing Boat and Canoe Rentals, Grocery Store.

TRINITY CENTER MARINA - Trinity Center 96091 - (530) 286-2225 - Paved Launch Ramp, Store, Fuel Dock, Slips, Mooring, Ski, Fishing and Boat Rentals.

PRIVATE RESORTS

(Prices Vary - Call Resort for Current Information)

RIPPLE CREEK CABINS - Box 4020, Star Rte. 2, Trinity Center 96091 - (530) 266-3505 - Housekeeping Cabins for 2 to 6 People, Secluded Area, Decks, Wood Stoves, Swimming, Hiking, Handicapped Cabin (sleeps 12) and Group Facilities, Panoramic Views, Pets Welcome, High and Low Season Rates - Open Year Around.

COFFEE CREEK GUEST RANCH - HC2, Box 4940, Trinity Center 96091 - (800) 624-4480 - On Coffee Creek in the Trinity Alps, 3-Star Diamond Dude Ranch, Secluded Cabins, Pool/Spa, Horseback Riding, Hayrides, Wilderness Pack Trips, Hunting, Stocked Fishing Pond, Gold Panning, Hiking, Summer Youth Programs, Square/Line Dancing, Reunions, Retreats, Small Meeting Planners, Complimentary Conference Room, Handicap Accessible, Spring/Fall/Senior Discounts, Open Year Around.

TRINITY ALPS RESORT - 1750 Trinity Alps Rd., Trinity Center 96091 - (530) 286-2205 - Rustic Housekeeping Cabins, Bar, Restaurant, General Store, Snack Bar, Horse Rides, Hiking Trails, Volleyball, Basketball, Horseshoes, Bingo, Bonfires, Movies and Talent Shows, Tennis Court, River Swim Beach, Square Dancing, High and Low Season Rates.

PINEWOOD COVE RESORT - 45110 State Highway 3, Trinity Center 96091 - (530) 286-2201 or (800) 988-LAKE (5253) 84 Tent/R.V. Sites, 43 Full Hookups, Disposal Station, Grocery Store, Ramp, Dock, Slips, Fishing Boat Rentals, Propane, Game Room, Recreation Hall, Cabin and Trailer Rentals, Laundromat, Swimming Pool, Organized Recreation Activities.

WYNTOON RESORT - Box 70, Trinity Center 96091 - (530) 266-3337 - Complete 90-Acre Destination Resort, 136 R.V. Sites, Full Hookups, 80 Tent Sites, Cabins, Grocery Store, Gas, Propane, Snack Bar, Rental Boats, Private Dock, Laundromat., Swimming Pool.

ENRIGHT GULCH CABINS and MOTEL - 3500 Highway 3, Box 244, Trinity Center 96091 - (530) 266-3600 or (888)) 383-5583 - Housekeeping Cabins and Motel Units, Quiet Private Road Surrounded by National Forest, Hiking Trails, Grocery Stores, Restaurants and Marina Nearby.

This is only a partial list of the excellent private facilities around Trinity Lake. For further information contact:

TRINITY COUNTY CHAMBER OF COMMERCE
P.O. BOX 517
WEAVERVILLE, CA 96093
(530) 623-6101 OR (800) 421-7259

Lewiston Lake is at an elevation of 1,902 feet in the Shasta-Trinity National Forest. This scenic Lake is 5 miles long and has a surface area of 610 acres with 15 miles of shoreline. It is open to all boating but subject to a 10 MPH speed limit. The very cold, constantly moving water flows into Lewiston Lake from the bottom waters of Trinity Lake providing an ideal habitat for large trout. Just below Lewiston Dam, the Trinity River, Rush Creek and other streams offer prize salmon and steelhead as well as trout. Lewiston Fish Hatchery is one of the world's most automated salmon and steelhead hatchery.

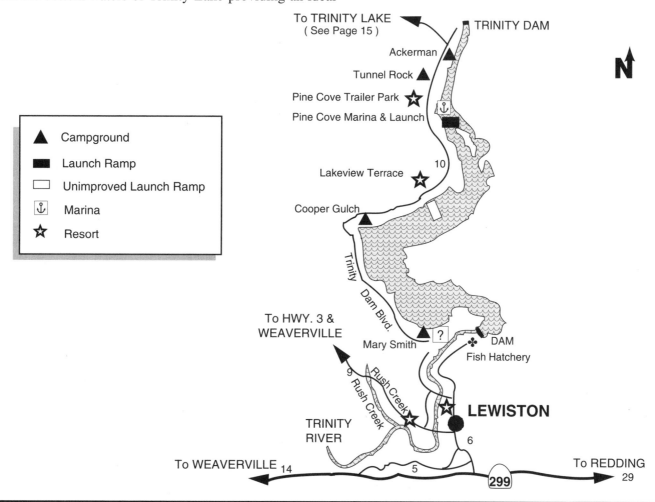

▲	Campground
■	Launch Ramp
▢	Unimproved Launch Ramp
⚓	Marina
☆	Resort

INFORMATION: Weaverville Ranger Station, Box 1190, Weaverville 96093—Ph: (530) 623-2121

CAMPING	BOATING	RECREATION	OTHER
Ackerman: 66 Dev. Sites R.V.s to 40 ft. Disposal Station Fee: $11 Tunnel Rock: 6 Sites - R.V.s to 15 ft. No Water Fee: $6 Cooper Gulch: 5 Dev. Sites R.V.s to 16 ft. - Fee: $12 Mary Smith: 18 Sites Tents Only - Fee: $10 Additional Campsites at Private Resorts	Power, Row, Canoe, Sail & Inflatable Speed Limit - 10 MPH Launch Ramps Rentals: Fishing Boats Docks, Gas Dry Storage	Fishing: Rainbow, Brook & Brown Trout, Kokanee Salmon Picnicking 5 Wildlife Viewing Areas Hunting: Deer, Bear, Fowl & Squirrel	Resorts: Contact: Trinity County Chamber of Commerce Box 517 Weaverville 96093 (530) 623-6101 or (800) 421-7259 Snack Bars Restaurants Grocery Stores Bait & Tackle

WHISKEYTOWN LAKE and KESWICK RESERVOIR

Whiskeytown Lake, at an elevation of 1,209 feet, has 36 miles of coniferous shoreline and is one of California's most diverse fisheries. Tree-shaded islands, numerous coves and 3,250 surface acres of clear blue water invite the watersport enthusiast. The boater will find complete marina facilities and over 5 square miles of open water. Houseboats or overnight boat camping are not allowed. The water is reasonably warm and there are some nice swimming beaches. Fishing is good from boat or shore for trout, kokanee salmon, bass and pan fish. The National Park Service maintains the facilities which include picnic areas and campgrounds. Approximately 50 miles of dirt roads and 40,000 acres of backcountry are open for visitor use. Keswick Reservoir is at an elevation of 587 feet and has a surface area of 630 acres. Fed by cold water released from Shasta Dam, Keswick provides the angler with large rainbow trout. Shore fishing at Keswick is difficult because of steep banks and heavy brush in most areas.

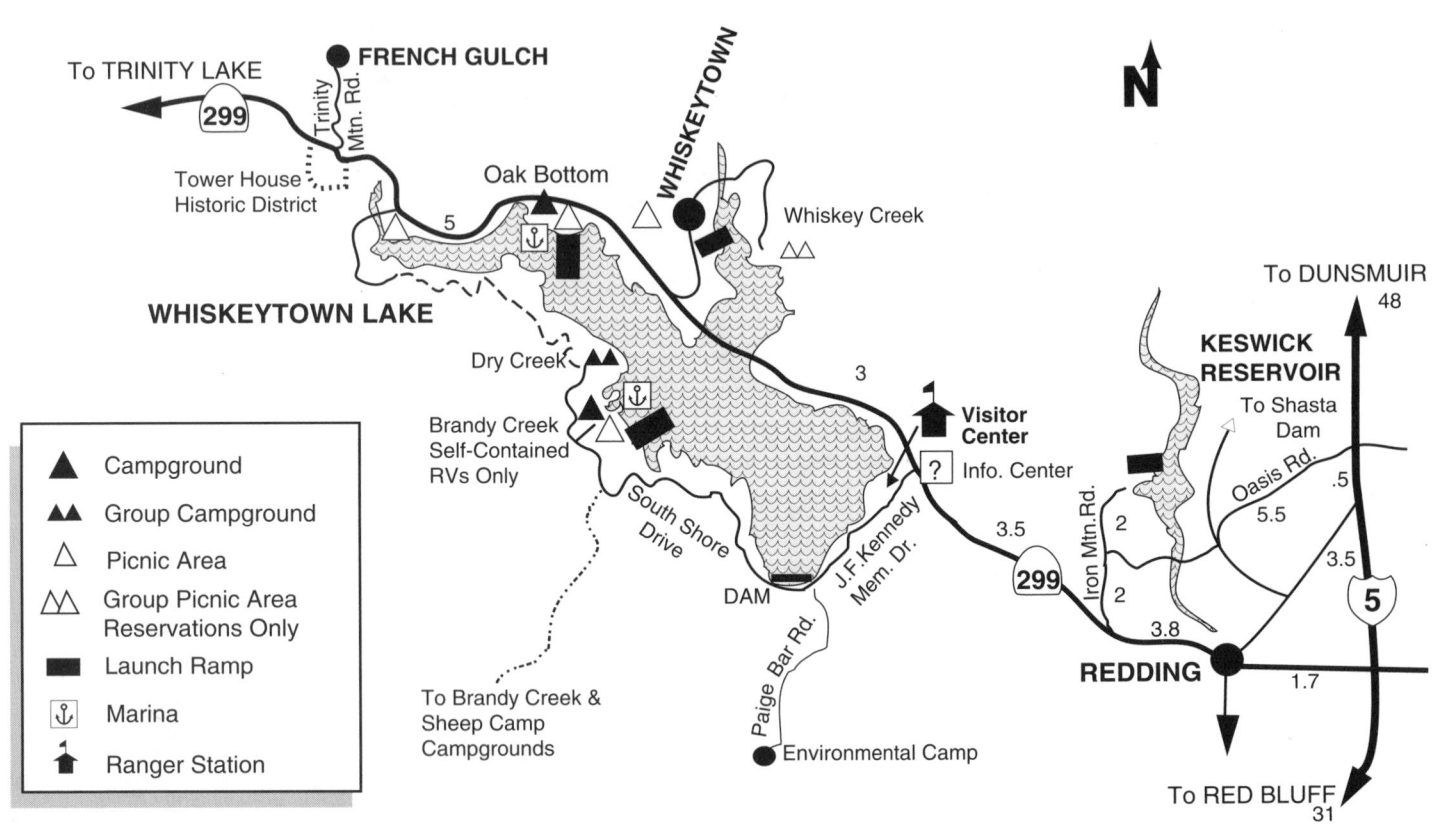

▲	Campground
▲▲	Group Campground
△	Picnic Area
⋀⋀	Group Picnic Area Reservations Only
▬	Launch Ramp
⚓	Marina
⬥	Ranger Station

INFORMATION: Whiskeytown National Rec. Area, P.O. Box 188, Whiskeytown 96095—Ph: (530) 241-6584			
CAMPING	**BOATING**	**RECREATION**	**OTHER**
National Park - Oak Bottom: 100 Dev. Walk-in Tent Sites & 22 R.V. Sites to 36 ft. Fees: $8 - $18 Disposal Station Reserve: (800) 365-CAMP Brandy Creek: 37 Self-Cont. R.V. Sites Fees: $7 - $14 Disposal Station Dry Creek: Group Camp to 160 People - Reserve at National Rec. Area	Whiskeytown : Open to All Boats Except Personal Watercraft Full Service Marina Rentals: Fishing, Ski, Sail, Canoe & Pontoon Boats Sailing Regattas Keswick: Open to All Boats Paved Launch Ramp	Fishing: Kokanee & Chinook Salmon, Brook & Rainbow Trout, Spotted, Large & Smallmouth Bass, Bluegill, Crappie & Catfish Swimming Scuba Diving Picnicking - Groups Reserve (800) 365-CAMP Hiking & Riding Trails Ranger Guided Tours	Whiskeytown NRA Day Use: $5 per Vehicle, $10/Week, $20/Year Campground Programs Gold Panning Grocery Store Snack Bar Bait & Tackle Keswick Reservoir: Bureau of Reclamation 16349 Shasta Dam Rd. Shasta Lake 96019 Ph: (530) 275-1554

Shasta Lake is one of California's prime recreation lakes. It is located on the northern tip of the Sacramento Valley just off Interstate 5 at an elevation of 1,067 feet. The four main arms of this huge 30,000 surface-acre Lake converge at the junction of the Cascade and Klamath Mountain Ranges and are fed by the Sacramento, McCloud and Pit Rivers and Squaw Creek. When at full water capacity, there are 370 miles of wooded and sometimes steep, red-rock shoreline. Shasta is California's largest man-made Lake and one of the most popular. With quiet sheltered coves ideal for houseboating and wide-open areas to enjoy water sports, Shasta is a great vacation destination. In addition to the many private marinas, there are 6 conveniently located public launch ramps. The angler will find over 16 species of fish from several varieties of bass to trout or sturgeon. Shasta is operated under the jurisdiction of the U. S. Forest Service which provides many developed and boat-in campsites. In addition, shoreline camping is permitted. *Call regarding possible low water levels as with all Lakes.*

....Continued....

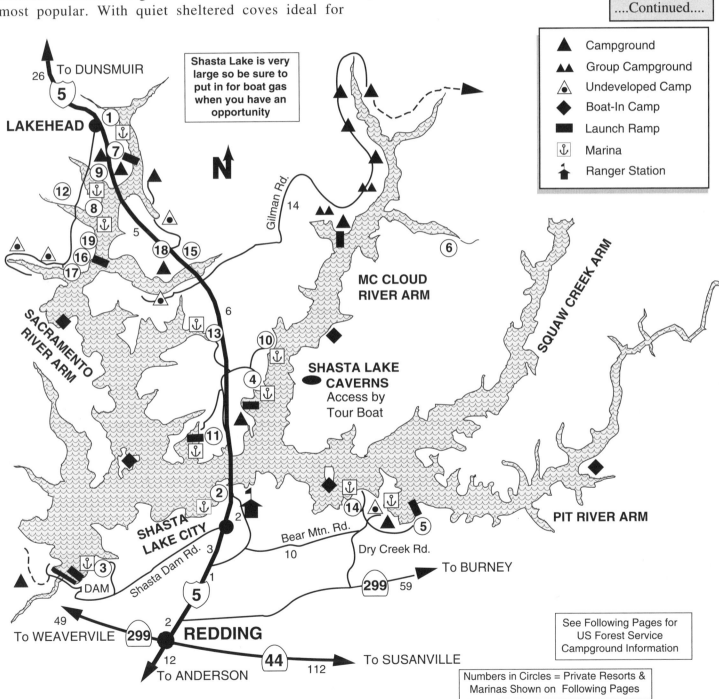

Shasta Lake is very large so be sure to put in for boat gas when you have an opportunity

▲	Campground
▲▲	Group Campground
⊙	Undeveloped Camp
◆	Boat-In Camp
▬	Launch Ramp
⚓	Marina
⚑	Ranger Station

SHASTA LAKE CAVERNS
Access by Tour Boat

MC CLOUD RIVER ARM

SACRAMENTO RIVER ARM

SQUAW CREEK ARM

PIT RIVER ARM

To DUNSMUIR

LAKEHEAD

N

Gilman Rd.

SHASTA LAKE CITY

Bear Mtn. Rd.

Shasta Dam Rd.

Dry Creek Rd.

To BURNEY

DAM

To WEAVERVILE

REDDING

To ANDERSON

To SUSANVILLE

See Following Pages for US Forest Service Campground Information

Numbers in Circles = Private Resorts & Marinas Shown on Following Pages

SHASTA LAKE..............Continued

U.S.F.S. CAMPGROUNDS

Reservations at Most Sites Shown Below:
Ph: (877) 444-6777
*Fees are Charged at all Campgrounds
and Boat Ramps*

FEES VARY WITH SEASON
Check Lake Level - Some Sites May Be Closed Because Of Low Water

PIT RIVER ARM:

From Interstate 5:
11 Miles NE - **Jones Valley** - 27 Tent/R.V. Sites to 30 feet, Boat Access, Launch Ramp
11 Miles NE - **Jones Inlet** - Primitive Shoreline Camp Sites for Tent/R.V.s to 30 feet
Campfire Permit Required.

McCLOUD ARM:

At O'Brien:
1 Mile E - **Bailey Cove** - 5 Single & 2 Double Tent/R.V. Sites to 30 feet, Launch Ramp -
Reservations Accepted
At Gilman Rd.:
9 Miles E - **Hirz Bay** - 38 Single & 10 Double Tent/R.V. Sites to 40 feet, Launch Ramp
Reservations Accepted
9 Miles E - **Hirz Bay Group Camp** - R.V. Sites to 30 feet
Camp #1 - Max. Capacity - 120 People
Camp #2 - Max. Capacity - 80 People
Reservations Required
10 Miles E - **Dekkas Rock Group Camp** - R.V. Sites tp 30 feet - Max. Capacity 60 People
Reservations Required
11 Miles E - **Moore Creek** - 12 Tent/R.V. Sites to 30 feet
15 Miles E - **Ellery Creek** - 19 Tent/R.V. Sites to 30 feet - Reservations Accepted
16 Miles E - **Pine Point** - 14 Tent/R.V. Sites to 30 feet
17 Miles E - **McCloud Bridge** - 20 Tent/R.V. Sites to 35 feet

....Continued....

INFORMATION: Shasta Lake Visitor Information Center, Mountain Gate/Wonderland Exit—Ph: (530) 275-1589

CAMPING	BOATING	RECREATION	OTHER
Dev. Sites for Tents & R.V.s	Power, Row, Canoe, Sail, Waterski,	Fishing: Trout, Bass, Catfish, Bluegill,	Motels & Cabins Snack Bars
Walk-In Sites	Jets, Windsurf	Perch, Crappie &	Restaurants
Boat-In Sites	& Inflatable	Kokanee Salmon	Grocery Stores
Group Camp Sites	Full Service Marinas	Shasta Caverns Tour	Bait & Tackle
	Launch Ramps	Swimming - Lake & Pools	Laundromats
See Following Pages	Rentals: Houseboats, Fishing & Ski Boats	Picnicking Hiking	Gas Stations Trailer Parks
	Docks, Berths, Gas, Moorings, Storage	Hunting: Deer, Elk, Bear, Turkey	Disposal Stations
	Overnight in Boat Permitted Anywhere	Cave Exploration	

U.S.F.S. CAMPGROUNDS: SACRAMENTO RIVER ARM

At Salt Creek:

1/2 Mile W - Nelson Point - 9 Primitive Tent/R.V. Sites to 40 feet
3 Miles NE - Gregory Creek - 18 Tent/R.V. Sites to 30 feet
Gregory Beach - Primitive Shoreline Camp Sites for Tent/R.V.s to 40 feet
Lower Salt Creek - Primitive Shoreline Camp Sites

At Lakehead:

1.7 Miles S - Antlers - 41 Single & 18 Double Tent/R.V. Sites to 40 feet - Reservations Accepted
Launch Ramp, Adjacent to Resort with Full Facilities
2.5 Miles S - Lakeshore - 20 Single & 6 Double Tent/R.V. Sites to 35 feet - Reservations Accepted
Adjacent to Resort with Full Facilities
4.6 Miles S - Beehive - Primitive Shoreline Camp Sites for Tent/R.V.s to 40 feet

PUBLIC LAUNCH RAMPS are located at Antlers, Sugarloaf, Centimudi, Hirz Bay, Bailey Cove, Packers Bay & Jones Valley

BOAT ACCESS ONLY CAMPING

Pit River Arm: Arbuckle Flat - 11 Sites, Ski Island - 29 Sites with Water
McCloud River Arm: Green Creek - 11 Sites
Sacramento River Arm: Gooseneck Cove - 10 Sites
Boat Launch Area Fees: $6 per Boat up to 29 feet, $15 for 30+ feet

DISPERSED CAMPING:

Jones Valley Inlet, Mariner's Point, Gregory Beach, Beehive - $6 - $8 Parking Fee per Night per Vehicle
Contact Shasta Recreation Company for Further Information - Ph: (530) 238-2824

SOME FACILITIES: See Map for Numbered Locations - (in Circles)
(Prices Vary - Call for Current Information)

1   **ANTLER'S RV PARK N CAMPGROUND** - P.O. Box 127, Lakehead 96051, Ph: (530) 238-2322 or (800) 642-6849
Campsites, Hookups, Showers, Laundry, Store, Snack Bar, Bait & Tackle, Swimming Pool.

1   **ANTLER MARINA RESORT** - P.O. Box 140, Lakehead 96051, Ph: (530) 238-2553 or (800) 238-3924 - Full Service Marina, Bait & Tackle, Fuel, Moorage, Ice, Conference Room for Rent, Cabins, Swimming Pool for Cabin Guests, Rentals: Houseboats, Sea Doos, Ski Boats & Competition Ski Boats.

2   **BRIDGE BAY RESORT** - 10300 Bridge Bay Road, Redding 96003, Ph: (530) 275-3021 or (800) 752-9669 - Full Service Marina, Ramp, Boat & Personal Watercraft Rentals, Motel, Restaurant, Lounge, General Store, Bait & Tackle, Swimming Pool.

3   **DIGGER BAY MARINA** - P.O. Box 1516, Central Valley 96019, Ph: (530) 275-3072 or (800) 752-9669 - Full Service Marina, Ramp, Boat & Personal Watercraft Rentals, General Store, Bait & Tackle, Gas, Private Moorage.

4   **HOLIDAY HARBOR RESORT** - P.O. Box 112, O'Brien 96070, Ph: (530) 238-2383 or (800) 776-BOAT - Full Service Marina, Ramp, Restaurant, Campsites, Hookups, Showers, General Store, Gas, All Types of Boat Rentals Including Houseboats, Jets, Parasailing.

5   **JONES VALLEY RESORT** - 22300 Jones Valley Marina Dr., Redding 96003, Ph: (800) 223-7950 - Full Service Marina, General Store, Bait & Tackle, Boat Rentals from Luxury Houseboats to Jet Skis, Gas.

6   **KAMPLOOPS CAMP** - Via Boat from Hirz Bay, P. O. Box 90133, Redding 96099, Ph: (530) 238-2472 - Campsites, Showers, Group Camps Available with Cook Shack, Equipment Included, Docks, Seasonal.

7   **LAKEHEAD CAMPGROUND and R.V. PARK** - 20999 Antlers Rd., P.O. Box 646, Lakehead 96051, Ph: (530) 238-8450, Campsites, Hookups, Laundry, Disposal Station, Showers, General Store, Swimming Pool, Basketball, Ping-Pong, Horseshoes, Volleyball, Pavilion for Groups.

...Continued...

SHASTA LAKE.............Continued

8 **LAKESHORE RESORT & MARINA - 20479 Lakeshore Dr., Lakehead 96051, Ph: (530) 238-2301** - Full Service Marina, Cabins, Restaurant & Lounge, Campsites, Hookups, Showers, General Store, Bait & Tackle, Swimming Pool, Gas, Camp Supplies, Rentals: Houseboats, Patio, Fishing & Ski Boats, Personal Watercraft.

9 **LAKE SHORE VILLA R. V. PARK - 20672 Lakeshore Dr., Lakehead 96051, Ph: (800) 238-8688** - 92 R.V. Sites, Full Hookups, 15 Pull Throughs over 70 Feet Plus, Laundry, Disposal Station, Showers, Docks, Cable T.V.

10 **LAKEVIEW MARINA RESORT - P.O. Box 992272, Redding 96099, Ph: (530) 223-3003 -** Full Service Marina, Private Boat Ramp, Rentals: Housboats, Fishing & Ski Boats, Patio Boat, PWC's, General Store, Ice, Bait & Tackle.

11 **PACKER'S BAY MARINA - P. O. Box 1105, Bella Vista 96008, Ph: (800) 331-3137 or (530) 275-5570** Boat Ramp, Houseboat Rentals, Boat Gas, Ice.

12 **SHASTA LAKE R.V. RESORT & CAMPGROUND - P.O. Box 450, 20433 Lakeshore Dr., Lakehead 96051, Ph: (800) 3-SHASTA or (530) 238-2370 -** 53 Full Hookup R.V. Sites, Secluded Tent Sites, On-Site Trailer Rentals, Store, Hot Showers, Laundry, Swimming Pool, Private Boat Dock.

13 **SHASTA MARINA RESORT - 18390 O'Brien Inlet Rd., Lakehead 96051, Ph: (800) 959-3359** - Full Service Marina, Boat Ramp, Gas, General Store, Bait & Tackle, Rentals: Houseboats, Patio, Ski & Fishing Boats, Moorage, Open All Year.

14 **SILVERTHORN RESORT - P.O. Box 1090, Bella Vista 96008, Ph: (530) 275-1571 -** Full Service Marina, Boat Ramp, Houseboats, Cabins, Rentals: Patio, Ski & Fishing Boats & Personal Watercraft, Pizza and Pub, Grocery Store.

15 **SALT CREEK RV PARK & CAMPGROUND - 19663 Solus Campground Rd., Lakehead 96051, Ph: (800) 954-1824 or (530) 238-8500** - 50 Campsites, 27 Full Hookups, Pull Throughs, Laundry, Showers, Pool, Playground, Store, Cabin, Video Game Room, Storage, Monthly Rental Space Available.

16 **SUGARLOAF COTTAGES - 19667 Lakeshore Dr., P.O. Box 768, Lakehead 96051, Ph: (530) 238-2448** - Lakeside Cabins, Free Moorage on Private Dock, Pool, Playground, Basketball, Volleyball.

17 **SUGARLOAF MARINA & RESORT, 19671 Lakeshore Dr., Lakehead 96051, Ph: (530) 238-2711** - Full Service Marina, Launch Ramp, General Store, Bait & Tackle, Fuel, Houseboats & Personal Watercraft Rentals.

18 **TRAIL IN Campground and Store, 19765 Gregory Creek Rd., Lakehead 96051, Ph: (530) 238-8533 -** Pull Through Campsites, Hookups, Pool, Laundry, Showers, Mini-Market, Playground, Bait & Tackle, R.V. Supplies.

19 **TSASDI RESORT - 19990 Lakeshore Dr., Lakehead 96051, Ph: (800) 995-0291 or (530) 238-2575** - Cabins, Cable TV, General Store, Bait, Heated Swimming Pool, Free Boat Slip on Private Dock, Playground.

*Full Service Marina = Boat Rentals, Moorage & Boat Gas

For Regional Information and Free Brochure
Ph: (800) 8-SHASTA

Shasta Recreation Company
14538 Wonderland Blvd., Mountain Gate 96003
Ph: (530) 275-8113

Shasta Lake Business Owners Association
P. O. Box 709
Lakehead 96051

MANZANITA, BUTTE, SUMMIT and JUNIPER LAKES and McCUMBER RESERVOIR

Manzanita, Butte, Summit and Juniper Lakes are within the 106,000 acre expanse of Lassen Volcanic National Park. There are over 150 miles of trails including a part of the Pacific Crest Trail for the hiker, backpacker and equestrian. Pets and vehicles are not allowed on trails. Pack and saddle stock must overnight in corrals by prior reservation and must have a Wilderness Permit for day use. Grazing is not permittted so you must pack in feed. The Lakes listed outside the Park boundaries are good fishing spots. McCumber Reservoir, Grace and Nora are P.G. & E. Lakes off Highway 44 while Diamond and Pear Lakes are reached by primitive roads south of Mineral.

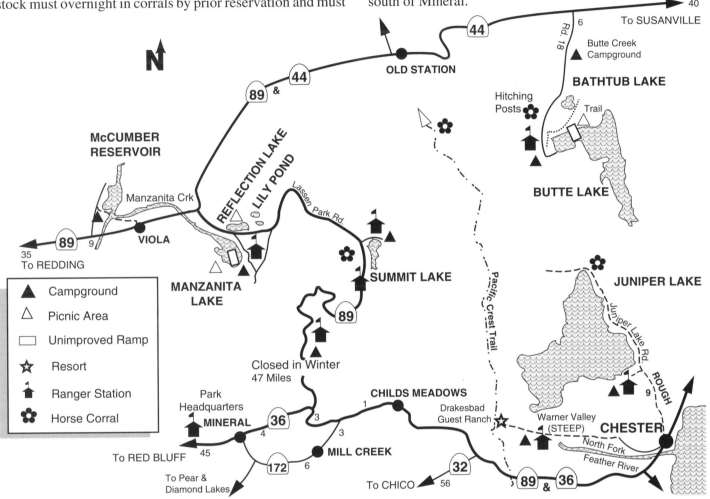

▲	Campground		
△	Picnic Area		
▭	Unimproved Ramp		
☆	Resort		
🔼	Ranger Station		
✿	Horse Corral		

INFORMATION: Lassen Volcanic National Park, P.O. Box 100, Mineral 96063—Ph: (530) 595-4444

CAMPING	BOATING	RECREATION	OTHER

Manzanita: 179 Sites
    Tents & R.V.s: $14
Summit: 94 Sites
    Tents & R.V.s: $12 - $14
Juniper: 18 Sites
    Tents Only: $10
    No Running Water
	No Power Motors
	Row, Sail, Windsurf
	    & Inflatables Only
	Unimproved
	    Launch Ramps:
	    Manzanita & Butte Only
		Fishing: Rainbow, Brook
		    & Brown Trout
		Manzanita:
		    Catch & Release
		    With Barbless Hooks Only
		Juniper: *No Fishing*
		Swimming - Picnicking
		Hiking, Backpacking
		Horseback Riding
		    Trails & Corrals
		Campfire Programs:
		    Summit & Manzanita
		    Lakes
			For Lodging Contact:
			    Lassen Volcanic
			    National Park
			
			P.G. & E.
			    Ph: (916) 386-5164
			McCumber Reservoir
			    7 Tent Sites
			    5 Walk-In Sites
			    Fee: $15
			
			No ORV's

CRATER, CARIBOU and SILVER LAKES

These Lakes are located in the Lassen National Forest. Crater Lake, at 6,800 feet elevation, has a surface area of 27 acres. This volcanic crater offers excellent fishing for trout. The Lakes near Silver Lake border the Caribou Wilderness, a gently rolling, forested plateau which can easily be explored by the hiker, backpacker or equestrian. Silver Lake and its neighbor, Caribou Lake, provide a quiet remote area for the small boater, camper and fisherman. The roads are dirt and rough, especially into Crater Lake, so large trailers are not advised.

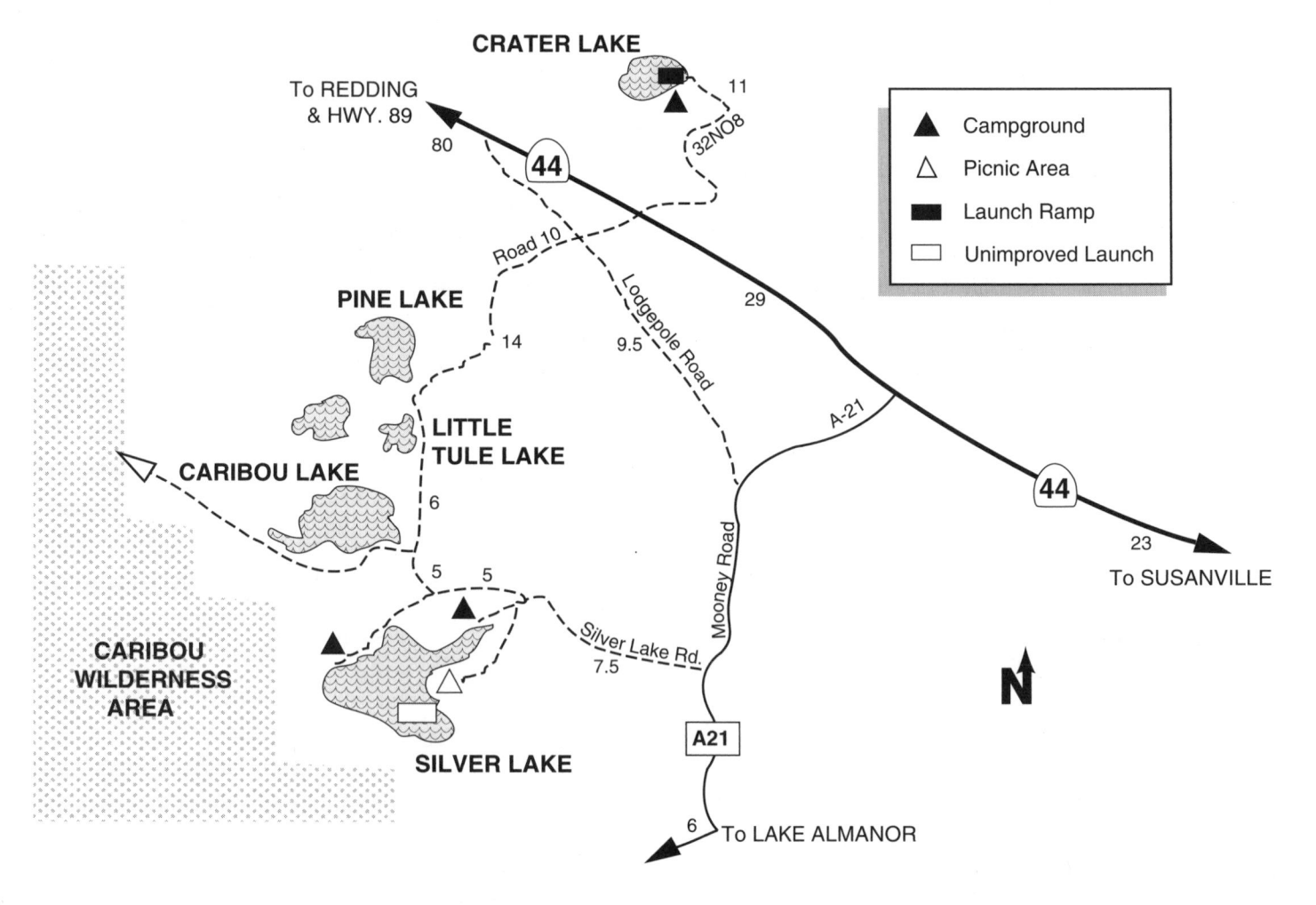

INFORMATION: Almanor Ranger District, P.O. Box 767, Chester 90620—(530) 258-2141			
CAMPING	**BOATING**	**RECREATION**	**OTHER**

Silver Lake:
   Rocky Knoll:
      7 Tent Sites
      11 Tent/R.V. Sites
      Fee: $10
   Silver Bowl:
      18 Tent/R.V. Sites
      Fee: $10
Crater Lake:
   17 Tent/R.V. Sites
   Fee: $12
   R.V.s Under 16 Feet
	Silver & Caribou Lakes:
	   Cartop Boats
	   Hand Launch Only
	
	Crater Lake:
	   No Gas Motors
	   Allowed
	   Launch Ramp
		Fishing: Rainbow
		   Trout
		Picnicking
		Swimming
		Hiking & Equestrian Trails
		Backpacking
		Hunting: Antelope, Deer,
		   Rabbit, Quail & Grouse
			Crater Lake Campground:
			Eagle Lake Ranger District
			477-050 Eagle
			Lake Rd.
			Susanville 96130
			(530) 257-4188

EAGLE LAKE

Eagle Lake is at an elevation of 5,104 feet in the Lassen National Forest. With a surface area of 27,000 acres and over 100 miles of timbered shoreline, it is the second largest natural Lake in California. The slightly alkaline water is the natural habitat for the famous Eagle Lake trout, a favorite of the fisherman for its size of 3 pounds or better. The water is warm and clear. There are 4 Forest Service campgrounds and 2 group campgrounds amid tall pines. Full hookups for R.V.s are located at Eagle Lake Park and Mariners Resort. McCoy Flat is a small Reservoir for fishing with brown and rainbow trout. *Contact USFS to check condition of McCoy as it may be dry.*

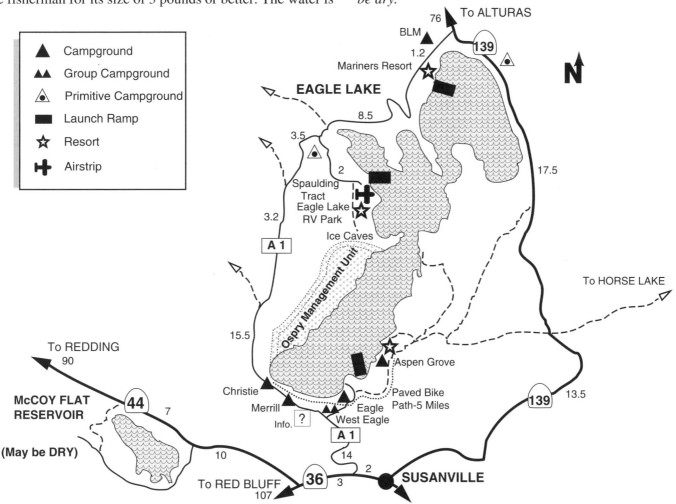

Legend:
- ▲ Campground
- ▲▲ Group Campground
- ⊙ Primitive Campground
- ▬ Launch Ramp
- ☆ Resort
- ✚ Airstrip

INFORMATION: Eagle Lake Ranger District, 477-050 Eagle Lake Rd., Susanville 96130—Ph: (530) 257-4188

CAMPING	BOATING	RECREATION	OTHER
300 Dev. Sites for Tents & R.V.s 11 Multiple Sites Reserve: Ph: (877) 444-6777 2 Group Camps #1 - 100 People #2 - 75 People Aspen Grove: 25 Dev. Sites for Tents Bureau of Land Management: 17 Dev. Sites	Power, Row, Canoe, Sail, Waterski, Jets, Windsurfing, Inflatables Launch Ramps Rentals: Fishing Boats & Motors, Pontoons Docks, Moorings, Berths	Fishing: Eagle Lake Trout Swimming Picnicking Hiking Nature Trails 5 Mile Paved Bicycle Path Campfire Programs Hunting: Deer & Waterfowl Birdwatching: Bald Eagles, Osprey, Grebes, Pelicans Airstrip	Mariners Resort 509 - 725 Stone Rd. Susanville 96130 Ph: (530) 825-3333 82 Full Hookups Cabins, Grocery Store Restaurant/Lounge Eagle Lake R.V. Park 687-125 Palmetto Way Susanville 96130 Ph: (530) 825-3133 46 Full Hookups Cabins & Grocery Store

RUTH LAKE

Ruth Lake is half way between Eureka and Red Bluff on Highway 36 within the boundaries of the Six Rivers National Forest. This is quite a drive on a narrow road at times but well worth the trip if you plan to stay awhile in this remote area. The Lake rests at an elevation of 2,654 feet and has a surface area of 1,200 acres. It was formed by damming the Mad River in 1962. This is now a popular recreation facility offering boating of all kinds, fishing and camping. The Mad River flows into and out of Ruth Lake and can provide good steelhead fishing. Call Ruth Lake Community Services for additional information.

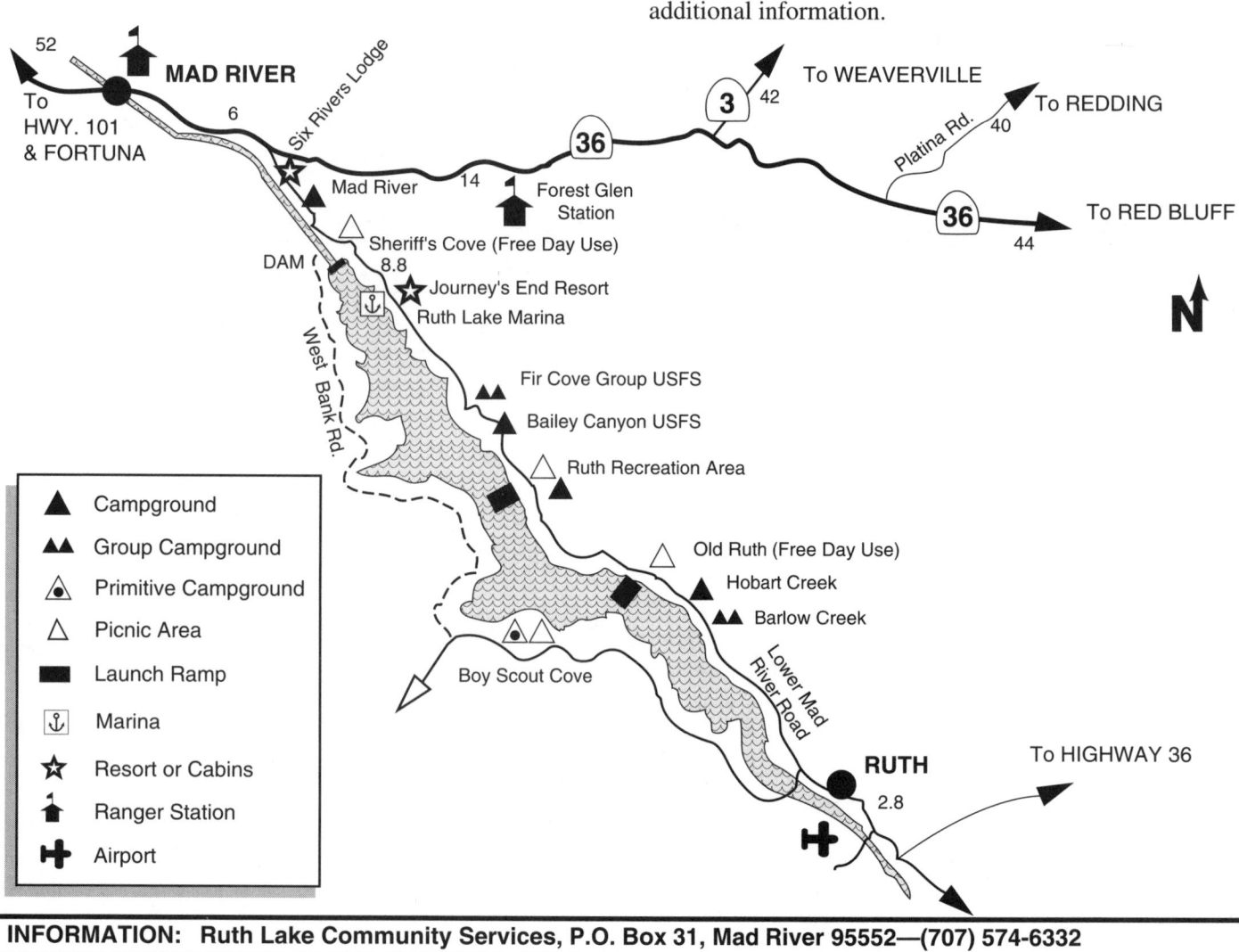

CAMPING	BOATING	RECREATION	OTHER

U.S.F.S.
  81 Dev. Sites for
  Tents & R.V.s
  Fee: $12
  1 Group Site - Reserve:
  (707) 574-6233
Ruth Lake Community
  85 Dev. Sites
  for Tents & R.V.s
  Fee: $13 per car
Barlow Group Camp &
  Picnic Area
Reserve: (800) 500-0285
	Power, Row, Canoe,
	  Sail, Waterski, Jets,
	  Windsurf & Inflatables
	Full Service Marina
	  Ph: (707) 574-6524
	Launch Ramps - Free
	Rentals: Fishing Boats &
	  Motors, Waterski
	  Boats & Pontoon
	Docks, Moorings, Slips
	  Boat Storage
		Fishing: Rainbow
		  Trout, Kokanee Salmon,
		  Large & Smallmouth
		  Bass, Catfish
		Picnicking
		Hiking
		Horseback Riding
		Wildlife Viewing
		Hunting: Bear, Boar, Deer,
		  Duck, Quail, Grouse,
		  Wild Turkey
			Annual Events
			  May:
			  Trap Shoot,
			  Kids Fishing Derby
			  Bass Tournaments
			
			  August:
			  Rodeo &
			  Summer Festival
			
			1st Sunday Each Month:
			  Community Breakfast

INFORMATION: Ruth Lake Community Services, P.O. Box 31, Mad River 95552—(707) 574-6332

Round Valley Reservoir, also known as Bidwell Lake, is at an elevation of 4,500 feet in the Plumas National Forest. Located 3 miles south of Greenville, this small, secluded Lake is the water supply for Greenville so water sports are limited to fishing. Body contact with the water is not permit-ted. Famous for black bass, Round Valley is an excellent warm water fishery. Good hiking, mountain biking, equestrian and nature study trails are numerous. Birdwatchers will enjoy over 100 species that reside in the area. Campsites are available at Greenville, Crescent Mills and Taylorsville.

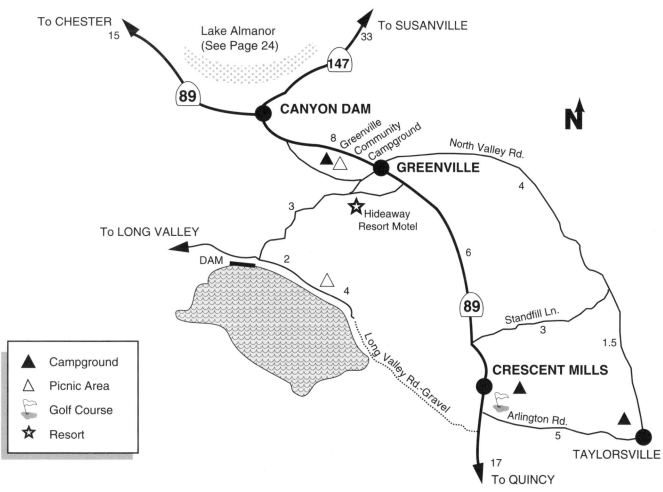

CAMPGROUND SYMBOL	
▲	Campground
△	Picnic Area
⛳	Golf Course
☆	Resort

INFORMATION: Plumas County Visitors Bureau, 550 Crescent St., Quincy 95971—Ph: (800) 326-2247

CAMPING	BOATING	RECREATION	OTHER
Greenville Community Campground Ph: (530) 284-7224 18 Dev. Sites for Tents & R.V.s Taylorsville Community Campground Ph: (530) 284-6646 24 Dev. Sites for Tents & R.V.s	Call Round Valley Lake for Current Info: Ph: (530) 258-7751	Fishing: Black Bass, Catfish & Bluegill Picnicking No Swimming 1 Mile Self-Guided Nature Walk at Dam Hiking Trails Mountain Bike Trails Equestrian Trails Bird Watching including Bald Eagle & Osprey	Hideaway Resort Motel Ph: (530) 284-7915 Spring Meadow Motel Ph: (530) 284-6768 Oak Grove Motor Lodge Ph: (530) 284-6671 Indian Valley Chamber of Commerce Ph: (530) 284-6633

LAKE ALMANOR

Lake Almanor rests at an elevation of 4,500 feet in the Lassen National Forest. There is an abundance of pine-sheltered campgrounds operated by P.G. & E., the Forest Service and private resorts. The Lake is 13 miles long and 6 miles wide with a surface area of 28,000 acres. It is one of the largest man-made Lakes in California. Almanor's clear, blue waters offer complete boating facilities. Caution is advised because small islands are exposed during low water levels. Gusty winds can also make boating hazardous. Fishing can be excellent for a variety of species in the Lake. Nearby streams are also productive. Mountain Meadow Reservoir is a small fishing Lake in a scenic area near Westwood. There are no facilities but it is surrounded by numerous hiking and equestrian trails.

....Continued....

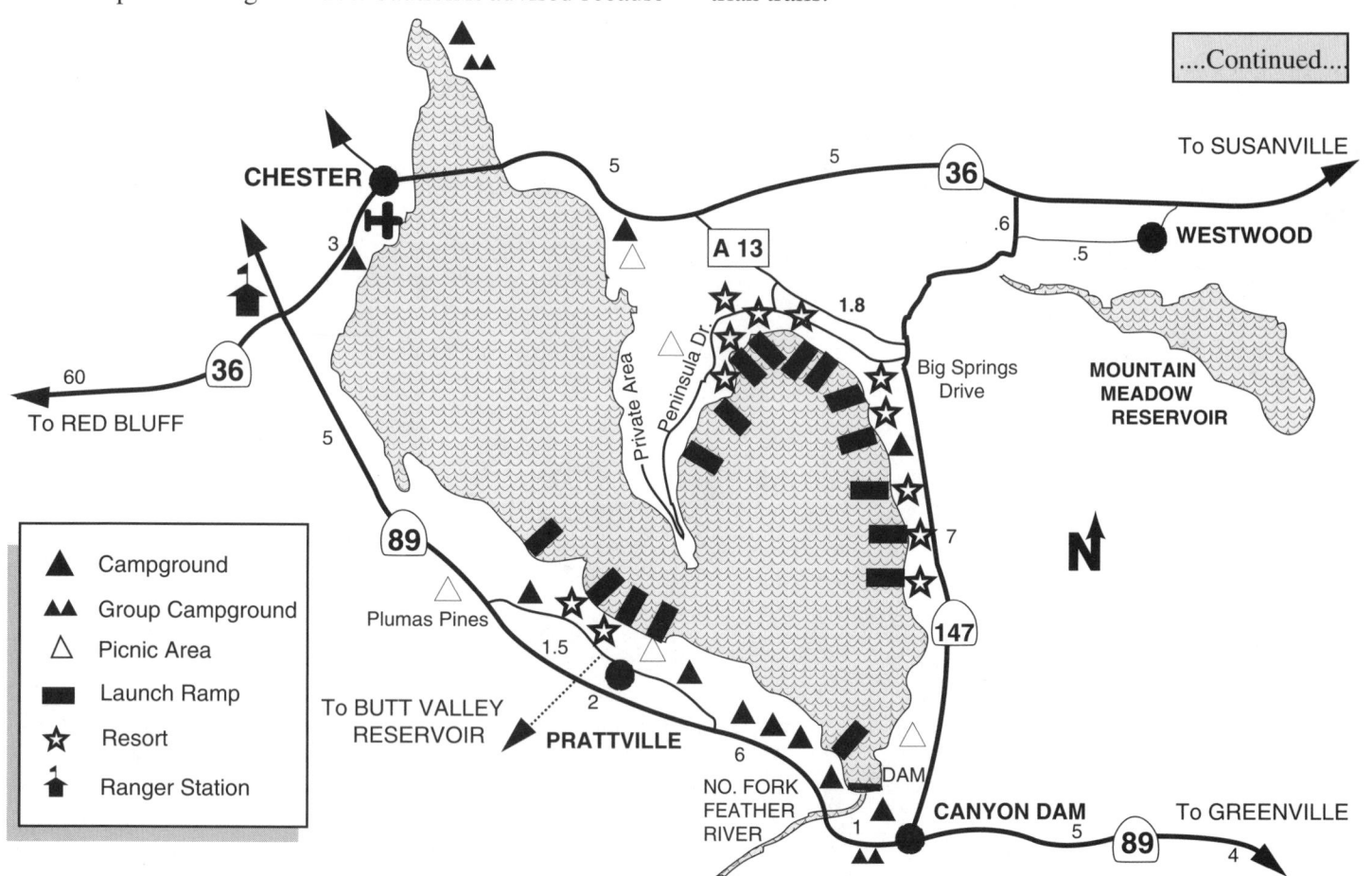

INFORMATION: P. G. & E. Land Projects, 2730 Gateway Oaks Dr., Sacramento 95833–Ph: (916) 386-5164			
CAMPING	**BOATING**	**RECREATION**	**OTHER**
P.G. & E.: 131 Dev. Sites for Tents & R.V.s Fee - $15 Plus 30 Overflow Sites Group Camp to 50 People Maximum U. S. F. S.: 101 Dev. Sites for Tents & R.V.s Fee: $14 *Private Campgrounds See Following Page*	Power, Row, Canoe, Sail, Waterski, Jets, Inflatables Full Service Marinas Launch Ramps Rentals: Fishing, Canoe, Patio & Ski Boats, Docks, Berths, Gas	Fishing: Rainbow & Brown Trout, Smallmouth Bass, Catfish & King Salmon Fishing Guides Swimming Picnicking Hiking Equestrian Trails Golf Hunting: Deer, Waterfowl	Cabins & Motels Snack Bars Restaurants Grocery Stores Bait & Tackle Laundromats Disposal Stations Gas Stations Plumas County Visitors Bureau Ph: (800) 326-2247

P.G.&E. CAMPGROUNDS - (916) 386-5164
Lake Almanor Campground - Off Highway 89 Westshore.
161 Tent/R.V. Sites - First Come, First Served
Yellow Creek Campground - Off Highway 89 Westshore.
10 Tent/RV Sites near Soda Springs Historic Site.
Camp Conery Group Camp - Off Highway 89 East of Dam.
50 People Maximum, Multi-purpose Utility Building with Cook Area, Grill, Refrigeration, Showers
and 5 Bunk Houses, Swimming Beach and Picnic Area - Reservations Only.
Last Chance Creek Campground - 4 miles northeast of Chester on Juniper Lake Road.
13 Tent/R.V. Group Sites - Reservations Only & 12 Tent/R.V. Family Sites, Horse Camping.

U. S. FOREST SERVICE - ALMANOR RANGER DISTRICT
P. O. Box 767, Chester 96020, Ph: (530) 258-2141
Reservations: (877) 444-6777
Almanor Campground - Off Highway 89 West Shore.
15 Tent Only Sites, 86 Tent/R.V. Sites to 22 Feet, Handicapped Facilities.
Almanor Group Camp - Off Highway 89 West Shore. Groups to 100 People by Reservation Only.

SOME PRIVATE RESORTS - Call for Current Prices

Plumas Pines Resort - 3000 Almanor Dr. West, Canyon Dam 95923, Ph: (530) 259-4343 - R.V. Sites with Full Hookups, No Tent Camping, Motel, Housekeeping Cottages, Laundromat, Boathouse, BBQ Grill, Marina, Boat Launch, Parasailing, Sailboat Regattas.

Knotty Pine Resort & Marina - 430 Peninsula Dr., Lake Almanor 96137, Ph: (530) 596-3348 - R.V. Sites with Full Hookups, Fully Equipped Log Cabins, Full Service Marina, Boat Rentals, Launch Ramp, Boat Slip Rentals.

Almanor Lakeside Resort - 300 Peninsula Dr., Lake Almanor 96137, Ph: (530) 596-3959 - 9 Housekeeping Units with Kitchens, Marina for Guests, Picnic & BBQ, Restaurant & Groceries Nearby - NO pets.

Northshore Campground - P.O. Box 1102, Chester 96020, Ph: (530) 258-3376 - 36 Tent Sites, 89 R.V. Sites, Water & Electric Hookups, Disposal Station, Laundromat, General Store, Library, Boat Rentals, Propane, Launch & Dock Facilities.

Lake Almanor Resort - 2706 Big Springs Rd., Lake Almanor 96137, Ph: (530) 596-3337 - 13 R.V. Sites, Full Hookups with Cable TV, 5 Cabins, Lodge with 8 Housekeeping Units, Showers, Laundry, Launch Ramp, Docks, Limited Boat Rentals, Grass Lawns with Group Barbercues, General Store, Bait & Tackle .

Lake Cove Resort and Marina - 3584 Highway 147, Lake Almanor 96137, Ph: (530) 284-7697 - 55 R.V. Sites, Full & Partial Hookups, Disposal Station, Showers, Laundry, Ramp, Slips, Rental Boats, General Store, Bait & Tackle, Propane

Lassen View Resort - 7457 Hwy. 147, Lake Almanor 96137, Ph: (530) 596-3437 - 45 R.V. Sites, 14 Tent Sites, Showers, Cabins, Snack Bar, General Store, Marina, Fuel Dock, Boat Rentals.

Little Norway Resort - 432 Peninsula Dr., Lake Almanor 96137, Ph: (530) 596-3225 - Cabins, Full Service Marina, Fishing, Ski, Pontoon and Wave Runner Rentals.

Wilson's Camp Prattville - 2932 Lake Almanor Dr. West, Canyondam 95923, Ph: (530) 259-2267 - 32 R.V. Sites, Full Hookups, Showers, 5 Cabins, Marina, Ramp, Docks, Cafe, General Store, Bait & Tackle.

The above are a random selection of facilities around the Lake. For additional information contact:
Chester - Lake Almanor Chamber of Commerce - (530) 258-2426 ..... or
Plumas Visitors Bureau - (800) 326-2247

BUTT VALLEY RESERVOIR

Butt Valley Reservoir rests at an elevation of 4,150 feet in the Lassen National Forest. This picturesque mountain Lake is five miles long and three-quarters of a mile at its widest point. It is connected to Lake Almanor by a tunnel. Butt Valley Reservoir is the second level of P.G. & E.'s "stairway of power" which flows down the Feather River into Lake Oroville. This is a nice boating Lake although marina facilities are limited to a launch ramp. There is a good fishery for planted rainbows as well as native brown and rainbow trout. The campground and picnic areas are under the jurisdiction of P.G. & E.

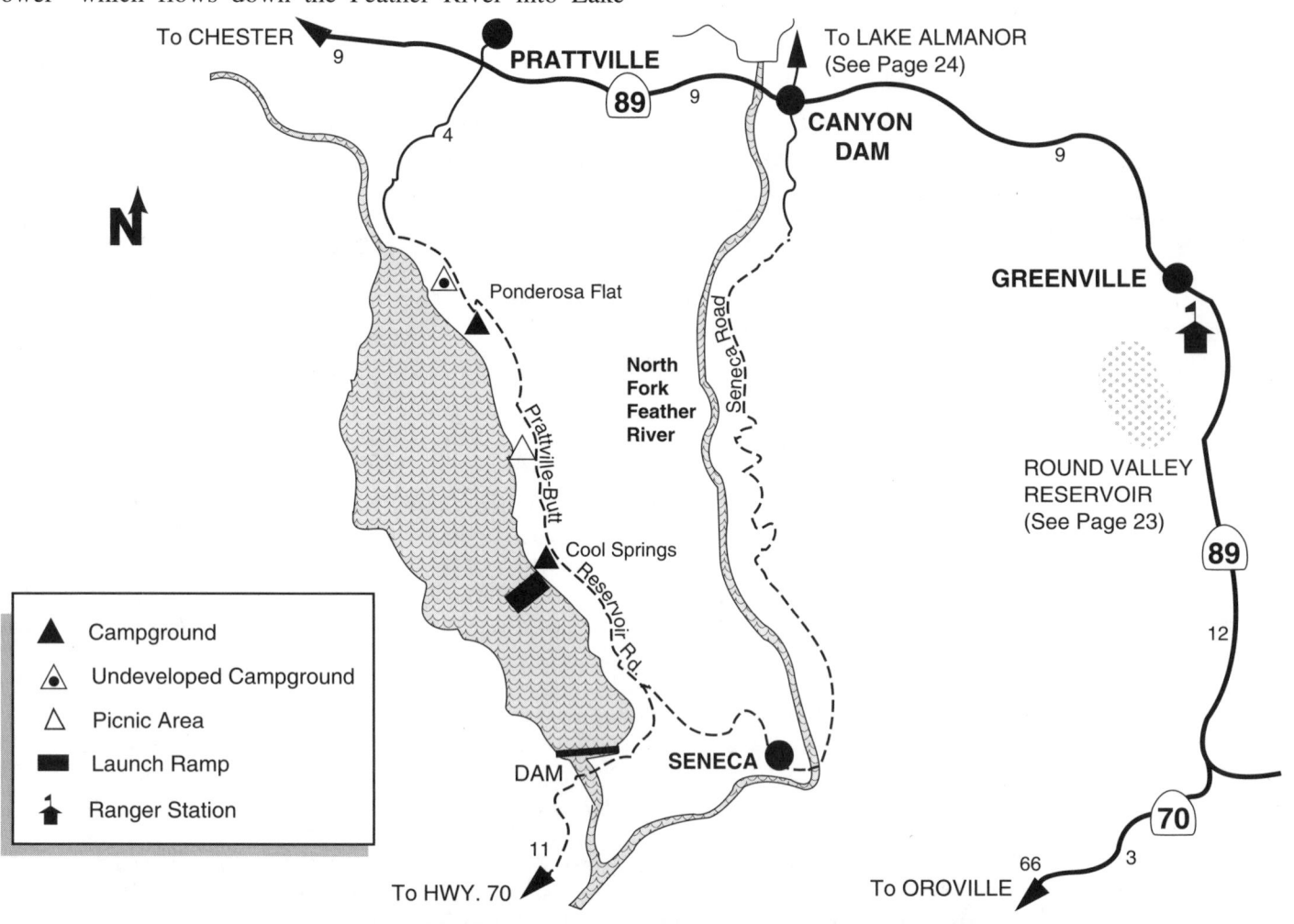

INFORMATION: P.G. & E. Land Projects, 2730 Gateway Oaks Dr., Sacramento 95833–Ph: (916) 386-5164

CAMPING	BOATING	RECREATION	OTHER
Cool Springs: 　30 Sites for Tents 　& R.V.s 　Fee: $15 Ponderosa Flat: 　63 Sites for Tents 　& R.V.s 　Fee: $15 Ponderosa Flat Overflow: 　20 Sites 　Fee: $15	Open to All Boating Launch Ramp No Waterskiing	Fishing: Rainbow & 　Brown Trout, Catfish Picnicking Swimming Hiking Nature Study Hunting: Waterfowl & Deer Horseback Riding	Full Facilities in Chester 　9 Miles Plumas County 　Visitors Bureau 　Ph: (800) 326-2247

The Antelope Lake Recreation Area rests at an elevation of 5,000 feet in the Plumas National Forest. The Lake has 15 miles of timbered shoreline and a surface area of 930 acres. The sheltered coves and islands make this beautiful Lake a boating haven. Forest Service campgrounds provide the camper with nice sites amid pine and fir trees. Good-sized Rainbow and Eagle Lake trout await the fisherman. Indian Creek, below the dam, has some large German Brown trout as well as Rainbows.

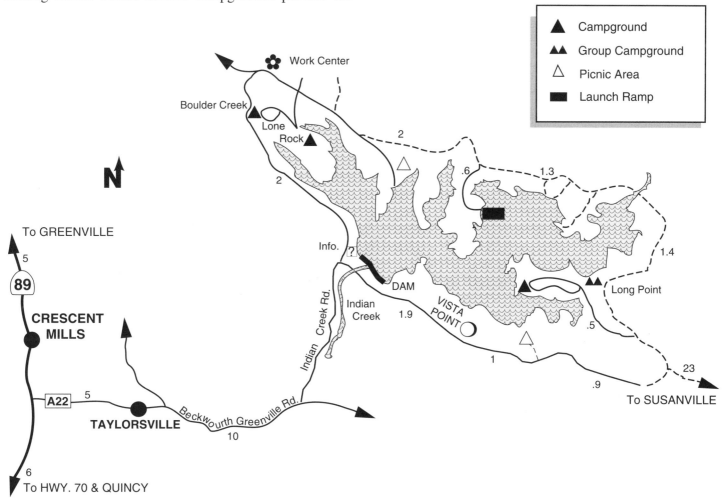

▲	Campground
▲▲	Group Campground
△	Picnic Area
■	Launch Ramp

INFORMATION: Mt. Hough Ranger District, 39696 State Highway 70, Quincy, 95971—Ph: (530) 283-0555

CAMPING	BOATING	RECREATION	OTHER
194 Dev. Sites for Tents & R.V.s Fee: $12 - $14 4 Dev. Sites - Can be used for Groups at Long Point Campground Reserve: (800) 280-CAMP	Power, Row, Canoe, Sail, Waterski, Windsurfing & Inflatables Launch Ramp	Fishing: Rainbow & German Brown Trout, Catfish & Largemouth Bass Swimming Hiking Nature Trail Campfire Programs Hunting: Deer	Grocery Store Bait & Tackle Disposal Station Full Facilities - 26 Miles at Taylorsville Plumas County Visitors Bureau P. O. Box 4120 Quincy 95971 Ph: (800) 326-2247

BENBOW LAKE

Benbow Lake State Recreation Area is at an elevation of 364 feet off Highway 101 in the Redwood Empire. This 230 acre Lake is created every summer by damming the South Fork of the Eel River. Boating is limited to small non-powered craft so this is a nice Lake for sailing and rowing. The California Department of Parks and Recreation maintains a 1,200 acre park with picnic areas, campgrounds and a swimming beach. The Benbow Inn, adjacent to the Lake, is a lovely old hotel and restaurant. The Benbow Valley R.V. Resort offers 112 campsites with full hook-ups, cable TV, swimming pool, jacuzzi and playgrounds. A 9-hole golf course is adjacent to the R.V. Park.

To GARBERVILLE 2.5

East Branch South Fork Eel River

Benbow Inn

Benbow Valley RV Resort

Off Ramp Benbow Dr.

N

DAM

Trails

Pratt Mill Site

Pioneer Trail Loop 2.8 Miles

101

Trails

1.5 Mile

South Fork Eel River

Entrance

Benbow Drive

101 4.2 To PIERCY

- ▲ Campground
- △ Picnic Area
- ■ Launch Ramp
- ☆ Resort

INFORMATION: Benbow Lake State Recreation Area, 1600 Hwy. 101, Garberville 95542—Ph: (707) 247-3318

CAMPING	BOATING	RECREATION	OTHER
State Park 77 Dev. Sites for Tents & Self-Contained Units including 2 Hookups Coin Showers Disposal Station Fee: $12 Hookups: $17 Reserve Ph: (800) 444-7275 Day Use - Fee: $2	Row, Sail, Canoe, Windsurfing & Inflatables No Motors Rentals: Canoes, Yak Boards Launch Ramp *Summer Only*	Fishing: Not Recommended in Summer due to Young Steelhead & Salmon Swimming Picnicking Hiking Nature Study Campfire Programs 9 Hole Golf Course	Benbow Valley R.V. Resort & Golf Course 7000 Benbow Dr. Garberville 95442 Ph: (707) 923-2777 112 R.V. Sites Full Hookups Fee: $33 - $48 Benbow Inn and Restaurant Ph: (707) 923-2124 Full Facilities in Garberville

Lake Cleone is at elevation of 20 feet within the MacKerricher State Park. This park along the scenic Mendocino Coast provides a variety of natural habitats including forests, wetlands, sand dunes and a 6-mile beach. Although swimming is not advised due to cold, turbulent waters, the 500 yard black, sandy beach is a popular attraction. Lake Cleone, 40 surface acres, is open to shallow draft non-powered boating. The angler can fish for trout and an occasional bass at the Lake. Steelhead and salmon are in nearby rivers. Surf fish, rock fish and ling cod can be caught in the ocean. Skin divers enjoy the nearby coves. Hikers and naturalists will find trails around the Lake and along the beach.

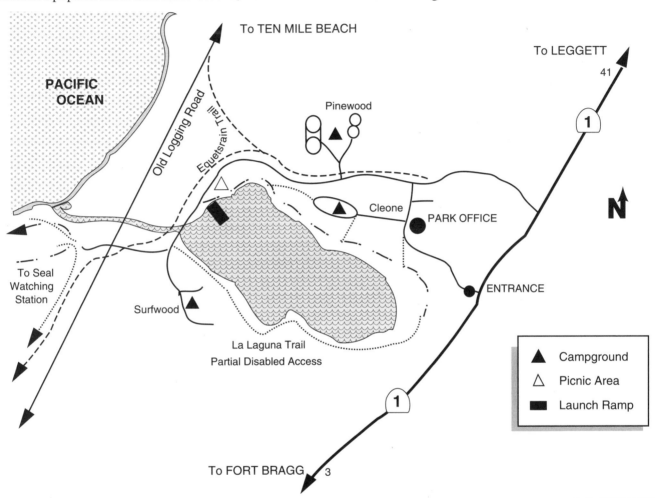

	Campground
△	Picnic Area
■	Launch Ramp

INFORMATION: MacKerricher State Park, P. O. Box 440, Mendocino 95460—Ph: (707) 937-5804

CAMPING	BOATING	RECREATION	OTHER
140 Dev. Sites for Tents & R.V.s to 35 Feet No Hookups Hot Showers Disposal Station Reserve: Ph: (800) 444-7275 10 Walk-In Camps	Open to Small, Shallow Draft, Non-Powered Boats Paved Launch Ramp	Fishing: Trout, Bass Picnicking Hiking & Nature Study Trails Disabled Access Trails Equestrian Trails Campfire Programs Bird Watching Beach Combing Skin Diving Seal Watching Station	Grocery Store Near Park Entrance Full Facilities at Fort Bragg

SNAG, PHILBROOK, De SABLA and PARADISE LAKES

These Lakes range in elevation from 3,000 feet at Paradise Lake to 5,000 feet at Philbrook Lake. Snag Lake does not have game fish but Philbrook is a good fishing Lake. Trailers, however, are not advised on this road. These two Lakes are part of the Lassen National Forest. P.G. & E. maintains a resort for its employees at De Sabla Reservoir but the public may fish for Rainbow and some Browns on the south and east sides of the Lake nearest Skyway Boulevard. A group picnic site is also available. Paradise Lake is popular for day use fishing. The angler will find planted rainbows, some brown trout, bass, and channel catfish. *Snag Lake is usually drained in mid-summer.*

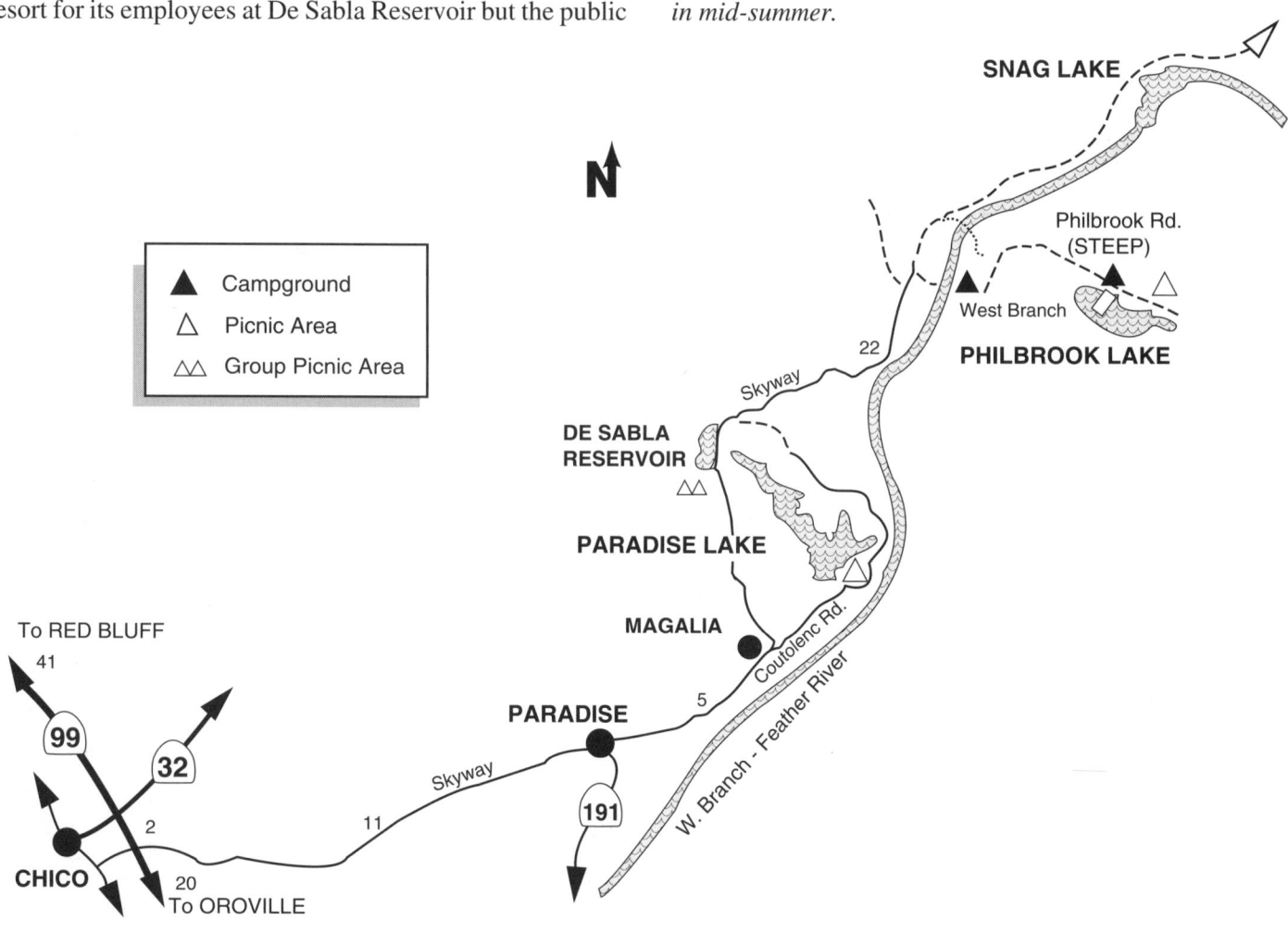

INFORMATION: Almanor Ranger District, P.O. Box 767, Chester 96020—Ph: (530) 258-2141			
CAMPING	**BOATING**	**RECREATION**	**OTHER**

U.S.F.S.
    West Branch
    15 Campsites
 	
P.G. & E.:
    Ph: (916) 386-5164
    Philbrook Lake
    20 Campsites
    Fee: $15
	Philbrook:
	    Cartop Launch Area
	    Fishing Access
	
	Paradise Lake:
	    Rowboats, Canoes &
	    Electric Motors
	    Minimal Facilities
	
	*Snag Lake is usually
	    Drained Mid-Summer*
		Fishing: Rainbow,
		    Brown & Eastern
		    Brook Trout, Small
		    & Largemouth Bass,
		    Channel Catfish
		Picnicking
		De Salba Reservoir:
		    Group Picnic Area
		    Reservations - PG&E:
		    Ph: (916) 386-5164
		Hiking & Backpacking
		Swimming - Philbrook
		    Lake Only
			Recreation Permits
			    and Fees are Required
			    at Paradise Lake

BUCKS, SILVER and SNAKE LAKES

The Bucks Lake Recreation Area in the Plumas National Forest is rich in wildlife and offers an abundance of outdoor recreation. Bucks Lake, at 5,155 feet elevation, has a surface area of 1,827 acres and holds State records for trout. There are facilities for all types of boating. Silver Lake, at 5,800 feet, offers excellent trout fishing. There is also good stream fishing. The Bucks Lake Wilderness Area of 24,000 acres and the Pacific Crest Trail welcome the hiker, horseback rider and backpacker to this area of gently rolling terrain, glaciated granite, forested meadows and perennial streams.

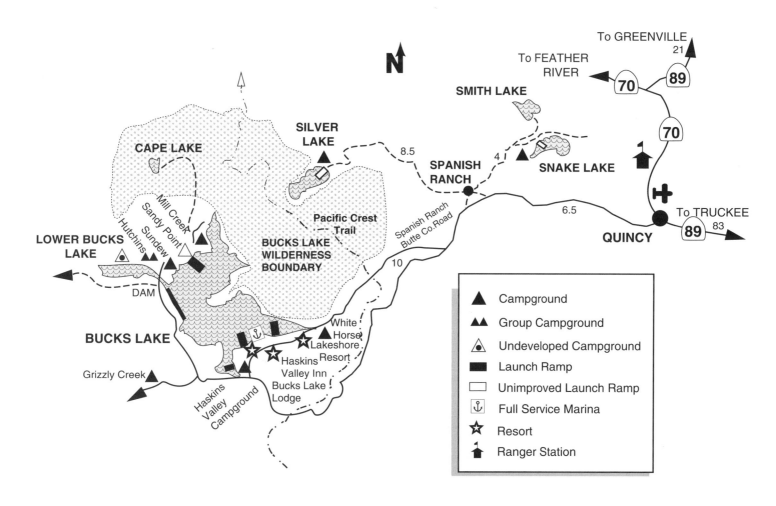

INFORMATION: Mt. Hough Ranger District, 39696 Highway 70, Quincy 95971—Ph: (530) 283-0555

CAMPING	BOATING	RECREATION	OTHER

U.S.F.S.
  64 Dev. Sites for
Tents & R.V.s to 22 feet
Plus Walk-in Sites
Hutchins Meadow:
  Reserve 3 Group Camps
    Ph: (877) 444-6777
P. G. & E.
  Ph: (916) 386-5164
Haskins Valley: 65 Dev.
  Sites for Tents & R.V.s
City of Santa Clara:
Grizzly Forebay: 7 Walk-Ins
	Bucks Lake:
	  Open to All Boats
	  Full Service Marina
	    64 Berths
	  Ph: (530) 283-4243
	  Rental Fishing Boats
	
	Silver Lake:
	  Rowboats & Canoes
	    Only
	  No Motors
	  Hand Launch
		Fishing: Rainbow,
		  German Brown,
		  Lake & Brook Trout,
		  Kokanee Salmon
		Swimming & Ski Beaches
		Hiking & Picnicking
		Backpacking [*Parking*]
		Horseback Riding
		  Trails & Rentals
		Hunting: Deer, Bear,
		  Rabbits, Waterfowl
			Lakeshore Resort
			  Ph: (530) 283-6900
			Tent & R.V. Sites-Hookups
			$12-$24 & Cabins on Lake
			  Restaurant & Bar, Marina
			Bucks Lake Lodge
			  Ph: (530) 283-2262
			  Cabins, Restaurant,
			  Store, Gas Station
			Haskins Valley Inn
			  Ph: (530) 283-9667
			Timberline Inn
			  Ph: (530) 283-2262

LAKE DAVIS

The Lake Davis Recreation Area is located in the Plumas National Forest, 7 miles north of Portola. The Lake is at an elevation of 5,775 feet and has a total surface area of 4,026 acres. A concessionaire, under permit from the Forest Service, maintains three campgrounds on the eastern shore of the Lake as well as launch ramps around the 32 miles of tree-covered shoreline. Steady winds make this an ideal Lake for sailing although afternoon winds can be a hazard for small craft. Lake Davis is open to all types of boating but water skiing is not permitted. There is a good warm water fishery along with an abundant population of both native and stocked trout. A threat to native trout and salmon are northern pike. The Department of Fish and Game are working to eliminate this problem. Call Beckwourth Ranger District for current information.

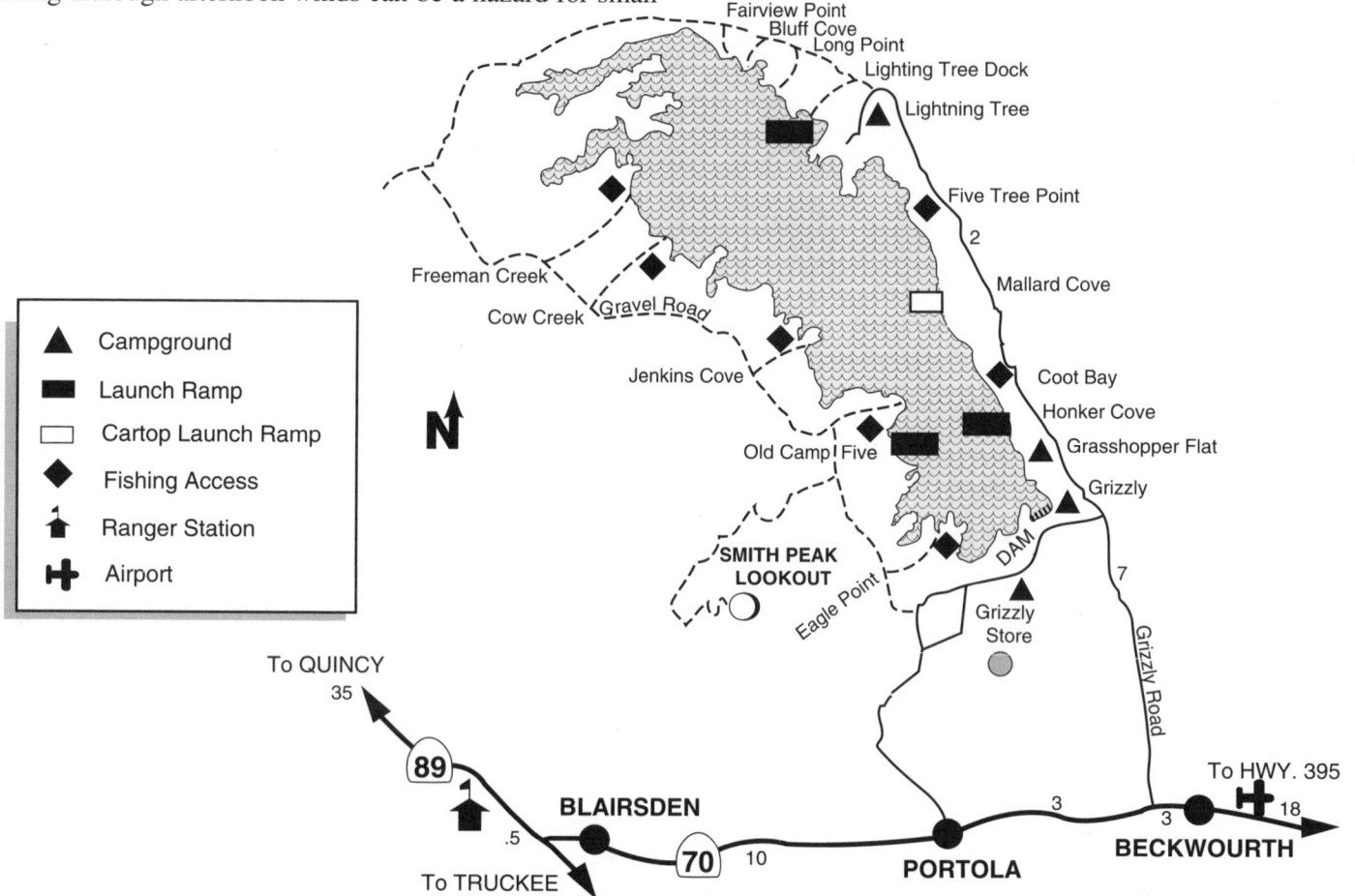

INFORMATION: Beckwourth Ranger District, Box 7, 23 Mohawk Rd., Blairsden 96103—Ph: (530) 836-2575

CAMPING	BOATING	RECREATION	OTHER
125 Dev. Sites for Tents & R.V.s Fee: $14	Power, Row, Canoe, Sail, Windsurf & Inflatables	Fishing: Rainbow, Brown, Eagle Lake, Kamloop Trout, Bass & Catfish	Grizzly Store & Camp P.O. Box 1498 Portola 96122
40 Sites for Self-Contained R.V.s Only: Nov. - April	*No Waterskiing or Jet Skis* Launch Ramps	Numerous Fishing Access Sites	Ph: (530) 832-0270 Store, Bait & Tackle
Disposal Station - Fee: $5 Reserve Above Sites: (877) 444-6777	Floating Boat Docks Cartop Boat Launch Areas Rentals: Fishing Boats	Swimming Picnicking Hiking	Propane & Firewood Boat Rentals R.V. & Boat Storage
Grizzly Camp: Ph: (530) 832-0270 34 Dev. Sites for Tents & R.V.s - Hookups Seasonal Rates	at Grizzly Store	Hunting: Deer, Waterfowl, Upland Game Birds Off Road Vehicles are Prohibited in Recreation Area	Airport & Full Facilities at Beckwourth

The Frenchman Recreation Area offers a variety of enjoyable outdoor activities from waterskiing to ice fishing in the winter. Frenchman Lake at an elevation of 5,588 feet, is within the Plumas National Forest. The 1,580 surface acres are surrounded by 21 miles of open sage and pine-dotted shoreline. There are five campgrounds managed by conces- sion permit from the Forest Service. There are also 15 picnic sites and 5 fishing access points around the Lake. All types of boats are permitted. Fishing is very good for rainbow and brook trout. This is a prime hunting area for the Rocky Mountain Mule Deer but it must be done beyond the bound- aries of the Recreation Area and the Game Refuge.

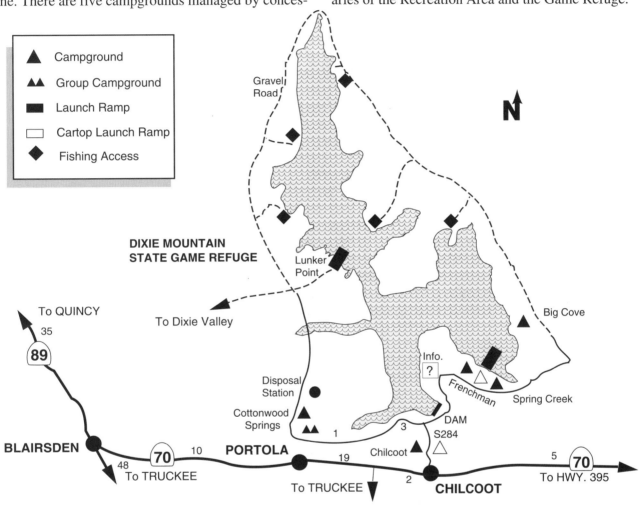

▲	Campground
▲▲	Group Campground
■	Launch Ramp
▢	Cartop Launch Ramp
◆	Fishing Access

INFORMATION: Beckwourth Ranger Dist. P.O. Box 7, 23 Mohawk Rd., Blairsden 96103—Ph: (530) 836-2575

CAMPING	BOATING	RECREATION	OTHER

Cottonwood Springs:
  20 Single Sites-Fee: $14
  2 Group Sites
    25 & 50 People Max.
    Fees: $44 & $87
Chilcoot: 5 Walk-in &
  35 Single Sites-Fee: $14
Spring Creek: 35 Sites - $14
Frenchman: 38 Sites - $14
Big Cove: 19 Singles - $14
  & 19 Double Sites - $28
Reserve:
  Ph: (877) 444-6777
	Power, Row, Canoe,
	  Sail, Waterski,
	  Jets, Windsurf,
	  Inflatables
	Launch Ramps
	
	*Check Current Water
	Levels*
		Fishing: Brown &
		  Rainbow Trout
		Swimming
		Picnicking: 15 Sites
		Hiking
		Backpacking [Parking]
		Hunting: Deer, Waterfowl,
		  Upland Game
		No Hunting on West Side
		of Lake in Game Refuge
			Supplies at Wiggens Store
			7 Miles in Chilcoot
			
			Handicapped Facilities
			Available at Lake
			
			*Off Road Vehicle Travel is
			Prohibited in Recreation
			Area*
			
			Plumas County
			Visitors Bureau
			Ph: (800) 326-2247

EAST PARK RESERVOIR - PLASKETT and LETTS LAKES

East Park Reservoir is operated by the Bureau of Reclamation. This warm water fishery is known for good bass fishing. All boating is allowed. Open primitive camping surrounds most of the Lake. Plaskett Lake, elevation 6,000 feet and Letts Lake at 4,500 feet, are within the boundaries of the Mendocino National Forest. These remote Lakes are good for trout fishing. Gas or electric powered boats are *not* allowed. Letts Lake is popular with hikers and backpackers who enjoy the Snow Mountain Wilderness. Summit Springs Trailhead is nearby. Trailers over 16 feet are not advised at Plaskett or Letts Lakes due to poor access roads.

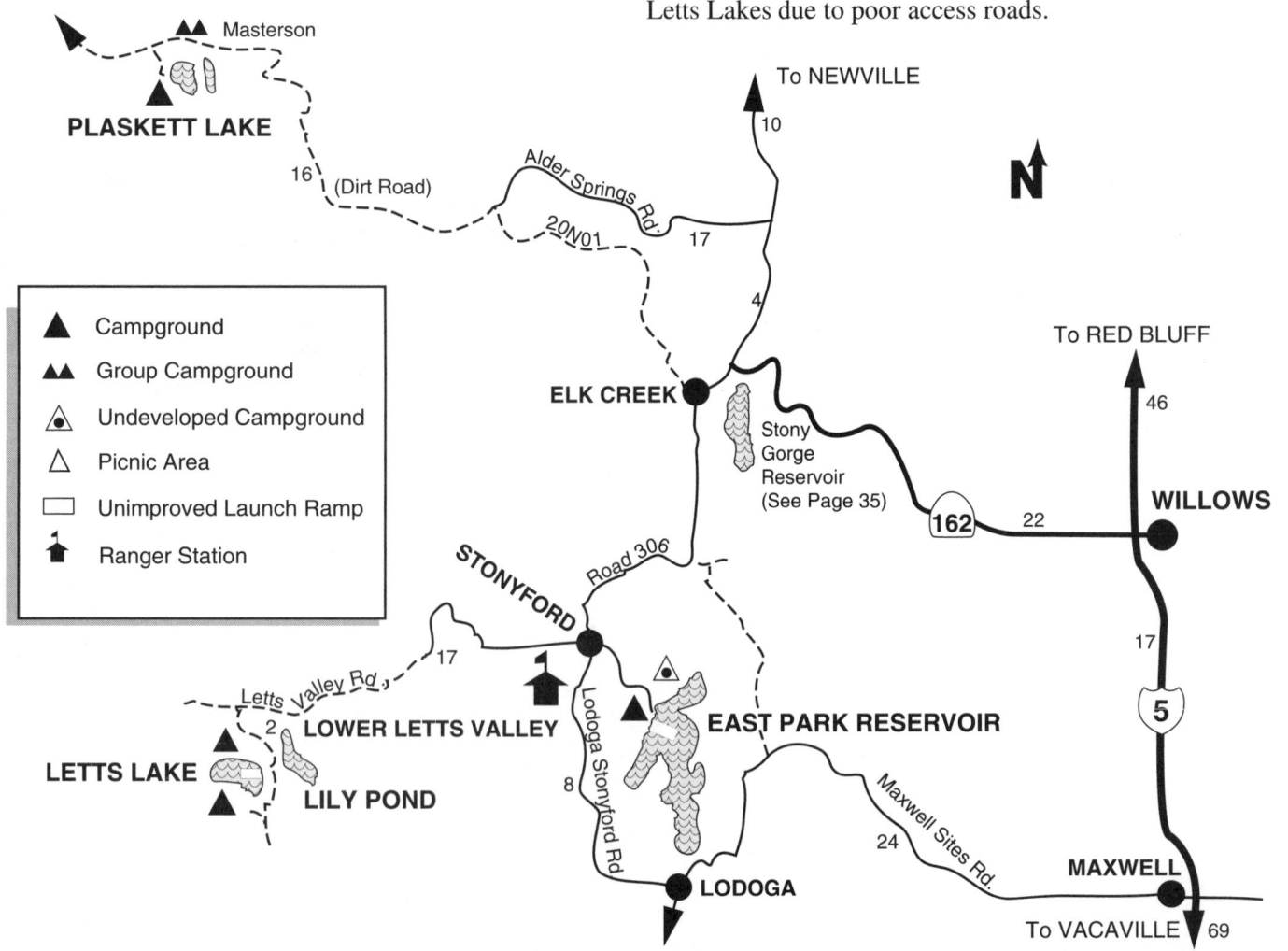

INFORMATION: East Park Reservoir, Bureau of Reclamation, P.O. Box 988, Willows 95988--Ph: (530) 275-1554

CAMPING	BOATING	RECREATION	OTHER
East Park Reservoir: Open Primitive Camping Around Most of the Lake No Water No Electricity Group Camp Available 15 Min. - 200 Max. Reservations	East Park Reservoir: Open to All Boats *Subject to Low* *Water Hazards* Unimproved Ramp 5 MPH Zone 100 feet from All Shorelines Boating Laws Strictly Enforced Ordinance Against Parasailing at East Park	Fishing: East Park Reservoir: Black Bass, Bluegill, Crappie & Catfish Plaskett Lake: Trout Letts Lake: Bass & Trout Swimming Hiking & Nature Trails *East Park:* *No Hunting, No Firearms* *No ORV's*	Plaskett & Letts Lakes: USFS-Stonyford R.D. P.O. Box 160 Stonyford 95979 Ph: (530) 963-3128 Camping (Dogs on Leash): Letts - 42 Sites - Fee: $8 Plaskett - 32 Sites - Fee: $8 Masterson Group Site by Reservation - Fee: $35 No Gas or Electric Boats

BLACK BUTTE LAKE

Black Butte is surrounded by rolling hills with basalt buttes and open grasslands spotted with oak trees. It rests at an elevation of 470 feet. This 4,500 surface-acre Lake has a shoreline of 40 miles. The U.S. Army Corps of Engineers administers the well-maintained campgrounds and facilities at the Lake. Water levels can change rapidly. Boaters are cautioned against possible hazards, such as sand bars, exposed during low water. This is a good warm water fishery especially in the spring when the crappie are hungry. There is abundant wildlife and the birdwatcher will find a wide variety of avian life.

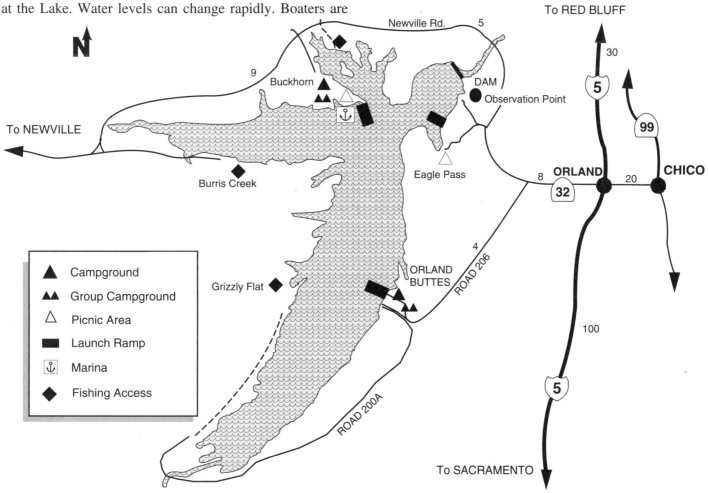

Legend:
- ▲ Campground
- ▲▲ Group Campground
- △ Picnic Area
- ■ Launch Ramp
- ⚓ Marina
- ◆ Fishing Access

INFORMATION: Park Manager, 19225 Newville Rd., Orland 95963—Ph: (530) 865-4781

CAMPING	BOATING	RECREATION	OTHER
Buckhorn: 65 Dev.Sites Tents & R.V.s-Fee: $14 Group Camp to 200 People - Fee: $85 Open Year Round Orland Buttes: 35 Dev. Sites Tents & R.V.s - Fee: $14 Group Camp to 100 People - Fee: $75 Open Late April-Sept. Reserve All Sites: Ph: (877) 444-6777	Power, Row, Canoe, Sail, Waterski, Jets, Windsurf, Inflatables Launch Ramps - Fee: $2 Black Butte Marina 500 Buckhorn Rd. Orland 95963 Ph: (530) 865-2665 Rentals: Fishing Boats & Paddle Boats Docks, Berths Storage, Gas	Fishing: Large & Smallmouth Bass, Blue, White & Channel Catfish, Crappie, Bluegill & Green Sunfish Swimming & Hiking Picnicking & Playground Campfire Programs Hunting: Deer, Dove, Quail, Waterfowl *(Shotgun & Archery Only)*	Supplies at Marina Store Bait & Tackle Hot Showers Disposal Station 75-Acre ATV Park Open May 20 through February Full Facilities - 8 Miles at Orland

STONY GORGE RESERVOIR

Stony Gorge Reservoir is at an elevation of 800 feet in the foothills west of Willows in the upper Sacramento Valley. The Lake has a surface area of 1,275 acres and is under the administration of the U. S. Bureau of Reclamation. The rolling hills surrounding the 25 miles of shoreline are dotted with oak, digger pine and brush. Although there are a number of campsites, they are relatively primitive. Boating facilities are limited to a 1-lane paved launch ramp which is unusable during late summer and fall . The fishing is good for warm water species in this scenic Lake.

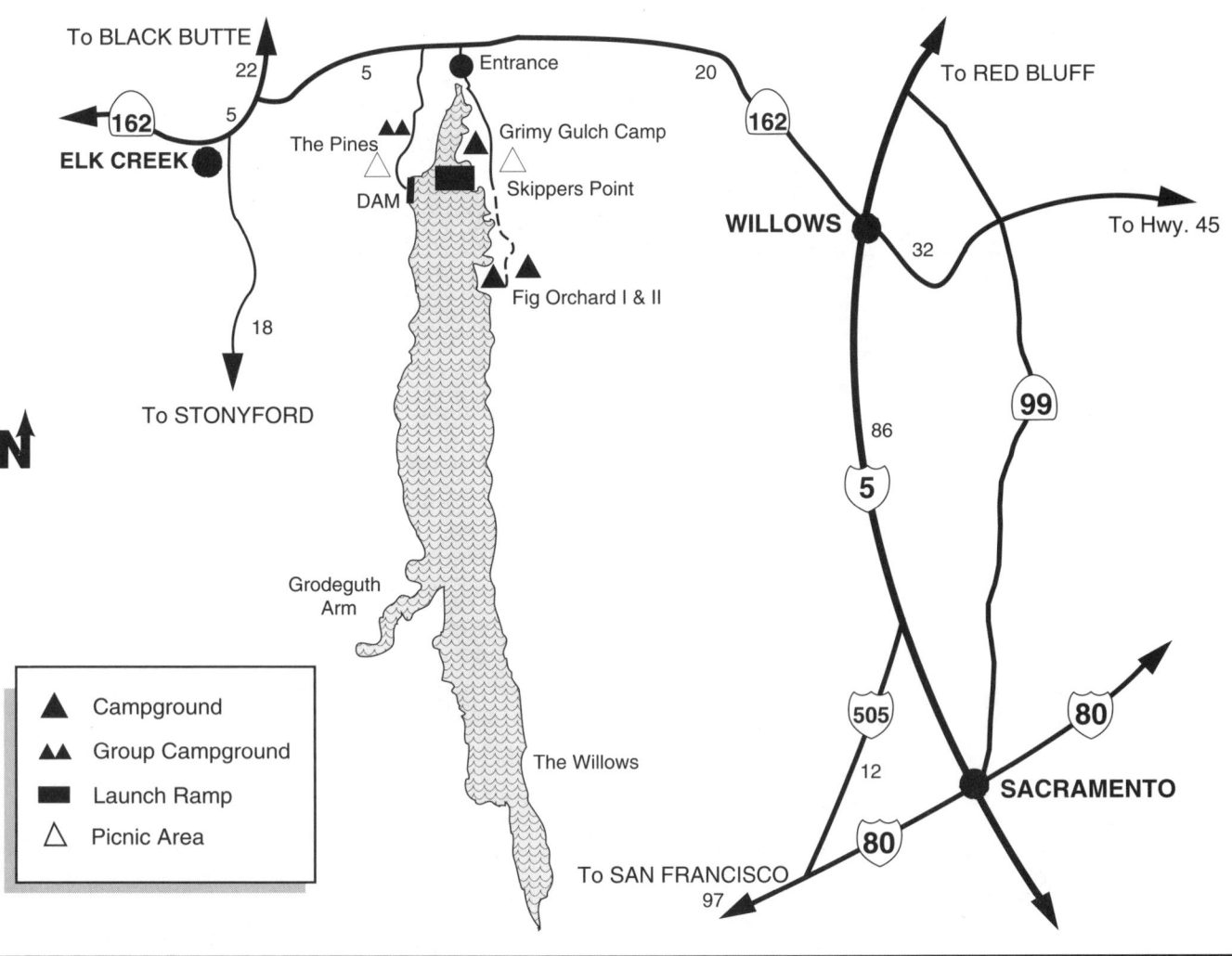

INFORMATION: Bureau of Reclamation, P.O. Box 988, Willows 95988—Ph: (530) 275-1554

CAMPING	BOATING	RECREATION	OTHER
150 Primitive Sites for Tents & R.V.s Group Camp or Day Use - 15 People Min. - 200 People Max. Reservations No Electricity No Water Figs Campground Closed Sept. 30 thru Mid April	Power, Row, Canoe, Sail, Waterski, Windsurf & Inflatables No Houseboats Permitted Launch Ramp *Underwater Hazards Due to Fluctuation in Lake Level*	Fishing: Catfish, Bluegill, Crappie, Bass & Perch Swimming Picnicking - Group Site 15 People Min. - 200 People Max. No ORV's and No Hunting	Elk Creek: Country Store Gas Station Full Facilities in Elk Creek or Willows

The Oroville Dam is the highest in the United States towering 770 feet above the City of Oroville. The Park encompasses 28,450 acres. Lake Oroville, at 900 feet elevation, has 15,500 surface acres with a shoreline of 167 miles. Although water levels drop late in the summer, the Lake offers unlimited recreation the year around. This is an excellent boating Lake with good marina facilities. Boat-in campsites and houseboat moorings are available for those who wish to spend the night on the Lake. The angler will find an extensive variety of game fish from smallmouth bass to king salmon. To the West, Thermalito Forebay includes 300 surface acres for boating, fishing and swimming.

....Continued....

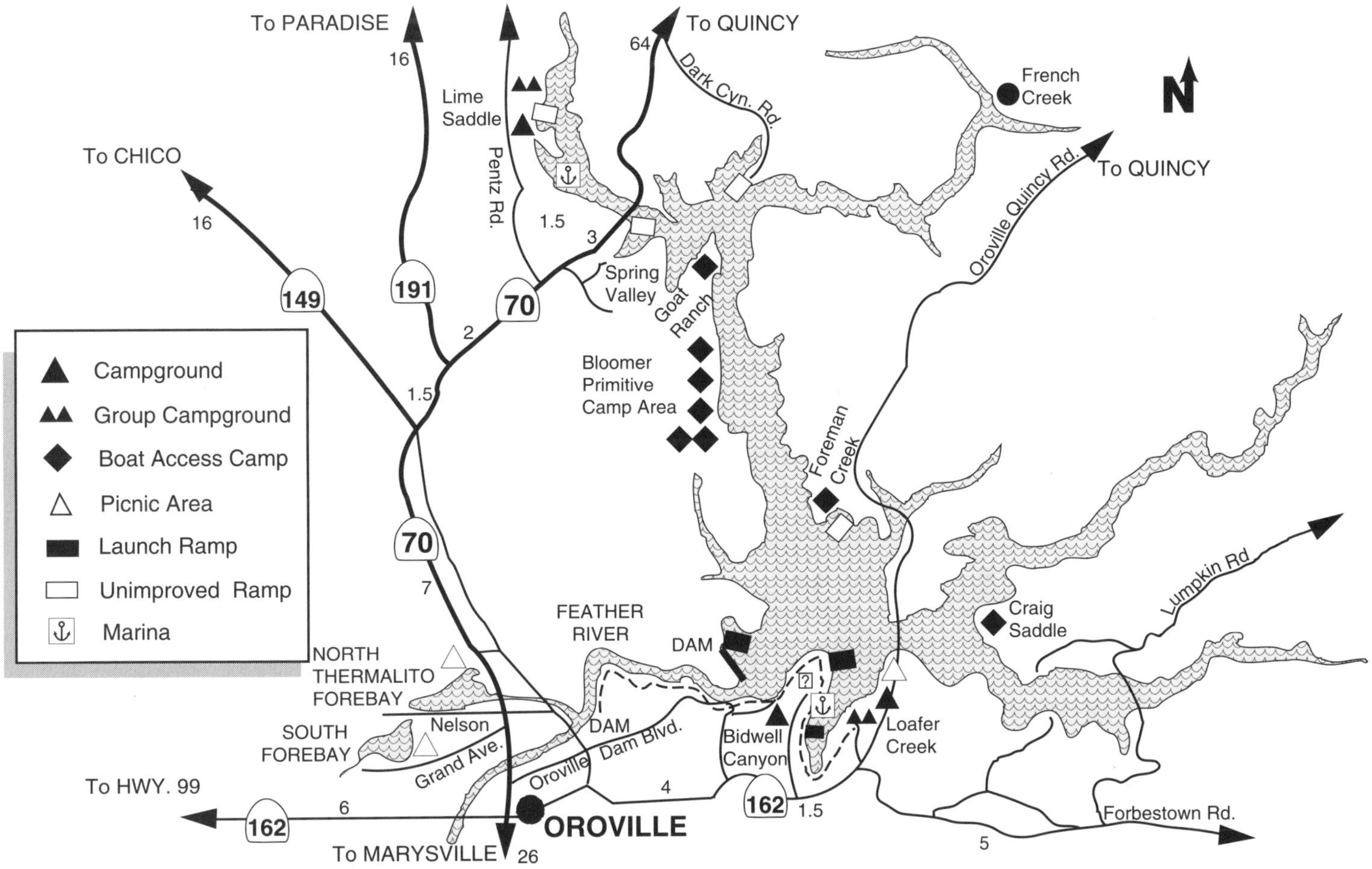

Map Legend:
- ▲ Campground
- ▲▲ Group Campground
- ◆ Boat Access Camp
- △ Picnic Area
- ■ Launch Ramp
- ▢ Unimproved Ramp
- ⚓ Marina

Map labels:

To PARADISE 16 · To QUINCY 64 · To CHICO 16 · To QUINCY · French Creek · N · Lime Saddle · Pentz Rd. · Dark Cyn. Rd. · Oroville Quincy Rd. · 149 · 191 · 70 · 1.5 · 3 · Spring Valley · Goat Ranch · Bloomer Primitive Camp Area · Foreman Creek · 2 · 1.5 · 70 · 7 · FEATHER RIVER · DAM · Craig Saddle · Lumpkin Rd · NORTH THERMALITO FOREBAY · SOUTH FOREBAY · Nelson · Grand Ave. · DAM · Oroville Dam Blvd. · Bidwell Canyon · Loafer Creek · To HWY. 99 · 162 · 6 · 4 · 162 · 1.5 · Forbestown Rd. · 5 · To MARYSVILLE 26 · OROVILLE

INFORMATION: State Recreation Area, 400 Glen Dr., Oroville 95966—Ph: (530) 538-2200

CAMPING	BOATING	RECREATION	OTHER
Family Campsites	All Boating Allowed	Fishing: Rainbow &	Full Facilities in
R.V. Hookup Sites	Full Service Marinas	Brown Trout, Large	Oroville & Paradise
Boat-In Campsites	Paved Launch Ramps	& Smallmouth Bass,	
Group Campsites	Hand Launch Ramps	Coho & King Salmon	Grocery Stores & Motels
Floating Campsites:	Docks, Berths &	Picnicking	7 Miles from
2-Story Structure	Moorings	Hiking & Equestrian Trails	Lime Saddle
Moored in a Cove	Rentals: Fishing,	Bicycle Trails	
Horse Camp	Waterskiing &	Hunting: Upland Game,	
Some Campsites:	Houseboats	Dove, Pheasant	
Reserve:		Swimming (No Diving)	
Ph: (800) 444-7275		Visitor Center	
		Fish Hatchery	
See Following Page			

36

LAKE OROVILLE..............continued

CAMPGROUNDS:

LOAFER CREEK:
137 Sites for Tents & R.V.s to 31 feet - Fee: $10.
Water, Showers, Laundry Tubs, Disposal Station, 100 Picnic Sites, Swim Beach, Launch Ramp.
Campground Ph: (530) 538-2217.
Group Camps: 6 Well-Developed Group Camps Each Accommodating 25 People - Fee: $20.
Campground Ph: (530) 538-2217.

BIDWELL CANYON:
75 R.V. Sites to 40 Feet (Include Boat Trailer in Total R.V. length) - Full Hookups - Fee: $16
Launch Ramp, Boat Rentals, Full Service Marina - Ph: (530) 589-3165)
Grocery Store, Laundry Tubs, Snack Bar - Campground Ph: (530) 538-2218.
Reserve: Ph: (800) 444-7275

LIME SADDLE:
44 R.V. Sites to 40 Feet - Hookups (No Sewer) - Fee: $16, Tent Sites: Fee: $10
Water, Showers, Disposal Station
Group Camps: 2 Sites with 4 Tent Pads Each Accommodating 25 People Each. - Fee: $20
Campground Ph: (530) 876-8516

BOAT-IN CAMPS: *NO Drinking Water Available*
109 sites at: Craig Saddle, Foreman Point, Goat Ranch, Bloomer,
Primitive Area - North Point, Knoll, South Cove, Bloomer. Fee: $7.
Group Camp for 75 People Located at South Bloomer : Fees: $30
Tables, Toilets,
Reserve: Ph: (800) 444-7275

LIME SADDLE MARINA, P.O. Box 1088, Paradise 95969—Ph: (530) 877-2414 or (800) 834-7517
Convenient location 1-1/2 miles off Hwy. 70 on Pentz Rd.
Full Service Marina, 5-Lane Launch Ramp, Gas, Boat Shop, OMC-Johnson Service.
Rentals: Houseboats, Ski Boats, Fishing & Patio Boats
Overnight Moorings, Docks, Covered & Open Slips, Water Ski Sales and Rentals, Marine Supplies
Grocery Store, Bait & Tackle, Ice, Propane & Pumpout Station.

BIDWELL CANYON MARINA, 801 Bidwell Canyon Road, Oroville 95966—Ph: (530) 589-3165 or (800) 637-1767
Full Service Marina, Gas.
Rentals: Fishing, Patio, Houseboats, Water Ski Sales and Rentals, Overnight Moorings,
Docks, Covered & Open Slips, Dry Storage,
Gift Shop, Grocery Store, Bait & Tackle Shop, Pumpout Station and Ice.

PAVED LAUNCH RAMPS ALSO LOCATED AT:

SPILLWAY: 3-Lane Launch Ramp, Parking, Toilets, Overnight Camping for Self-Contained R.V.s.
ENTERPRISE: Free 2-Lane Launch Ramp, Cartop Launch During Low Water.

THERMALITO FOREBAY

The *North End of the Forebay* is for Day Use. There are 300 Surface Acres. Facilities include a 2-lane launch ramp, sandy swim beach, picnic tables, shade ramadas, potable water and many lovely trees. This area is for sailboats and other non-power boats only. *The Group Area is by Reservation at Park Headquarters.*
The *South End of the Forebay* has a 4-lane launch ramp. There is no shade or potable water.

LITTLE GRASS VALLEY, SLY CREEK and LOST CREEK RESERVOIRS

Little Grass Valley, at 5,040 feet elevation, and Sly Creek, at 3,560 feet elevation, are scenic Lakes in the Plumas National Forest. Little Grass Valley, with 1,615 surface acres and 16 miles of shoreline, is a good boating lake. There is an abundance of developed campsites in this forested area. Sly Creek Reservoir has 562 surface acres with facilities for boating and camping. Its neighbor, Lost Creek Reservoir, is surrounded by private land except for a small portion of Forest Service land on the north side which is relatively unusable due to the steep slopes.

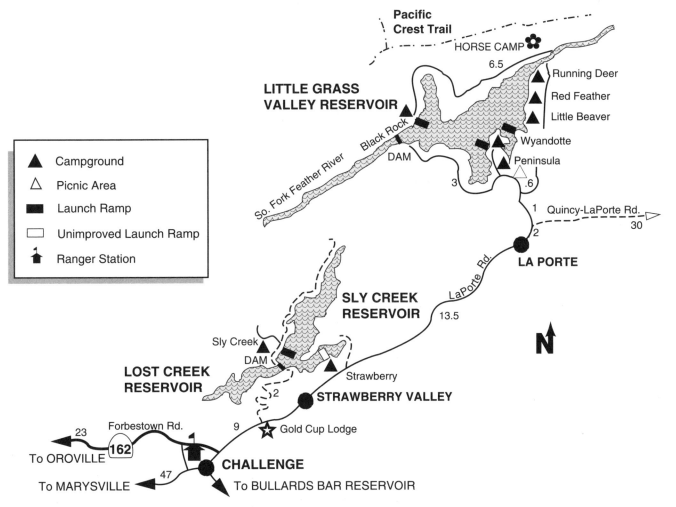

INFORMATION: Feather River Ranger District, 875 Mitchell Ave., Oroville 95965—Ph: (530) 534-6500			
CAMPING	**BOATING**	**RECREATION**	**OTHER**

Little Grass Valley:
   320 Dev. Sites for
   Tents & R.V.s to 30 feet
   Plus Horse Camp
   Fee: $8 - $12
   2 Disposal Stations
Reserve Some Sites:
   Ph: (877) 444-6777
 	
Sly Creek:
   53 Dev. Sites for Tents
   & R.V.s
   Fee: $12 - $14
	Little Grass Valley:
	   Open to Small Boats
	   3 Paved Launch
	   Ramps
	Sly Creek:
	   Open to Small Boats
	   1 Paved Launch Ramp
	   1 Cartop Launch Ramp
		Fishing: Rainbow,
		   Brook & Brown Trout
		Swimming
		Picnicking
		Hiking & Riding
		Backpacking
		Nature Study
		Hunting: Waterfowl
		   Upland Game & Deer
			Facilities: 3-1/2 Miles
			   at La Porte
			Abandoned Mining
			   Towns
			
			Nearby Access to
			   Pacific Crest Trail

GOLD LAKE and THE LAKES BASIN RECREATION AREA

More than 50 small glacial lakes and numerous streams filled with trout are located in this scenic area. Gold Lake is the largest. Elevations range from 5,000 to 6,000 feet. Several of the Lakes can be reached by car but many can only be reached by trail. This is a popular fly fishing area especially along the Middle Fork of the Feather River which has been designated a natural Wild and Scenic River. The Lakes Basin is in both the Plumas and Tahoe National Forests. The hiker and packer will find trails leading to the Pacific Crest Trail. Although this area remains relatively unspoiled, there are a number of resorts and facilities that complement the natural setting of this beautiful countryside. ...Continued....

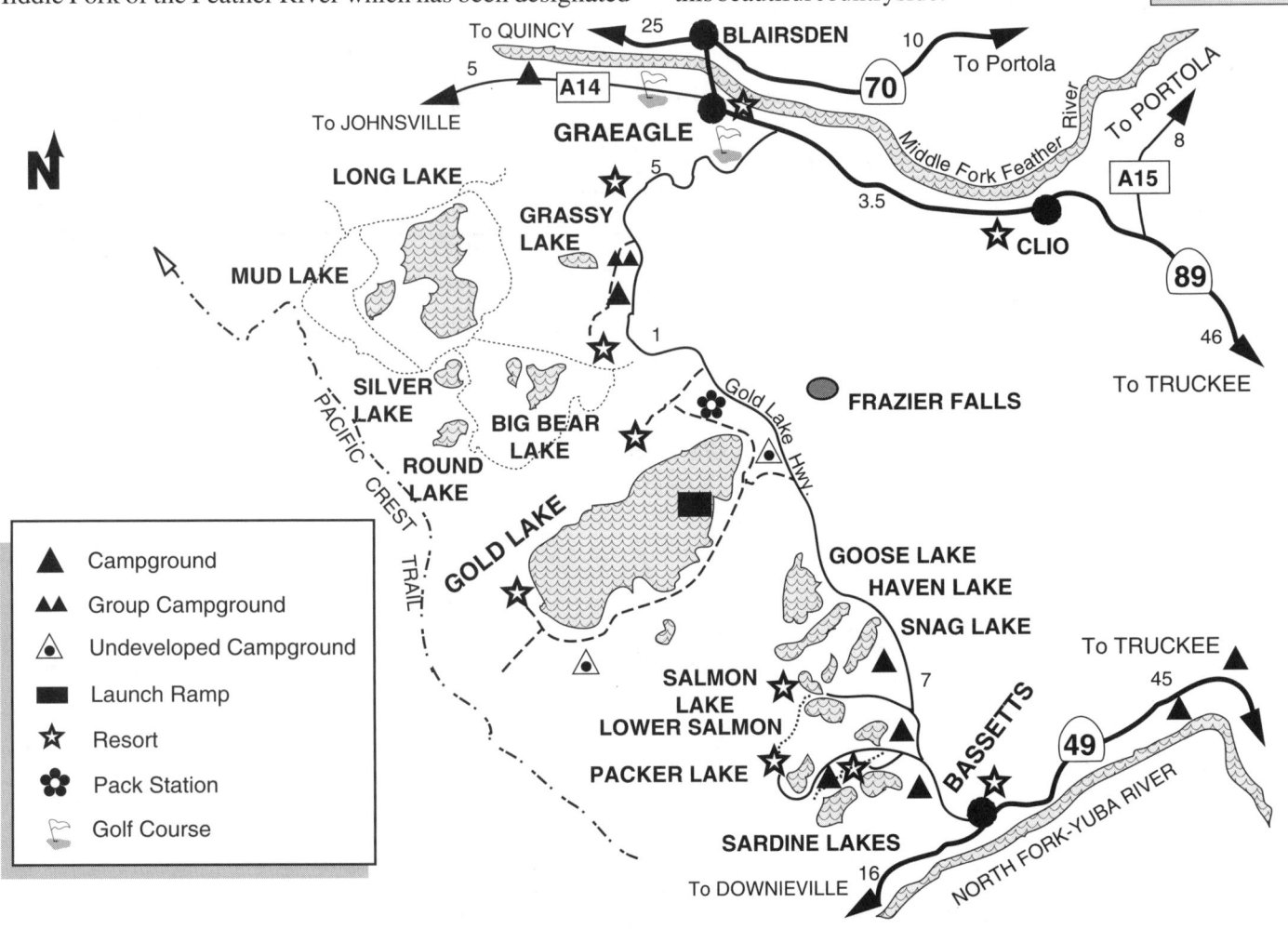

INFORMATION: Beckwourth Ranger Station, P.O. Box 7, 23 Mohawk Rd., Blairsden 96103—Ph: (530) 836-2575

CAMPING	BOATING	RECREATION	OTHER
US Forest Service Campgrounds in Area Fee: $13 Lakes in North Area: Beckwourth Ranger Sta. Ph: (530) 836-2575 Group Camp to 25 People - Fee: $45 Reserve: Ph: (877) 444-6777 Lakes in South Area: North Yuba Ranger Dist. Ph: (530) 288-3231	Gold Lake: Power, Row, Sail, Windsurfing & Waterskiing Launch Ramp with Dock	Fishing: Rainbow, Brown & Brook Trout, Mackinaw Picnicking Hiking & Riding Trails Backpacking Gold Lake Pack Station Ph: (530) 836-0940 Swimming Hunting: Deer Golf Courses: 9-Hole & 18-Hole	Numerous Facilities & Resorts in this Area *See Following Page* Plumas County Visitors Bureau Ph: 800-326-2247 Sierra County Chamber of Commerce Ph: 800-200-4949

GOLD LAKE and THE LAKES BASIN RECREATION AREA............Continued

The following is a list of some accommodations in the Lakes Basin Recreation Area, in alphabetical order. Many of the lodges and resorts are fully booked one year in advance in season so reservations are imperative.

CLIO'S RIVERS EDGE R V PARK - Box 111, 3754 Highway 89, Clio 96106—Ph: (530) 836-2375
R.V.s to 45 feet, Full Hookups, Showers, Cable TV, Open April 15 to October 30.

ELWELL LAKES LODGE - Box 68, Gold Lake Rd., Blairsden 96103—Ph: (530) 836-2347
10 Housekeeping Cabins, B&B Rooms, Main Lodge with Recreation Room, Complimentary Boats for Guests, Creek-filled Swimming Pool, Picnic Area, BBQ, No Pets, Open June-September.

FEATHER RIVER INN - Box 67, Blairsden 96103—Ph: (530) 836-2623 OR (888) 324-6400
3/4 mile west of Blairsden, 50 Units, Conference Facilities, Catering, Golf Course, Golf Package Available, No Pets.

FEATHER RIVER PARK RESORT, Box 37, Highway 89, Blairsden 96103—Ph: (530) 836-2328
35 Housekeeping Log Cabins, Weekly Rental Only from mid-June to Labor Day, 3 Swimming Pools, 9-Hole Golf Course, Tennis Court, Playground, Bicycle Rental, Lodge with Games & Snacks, Pets OK, Open May to mid-October.

GOLD LAKE BEACH RESORT, 5920 Butler Rd., Penryn 95663—Ph: (530) 836-2491
On Gold Lake, Pick-up at Dock, Cabins, Complete Meal Service, 3-Night Minimum, Open June-September.
GOLD LAKE PACK STATION & STABLES, 1540 Chandler Rd., Quincy 95971—Ph: (530) 836-0940

GOLD LAKE LODGE, Box 25, Graeagle 96103—Ph: (530) 836-2350
11 Cabins, Breakfast & Dinner Included, Maid Service, Family Discounts, Daily/Weekly Rates, Lodge, Restaurant, No Pets, Open mid-June to Early October.

GRAY EAGLE LODGE, Box 38, Gold Lake Rd., Graeagle 96103—Ph: (530) 836-2511
18 Cabins, Breakfast & Dinner Included, 3-Night Min., Lodge, Restaurant, Game Room, Pets OK, Open May-October.

HIGH COUNTRY INN, Highway 49 & Gold Lake Rd., Sierra City 96125—Ph: (530) 862-1530 or (800) 862-1530
5 Rooms, Views of Sierra Buttes & River, Deck, No Pets, Open All Year.

LAYMAN RESORT, Box 8, Highway 70, Blairsden 96103—Ph: (530) 836-2356
13 Housekeeping Cabins, Picnic & BBQ Area, Off-Season Rates, Open April to early November.

LITTLE BEAR R.V. PARK, Box 103, Blairsden 96103—Ph: (530) 836-2774
R.V.s to 40 ft., Hookups, Satellite TV, Showers, Store, Open April 15 to October 31.

MOVIN' WEST TRAILER RANCH, Box 1010, 305 Johnsville Rd., Graeagle 96103—Ph: (530) 836-2614
R.V.s to 40 Feet, Hookups, Showers, Cable TV, Open May 1 to October 31.

PACKER LAKE LODGE, Box 237, 3901 Packer Lake Rd., Sierra City 96125—Ph: (530) 862-1221
14 Cabins, 8 with Kitchens, Complimentary Boat Included, Store, Restaurant, Bar, Pets OK, Open May-October.

RIVER PINES RESORT, Box 249, Highway 89, Clio 96106—Ph: (530) 836-2552 or in California (800) 696-2551
1/4 Mile North of Graeagle, 62 Units, Motel Rooms, Some with Kitchens, Housekeeping Cottages, Pool, Jacuzzi, Playground, Recreation Room, BBQ Area, Restaurant, Lounge, Golf Packages, Open All Year.

SALMON LAKE LODGE, Box 121, Sierra City 96125—Ph: (530) 757-1825
Tent Cabins, Central Utility House with Refrigerator & Showers, Bring Own Sleeping Bags, Pans & Groceries, Parking at East End of Lake, Barge Transports Guest & Baggage Across Lake, Fishing Boats, Sailboats and Canoes for Guests.

SARDINE LAKES RESORT—Ph: (530) 862-1196 - Cabins, Lunch & Dinner by Reservations, Rental Boats.

BULLARDS BAR RESERVOIR

Bullards Bar Reservoir is at an elevation of 2,000 feet in the Tahoe and Plumas National Forests surrounded by rugged countryside. This beautiful large Lake of 4,700 surface acres has 56 miles of shoreline. The area is heavily wooded so all campsites are shaded by trees. All boating is allowed and the waterskiing is some of the best in California. Fishing is open year around for both warm and cold water fish. This is a prime Lake for Kokanee salmon. The Yuba County Water Agency and the U.S. Forest Service maintain 30 boat access camps and lakeside camping. The Emerald Cove Marina is a full service facility offering rental houseboats and fishing boats along with private houseboat moorings. The Emerald Cove Resort & Marina make Bullards Bar Reservoir a good place to visit for a variety of outdoor recreation.

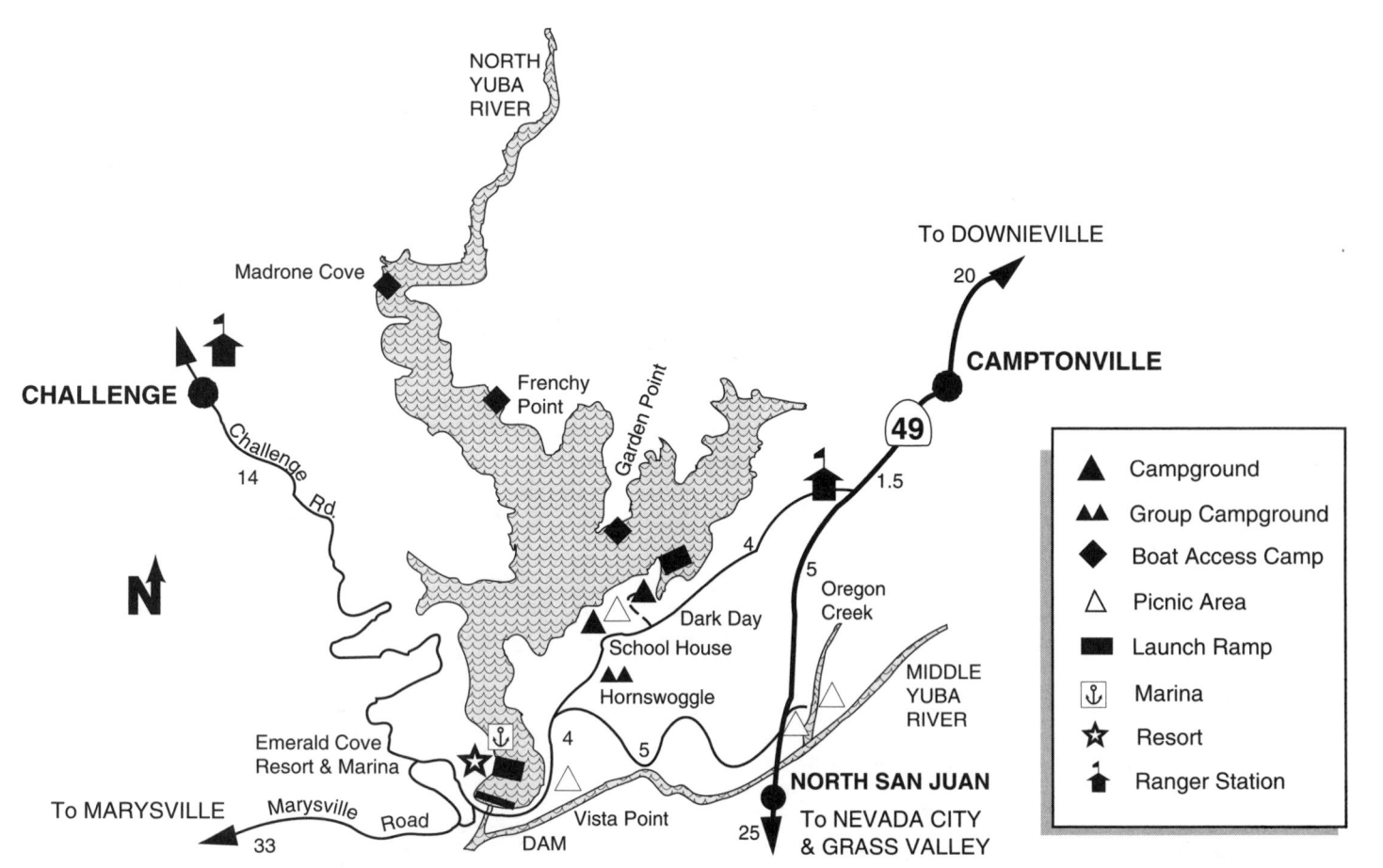

▲	Campground
▲▲	Group Campground
◆	Boat Access Camp
△	Picnic Area
▬	Launch Ramp
⚓	Marina
★	Resort
⚑	Ranger Station

INFORMATION: Emerald Cove Resort & Marina, P.O. Box 1954, Nevada City 95959—Ph: (530) 692-3200

CAMPING	BOATING	RECREATION	OTHER
Emerald Cove Resort: Accepts Reservations Dev. Sites for Tents & R.V.s Boat Access Camps Shoreline Camping Fee: $14 up to 6 People Hornswoggle Group Camps 4 Sites - 15-25 People Fee: $50 1 Site - 35-50 People Fee: $100 Plus $5 Reservation Fee	Open to All Boating Waterskiing Launch Ramps - No Fee Full Service Marina Gas - Propane Rentals: Fishing, Ski, Patio, Paddle & Houseboats Private Houseboat Moorings Overnight Slips & Dry Storage	Fishing: Rainbow & Brown Trout, Bluegill, Catfish, Crappie, Large & Smallmouth Bass, Kokanee Salmon Swimming Picnicking Hiking Trails	Snack Bar Groceries Beer, Wine, Ice Bait & Tackle USFS-N. Yuba Ranger Station Ph: (530) 288-3231

Bowman Lake is the largest of several small Lakes in the scenic Bowman Road Area of the Tahoe National Forest. Bowman is 6 miles south of Jackson Meadows Reservoir and 16 miles north of Highway 20. These are often steep and rocky roads; 4-wheel drive vehicles are advised. The Lakes range in altitude from 5,600 feet to 7,000 feet in this beautiful high Sierra country. The Forest Service maintains a number of campsites in this area but be sure to bring your own drinking water. Stream and lake fishing can be excellent in this rugged and remote but scenic environment.

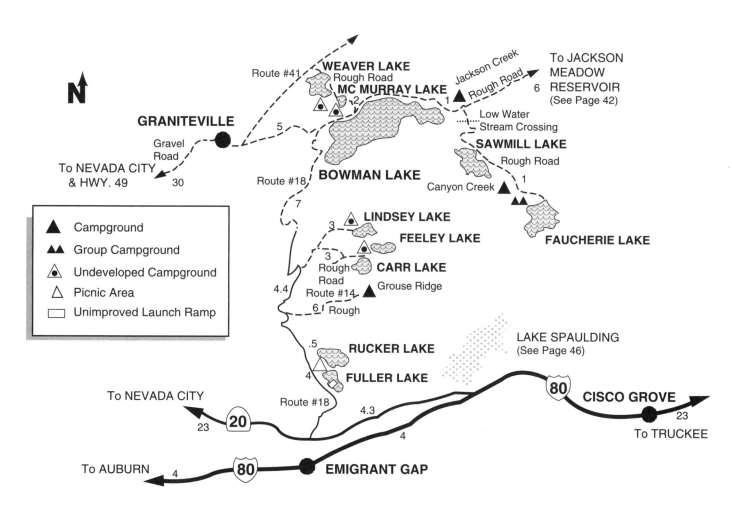

INFORMATION: USFS, Nevada City Ranger Dist., 631 Coyote St., Nevada City 95959—Ph: (530) 265-4531			
CAMPING	**BOATING**	**RECREATION**	**OTHER**
Primitive Camping In Area No Fee Faucherie Lake: Group Camp - 25 People Maximum Fee: $50 Reserve: Ph: (877) 444-6777 *Rucker & Fuller Lakes: No Trailers - No Turnaround*	Small Boats Only 10 MPH Speed Limit Fuller Lake: Cartop Launch Ramp Rucker Lake: No Motors	Fishing: Rainbow, Brook & Brown Trout Swimming Picnicking Hiking, Bicyling & Equestrian Trails Backpacking Nature Study Hunting: Deer	Full Facilities in Truckee or Along Highway 80 *Rough Roads Not Recommended for Trailers or R.V.s 4-Wheel Drive Only*

FORDYCE, STERLING, EAGLE, KIDD, CASCADE, LONG and SERENE LAKES

These Lakes, off Interstate Highway 80 near Soda Springs, rest at elevations of about 7,000 feet in the Tahoe National Forest. This beautiful high Sierra country offers a variety of recreational opportunities. Boating is limited to non-powered craft with limited facilities, but rentals are available at Serene Lake. The angler will find trout and catfish. Numerous trails invite the hiker, backpacker and equestrian to get away from it all in this remote natural area. The roads into Eagle, Fordyce, and Sterling are not advised for any vehicles but 4-wheelers.

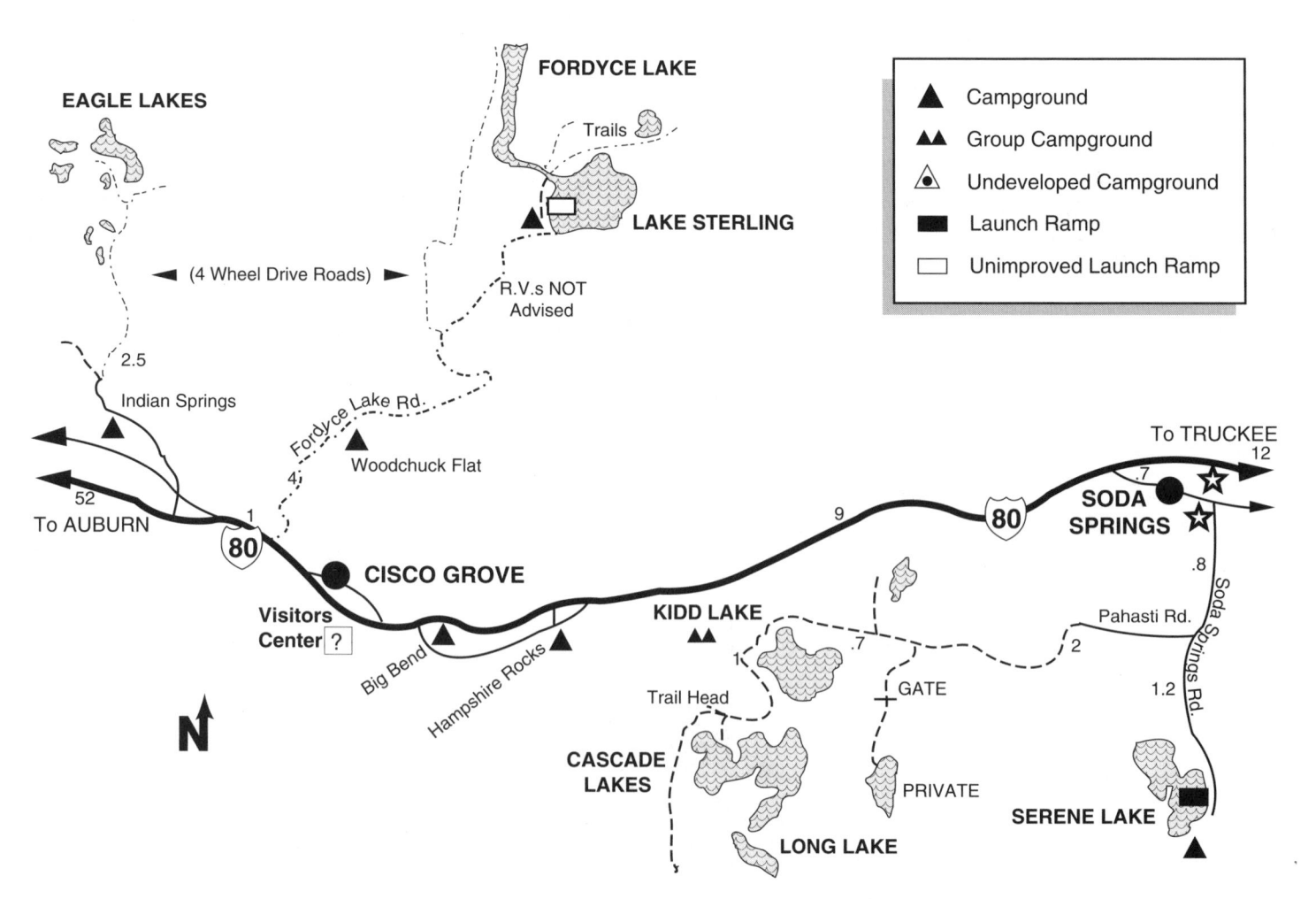

▲	Campground
▲▲	Group Campground
⌖	Undeveloped Campground
▬	Launch Ramp
▭	Unimproved Launch Ramp

INFORMATION: Chamber of Commerce 10065 Donner Pass Rd., Truckee 96161—Ph: (530) 587-2757

CAMPING	BOATING	RECREATION	OTHER
U.S.F.S. Nevada City Ranger District Sites for Tents & R.V.s - Call for Fees Ph: (530) 265-4531 P.G.&E. Kidd Lake: Group Campground to 100 People Maximum 10 People per Site Call for Fee Reserve: Ph: (916) 386-5164	Electric Motors Allowed at Sterling Lake No Motors at All Other Lakes Rentals at Serene Lake	Fishing: Trout & Catfish Swimming Picnicking Numerous Hiking & Equestrian Trails Mountain Bicycling Backpacking Nature Study Photography	USFS Visitor Center at Big Bend Ph: (530) 426-3609 Facilities at Cisco Grove & Soda Springs

JACKSON MEADOW RECREATION AREA

The Jackson Meadow Recreation Area is at an elevation of 6,200 feet in the Tahoe National Forest. This area of forested slopes, alpine meadows, lakes and streams provides an abundance of recreational opportunities. Jackson Meadows Reservoir offers well-maintained camping and recreational facilities along its 11 miles of shoreline. Nearby Milton Reservoir and the Middle Fork of the Yuba River between Jackson Meadow and Milton are subject to specific artificial lures, and size limitations. Refer to the California Sport Fishing Regulations for details. The hiker, backpacker and equestrian will find a trailhead to the Pacific Crest Trail nearby.

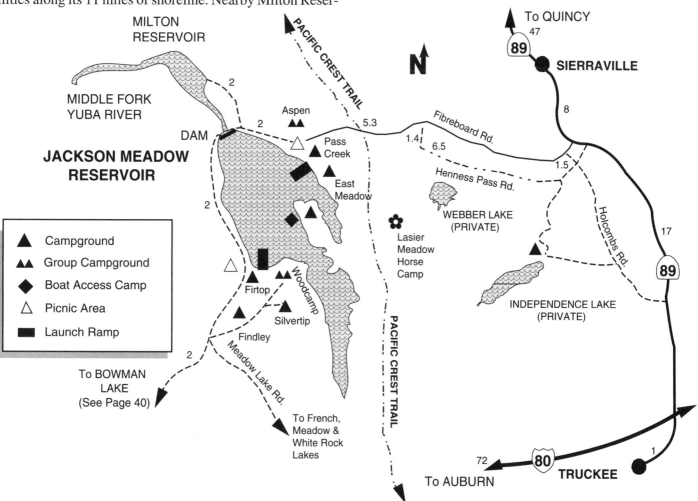

	Campground
▲▲	Group Campground
◆	Boat Access Camp
△	Picnic Area
▬	Launch Ramp

INFORMATION: Sierraville Ranger District, P.O. Box 95, Hwy. 89, Sierraville 96126—Ph: (530) 994-3401

CAMPING	BOATING	RECREATION	OTHER
130 Dev. Sites for Tents & R.V.s Fee: $11 - $13	Power, Row, Canoe, Sail, Waterski, Jets, Windsurf	Fishing: Rainbow, Brook & Brown Trout	Full Facilities 28 Miles at Sierraville or
2 Group Camps 2 - 25 People Max. $55 1 - 50 People Max. $111	& Inflatables Noise Level Laws Enforced	2 Swimming Beaches With Dressing Rooms Picnicking	31 Miles at Truckee
Disposal Station Fee: $5	2 Launch Ramps	Backpacking [Parking] Hiking, Equestrian & Nature Trails	
Reserve: Ph: (877) 444-6777		Hunting: Deer Only in Season Outside Recreation Area	
10 Boat Access Only Sites			

STAMPEDE RESERVOIR

Stampede Reservoir is at an elevation of 5,949 feet in the Tahoe National Forest northeast of Truckee. Stampede has a surface area of 3,440 acres with 25 miles of sage and coniferous covered shoreline. This large open Lake offers westerly winds for the sailor. Vast open waters are enjoyed by the waterskier. Fishing is very popular and anglers will find rainbow and brown trout. While the campground at Davies Creek has limited facilities, a concessionaire, under permit from the Forest Service, maintains developed campsites near the Lake at Logger Campground. The Reservoir water level is lower during the end of the season and in drought years.

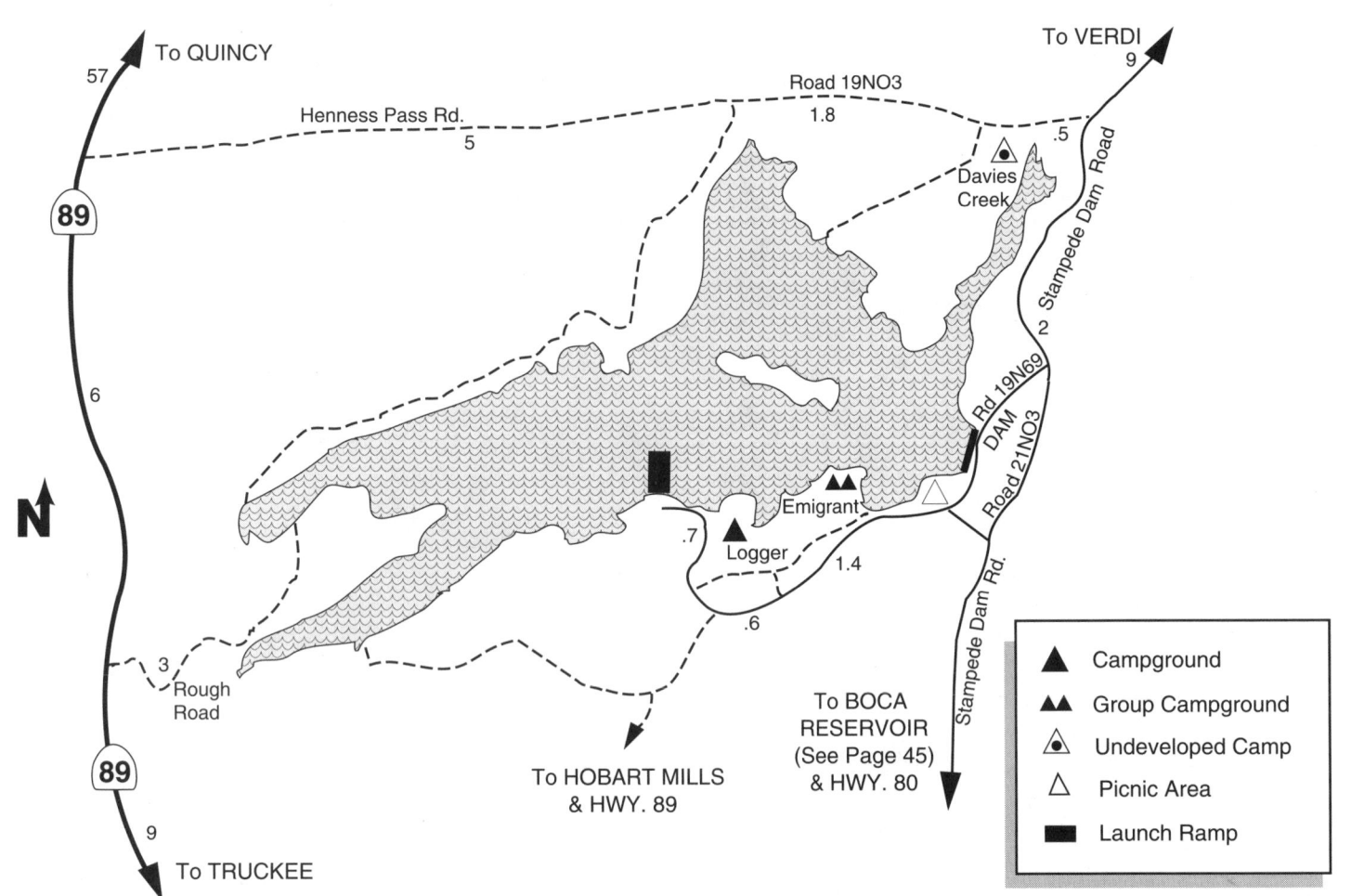

INFORMATION: Truckee Ranger District, 10342 Highway 89 North, Truckee 96161—Ph: (530) 478-6257

CAMPING	BOATING	RECREATION	OTHER
U.S.F.S. - Logger: 252 Dev. Sites for Tents & R.V.s - Fee: $15 Disposal Station Emigrant Group Camps: 2-25 People - Fee: $63 2-150 People - Fee: $127 Reservations: Ph: (877) 444-6777 Davies Creek: 8 Primitive Sites No Water - No Fee Horses Allowed	Power, Row, Canoe Sail, Waterski, Jets, Windsurf & Inflatables *Water Low In Fall* Launch Ramp Extended for Low Water Launching	Fishing: Rainbow Brown Trout, Kokanee Salmon Swimming Picnicking Mountain Bicycling Hunting: Deer - By Special Draw Only Away from Developed Recreation Areas	Full Facilities 14 Miles at Truckee

PROSSER CREEK RESERVOIR

Prosser Creek Reservoir is at an elevation of 5,711 located in the scenic Tahoe National Forest. This 740 surface acre Lake rests in an open canyon surrounded by 11 miles of sage and coniferous-covered hills. The Donner Camp picnic area was the site of the Donner Party tragedy of the winter of 1846-47.

Boating is limited to 10 MPH. Waterskiing, power boating and jets are not allowed at this facility. Launching can be difficult in the fall with low water levels. You can fish for trout and the scenery is beautiful with grassy open meadows at this high elevation Reservoir.

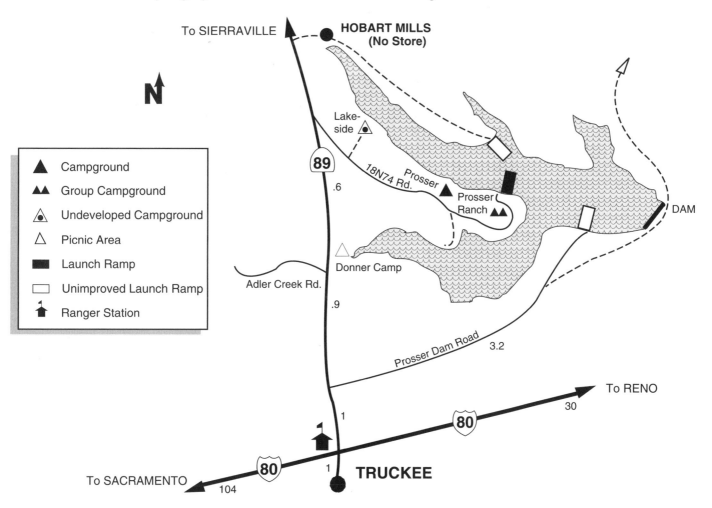

Legend	
▲	Campground
▲▲	Group Campground
⊙	Undeveloped Campground
△	Picnic Area
■	Launch Ramp
☐	Unimproved Launch Ramp
⚑	Ranger Station

INFORMATION: Truckee Ranger District, 10342 Highway 89 North, Truckee 96161—Ph: (530) 478-6257

CAMPING	BOATING	RECREATION	OTHER

Prosser Family:
    29 Dev. Sites for
    Tents & R.V.s to 24 Feet
    Fee: $12
Prosser Ranch Group
    Camp to 50 People
     Fee: $86
    Reserve: (877) 444-6777
Lakeside:
    24 Sem-Developed Sites
    for Tents & R.V.s, Water
    Fee: $12
	Power, Row, Canoe,
	    Sail, Windsurf, &
	    Inflatables
	Speed Limit- 10 MPH
	Launch Ramps
		Fishing: Rainbow Trout
		Swimming
		Picnicking at
		    Donner Camp
		Hiking
		Interpretive Trail at
		    Donner Camp
		Mountain Bicycling
		Hunting: Deer
			Full Facilities - 5
			    Miles at Truckee

BOCA RESERVOIR

Boca Reservoir is in the Tahoe National Forest at an elevation of 5,700 feet. The Lake has a surface area of 980 acres with 14 miles of shoreline. Steep bluffs and low grassy areas amid tall pine trees make for a scenic setting. Campgrounds include U.S. Forest Service sites which all charge fees. The many inlets and prevailing winds create an excellent atmosphere for sailing and boating. *The speed limit in all inlets is 5 mph.* The water level lowers at the end of the season. Boca is fed by Stampede Reservoir, 5 miles above. *During drought conditions boat ramp can be completely out of the water. Always check water levels before leaving home.*

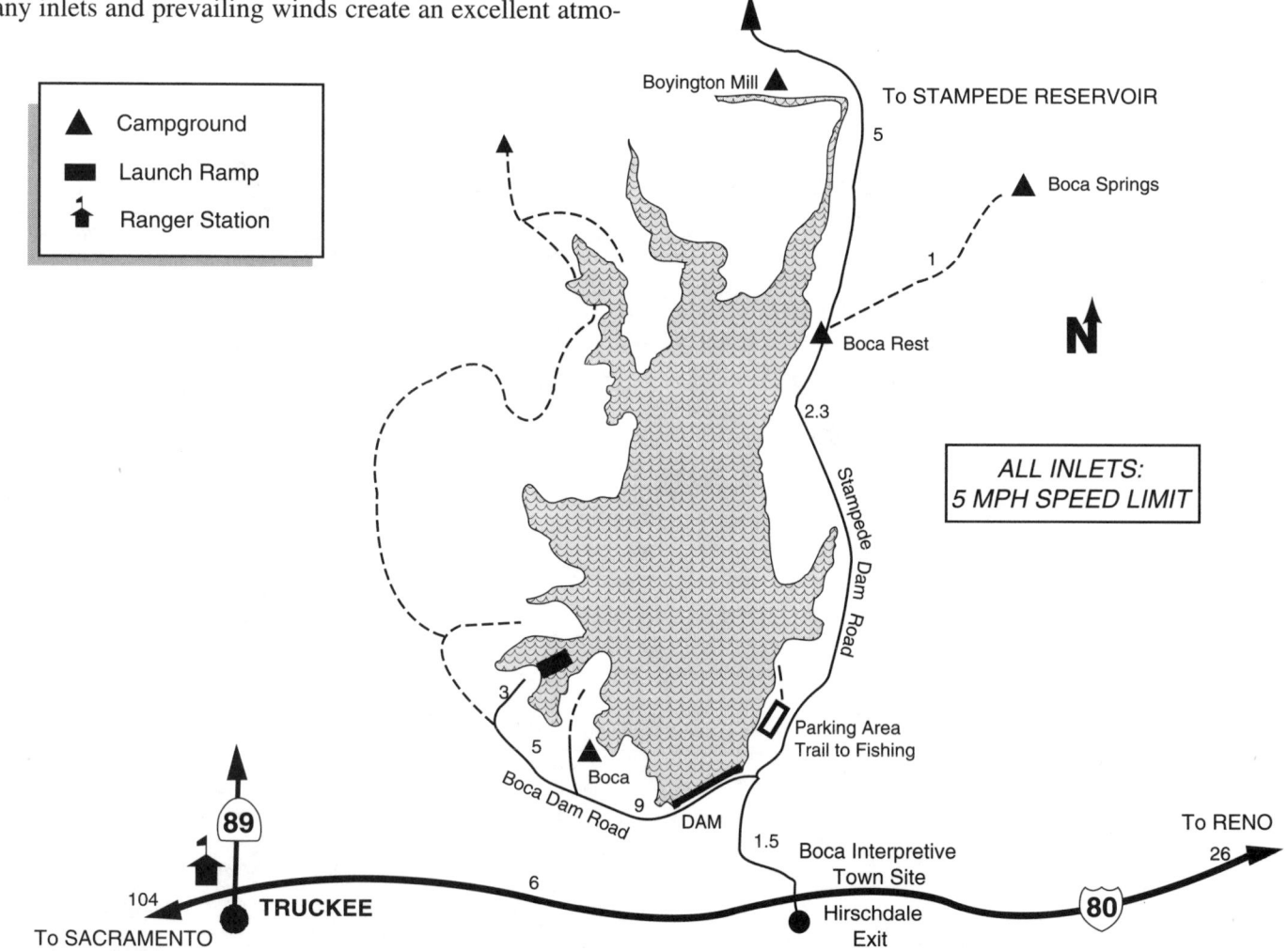

▲ Campground

■ Launch Ramp

🛈 Ranger Station

ALL INLETS: 5 MPH SPEED LIMIT

INFORMATION: Truckee Ranger District, 10342 Highway 89 North, Truckee 96161—Ph: (530) 478-6257

CAMPING	BOATING	RECREATION	OTHER

Boca: 20 Sites
    Fee: $12 - No Water
Boca Rest: 25 Sites
    Fee: $12 - Water
Boca Springs: 17 Sites
    Fee: $12 - Water
    Horses Permitted
Boyington Mill: 13 Sites
    Fee: $12 - No Water
 	
Call USFS for R.V. and Trailer Access Information
	Power, Row, Canoe,
	    Sail, Waterski,
	    Jets, Windsurf
	    & Inflatables
	Launch Ramp
		Fishing: Rainbow Trout
		Swimming
		Picnicking
		Hiking
		Horseback Riding
		Hunting: Deer
		
		Fish Trail: Parking -
		    2 Handicap Spaces
			Full Facilities - 7
			    Miles in Truckee
			Limited Facilities at
			    Hirschdale Exit

Lake Spaulding rests at an elevation of 5,014 feet in a glacier carved bowl of granite. The Lake has a surface area of 698 acres surrounded by giant rocks and conifers. Now a part of Pacific Gas and Electric Company's Drum-Spaulding Project, the dam was originally built in 1912 for hydraulic mining. P.G. & E. operates the facilities at this scenic Lake which includes a campground and launch ramp. The Lake is open to all types of boating although launching large boats can be difficult. Fishing from the bank or boat is often rewarding. This is a good Lake for a family outing with a spectacular setting of granite boulders dipping into the clear, blue waters.

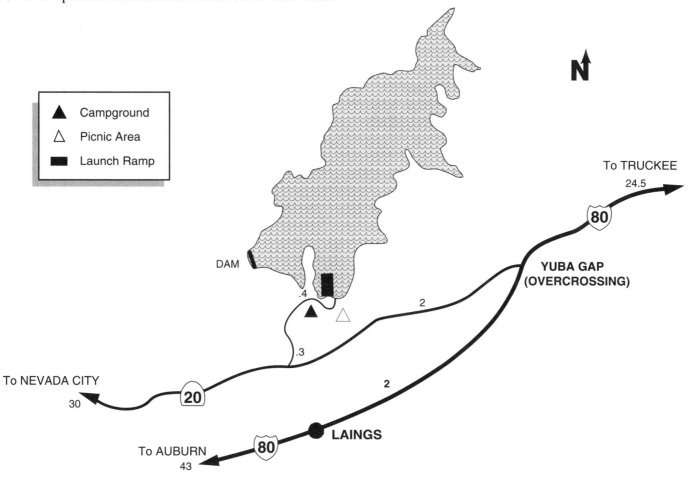

▲ Campground
△ Picnic Area
■ Launch Ramp

DAM

N

To TRUCKEE
24.5

80

YUBA GAP
(OVERCROSSING)

.4

2

.3

To NEVADA CITY
30

20

2

LAINGS

To AUBURN
43

80

INFORMATION: P.G. & E. Land Projects, 2730 Gateway Oaks Dr., Sacramento 95833–Ph: (916) 386-5164

CAMPING	BOATING	RECREATION	OTHER
25 Dev. Sites for Tents & R.V.s Fee: $15 Pets - Fee Plus 10 Overflow Sites	Power, Row, Canoe, Sail, Waterski, Jets, Windsurf & Inflatables Launch Ramp - Fee Summer Use Only *Hazardous Rocks In Late Summer As Water Level Drops*	Fishing: Rainbow & Brown Trout Swimming - Beaches Picnicking Hiking Backpacking [Parking]	Full Facilities at Nevada City

Donner Lake is at an elevation of 5,963 feet in the Tahoe National Forest next to Interstate 80 and west of Truckee. The Lake is 3 miles long and 3/4 mile wide with a shoreline of 7-1/2 miles of high alpine woods. Donner has numerous private homes (no access) on the south shore and portions of the north shore. The Donner State Memorial Park, on the east shore, was named after the tragic Donner Party whose fate in the winter of 1846 attests to the hardships encountered by California's early settlers. This well-maintained park has 150 developed campsites with campfire programs and nature trails. The Emigrant Trail Museum is open daily from 10 a.m. to 4 p.m. The water in the Lake is clear and cold. A popular sailing Lake, Donner has its own local Sailing Club. *Beware of periodic afternoon winds that can be hazardous.*

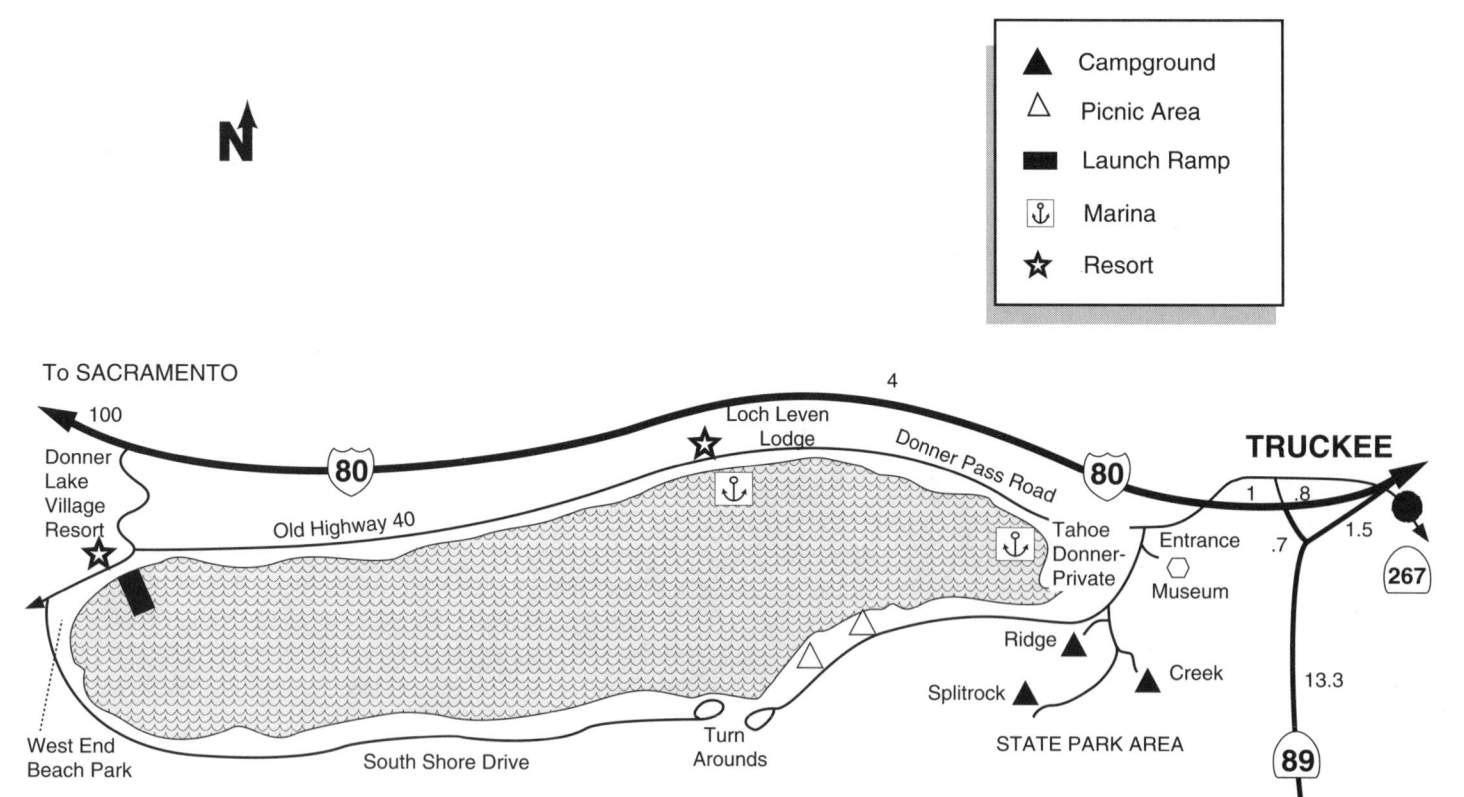

INFORMATION: Donner Memorial State Park, 12593 Donner Pass Rd., Truckee 96161—Ph: (530) 582-7892

CAMPING	BOATING	RECREATION	OTHER
Donner Memorial State Park 150 Dev. Sites for Tents & R.V.s Fee: $12 Ph: (530) 582-7892 or Reserve: Ph: (800) 444-7275 (On First Come Basis at Times) Day Use - Fee: $2	Power, Row, Canoe, Sail, Waterski, Jets, Windsurf & Inflatables No Launching From State Park Public Launch Ramp At West End Rentals: Fishing, Pontoon & Paddleboats	Fishing: Rainbow Trout, Mackinaw, Kokanee Salmon Swimming - Beaches Picnicking Hiking Bicycle Trails Campfire Programs Nature Study Tennis Golf	Motels, Cabins Snack Bar Restaurant Cocktail Lounge Grocery Store Bait & Tackle Laundromat Gas Station Airport With Auto Rentals - 5 Miles Movies Emigrant Trail Museum

Martis Creek Lake, 70 surface acres at minimum pool, was California's first "Wild Trout Lake" and probably one of its most unique. Originally built in 1972 by the U. S. Army Corps of Engineers for flood control and a water supply for Reno, this Lake was selected by the California Department of Fish and Game as an exclusive, naturally producing, trophy trout fishery for the endangered Lahontan Cutthroat Trout. Martis Creek is a trophy German Brown fishery in the catch and release program. The facilities and nearby 1,000 acre wildlife area are administered by the Corps of Engineers.

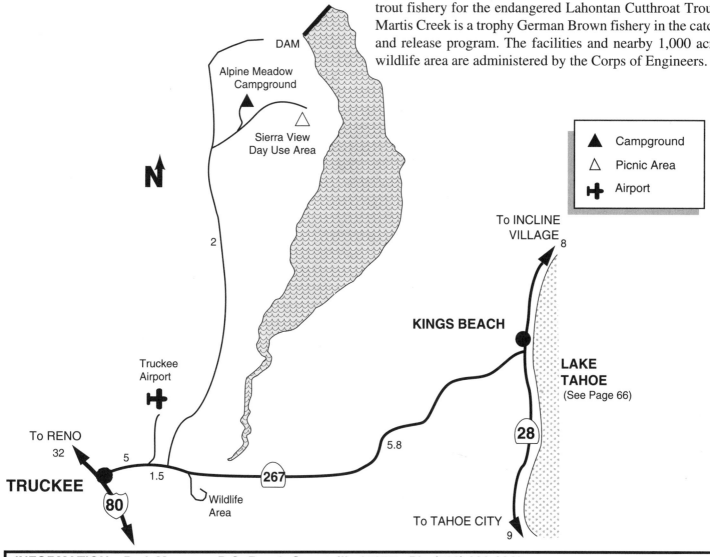

INFORMATION: Park Manager, P.O. Box 6, Smartville 95977—Ph: (530) 639-2342

CAMPING	BOATING	RECREATION	OTHER
25 Dev. Sites for Tents and R.V.s Fee: $10 First Come, First Serve 2 Handicap Sites May Be Reserved Campground Closed in Winter	No Gas or Electric Motor Powered Boats Allowed Sail, Row, Canoe, Inflatables & Windsurf Only Hand Launch Only	Fishing: Brown & Rainbow Trout *Artificial Lures and Flies Only* *Barbless Hooks* *Catch & Release Only* Picnicking Hiking Nature Trails Campfire Programs	Full Facilities 6 Miles at Truckee Airport Within 3 Miles

MARLETTE & SPOONER LAKES, HOBART RESERVOIR

The Lake Tahoe Nevada State Park has jurisdiction over these Lakes and the surrounding backcountry spanning over 13,000 acres. Marlette Lake is one of the most beautiful in the Sierras. No fishing is permitted as it is a fish hatchery for rainbow trout. Fishing is allowed at Hobart Reservoir. Check for fishing conditions at Spooner Lake. This Lake is a trailhead for equestrians, hikers and mountain bikers including connections to the spectacular Tahoe Rim Trail - 165 miles. Numerous trails are throughout this entire area. For details contact the State Park. A great array of wildlife and wildflowers can be viewed.

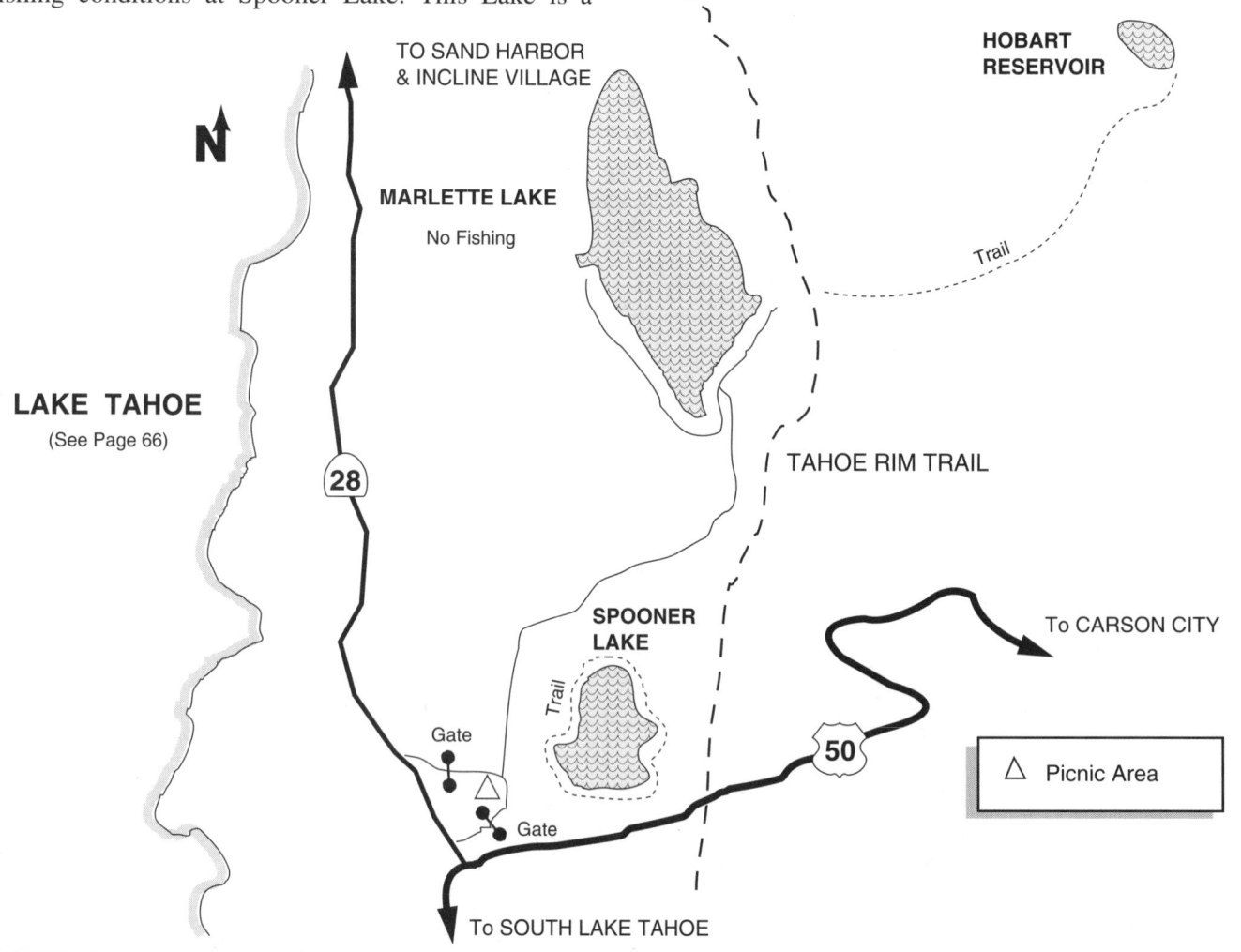

TO SAND HARBOR & INCLINE VILLAGE

N

MARLETTE LAKE
No Fishing

HOBART RESERVOIR

Trail

LAKE TAHOE
(See Page 66)

28

TAHOE RIM TRAIL

SPOONER LAKE

Trail

To CARSON CITY

Gate

50

△ Picnic Area

Gate

To SOUTH LAKE TAHOE

INFORMATION: Lake Tahoe Nevada State Parks, P.O. Box 8867, Incline, NV 89452—Ph: (775) 831-0494

CAMPING	BOATING	RECREATION	OTHER
Backcountry Camping In Designated Areas 2 Overnight Cabin Rentals Mountain Bike Rentals Guide Service Ph: (775) 749-5349	No Boating Allowed For Lake Tahoe Boating Facilities See Page 66	Fishing: Trout Spooner Lake: Catch & Release Barbless Artificial Lures Only Fishing Clinics Hiking & Equestrian Trails Mountain Bike Trails 20 mph Max. 5 mph on Curves Picnicking Spooner Lake: 25 Sites	Tahoe Rim Trail Assn. DWR Community Non-Profit Center 948 Incline Way Incline Village, NV 89451 Ph: (775) 298-0012 Information for Volunteers Memberships Trail Maps

COLLINS LAKE

The Collins Lake Recreation Area is at an elevation of 1,200 feet in the scenic Mother Lode Country. The Lake has a surface area of over 1,000 acres with 12-1/2 miles of shoreline. The modern campground and R.V. Park provide well separated sites under oak and pine trees. There is a broad, sandy beach and many family and group picnic sites. All boating is allowed. Unmuffled boats and small personal watercraft such as jet skis are *not permitted.* Waterskiing is permitted from May 15 to September 30. One of the finest fishing Lakes in California, Collins is famous for trophy trout along with a variety of warm water species. There are zones for the exclusive use of fishermen throughout the year.

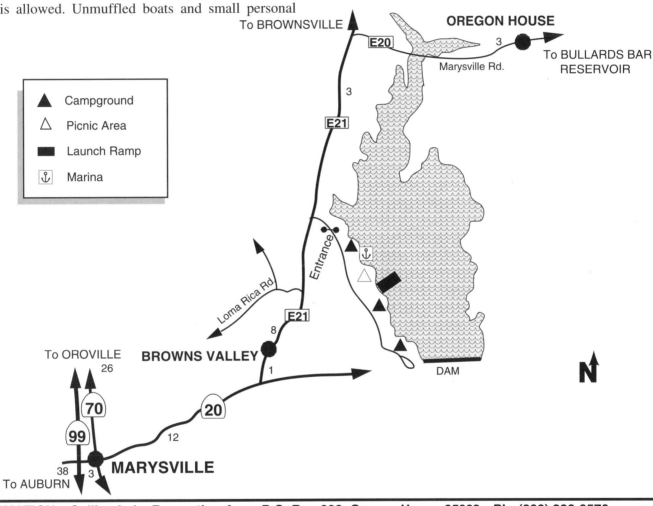

▲	Campground
△	Picnic Area
■	Launch Ramp
⚓	Marina

INFORMATION: Collins Lake Recreation Area, P.O. Box 300, Oregon House 95962—Ph: (800) 286-0576

CAMPING	BOATING	RECREATION	OTHER
183 Dev. Sites for Tents & R.V.s	Power, Row, Canoe, Sail, Waterski,	Fishing: Trout, Catfish, Bluegill,	Snack Bar Grocery Store
Fee: $20 - $32 Electric, Water, & Sewer Hookups Available Reservations Recommended	Windsurf & Inflatables No Jets or Unmuffled Boats Launch Ramp or Boat Use Fee: $6 Rentals : Outboard Fishing,	Crappie, Bass Swimming - Sand Beach Picnicking - Families & Groups Playgrounds	Bait & Tackle Hot Showers Disposal Station Gas Station Propane
Open Camp Areas Along Shoreline Fee: $18	Row, Paddle, Kayaks & Patio Boats Docks, Berths, Moorings, Dry Storage		Full Facilities Within 6 Miles

LAKE FRANCIS

Located in the foothills of the Motherlode country, Lake Francis is at an elevation of 1,700 feet. The Lake has approximately 40 surface acres. The 32-acre Resort offers full vacation facilities including cabins and campsites for R.V.s and tents. No motors are allowed on the Lake so it is good for non-powered craft. Campsites are spotted with 100-foot pines, large oaks and madrones. Canadian geese and abundant wildlife can often be enjoyed at the Lake. There is a launch ramp and nice picnic areas around the water. This is a good spot to bring the whole family.

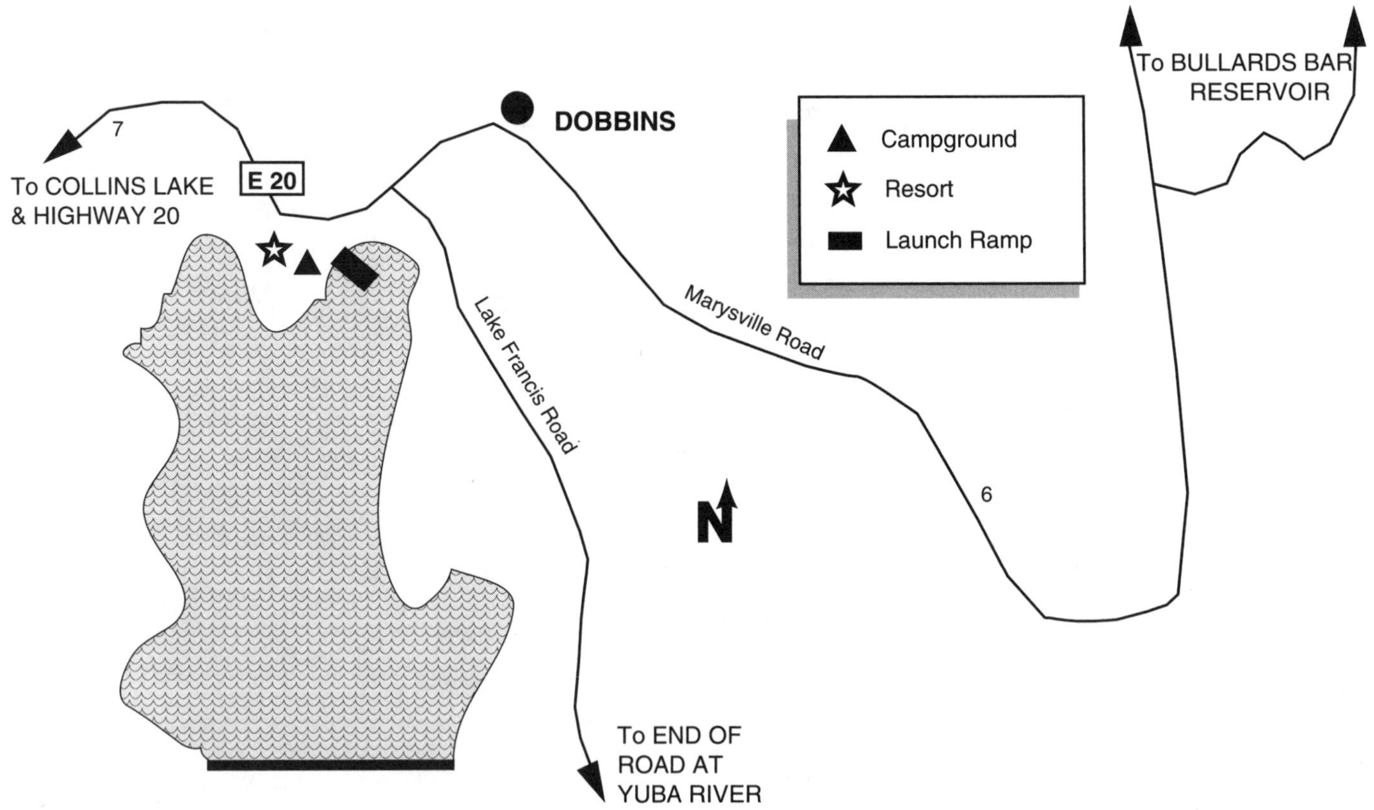

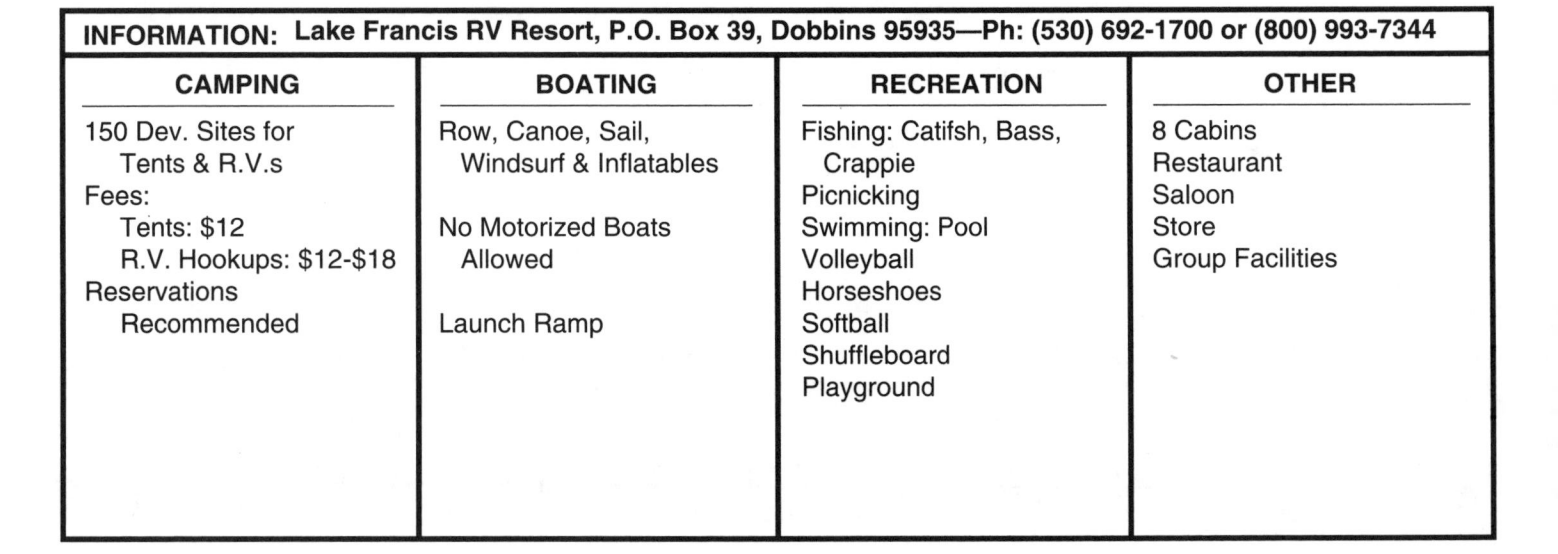

INFORMATION: Lake Francis RV Resort, P.O. Box 39, Dobbins 95935—Ph: (530) 692-1700 or (800) 993-7344			
CAMPING	**BOATING**	**RECREATION**	**OTHER**
150 Dev. Sites for Tents & R.V.s	Row, Canoe, Sail, Windsurf & Inflatables	Fishing: Catifsh, Bass, Crappie	8 Cabins
Fees:		Picnicking	Restaurant
Tents: $12	No Motorized Boats	Swimming: Pool	Saloon
R.V. Hookups: $12-$18	Allowed	Volleyball	Store
Reservations		Horseshoes	Group Facilities
Recommended	Launch Ramp	Softball	
		Shuffleboard	
		Playground	

ENGLEBRIGHT RESERVOIR

Englebright Reservoir, located northeast of Marysville, is at an elevation of 527 feet. The Lake has a surface area of 815 acres with a shoreline of 24 miles. Englebright is a boat camper's bonanza. Boats can be launched near the dam or at Joe Miller. A variety of boats can be rented at Skippers Cove.

You can then proceed by boat up the Lake to a campsite. The shoreline is steep and rocky except at the campgrounds where there are some sandy beaches with pine and oak trees above the high water line. Fishing is good in the quiet, narrow coves. *Waterskiing is not allowed at the North end as noted on map.*

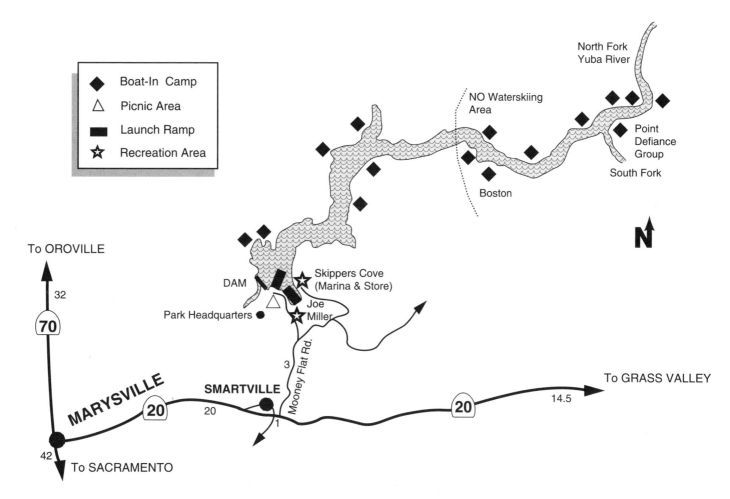

INFORMATION: U.S. Army Corps of Engineers, P. O. Box 6, Smartville 95977—Ph: (530) 639-2342

CAMPING	BOATING	RECREATION	OTHER
100 Developed Boat-In Sites Fee: $10 First Come, First Served	Power, Row, Canoe, Sail, Waterski, Jets, Windsurf & Inflatables	Fishing: Trout, Bass, Catfish, Bluegill, Bass & Kokanee	Skippers Cove Marina 13104 Marina Smartville 95977
	Full Service Marina	Swimming	Ph: (530) 639-2272
Group Campground at Point Defiance Can be Reserved	Launch Ramps Fee: $2 Rentals: Fishing, Canoe & Waterski	Picnicking Hiking	Grocery Store Hot Sandwiches Gas - Propane Bait & Tackle
Water levels may fluctuate Use caution when you boat camp as low water levels may occur overnight	Boats, Houseboats & Patio Boats Docks, Berths, Moorings, Gas		

SCOTTS FLAT LAKE

Scotts Flat Lake is at an elevation of 3,100 feet at the gateway to the Tahoe National Forest. The Lake has a surface area of 850 acres with 7-1/2 miles of coniferous shoreline. This is a good boating Lake with two launch ramps and marina facilities. Anglers will find trout and warm water fish. The Scotts Flat campground includes a picnic area, sandy beaches and a store. Scotts Flat is a quiet, relaxing facility where nature provides a beautifully forested environment.

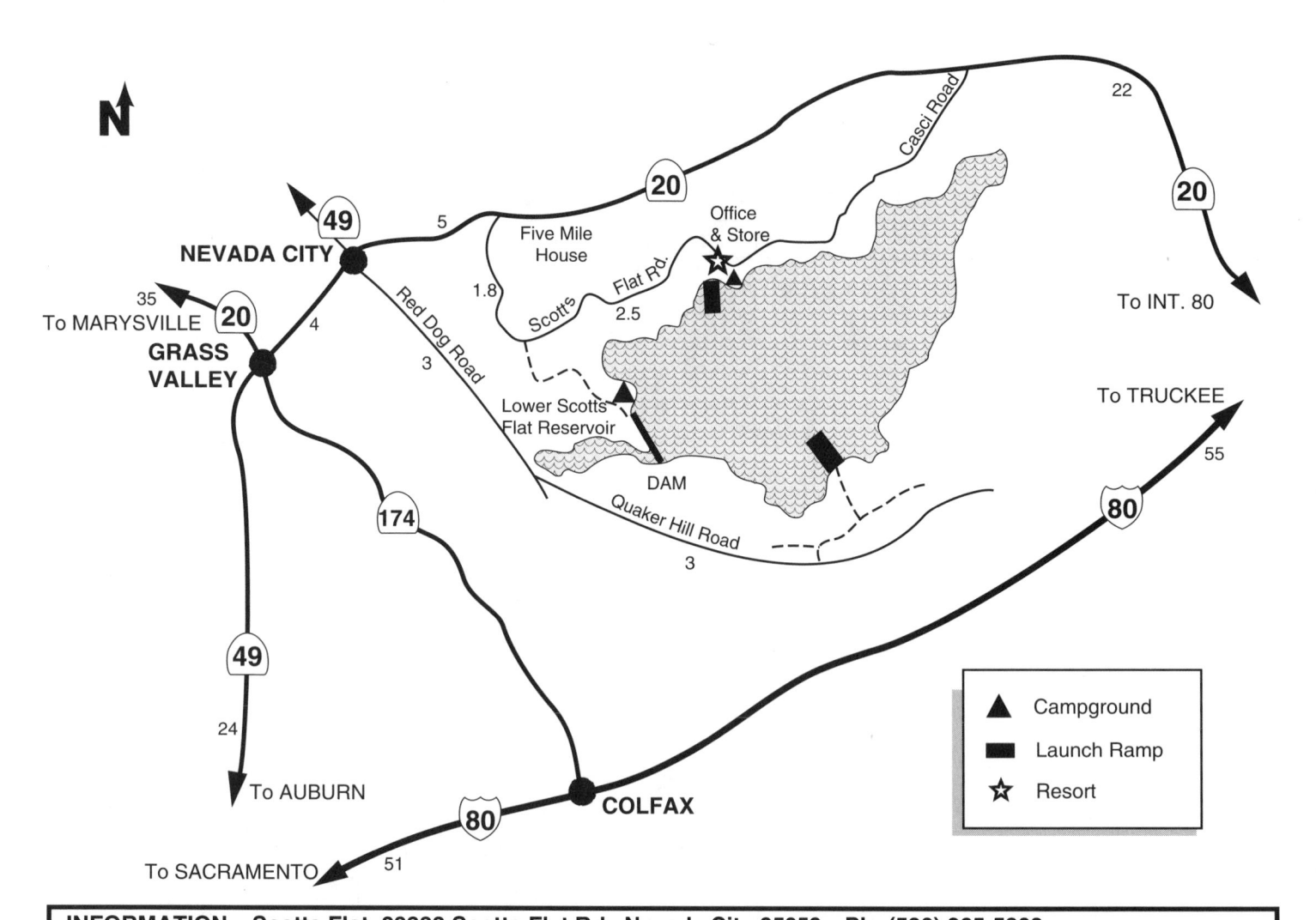

INFORMATION: Scotts Flat, 23333 Scotts Flat Rd., Nevada City 95959—Ph: (530) 265-5302

CAMPING	BOATING	RECREATION	OTHER
20 Dev. Sites for Tents 165 Dev. Sites for R.V.s Fees: Sept.15 to May 15 　　All Sites - $14 - $16 May 15 to Sept. 15 　　Water Sites - $23 　　Inland Sites - $17 Reservations Accepted	Power, Row, Canoe, 　Sail, Waterski & 　Inflatables *No PWC's* Full Service Marina Launch Ramps Rentals: Fishing 　& Pedal Boats Moorings Dry Storage	Fishing: Rainbow & 　German Brown 　Trout, Large & 　Smallmouth Bass, 　Kokanee Barrier Free Fishing 　Platform Swimming Picnicking Hiking Volleyball Goldpanning Horseshoes	Grocery Store Bait & Tackle Hot Showers Disposal Station Children's Playground *No ATVs or 　Horses*

Rollins Lake, situated in the heart of the Gold Country at an elevation of 2,100 feet, is right off Interstate 80 near Colfax and Grass Valley. The Lake has approximately 825 surface acres of water and 26 miles of wooded shoreline. Rollins Lake offers 4 unique individual, family-owned and operated campgrounds. Each has their own convenience store, boat ramp, sandy beach and roped off swim area. The individual campgrounds take their own reservations. Each arm of the Lake provides many coves and long stretches of open water for boating and waterskiing. Fishing is good from both boat and shore for a wide variety of trout and warm water species.

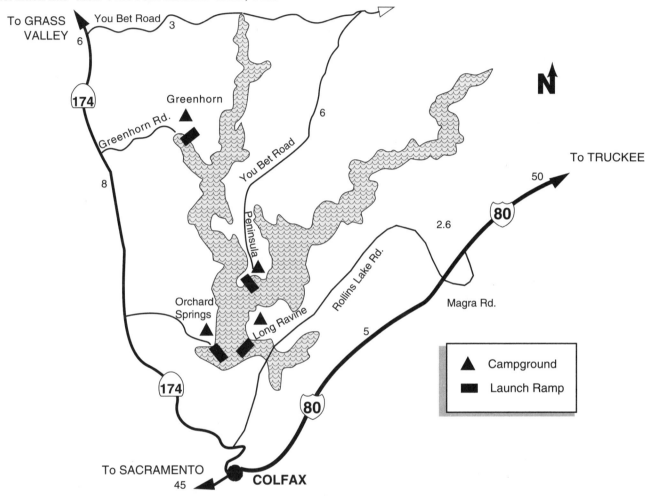

INFORMATION: Each Campground has its own Phone Number - See Below			
CAMPING	**BOATING**	**RECREATION**	**OTHER**

Dev. Sites for Tents & R.V.s
    Fees: $18 - $25
    Some Full Hookups
Greenhorn: 84 Sites
Orchard Springs: 60 Sites
Long Ravine: 58 Sites
Peninsula: 78 Sites
Group Camping
R.V. & Trailer Storage
Disposal Station
Additional Fees for
    Watercraft, Pets and
    Extra Vehicles
	Power, Row, Canoe,
	    Sail, Waterski,
	    Jets, Windsurfers
	Boat Gas Dock
	4 Launch Ramps
	Rentals: Fishing
	    Boats, Kayaks,
	    Paddle Boats
	    & Hydro Bikes
	Boat Slips
	Dry Storage
		Fishing: Rainbow
		    & Brown Trout,
		    Small & Largemouth
		    Bass, Crappie,
		    Catfish & Sunfish
		Picnicking
		Swimming
		Bicyling
		Hiking Trails
		Volleyball Court
			Snack Bar & Grill
			Restaurant & Lounge
			Bait & Tackle
			Fishing Licenses
			
			Reservations - Phone:
			Greenhorn: (530) 272-6100
			Orchard Springs:
			    (530) 346-2212
			Long Ravine:(530) 346-6166
			Peninsula: (530) 477-9413

LAKE VALLEY RESERVOIR and KELLY LAKE

Lake Valley Reservoir is at an elevation of 5,800 feet. The shoreline is surrounded by tall trees and granite boulders. The campsites are situated under the trees near the Lake and accommodate both tents and R.V.s. The steep shoreline combined with the steady west wind allows for good sailing.

Waterskiing is not permitted at Lake Valley. Kelley Lake is a small day-use facility well worth a visit. 5 picnic sites, tables and firepits are available. Small boats without motors are allowed. Trout fishing can be excellent at both these High Sierra Lakes.

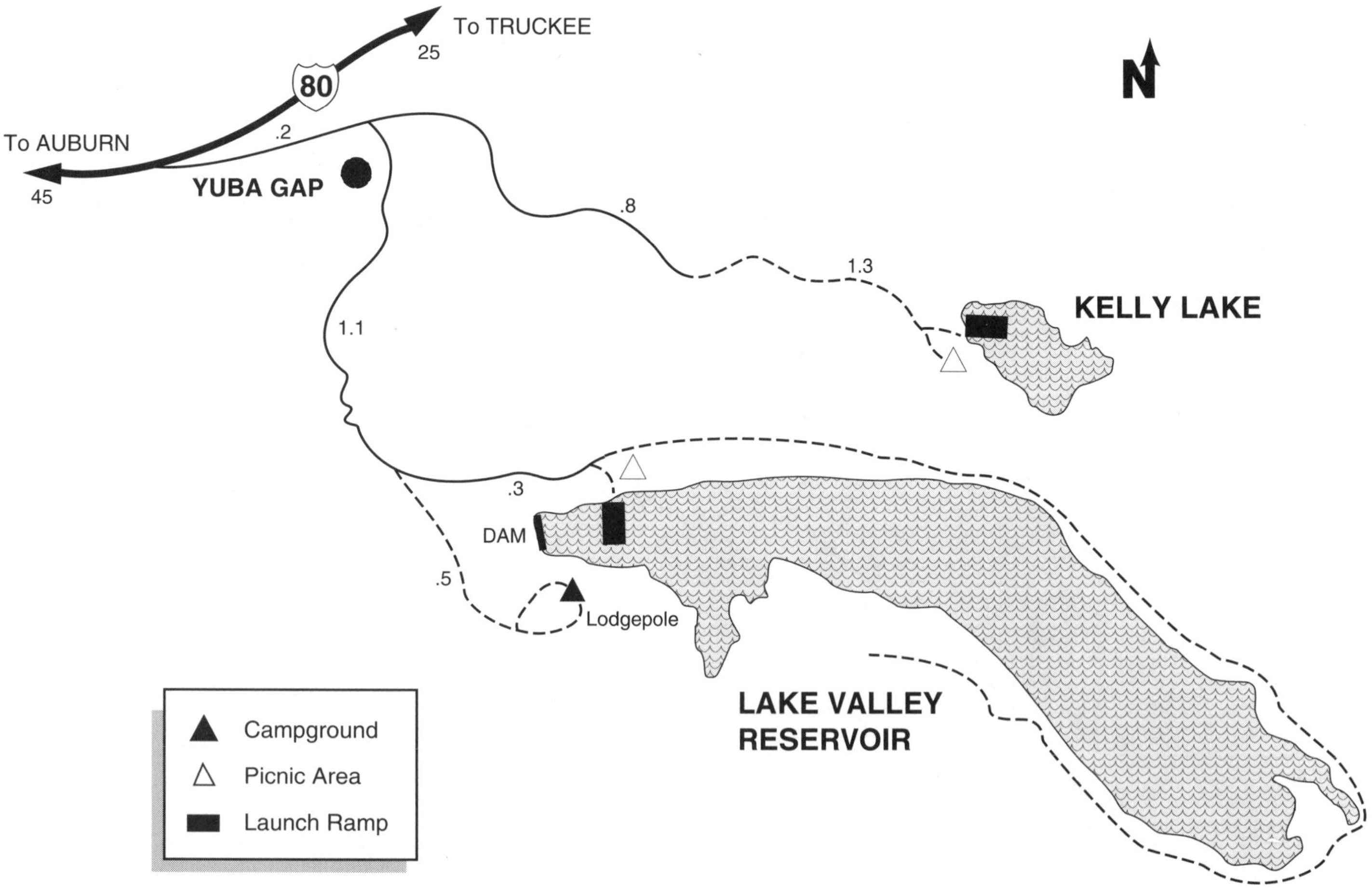

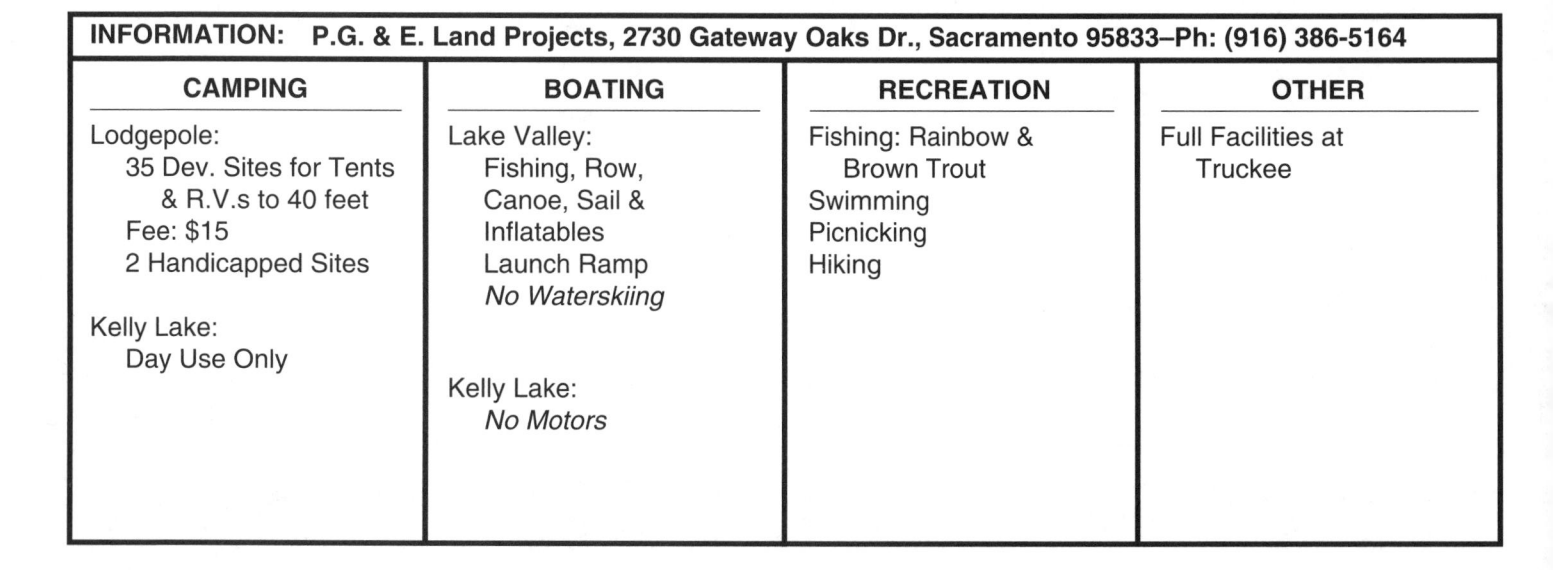

CAMPING	BOATING	RECREATION	OTHER
Lodgepole: 　35 Dev. Sites for Tents 　　& R.V.s to 40 feet 　Fee: $15 　2 Handicapped Sites Kelly Lake: 　Day Use Only	Lake Valley: 　Fishing, Row, 　Canoe, Sail & 　Inflatables 　Launch Ramp 　*No Waterskiing* Kelly Lake: 　*No Motors*	Fishing: Rainbow & 　Brown Trout Swimming Picnicking Hiking	Full Facilities at 　Truckee

INFORMATION: P.G. & E. Land Projects, 2730 Gateway Oaks Dr., Sacramento 95833–Ph: (916) 386-5164

The Lake Pillsbury Recreation Area provides a wide range of outdoor recreation. Located in a mountainous setting at an elevation of 1,818 feet in the Mendocino National Forest, this 2,003 surface acre Lake has 65 miles of shoreline. It is open to all types of boating including boat camping in designated areas. Anglers will find trout, steelhead and salmon in season in the nearby Eel River and its tributaries. The Bloody Rock Area is popular with equestrians. Hang gliding at Hull Mountain (elevation 6,873 feet) offers spectacular views of the surrounding countryside. *For further information: Lake County Visitor Center, 875 Lakeport Blvd., Lakeport 95453, Ph: (800) LAKESIDE.*

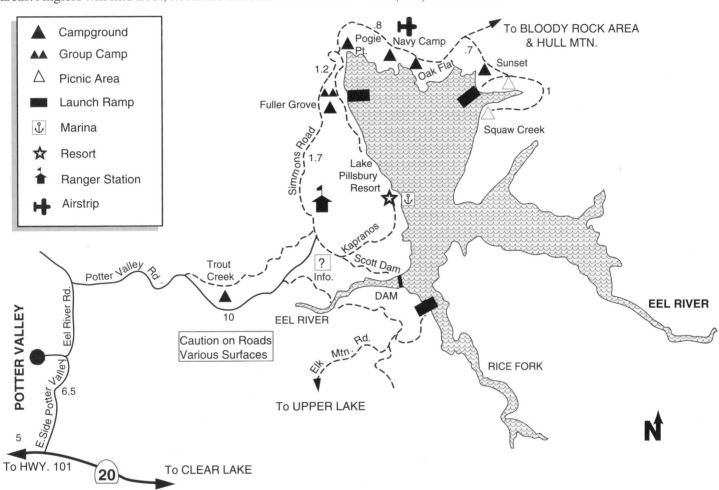

INFORMATION: Upper Lake Ranger District, 10025 Elk Mountain Rd., Upper Lake 95485—Ph: (707) 275-2361

CAMPING	BOATING	RECREATION	OTHER
U.S.F.S.: 141 Tent & R.V. Sites Fee: $12	Open to All Boating Boat Camping in Designated Areas	Fishing: Largemouth & Black Bass, Rainbow Trout, Bluegill & Sunfish	Snack Bars Groceries Restaurant & Lounge
PG&E Sites: Sunset: 54 Dev. Sites Navy Camp: 20 Dev. Sites Pogie Point: 45 Dev. Sites Fuller Grove: 30 Dev. Sites Trout Creek: 15 Dev. Sites Fees for PG&E Sites: $15 Plus Fuller Grove Group to 60 People Max. $100 Reserve:Ph: (916) 386-5164	Launch Ramps Rentals: Fishing Boats & Canoes Marina: Fuel, Slips & Supplies	Eel River: Salmon & Steelhead Swimming Picnicking Hiking & Equestrian Trails Backpacking Hang Gliding	Bait & Tackle Gas Station Lake Pillsbury Resort P.O. Box 37 Potter Valley 95469 Ph: (707) 743-1581 40 Tent & R.V. Sites 8 Cabins

LAKE MENDOCINO

Lake Mendocino is at an elevation of 748 feet above Coyote Dam on the East Fork of the Russian River. This is wine country with many small valleys of vineyards and pear trees. The Lake has a surface area of 1,740 acres with 15 miles of oak-wooded shoreline. The U.S. Army Corps of Engineers maintain the facilities which include numerous campsites, picnic sites and 7 group picnic shelters, each with a massive stone barbecue pit. There is a large protected swim beach and a 5-kilometer hiking trail. Equestrians will find a staging area and riding trails. The fishing is good with Channel catfish going to 30 pounds and Stripers to 40 pounds. A Fish Hatchery is open to the public from November to March.

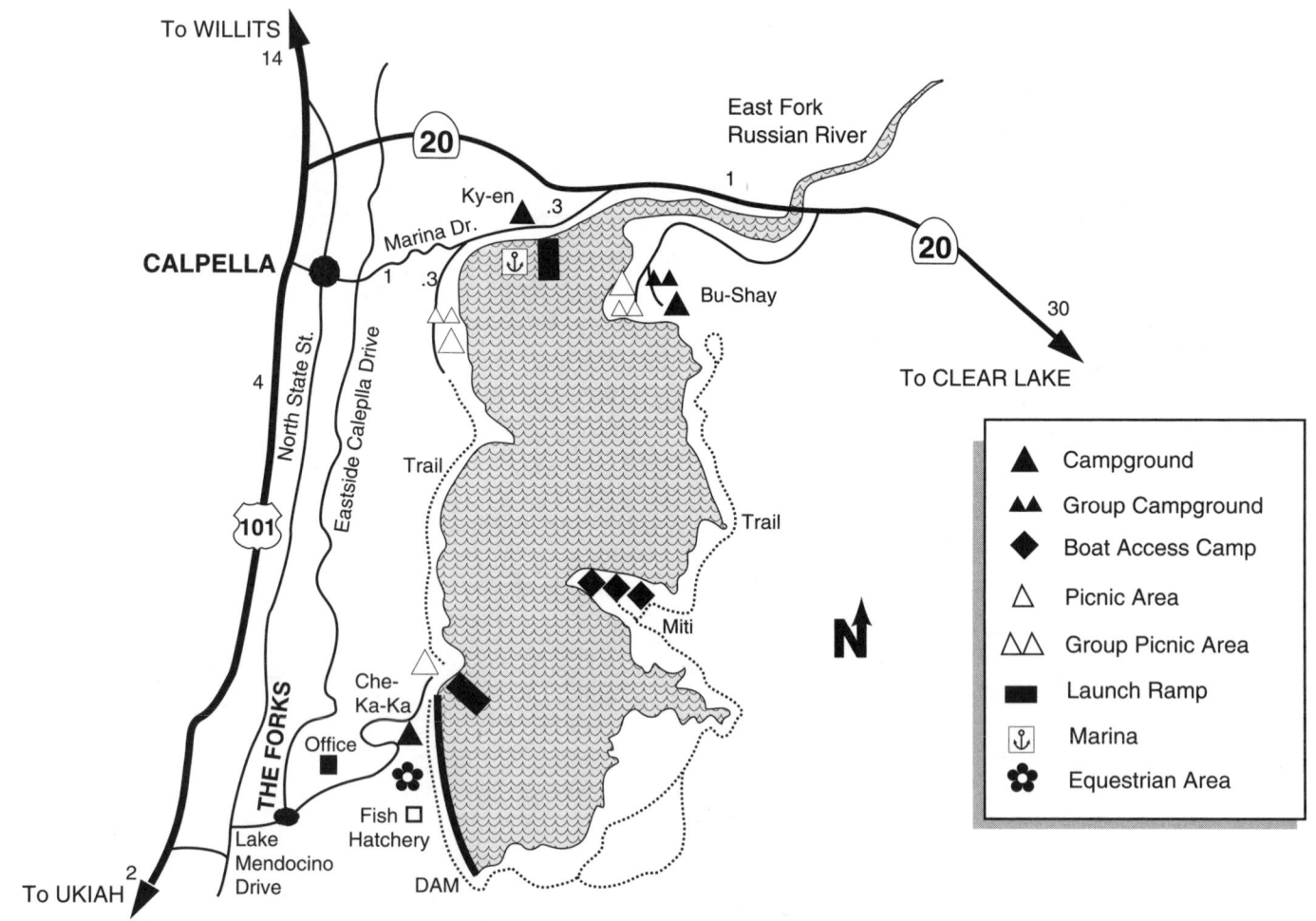

INFORMATION: Park Manager, 1160 Lake Mendocino Dr., Ukiah 95482—Ph: (707) 462-7581

CAMPING	BOATING	RECREATION	OTHER
319 Dev. Sites for Tents & R.V.s Fee: $14 to $16	Power, Row, Canoe, Sail, Waterski & Inflatables	Fishing: Catfish, Bluegill, Crappie, Large, Smallmouth & Striped Bass	Lake Mendocino Marina: P.O. Box 13 Calpella 95418
22 R.V.s Only Sites	Full Service Marina	Swimming	Ph: (707) 485-8644
3 Group Camps 165 People Maximum	Launch Ramps Rentals:	Picnicking	(Off Highway 20 at North End)
Reserve: Ph: (877) 444-6777	Power, Canoe, Waterski & Pontoon Boats	Hiking Junior Ranger & Interpretive	33 R.V. Site No Hookups
18 Boat Access Only Sites	Docks, Berths Dry Storage	Programs Hunting: Waterfowl Special Seasonal Turkey Hunts	Snack Bar Ice, Firewood Boat & Slip Rentals

The Blue Lakes are at an elevation of 1,320 feet off Highway 20 between Clear Lake and Lake Mendocino. These popular Lakes are nestled in a beautiful setting of dense groves of madrones, oaks and evergreens. They are spring fed and have existed for over 10,000 years. The clear blue waters and relaxed environment make this a delightful retreat for fishing, swimming and boating. The private resorts surrounding the Lakes provide complete vacation facilities including shaded campsites, cabins, restaurants, boat rentals, swim beaches and picnic areas.

...Continued...

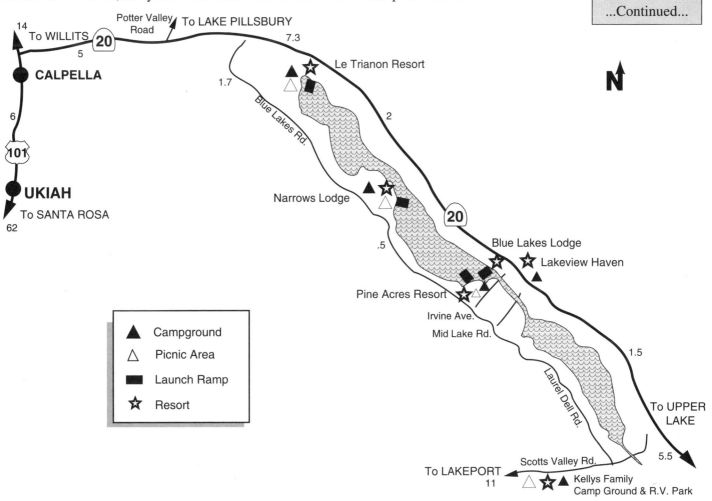

INFORMATION: Lake County Visitor Info. Center, 875 Lakeport Blvd., Lakeport 95485—Ph: (800) 525-3743

CAMPING	BOATING	RECREATION	OTHER
Private Resorts: Sites for Tents & R.V.s *See Following Page*	Power, Row, Canoe, Sail, Windsurf & Inflatables 5 MPH Speed Limit Launch Ramps Rentals: Rowboats, Motorboats, Canoes & Paddleboats (Check following page) Docks	Fishing: Trout, Small and Largemouth Bass, Catfish, Bluegill, Crappie Swimming - Beaches Picnicking	*See Following Page*

58

LE TRIANON RESORT: 5845 E. Hwy. 20, Ukiah 95482
Ph: (707) 275-2262

Le Trianon Resort offers housekeeping cabins as well as 200 sites for tent camping, R.V.s or trailers. Electric and water hookups, disposal station, laundry and showers are available. Also provided are a launch ramp, dock, swim area and boat rentals. Open April 1 to October 31, First Come, First Served.

NARROWS LODGE: 5690 Blue Lakes Road
Upper Lake 95485—Ph: (707) 275-2718

The Narrows Lodge Resort provides all the comforts of modern conveniences in a lovely forest setting. There are fully equipped housekeeping cabins and motel units with coffee service. The R.V. Park has 20 sites with complete hookups. 10 sites have water and electric hookups. Tent sites are also available. The Resort has a launch ramp, fishing dock, swim area, BBQ's, picnic tables, disposal station, bait and tackle shop and game room. Rowboats, motorboats, kayaks, canoes and paddleboats can be rented. Open year around.

PINE ACRES RESORT: 5328 Blue Lakes Road
Upper Lake 95485—Ph: (707) 275-2811
FAX (707) 275-9549

Pine Acres Resort offers a motel and fully equipped cottages. 30 R.V. sites are available, 26 with water and electric hookups and 4 with full hookups. There are shaded lawns, BBQs, picnic tables, horseshoe court, swimming beach with float, fishing pier, launch ramp, boat rentals, bait and tackle shop and disposal station. A gazebo is available for pot lucks, square dancing, conferences, family reunions and other uses for R.V. groups. Open year around.

BLUE LAKES LODGE: 5135 W. Highway 20
Upper Lake 95485—Ph: (707) 275-2178

This Resort has a motel with housekeeping units with T.V.s including free HBO, complimentary coffee and air conditioning. A restaurant and cocktail bar are open year around with live entertainment and dancing on the weekends. There is a launch ramp along with fishing docks, swim area and boat rentals including a patio boat rental for parties. Picnic tables, barbecues, horseshoes and a large parking area for R.V.s (no hookups) are also available. There are facilities for banquets, weddings and seminars.

KELLY'S KAMP: 8220 Scotts Valley Road
Upper Lake 95485—Ph: (707) 263-5754

Kelly's Family Kamp Ground and R.V. Park offers quiet family camping on spacious sites with frontage on Scotts Creek. There are 48 Tent/R.V. sites with water and electric hookups. Also available are the Kamp Store, modern restrooms, laundromat, disposal station, hot showers, firewood, picnic tables, fire pits and BBQ grills. Recreational facilities include swimming, 2-acre Lake with floats, fishing, volleyball, basketball, horseshoes and hiking. A horseback riding trail is nearby. R.V. storage is available and a pavilion area with a built-in barbecue for large groups.

LAKEVIEW HAVEN R.V. PARK: 5178 WestHighway 20
Upper Lake 95485—Ph: (707) 275-2105

Lakeview Haven has a 46 site R.V. park with full hookups. Nearby there is a restaurant, cocktail lounge and game room, launch ramp and fishing dock.

By: Greg Dirksen

Call Resorts for Current Prices

Clear Lake is at an elevation of 1,320 feet with a surface area of 43,000 acres. The Lake has a shoreline of 100 miles and offers a huge variety of recreational activities. This was once the home of the Pomo and Lile'ek tribes who were drawn here by the abundant fish and game. Often called "Bass Capital of the West," Clear Lake provides the angler with a productive warm water fishery. Miles of open water, many coves and inlets entice the boater and waterskiier. This Lake is also known for excellent sailing conditions. Numerous launch ramps, marinas, beaches, campgrounds and resorts dot the shoreline. Nearby Highland Springs Reservoir offers warm water fishing and non-powered boating.

...Continued.....

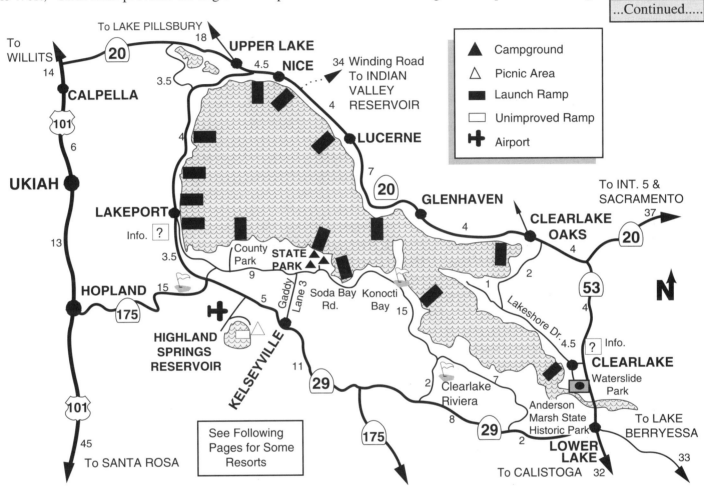

▲	Campground
△	Picnic Area
■	Launch Ramp
▭	Unimproved Ramp
✈	Airport

INFORMATION: Lake County Visitor Info. Center, 875 Lakeport Blvd., Lakeport 95453—Ph: (800) 525-3743

CAMPING	BOATING	RECREATION	OTHER
Clear Lake State Park 5300 Soda Bay Rd. Kelseyville 95451 Ph: (707) 279-4293 147 Dev. Sites for Tents & R.V.s to 35 Feet Fee: $12 Reservations Ph: (800) 444-7275 *For Additional Campgrounds, See Following Pages*	Open to All Boating Full Service Marinas Public Launch Ramps Boat Rentals: Fishing, Waterski Boats & Pontoons Clear Lake Queen Cruise Boat	Fishing: Florida & Northern Bass, Yellow & Blue Channel Catfish, Trout, Crappie & Bluegill Swimming: Beaches & Pools Picnicking at State Parks Hiking & Nature Trails Rock Hounding Hunting Nearby: Deer, Dove, Quail, & Waterfowl, Turkey	Winery Tours Water Park Glider Flights Golf Courses Complete Facilities in Nearby Towns Anderson Marsh State Historical Park: Archeological Sites of Indian Villages and Sanctuary for Water Birds and Fish Gaming Casinos

CLEAR LAKE.............Continued

**THERE ARE OVER 50 PRIVATE CAMPGROUNDS AND RESORTS ON CLEAR LAKE.
THE FOLLOWING ARE RANDOMLY SELECTED FACILITIES, MANY WITH LAUNCH RAMPS**

NORTHSHORE, NICE, LUCERNE

HOLIDAY HARBOR
P.O. Box 26, 3605 Lakeshore Blvd., Nice 95464—Ph: (707) 274-1136
33 Sites, Hookups, Disposal Station, Hot Showers, Laundry, Concrete Ramp, Marine Gas, 130 Boat Slips.

ARROW TRAILER PARK
P.O. Box 1735, 6720 E. Hwy. 20, Lucerne 95458—Ph: (707) 274-7715
24 Sites, 18 Full Hookups, 2 Pull-Throughs, Disposal Station, Hot Showers, Laundry, BBQ Area, Ramp, Pier,
Mooring, Storage, Bait & Tackle, Guest Suite for 2.

GLENHAVEN - CLEARLAKE OAKS

INDIAN BEACH RESORT
9945 E. Hwy. 20, Glenhaven 95443—Ph: (707) 998-3760
Housekeeping Cabins with Fully Equipped Kitchenettes, 300 feet of Sandy Beach, Large Oak Trees,
Lighted Pier, Launch Ramp, Boat Slips, BBQ Areas, Children's Playground, Cabana, Mini-Store, Bait.

LAKE MARINA MOTEL/RESORT
10215 E. Hwy. 20, Clearlake Oaks 95423—Ph: (707) 998-3787
12 Units with Kitchens, Boat Launch, Pier, Catfishing Area, Boat Rentals, Party Room, BBQs, Group Rates.

BLUE FISH COVE
10573 E. Hwy. 20, Clearlake Oaks 95423—Ph: (707) 998-1769
Housekeeping Units on the Lake, Hot Tub, Pier, Beach, Game Room, Rentals: Fishing Boats.

GLENHAVEN BEACH CAMPGROUND & MARINA
P.O. Box 406, 9625 E. Hwy. 20, Glenhaven 95423—Ph: (707) 998-3406
23 Tent/R.V. Sites, Hookups, Hot Showers, Laundry, Launch Ramp, Mooring, Slips, Fuel Dock, Groceries.

ISLAND RV PARK
P.O. Box 126, 12840 Island Dr., Clearlake Oaks 95423—Ph: (707) 998-3940
19 R.V. Sites, Hookups, Tent Sites Available, Showers, Laundry, Boat Launch, Docks with Electric Hookups.

HARBOR MOTEL
P. O. Box 1192, 130 Short St., Clearlake Oaks 95423—Ph: (707) 998-3587
7 Units with Kitchenettes, Launch Ramp, Pier, Boat Mooring.

SEA BREEZE RESORT
P. O. Box 653, 9595 Harbor Dr., Glenhaven 95443—Ph: (707) 998-3327
Small Resort with Kitchenette Units, Well Landscaped, Lighted Pier, Launch Ramp, Boat Docks.

CLEARLAKE - SOUTH SHORE

FUNTIME RV PARK AND WATERSPORTS
P.O. Box 509, 6035 Old Hwy. 53, Clearlake 95422—Ph: (707) 994-6267
92 Tent/R.V. Sites, Hookups, Pull Throughs, 50 amp Service, Disposal Station, 6 Cabins, Sleeps 4 to 8 People, A/C,
Cable TV, Groceries, Bait & Tackle, Pool, Beach, Horseshoes, Volley Ball, Ramp, Rental Boats, Fuel Dock, Slips.

ALBATROSS ACRES
P. O. Box 4115, 5545 Old Hwy. 53, Clearlake 95422—Ph: (707) 994-1194
15 R.V. Sites, Hookups, Launch Ramp, Docks, Fishing Area.

....Continued....

KELSEYVILLE - SODA BAY - KONOCTI BAY

EDGEWATER RESORT
1 Mile East of Clear Lake State Park
6420 Soda Bay Rd., Soda Bay, Kelseyville 95451—Ph: (707) 279-0208
Reserve: (800) 396-6224
61 R.V./Tent Sites, 59 Full Hookups with Water, Sites up to 40 ft. with Slide Outs, Hot Showers,
8 Cabins for 2-12 People, Full Kitchens, AC & Cable TV,
Lighted Fishing Pier, Dock, Launch Ramp, Rental Boats, 300 ft. Swim Beach, Swimming Pool,
Clubhouse, General Store, Bait and Tackle, Laundry, Game Room, Volleyball Court,
Ping-Pong & Horseshoe Pits, Group Camping, Pets on Leash Welcome.

RICHMOND PARK
9435 Konocti Bay Rd., Kelseyville 95451—Ph: (707) 277-7535
30 R.V. Sites, Hookups, Launch Ramp, Rental Boats, Snack Bar, Lounge.

FERNDALE RESORT
6190 Soda Bay Rd., Kelseyville 95451—Ph: (707) 279-4866
19 Motel Suites w/ 2 Queen Beds, 5 w/Kitchens, 2 Cottages, 4 Mobile Homes - 1 & 2 Bedrooms w/Kitchen,
No Pets, A/C, Cable T.V.,
Launch Ramp, Slips, Pier, Large Rental Fleet,
Tackle Shop, Fuel Dock, Marine Parts, Repair Shop, Snack Bar.

KONOCTI HARBOR RESORT & SPA
8727 Soda Bay Rd., Kelseyville 95451—Ph: (707) 279-4281 or (800) 660-LAKE
250 Rooms, Restaurant & Lounge, 4 Swimming Pools, Tennis, Launch Ramps, Piers, Slips,
Full Service Marina, Conference Facilities, Theatre.

LAKEPORT

ANCHORAGE INN
950 N. Main St., Lakeport 95453—Ph: (707) 263-5417
34 Units, 20 w/ Kitchens, TV, Laundry, Pool, Sauna, Jacuzzi, Boat Berths, Dock.
CLEAR LAKE INN
1010 N. Main St., Lakeport 95453—Ph: (707) 263-3551
40 Units, TV, Pool, Dock, Fishing Pier.
MALLARD HOUSE, 970 N. Main St., Lakeport 95453—Ph: (707) 262-1601
13 Units, 9 w/Kitchens, Boat Dock
SKYLARK SHORES RESORT/MOTEL
1120 N. Main St., Lakeport 95453—Ph: (707) 263-6151
45 Units, 18 w/Kitchens, TV, Swimming Pool, Boat Dock, Playground.

Along with other resorts not mentioned, there are public launch ramps shown on our map. The State Park is shown on the graph. For information on additional resorts and other attractions, contact:

Lake County Visitor Information Center
875 Lakeport Blvd., Lakeport 95453
Ph: (707) 263-9544 or 800-LAKESIDE (525-3743)

Lakeport Regional Chamber of Commerce
560 Lakeport Blvd., Lakeport 95453
Ph: (707) 263-5092

Clear Lake Chamber of Commerce
4700 Golf Ave., Clearlake 95422
Ph: (707) 994-3600

INDIAN VALLEY RESERVOIR

Indian Valley Reservoir is under the jurisdiction of the Yolo County Flood Control District. Resting at an elevation of 1,476 feet, this very remote 3,800 acre Lake has 39 miles of shoreline. Access is by a 10 mile dirt road. The Lake is an excellent Rainbow trout fishery and a developing warm water fishery. Since there is a 10 MPH speed limit, this is a quiet place for sailing, canoeing and fishing. High winds, however, can occur, particularly in the afternoon. The concessionaire at Indian Valley Store operates a developed campground. The area surrounding the Reservoir is an important winter habitat for both bald eagles, golden eagles and waterfowl.

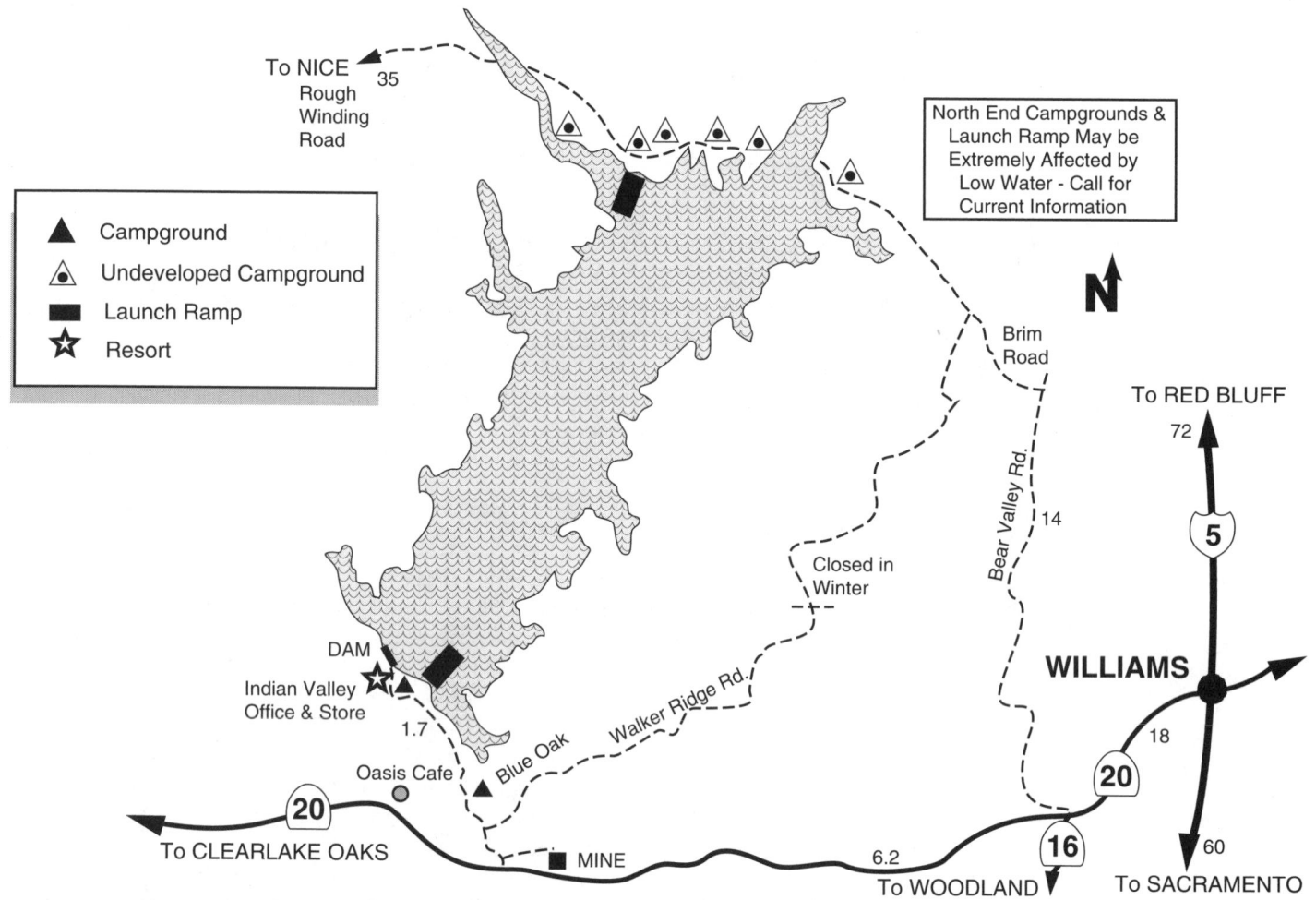

North End Campgrounds & Launch Ramp May be Extremely Affected by Low Water - Call for Current Information

Legend:
- ▲ Campground
- ⚲ Undeveloped Campground
- ■ Launch Ramp
- ★ Resort

To NICE 35 — Rough Winding Road

To RED BLUFF 72
5

Brim Road

Bear Valley Rd. 14

Closed in Winter

WILLIAMS

DAM
Indian Valley Office & Store
1.7
Oasis Cafe
Blue Oak
Walker Ridge Rd.

20 To CLEARLAKE OAKS

MINE

6.2

To WOODLAND

16

20

18

To SACRAMENTO 60

INFORMATION: Yolo Flood Control Fish Report—Ph: (530) 662-0265

CAMPING	BOATING	RECREATION	OTHER
15 Dev. Sites for Tents 20 Dev. Sites for R.V.s 　Fee: $12 - Plus 　$1 Extra Per Person Disposal Station Day Use Fee: $5.50 　3 People per Vehicle 　Plus $1 Extra Per 　Person	Open to All Boating 10 MPH Speed Limit Paved Launch Ramp *Beware of Underwater Hazards and Afternoon Winds*	Fishing: Eagle Lake & 　Rainbow Trout, Large 　& Smallmouth Bass, 　Catfish, Blue Gill, Red 　Ear Perch & Crappie Picnicking Swimming Hiking Birdwatching & Nature Study Hunting on Nearby Bureau of Land Management Area: 　Waterfowl, Quail, Dove, 　Turkey, Pig & Bear	Grocery Store Bait & Tackle Propane On Hwy. 20: 　Oasis Cafe Access: 10 Mile Dirt Road

Numbers around highways represent lakes in numerical order in this book. *See Index for complete listing.*

Highways
- Interstate
- United States
- California

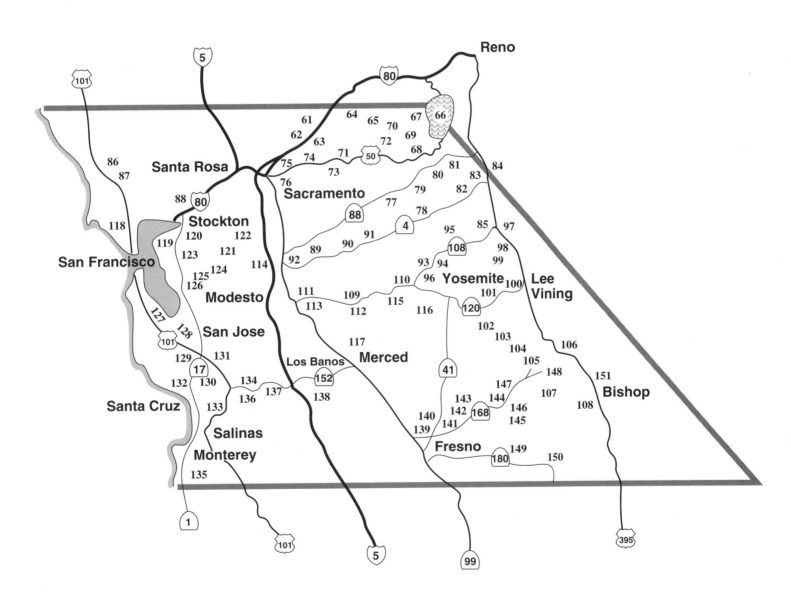

SUGAR PINE and BIG RESERVOIRS—LAKE CLEMENTINE

Sugar Pine Reservoir, at an elevation of 3,618 feet, has 160 surface acres and is located in the Tahoe National Forest. The complex offers handicapped facilities and will accommodate R.V.s and trailers up to 40 feet. Its neighbor, Big Reservoir, sometimes called Morning Star Lake, rests at 4,092 feet in a heavily forested area. Facilities at this privately owned 80-acre Lake include Morning Star Resort. Down the road in the foothill canyons of the American River, Lake Clementine is a part of the Auburn State Recreation Area. The Lake is a 3-1/2 mile long stretch of the North Fork of the American River. Campgrounds are undeveloped but there is a launch ramp. This Lake is open to all boating.

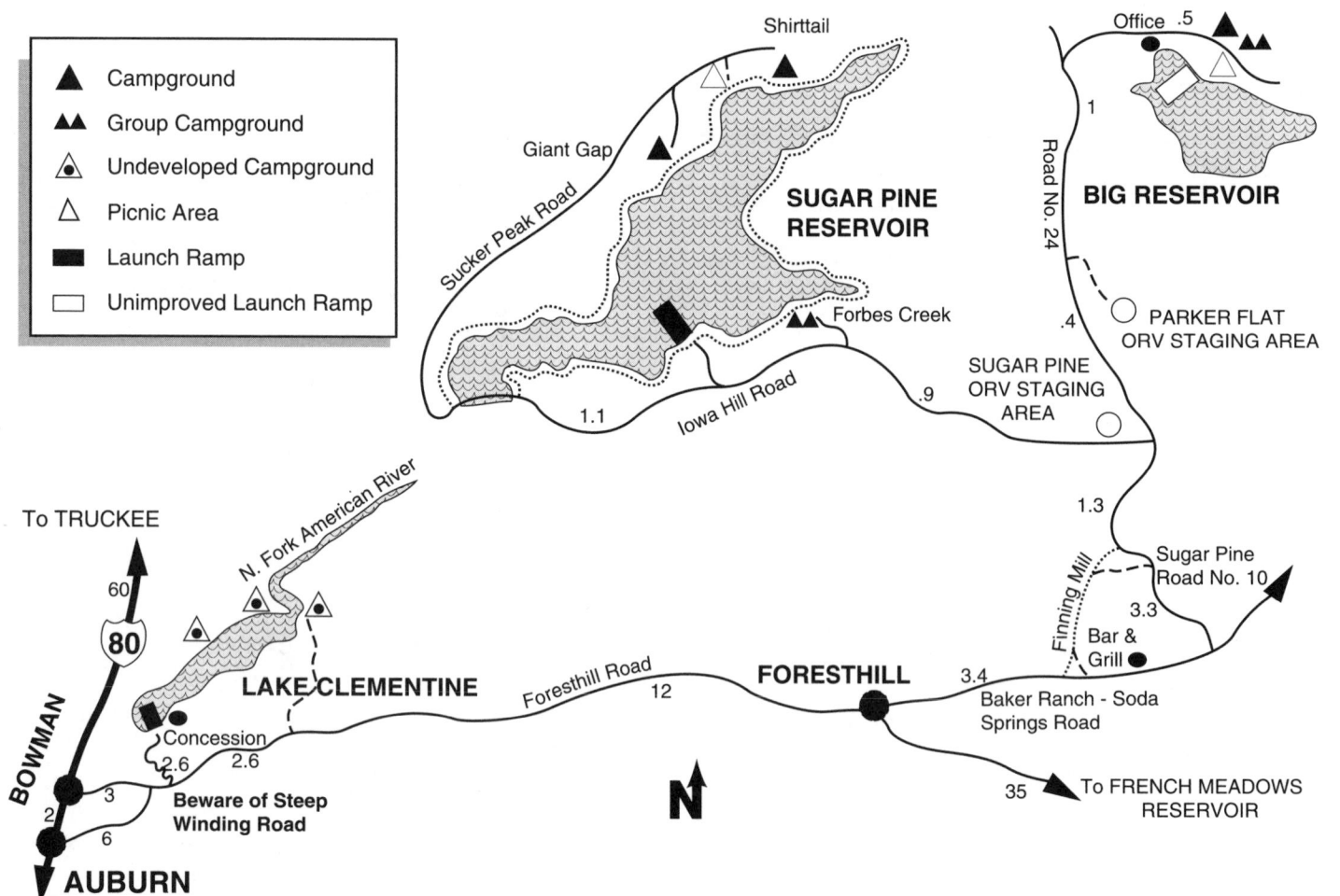

INFORMATION:Foresthill Ranger Station, 22830 Foresthill Rd., Foresthill 95631—Ph: (530) 367-2224 or 478-6254

CAMPING	BOATING	RECREATION	OTHER

Sugar Pine: 60 Dev. Sites Tents & R.V.s
Fees: $12, $24, $35
Forbes Group Campground Reserve: Ph:(877) 444-6777
Big Reservoir:
   19 Dev. Sites for Tents & R.V.s - Fee: $18-$25
   Plus 2 Group Sites for Tents
Lake Clementine:
   Undeveloped Campground Fees: $9 & $11
	Sugar Pine:
	   Open to All Boating
	   10 MPH Speed Limit
	   Launch Ramp
	Big Reservoir:
	   Open to Non-
	      Powered Boating
	   Electric Motors Permitted
	   Dock
	   Fishing by Permit
	Lake Clementine:
	   25 MPH Speed Limit
		Fishing: Rainbow & Brown Trout, Black Bass, Bluegill & Perch
		Picnicking
		Paved & Unpaved Trails
		Swimming
		Hiking & Backpacking
		ORV Trails Nearby
		Hunting: Deer & Bear
			Morning Star Lake Resort at Big Reservoir Campsites
			P.O. Box 119
			Foresthill 95631
			Reservations:
			Ph: (530) 367-2129
			Lake Clementine
			   Auburn State Rec. Area
			   501 El Dorado St.
			   Auburn 95603
			   Ph: (530) 885-4527
			Facilities at Foresthill

Camp Far West Lake is at an elevation of 320 feet in the Sierra foothills northeast of Roseville. The Lake has a surface area of 2,000 acres, 29 miles of shoreline plus 800 acres of camping, hiking, bicycle and equestrian trails. The water temperature rises up to 85 degrees in the summer when the climate can be quite hot although there are many oak trees providing ample shade. The Lake is open year around but the south entrance is closed at the end of summer. This is a good Lake for all types of boating and waterskiing. The boater should be aware of the rocky area as noted on the map. The water level of the Lake can fluctuate. There is a warm water fishery for landlocked smallmouth and black bass at the Bear River and Rock Creek Arms. A horse camp is also available.

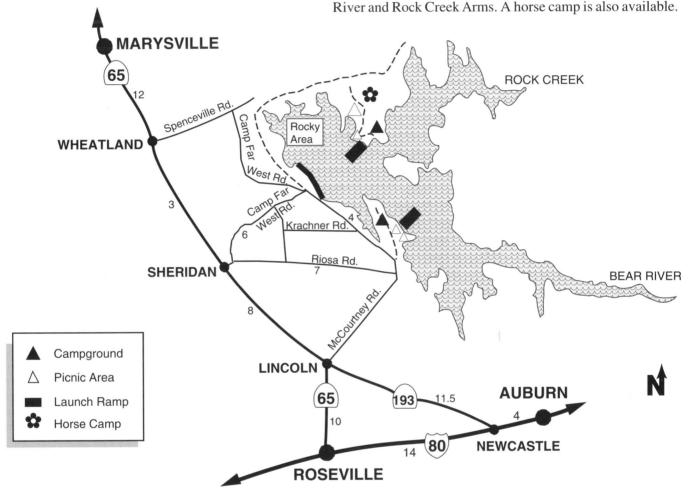

CAMPING	BOATING	RECREATION	OTHER
143 Dev. Sites for Tents & R.V.s 10 with Full Hookups Fees: $12 - $18 Overflow Area Horse Camp Disposal Stations 3 Group Camps - to 250 People Reservations Accepted Day Use: $5 $10 with Boat	Power, Row, Canoe, Sail, Waterski, Jets, Windsurf & Inflatables 2 Launch Ramps Gas, Dry Storage Water Toys & Equipment Rentals at North Shore	Fishing: Florida Largemouth, Black, Striped & Smallmouth Bass, Crappie & Catfish Swimming Picnicking Bicycling Hiking Equestrian Trails	Grocery Stores Bait & Tackle

INFORMATION: Camp Far West, Box 385, Sheridan 95681—South Ph:(916) 645-0484, North Ph:(530) 633-0803

FRENCH MEADOWS RESERVOIR

French Meadows Reservoir rests at an elevation of 5,200 feet on the western slope of the Sierra Nevada. This man-made reservoir of 1,920 surface acres is often subject to low water levels late in the season. Although open to all types of boating, these low water conditions along with underwater hazards, including tree stumps, make waterskiing and speed boating extremely dangerous. If the angler can suffer through the loss of tackle from these hazards, you are sometimes rewarded with a beautiful German brown or rainbow trout up to 7 pounds. The U.S. Forest Service maintains numerous campsites around the lake along with picnic areas and two launch ramps. There are several natural swimming beaches. This is a nice family camping area but remote so plan on staying awhile.

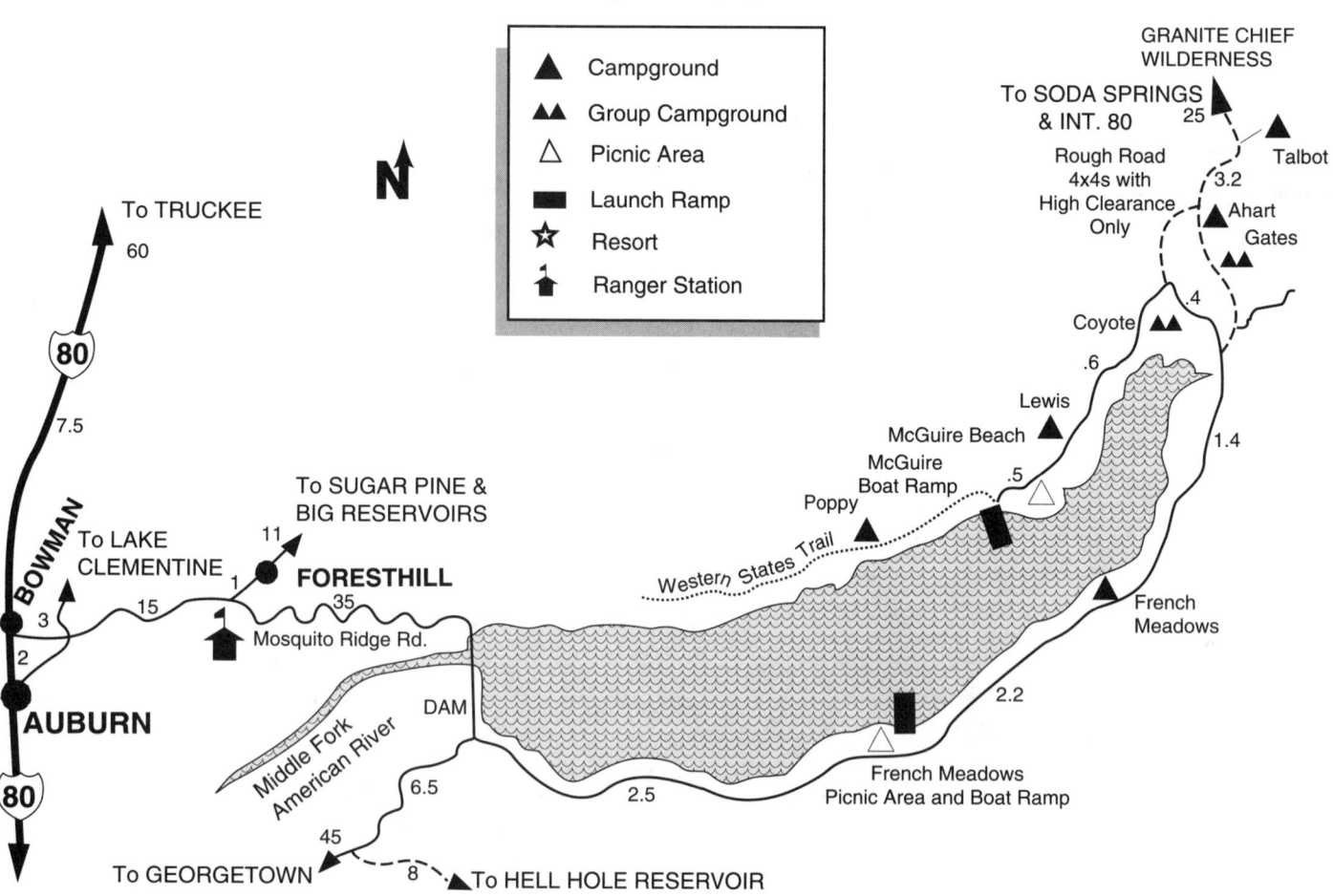

CAMPING	BOATING	RECREATION	OTHER

115 Dev. Sites
Fee: $10 - $12
12 Boat or Walk-In
Sites at Poppy
7 Group Sites
Fees: $50 - $65
 	
Reservations for
French Meadows &
Coyote Group Camps:
Ph: (877) 444-6777
	Open to All Boats
	
	*Speed Boats &
	Waterskiing Not
	Advised Due to
	Submerged Hazards*
		Fishing: Rainbow &
		    Brown Trout
		Picnicking
		Swimming
		Hiking
		Backpacking [Parking]
		
		Granite Chief Wilderness
		    7 Miles East
		    No Mountain Bikes,
		    Motorcycles or
		    Mechanized Vehicles
			Nearest Supplies and
			    Facilities
			39 Miles in Foresthill

INFORMATION: Foresthill Ranger District, 22830 Foresthill Rd., Foresthill 95631—Ph: (530) 367-2224

Hell Hole Reservoir is in the Eldorado National Forest at an elevation of 4,700 feet. The facilities are operated and maintained by the U.S. Forest Service. Hell Hole is 15 miles south of French Meadows Reservoir in a rugged, rocky area on the Rubicon River. The Lake, 1,300 surface acres, is in a deep gorge surrounded by granite boulders with cold, clear water, creating a beautiful setting. It is especially scenic where the water leaves the power house and drops into the Lake. Be sure to bring a camera. Extreme water fluctuations can occur seasonally. Call for information on Lake levels. There are no facilities other than the launch ramp and campgrounds so come well supplied. Ralston Afterbay is on the Middle Fork of the American River with a nice picnic area and gravel launch ramps. *Campers should be aware that bears inhabit this area.*

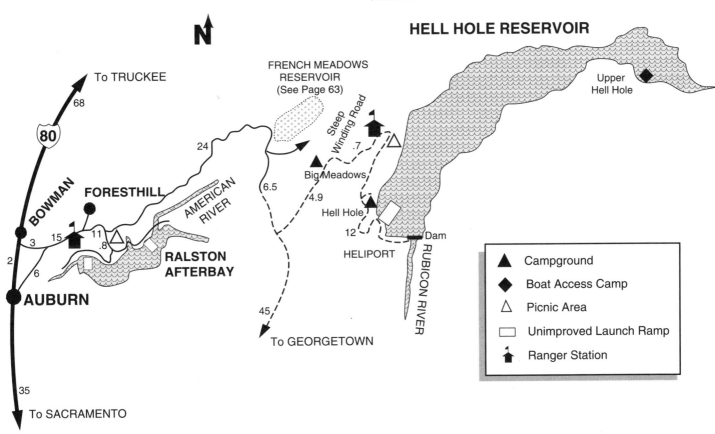

INFORMATION: Georgetown Ranger Dist., 7600 Wentworth Springs Rd., Georgetown 95634—Ph: (530) 333-4312

CAMPING	BOATING	RECREATION	OTHER

Hell Hole:
   10 Tent Sites
   No Reservations
Upper Hell Hole:
   15 Boat Access or
   Hike-In Sites
    No Fee - No Water
Big Meadows:
   54 Tent/R.V. Sites
No Reservations
 	
Ralston Afterbay:
   No Campgrounds
	Hell Hole:
	   Power, Row, Canoe,
	   Sail, Waterski &
	   Inflatable
	Launch Ramp
	*Caution - Afternoon
	   Winds Can Be
	   Hazardous*
	
	Ralston Afterbay:
	   Small Craft Only
	   Hand Launch
		Fishing: Rainbow,
		   Brown, Cutthroat
		   & Kamloop Trout,
		   MacKinaw, Kokanee
		   Salmon
		Picnicking
		Hiking, Backpacking
		Equestrian Trails
		Hunting: Deer, Bear,
		   Turkey
		4 Wheel Drive Trails in
		   Area
			Nearest Facilities
			   From Hell Hole
			   Reservoir: 48 Miles at
			   Foresthill

STUMPY MEADOWS RESERVOIR and FINNON LAKE

Stumpy Meadows is at an elevation of 4,260 feet in the Eldorado National Forest. This Lake has 320 surface acres and is surrounded by conifers. The water is clear and cold. Boating is restricted to 5 MPH so waterskiing is not allowed. The angler will often find German Brown and Rainbow Trout. Finnon Lake, at 2,420 feet, is a small Lake administered by the Mosquito Volunteer Fire Department. They are developing a family campground. Boating is limited to rowboats. Fishing, swimming, hiking and horseback riding are the primary activities. Lake levels can fluctuate so call for current information.

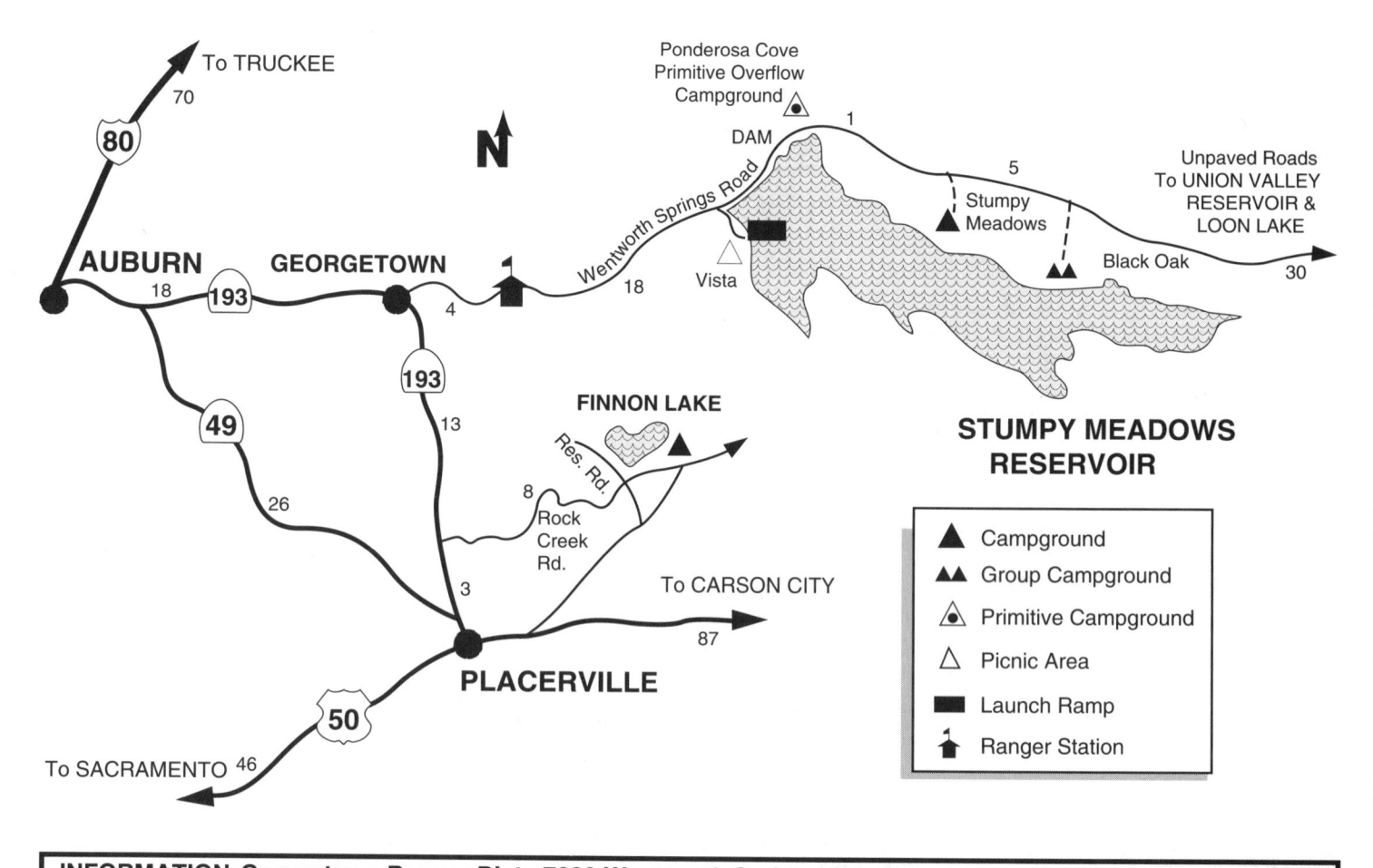

INFORMATION: Georgetown Ranger Dist., 7600 Wentworth Springs Rd., Georgetown 95634—Ph: (530) 333-4312

CAMPING	BOATING	RECREATION	OTHER

Stumpy Meadows:
  40 Dev. Sites for
  Tents & R.V.s to 45 Feet
  Fee: $13 - No Hookups
  Disposal Station
Black Oak:
  4 Group Sites to
    200 People
  Fee: $55 up to 75 People
Reserve All Sites:
    Ph: (877) 444-6777
Ponderosa Cove: Overflow
  Primitive Campground
	Stumpy Meadows:
	  Open to All Boats
	  5 MPH Speed Limit
	Improved Launch Ramp
	
	Finnon Lake:
	  Rowboats Only
		Fishing: Rainbow &
		  Brown Trout
		Finnon Lake: Largemouth
		  Bass & Sacramento
		    Perch
		Picnicking
		Swimming
			Finnon Lake:
			  Mosquito Volunteer
			    Fire Department
			  9100 Rock Creek Rd.
			  Placerville 95667
			  Ph: (530) 626-9017
			  Family Campground -
			    up to 50 Dev. Tent
			     Sites
			  Store
			  Snack Bar
			  Restaurant

At 6,225 feet elevation, Tahoe is one of America's largest and most beautiful mountain Lakes. It is 22 miles long, 12 miles wide and 72 miles around. Tahoe is a prime recreation lake with a variety of opportunities and facilities. Boaters, waterskiers and sailors make great use of the vast expanse of clear open water. The varied trout fishery ranges from planted rainbows to the huge lake trout or mackinaw and salmon. Hikers, backpackers and equestrians can enjoy the numerous trails, including the Tahoe Rim Trail, within the surrounding mountains and nearby Desolation Wilderness. Add these outdoor activities to the excitement and luxury of Nevada's casinos, "The Lake" has it all.

....Continued.....

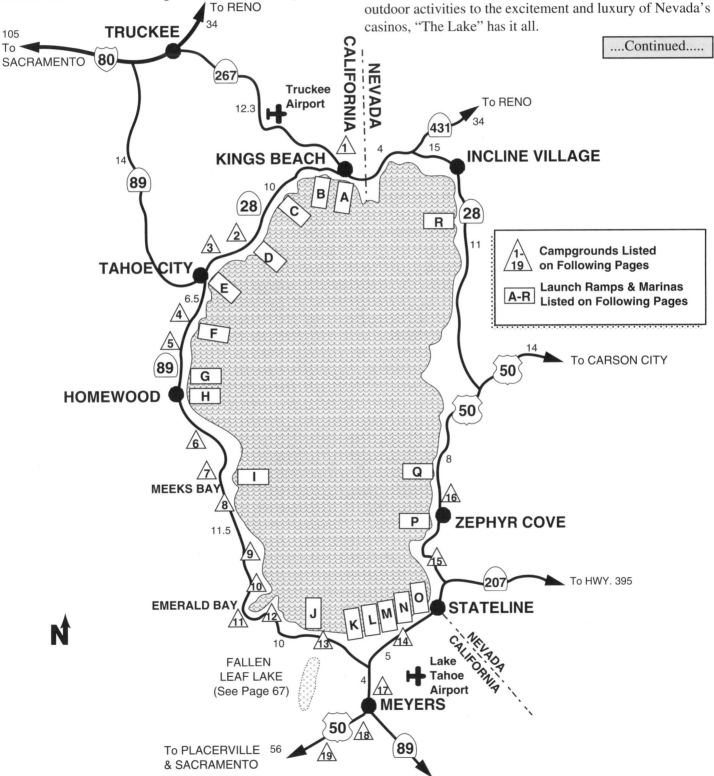

△ 1- 19 Campgrounds Listed on Following Pages

A-R Launch Ramps & Marinas Listed on Following Pages

LAKE TAHOE.............Continued

Managed by California Land Management by Special Use Permit of the USDA Forest Service, Lake Tahoe Basin Management Unit Information Ph: (530) 544-5994
Reserve the following Sites Except for Bayview Ph: (877) 444-6777

4. WILLIAM KENT - 2 Miles South of Tahoe City on Hwy. 89, - *Fee: $16* - 91 Tent/R.V. Sites to 40 Feet, Disposal Station, Swim Beach.
5. KASPIAN - 1 Miles North of Tahoe Pines on Hwy. 89 - *Fee: $10* - 9 Tent/R.V. Sites to 20 Feet, Picnic Area.
8. MEEKS BAY - 2 Miles South of Tahoma on Hwy. 89, - *Fee: $16* - 40 Tent/R.V. Sites to 20 Feet, Handicapped Access, Swim Beach.
15. NEVADA BEACH - 2 Miles North of Stateline off Hwy. 50, -*Fee: $20-22* - 54 Tent/R.V. Sites to 45 Ft, Handicapped Access, Boat-In Picnic Area, Group Picnic Area to 100 People.
11. BAYVIEW - On Hwy. 89 at Emerald Bay - *Fee: $10* - 10 Tent Sites, No Water, 2-Days Stay Limit.
(Pets okay on Leash at Above Sites)

Operated by California State Parks
Reserve Ph: (800) 444-7275
Family Sites - Up to7 Months in Advance
Group Sites - Up to 7 Months in Advance.

3. TAHOE STATE RECREATION AREA - 1/4 Mile East of Tahoe City - *Fee: $12* - 38 Tent/R.V. Sites to 24 Feet, Pets - Free, Picnic Sites, Showers, Groceries, Laundromat, Fishing Pier - Information: (530) 583-3074.
6. GENERAL CREEK - SUGAR PINE POINT - One Mile South of Tahoma off Hwy. 89 - *Fee: $12* - 175 Tent/R.V. Sites to 30 Feet, Showers
Group Camps (Limit 6 R.V.s Over 15 Feet per Camp) - Fee: $75 - Open All Year.
All Camps can Accommodate up to 400 People - Information: (530) 525-7982.
9. D. L. BLISS STATE PARK - 3 Miles North of Emerald Bay, off Hwy. 89 - *Fee: $16 - $20* - 168 Tent/R.V. Sites to 18 Feet, Group Camp, Pets $1 a Day, Showers, Information: (530) 525-7277.
10. EMERALD BAY STATE PARK - 8 Miles North of South Lake Tahoe off Hwy. 89 - *Fee: $10* - 20 Tent Sites
Boat-In Camp - First Come, First Served
Information: (530) 525-7277.
12. EAGLE POINT - Off Hwy. 89 at Emerald Bay-*Fee: $12* -100 Tent/R.V. Sites to 21 Feet,
Pets $1 a Day, Showers, Information: (530) 525-7277

Operated by the City of South Lake Tahoe
1180 Rufus Allen, South Lake Tahoe, CA 96150
Information: (530) 542-6096
Open April 1 to October 31

14. CAMPGROUND BY THE LAKE
2.3 Miles West of Stateline on
Hwy. 50 & Rufus Allen Blvd.

Fee: $18-$25 per Vehicle & 4 People per Night
$2 for Extra Person, $1 a Day for Pets
157 Tent/R.V. Sites, 50 Sites w/ Electric Hookups,
Group Sites, Disposal Station, Showers
Free Casino Shuttles
Reservations by Phone or Mail
Adjacent to Complex with Swimming Pool,
Horseshoes, Volleyball
Gym Ph: (530) 542-6056
Bijou 9-Hole Golf Course Ph: (530) 542-6097

Operated by Tahoe City Parks and Recreation
380 North Lake Blvd., Tahoe City 96145
Information: (530) 583-5544

2. LAKE FOREST CAMPGROUND
2 Miles East of Tahoe City
Fee: $15
18 Tent/R.V. Sites to 20 Feet
Boat Ramp, Swim Beach
Pets Okay on Leash.

....Continued....

PRIVATELY OPERATED CAMPGROUNDS: SEE NUMBER IN TRIANGLE ON MAP

1. SANDY BEACH - at Kings Beach on Hwy. 28 - *Fees: From $20-$25 - Ph: (530) 546-7682* - 44 Tent/R.V. Sites to 40 Feet, Hookups, Pets $1.50 a Day, Showers, Boat Ramp.

7. MEEKS BAY RESORT & MARINA, P.O. Box 787, Tahoma 96142 - 10 Miles South of Tahoe City - *Fees: From $20 Ph: (530) 525-6946 or Toll Free (877) 326-3357* - 10 R.V. Sites, Full Hookups, 25 Tent Sites, No Pets, Cabins & Lodge Units, Launch Ramp. (Under USFS Permit)

13. CAMP RICHARDSON RESORT, P. O. Box 9028, South Lake Tahoe 96158 - 3 Miles West of the "Y" - *Fee: From $17-$26 - Ph: (530) 541-1801 or (800) 544-1801* - 333 Tent/R.V. Sites, Group Sites, Hookups, No Pets, Showers, Disposal Station, Lodge Units, Beach Motel, Groceries, Propane, Supplies, Boat Ramp, Horse Stables, Bicycle Rentals, Open All Year. (Under USFS Permit)

16. ZEPHYR COVE RESORT - 4 Miles North of Stateline - *Fee: From $25 - Ph: (775) 589-4981* - 150 Tent/RV Sites to 40 Feet, Group Sites, Pets OK, Showers, Cabins, Lodge, Marina, Groceries, Propane, Restaurant, MS Dixie II Paddlewheeler, Open All Year. (Under USFS Permit)

17. TAHOE VALLEY CAMPGROUND, P. O. Box 9026, South Lake Tahoe 96158 - 1/4 Mile South of Highway 89 - *Fee: From $24-$38 - Ph: (530) 541-2222* - 413 Tent/R.V. Sites, Full Hookups, Group Sites, Pets OK, Disposal Station, Showers, Playground, Laundromat, Groceries, Propane, Recreation Room, Cable T.V., Open All Year, Swimming Pool in Season.

18. TAHOE PINES CAMPGROUND AND RV PARK, Box 550987, South Lake Tahoe 96155 - Off Hwy. 50, West of Meyers *Fee: From $28-$60 - Ph: (530) 577-1653* - 50 Tent Sites, 21 R.V. Sites with Full Hookups to 40 Feet, Pets $3.50 a Day, Disposal Station, Showers, Laundromat, Groceries, Playground, Secluded Wooded River & Creek Sites.

19. KOA KAMPGROUND, Box 550967, South Lake Tahoe 96155 - Off Hwy. 50 West of Meyers - *Fee: From $28-$36 Ph: (530) 577-3693* **or (800) 562-3477 -** 16 Tent Sites, 52 R.V. Sites to 40 Feet, Full Hookups, Pets $3.50 a Day, Disposal Station, Showers, Laundry, Mini-Market, Propane, Swimming Pool, Recreation Room, Playground, Picnic Tables, Campfire Rings and BBQ Grills, Wooded Area.

LAUNCH RAMPS AND MARINA FACILITIES: SEE LETTER IN RECTANGLE ON MAP

A. KINGS BEACH STATE RECREATIONAL AREA - North Tahoe Parks & Recreation, P.O. Box 139, Tahoe Vista 96148 Ph: (530) 546-7248 - *Launch & Parking Fee: $5* - Launch Ramp - Water Can Be Low - Rentals: 12 & 14 Feet Sailboats, Jetskis, Pedal Boats, Kayaks.

B. NORTH TAHOE MARINA - 7360 N. Lake Blvd., Tahoe Vista 96148—Ph: (530) 546-8248 - *Launch Fees: To 20 Feet $22; Over 20 Feet $1.50 per Foot* - Paved Ramp - *Power Boats Only,* Full Service Marina, Buoys, Fuel and Repairs, Accessory Sales, Power Boat & Ski Equipment Rentals.

C. SIERRA BOAT CO. - 5146 North Lake Blvd., Carnelian Bay 96146—Ph: (530) 546-2552 - *Fees: Sailboats $3 per Foot; Boats to 24 Feet $25; Over 24 Feet $30-$35* - Hoist, Buoys, Slips, Fuel and Repairs, Supplies, Dry Storage.

D. LAKE FOREST BOAT RAMP - Hwy. 28 at end of Lake Forest Rd. near U. S. Coast Guard Station - Ph: (530) 583-3796 - May be closed - Call for Information.

....Continued....

LAUNCH RAMPS AND MARINA FACILITIES: SEE NUMBER IN RECTANGLE ON MAP

E. TAHOE BOAT COMPANY - 700 N. Lake Blvd., Box 6651, Tahoe City 96145—Ph: (530) 583-5567, Hoist (No Ramp), Full Service Marina, Fuel, Repairs, Marine Accessories, Ski Boat Rentals, Winter Storage, Boat Sales.

F. SUNNYSIDE RESORT - P.O. Box 5969, Tahoe City 95730—Ph: (530) 583-7200, Hoist, Slips, Buoys, Pump Station, Fuel, Repairs, Restaurant, Ski & Sail Boat Rentals & Sales, Ski School, General Store.

G. HIGH & DRY MARINA - P.O. Box 1735, Tahoe City 96145 @ 5190 Hwy. 89, Homewood —Ph: (530) 525-5966, Hoist (No Ramp), Fuel, Power Boat Rentals, Complete Service and Chandlery.

H. OBEXERS, 5355 West Lake Blvd., Homewood 96141—Ph: (530) 525-7962, Paved Ramp and Travel Lift, Fork Lift, Fuel, Marine Accessories, Boat Repairs, Groceries.

I. MEEKS BAY RESORT & MARINA - 7941 Emerald Bay Rd., Meeks Bay 96142—Ph: (530) 525-6946 or (877) 326-3357, Paved Ramp, Slips, Row, Power & Sail Boat Rentals, Groceries, Bait & Tackle, Snack Bar, Cabins, R.V. Park, Campsites.

J. RICHARDSON'S RESORT, ANCHORAGE MARINA - Off Hwy. 89, 2 Miles Northwest of "Y"—Ph: (530) 542-6570 - *Fees: Call for Information* - Launch Ramp, Gas, Supplies, Repairs, Rentals, Moorings.

K. TAHOE KEYS MARINA - 2435 Venice Dr. East, South Lake Tahoe 96150—Ph: (530) 541-2155 - *Fees: $25 Round Trip* Double Paved Ramp, 45 Ton Capacity Travel Lift, Paved Full Service Marina, Sail & Power Boat Rentals, Fuel, Repairs, Boat Supplies, Mini-Mart, 300 Slips, Largest Marina on the Lake, Overnight Parking, Restaurant.

L. EL DORADO BEACH PUBLIC BOAT RAMP - Hwy. 50 & Lakeview Ave., South Lake Tahoe 96150—Ph: (530) 542-6056, *Launch Fee: $13*, Public Use Facility, Paved Ramp, Swim Beach, Picnic Area with BBQ's, Campground across Street on Rufus Allen Blvd.

M. TIMBER COVE MARINA - 3411 Lake Tahoe Blvd., South Lake Tahoe 96150—Ph: (530) 544-2942 - *Fees: Call for Information* - Unpaved Ramp, Hoist, Mooring, Fuel, Repairs, Power, Sail Boat and Jet Ski Rentals, Snack Bar, Gift Shop, Boat Charters.

N. SKI RUN MARINA - 900 Ski Run Blvd., South Lake Tahoe 96150—Ph: (530) 544-0200 - *Fees: Call for Information* - Moorings, Slips, Power & Sail Boat Rentals, Fuel, Repairs, Cafe, Beer Garden, On the Water Restaurant, Shops, Home of the Hornblower Cruises and Events, Plus the All New Lake Link Meteor High Speed Shuttle, 500 Passenger *Tahoe Queen*.

O. LAKESIDE MARINA - Hwy. 50 at end of Park Ave., South Lake Tahoe - Ph: (530) 541-6626 - *Fees: $10 In - $10-Out* - Ramp Access - Boats Under 27 Feet Only, Slips, Gas, Supplies, Slips, Moorings, Dry Storage.

P. ZEPHYR COVE MARINA - 760 US 50, Zephyr Cove, NV 89448—Ph: (775) 588-3833, *Fees: Call for Information* - Moorings, Fuel, Power & Sail Boat Rentals, Full Resort Facilities, Picnic Area, Cabins, Campground, Restaurant.

Q. CAVE ROCK PUBLIC LAUNCH FACILITY - Off Hwy. 50, North of Zephyr Cove - Ph: (775) 831-0494 - *Fees: Launch $10 - Day Use $5* - Paved Ramp, Swim Beach, Fishing Area.

R. SAND HARBOR - 4 Miles South of Incline Village - Ph: (775) 831-0494 - *Fees: Launch $12 - Day Use $6* - Paved Launch Ramp, Swim Beach, Picnic Areas, Group Use Picnic Area, Nature Trai.

....Continued....

GENERAL INFORMATION

Lodging and accommodations are extensive throughout the Lake Tahoe Basin. The casinos offer luxurious hotel rooms with complete facilities. Condominiums, bed & breakfasts, cabins and houses are available for rent. In addition to the enormous variety of lodging available, there is an abundance of recreational and service facilities.

For Further Information Contact:

Lake Tahoe Basin Management Unit
USDA, Forest Service
870 Emerald Bay Road, Suite 1
South Lake Tahoe, CA 96150
Ph: (530) 573-2600

Eldorado National Forest
Information Center
3070 Camino Heights Drive
Camino, CA 97509
Ph: (530) 644-6048

Toiyabe National Forest
Carson Ranger Station
1536 S. Carson Street
Carson City, NV 89701
Ph: (775) 882-2766

California State Parks
Sierra District
P. O. Drawer D
Tahoma, CA 96142
Ph: (530) 525-7232

Nevada State Parks
Sand Harbor
P. O. Box 8867
2005 Highway 28
Incline Village, NV 89450
Ph: (775) 831-0494

Chambers of Commerce:

South Lake Tahoe
3066 Lake Tahoe Blvd.
South Lake Tahoe, CA 96150
Ph: (530) 541-5255

North Lake Tahoe
P.O. Box 884
Tahoe City, CA 96145
Ph: (530) 583-3494

Tahoe - Douglas
P. O. Box 401
Zephyr Cove, NV 89448
Ph: (775) 588-4591

Lake Tahoe Incline Village
Crystal Bay Visitors Bureau
969 Tahoe Blvd.
Incline Village, NV 89451
*Ph: (775) 832-1606 or
       (800) GO TAHOE*

Lake Tahoe Visitors Authority
        at South Shore
1156 Ski Run Blvd.
South Lake Tahoe, CA 96150
*Ph: (800) AT TAHOE (288-2463)
        Reservations*
Ph: (530) 544-5050 - Information

North Lake Tahoe
        Resort Association
P.O. Box 5459
Tahoe City, CA 96145
Ph: (530) 583-3494 - Reservations
Ph: (800) 824-6348 - Information

FALLEN LEAF LAKE

Fallen Leaf Lake is at an elevation of 6,400 feet and is part of the Lake Tahoe Basin Management Unit. The property around this Lake is divided between private and National Forest land. The shoreline is heavily forested with pine trees to the water's edge. It is within easy access to the Desolation Wilderness and near the numerous attractions at South Lake Tahoe with casinos at Stateline. The Forest Service maintains a campground on the north end of the Lake.

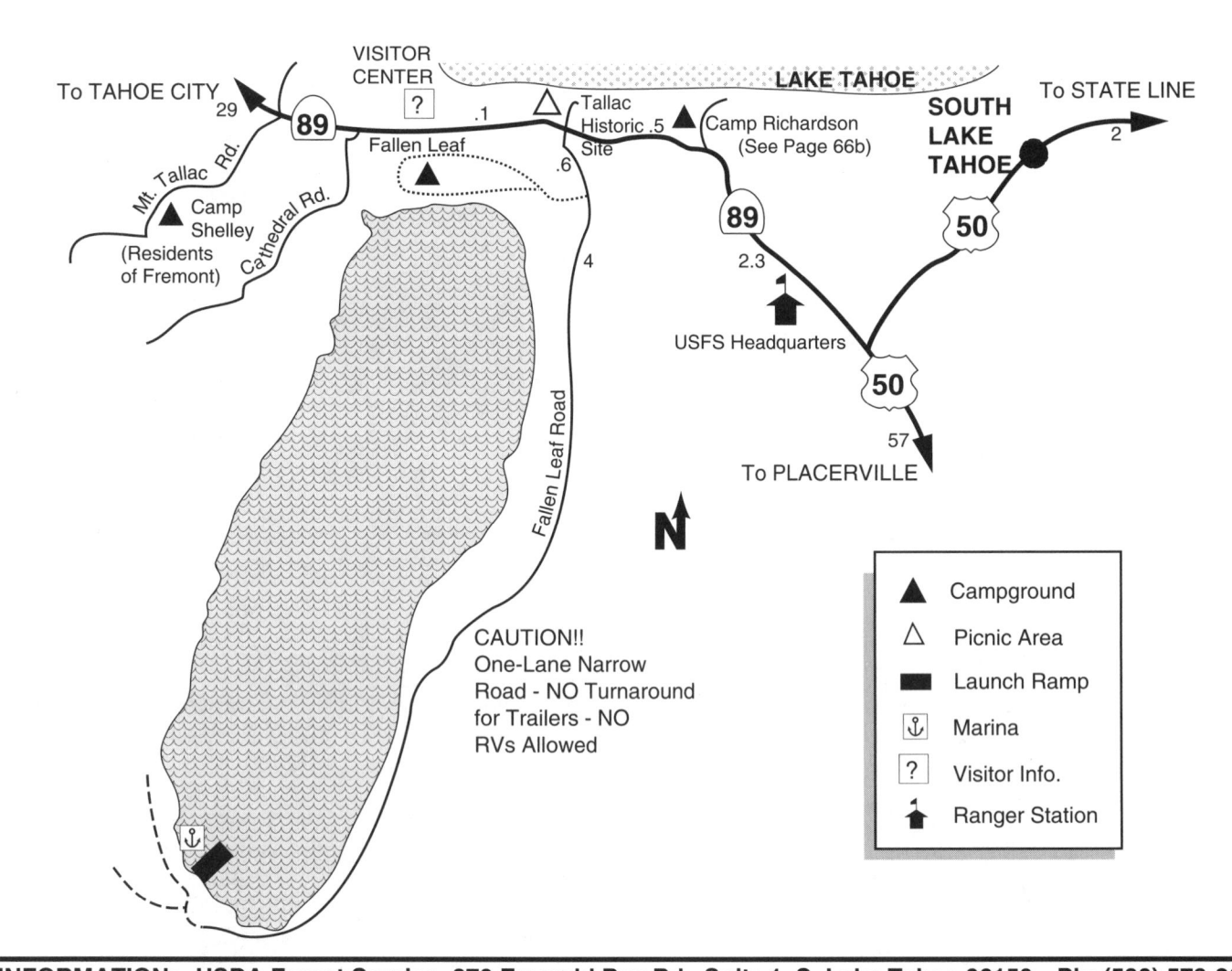

CAUTION!!
One-Lane Narrow Road - NO Turnaround for Trailers - NO RVs Allowed

▲	Campground
△	Picnic Area
■	Launch Ramp
⚓	Marina
?	Visitor Info.
⛪	Ranger Station

INFORMATION: USDA Forest Service, 870 Emerald Bay Rd., Suite 1, S. Lake Tahoe 96150—Ph: (530) 573-2600

CAMPING	BOATING	RECREATION	OTHER

U.S.F.S.
    205 Dev. Sites for
    Tents & R.V.s to 40 Feet
    Fee: $18
    Reserve:
        Ph: (877) 444-6777
 	
Camp Shelley:
    For Residents of
    City of Fremont Only
Ph: (530) 541-6985
	Power, Row, Canoe,
	    & Sail
	Launch Ramp
	Marina
	Rentals: Rowboats, Fishing
	    Boats with Motors
	    & Ski Boats
	
	*NO R.V.s on Road
	    to Marina & Launch
	    Ramp*
		Fishing: Rainbow,
		    German Brown &
		    Mackinaw Trout
		Swimming
		Picnicking
		Hiking
		Backpacking
		Equestrian Trails
		Mountain Biking
		Nature Study
			Visitor Center on
			    Highway 89

Echo Lake is nestled at 7,414 feet in between high mountains near Echo Summit off Highway 50. This is one of the most beautiful natural Lakes in the High Sierra. All boating is allowed but waterskiing is not permitted on Upper Echo Lake. The bordering Desolation Wilderness has 63,475 acres of trails, lakes and streams easily accessible for the back-packer or equestrian. Echo Chalet, the only facility on the Lake, provides a taxi service to the Upper Lake which shortens the hike into the Wilderness Area by 3-1/2 miles. The Rubicon and American Rivers along with over 50 Lakes and streams welcome anglers to the uncrowded waters of this area. *(Cover Photo)*

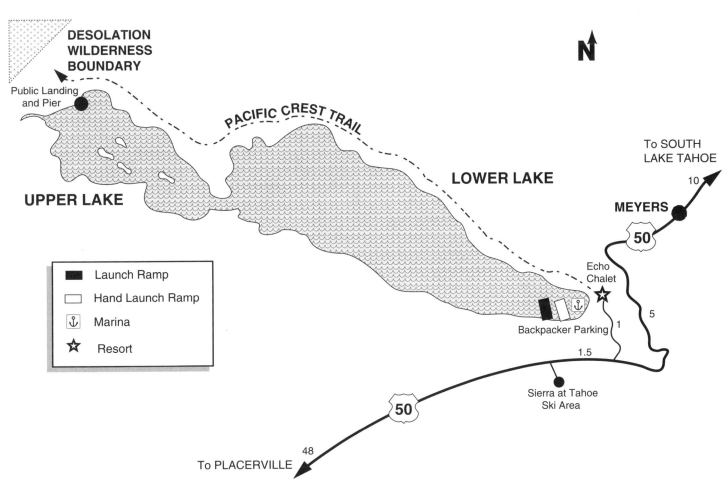

INFORMATION: Echo Chalet, Echo Lake 95721—Ph: (530) 659-7207			
CAMPING	**BOATING**	**RECREATION**	**OTHER**
No Overnight Camping or Trailers Allowed in Echo Lake Basin Camping Allowed in Desolation Wilderness Area with Permit from U.S.F.S.	Power, Row, Canoe, Sail, Waterski, Windsurf & Inflatable Full Service Marina Launch Ramp - $15 Cartops and Inflatables - $6 Rentals: Fishing Boats, Canoes & Kayaks Docks, Berths, Gas, Storage	Fishing: Rainbow, Brook & Cutthroat Trout, Kokanee Salmon Swimming Picnicking Hiking Backpacking [Parking] Equestrian Trails Hunting: Deer, Quail	Housekeeping Cabins Snack Bar Grocery Store Hardware & Sporting Goods Bait & Tackle Fishing Licenses Gas Station Day Hike Permits to Wilderness Area

WRIGHTS LAKE

Wrights Lake has a surface area of 65 acres. It is at an elevation of 7,000 feet in the Eldorado National Forest, one of many Lakes in this area. The high Sierra setting provides a unique retreat for the outdoorsman. Two Trailheads for Desolation Wilderness Area border the Lake, making it popular for the equestrian, hiker and backpacker. Wrights Lake offers good fishing. The other Lakes and streams in this vicinity are equally inviting to the angler. Boating is restricted to hand launching. Motors are not allowed. Permits are required for entry into the Desolation Wilderness Area.

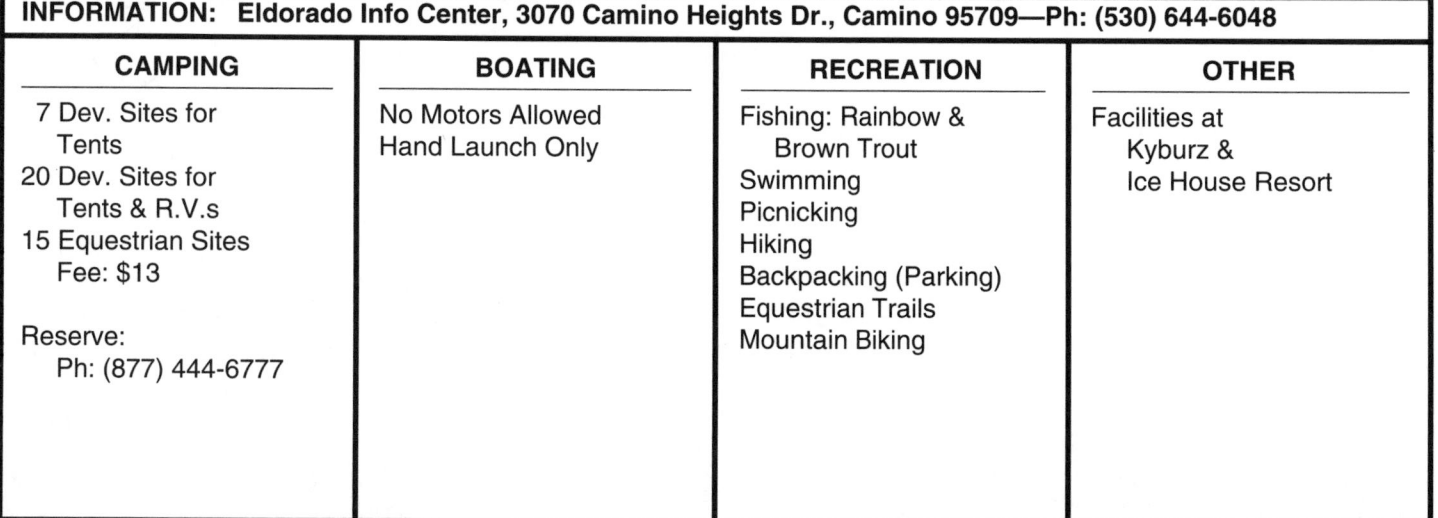

▲ Campground

✿ Equestrian Camping

△ Picnic Area

⚑ Ranger Station

BEAUTY LAKE

DESOLATION WILDERNESS BOUNDARY

Barrett OHV Trail

DARK LAKE

WRIGHTS LAKE

To UNION VALLEY RESERVOIR

Ice House-Wrights Lake Rd.

Ice House Rd.

Silver Creek

Ice House Reservoir (See Page 71) (NOT TO SCALE)

Wrights Lake Rd

N

3

Check Road Conditions

3

To SOUTH LAKE TAHOE

INFO

?

RIVERTON

50

To PLACERVILLE

2

9

10

5

50

29

13

POLLOCK PINES

KYBURZ

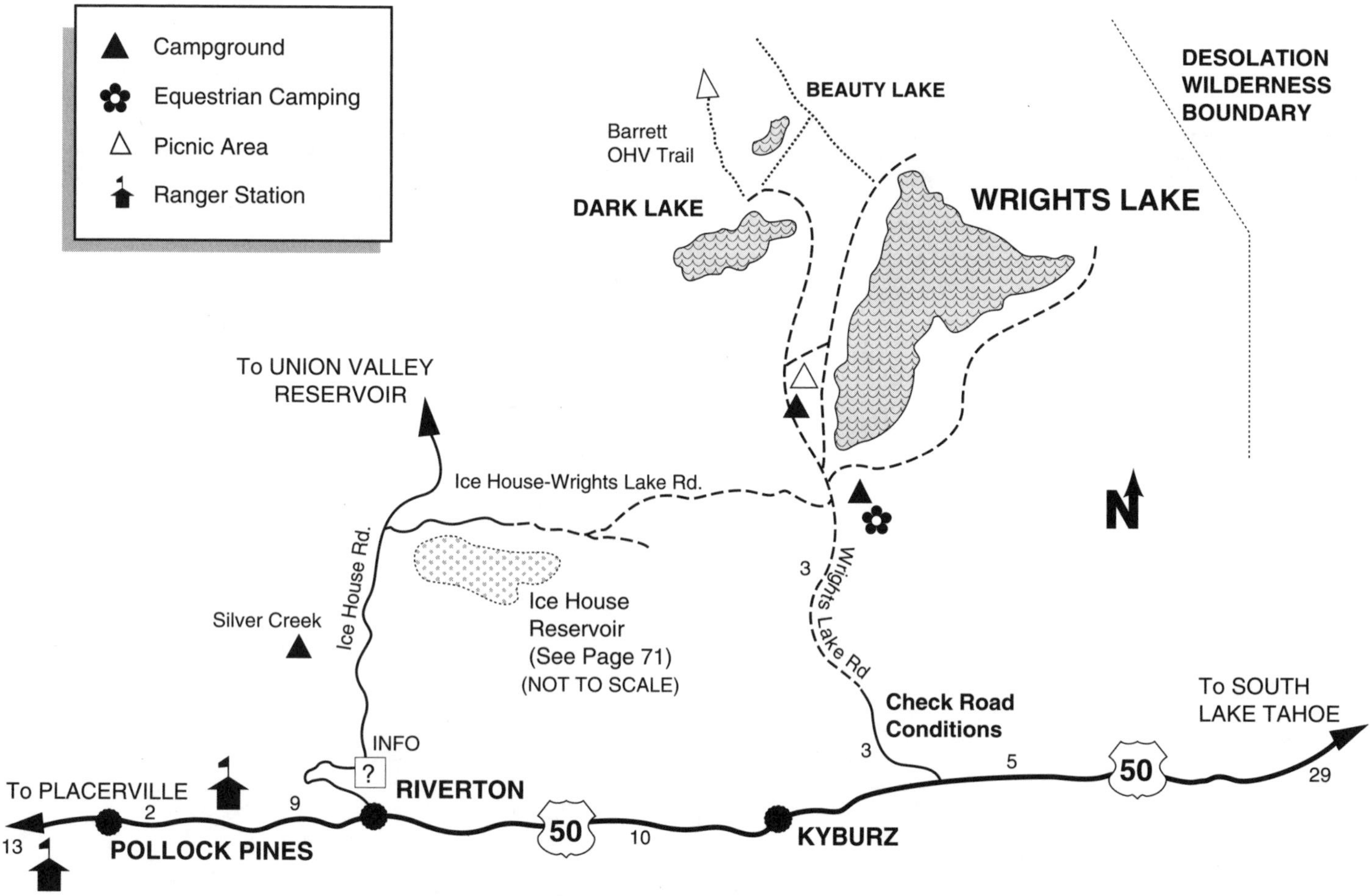

INFORMATION: Eldorado Info Center, 3070 Camino Heights Dr., Camino 95709—Ph: (530) 644-6048

CAMPING	BOATING	RECREATION	OTHER
7 Dev. Sites for Tents 20 Dev. Sites for Tents & R.V.s 15 Equestrian Sites Fee: $13 Reserve: Ph: (877) 444-6777	No Motors Allowed Hand Launch Only	Fishing: Rainbow & Brown Trout Swimming Picnicking Hiking Backpacking (Parking) Equestrian Trails Mountain Biking	Facilities at Kyburz & Ice House Resort

LOON LAKE and GERLE CREEK RESERVOIR

Loon Lake is at an elevation of 6,500 feet in the Crystal Basin Recreation Area of the Eldorado National Forest. This beautiful high mountain Lake, with crystal clear water, appears carved out of granite. The Forest Service maintains the campgrounds, picnic areas, paved launch ramp and a walk-in or boat-in campground. This is a good Lake for sailing and boating in general but waterskiing is not advised due to extremely cold water. Fishing can be excellent for Rainbow and German Brown trout. There is trailhead parking for the Desolation Wilderness. Trail conditions are good for hikers and horses. Wilderness Permits are required for entry into Desolation Wilderness. Gerle Creek Reservoir has a 50-site campground and picnic area with a handicap fishing pier. Boats with motors are not allowed at this facility.

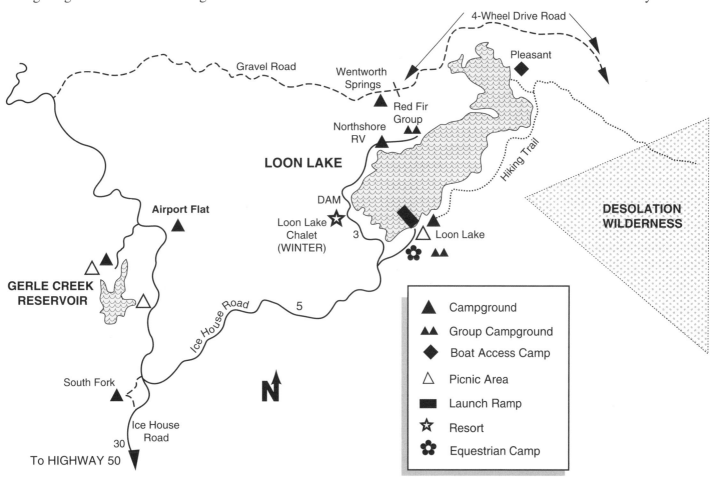

INFORMATION: Eldorado Info Center, 3070 Camino Heights Dr., Camino 95709—Ph: (530) 644-6048

CAMPING	BOATING	RECREATION	OTHER
Loon Lake Complex: 53 Dev. Sites for Tents & R.V.s - Fee: $13, 3 Group Camps: 25, 35 & 50 People (1 Equestrian)Fee: $50-$75 9 Equestrian Units: $13 Red Fir Group: 25 People No Trailers - Fee: $35 Reserve Above: Ph: (877) 444-6777 Northshore: 15 R.V. Sites Fee: $5 - No Water Pleasant: 10 Sites No Water	Power, Row, Canoe & Sail Launch Ramp *Waterskiing is NOT Recommended* Gerle Creek Reservoir: No Motorboats	Fishing: Rainbow & German Brown Trout Picnicking Hiking Backpacking [Parking] Entrance to Desolation Wilderness Equestrian Trails ORV Trails Mountain Biking	Gerle Creek: 50 Dev. Sites for Tents & R.V.s - Fee: $13 Reserve: Ph: (877) 444-6777 Airport Flat: 16 Units No Fee, No Water OHVs Allowed Wentworth Springs: 8 Sites 4WD - No Fee, No Water South Fork: 17 Sites No Fee, No Water Full Facilities: 23 Miles

Ice House Reservoir is at an elevation of 5,500 feet in the Crystal Basin Recreation Area of the Eldorado National Forest. The surface area of this Lake is 678 acres with clear, cold water. The surrounding shoreline is covered with conifers. The Ice House campground, launch ramp and picnic facilities are run by a concessionaire. The Forest Service operates Northwind and Strawberry Point campgrounds. There are nice swimming areas. The roads are paved and well maintained but beware of logging trucks. This is an excellent boating Lake especially for sailing. The Reservoir is stocked during the summer months and the angler will find good fishing for trout and Kokanee.

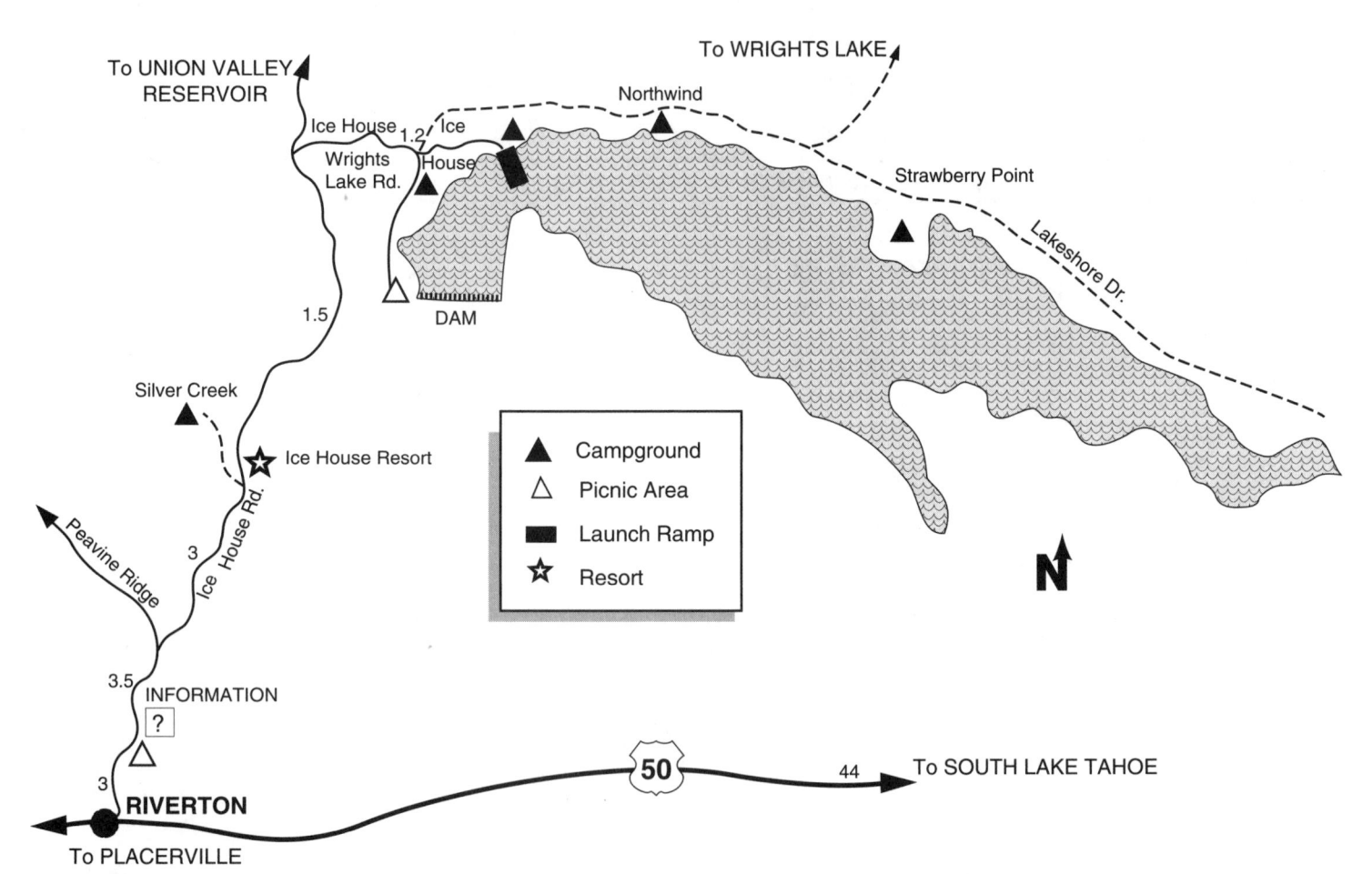

INFORMATION: Eldorado Info Center, 3070 Camino Heights Dr., Camino 95709—Ph: (530) 644-6048

CAMPING	BOATING	RECREATION	OTHER

Ice House:
    83 Dev. Sites for
Tents & R.V.s - Fee: $13
3 Handicapped - Reserve:
    Ph: (877) 444-6777
    8 Walk-Ins for Tents
No Water at:
Silver Creek: 12 Sites
    No R.V.s - Fee: $6
Northwind: 9 Sites
    Tents & R.V.s - Fee: $5
Strawberry Point: 10 Sites
    Tents & R.V.s - Fee: $5
	Power, Row, Canoe,
	    Sail, Windsurf &
	    Inflatables
	Launch Ramp
		Fishing: Rainbow &
		    Brown Trout,
		    Kokanee Salmon
		Swimming
		Picnicking
		Hiking
		Mountain Biking
			Ice House Resort:
			    Ph: (530) 293-3321
			Motel
			Restaurant
			Grocery Store
			Gas Station

UNION VALLEY RESERVOIR

Union Valley Reservoir is located at an elevation of 4,900 feet in the Crystal Basin Recreation Area of the Eldorado National Forest. This area is in the pine and fir forests of the western Sierra and is dominated by the high granite peaks of the Crystal Range. The Reservoir has a surface area of 2,860 acres. The Forest Service maintains 3 launch ramps at the Lake as well as a picnic area and campgrounds. Union Valley is an excellent Lake for sailing and many clubs use this facility during the summer. Fishing can be excellent from your boat or along the shoreline.

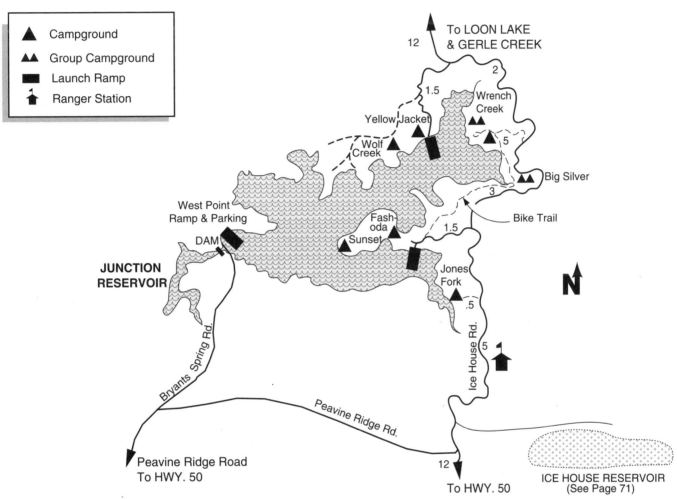

INFORMATION: Eldorado Info Center, 3070 Camino Heights Dr., Camino 95709—Ph: (530) 644-6048

CAMPING	BOATING	RECREATION	OTHER
Sites for Tents & R.V.s:	Power, Rowboats,	Fishing: Rainbow &	Disposal Station
Yellowjacket-40 Sites - $13	Sail, Canoes, Windsurf,	Brown Trout	
Wolf Creek-42 Sites - $13	Inflatables	Swimming	Facilities - 7 Miles
Sunset-131 Sites - $13	Launch Ramps	Picnicking	at Ice House Resort
Jones Fork-10 Sites - $5		Hiking	
No Water at this Site		Bicycle Trails	
Wench & Big Silver Group			Big Silver, Wolf Creek,
Sites for Tents & R.V.s			Yellowjacket, Sunset &
Group - Fee: $60			Wench Campgrounds:
Fashoda - 30 Tents *Only*			Reserve:
1 Handicapped Site			Ph: (877) 444-6777
Camino, W.Point-No Water			
First Come Basis			

JENKINSON LAKE - SLY PARK RECREATION AREA

Jenkinson Lake is at an elevation of 3,478 feet in the Sly Park Recreation Area south of Pollock Pines. The Lake has a surface area of 640 acres with 8 miles of coniferous tree-covered shoreline. The Eldorado Irrigation District has jurisdiction over the modern facilities at this scenic Lake. Facilities include 2 launch ramps with floats. There are a variety of individual and group campsites offering equestrian, handicapped and youth facilities. The water is clear and fishing can be good along the coves. Winds are usually favorable for sailing. Waterskiing is in a counterclockwise direction in the central section of the Lake.

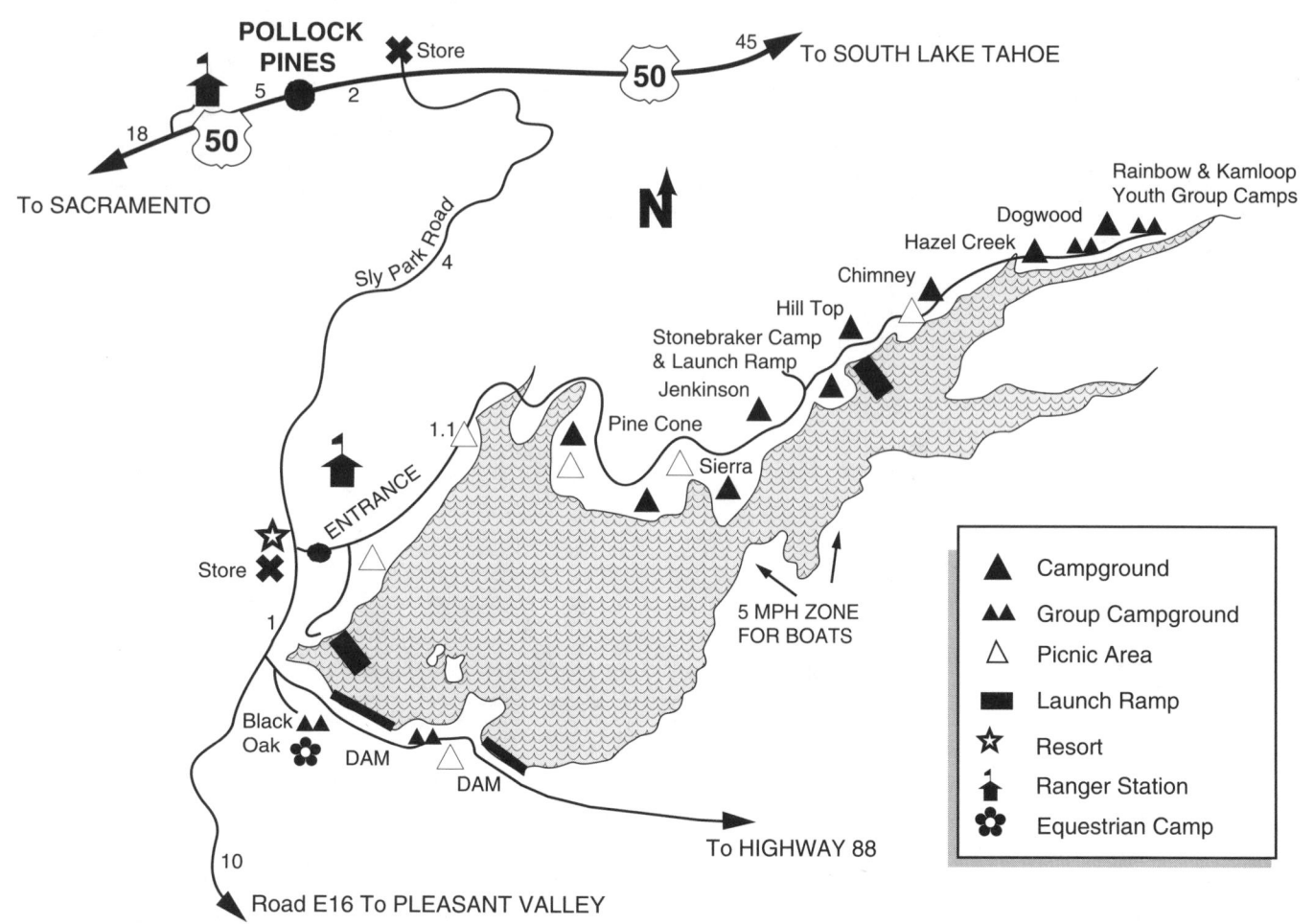

▲	Campground
▲▲	Group Campground
△	Picnic Area
■	Launch Ramp
☆	Resort
⚑	Ranger Station
❁	Equestrian Camp

INFORMATION: Sly Park Recreation Area, P.O. Box 577, Pollock Pines 95726—Ph: (530) 644-2545

CAMPING	BOATING	RECREATION	OTHER
191 Dev. Sites for Tents & R.V.s Fee: $16 - $21	Power, Row, Canoe, Sail, Waterski, Windsurf & Inflatables *No Jets*	Fishing: Rainbow, Brown & Mackinaw Trout, Smallmouth Bass & Bluegill	Sly Park Store 4782 Sly Park Road Pollock Pines 95726 Ph: (530) 644-1113
Handicapped & Equestrian Facilities	2 Launch Ramps Fee: $6	Swimming	Motel Bar & Grill
Group & Youth Camp Areas	Courtesy Docks	Picnicking	Grocery Store
Day Use: $7 or with a Boat $13	Rentals - May-September: Pedal Boats, Kayaks,	Hiking & Bicycle Trails Equestrian Trails	Bait & Tackle Gas Station
Reservations Recommended for All Campsites Ph: (530) 644-2792	Canoes, Row Boats $8 an Hour	Nature Trails Small Museum	R.V. Space Additional Facilities in Pollock Pines - 5 Miles

The Folsom Lake State Recreation Area is one of the most complete recreation parks in California. This 18,000 acre Recreation Area offers an abundance of campsites, picnic areas, swimming beaches and marina facilities. With excellent waters for sailing and other types of boating, Folsom Lake has 11,930 surface acres with 75 miles of shoreline. You may camp aboard your self-contained boat after registering at the Marina, off Green Valley Road, or at Granite Bay. This is a popular equestrian area with 80 miles of trails. There is a bicycle trail that links Beals Point via the American River Bike Trail to downtown Sacramento.

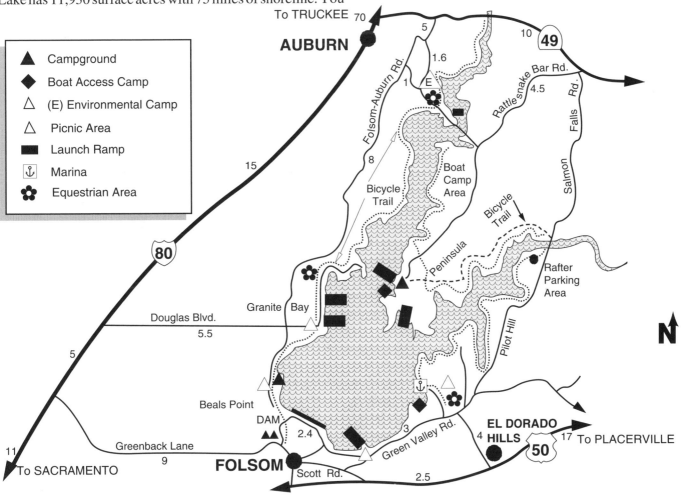

Map Legend:
- ▲ Campground
- ◆ Boat Access Camp
- △ (E) Environmental Camp
- △ Picnic Area
- ■ Launch Ramp
- ⚓ Marina
- ✿ Equestrian Area

INFORMATION: Folsom Lake, 7806 Folsom-Auburn Rd., Folsom 95630—Ph: (916) 988-0205

CAMPING	BOATING	RECREATION	OTHER
149 Dev. Sites Tents & R.V.s to 31 Feet Fee: $12 Reserve: Ph: (800) 444-7275 Environmental Camp Reached by Foot or Horseback Boat Camping Equestrian Area up to 50 Riders & Horses Contact Park Hdqtrs.	Open to All Boating Full Service Marina Launch Ramps - Fees Charged Rentals: Fishing, Canoe, Sail & Windsurfing Docks, Berths, Dry Storage & Gas Windsurfing Lessons Low Water Hazards	Fishing: Rainbow Trout, Coho Salmon, Catfish, Bluegill, Crappie, Bass, Perch & Sturgeon Picnicking Swimming - Beaches Bicycle, Hiking & Equestrian Trails Campfire Programs	Snack Bar Bait & Tackle Day Use Fee Full Facilities in Folsom

LAKE NATOMA

Lake Natoma is a part of the Folsom Lake Recreation Area. Resting at an elevation of 126 feet just below Folsom Dam, Natoma is the regulating Reservoir for Folsom Lake. The water is very cold and levels can fluctuate 3 or 4 feet in a day. This small Lake of 500 surface acres flows over dredger piles.

While the piles can create a good fish habitat, they are a boating hazard. Fishing may be difficult, but for those who know the Lake, it can be rewarding. Good trails are available for the equestrian, bicyclist and hiker.

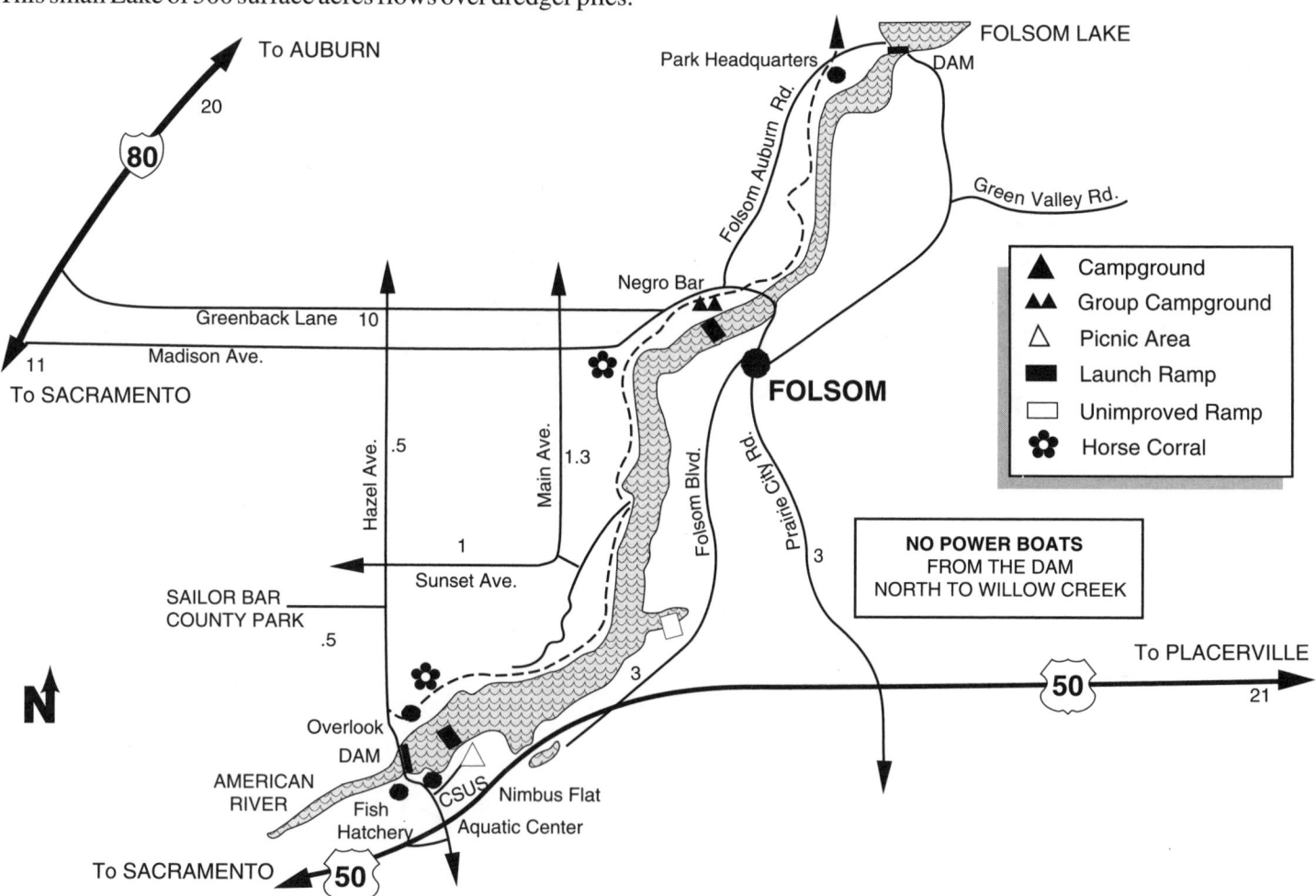

Legend	
▲	Campground
▲▲	Group Campground
△	Picnic Area
■	Launch Ramp
▭	Unimproved Ramp
✿	Horse Corral

NO POWER BOATS
FROM THE DAM
NORTH TO WILLOW CREEK

INFORMATION: Folsom Lake, 7806 Folsom-Auburn Rd., Folsom 95630—Ph: (916) 988-0205

CAMPING	BOATING	RECREATION	OTHER
3 Group Camps at Negro Bar A & B to 50 People $32 C to 25 People $18 Reserve: Ph: (800) 444-7275	Power, Row, Canoe, Sail, Windsurf & Inflatables Speed Limit - 5 MPH Launch Ramps - Fee CSUS Aquatic Center: Ph: (916) 985-7239 Rowing, Sail, Canoe, Kayak & Windsurfing Lessons	Fishing: Rainbow Trout, Bluegill, Catfish, Crappie, Large & Smallmouth Bass Swimming - Beaches Picnicking Hiking Horse Rentals Bicycle Trails Home of the Pacific Coast Rowing Championships	Day Use Fee Entrance Fees Enforced Year Around When Park-Ur-Self Machines are in Use Correct Change is Necessary Full Facilities at Folsom

GIBSON RANCH AND ELK GROVE PARKS - RANCHO SECO REC. AREA

With all the qualities of a working ranch, Gibson Ranch Regional Park, 325 acres, is an unique facility. A fishing lake and numerous equestrian activities and trails make it an ideal day use area for families. It offers 5 large picnic sites for groups. Elk Grove Regional Park, 125 acres, includes a 3 acre fishing lake, a swimming pool and numerous ball diamonds and picnic areas. Both these Parks are maintained by the County of Sacramento.

Under the jurisdiction of the Sacramento Municipal Utility District, the 400-acre Rancho Seco Recreational Area surrounds a 160-acre, warm-water lake fed by the Folsom South Canal. The water is recirculated daily and maintained at a constant level year around, providing ideal conditions for swimming, fishing, windsurfing and boating. No gas-powered motorboats are permitted. The camping facilities include a group campsite and reservations are available. There is a good swim area with a sandy beach and lifeguards on duty from Memorial Day through Labor Day.

INFORMATION: County Regional Parks, 3711 Branch Center Rd., Sacramento 95827—Ph: (916) 875-6336

CAMPING	BOATING	RECREATION	OTHER
Gibson Ranch & Elk Grove: Day Use Only	Gibson Ranch & Elk Grove - No Boating	Fishing: Rainbow Trout, Florida Bass Bluegill, Sunfish, Catfish & Crappie	General Store Fish Cleaning Station Coin-Operated Solar Showers
Rancho Seco Park: Sites for Tents & R.V.s Electric & Water Hookups Group Camping Area Disposal Station Reservations: Ph: (916) 732-4913	Rancho Seco: Electric Motorboats, Sailboats & Rowboats Rentals: Kayak & Paddleboat s 2 Launch Ramps	Fishing Docks Trout Derby: March & Dec. Family & Group Picnic Areas - Reserve Pool - Elk Grove Horseshoe Pits	Sacramento Utility District P.O. Box 15830 Sacramento 95852 Ph: (916) 732-4913 Full Facilities in Sacramento

SALT SPRINGS RESERVOIR

Salt Springs Reservoir is at an elevation of 3,900 feet in the spectacular Mokelumne River Canyon of the Eldorado National Forest. This P.G. & E. Reservoir has a surface area of 961 acres. High afternoon winds may be hazardous for small boats. Fishing is often productive in both the Lake and the Mokelumne River as well as other nearby streams. The Forest Service maintains three campgrounds along the river just below the dam. A trailhead into the 105,000 acre Mokelumne Wilderness is located just above the dam. *This is a high fire hazard area - NO campfires allowed - use portable stoves.*

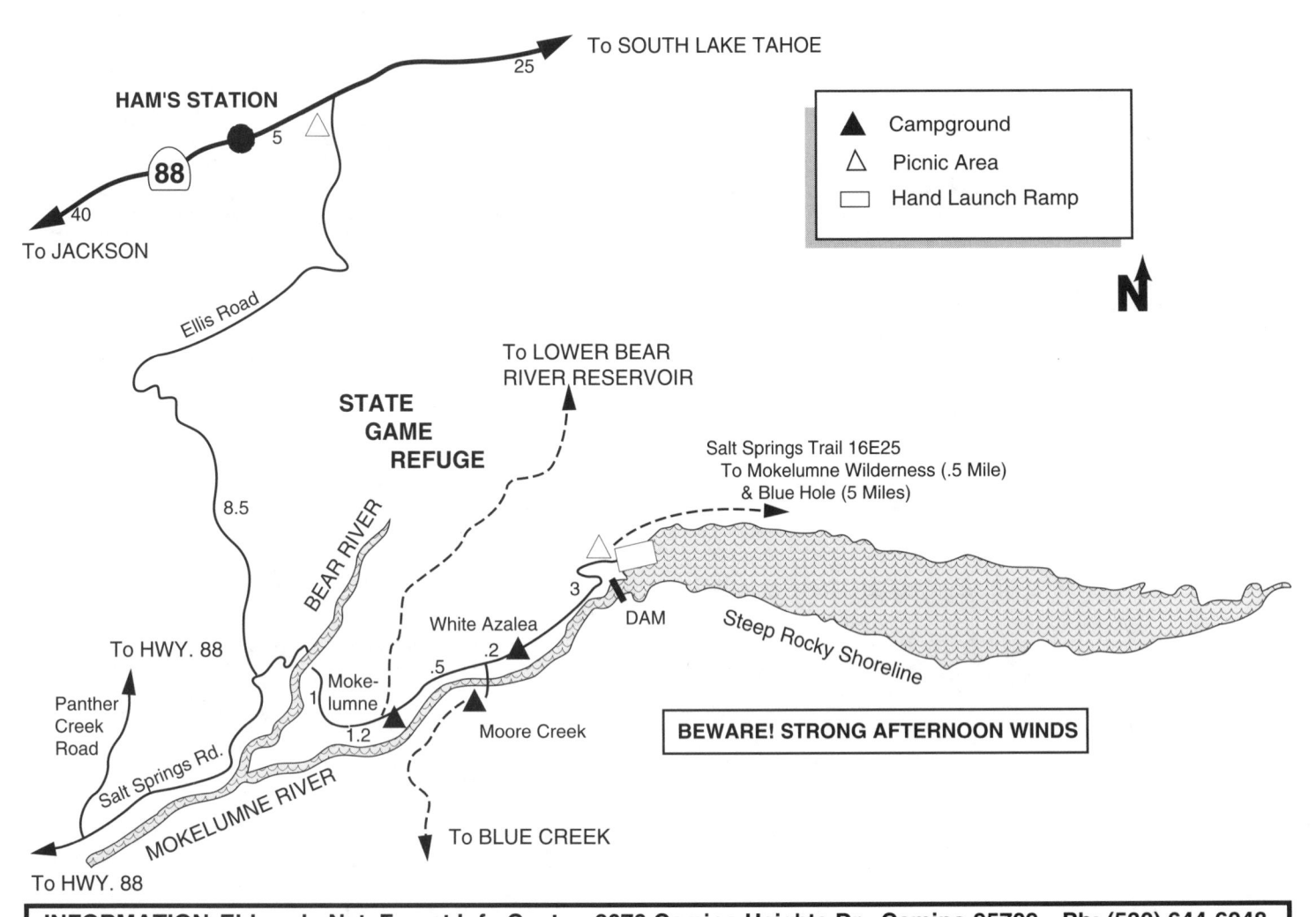

INFORMATION: Eldorado Nat. Forest Info Center, 3070 Camino Heights Dr., Camino 95709—Ph: (530) 644-6048

CAMPING	BOATING	RECREATION	OTHER

22 Sites for Tents & R.V.s
  Mokelumne: 8 Sites
  Moore Creek: 8 Sites
  White Azalea: 6 Sites
No Drinking Water
No Fee
	Power, Row, Canoe
	  & Sail
	Hand Launch Only
	
	Winds Can be Hazardous
	* in the Afternoon*
	* in Afternoon*
		Fishing: Rainbow,
		  Brown & Brook
		  Trout
		Swimming
		Picnicking
		Hiking
		Backpacking [Parking]
		Equestrian Trails
		Hunting: Deer,
		  Upland Game
			Nearest Facilities & Gas
			  at Ham's Station
			
			No Hunting in State
			* Game Refuge*
			
			No ORVs within
			* the Mokelumne River*
			* Canyon below areas*
			* on Panther Creek and*
			* Ellis Roads*

LOWER BEAR RIVER RESERVOIR

Lower Bear River Reservoir rests at an elevation of 5,849 feet in the Eldorado National Forest. This scenic Lake of 727 surface acres is surrounded by a coniferous forest reaching to water's edge. There are good vacation and boating facilities. Afternoon breezes make sailing a delight. The Lake is regularly stocked, and fishing is usually productive. The Forest Service campgrounds are operated by a concessionaire. Overnight camping is limited to designated sites only. The Bear River Resort has complete camping and marina facilities with hot showers, groceries, bait and tackle, snack bar, trailer rentals and storage.

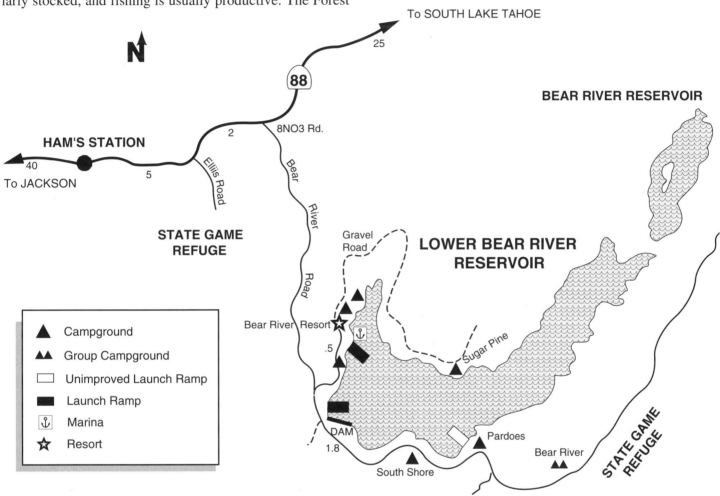

INFORMATION: ElDorado Nat. Forest Info Center, 3070 Camino Heights Dr., Camino 95709—Ph: (530) 644-6048

CAMPING	BOATING	RECREATION	OTHER

South Shore:
  22 Dev. Sites for
  Tents & R.V.s
  Fee: $11 (Extra Veh. $5)
Pardoes Pt. & Sugar Pine:
  10 Sites Each for Tents
  & R.V.s - No Water
  Fee: $8 (Extra Veh. $4)
Bear River Group Camps:
2 Sites - 25 People - $50
1 Site - 50 People - $100
Group Reservations:
  Ph: (209) 295-4512
	Open to All Boating
	Full Service Marina
	Paved Launch Ramp
	
	Rentals:
	  Fishing Boats
	
	*Low Water Hazards
	Late in Season*
		Fishing: Rainbow,
		  Macinaw &
		  Brown Trout
		Picnicking
		Swimming - No Lifeguards
		Hiking - Backpacking
		Hunting: Deer
			Lower Bear River Resort
			  40800 Hwy. 88
			  Pioneer 95666
			  Ph: (209) 295-4868
			  125 Dev. Sites with
			    Hookups
			    Fee: $22
			  Group Camp to 60
			    People
			  Disposal Station
			  Laundromat

SILVER LAKE

Silver Lake rests at an elevation of 7,200 feet in a large granite basin just west of the Sierra Summit in the Eldorado National Forest. This exceptionally beautiful Lake was once a resting place on the Emigrant Trail leading to the gold fields. You can still see the trail markers carved in the trees. The descendants of Raymond Peter Plasse, who established a trading post in 1853, operate a good resort at the Lake from June through September. They offer campsites, horse camping and several recreational acitivties including horse rentals. A dining room and bar are also available. Silver Lake has been a popular recreation area for over a century, offering a variety of natural resources and facilities for the camper, angler, boater, hiker and equestrian.

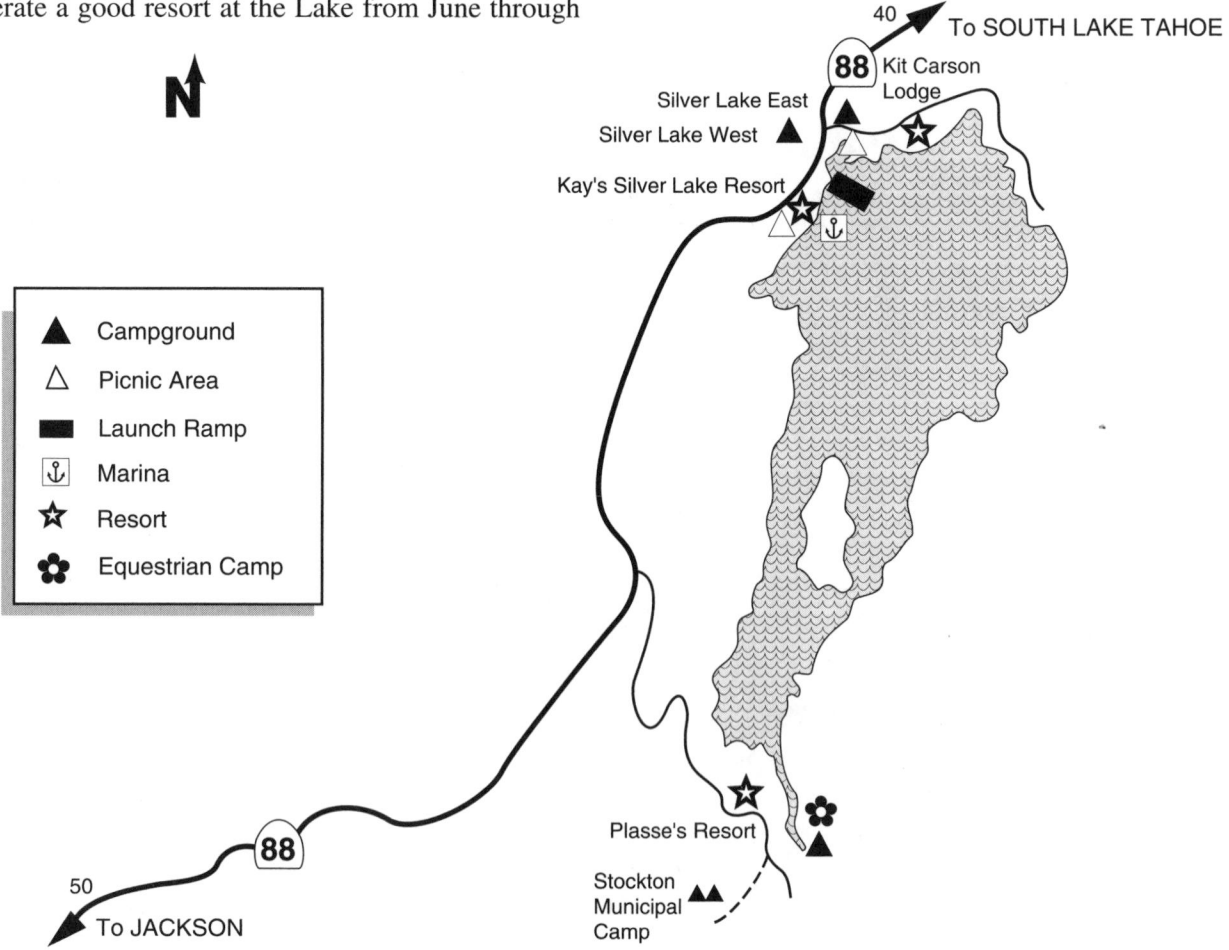

INFORMATION: Eldorado Nat. Forest Info Center, 3070 Camino Heights Dr., Camino 95709—Ph: (530) 644-6048

CAMPING	BOATING	RECREATION	OTHER
U.S.F.S. - 62 Dev. Sites for Tents & R.V.s - Fee: $12 17 Sites can be Reserved Ph: (877) 444-6777 Eldorado Irrigation Dist. Ph: (530) 644-1960 35 Dev. Sites for Tents & R.V.s - Fee: $15 Plasse's Resort Ph: (209) 258-8814 Dev. Sites for Tents & R.V.s Horse Trailers - Group Area Fees: $15 and up	Power, Row, Canoe, Sail, Inflatables Full Service Marina Launch Ramps Rentals: Fishing Boats & Motors Docks, Moorings	Fishing: Rainbow Trout Swimming Picnicking Hiking Equestrian Trails Horse Rentals at Plasse's Resort	Cabins Located at: Kit Carson Lodge Ph: (209) 258-8500 Kay's Silver Lake Resort Ph: (209) 258-8598 Snack Bars Restaurants Grocery Stores Bait & Tackle Laundromat Gas Station Propane Disposal Station

CAPLES and KIRKWOOD LAKES

Caples Lake is at an elevation of 7,950 feet in the Eldorado National Forest near the summit of Carson Pass. The nights and mornings are coo, and the water is cold in this 600 surface acre Lake. Kirkwood Lake is 3 miles to the west of Caples Lake at an elevation of 7,600 feet. The road is not suitable for larger R.V.s or trailers. Gas or electric motor boats are not allowed on Kirkwood but you may use a motor up to 5 mph on Caples. Fishing is good for a variety of trout in these Lakes as well as other nearby lakes and streams. Trails lead into the Mokelumne Wilderness for the hiker or backpacker. Permits are required for overnight trips into the Wilderness year around. This entire area is a photographer's delight.

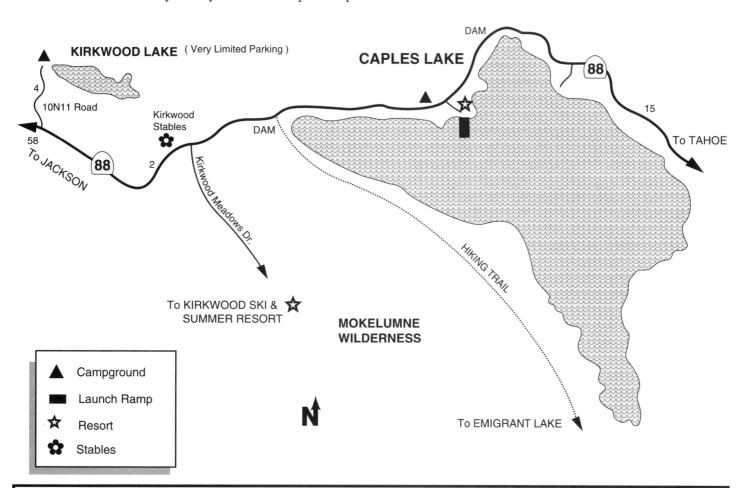

KIRKWOOD LAKE (Very Limited Parking)

CAPLES LAKE

4

10N11 Road

58

To JACKSON

88

Kirkwood Stables

2

DAM

Kirkwood Meadows Dr.

To KIRKWOOD SKI & SUMMER RESORT

MOKELUMNE WILDERNESS

DAM

88

15

To TAHOE

HIKING TRAIL

To EMIGRANT LAKE

N

▲ Campground

■ Launch Ramp

☆ Resort

✿ Stables

INFORMATION: ElDorado Nat. Forest Info Center, 3070 Camino Heights Dr., Camino 95709—Ph: (530) 644-6048

CAMPING	BOATING	RECREATION	OTHER

Caples Lake:
    35 Dev. Sites for
    Tents & R.V.s
    Fee: $14
        Extra Vehicle: $5
 	
Kirkwood Lake:
    12 Dev. Sites for
    Tents & Small R.V.s
    Fee: $10
        Extra Vehicle: $4
	Caples Lake:
	    Power, Row, Canoe,
	    Sail & Inflatables
	    5 MPH Speed Limit
	    Launch Ramp
	    Rentals: Fishing Boats
	    Water Taxi
	
	No Motors of Any Kind
	    on Kirkwood
		Fishing: Rainbow,
		    Brown, Brook &
		    Cutthroat Trout
		Swimming
		Picnicking
		Hiking
		Backpacking
		Equestrian Trails
		Hunting: Deer
		Horse Rentals at
		    Kirkwood Stables
			Caples Lake Resort
			    Ph: (209) 258-8888
			    Lodge & Restaurant
			    Housekeeping Cabins
			    Grocery Store, Bait &
			        Tackle, Boat Rentals
			Kirkwood Resort
			    Ph: (209) 258-6000
			    Lodge & Restaurant
			    Condo Rentals
			    Store, Gas Station
			    Tennis Courts
			    Mountain Bike Rentals

WOODS and RED LAKES

Woods Lake is at an elevation of 8,200 feet southwest of the Carson Pass in the Eldorado National Forest. This scenic hidden retreat, just 2 miles south of Highway 88, offers a variety of recreational opportunities. In addition to the campground, the Forest Service provides a picnic area at the water's edge with facilities for the handicapped. Fishing can be good from a boat or along the bank as well as in the streams throughout the area. Motorboats are not permitted on the Lake. Trails lead to Winnemucca, Round Top Lakes and other sites within the Mokelumne Wilderness. Permits are required for overnight trips into the Wilderness areas year around. The Pacific Crest Trail runs to the east of Woods Lake. Most of Red Lake is State land (Department of Fish & Game). Facilities are limited.

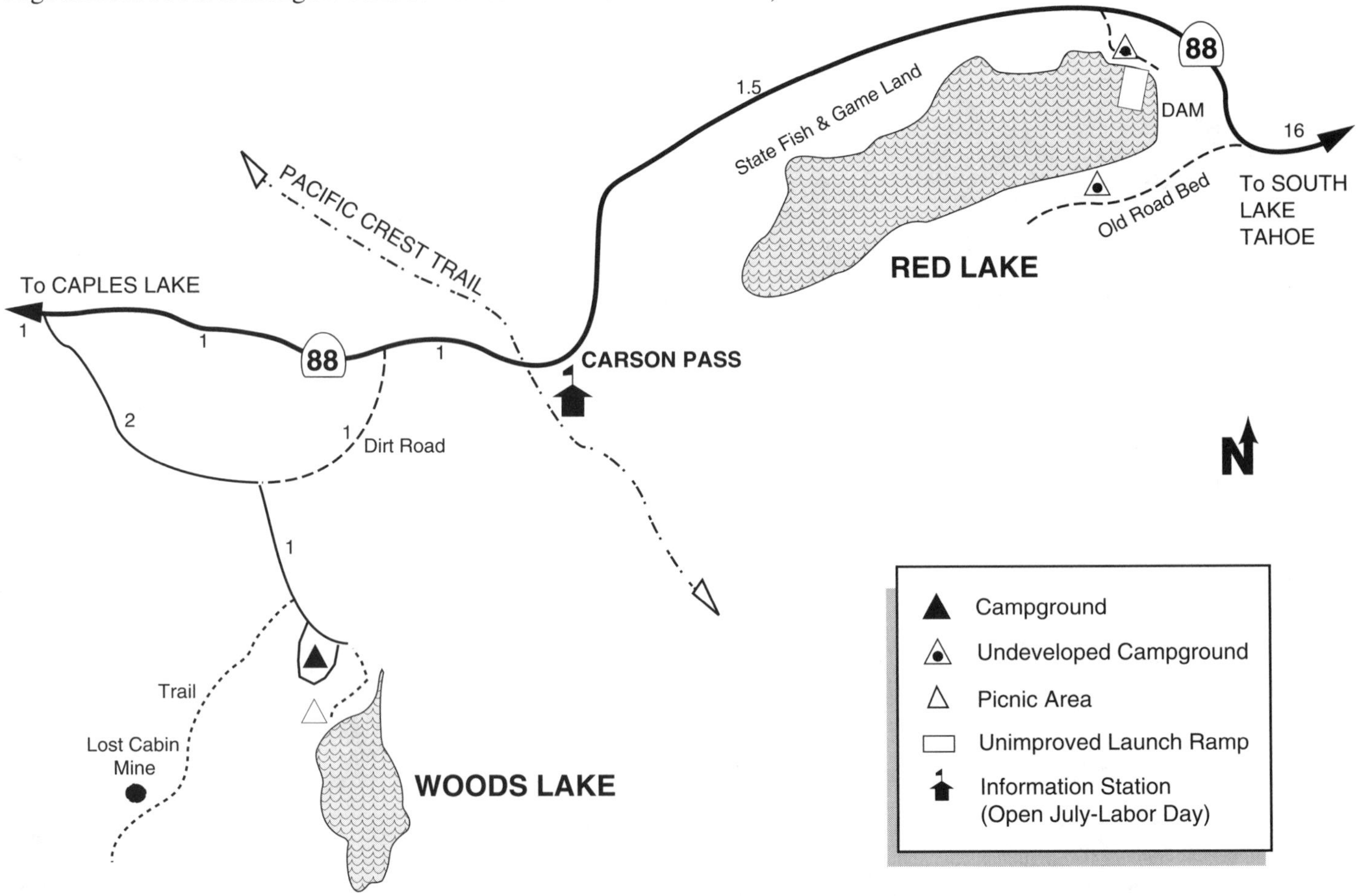

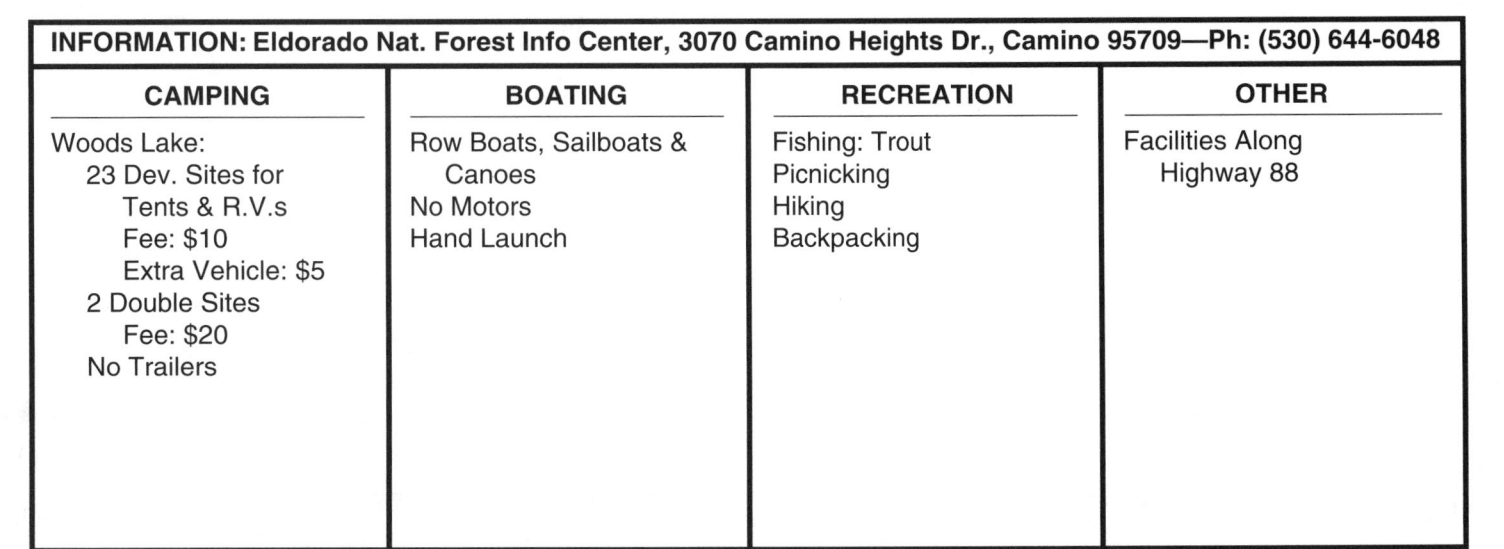

CAMPING	BOATING	RECREATION	OTHER
Woods Lake: 23 Dev. Sites for Tents & R.V.s Fee: $10 Extra Vehicle: $5 2 Double Sites Fee: $20 No Trailers	Row Boats, Sailboats & Canoes No Motors Hand Launch	Fishing: Trout Picnicking Hiking Backpacking	Facilities Along Highway 88

INFORMATION: Eldorado Nat. Forest Info Center, 3070 Camino Heights Dr., Camino 95709—Ph: (530) 644-6048

BLUE LAKES - ALPINE COUNTY

The Blue Lakes are at an elevation of 8,000 feet in this remote area of the Eldorado National Forest. The mornings and evenings are cool and the water is clear and cold. Boating is limited to small craft and fishing can be good. There are numerous hiking trails, with some leading into the Mokelumne Wilderness. The campgrounds are maintained by P.G. & E. except for Hope Valley which is operated by the U.S.F.S., Carson Ranger District, Toiyabe National Forest. Facilities are limited, so come well prepared. Only the first 7 miles of road are paved from Highway 88.

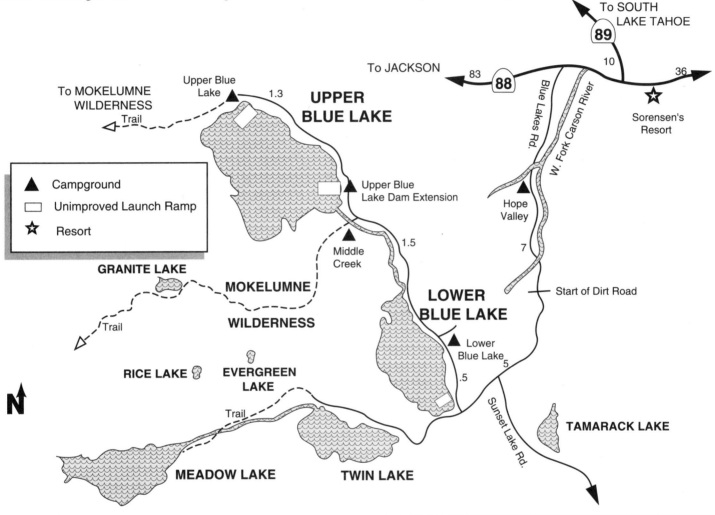

INFORMATION: P.G. & E. Land Projects, 2730 Gateway Oaks Dr., Sacramento 95833—Ph: (916) 386-5164

CAMPING	BOATING	RECREATION	OTHER

P.G.&E.:
Upper Blue Lake:
  32 Dev. Sites for
  Tents & R.V.s
Upper Blue Lake Dam:
  25 Dev. Sites
Middle Creek: 5 Dev. Sites
Lower Blue Lake:
  16 Dev. Sites
  Fees: $15
USFS - Hope Valley:
  26 Dev. Sites
  Fee: $10
	Small Boats Only
	Unimproved Launch
	  Ramps
		Fishing: Rainbow
		  Trout
		Swimming
		Picnicking
		Hiking
		Backpacking [Parking]
			Sorensen's Resort
			Hope Valley 96120
			Ph: (530) 694-2203
			  30 Cabins
			  Restaurant
			  Fly Fishing &
			    Tying Lessons
			  Fishing Supplies &
			    Licenses
			  Guide Service
			  For Reservations:
			    (800) 423-9949

INDIAN CREEK RESERVOIR and HEENAN LAKE

Indian Creek Reservoir is at an elevation of 5,600 feet on the eastern slope of the Sierras. The Bureau of Land Management maintains more than 7,000 acres in this beautiful area of Jeffrey and Pinon Pines. The 160 surface-acre Lake offers good fishing and small craft boating. Check current water levels. Nearby Heenan Lake, 129 surface acres, provides a good catch and release fishery. Only artificial lures and barbless hooks can be used. *Contact the California Department of Fish and Game at (916) 358-2900 for specific regulations.* A popular attraction nearby is Grover Hot Springs State Park where a hot mineral bath can be enjoyed. Camping reservations are advised.

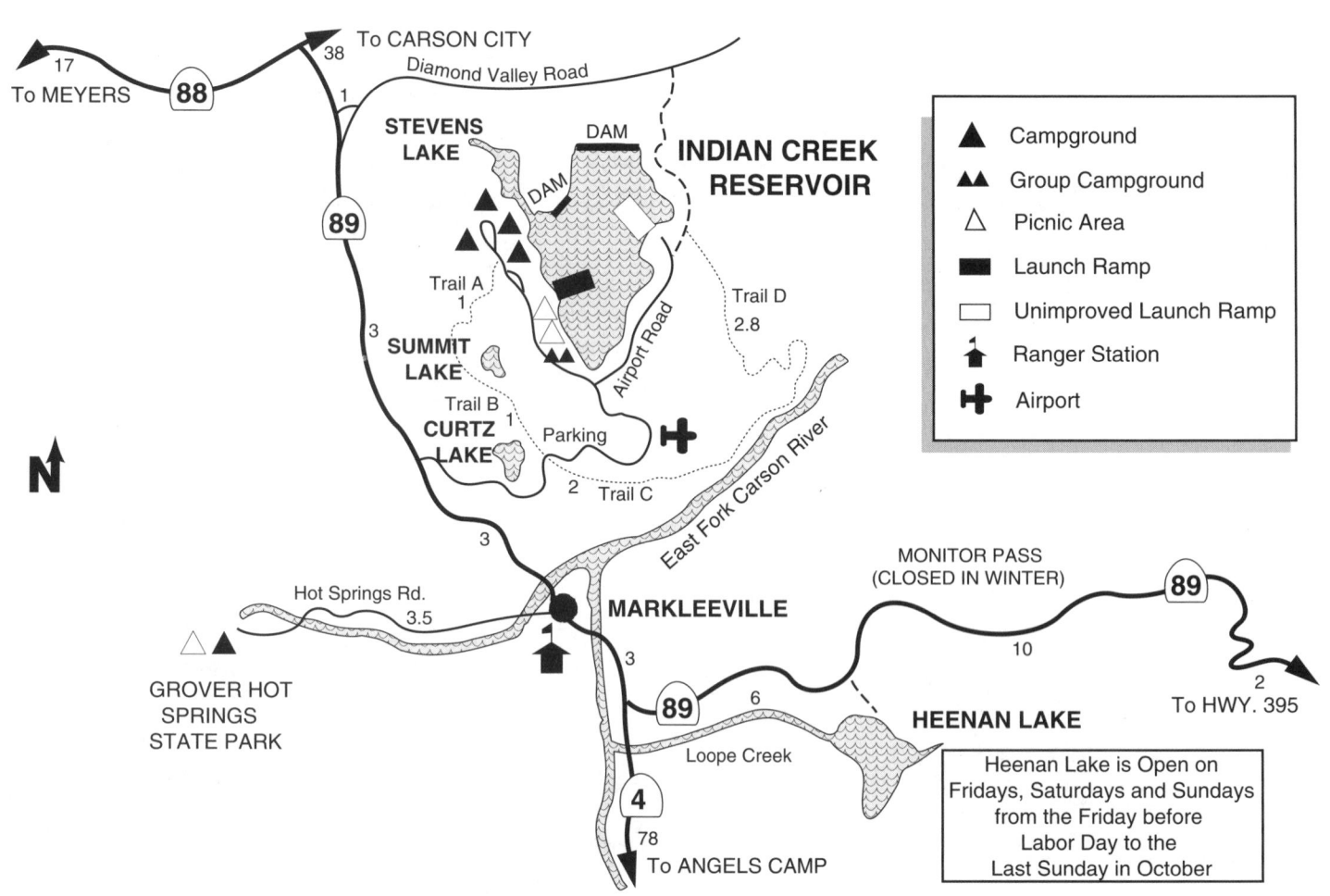

INFORMATION: Bureau of Land Management, 5665 Morgan Mill Rd., Carson City, NV 89701—Ph: (775) 885-6000

CAMPING	BOATING	RECREATION	OTHER

Indian Creek:
    19 Dev. Sites for
    Tents & R.V.s to 30 Ft.
    Plus 10 Tent Only Sites
    No Hookups
        Fees: $8 - $12
    No Reservations
Group Camp to 40 People
    Fee: $35
    Reservations:
        Ph: (775) 885-6000
Disposal Station
	Indian Creek:
	    Open to All Small Boats
	    Launch Ramp
	
	Heenan Lake:
	    Small Hand Launch
	        Boats Only
	    Electric Motors Only
	    Call for Specific
	    Fishing Regulations
	    Ph: (916) 358-2900
		Fishing :
		    Indian Creek:
		        Rainbow & Brown
		        Trout
		    Heenan: Lahontan
		        Cutthroat Trout
		        Catch & Release
		Picnicking
		Hiking & Nature Trails
		Backpacking
		Curtz Lake: Environmental
		    Study Area
			Grover Hot Springs
			    P.O. Box 188
			    Markleeville 96120
			    Ph: (530) 694-2248
			    76 Dev. Sites for Tents
			        & R.V.s to 24 Feet
			    Fee: $12
			    Reservations:
			        Ph: (800) 444-7275
			
			Alpine Chamber of
			    Commerce
			    Ph: (530) 694-2475

Topaz Lake rests on the California-Nevada State Line at an elevation of 5,000 feet. This 1,800 surface-acre Reservoir is nestled amid sage-covered mountains and has 25 miles of sandy shoreline. The Lake is open to all types of boating, including boat camping, but beware of potential heavy after-noon winds. California and Nevada Fish and Game Departments stock the Lake which is closed to fishing for three months beginning October 1. As a result, trophy sized trout up to 8 pounds are no surprise. Half of Topaz Lake is in Nevada so there are nearby casinos to enjoy.

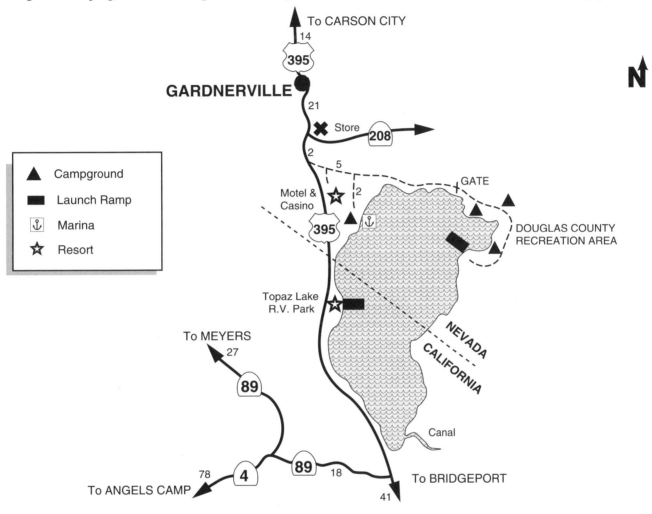

▲	Campground
◼	Launch Ramp
⚓	Marina
★	Resort

INFORMATION: Douglas County, 3700 Topaz Park Rd., Gardnerville, NV 89410—Ph: (775) 266-3343

CAMPING	BOATING	RECREATION	OTHER
Douglas County Park: 28 R.V. Sites - Water & Electric Hookups - $15 39 Sites - Fee: $10 Disposal Station Topaz Lake RV Park: 50 R.V. Sites Full Hookups Topaz Marina: 28 Dev. Sites for Tents & R.V.s, Some Hookups	Power, Row, Canoe, Sail, Waterski, Jets, Windsurf, & Inflatables Full Service Marina County Launch Ramp - $5 Rentals: Fishing Boats Docks, Berths, Dry Storage, Moorings & Gas Boat Camping	Fishing: Rainbow, Brown & Cutthroat Trout Swimming - Beaches Picnicking Hiking Playgrounds	Douglas County Park Ph: (775) 266-3343 Topaz Lake R.V. Park Ph: (530) 495-2357 Topaz Marina Ph: (775) 266-3236 Motel Restaurant & Lounge Casinos Bait & Tackle at Topaz Marina

LAKE ALPINE

Lake Alpine is at an elevation of 7,303 feet in the Stanislaus National Forest. The Lake has a surface area of 180 acres and is regularly stocked with rainbow trout. The water is crystal clear and very cold. All boating is allowed within a 10 mph speed limit. The steady breezes make this a good sailing Lake. For the hiker and equestrian, there are trails leading to Carson-Iceberg Wilderness, located south of Lake Alpine, and to the Mokelumne Wilderness, a few miles to the north. The Forest Service maintains campgrounds near the Lake plus a special area set aside for backpackers. The historic Lake Alpine Lodge overlooks this beautiful Lake and the heavily timbered mountains.

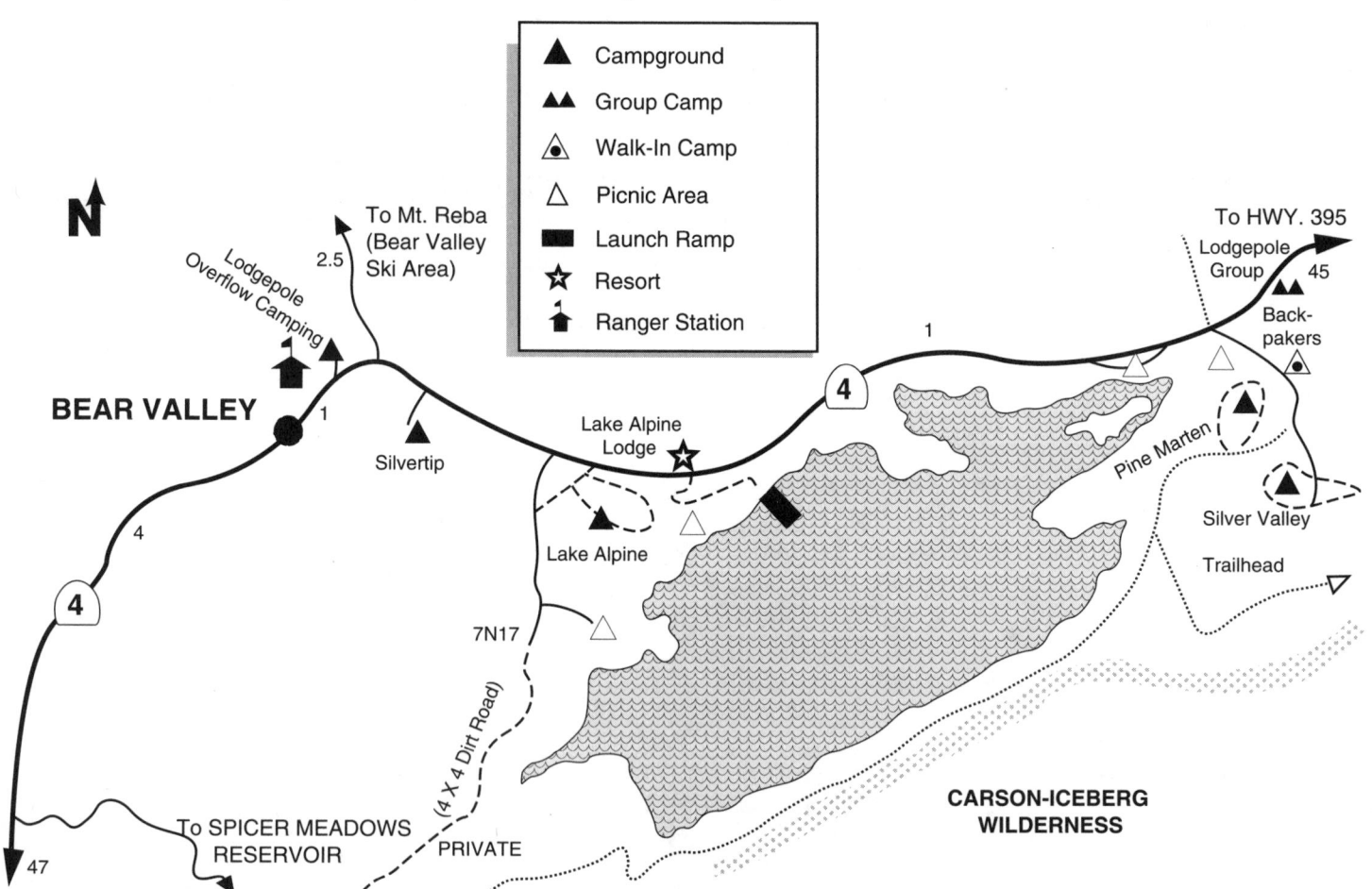

INFORMATION: Calaveras Ranger District, P.O. Box 500, Hathaway Pines 95233—Ph: (209) 795-1381

CAMPING	BOATING	RECREATION	OTHER
112 Dev. Sites for Tents & R.V.s to 27 feet Fee: $14.50 Group Camp Backpacker's Camp Reserve: Ph: (877) 444-6777 Plus Overflow Area Nearby - Open on Busy Weekends Only	Power, Row, Sail, Canoe & Inflatable Speed Limit - 10 MPH Launch Ramp Rentals: Fishing & Motor Boats, Canoes, Rowboats & Kayaks	Fishing: Rainbow Trout Handicap Access Swimming Picnicking Hiking Backpacking [Parking] 4-Wheel Drive & Motorcycle Trails Mountain Biking Bike Trail from Bear Valley to the End of the Lake	Lake Alpine Lodge: P.O. 5300 Bear Valley 95223 Ph: (209) 753-6358 Cabins Showers & Laundromat Restaurant Grocery Store Gift Shop Bait & Tackle Boat & Bike Rentals Full Services & Gas Station
Marmot Picnic Area Suitable for Handicapped		Hunting: Deer & Bear	at Bear Valley

LAKE SONOMA

Lake Sonoma is nestled amid the rolling foothills of Northern California's coastal mountain range at an elevation of 451 feet. Located in the "wine country" just west of Healdsburg, this scenic Lake offers 2,700 surface acres of prime recreational waters. There are many quiet, secluded coves for the boater, sailor or angler. Waterskiers are allowed only in designated areas. The U.S. Army Corps of Engineers has developed a variety of facilities. The 53 miles of oak-shaded hilly shoreline have almost 40 miles of lake access trails for the hiker or equestrian. There are primitive walk-in or boat-in areas with a total of 109 individual sites. The Liberty Glen Campground offers shaded, modern campsites. There is a 5-lane public launch ramp. The privately operated marina has complete facilities.

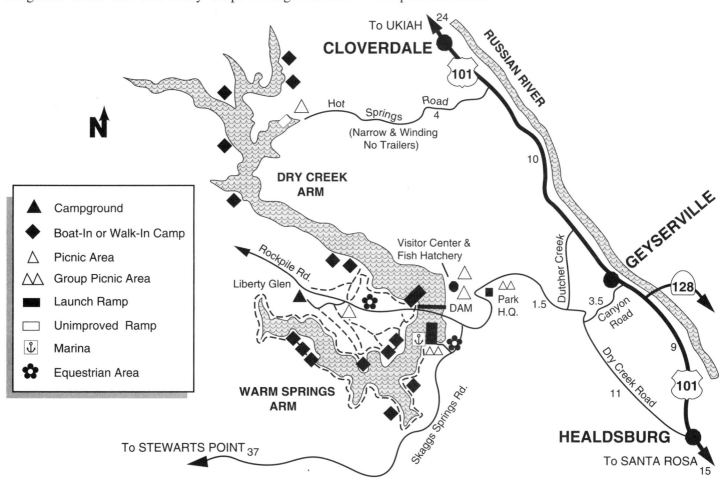

Legend:
- ▲ Campground
- ◆ Boat-In or Walk-In Camp
- △ Picnic Area
- △△ Group Picnic Area
- ■ Launch Ramp
- ☐ Unimproved Ramp
- ⚓ Marina
- ✿ Equestrian Area

INFORMATION: Lake Sonoma Rec. Area, 3333 Skaggs Springs Rd., Geyserville 95441—Ph: (707) 433-9483

CAMPING	BOATING	RECREATION	OTHER
Liberty Glen: 97 Dev. Sites for Tents & R.V.s Disposal Station 2 Group Use Sites 109 Boat-in or Walk-in Primitive Sites No Water Permits Required Reserve All Sites: Ph: (877) 444-6777	Open to all Boating Designated Areas for Waterskiing Public Launch Ramp Fee: $2 Full Service Marina Boat Gas Slip Rentals Boat Storage Boat Rentals Launch Ramp: $10 Hand Launch at Hot Springs - Fee: $2	Fishing: Large & Smallmouth Bass, Sacramento Perch, Channel Catfish & Redear Sunfish Picnic Areas Group Picnic Sites-Reserve Swim Beach Hiking & Equestrian Trails 2 Equestrian Staging Areas Visitor Center Fish Hatchery	Lake Sonoma Resort 520 Mendocino Ave. Suite 200 Santa Rosa 95401 Ph: (707) 433-2200 Snack Bar General Store Beer & Wine Gardens Bait & Tackle Day Use Fee: $5

SPRING LAKE and LAKE RALPHINE

Spring Lake is under the jurisdiction of the Sonoma County Regional Parks Department. The 320-acre Park has a visitors center including a museum, picnic areas, campground, summer swim lagoon and well-maintained trails. This is a popular equestrian area. The 75 surface-acre Lake is open to non-powered boating except for electric motors. Lake Ralphine is within the City of Santa Rosa's Howarth Park. This day-use facility has numerous children's attractions and various boat rentals. Lake Ralphine allows non-powered boating with sailing being a special attraction. There is a warm water fishery in addition to planted trout in the winter at both Lakes. A bicycle path connects these parks.

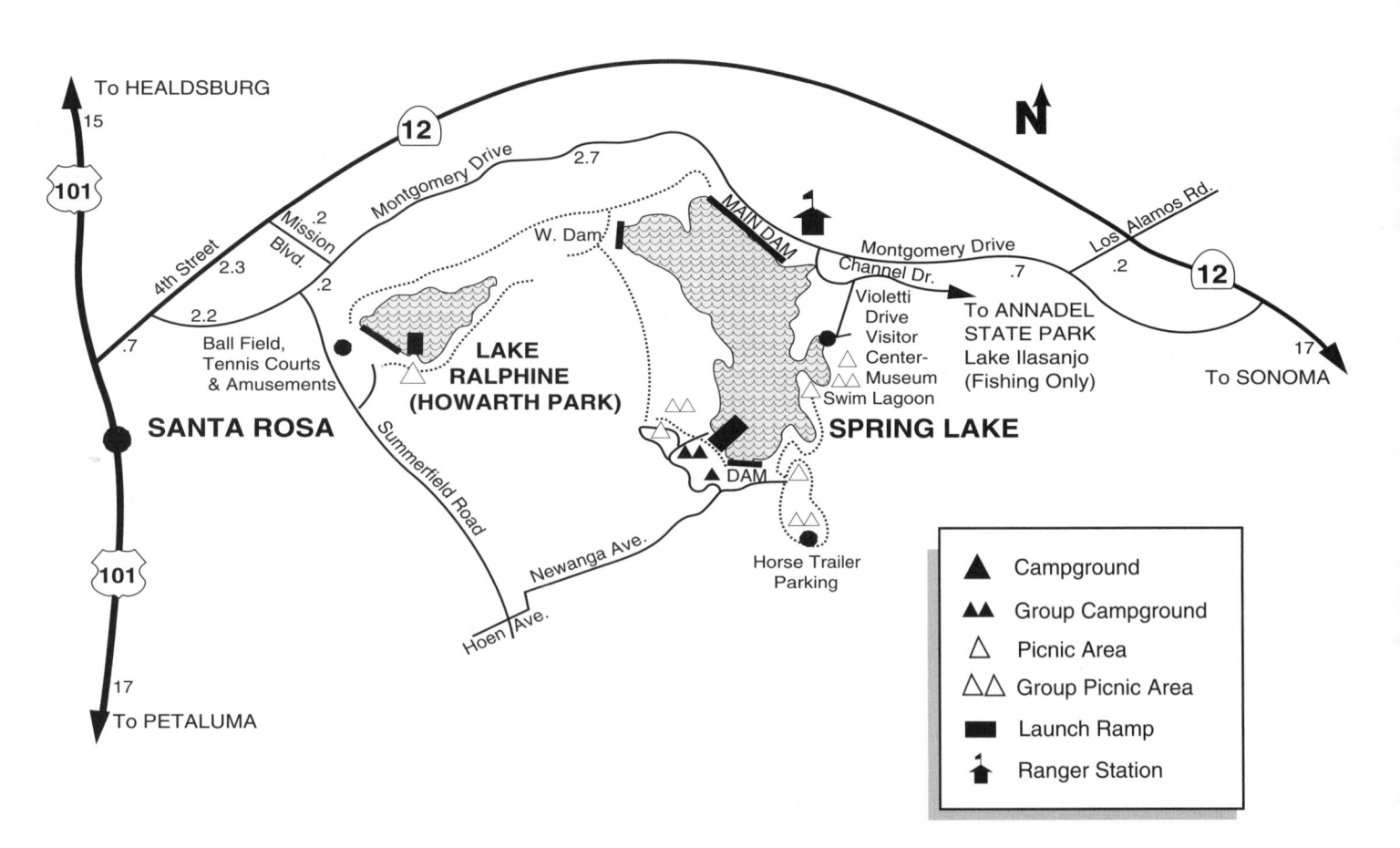

▲	Campground
▲▲	Group Campground
△	Picnic Area
△△	Group Picnic Area
■	Launch Ramp
⚑	Ranger Station

INFORMATION: Spring Lake, 5390 Montgomery Dr., Santa Rosa 95409—Ph: (707) 539-8092

CAMPING	BOATING	RECREATION	OTHER
29 Dev. Sites for Tents & R.V.s No Hookups Fee: $15 Reservations: Ph: (707) 565-2267 Disposal Station Group Camp to 100 People No R.V.s Reservations Ph: (707)539-8082 Day Use Only at Ralphine Dogs on Leash OK	Spring Lake: Row, Sail, Canoe, Inflatables (2 Chamber), Electric Motors Rentals: Row, Canoe, Paddle Boats, Sailboats (Summer) Life Jackets Required Lake Ralphine: Rentals: As Above Open Tues-Sunday in Summer (Weekends in Fall & Spring)	Fishing: Trout, Bluegill, Redear Sunfish & Bass Swim Lagoon (Summer) Picnic Areas: Group Reservations Available Hiking Trails Paved Bicycle Trails Equestrian Trails Tennis Courts - Ralphine No Swimming in Lake Ralphine	Howarth Park: Santa Rosa Rec. & Parks Dept. Ph: (707) 543-3282 Miniature Steam Train Pony Rides Merry-Go-Round Land of Imagination Play Area for Children of All Ages

LAKE BERRYESSA, LAKE HENNESSY and LAKE S0LAN0

Lake Berryessa is one of Northern California's most popular recreation Lakes. One of the State's largest man-made Lakes, it covers over 13,000 surface acres with 165 miles of shoreline. Surrounding hills are covered with oak and madrone trees. Known for excellent year-around fishing, the angler will find trophy trout, three species of bass and a good warm water fishery. The average water temperature of 78 degrees attracts the waterskier and swimmer. Light and variable winds are good for sailing. Complete resort, camping and marine facilities complement the Lake's natural attrractions.

To the west of Lake Berryessa, off Highway 128, is Lake Hennessy. Under the jurisdiction of the City of Napa, this Lake is for day use only and has limited facilities. Lake Solano, southeast of Berryessa, provides swim lagoons, picnic sites, boat rentals and a campground for tents and R.V.s. The water can be cold as it comes out from Lake Berryessa Dam. Non-powered boating and trout fishing are popular.

....Continued....

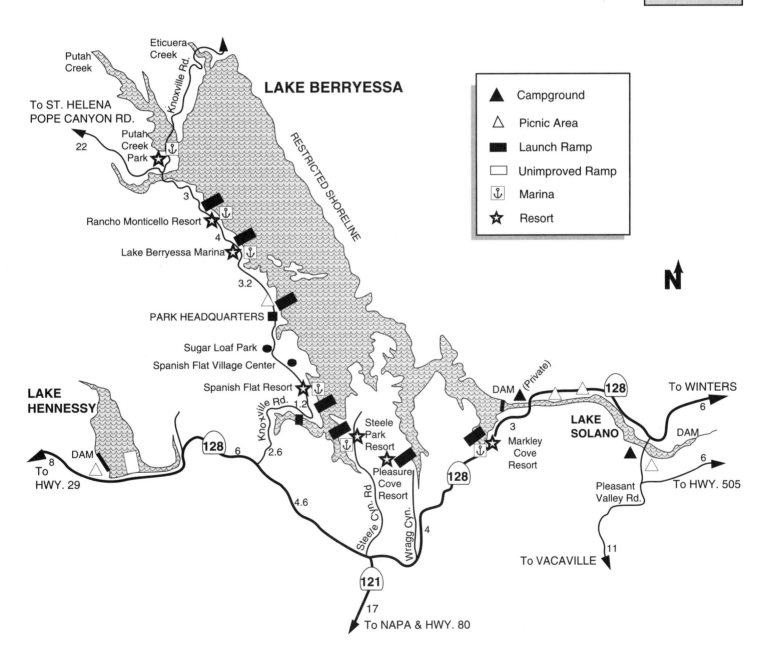

LAKE BERRYESSA.............Continued

LAKE BERRYESSA MARINA RESORT - 5800 Knoxville Rd., Napa 94558—Ph: (707) 966-2161 - Tent & R.V. Sites, Full Hookups, Disposal Station, Courtesy Pumpouts, Hot Showers, Picnic Area, Grocery Store, Laundromat, Restaurant & Lounge, Swim Beach, Full Service Marina, Fishing, Patio & Ski Boat Rentals, Fuel Dock, Launch Ramp, Courtesy Dock.

MARKLEY COVE RESORT - P.O. Box 987, Winters 95694—Ph: (707) 966-2134 - Fishing Boat Rentals, Launch Ramp, Berths, Boat Pumpout Station, Fuel Dock, Private Houseboat Moorage, Store, Bait & Tackle, Snack Bar.

PUTAH CREEK PARK - 7600 Knoxville Rd., Napa 94558—Ph: (707) 966-2116 - Tent & R.V. Sites, Partial and Full Hookups, Disposal Station, Hot Showers, Picnic Area, Motel, Full Service Marina, Ski Boat Rentals, Storage, Bait & Tackle, Store, Restaurant & Lounge, Snack Bar.

RANCHO MONTICELLO RESORT - 6590 Knoxville Rd., Napa 94558—Ph: (707) 966-2188 - Tent & R.V. Sites, Full Hookups, 2 Disposal Stations, Hot Showers, Picnic Areas, Store, Snack Bar, Launch Ramp, Laundromat.

PLEASURE COVE RESORT- 6100 Hwy. 128, Napa 94558—Ph: (707) 966-2172 - Tent & R.V. Sites, Full Hookups, Disposal Station, Hot Showers, Cabin Rentals, Slips, Storage, Fuel Dock, Launch Ramp, Private Houseboat Moorage, Grocery Store, Restaurant & Lounge, Picnic Area, Barbecues, Laundromat.

SPANISH FLAT RESORT - 4290 Knoxville Rd., Napa 94558—Ph: (707) 966-7700 - Tent & R.V. Sites, Hot Showers, Disposal Station, Electric and Water Hookups, 12 Cabins, Full Service Marina, Launch Ramp, Berths, Fishing and Patio Boat Rentals, Grocery Store, Picnic Sites, Barbecues, Swim Beach.

STEELE PARK RESORT - 1605 Steel Canyon Rd., Napa 94558—Ph: (707) 966-2123 - For Reservations—Ph: (800) 522-2123 - Largest Resort on Lake, R.V. Sites, Full Hookups, Disposal Station, Hot Showers, Motel, Housekeeping Cottages, Full Service Marina, Launch Ramp, Covered and Open Berths, Dry Storage, Fuel Dock, Motel & Cottage Courtesy Dock, Jet Skis & Patio Boat Rentals, Ski School, Swim Beach, Tennis Courts, Swimming Pool for Motel Guests, Ice Cream Parlor, Arcade Room, 2 Restaurants, Cocktail Lounge, Grocery Store, Large Picnic Area.

For further information on facilities contact:

NAPA CHAMBER OF COMMERCE
1556 - 1st Street
Napa 94559
Ph: (707) 226-7455

INFORMATION: See Above

CAMPING	BOATING	RECREATION	OTHER

Lake Berryessa
  Tent & R.V. Sites
  at Resorts
  See Above for Details
 	
Lake Solano
  50 Tent & R.V. Sites
 	
Lake Hennessy
  No Camping
	Lake Berryessa
	  Open to All Boating
	  Full Service Marinas
	  Rentals: Houseboats,
	  Waterski, Fishing
	  & Patio Boat
	Lake Solano
	  Non-Power Boating
	  Only
	Lake Hennessy
	  10 HP Max. Limit
	  No Kayaks or
	  Windsurfers
		Fishing: Rainbow &
		  Brown Trout, Large
		  & Smallmouth Bass,
		  Catfish, Bluegill,
		  Crappie
		
		Swimming - Lakes & Pools
		Picnic Areas
		Hiking & Equestrian
		  Trails
		Wine Country
		  Excursions
			Lake Solano:
			  County of Solano
			  Parks Department
			  603 Texas Street
			  Fairfield 94533
			  Ph: (707) 421-7925

LAKE AMADOR

Lake Amador is at an elevation of 485 feet in the Sierra foothills, one mile east of historic town of Buena Vista. The surface area of the Lake is 400 acres with 14 miles of shoreline surrounded by black oak-covered hills. Brush along the water's edge provides a thriving warm water fishery. Northern California records have been set for bass. Trout and catfish are also large and plentiful. This is a nice boating facility with good winds for sailing. No waterskiing or jet skis are allowed. The Lake is open to boating and fishing 24 hours a day and fishing boats with motors can be rented. Camping facilities include full hookups for R.V.s. Amador is a good family recreation area and the angler's dream.

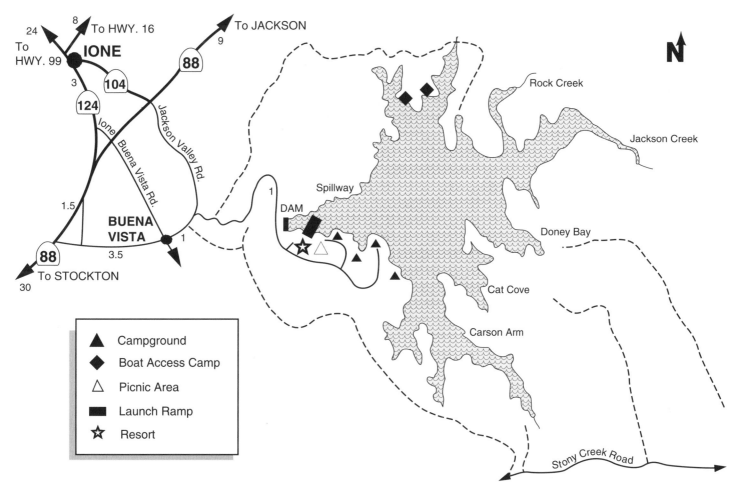

| Campground |
| Boat Access Camp |
| Picnic Area |
| Launch Ramp |
| Resort |

INFORMATION: Lake Amador Resort, 7500 Amador Dr., Ione 95640—Ph: (209) 274-4739

CAMPING	BOATING	RECREATION	OTHER
150 Dev. Sites for Tents & R.V.s to 40 feet Fee: $18	Power, Row, Canoe, Sail, Windsurf & Inflatables	Fishing: Trout, Largemouth Bass, Catfish, Bluegill, Crappie & Perch	Restaurant General Store Bait & Tackle
73 Full Hookups for R.V.s & Trailers Fee: $23	*No Waterskiing or Jets*	Fishing Fee: $6 per Day per Person	Hot Showers
Disposal Station	Launch Ramp - $5	Swimming - Pond	Gas Station & Propane
Boat Access Camp	Rentals: Fishing Boats	Free Waterslide	Club House &
Group Camp to 50 Vehicles	Docks, Storage	Picnicking	Recreation Room
Reservations for All Sites Suggested Reservation Fee: $5	Fishing Floats Around Shoreline	Hiking Mountain Biking	
Day Use Fee: $7			

LAKE PARDEE

Lake Pardee rests at an elevation of 568 feet in the heart of the "Mother Lode Country" and its historic gold towns. Under the jurisdiction of East Bay Municipal Water District, this popular fishing Lake in the Sierra foothills has a surface area of 2,200 acres surrounded by 43 miles of rolling woodland. Trout and Kokanee are the primary gamefish. The angler will find a good smallmouth and largemouth bass fishery along with abundant catfish. Boating is generally related to fishing. Waterskiing and jet skis are not allowed. There are marine support facilities. This is a nice family area with a large campground, a swimming pool (no lake swimming), picnic area, playground and store.

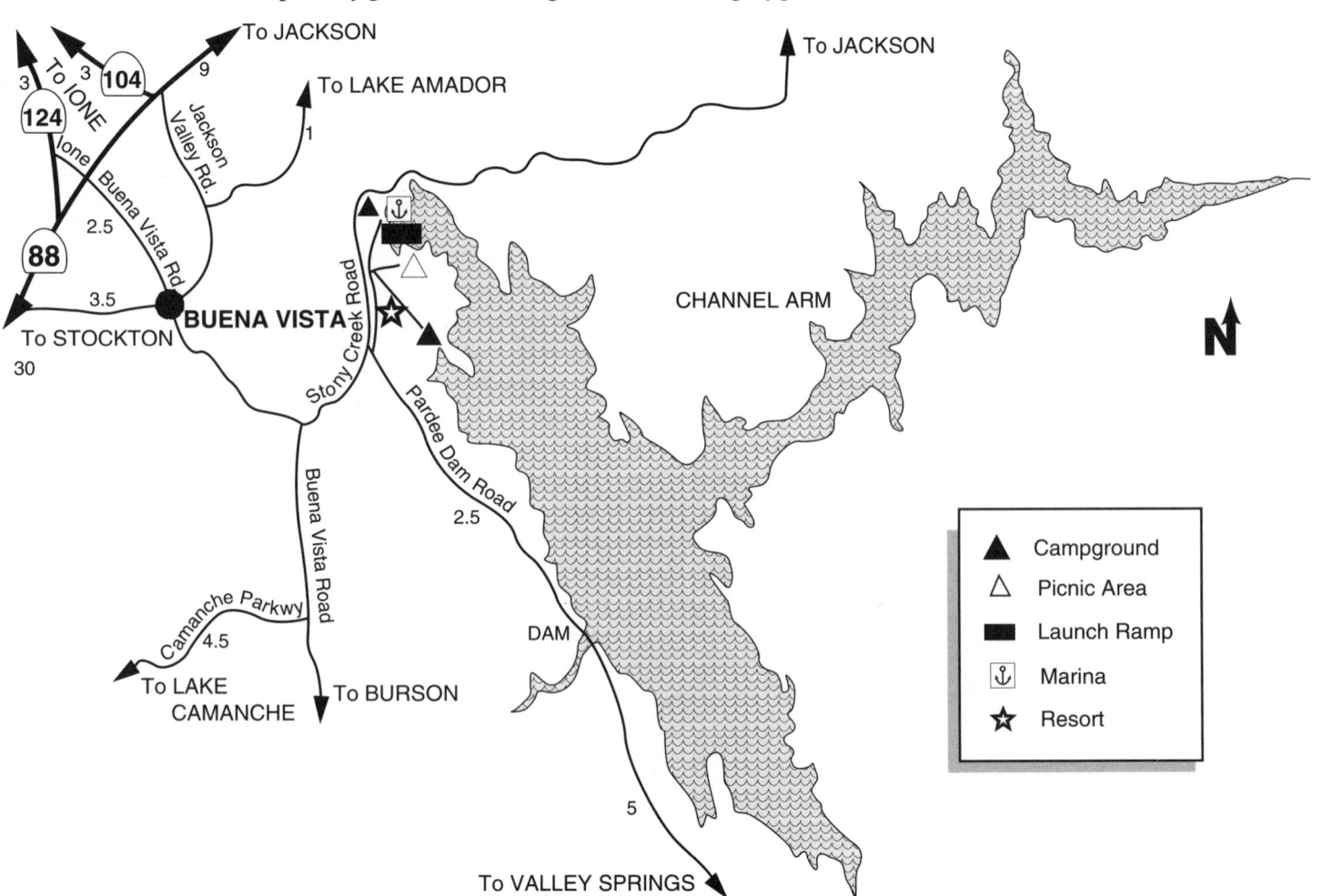

INFORMATION: Lake Pardee Marina, Inc., 4900 Stony Creek Rd., Ione 95640—Ph: (209) 772-1472

CAMPING	BOATING	RECREATION	OTHER
141 Dev. Tent Sites Fee: $16	Power, Row, Canoe, Sail & Inflatables	Fishing: Rainbow & Brown Trout,	Snack Bar Restaurant
12 Dev. R.V. Sites With Full Hookups Fee: $22	Fuel Must be MTBE Free *No Waterskiing or Jet Skis* *No Body Contact*	Kokanee Salmon, Catfish, Bluegill, Crappie, Small	Grocery Store Laundromat Gas & Propane
Disposal Station Additional Monthly R.V. Sites	*With the Water* Full Service Marina Launch Ramp: $5.50	& Largemouth Bass Fishing Permit: $2.50 16 and Older	Fish Cleaning Station
at Trailer Park Reservations at R.V. Sites Only	Rentals: Fishing Boats & Pontoons Docks, Berths,	Fishing Float Swimming in Pool Picnicking	
Day Use: $6 - $12 Dog: $1	Moorings, Gas Dry Storage	Bicycle Trails Playground	

Lake Camanche is at an elevation of 235 feet in the foothills of the Sierra Nevada. This large Reservoir, part of the East Bay Municipal Utility District, has a surface area of 12 square miles with a shoreline of 53 miles. Camanche is ocated in the famous "Mother Lode Country," and panning for gold is still popular in the spring when streams are high. Indian grave sites are visible along the shoreline. The water is warm and clear making water sports a delight. Known for bass fishing, there is also a variety of other good catches. The Resorts at Northshore and Southshore offer complete camping, marine and recreation facilities. There are over 15,000 acres of park lands for the hiker and equestrian. Lake Camanche has complete facilities and easy access from the San Francisco Bay Area.

...Continued....

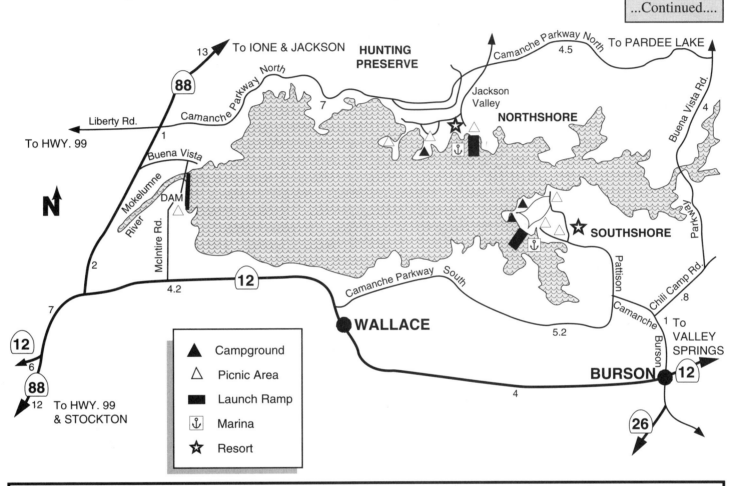

INFORMATION: Camanche Recreation Company Northshore and South Shore - See Next Page

CAMPING	BOATING	RECREATION	OTHER
Over 600 Dev. Sites for Tents & R.V.s	Power, Row, Canoe, Sail, Waterski, Jets, & Inflatables	Fishing: Black Bass, Catfish, Bluegill, Crappie, Kokanee,	Cottages & Motels from $55 to $230
Tents & R.V.s: $18 With Hookups at South Shore Only Fee: $25	*No Waterskiing in Upper Lake* Full Service Marinas	Sunfish, Trout Trout Pond at South Shore Fishing Permit: $2.50	Extensive Vacation Facilities
Group Sites: Fee: $33 to $160	Launch Ramps Rentals: Fishing &	Swimming Picnicking	See Next Page For Details
Disposal Stations Laundromats & Propane Day Use Fee: $6.50 Dog: $1	Patio Boats Fishing Rods & Reels Dry Storage Covered Slips	Tennis Courts Hiking & Equestrian Trails	

CAMANCHE RECREATION COMPANY
NORTHSHORE
2000 Camanche Rd., Ione, 95640
Ph: (209) 763-5121

219 Dev. Sites for Tents & R.V.s
No Hookups
Fee: $18
Water, Showers, Disposal Station, Trailer Storage,
Laundromat, Playgrounds, Store, Coffee Shop.
Group Reservations for Camping or Picnicking.

Full Service Marina—Ph: (209) 763-5166
6 Lane Launch Ramp - Fee: $6,
Boat Rentals: Fishing & Patio Boats,
Storage, Berths, Moorings.

Information—Ph: (209) 763-5166.
Deluxe Housekeeping Cottages for 2 to 12 People
Motel Rooms
From $55 to $230

Tennis Courts, Golf Courses, Wineries, Special Events.
Nearby: Bird Hunting Preserve and Club,
Two Mobile Home Parks.

CAMANCHE RECREATION COMPANY
SOUTHSHORE
11700 Wade Lane
Burson, 95225
Ph: (209) 763-5178

263 Dev. Sites for Tents & R.V.s
Full Hookups
Fee: $25
120 Sites for Tents and Self-Contained R.V.s
Fee: $18
Showers, Laundromat, Disposal Station,
Store, Snack Bar.

Full Service Marina
Ph: (209) 763-5915
6-Lane Launch Ramp - Fee: $6
Boat Rentals: Fishing & Pontoon Boats,
Storage, Berths, Moorings.

Housekeeping Cottages,
Tennis Courts, Amphitheater with
Movies on Saturdays during High Season,
Recreation Hall, Trout Pond, Mobile Home Park.

NEW HOGAN LAKE

New Hogan Lake is at an elevation of 713 feet in the foothills east of Stockton. The U.S. Army Corps of Engineers hold jurisdiction over the Lake and maintain the marine and camping facilities. The surface area of the Lake is 4,400 acres with 50 miles of shoreline covered with oak, digger pine and brush of chamise and manzanita. In the spring a variety of colorful wildflowers are on display. Wildlife is abundant with over 153 species of birds. New Hogan is ideal for water-oriented recreation. The Florida strain of largemouth bass is a prime target for anglers. Waterskiing is allowed in the central Lake although many coves and the swimming beaches are restricted.

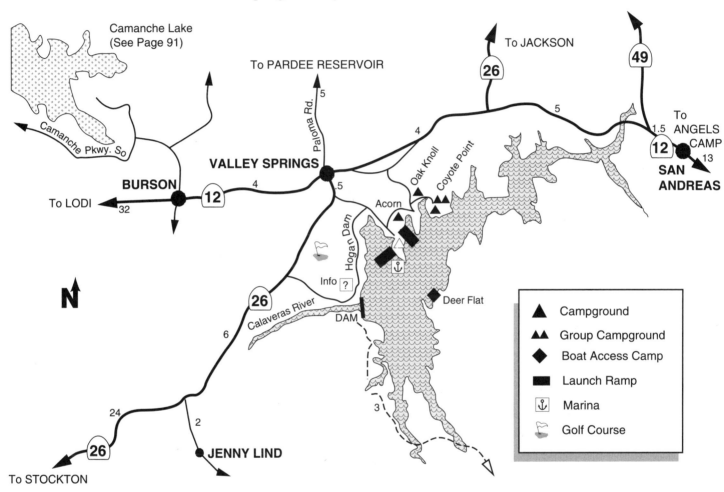

INFORMATION: New Hogan Lake, 2713 Hogan Dam Rd., Valley Springs 95252—Ph: (209) 772-1343

CAMPING	BOATING	RECREATION	OTHER
Acorn West: 58 Dev. Sites for Tents & R.V.s - $16 Acorn East: 70 Dev. Sites for Tents & R.V.s - $16 Oak Knoll: 50 Dev. Sites for Tents & R.V.s - $10 (No Showers) Reserve: (877) 444-6777 30 Boat Access Camps at Deer Flat - No Water Fee: $8	Power, Row, Canoe, Sail, Waterski, Jets, Windsurf & Inflatable Night Boating: 15 MPH Full Service Marina Launch Ramps Rentals: Fishing Boats & Motors, Patio Boats Docks, Moorings, Dry Storage	Fishing: Catfish, Bluegill, Crappie, Largemouth, Smallmouth & Striped Bass Swimming Picnicking Hiking, Nature & Equestrian Trails Campfire Program Bird Watching Hunting: Deer, Quail, Dove, Upland Game Birds *Shotgun or Bow Only*	Grocery Store Bait & Tackle Hot Showers Disposal Station Gas Station La Contenta Golf Course Nearby Full Facilities in Valley Springs

HIGHLAND and MOSQUITO LAKES - UTICA, UNION and SPICER MEADOW RESERVOIRS

These relatively remote Lakes in the Stanislaus National Forest are often passed by when people visit the more popular and developed Lake Alpine. For those who enjoy a rustic and quiet environment, these Lakes are well worth the visit. The elevation is high, ranging from 6,460 feet at Big Meadow Campground to 8,730 feet at Ebbetts Pass. Mosquito and Highland Lakes have several campgrounds nearby. Spicer

Meadow Reservoir, at 6,600 feet elevation, has a surface area of 2,000 acres. Facilities include campgrounds and a launch ramp. The eastern portion of this Reservoir is surrounded by the Carson-Iceberg Wilderness. There is often good fishing at the lakes, rivers and streams. This is a popular area for deer and bear hunting in season.

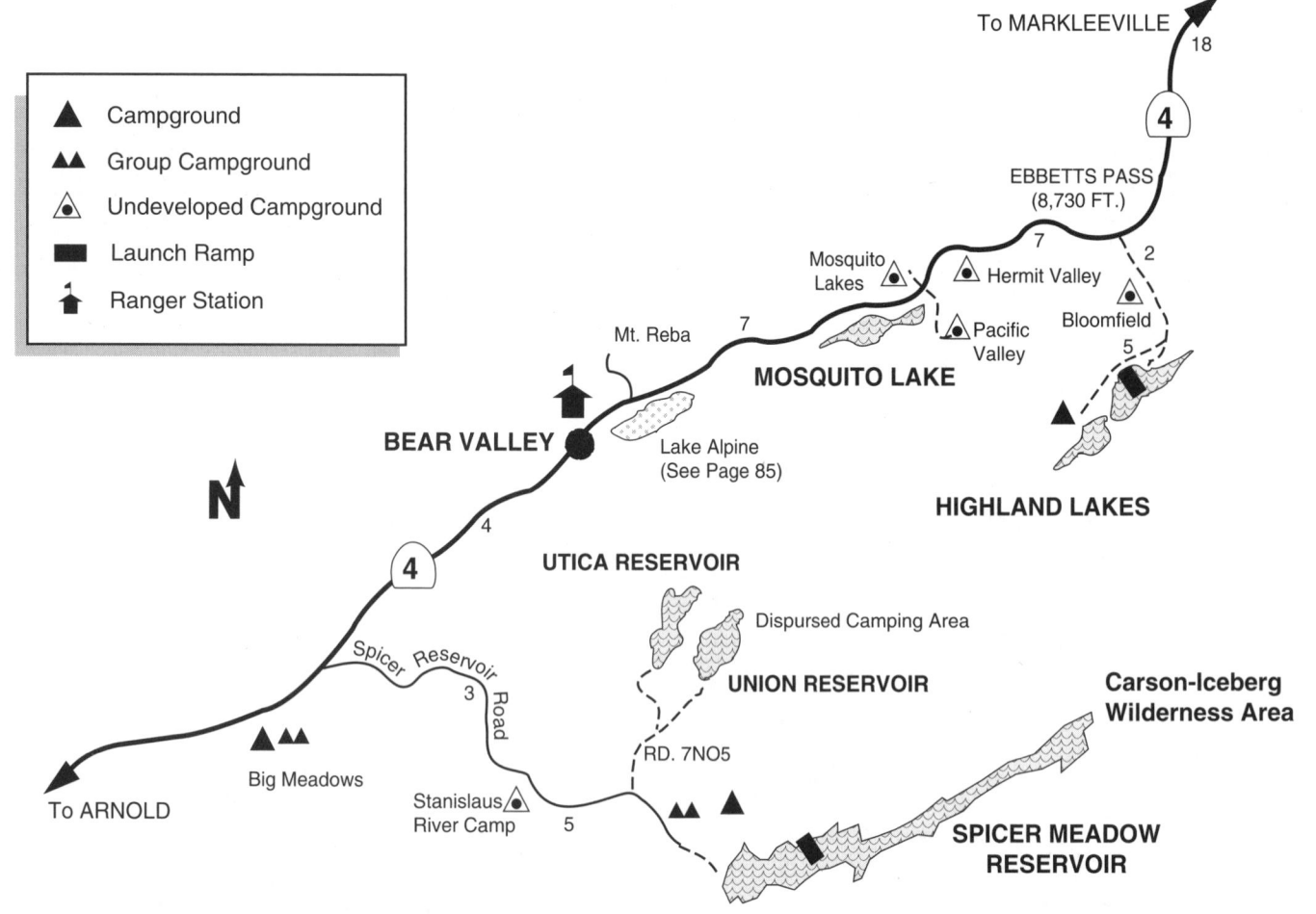

INFORMATION: Calaveras Ranger District, P.O. Box 500, Hathaway Pines 95233—Ph: (209) 795-1381

CAMPING	BOATING	RECREATION	OTHER
Highland Lakes: 35 Dev. Sites - Fee: $8	Highland Lakes: Open to All Boats 15 MPH Speed Limit	Fishing: Rainbow, Eastern Brook & German Brown Trout	Limited Facilities
Mosquito Lakes: 8 Sites No Water - Fee: $5	Mosquito, Union & Utica: Small Hand Launch Only No Motors	Hiking Trails to Carson-Iceberg Wilderness	Stanislaus River Camp: 8 Tent/R.V. Sites No Water - Fee: $8
Big Meadows: 65 Tent/R.V. Sites to 27 feet-Fee: $11 & Group Campground Some Equestrian Sites	Spicer: Launch Ramp - Free 10 MPH Western Arm *No Motorized Boating in Eastern Arm of Reservoir*	Backpacking [Parking] No Swimming	Other Undeveloped Sites: Fees to $8
Spicer: 60 Tent/R.V. Sites to 50 feet - Fee: $12 Group Campground 75 People Capacity Reserve: (209) 295-4512		*Protect Fragile Shoreline Zone Camp at Least 100 Feet From Water's Edge*	Reservations for Big Meadows Group Campground Ph: (877) 444-6777

Pinecrest Lake is at an elevation of 5,600 feet in the Stanislaus National Forest. Also known as Strawberry Reservoir, Pinecrest has a surface area of 300 acres with 4 miles of mountainous, tree-covered shoreline. The U.S. Forest Service has jurisdiction over 300 campsites, a group camp, picnic sites next to the beach, a paved launch ramp and a fishing pier. Pinecrest Lake Resort is a complete destination facility with extensive accommodations. Reservations for Pinecrest and Pioneer Group Campgrounds are required during the summer season. Meadowview is on a first come basis and is always full on weekends. In season, trout are planted weekly at Pinecrest Lake. There are a number of other lakes and streams within easy walking distance for the angler. Boating is limited to 20 MPH. Waterskiing and jets are not permitted. A designated swim beach is adjacent to the picnic area. Lyons Lake, a separate facility, is operated by P.G.&E. and offers fishing access only. *R.V.s and trailers not advised due to road conditions to Lyons Lake.*

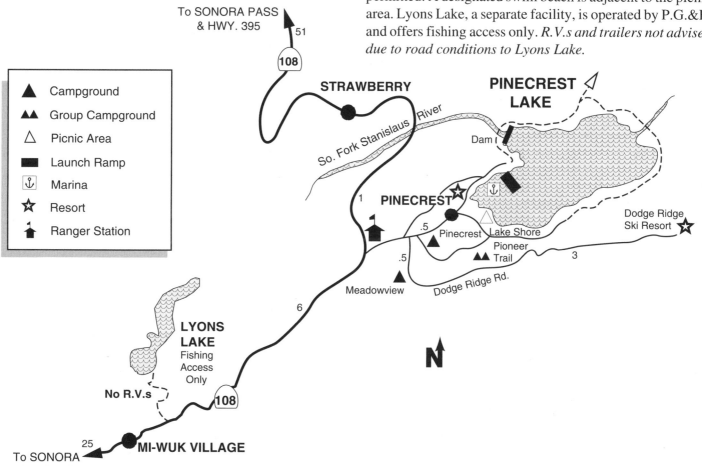

INFORMATION: Summit Ranger District, #1 Pinecrest Lake Rd., Pinecrest 95364—Ph: (209) 965-3434

CAMPING	BOATING	RECREATION	OTHER
300 Dev. Sites for Tents & R.V.s Fee: $10 - $12.50 Ph: (209) 965-3116 Pioneer Trails Group Camp 200 People Maximum No Trailers Reserve: Ph: (877) 444-6777 Meadowview - 100 Sites First Come Basis	Power, Row, Canoe, Sail, Windsurf & Inflatables *No Waterskiing or Jets* Speed Limit - 20 MPH Full Service Marina at Pinecrest Lake Resort Launch Ramp Rentals: Fishing, Sail, Paddle & Motor Boats, Windsurfers Docks, Berths, Gas *No Boating at Lyons Lake*	Fishing: Rainbow, Brown & Eastern Brook Trout Swimming - Beaches *No Swimming at Lyons* At Pinecrest Lake: Picnicking Hiking, Bicycling & Equestrian Trails Backpacking [Parking] Bicycle Rentals Amphitheatre: Campfire Programs & Movies	Pinecrest Lake Resort P.O. Box 1216 Pinecrest 95364 Ph: (209) 965-3411 Cabins, Condos & Motel Restaurant, Snack Bar, Groceries, Bait & Tackle, Sports Store, Tennis, Art Gallery Lyons Lake: P.G.&E. Ph: (916) 386-5164 for Information

HARTLEY (BEARDSLEY), DONNELLS, LEAVITT and KIRMAN LAKES

Ascending the western slopes of the Sierra Nevada above Sonora, these Lakes are along Highway 108 and range in elevation from 3,400 at Hartley (Beardsley) to 7,000 feet at Leavitt Lake. The fishing is often good although some areas are a bit difficult to reach. Donnells Reservoir and Leavitt Lake are undeveloped with no facilities. *The road into Donnells is rough and not recommended for trailers or any large-sized vehicles.* Hartley Lake has picnic sites and a launch ramp. There is an undeveloped campground on the northwest side of the dam that has limited facilities. Kirman Lake is a designated Wild Trout Lake where barbless hooks are required. There is a two trout limit. Numerous trails throughout the area invite the equestrian, hiker and backpacker to this beautiful high Sierra area within the Stanislaus and Toiyabe National Forests.

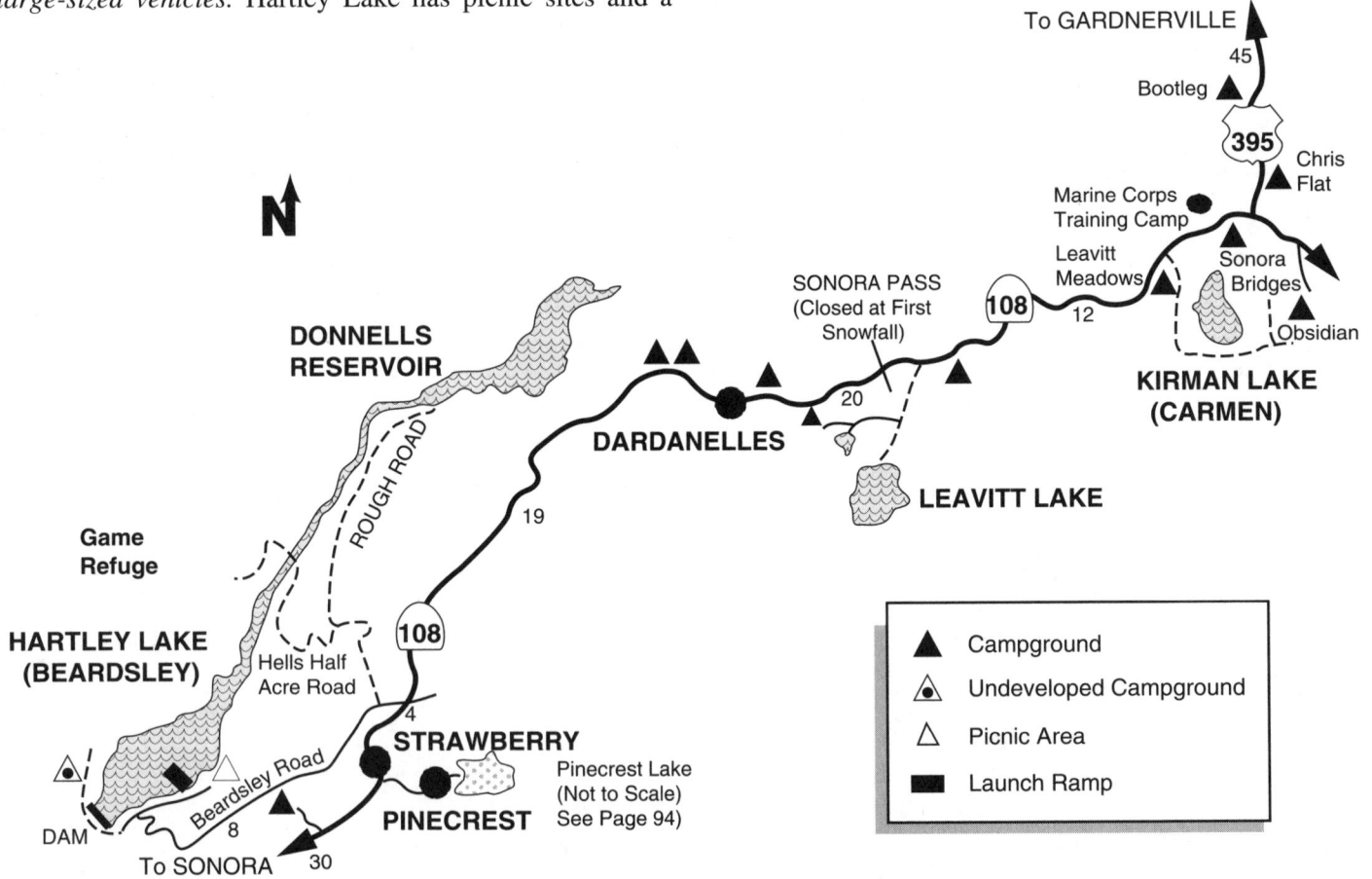

| INFORMATION: Summit Ranger District, #1 Pinecrest Lake Rd., Pinecrest 95364—Ph: (209) 965-3434 |

CAMPING	BOATING	RECREATION	OTHER
Numerous U.S.F.S. Campgrounds Along Highway 108 - Contact Summit Ranger District East of Sonora Pass: Toiyabe National Forest Bridgeport Ranger Dist. Ph: (760) 932-7070 Leavitt Meadows: 20 Tent/R.V. Sites Sonora Bridge: 23 Tent/R.V. Sites	Hartley Lake: Open to All Boats 2-Lane Paved Launch Ramp Leavitt Lake: Small Hand-Launch Boats Donnells: Boating Not Advised *Difficult to Impossible Access*	Fishing: Rainbow, German Brown & Brook Trout Picnicking Swimming Hiking Trails Equestrian Trails Backpacking Hunting: Deer & Bear *No Hunting in Game Refuge Near Hartley*	Limited Facilities Sonora Pass Closed at First Snowfall

Cherry Lake, sometimes called Cherry Valley Reservoir, is at an elevation of 4,700 feet in the rugged back country of the Stanislaus National Forest. This remote mountain Lake offers a good trout fishery. Boating is limited and subject to low water levels. This is truly a place to get away from it all. There is a campground and launch ramp but other facilities are limited. Numerous small lakes and streams are within hiking distance. Backpackers will enjoy the expanse of this area. The roads into Cherry Lake are winding and long so extra caution should be taken.

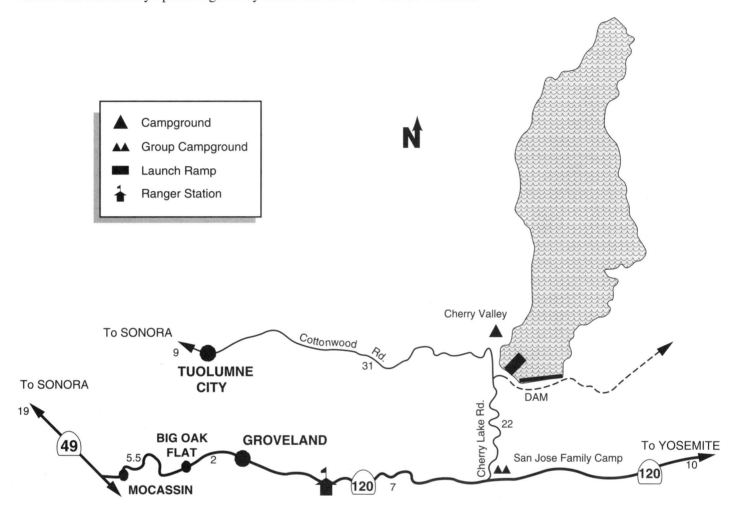

	CAMPING	BOATING	RECREATION	OTHER
INFORMATION: Groveland Ranger District, 24545 Highway 120, Groveland 95321—Ph: (209) 962-7825	46 Dev. Sites for Tents & R.V.s to 22 feet Fees: $12 - $24 Boat Camping Allowed on East Side of Lake	Power, Row, Canoe, Sail & Waterski Paved Launch Ramp High Water Only	Fishing: Rainbow, Brown & Brook Trout, Coho Salmon Swimming Backpacking Hiking Trails Equestrian Trails Hunting Nearby: Deer & Bear	No Services Available at Cherry Lake Full Facilities - 31 Miles at Tuolumne City

LAKES ON HIGHWAY 395 FROM BRIDGEPORT TO BISHOP

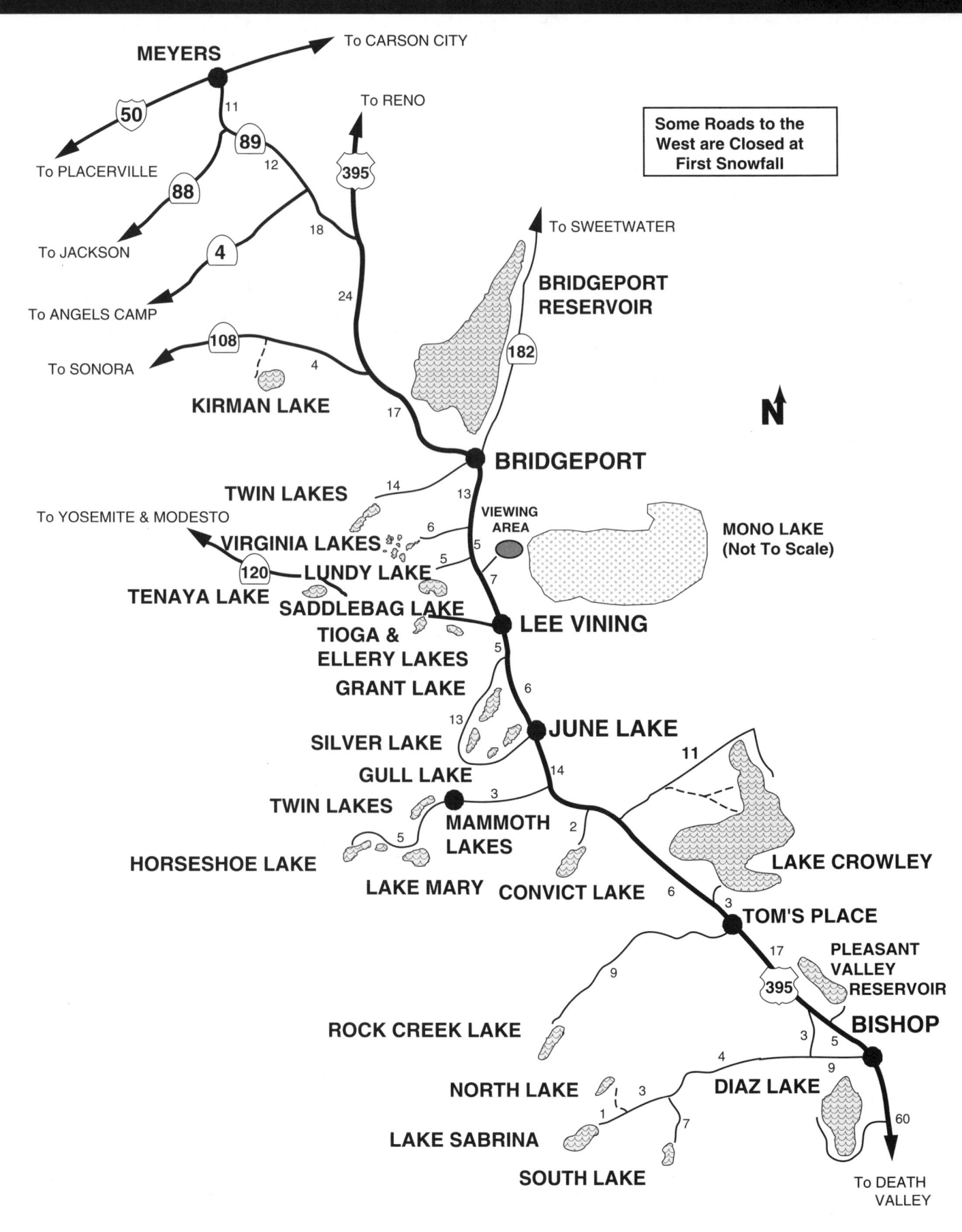

BRIDGEPORT RESERVOIR

Bridgeport Reservoir rests at an elevation of 6,500 feet in a large mountain meadow. This expansive 4,400 surface acre Lake is famous for large trout, especially when trolling early in the season. In addition to the Reservoir, the angler will find 35 lakes and streams within 15 miles. The East Walker River, designated as a Wild Trout Stream, is considered prime waters for large German Browns. Artificial lures or flies are required. 18-inches is the minimum size with a 1-fish limit from the Dam to the bridge and a 2-fish limit from the bridge to the Nevada Border. The Lake is open to all boating. In addition to the facilities at Bridgeport Reservoir, the U.S. Forest Service operates many campgrounds in this area.

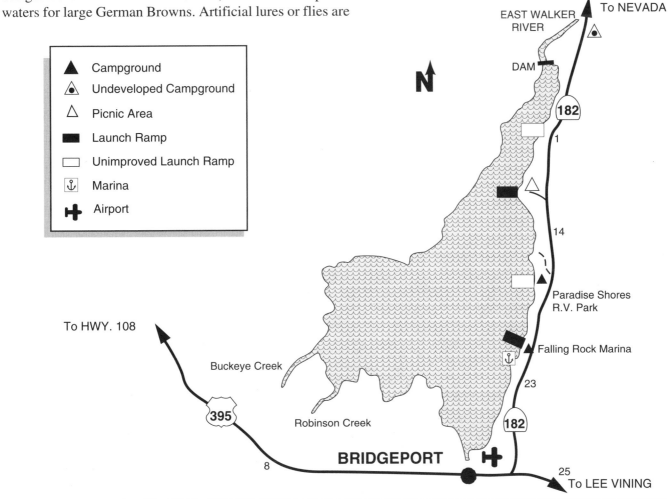

Legend:
- ▲ Campground
- ⚑ Undeveloped Campground
- △ Picnic Area
- ▬ Launch Ramp
- ☐ Unimproved Launch Ramp
- ⚓ Marina
- ✈ Airport

INFORMATION:	Falling Rock Marina or Paradise Shore Park, Bridgeport 93517		
CAMPING	**BOATING**	**RECREATION**	**OTHER**

Falling Rock Marina
  Ph: (760) 932-7001
  23 Dev. Tent Sites
  18 R.V. Sites with
    Full Hookups
 	
Paradise Shores R.V. Park
  Ph: (760) 932-7735
  38 R.V. Sites with
  Full Hookups Plus
    6 with No Hookups
 	
Call for Fees
	Power, Row, Canoe,
	  Sail & Inflatables
	Full Service Marina
	2 Improved Ramps
	2 Unimproved Ramps
	Rentals: Fishing
	  Boats & Motors
	Docks, Berths,
	Moorings, Storage
	Overnight in Boat
	  Permitted Anywhere
		Fishing: Rainbow,
		  German Brown &
		  Cutthroat Trout,
		  Sacramento Perch,
		  Carp
		Swimming
		Backpacking [Parking]
		Bicycle Trails
		Hunting: Deer &
		  Waterfowl
			Bait & Tackle
			Laundromat
			Trailer Rentals
			Gas Station
			Airport
			
			Full Facilities at
			  Bridgeport

TWIN LAKES

Twin Lakes are 12 miles southwest of Bridgeport in the Eastern Sierra at an elevation of 7,000 feet. The private campgrounds at the Lake are in a pine forest. Complete resort and marine facilities are available. There are 5 U.S. Forest Service Campgrounds along Robinson Creek. These Lakes provide excellent fishing for large rainbow and brown trout.

Doc and Al's Resort is a pleasant angler's retreat. The Hunewill Guest Ranch is a working cattle ranch offering excellent accommodations, food and excursions on horseback into this beautiful area. The backpacker can enjoy the nearby Hoover Wilderness with its many scenic trails, lakes and streams.

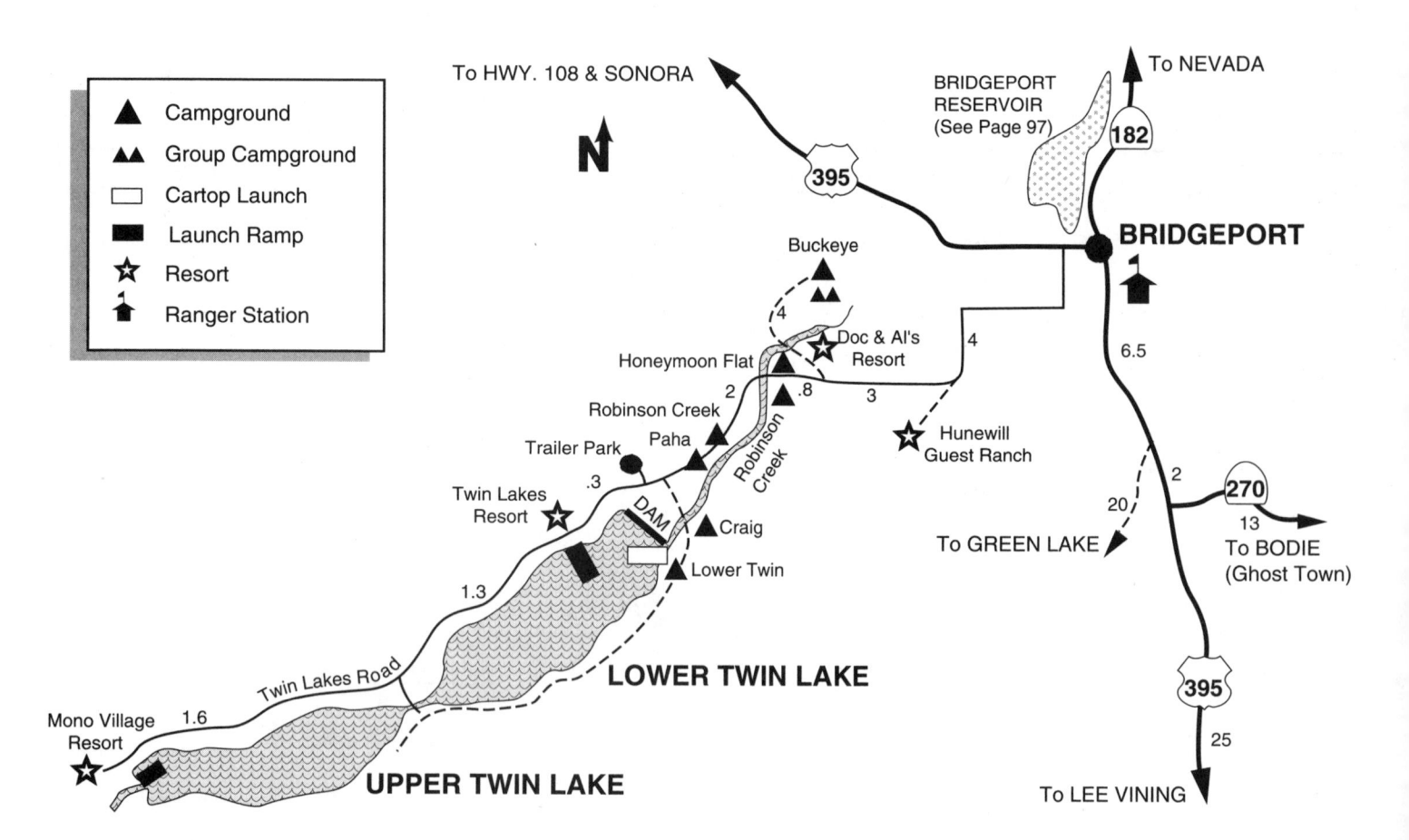

▲	Campground
▲▲	Group Campground
▢	Cartop Launch
▮	Launch Ramp
☆	Resort
⌂	Ranger Station

INFORMATION: Bridgeport Ranger District, P.O. Box 595, Bridgeport 93517—Ph: (760) 932-7070

CAMPING	BOATING	RECREATION	OTHER

U.S.F.S.
  400 Dev. Sites for
    Tents & R.V.s
  Fee: $11-$13
  Group Site: $65
  30 People
Reservations:
  Ph: (877) 444-6777
Privately Owned Campsites:
  Mono Village Resort
  Ph: (760) 932-7071
  Twin Lakes R.V. Park
  Ph: (760) 932-7751
	Power, Row, Canoe,
	  Sail & Inflatables
	Waterskiing at
	  Upper Lake Only
	Full Service Marina
	Launch Ramps
	Boat Rentals
	Docks
		Fishing: Rainbow, German
		  Brown, Eastern
		  Brook & Kokanee
		  Trout
		Picnicking
		Backpacking [Parking]
		  Hoover Wilderness
		Horseback Riding
		Hunting: Deer &
		  Waterfowl
			Cabins
			Restaurant
			Grocery Store
			Bait & Tackle
			
			Doc & Al's Resort
			  Ph: (760) 932-7051
			Hunewill Guest Ranch
			  Ph: (760) 932-7710
			  Reservations Only
			
			Full Facilities at Bridgeport

Within the Virginia Lakes area are numerous small Lakes at 9,700 feet elevation located west of Highway 395. No swimming is allowed in these Lakes. Virginia Lake Resort has cabins, a grocery store, fishing supplies and restaurant. The U. S. Forest Service operates campsites near Trumbull Lake.

There is a Pack Station with horses available for scenic rides into the Hoover Wilderness and Yosemite National Park. This is a fisherman's paradise. The Lakes and many streams are within easy distance of the Resort.

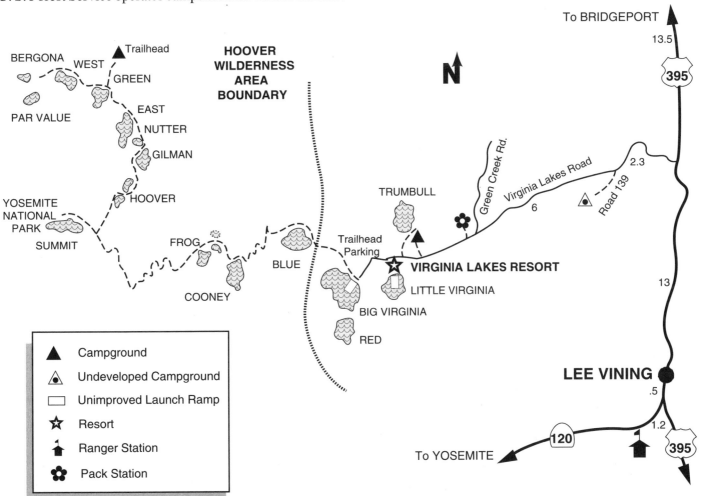

INFORMATION: Bridgeport Ranger District, HCR1 Box 1000, Bridgeport 93517—Ph: (760) 932-7070			
CAMPING	**BOATING**	**RECREATION**	**OTHER**
45 Dev. Sites for Tents & R.V.s No Hookups No Disposal Station Fee: $11 Group Camp to 18 People Reservations or First-Come Basis Undeveloped Camping Fire Permit Req'd. Reserve Some Sites: Ph: (877) 444-6777	Electric Motors, Row, Canoe & Inflatables *No Gas Motors* 10 MPH Speed Limit Unimproved Launch Ramp Rentals: Fishing & Row Boats	Fishing: Rainbow, Golden, German Brown & Eastern Brook Trout Picnicking Hiking Backpacking [Parking] Horse Rentals Equestrian Trails	Virginia Lakes Resort HCR 1, Box 1065 Bridgeport 93517 Ph: (760) 647-6484 Cabins, Store Bait & Tackle Virginia Lakes Pack Outfit HCR 1, Box 1070 Bridgeport 93517 Summer Phone: Ph: (760) 937-0326 Winter Phone: Ph: (775) 867-2591

LUNDY LAKE

Nestled in a high valley at an 7,800 feet elevation, Lundy Lake is the trailhead to the 20 Lakes Basin. High, majestic mountains and a rocky, aspen and pine-covered shoreline provide for spectacular scenery. The Lake is 1 mile long and 1/2 mile wide. The water is clear and cold. This is a popular fishing Lake. The rustic atmosphere is relaxed with good facilities at the Resort. Mono Lake rests just off Highway 395. This huge, barren salt water Lake is the nesting site for 95 percent of California's gulls. Towers of formations of calcium carbonate can be viewed along guided walking tours on the weekends in season. No other recreation activities are permitted at Mono Lake.

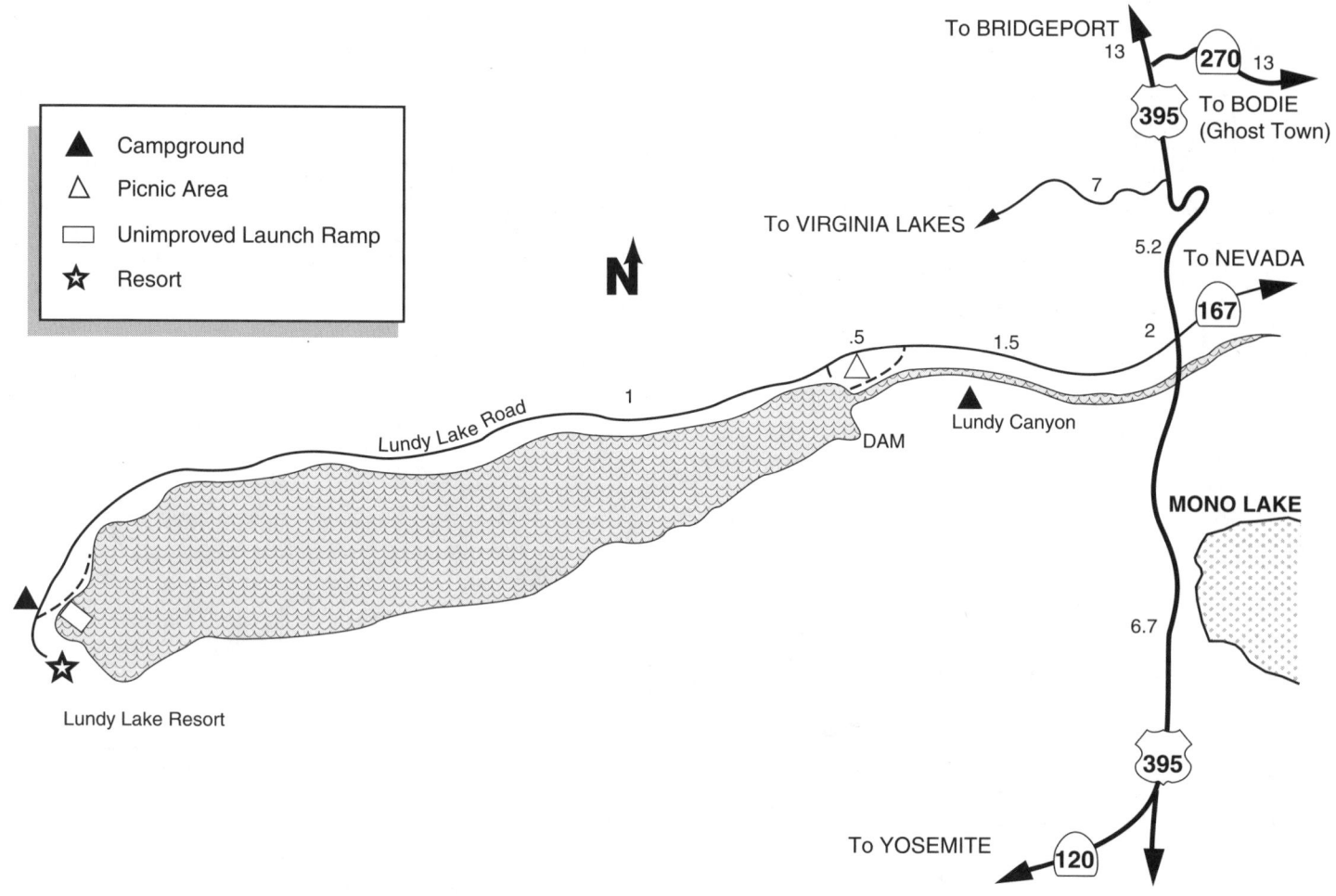

▲	Campground
△	Picnic Area
▢	Unimproved Launch Ramp
☆	Resort

INFORMATION: Lundy Lake Resort, P.O. Box 265, Lee Vining 93541–No Phone - Write & Send Your Phone No.

CAMPING	BOATING	RECREATION	OTHER
Lundy Lake Resort: 27 Tent Sites 3 Camp Huts 8 R.V. Sites with Full Hookups Mono County Parks P.O. Box 457 Bridgeport 93517 Ph: (760) 932-5450 Lundy Canyon: 50 Sites	Fishing Boats, Canoes & Inflatables Speed Limit - 10 MPH Hand Launch Only Rentals: Fishing Boats & Motors	Fishing: Rainbow, German Brown & Eastern Brook Trout Picnicking Hiking Backpacking Bird Watching Hunting: Deer	Housekeeping Cabins Grocery Store Bait & Tackle Hot Showers Laundromat Camping Supplies Mono Lake Walking Tours

Saddlebag Lake, at an elevation of 10,087 feet, is the highest Lake in California reached by public road. The 2-mile partially paved road north of Highway 120 is steep. Large R.V.s and trailers are not advised. The Lake is surrounded by rugged mountain peaks and the alpine setting is spectacular. Fishing from boat, bank or stream can be excellent. Located near the trailhead into the Hoover Wilderness Area, an hour or less of easy hiking from Saddlebag will bring you to the first lake and streams of the 20 Lakes Basin. This wilderness area is a good destination for backpackers who can overnight in the area with a permit. Open fires are prohibited so bring your own stove. Mt. Conness Glacier is a popular destination for experienced climbers.

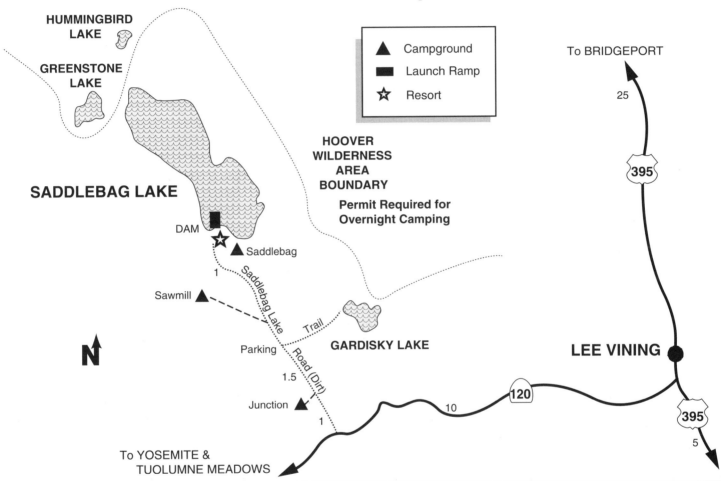

CAMPING	BOATING	RECREATION	OTHER
Saddlebag Campground 20 Sites for Tents & Small R.V.s Fee: $15 1 Trailhead Group Site - Reserve Ph: (877) 444-6777 Sawmill: 12 Walk-In Sites Junction: 13 Sites Fee: $7	Fishing Boats, Sailboats, Canoes & Inflatables Unimproved Launch Ramp for Boats to 16 Feet Fees: Boats: $5 Inflatables: $2 Rentals: Fishing Boats & Motors	Fishing: Rainbow, Cutthroat, Brook, Kamloop & Golden Trout Hiking Backpacking [Parking] Mountain Climbing Nature Study Obtain Wilderness Permits at Mono Lake Forest Service Visitor Center	Saddlebag Lake Resort P.O. Box 303 Lee Vining 93541 (No Phone - Send for Brochure) Snack Bar Grocery Store Bait & Tackle Water Taxi Across Lake for Hikers, Backpackers & Dogs on Leash Fees Charged

INFORMATION: Mono Lake Ranger District, Box 429, Lee Vining 93541—Ph: (760) 647-3044

ELLERY, TIOGA and TENAYA

These Lakes are in the spectacular Eastern Sierra along Highway 120, west of Tioga Pass. Ellery and Tioga Lakes are 2 miles outside the eastern entrance to Yosemite National Park. Tenaya is 15 miles inside the park. There are many natural attractions in this scenic area. An interesting trip is the mining site at Bennettville, a 20-minute hike from Junction Campground. The water in these Lakes is clear and cold, providing the angler with some good opportunities to catch trout. There are also numerous streams and other small lakes in this area. The Nunatak Trail is nearby.

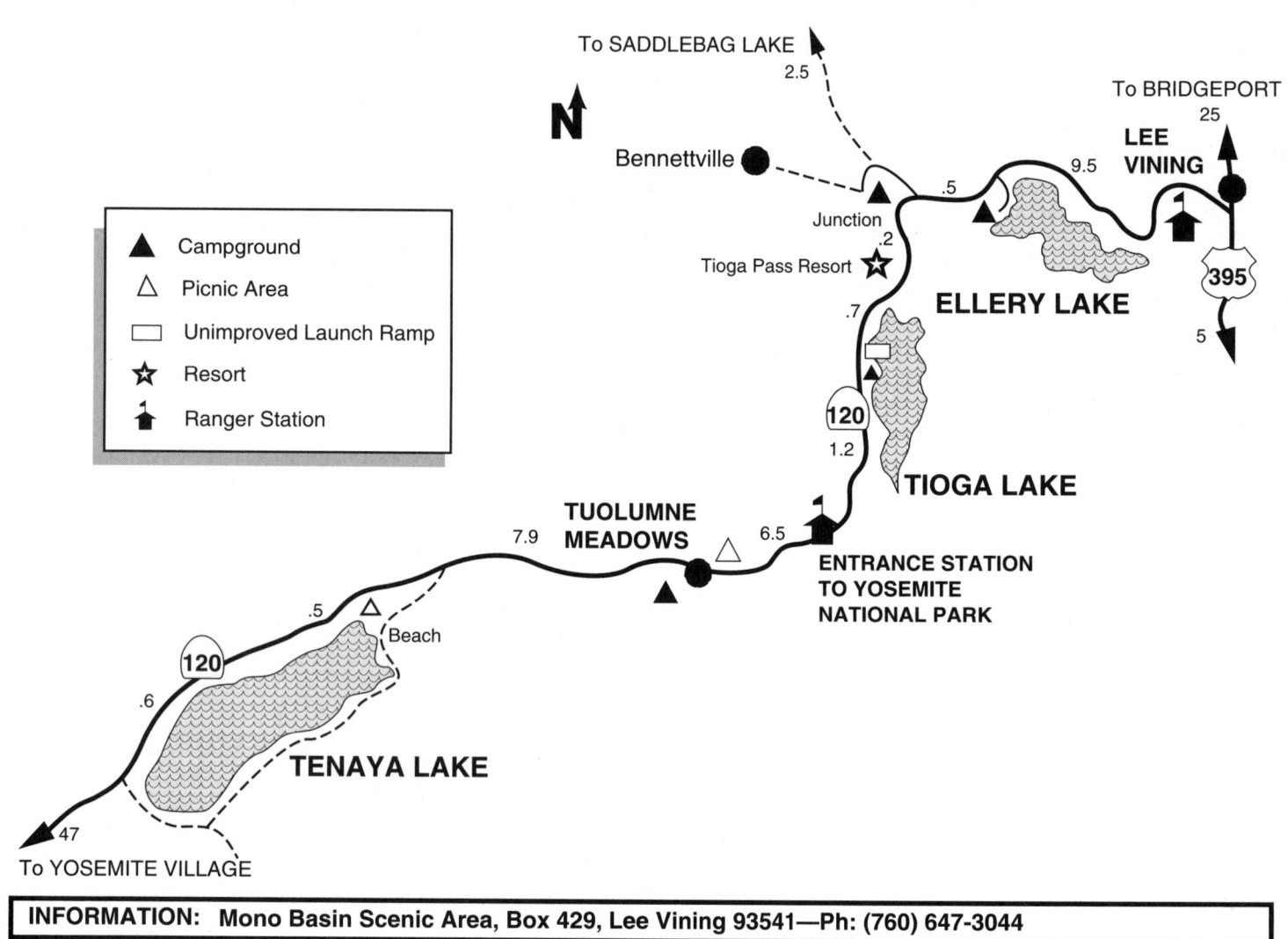

INFORMATION: Mono Basin Scenic Area, Box 429, Lee Vining 93541—Ph: (760) 647-3044

CAMPING	BOATING	RECREATION	OTHER

U.S.F.S.
   Ellery Lake:
     12 Dev. Sites
     Fee: $12
   Tioga Lake:
     13 Dev. Sites
     Fee: $12
   Junction Camp:
     13 Dev. Sites
     Fee: $7
Yosemite National Park:
   Tuolumne Meadows:
     304 Dev. Sites
	Ellery and Tioga Lakes:
	   Motors Permitted
	   Hand Launch at
	     Ellery
	   Small Trailered
	     Boats at Tioga
	Tenaya Lake:
	   No Motors
	   Hand Launch Only
	   (No Camping)
		Fishing: Rainbow,
		   Brook, Brown &
		   Golden Trout
		Picnicking
		Hiking & Rock
		   Climbing
		Nature Trail
		Horseback Riding
		Hunting *Outside Park:*
		   Deer,
		   Upland Game
			Yosemite National Park
			   Box 577
			   Yosemite 95389
			   Ph: (209) 372-0265
			Tioga Pass Resort
			   Box 7
			   Lee Vining 93541
			   All Inquiries by Mail
			   Cabins, Lodge
			   Cafe: 7 am - 9 pm
			   Groceries, Tackle,
			   Sporting Goods, Gas

JUNE, GULL, SILVER and GRANT LAKES

The June Lake Loop consists of 4 scenic mountain Lakes on the eastern slope of the high Sierras. Resting at an elevation of 7,600 feet in the Inyo National Forest, these popular Lakes provide outstanding recreational opportunities. Grant is the largest Lake on the loop with 1,000 surface acres. Silver has 80 acres; Gull, the smallest, has 64 acres and June has 400 acres. Each of these Lakes is interconnected by stream or creek and all are prime trout waters. Hikers, equestrians and backpackers can enjoy the nearby Ansel Adams Wilderness area with its spectacular scenery and many small lakes and streams. The June Lake Loop has numerous Forest Service campsites in addition to private facilities.

....Continued....

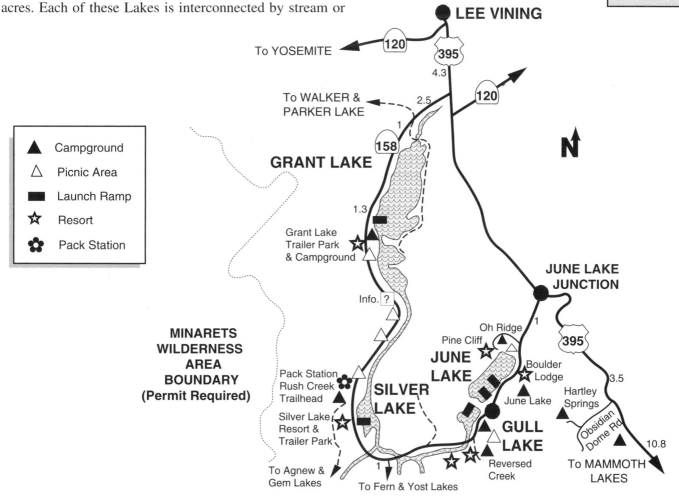

INFORMATION: Mono Basin Scenic Area, P.O. Box 429, Lee Vining 93541—Ph: (760) 647-3044

CAMPING	BOATING	RECREATION	OTHER
U. S. Forest Service 300 Plus Campsites for Tents & R.V.s Fee: $14 See Following Page for Details	Power, Row, Canoe, Sail, Windsurf & Inflatables Waterskiing at Grant Lake Only Other Lakes: 10 MPH Speed Limit Launch Ramps Rentals: Fishing Boats & Motors, Paddleboats, Canoes Docks, Gas, Repairs	Fishing: Rainbow, Brown, Cutthroat & Brook Trout Swimming - June Lake Backpacking [Parking] Equestrian Trails & Pack Station Hunting: Deer, Geese, Duck & Quail	Housekeeping Cabins Motels, Rental Condos Snack Bars Restaurants Grocery Stores Bait & Tackle Laundromats Further Info: June Lake Chamber of Commerce P.O. Box 2 June Lake 93529 Ph: (760) 648-7584

GRANT LAKE

GRANT LAKE MARINA, P.O. Box 627, June Lake 93529—Ph: (760) 648-7964
70 Developed Sites for Tents & R.V.s, Water & Sewer Hookups.- *Fee: $13* - Water, Fire Pits, Hot Showers,
Disposal Station, Store, Cafe, Bait & Tackle, Beer & Wine, Ice, Propane, Launch Ramp, Boat Rentals & Dock Rental,
Trailer Rentals. Waterskiing Approximately June - August.

SILVER LAKE
10 MPH Speed Limit on Lake.

U. S. FOREST SERVICE CAMPGROUND
63 Developed Sites for Tents & R.V.s. - *Fee: $15* - Water & Barbecues.

SILVER LAKE RESORT, P.O. Box 116, June Lake 93529—Ph: (760) 648-7525
Full Housekeeping Cabins, Complete Country General Store, Groceries, R.V.Hardware, Gift Shop, Bait & Tackle,
Restaurant, Boat Gas, Launch Ramp, Rental Boats, 75-Unit Trailer Park with Full Hookups.

FRONTIER PACK TRAIN, Route 3, Box 18, June Lake 93529—Ph: (760) 648-7701
Horseback & Pack Trips to Remote Lakes & Streams, 2 Miles High, in the Minaret Wilderness
Hour Rides & 1/2 Day Rides.

GULL LAKE

U. S. FOREST SERVICE CAMPGROUND
Gull Lake Campground -11 Sites - *Fee: $15* - Ramp. **Reversed Creek Campground** -17 R.V. Sites -*Fee: $15.*

GULL LAKE MARINA, P.O. Box 65, June Lake 93529—Ph: (760) 648-7539
Full Service Marina, Rental Boats & Motors, Row Boats, Canoes, Paddleboats,
Docks, Launch Ramps, Bait & Tackle, Store, Ice, Gifts.
Gull Meadows Cartop Launch Ramp & Picnic Area

JUNE LAKE

U. S. FOREST SERVICE CAMPGROUNDS
Ph: (877) 444-6777 - USFS Reservation Center
Oh! Ridge - 148 Developed Sites for Tents & R.V.s. - *Fee: $15.* Half can be Reserved.
June Lake - 28 Developed Sites for Tents & R.V.s. - *Fee: $15.* 15 can be Reserved
Hartley Springs - South on Highway 395 - 20 Sites for Tents & R.V.s - *No Fee, No Reservations*

JUNE LAKE MARINA, P.O. Box 26, June Lake 93529—Ph: (760) 648-7726
Full Service Marina, Boat Rentals, Docks, Bait & Tackle, Launch Ramp, Gas, Motor Repairs.

For Other Resorts and Reservations Contact:

June Lake - June Mountain Reservation Service
P. O. Box 694
June Lake 93529
Ph: (800) 648-2211 or (760) 648-7794

Rainbow Ridge Realty and Reservations
P. O. Box C
June Lake 93529
Ph: (800) 462-5589 or (760) 648-7811

June Lake Properties Reservations
P. O. Box 606
June Lake 93529
Ph: (800) 648-JUNE or (760) 648-7705

The Mammoth Lakes Basin is located in the high Sierras. These small glacial-formed Lakes range in elevation from 8,540 feet to 9,250 feet. They are easily accessible by road or pine-shaded trails. Fishing in the Lakes or streams is often excellent. The hiker and equestrian can enjoy the scenic landscape with trails leading the John Muir or Ansel Adams Wilderness areas. Numerous resorts and campgrounds are available and complete facilities are located in the town of Mammoth Lakes. While Sotcher and Starkweather Lakes are outside the Lakes Basin, they share the same abundance of natural beauty and recreation.

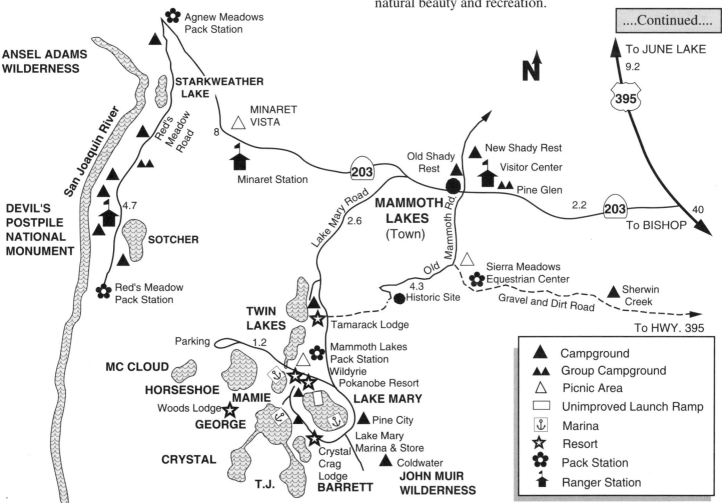

....Continued....

INFORMATION: Mammoth Lakes Visitors Center, Box 148, Mammoth Lakes 93546—Ph: (760) 924-5500

CAMPING	BOATING	RECREATION	OTHER
Dev. Tent/R.V. and Group Sites - U.S.F.S. Resorts See Following Pages Wilderness Permits Required for Overnight Stays in Ansel Adams and John Muir Wilderness Areas	Power, Row, Canoe & Sailboats 10 MPH Speed Limit Rentals: Fishing Boats & Motors Starkweather Lake & Sotcher Lake: Rowboats & Canoes Only	Fishing: Rainbow, Brown & Brook Trout Hiking Trails Equestrian Trails Nature Study Backpacking Picnicking Hunting: Deer Pack Stations & Horse Rentals	Numerous Resorts & Full Facilities In Town of Mammoth Lakes Nature Guided Activities Provided by Mammoth Visitor Center Shuttle into Red's Meadow & Devil's Postpile Areas Mandatory Day Use Fee

MAMMOTH LAKES BASIN............Continued

U.S. FOREST SERVICE CAMPGROUNDS

Fees Vary
Reservations Required for Group Camps and
Available for Some Individual Sites Shown Below: Ph: (877) 444-6777

NEW SHADY REST
94 Tent/R.V. Sites
Disposal Station
Fee: $15 - 14 Day Limit

OLD SHADY REST
51 Tent/R.V. Sites
Fee: $15 - 14 Day Limit

SHERWIN CREEK
87 Tent/R.V. Sites
Fee: $15 - 21 Day Limit

TWIN LAKES
95 Tent/R.V. Sites
Fee: $16 - 7 Day Limit

LAKE GEORGE
16 Tent/R.V. Sites
Fee: $16 - 7 Day Limit
Boat Ramp and Rentals Nearby

REDS MEADOW
56 Tent/R.V. Sites
Fee: $16 - 14 Day Limit

PINE GLEN
20 Tent/R.V. Family Sites for
Handicapped use or as
overflow during holiday
weekends only. Fee: $13
Campers must obtain
permission to use these Sites.

6 Group Tent/R.V. Sites
Maximum Persons per Site
varies from 15 to 30 - Fees: $35 - $50
Must Reserve: Ph (877) 444-6777

LAKE MARY
48 Tent/R.V. Sites
Fee: $16 - 14 Day Limit

COLDWATER
77 Tent/R.V. Sites
Fee: $16 - 14 Day Limit
Trailhead into the John Muir Wilderness

PINE CITY
10 Tent/R.V. Sites
Fee: $16 - 14 Day Limit

Overnight visitors into the Sotcher Lake/Red's Meadow/Devil's Postpile Areas MUST obtain an access pass at Minaret Station between 6:30 am to 8:30 pm.
There is a mandatory shuttle bus system for all users from 7:00 a.m. to 7:00 p.m.
Inquire at the Visitors Center for further details. The Visitors Center also provides a number of interpretive programs.

Wilderness Permits are required year around for any overnight camping in the John Muir or Ansel Adams Wildernesses. Obtain Permits from the Visitor Center.

For Further Information Contact:
Mammoth Lakes Visitors Center & Ranger Station
P.O. Box 148
Mammoth Lakes 93546
24 Hour Info: (760) 924-5500
Hearing Impaired: (760) 924-5531

....Continued....

SOME PRIVATE FACILITIES NEAR THE LAKES:

TWIN LAKES:

TAMARACK LODGE RESORT - P.O. Box 69, Mammoth Lakes 93546—Ph: (760) 934-2442
Fully Equipped Housekeeping Cabins, Historic Lodge Accommodations, Restaurant, Boat Rentals.

LAKE MAMIE:

WILDYRIE LODGE - P.O. Box 108, Mammoth Lakes 93546—Ph: (760) 934-2444
Housekeeping Cabins, Grocery Store, Boat Rentals.

LAKE GEORGE:

WOODS LODGE - P.O. Box 108, Mammoth Lakes 93546, Ph: (760) 934-2261
Housekeeping Cabins, Bait & Tackle, Unimproved Ramp, Dock, Boat & Motor Rentals.

LAKE MARY:

CRYSTAL CRAG LODGE - P.O. Box 88, Mammoth Lakes 93546—Ph: (760) 934-2436
Housekeeping Cabins, Most with Fireplace, Boat & Motor Rentals.

POKONOBE RESORT - P.O. Box 72, Mammoth Lakes 93546—Ph: (760) 934-2437
Camp Sites, Grocery Store, Launch Ramp, Dock, Boat Rentals.

LAKE MARY MARINA & STORE - 482 Cottonwood Dr., Bishop 93514—Ph: (760) 934-5353
Grocery Store, Tackle, Hot Showers, Laundromat, Cafe, Ramp and Docks, Boat Rentals: Boat & Motor Rentals, Pontoons, Paddleboats, Canoes.

MAMMOTH MOUNTAIN R.V. PARK: P.O. Box 288, Mammoth Lakes 93546—Ph: (760) 934-3822
130 R.V. Sites, Electric & Water Hookups, Hot Showers, Disposal Station, Spa, Cable TV Hookups, Pool.

....Continued....

BY: GREG DIRKSEN 2002©

Mammoth Lakes is a complete resort town. There are major grocery stores as well as small retail outlets. Gourmet restaurants, fast food chains, resorts, motels and condominiums are all too numerous to mention. Listed below are reservation services in this area that can help find the best place to suit your needs.

**Mammoth Lakes Visitor Center
& Ranger Station**
P.O. Box 148, Mammoth Lakes 93546
Ph: (760) 924-5500

Mammoth Reservation Bureau
P.O. Box 1608, Mammoth Lakes 93546
Ph: (800) 462-5571
Complete Visitor's Information
Over 250 Condos Can Be Reserved

**Town of Mammoth Lakes
Visitors Bureau**
P.O. Box 48, Mammoth Lakes 93546
Ph: (760) 934-2712 or
Ph: (888) GO-MAMMOTH
Reservation Assistance
and Complete Visitor Resort Information

Convict Lake is one of the most beautiful lakes in California (and our personal favorite). The crystal clear waters are surrounded by steep, rugged granite peaks. Resting at an elevation of 7,583 feet, this small mountain Lake is 1 mile long and 1/2 mile wide. The 3 miles of shoreline are shaded by pine trees. A great trail goes all the way around the Lake. Boating is popular and the fishing can be excellent in both the Lake and creek. The backpacker and equestrian will find a trail leading through a rock-walled canyon to 9 lakes in the nearby John Muir Wilderness Area. The Inyo National Forest maintains the developed campground next to Convict Creek. The Resort includess rustic cabins, rental houses for large groups, other deluxe accommodations and an excellent dinner house. Be sure to visit this Lake when you are travelling along Highway 395.

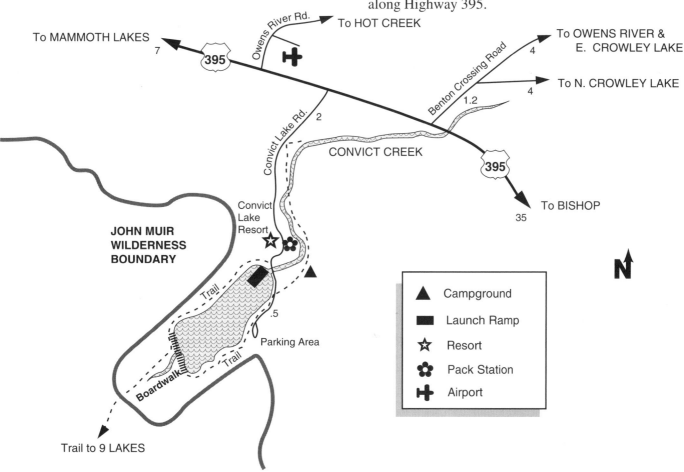

INFORMATION: Convict Lake Resort, Rt. 1 Box 204, Mammoth Lakes 93546—Ph: (760) 934-3800-(800) 992-2260

CAMPING	BOATING	RECREATION	OTHER

88 Dev. Sites for Tents & R.V.s
No Hookups
2 Vehicles Max. per Site
Fee: $15
7-Day Limit
No Reservations
 	
Open: End of April to November 15
 	
Free Disposal Station
	Power, Row, Canoe, Sail & Inflatables
	Rentals:
	  Fishing Boats & Motors,
	  Canoes, Rowboats,
	  Pontoon Boats for
	    up to 10 Adults
	Dry Storage
	Guided Scenic Lake Rides:
	  $30 per Person
		Fishing: Rainbow & German Brown Trout
		Picnicking
		Hiking Trails
		Backpacking [Parking]
		Bicycle Rentals
		Equestrian Trails
		Hunting: Deer, Rabbit
			Housekeeping Cabins & Deluxe Accommodations
			Rates: $90 to $695
			Some Open Year Around
			Gourmet Restaurant with Award Winning Wine List
			Cocktail Lounge
			Grocery Store
			Bait & Tackle
			Pets: $15 per Stay
			Airport with Auto Rentals - 5 Miles

CROWLEY LAKE

Crowley Lake is one of California's most popular and productive fishing Lakes. Resting at an elevation of 6,500 feet on the eastern side of the high Sierra, the Lake is situated in Long Valley surrounded by the Glass Mountains and the White Mountains. Anglers jam its shores and waters on opening weekends. This 650 surface acre Lake has held State records for German brown trout and Sacramento perch. Trophy-sized fish are common. Guided fishing trips are available. Boating and waterskiing are also popular. Numerous resorts and other recreational facilities are nearby.

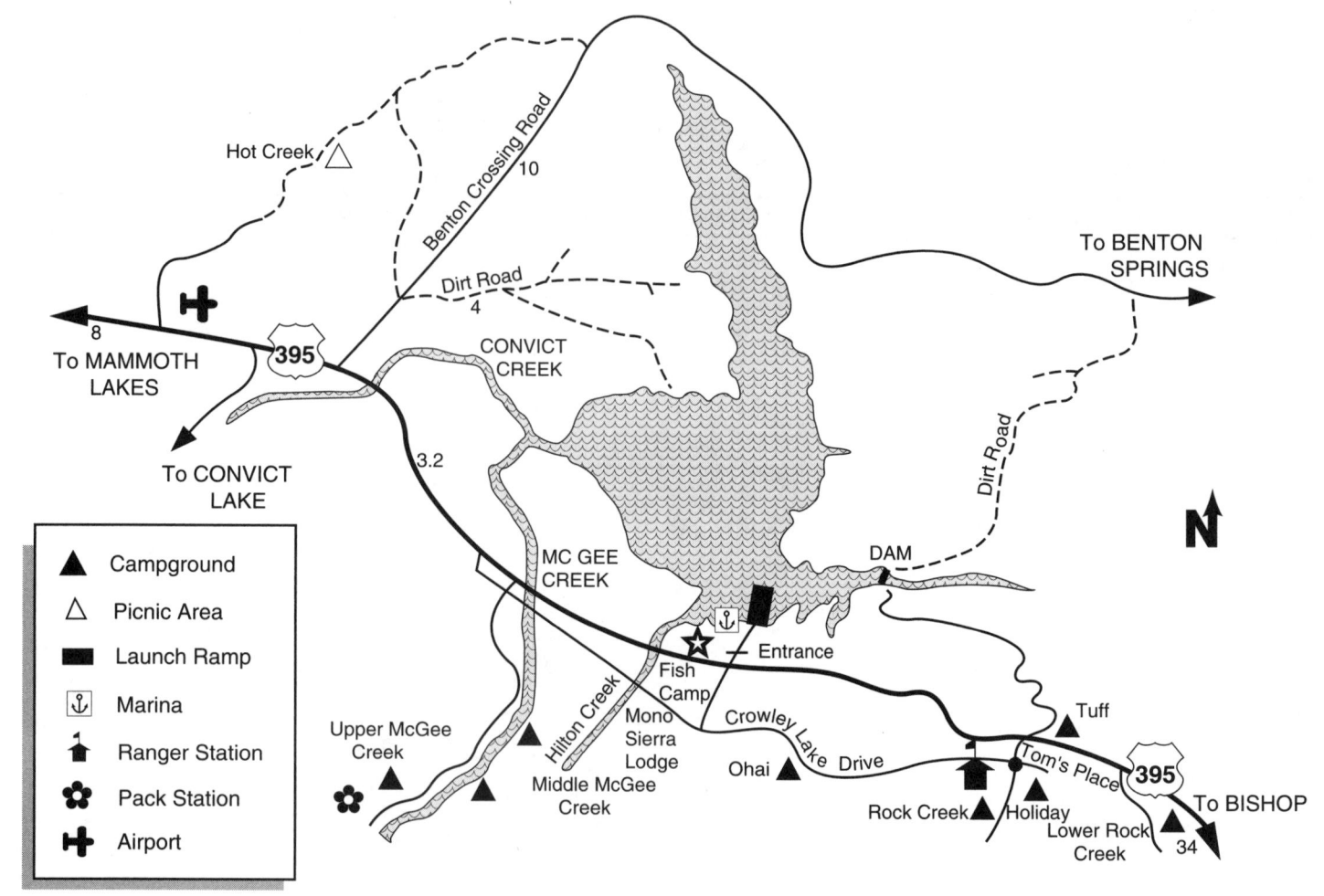

INFORMATION: Crowley Lake Fish Camp, P.O. Box 1268, Mammoth Lakes 93546—Ph: (760) 935-4301

CAMPING	BOATING	RECREATION	OTHER

Fish Camp:
  30 Dev. Sites for
  Tents & R.V.s
  Some Full Hookups
 	
Bureau of Land
  Management
  47 Sites for Tents & R.V.s
  First Come Basis
  No Fee - No Water
 	
Other USFS Campgrounds
  Nearby
	Power, Waterskiing,
	  Sail, Windsurf &
	  Inflatable
	All Craft Must Register
	Permit Fee Required
	Launch Ramp
	Boat Slips
	Full Service Marina
	Rentals: Boats & Motors
		Fishing: Rainbow &
		  German Brown Trout,
		  Sacramento Perch
		Season: May through
		  October
		  Check Regulations
		Waterskiing Season
		Picnicking
		Hiking & Backpacking
		Special Events
		Fishing Derbies
			Grocery Store
			Bait & Tackle
			Mono Sierra Lodge
			  Ph: (800) 723-5387
			Tube Tenders
			  Ph: (760) 934-6922
			  24 ft. Pontoon Boat
			  Guided Fishing Trips
			
			Chamber of Commerce
			  Ph: (760) 935-4666
			Full Facilities at
			  Mammoth Lakes

ROCK CREEK LAKE

Rock Creek Lake, at an elevation of 9,682 feet, is one of the highest lakes in California. Located in the Rock Creek Canyon of Inyo National Forest, this area has over 60 lakes and streams for the equestrian, backpacker and angler. Snow-fed streams flow into Rock Creek, a natural Lake of 63 surface acres. Rainbow and German brown trout are planted throughout the season. Native Eastern brook and golden trout are found in the waters of the John Muir Wilderness. There are several U.S. Forest Service campgrounds along Rock Creek. The speed limit for boating is limited to 5 MPH. Rock Creek Pack Station offers rental horses for a day or extended trips.

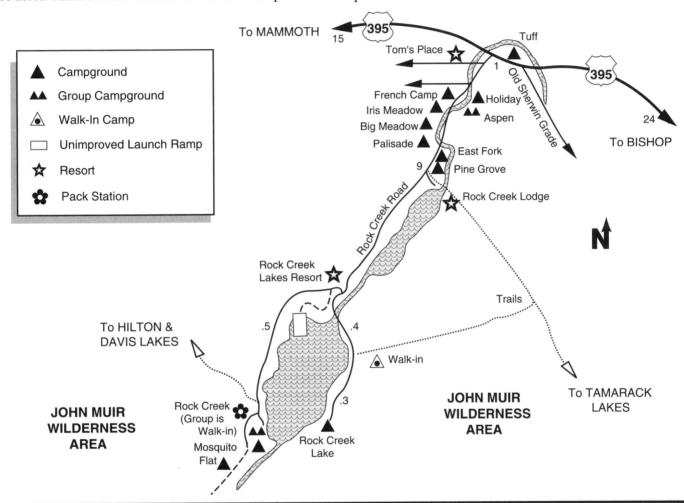

▲	Campground
▲▲	Group Campground
◬	Walk-In Camp
▭	Unimproved Launch Ramp
☆	Resort
❀	Pack Station

INFORMATION: White Mountain Ranger District, 798 N. Main St., Bishop 93514—Ph: (760) 873-2500

CAMPING	BOATING	RECREATION	OTHER

Dev. Sites - $15
  French Camp: 86 Sites
  Tuff: 34 Sites
  East Fork: 133 Sites
Group Sites - $55
  Aspen & Rock Creek
Reservations for Above:
  Ph: (877) 444-6777
Mosquito Flat Trailhead
  10 Sites Free - 1 Day
Other Sites - $15-$16
  No Reservations
  First-Come Basis
	Power, Row, Canoe,
	  Sail & Inflatables
	Speed Limit - 5 MPH
	Unimproved Launch
	  Ramp
	Rentals at Rock Creek
	  Lakes Resort:
	  Fishing Boats &
	  Motors
		Fishing: Rainbow,
		  Eastern Brook,
		  German Brown &
		  Golden Trout
		  in Lake & Streams
		Picnicking
		Hiking Trails
		Equestrian Trails
		Horse Rentals
		
		John Muir Wilderness
		  Permit Required
			Rock Creek Lakes Resort
			  Cottages,
			  Store, Cafe,
			  Boat Rentals
			  Ph: (760) 935-4311
			Rock Creek Lodge
			  Ph: (760) 935-4170
			Tom's Place Resort
			  Ph: (760) 935-4239
			Rock Creek Pack Station
			  Ph: (760) 935-4493

Bishop Creek Canyon is on the eastern slope of the Sierra Nevada at elevations ranging from 7,500 feet to 9,500 feet. This area is popular with backpackers and equestrians who can enjoy the nearby John Muir Wilderness Area. Lake Sabrina has a surface area of 150 acres. South Lake has 180 acres and North Lake is much smaller. These Lakes, along with Bishop Creek, are planted weekly with trout during the season. The U.S. Forest Service offers numerous campsites. In addition, there are private resorts with full facilities.

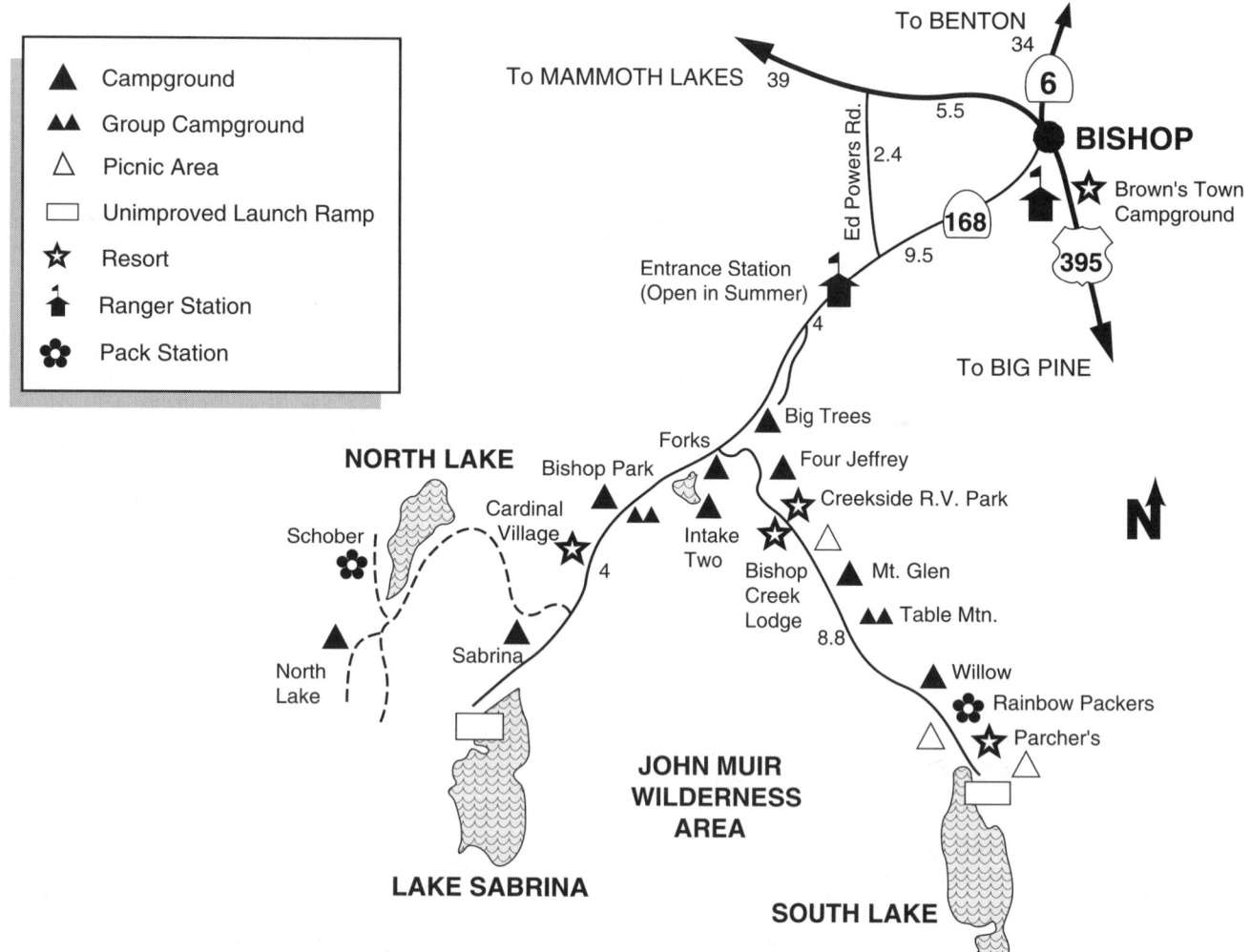

INFORMATION: White Mountain Ranger District. 798 N. Main St., Bishop 93514—Ph: (760) 873-2500

CAMPING	BOATING	RECREATION	OTHER
Dev. Sites: $13 - $14	Power, Row, Canoe,	Fishing: Rainbow &	Brown's Town Campground:
Big Trees - 9 Sites	Sail & Inflatables	German Brown	Ph: (760) 873-8522
Four Jeffrey - 106 Sites	5 MPH Speed Limit	Trout	150 Dev. Sites for
Forks - 9 Sites	Unimproved Launch	Picnicking	Tents & R.V.s, Hookups
Intake Two - 5 Walk-Ins	Ramps at South	Hiking Trails	Creekside R.V. Park
Plus 8 Sites	Lake and Sabrina	Equestrian Trails	Ph: (760) 872-3044
Bishop Park - 21 Sites	Rentals: Fishing	Horse Rentals	Bishop Creek Lodge
Sabrina - 18 Sites	and Motorboats	Rainbow Packers:	Ph: (760) 873-4484
North Lake - 11 Sites	Boat Gas Only	Ph: (760) 873-8877	Parcher's Resort
Groups: $45 to 25 People			Ph: (760) 873-4177
Bishop Park & Table Mtn.			Cabins, Restaurants, Stores
Reserve Some Sites:		John Muir Wilderness	
Ph: (877) 444-6777		Permit Required	Full Facilities in Bishop

NEW MELONES LAKE

New Melones Lake is at an elevation of 1,088 feet in the Mother Lode Gold Country of Central California. The damming of the Stanislaus River has created the largest Lake in this area with 12,500 surface acres and over 100 miles of tree-covered shoreline. This is one of California's prime recreational Lakes. Extensive facilities have been developed un-der the management of the U. S. Bureau of Reclamation. There are 2 large campgrounds as well as day use areas. The boater will find launch ramps and a full service marina. Fishing for a variety of species is considered good. *Call for information regarding water levels.*

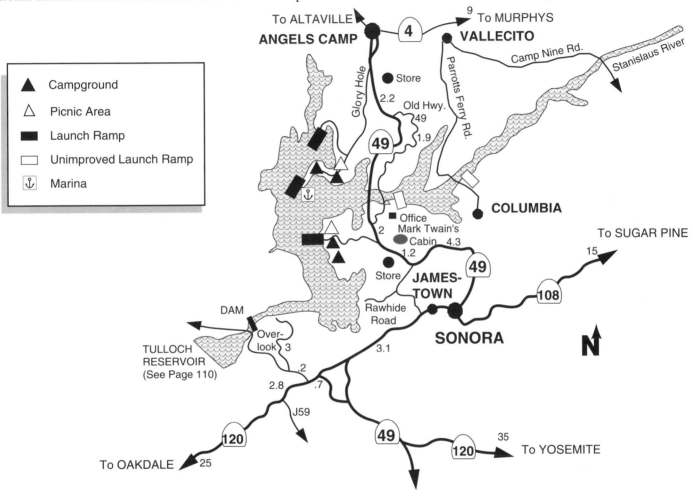

▲	Campground
△	Picnic Area
■	Launch Ramp
☐	Unimproved Launch Ramp
⚓	Marina

INFORMATION: Resource Manager, 6850 Studhorse Flat Road, Sonora 95370—Ph: (209) 536-9094

CAMPING	BOATING	RECREATION	OTHER

Glory Hole:
   144 Dev. Sites for
     Tents & R.V.s
Tuttletown:
   158 Dev. Sites for
     Tents & R.V.s
Disposal Station
Fee: $14
 	
2 Group Sites:
   Reservations Only
	Open to All Boating
	Launch Ramps
	Full Service Marina
	   Ph: (209) 785-3300
	Fuel Dock
	Boat Pumpout
	Rentals: Fishing Boats
	   Pontoon, Houseboats
		Fishing: Rainbow &
		   Brown Trout, Large
		   & Smallmouth Bass,
		   Bluegill, Catfish &
		   Crappie
		Picnicking
		Hiking Trails
		Bicycle Trails
		Gold Panning
		Mark Twain's Cabin
		
		No ORVs
			Visitors Center
			Stores
			
			Angel's R.V. Park
			   Dev. Sites for Tents &
			   R.V.s - Hookups
			   Ph: (209) 736-0404
			
			Full Facilities in
			   Nearby Towns

LAKE TULLOCH

Lake Tulloch, at an elevation of 510 feet, is on the western slope of the Sierras just east of Modesto. The 55 miles of shoreline encompass two submerged valleys surrounded by rolling hills dotted with oak trees. This "Gold Country" Lake is open to all types of boating and offers good marine facilities. Fishing for trout and warm water species is popular. Tulloch is known as one of California's prime smallmouth bass Lakes. The South Shore offers developed and open camping. The Marina provides a launch ramp, boat rentals, gas dock, snack bar, groceries and a campground. Lake Tulloch Resort has a luxury motel on the water with a launch ramp, swimming pool and beach, restaurant and bar.

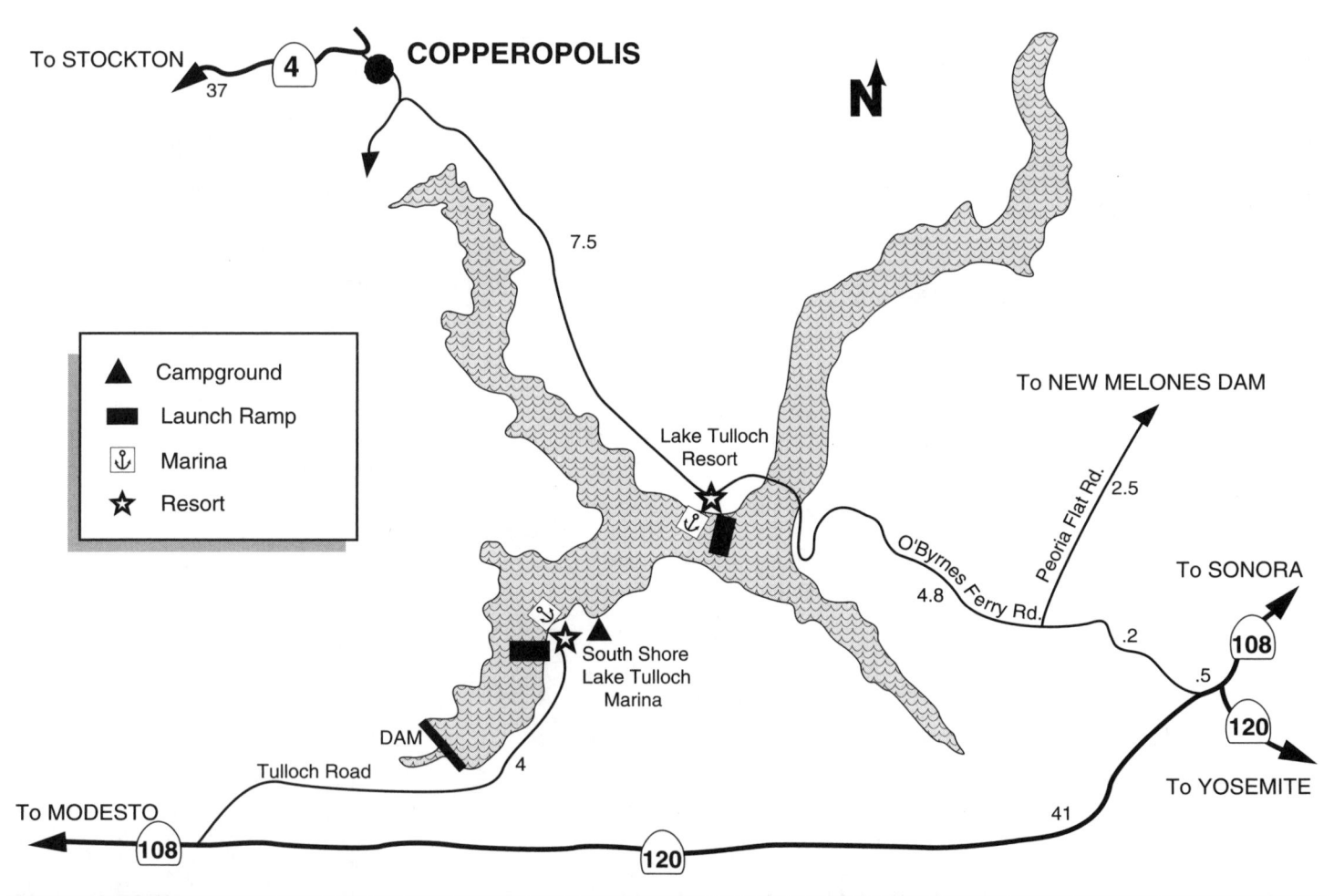

CAMPING	BOATING	RECREATION	OTHER
130 Dev. Sites for Tents & R.V.s Full Hookups Lakefront Cabanas with Electricity Fees: $17.50 - $27.50 Reservations: Ph: (800) 894-2267 Lakefront Cabins with Dock	Power, Row, Canoe, Sail, Waterski, Jets, Windsurf & Inflatables Launch Ramp: $2 Rentals: Fishing, Waterski & Patio Boats, Kayaks, Waverunners Overnight Boating Allowed Lake Tulloch Resort: Marina Launch Ramp: $10	Fishing: Rainbow Trout, Small & Largemouth Bass, Bluegill, Catfish, Crappie Picnicking Swimming - Beaches Hiking Trails Equestrian Trails Gold Panning	Lake Tulloch Resort 7260 O'Byrnes Ferry Rd. Copperopolis 95228 Ph: (209) 785-8200 or (888) 785-8200 Lake View Rooms Restaurant & Lounge Grocery Store Bait & Tackle Snack Bars

WOODWARD RESERVOIR

Woodward Reservoir is at an elevation of 210 feet and located in rolling foothills 6 miles north of Oakdale. This 2,900 surface acre irrigation Reservoir is under the jurisdiction of Stanislaus County. The 23 miles of shallow shoreline provides many quiet coves and inlets for the boater and angler. The Lake is divided by speed limit restrictions with a few "No Boat" areas. Ample space allows all boaters to enjoy their sport. There is a good warm water fishery. The County maintains a campground on the edge of the Lake and a large overflow primitive camping area with limited facilities. This is a popular family area with approximately 3,240 acres of park land.

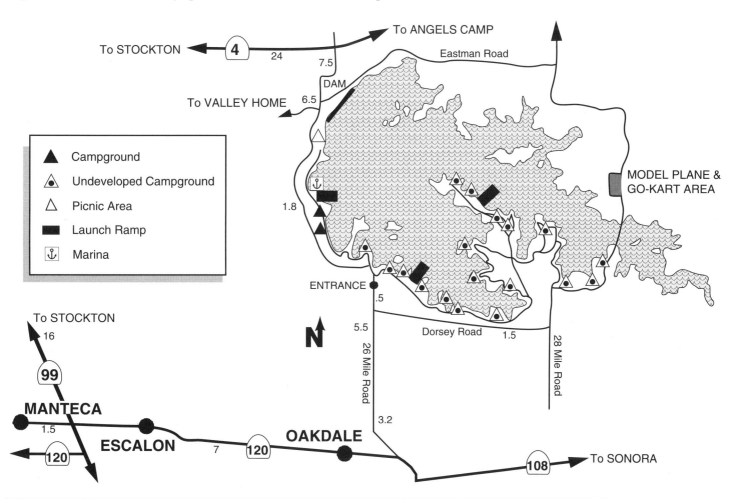

Legend:
- ▲ Campground
- ⊛ Undeveloped Campground
- △ Picnic Area
- ▬ Launch Ramp
- ⚓ Marina

MODEL PLANE & GO-KART AREA

INFORMATION: Woodward Reservoir, 14528 - 26 Mile Rd., Oakdale 95361—Ph: (209) 847-3304

CAMPING	BOATING	RECREATION	OTHER
154 Dev. Sites for Tents & R.V.s Fees: $14 Full Hookups: $16 Disposal Station	Power, Row, Canoe, Sail, Waterski, Jet Skis, Windsurf, Inflatables	Fishing: Rainbow Trout, Catfish, Perch, Bluegill, Crappie, Large & Smallmouth Bass	Snack Bar Grocery Store Bait & Tackle
No Reservations 13 Miles of Shoreline for Primitive Camping Fee: $12	Restricted Speed Limit Areas MTBE-Free Fuel Only Launch Ramps Full Service Marina Docks & Gas	Swimming Picnicking: Large Shelter Can Be Reserved Hiking Trails Equestrian Trails Volleyball Court	No ORVs Full Facilities at Oakdale
Dog or Horse: $2 Day Use Fee: $6	Rentals: Fishing Boats & Canoes	Horseshoe Pits Hunting: Waterfowl With Permit	

Don Pedro Lake is at an elevation of 800 feet in the Sierra foothills of the southern region of the Gold Country. This huge Lake has a surface area of 12,960 acres with 160 miles of pine and oak-covered shoreline. The extensive facilities which include three recreation areas and two full service marinas are under the jurisdiction of the Don Pedro Recreation Agency. The vast size and irregular shoreline provides a multitude of opportunities from boat-in camping to waterskiing. The angler, whether novice or on the Pro Bass Tour, will find a good varied fishery. *Be aware, due to fluctuating water levels, emerging rocks and islands are potential boating hazards.*

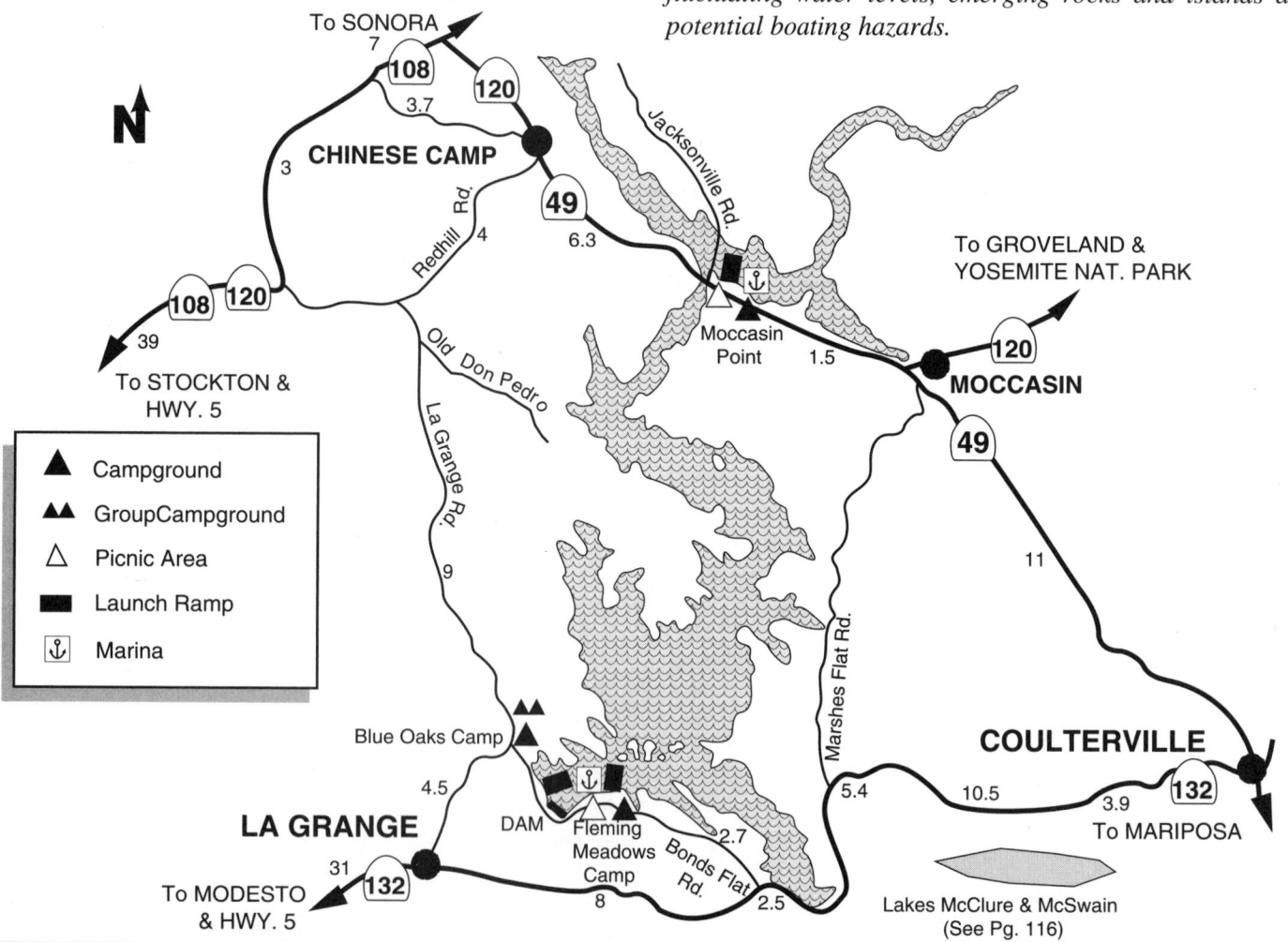

N

To SONORA
108 **120**
3.7
CHINESE CAMP
3
Redhill Rd.
4
49
6.3
Jacksonville Rd.
To GROVELAND & YOSEMITE NAT. PARK
108 **120**
39
To STOCKTON & HWY. 5
Old Don Pedro
La Grange Rd.
Moccasin Point
1.5
120
MOCCASIN
49
11
Marshes Flat Rd.

▲ Campground
▲▲ GroupCampground
△ Picnic Area
■ Launch Ramp
⚓ Marina

9

Blue Oaks Camp
4.5
LA GRANGE
31 **132**
To MODESTO & HWY. 5
DAM
Fleming Meadows Camp
Bonds Flat Rd.
8
2.7
2.5

COULTERVILLE
5.4   10.5   3.9 **132**
To MARIPOSA
Lakes McClure & McSwain
(See Pg. 116)

INFORMATION: Don Pedro Recreation Agency, 31 Bonds Flat Rd., La Grange 95329—Ph: (209) 852-2396

CAMPING	BOATING	RECREATION	OTHER
550 Dev. Sites for Tents & R.V.s Fees: Tents - $15 - $17 Full Hookups - $22 - $25 Group Camp Facility Walk-In Sites Reservations: $5 Fee per Site Boat-in Camping Most Anywhere Except Near Campgrounds *No Pets Allowed* Day Use Fee: $5	Power, Row, Canoe, Sail, Waterski, Jets, Windsurf & Inflatable Sailing Slalom Course Full Service Marinas 3 Launch Ramps - $5 Rentals: Fishing & Ski Boats, Houseboats, Pontoons & PWCs Docks, Berths, Moorings Dry Storage & Gas Private Houseboats Require Permit	Fishing: Trout, Catfish, Bluegill, Crappie, Perch, Silver Salmon, Florida Black Bass Swimming Lagoon Handicap Access Picnicking Group Picnic Area Hiking Trails	Snack Bars Restaurant Grocery Store Bait & Tackle Hot Showers Laundromat Disposal Stations Gas Station Propane

MODESTO RESERVOIR

Modesto Reservoir is at an elevation of 210 feet in the low hills and pasturelands northeast of Modesto. The Lake has a surface area of 2,700 acres with 31 miles of shoreline. The facilities are under the jurisdiction of the Stanislaus County Parks Department. This is a good boating Lake with westerly breezes for sailing and vast open water for the waterskier.

Many coves are available for unlimited boat camping. Boaters should note there is a 5 MPH speed limit on the southern area of the Lake and near the facilities. There are also several no boating zones; refer to posted rules or ask a park aide for specifics. The many coves have submerged trees which provide for a good warm water fishery.

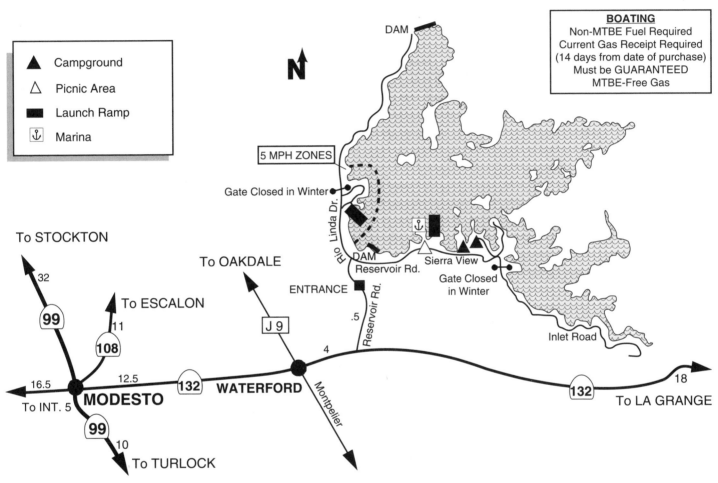

BOATING
Non-MTBE Fuel Required
Current Gas Receipt Required
(14 days from date of purchase)
Must be GUARANTEED
MTBE-Free Gas

▲ Campground
△ Picnic Area
■ Launch Ramp
⚓ Marina

INFORMATION: Modesto Reservoir, 1716 Morgan Rd., Modesto 95351—Ph: (209) 874-9540			
CAMPING	**BOATING**	**RECREATION**	**OTHER**
150 Dev. Sites for Tents & R.V.s Fees: $14 Full Hookups: $16 Disposal Station No Reservations Unlimited Primitive Sites Fee: $12 Day Use Fees Cars: $6 Boats: $5 *No Pets or Horses Permitted*	Power, Row, Canoe, Sail, Waterski, PWCs, Windsurfing & Inflatables Launch Ramps Full Service Marina Docks Rentals: Paddleboats	Fishing: Black, Large & Smallmouth Bass, Trout, Catfish, Carp, Bluegill, Crappie, Swimming - Beaches Picnicking Hiking Trails Backpacking [Parking] Hunting By Permit Only: Duck	Snack Bar Grocery Store Bait & Tackle Hot Showers Gas Full Facilities at Modesto *Call for Current Water Level Conditions*

OAKWOOD LAKE

Bordering the San Joaquin River, just off the junction of Interstate 5 and Highway 120, Oakwood Lake is very unique. With over one mile of waterslides, this is one of North America's biggest waterparks. Boating on the Lake is restricted to canoes and inflatables. 100 campsites, located on shaded lawns, have full hookups. Power boats can be enjoyed along the San Joaquin River which also provides a more diverse fishery. This is a great family park for those who enjoy a multitude of activities.

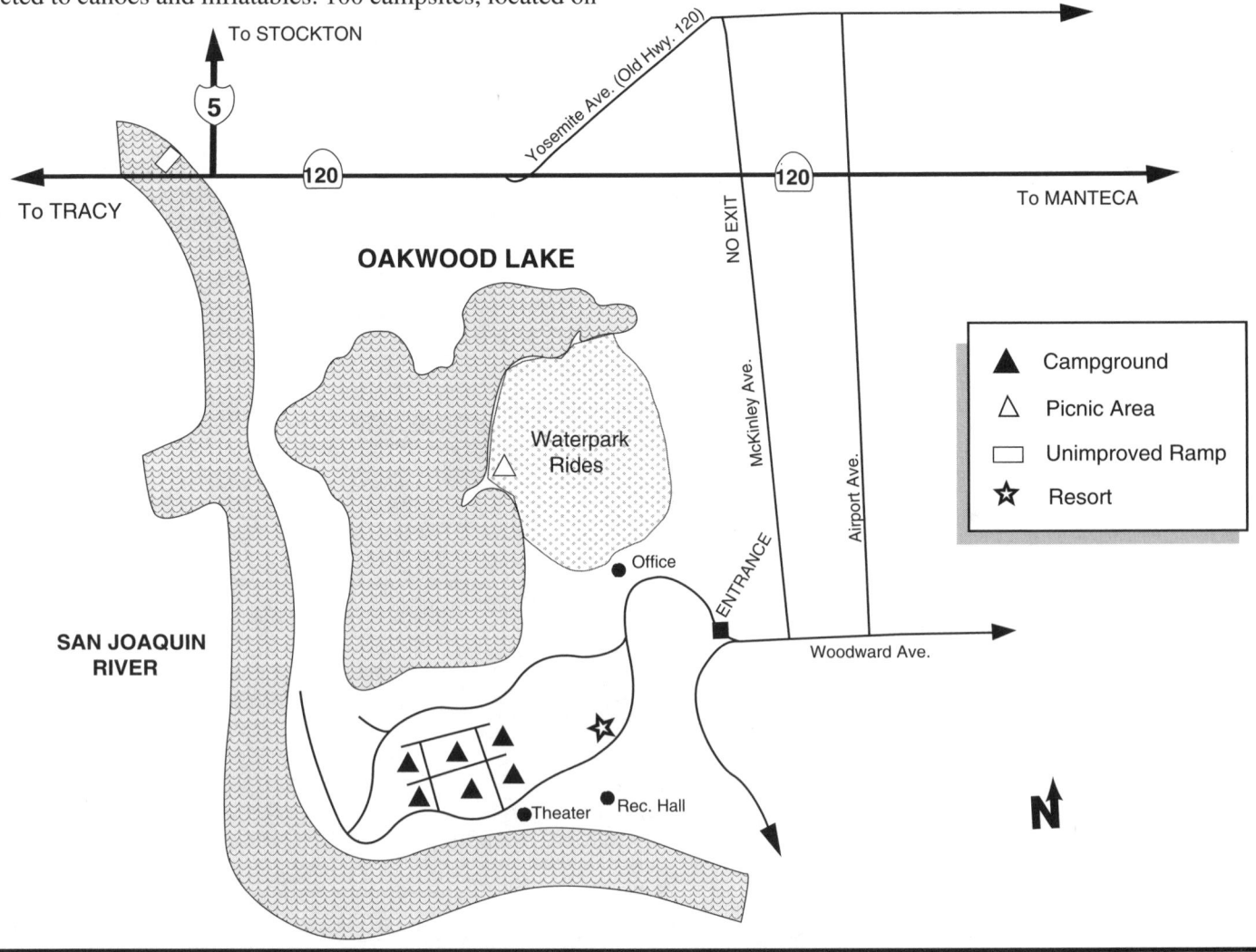

INFORMATION: Oakwood Lake, 874 E. Woodward, Manteca 95337—Ph: (209) 239-2500			
CAMPING	**BOATING**	**RECREATION**	**OTHER**

100 Dev. Sites for
  Tents & R.V.s
    Full Hookups
  Fees Start at $28
Group Sites
  Discount Rates for
  R.V. Clubs
Disposal Station
 	
Reservations Only:
  Ph: (209) 249-2500
	Oakwood Lake:
	  Small Boats &
	    Inflatables
	Electric Motors Only
	No Rental Boats
	
	San Joaquin River:
	  Power Boats and
	    Waterskiing
	  Launch Ramp off
	    Hwy. 120
		Fishing: Catfish &
		  Bass - Campers Only
		Picnicking
		  2 Large Day Use Areas
		Manteca Waterslides
		Basketball Courts
		Horseshoe Pits
		Playground
		Arcades
		Movies & Bingo
			Snack Bar
			Grocery Store
			Bait & Tackle
			Hot Showers
			Laundromat
			Gas
			
			Day Use - Call for Rates

TURLOCK LAKE

Turlock Lake, at an elevation of 250 feet, is nestled in the foothills 25 miles east of Modesto. The State Recreation Area is included in the California State Park System. The Lake has a surface area of 3,500 acres 26 miles of shoreline. Open year around, this is a popular recreation area. The Lake is open to all types of boating but in late summer, low water levels can be a hazard. There is a good warm water fishery and trout are planted on a regular basis in season. Swimming is popular and several beaches are available. The shaded campground is located along the Tuolomne River. Reservations are advised.

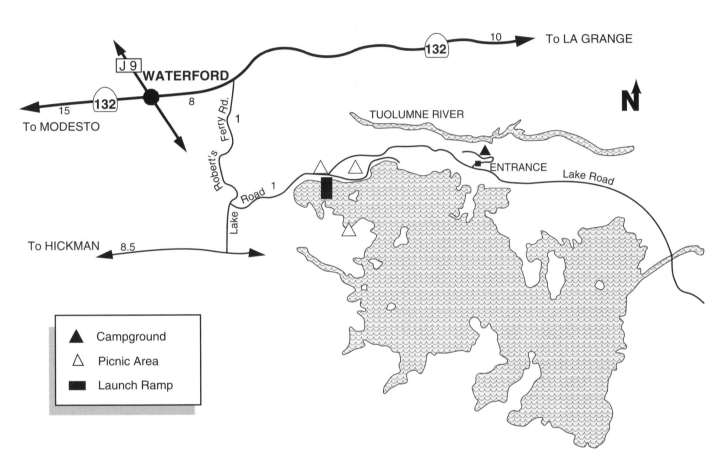

▲	Campground
△	Picnic Area
■	Launch Ramp

INFORMATION: Turlock State Recreation Area, 22600 Lake Rd., La Grange 95329—Ph: (209) 874-2056

CAMPING	BOATING	RECREATION	OTHER
State Recreation Area: 63 Dev. Sites for Tents & R.V.s to 27 Feet Fees: $12 Reservations: Ph: (800) 444-7275	Power, Row, Canoe, Sail, Waterski, Jets, Windsurf & Inflatable Launch Ramp - Free	Fishing: Trout, Catfish, Bluegill, Crappie, Large & Smallmouth Bass Swimming - Beaches Picnicking	Campfire & Junior Ranger Program Full Facilities at Waterford
	Low Water Levels Late in Summer	Hiking Trails Hunting in Season Waterfowl Only - In Designated, Pre-assigned Blinds	
Day Use Fee: $2			

LAKE MC CLURE and LAKE MC SWAIN

Located in the Mother Lode Country of the Sierra foothills, these Lakes are at an elevation of 867 feet. Lake McClure has a surface area of 7,100 acres with 82 miles of pine and oak-covered shoreline. Lake McSwain, with 7-1/2 miles of shore-line, is the forebay of Lake McClure. Both these Lakes have campgrounds, marinas and full recreation facilities. Many coves are popular for houseboats at Lake McClure and the waterskiier will find 26 miles of open water. The very cold water flowing from the dam into Lake McSwain has created a good fishery, enhanced by weekly trout plants in season. There is a 10 MPH speed limit for boaters on Lake McSwain. Campsites next to the water are available and this Lake remains full year around. Waterskiing and houseboats are not allowed at McSwain.

....Continued....

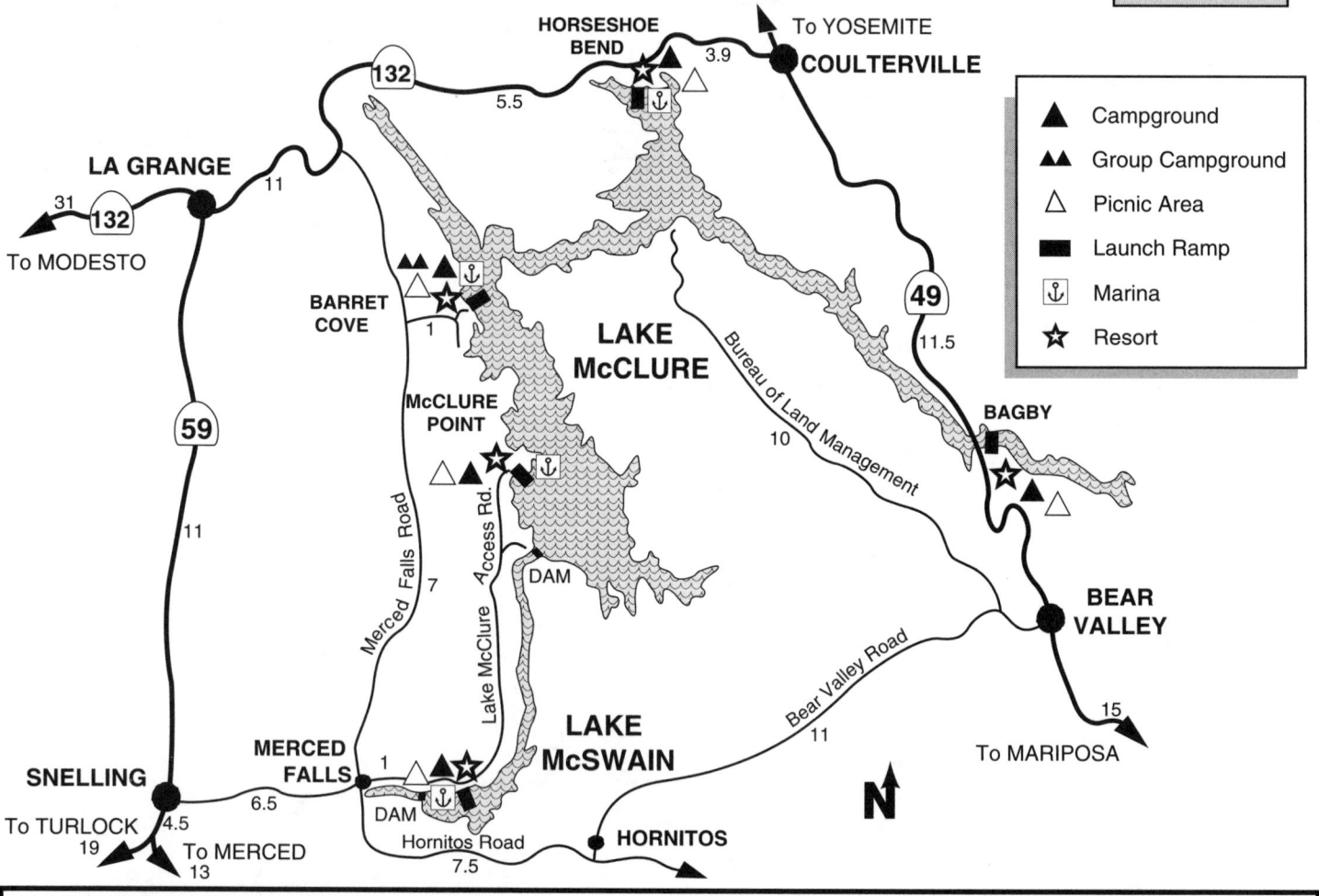

LEGEND

▲	Campground
▲▲	Group Campground
△	Picnic Area
■	Launch Ramp
⚓	Marina
☆	Resort

INFORMATION: See Following Page for Recreation Areas - Park Headquarters Ph: (800) 468-8889

CAMPING	BOATING	RECREATION	OTHER
614 Dev. Sites for Tents & R.V.s Fee: $16	All Boating Allowed at Lake McClure	Fishing: Trout, Catfish, Bluegill, Crappie, Perch,	Snack Bars Grocery Stores Bait & Tackle
167 Electric & Water Hookups Fee: $22	No Waterskiing or Houseboats at Lake McSwain	Black & Florida Bass Swim Lagoons at Lake McClure	Hot Showers Laundromats Disposal Stations
84 Electric & Water & Sewer Hookups Fee: $22	Full Service Marinas Launch Ramps Rentals: Fishing &	Beaches Picnicking Group Picnic Shelter	Gas Stations Propane
Day Use Fees: Vehicle: $5.50 Boat: $5 Pet: $2	Pontoon Boats, Houseboats Docks, Berths Moorings, Gas Boat Storage	Hiking Trails Playgrounds Sightseeing - Gold Rush Towns	

Mc CLURE POINT:

M I D Parks Department
9090 Lake McClure Rd.
Snelling 95369
Ph: (209) 378-2521

McClure Point Marina
Call for Information at
Barrett Cove Marina
Ph: (209) 378-2441

100 Developed Campsites for Tents & R.V.s, 52 Water & Electric Hookups. Fees: $14 - $22. 64 Picnic Sites. Full Service Marina with Gas for Boats & Cars, 3-Lane Launch Ramp, Docks, Berths, Moorings, Storage. Swim Lagoon, Grocery Store, Laundromat, Showers. *Reservations through Parks Department Office at (800) 468-8889. Reservation Fee: $5.*

BARRETT COVE:

M I D Parks Department
Barrett Cove Rec. Area
Star Route
La Grange 95329
Ph: (209) 378-2611

Barrett Cove Marina
Star Route
La Grange 95329
Ph: (209) 378-2441

275 Developed Campsites for Tents & R.V.s, 55 Full Hookups, 34 Water and Electric Hookups. Fees: $14 - $22. 100 Picnic Sites Plus Group Picnic Facility to 100 People Maximum. Full Service Marina with Gas for Boats & Cars, 3-Lane Launch Ramp, Boat Rentals: Fishing, Houseboats, Pontoons. Moorings, Storage. Swim Lagoon, Playground, Snack Bar, Grocery Store, Laundromat, Showers. *Reservations through Parks Department Office at (800) 468-8889. Reservation Fee: $5.*

HORSESHOE BEND:

M I D Parks Department
Horseshoe Bend Rec. Area
4244 Highway 132
Coulterville 95311
Ph: (209) 878-3452

Horseshoe Bend Marina
Call for Information at
Barrett Cove Marina
Ph: (209) 378-2441

110 Developed Campsites for Tents & R.V.s, 7 Full Hookups, 28 Water & Electric Hookups. Fees: $14 - $22. 32 Picnic Sites, 2-Lane Launch Ramp, Swim Lagoon, Laundromat, Showers. *Reservations through Parks Department Office at (800) 468-8889. Reservation Fee: $5.*

BAGBY:

Bagby Recreation Area
8324 Highway 49 North
Mariposa 95338

30 Developed Campsites for Tents & R.V.s., 10 Water & Electric Hookups, Fees: $13 - $21
25 Picnic Sites, Launch Ramp.

LAKE MC SWAIN:

M I D Parks Department
9090 Lake McClure Rd.
Snelling 95369
Ph: (209) 378-2521

Lake McSwain Marina
8044 Lake McClure Road
Snelling 95369
Ph: (209) 378-2534

99 Developed Campsites for Tents & R.V.s, 22 Full Hookups, 43 Water & Electric Hookups. Fees: $14 - $22. Picnic Sites and Group Picnic Facility up to 200 People. Full Service Marina with Gas for Boats & Cars, 2-lane Launch Ramp, Rentals: Fishing Boats. Moorings, Snack Bar, Grocery Store, Laundromat, Showers, Playground Area. *Reservations through Parks Department Office at (800) 468-8889. Reservation Fee: $5.*

LAKE YOSEMITE

Located in the rolling foothills of the Sierra Nevada, Lake Yosemite is east of Merced and under the jurisdiction of the County of Merced. This Lake has 387 surface acres and offers good marine facilities, beaches and shaded picnic sites for groups up to 200 people. All types of boating are allowed with designated areas for waterskiing, sailing and rowing. Fishing can be productive at this scenic Lake in the San Joaquin Valley. Facilities are for day use only except for Youth Group camping with reservations.

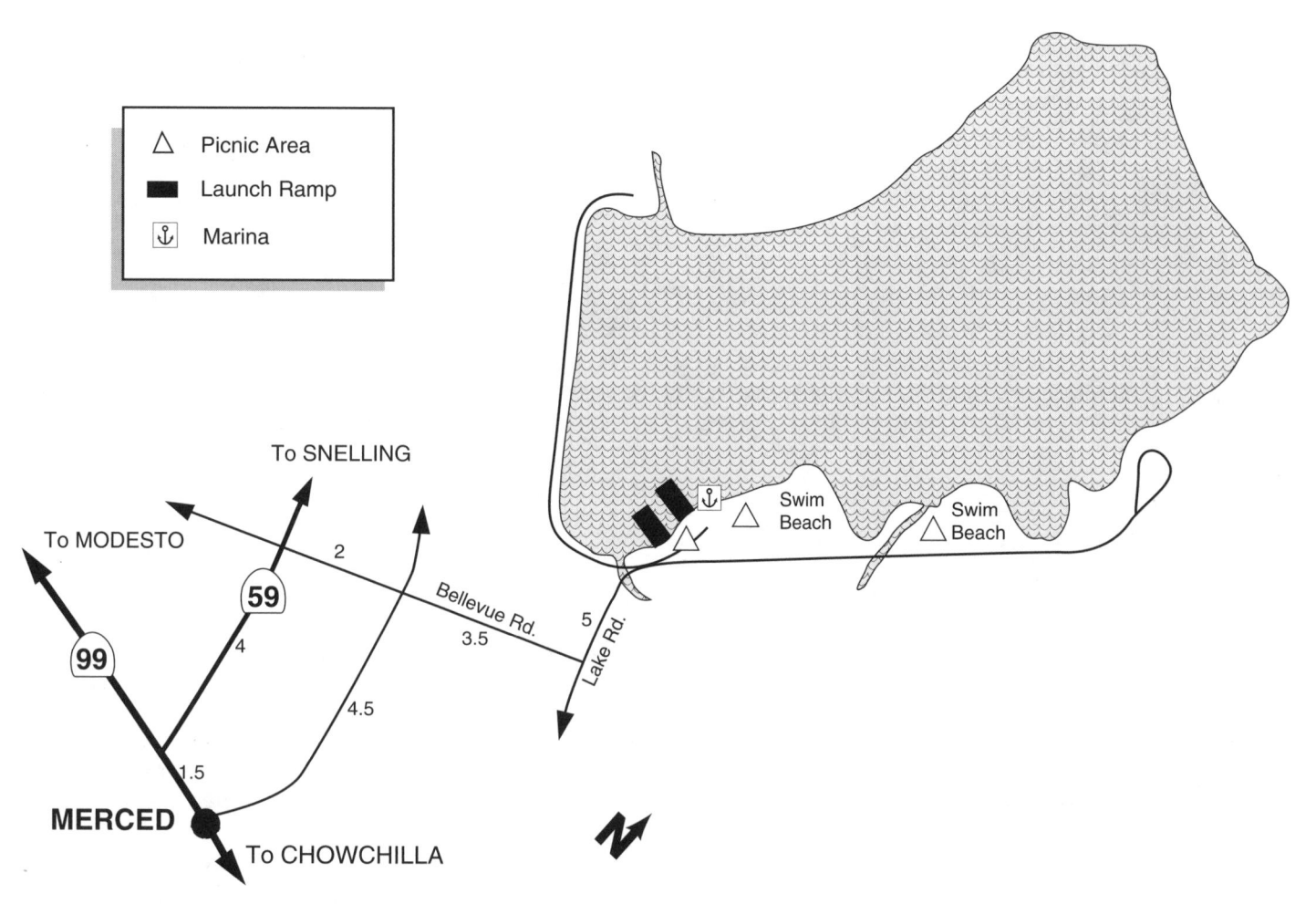

	Picnic Area
	Launch Ramp
⚓	Marina

To SNELLING
To MODESTO
59
2
4
Bellevue Rd.
3.5
99
4.5
5
Lake Rd.
1.5
MERCED
To CHOWCHILLA

Swim Beach
Swim Beach

N

INFORMATION: Parks & Recreation, Merced County Courthouse, Merced 95340—Ph: (209) 385-7426

CAMPING	BOATING	RECREATION	OTHER
Youth Groups Only Reservations: Ph: (209) 385-7426	All Boating Allowed with Designated Areas for Sailboats, Waterskiing, Rowboats & Powerboats Launch Ramps Fee: $4 Docks and Marina Boat Rentals	Fishing: Trout, Largemouth Bass, Bluegill & Catfish Swimming - Beaches Picnicking Group Picnic Facility with Reservations	Snack Bar Sailing Club Day Use Park Fees: $4 per Vehicle

SOULAJULE, STAFFORD, NICASIO, PHOENIX, LAGUNITAS, BON TEMPE, ALPINE and KENT LAKES

These Lakes, along the slopes of Mt. Tamalpais, are under the jurisdiction of the North Marin Municipal Water District except for Stafford Lake Park which is operated by the Marin County Department of Parks. Shaded hiking trails are numerous. Boating and swimming are not permitted at any Lake. Nicasio and Soulajule have warm water fisheries. Stafford contains largemouth bass but the use of live bait (except worms) is not allowed. Stafford Lake Park offers two large group picnic areas. Lagunitas Lake has special restrictions including the use of only artificial lures with single barbless hooks with a limit of 2 fish. Samuel P. Taylor State Park includes single and group sites for camping.

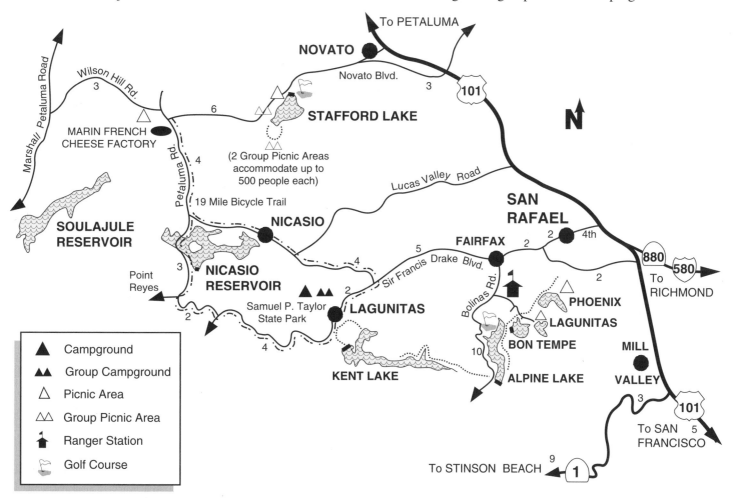

INFORMATION: Marin Municipal Water District, 200 Nellen Ave., Corte Madera 94903—Ph: (415) 924-4600

CAMPING	BOATING	RECREATION	OTHER
No Camping on Marin Water District Land	No Boating Allowed	Fishing: Trout, Bass, Bluegill, Catfish & Crappie	Stafford Lake: Marin County Dept. of Parks Open Space & Cultural Services
Lakes: Day Use Only		Stafford: Largemouth Bass	3501 Civic Center Dr. #415
Vehicle Fee: $5 Daily		*Live Bait Prohibited (except worms)*	San Rafael 94903 Ph: (415) 499-6387
Nearby: Samuel P. Taylor Park		Hiking & Equestrian Trails	
Ph: (415) 488-9897		Bicycles - *Fire Roads Only*	Cheese Factory:
Family & Group Sites		Nature Study	4 Miles North of
Tents & R.V.s to 27 Feet		Picnicking	Nicasio Reservoir
Fee: $14 Single $75 Group		*No Swimming or Wading* Pets To Be Leashed	
Reserve Ph:(800) 444-7275		At All Times	Full Facilities Nearby

LAKES ANZA, MERRITT and TEMESCAL, BERKELEY AQUATIC PARK

Lake Anza is a small Lake within the beautiful Charles Lee Tilden Regional Park, one of the most extensively developed facilities in the Bay Area. With over 2,077 acres, this Park includes a public golf course, botanical gardens, a carousel, pony rides and a scaled-down steam train. Temescal Recreation Area, 48 acres, includes a small 10-acre Lake. This facility is popular for swimming, fishing and picnicking. The City of Oakland administers the 160-acre saltwater Lake Merritt. The surrounding Lakeside Park provides expansive shaded lawns, picnic areas, playground and North America's oldest bird sanctuary. Boating, biking and picnicking can be enjoyed at the Berkeley Aquatic Park.

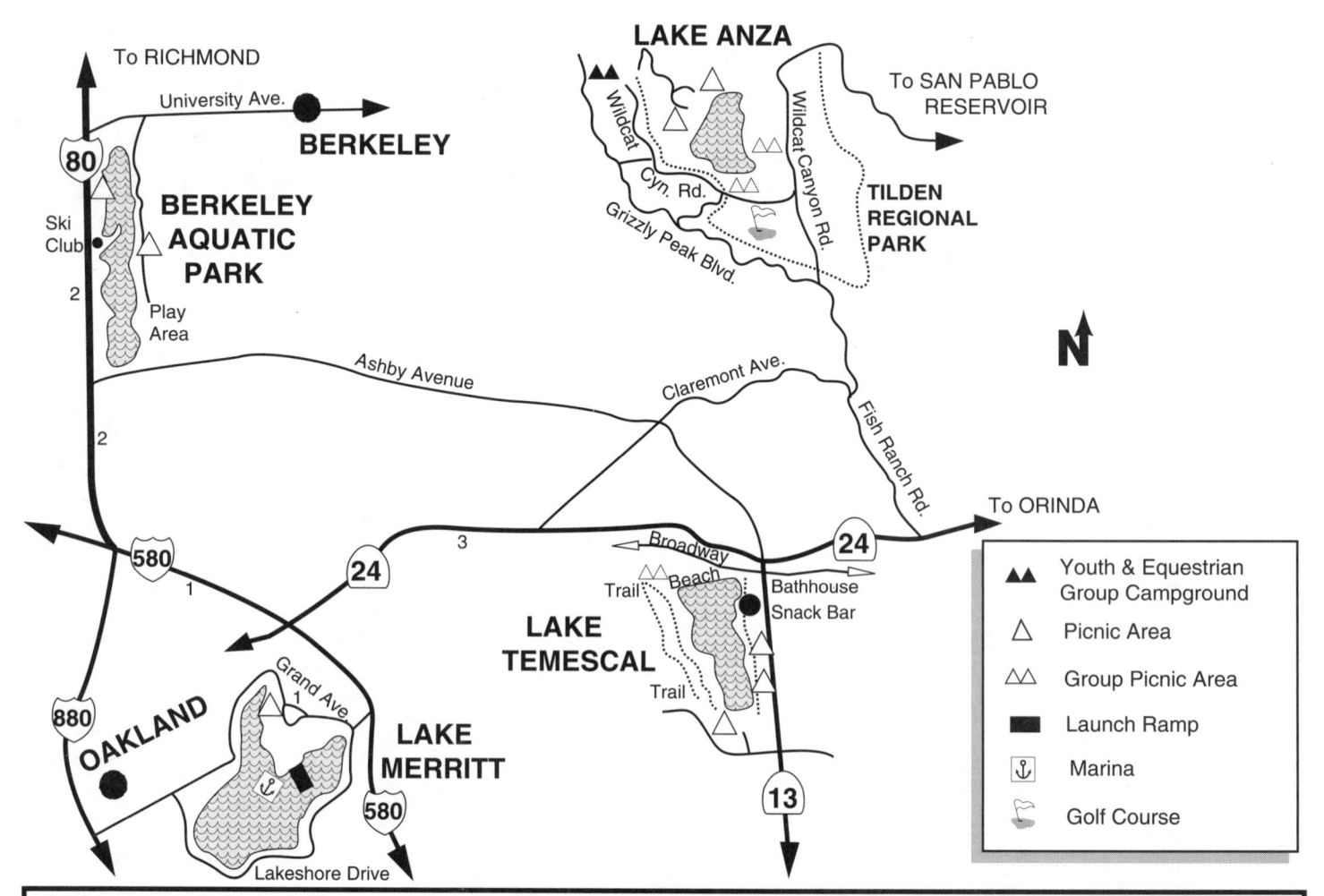

INFORMATION: Anza & Temescal East Bay Reg. Parks, 2950 Peralta Oaks, Oakland 94605- Ph: (510) 562-PARK

CAMPING	BOATING	RECREATION	OTHER
Tilden Regional Park: 　Non-Profit Groups and 　Equestrian Groups 　Only 　Reservations 　Ph: (510) 562-CAMP No Camping at Merritt, Temescal or Berkeley Aquatic Park Lake Temescal Day Use 　Parking: $4 　Dog on Leash: $1	Anza & Temescal: 　No Boating Berkeley Aquatic Park: 　Sail, Windsurf & Row Lake Merritt: 　Sail & Row Boats 　Launch Ramp & Hoist 　Rental: Sail, Row 　　Canoe & Pedal Boats 　Sailing Instructions 　Indoor Boat Storage	Fishing: Trout, Bass, 　Catfish, Crappie & 　Sunfish Picnicking 　Group Sites - Temescal 　Reserve: (510) 636-1684 Hiking & Equestrian Trails Playgrounds Nature Study Bird Sanctuary at Merritt Boat Tour at Merritt Swimming - Beaches: 　Anza & Temescal Only	Lake Merritt: 　City of Oakland 　　Sailboat House 　Oakland Office of 　　Parks & Recreation 　568 Bellevue Ave. 　Oakland 94610 　Ph: (510) 444-3807 Berkeley Aquatic Park 　Ph: (510) 981-5150

SAN PABLO RESERVOIR

East of the Berkeley hills, San Pablo Reservoir is located at an elevation of 314 feet. With 866 surface acres and 14 miles of shoreline, this Reservoir is under the jurisdiction of the East Bay Municipal Utility District. The winds allow for good sailing. Although windsurfing, waterskiing or swimming are not permitted, this is a popular boating Lake with good marine facilities. An extensive fishery habitat along with a tremendous annual trout planting schedule make this one of the best lakes in the State for anglers. There are 142 picnic sites with barbecues overlooking the water plus a children's play area. In addition, there is one large group picnic area which can be reserved. Hiking and riding trails, available by permit, lead to Briones and Tilden Regional Park.

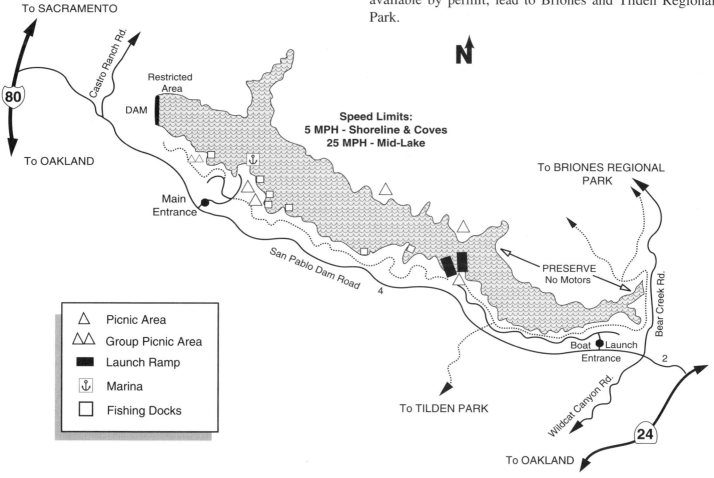

	Picnic Area
	Group Picnic Area
	Launch Ramp
	Marina
	Fishing Docks

INFORMATION: San Pablo Reservoir, 7301 San Pablo Dam Rd., El Sobrante 94803—Ph: (510) 223-1661

CAMPING	BOATING	RECREATION	OTHER

No Camping
 	
Day Use Only
  Fee: $5.50
 	
Group Picnic Area for
  up to 100 People
  By Reservation Only
  Ph: (510) 223-1661
	All Boating Requires
	  Permit
	MTBE Free Fuel Only
	*Waterskiing, Windsurfing
	  & Racing Boats Not
	  Allowed*
	Launch Ramp Fee: $5
	Full Service Marina
	Docks
	Rentals: Fishing, Row &
	  Patio Boats
		Fishing: Trophy Trout,
		  Large, Smallmouth &
		  Spotted Bass, Sturgeon,
		  Channel Catfish,
		  Crappie & Bluegill
		Fishing Fee: $3.25
		Fishing Docks
		Fishing Access Trail
		Picnic Areas
		Hiking, Bicycle &
		  Equestrian Trails
		Playground
		No Swimming or Wading
			Restaurant
			Bait & Tackle
			Fish Cleaning Stations
			
			Briones Regional Park:
			  Group Camping
			  Group Picnic Sites
			  For Information:
			    East Bay
			      Regional Parks
			  Ph: (510) 636-1684

LAFAYETTE RESERVOIR

Lafayette Reservoir provides a scenic retreat from the urban areas that surround it. Nestled amid the rolling oak-covered hills of Contra Costa County and within the city limits of Lafayette, this popular Reservoir has 126 surface acres and is for day use only. Electric motors are permitted. Although you must hand launch your boat, there is a dock for small boats.

Rental boats are available. In addition to planted trout, the angler will find a warm water fishery. Most of the picnic sites around the Lake have barbecues. Two group picnic areas can be reserved. A paved walking trail surrounds the Lake. A self-guided nature trail goes through 928 acres of open space. The facilities are under the jurisdiction of the East Bay Municipal Utility District. No body contact with the water is permitted.

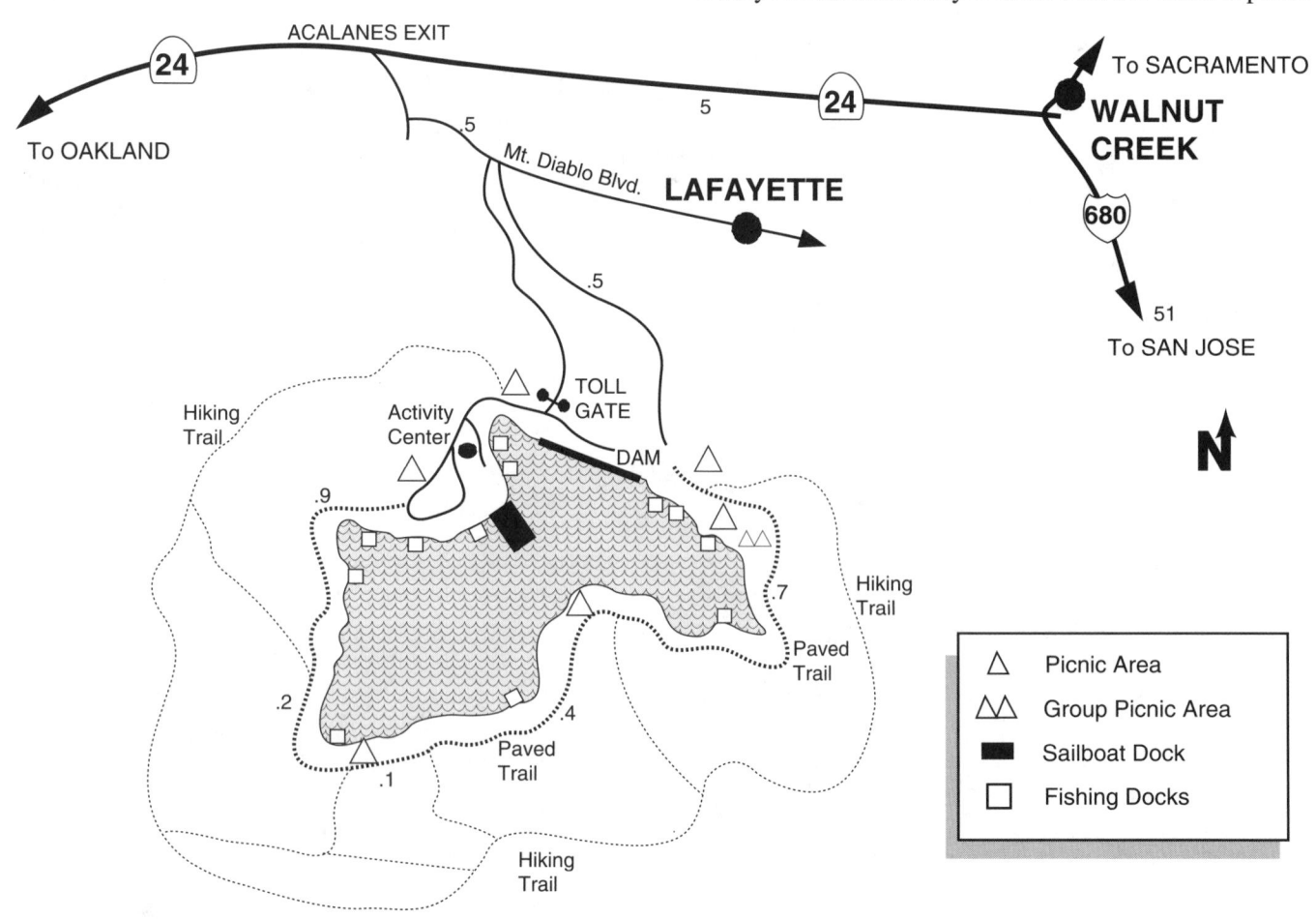

△	Picnic Area
△△	Group Picnic Area
■	Sailboat Dock
□	Fishing Docks

INFORMATION: East Bay Muni. Utility District. P.O. Box 24055, Oakland 94623—Ph: (925) 284-9669-Reservoir

CAMPING	BOATING	RECREATION	OTHER
No Camping	Cartop Boats Only	Fishing: Rainbow Trout,	Bait & Tackle
	Hand Launch with Permit	Black Bass, Bluegill,	Fishing Licenses
Day Use Only	Electric Motors Only	Crappie & Catfish	Fish Cleaning Station
Fee: $5	Sailboat Dock	Fishing Docks	
	Rentals:	Picnic Areas	Bicycles, Rollerskates
2 Group Picnic Areas	Pedal & Row Boats	Group Picnic Sites	& Scooters Permitted:
By Reservation	Boat Launch: $3	Hiking Trails	Tues. & Thurs.
50 & 250 People		Bicycle Trails	Noon to Closing
		Nature Walks	Sunday
Complete Handicap		*No Swimming*	Opening to 11:00 am
Facilities			

CONTRA LOMA RESERVOIR

Located in the rolling hills of eastern Contra Costa County, Contra Loma Reservoir has 80 surface acres within the 776-acre Contra Loma Regional Park. Hiking and equestrian trails run through the open grasslands of the Park into the adjoining Black Diamond Mines Regional Preserve. Large shaded lawns with picnic areas and playgrounds await the visitor. There is a sandy swim beach and a handicap accessible swim ramp. Contra Loma is very popular with windsurfers. Row boats and electric powered boats are also allowed. The angler will find catfish, bluegill and largemouth bass along with a good striped bass population. This facility is under the jurisdiction of the East Bay Regional Park District.

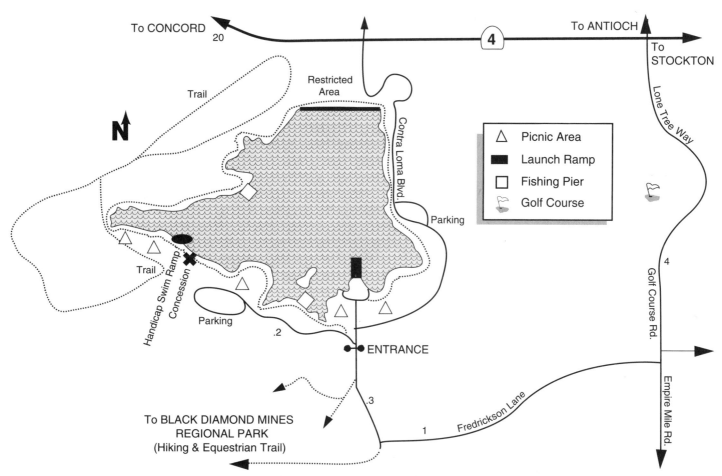

INFORMATION: East Bay Regional Parks, 2950 Peralta Oaks Ct., Oakland 94605—Ph: (510) 562-PARK

CAMPING	BOATING	RECREATION	OTHER

Day Use Only
  Fee: $4
  Dog: $1
 	
Group Picnic Reservations:
  Ph: (510) 636-1684
 	
Park Headquarters:
  Ph: (925) 757-0404
	Electric Motors, Row,
	  Sail & Windsurfing
	Boats up to 17 feet
	No Gas Motors
	Launch Ramp Fees:
	  Cartop: $2
	  Trailer: $3
	Rentals: Windsurfing,
	  Pedal Boats & Kayaks
		Fishing: Largemouth &
		  Striped Bass, Trout,
		  Bluegill & Sunfish
		Fishing Permit: $4 for
		  16 years and older
		Fishing Piers
		Picnic Area
		  Group Sites
		Hiking & Equestrian
		  Trails
		Swimming in
		  Lagoon - Fee
		Playground
			Snack Bar
			Bait & Tackle
			Golf Course Nearby

CHABOT, CULL CANYON, DON CASTRO and JORDAN POND

These four small Lakes are within the East Bay Regional Park District. The angler will find a warm water fishery at all of these facilities along with trout at Lake Chabot and Don Castro. Boating is limited to rentals at Lake Chabot. Each of these Regional Parks provides numerous attractions along with picnic facilities. Anthony Chabot Regional Park, 4,972 acres, offers camping at Lake Chabot and hiking, equestrian and bicycle trails. Facilities at Cull Canyon include a swim complex with a sandy beach. The angler will find bass and catfish. Don Castro has a swim lagoon, numerous picnic areas and large lawns. This Lake is regularly stocked with trout and catfish. Jordan Pond is within the scenic 2,685 acre Garin Regional Park and has an interpretive center with programs conducted by park naturalists.

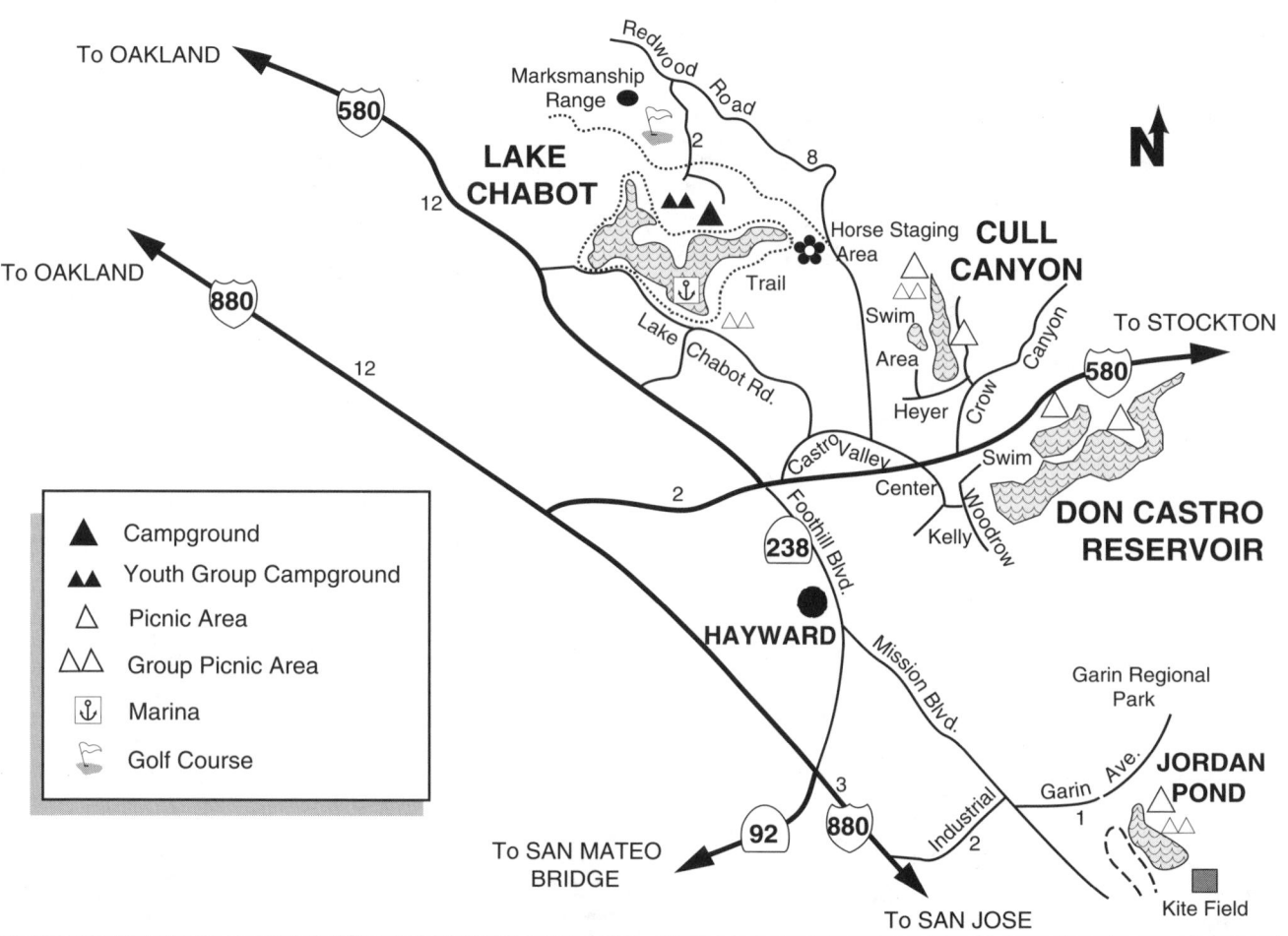

	Legend
▲	Campground
▲▲	Youth Group Campground
△	Picnic Area
△△	Group Picnic Area
⚓	Marina
⛳	Golf Course

INFORMATION: East Bay Regional Parks, 2950 Peralta Oaks Ct., Oakland 94605—Ph: (510) 562-PARK

CAMPING	BOATING	RECREATION	OTHER
Lake Chabot: 　75 Tent & R.V. Sites 　　Walk-In Sites 　Youth Group Camp 　Reservations: 　　Ph: (510) 562-2267 　Day Use Fee: $4 Don Castro: Day Use Only 　Parking: $4 　Dog: $1 Cull Canyon: Day Use Only 　No Fees	Lake Chabot: 　Rentals Only: Electric, 　　Row, Paddle & 　　Canoe 　"Chabot Queen" 　　Seasonal Boat Tour No Boating at Other Lakes	Fishing: Trout, Black Bass, 　Bluegill, Catfish & Crappie Fishing Fees: $3 - $4 Hiking & 　Equestrian Trails Swim Lagoons: 　Don Castro 　& Cull Canyon Nature Study & 　Interpretive Center Group Picnic Reservations: 　Ph: (510) 562-2267 Playgrounds	Lake Chabot: 　Coffee Shop 　Golf Course 　Equestrian Center 　Chabot Gun Club & 　Marksmanship Range 　　Open to the Public 　　Wed. - Sun. 　Horse Rentals 　　Off Skyline Blvd. 　　Ph: (510) 569-4428

BETHANY and SHADOW CLIFFS RESERVOIRS, QUARRY LAKES and LAKE ELIZABETH

Within the greater Bay Area, these day-use Lakes provide numerous recreational opportunities. Bethany Reservoir is a State Recreation Area and is open to boating with a 5 mph speed limit. Shadow Cliffs Reservoir offers various activities within the 296-acre park including a swim beach for families with children. Quarry Lakes includes Horseshoe and Rainbow Lakes. This is the Bay Area's newest facility within the East Bay Regional Park District. Lake Elizabeth is popular with boaters and anglers. The large park offers numerous activities including various sports fields. *See following page for detailed information.*

....Continued....

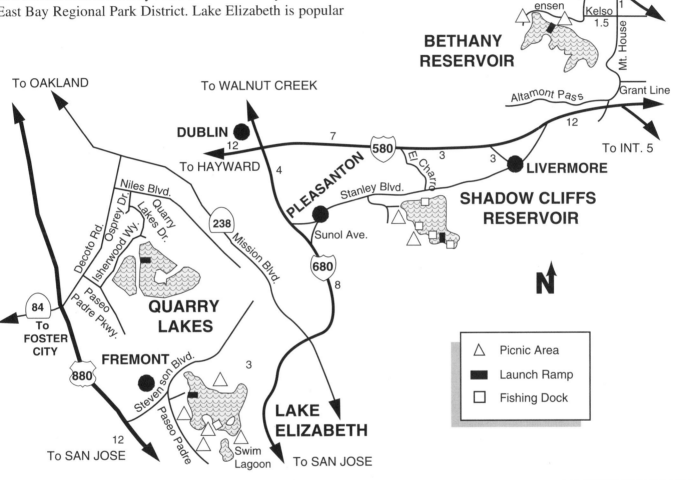

| | Picnic Area |
| Launch Ramp |
| Fishing Dock |

INFORMATION: See Following Page for Individual Lake Information			
CAMPING	**BOATING**	**RECREATION**	**OTHER**
Day Use Only	Varies at Each Lake *See Following Page*	Fishing: Trout, Largemouth & Striped Bass, Catfish, Bluegill & Crappie Picnicking Hiking Trails Bicycle Trails Swimming Beaches & Lagoons Playgrounds	Athletic Fields Waterslide Concessions at Shadow Cliffs & Lake Elizabeth Full Facilities Near Each Lake

124a

BETHANY and SHADOW CLIFFS RESERVOIRS, QUARRY LAKES, LAKE ELIZABETH...Cont.

BETHANY RESERVOIR
State Recreation Area
Mailing Address:
22600 Lake Rd.
La Grange 95329
Ph: (209) 874-2056
Day Use Only

Bethany Reservoir State Recreation Area rests in gently rolling, grass-covered hills overlooking the vast Delta of the Sacramento and San Joaquin Rivers. This 58 surface acre Reservoir is open to boating with a 5 MPH speed limit. Windsurfing is very popular. Strong winds can be a hazard at times. This is a good warm water fishery for striped bass and catfish. Bethany is the northern terminus for the California Aqueduct Bikeway.

SHADOW CLIFFS RESERVOIR
East Bay Regional Park District
2950 Peralta Oaks Ct., Oakland 94605
Ph: (510) 635-0135 - Parking Fee
Marina Ph: (510) 562-PARK
Group Picnic Reservations: (510) 636-1684

This facility has been transformed from a sand and gravel quarry to a complete 296-acre park with a 74 surface-acre Lake. Visitor's boats are limited to a maximum of 17 feet and only electric motors are permitted. Fishing and electric motorboats and pedal boats can be rented. There are also windsurfer rentals and lessons. The angler can fish for trout, black bass, channel and white catfish and bluegill. There is a sandy swim beach with a bathhouse and snack bar. A four-flume waterslide is in a separate area of the park. Picnic aites, lawn areas, hiking and equestrian trails and a food concession, along with handicap facilities, are available.

QUARRY LAKES
East Bay Regional Park District
2250 Isherwood Way
Fremont 94535
Ph: (510) 562-PARK
Reservations Ph: (510) 562-2267
Park Headquarters Ph: (510) 795-4883
Day Use and Lake Use Fees.

Horseshoe and Rainbow Lakes along with nearby surrounding ponds and lagoons cover about 350 surface acres in this 458 acre park. The Lake's water is eventually used for drinking so gasoline-powered engines are not allowed. This facility offers close, easy access for swimming and fishing. Fees are collected for parking, dogs, fishing, swimming and boat launching. The park was opened to the public for the first full year in 2002. Vending machines offer everything from bait and tackle to snacks and drinks. Change rooms, showers, biking and equestrian trails, group picnic sites with BBQs, two sand-filled volleyball courts and a large white sandy beach make this park a great family facility. For the angler, Horseshoe Lake includes a launch ramp, handicap fishing area and a fish cleaning station. Planted trout and catfish inhabit the Lake. Also the East Bay Regional Park District promotes the reproduction and growth of largemouth and smallmouth bass, bluegill, sunfish and crappie. No lead fishing weights are allowed.

LAKE ELIZABETH
Central Park
Visitor Services Center
40000 Paseo Padre Parkway
Fremont 94538
Ph: (510) 791-4340
Sports Fields Information Ph: (510) 791-4372
Day Use and Lake Use Fees.

This Lake, 80 surface acres, is within Fremont Central Park. There are complete facilities for non-powered boating including ramps, docks, storage and rental canoe and paddle boats. This is a good sailing lake with westerly winds which can become strong in the afternoons. The Lake contains populations of black bass, bluegill and catfish. The well-maintained park of nearly 500 acres has several recreational facilities with open lawn areas, snack bars, picnic areas, tennis courts, athletic fields, a golf driving range, volleyball courts and a swim lagoon. There are dozens of picnic tables and four group picnic sites which can accommodate between 125 and 350 people each. The 1.96 mile path around the Lake accommodates joggers, hikers and bicyclists at this complete city facility.

RECREATION LAKES OF CALIFORNIA
BEST LIVE BAIT
"IT'S WHERE THE ACTION IS"

DEL VALLE RESERVOIR

Del Valle Reservoir, at an elevation of 700 feet, is located in oak-covered, rolling hills near Livermore. The Lake has a surface area of 750 acres with 16 miles of shoreline. Del Valle Park, 3,997 acres, is under the jurisdiction of the East Bay Regional Park District. In addition to the large tree-shaded campgrounds, there are group campsites, picnic areas, equestrian staging and marina facilities. Miles of scenic trails are available for the hiker or equestrian. Boating is limited to 10 miles per hour. This is a very popular windsurfing Lake. Westerly winds can be strong in the afternoon.

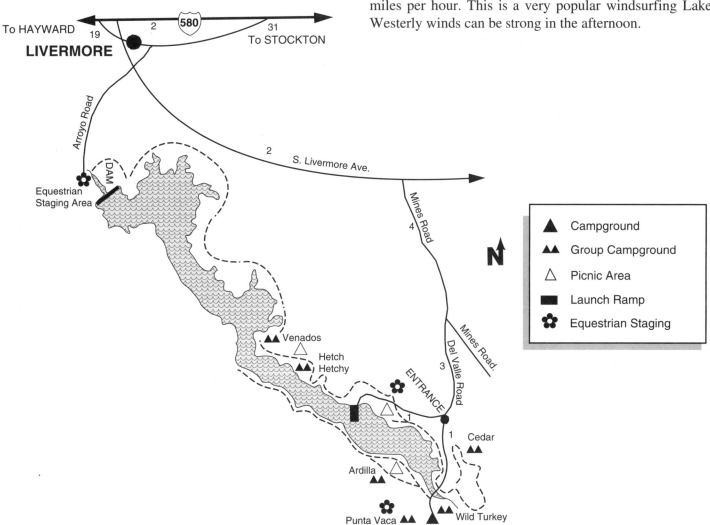

	Legend
▲	Campground
▲▲	Group Campground
△	Picnic Area
■	Launch Ramp
✿	Equestrian Staging

INFORMATION: Del Valle Park, 7000 Del Valle Rd., Livermore 94550—Ph: (925) 373-0332

CAMPING	BOATING	RECREATION	OTHER
150 Dev. Sites for Tents & R.V.s 21 with Water & Sewer Hookups No Electric Hookups Fee: $18 Disposal Station Youth Group Campgrounds Reservations: Ph: (510) 636-1684 Day Use Fee:$6 Dogs: $1	Power, Row, Canoe, Sail, Windsurf & Inflatables Speed Limit - 10 MPH Launch Ramp Rentals: Fishing Boats with Motors, Row, Paddle, Canoe & Patio Boats	Fishing: Trout, Catfish, Bluegill, Large & Smallmouth Bass, Striped Bass Swimming - 2 Beaches Picnicking Group Sites Hiking Trails Bicycle & Equestrian Trails Summer Weekends Only: Campfire Program Boat Tour of Lake	Snack Bar Bait & Tackle Campground Store Visitor Center Group Picnic Reservations Ph: (510) 636-1684 Full Facilities in Livermore

LOS VAQUEROS RESERVOIR

With 1,500 surface acres, Los Vaqueros Reservoir is one of California's newest prime fisheries. The Department of Fish and Game, Contra Costa County and the concessionaire plant rainbow trout. Bass and Kokanee are also established. Due to the tremendous amount of feed in the Lake, expect to catch some good- sized fish. Body contact with the water is not allowed because this is a watershed for drinking water. Over 55 miles of open trails are available for hikers including 13 miles of bicycle and equestrian trails. Oak trees and brush are scattered throughout the rolling pastures surrounding the Reservoir. This well-maintained facility includes a marina, rental boats and a fish cleaning station.

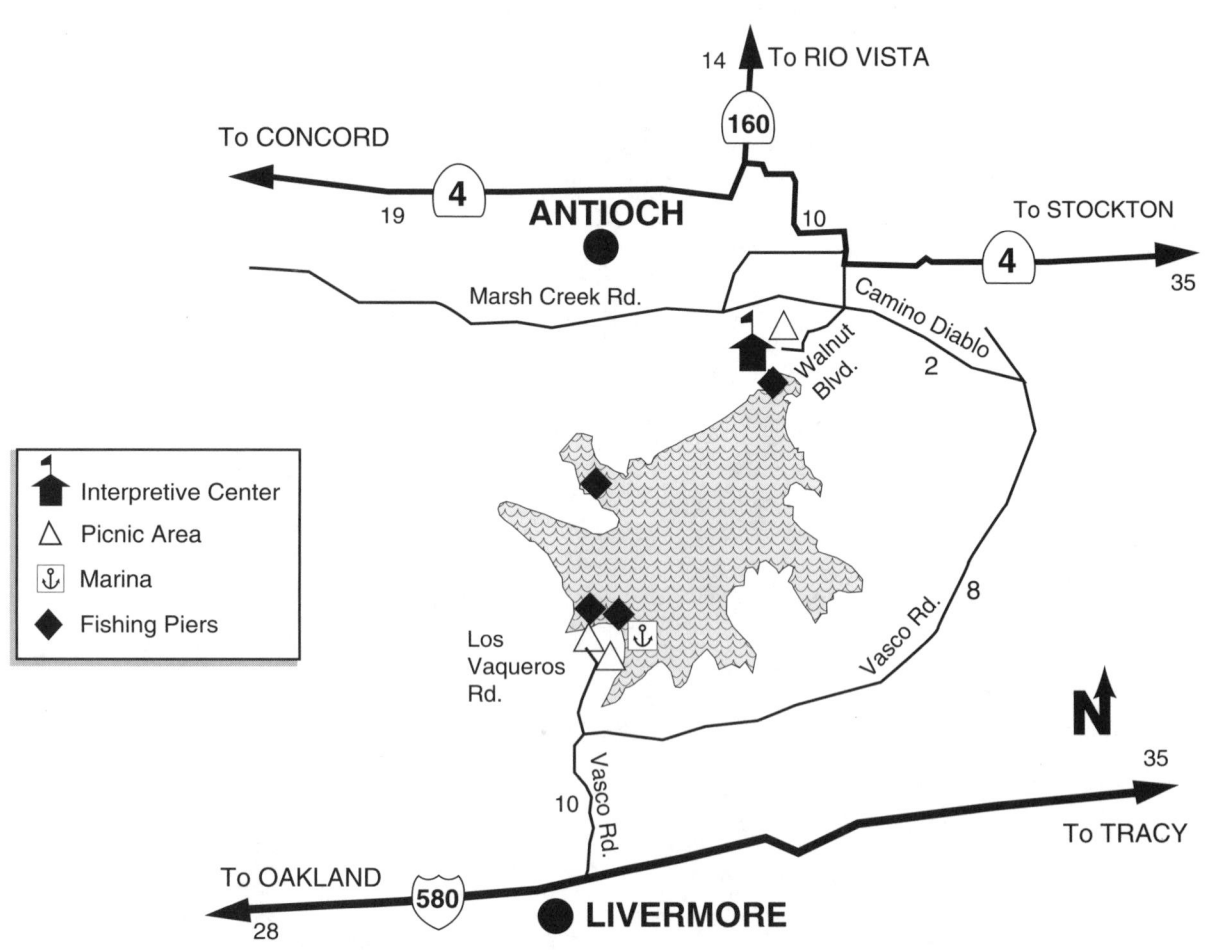

Interpretive Center
Picnic Area
Marina
Fishing Piers

INFORMATION: Contra Costa Water District, 1331 Concord Ave., Concord 94524—Ph: (925) 688-8000

CAMPING	BOATING	RECREATION	OTHER

No Camping
Day Use Only
 	
Parking Fee: $6
Annual Pass: $85
 	
No Pets Allowed
	Rental Boats:
	  Fishing Boats
	    with Electric Motors
	  Pontoon Boat
	Marina Ph: (925) 371-2628
	
	No Private Boats Allowed
		Fishing: Rainbow Trout,
		  Largemouth Black &
		  Striped Bass, Kokanee,
		  Channel Catfish,
		  Perch & Sunfish
		Fishing Permit: $3
		Fishing Piers
		  One for Handicapped
		Hiking, Bicycling &
		  Equestrian Trails
		Covered Picnic Tables
			Loacted at North End:
			  Interpretive Center
			
			Located at South End:
			  Fish Cleaning Station
			  Bait & Tackle
			  Snack Bar
			
			Bird Watchers - Look for
			  Bald Eagles & Hawks
			
			Group Picnic Reservations:
			  Ph: (925) 426-3060

SHORELINE PARK, LAKE MERCED and STEVENS CREEK RESERVOIR

These three urban Lakes provide a variety of recreational opportunities. Shoreline Lake offers the windsurfer and sailor a 50-acre expanse of saltwater along with protected wildlife areas reached by paved trails. This is a popular windsurfing Lake with prevailing northwesterly winds. Lake Merced, adjacent to San Francisco, is actually two small lakes. Water levels have become low in recent years so call for current information. Restoration is expected in the future. Stevens Creek Reservoir with 91 surface acres when full, provides the angler with a warm water fishery. There are oak-shaded trails for the hiker and equestrian. Mountain bikers can use the multiple trail system which allows access to adjacent park lands. Family and group picnic sites are available.

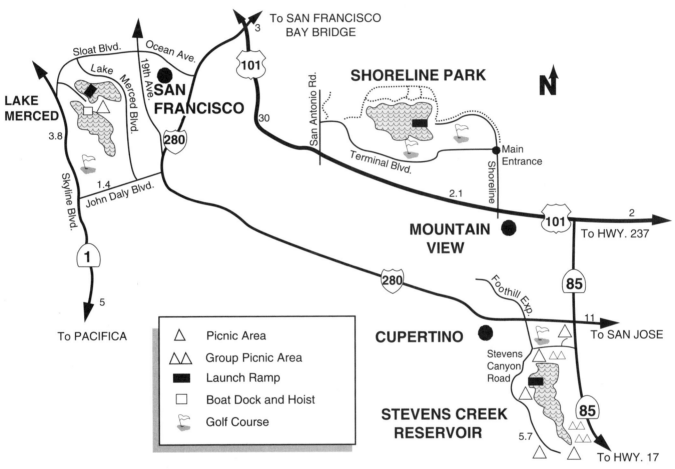

INFORMATION: Shoreline Aquatic Center, 3160 N. Shoreline Blvd., Mountain View 94043—Ph: (650) 965-7474

CAMPING	BOATING	RECREATION	OTHER
Day Use Only - Fees No Camping	Shoreline Park: Windsurf, Sail Boats Canoes, Kayaks Rentals, Lessons, Sales Launch Ramp: $4-$5	Fishing: Rainbow & Brook Trout, Bass, Bluegill, Catfish & Crappie	Shoreline Park: Showers Store Lakeside Cafe Ph: (650) 965-1745
Stevens Creek Park: Group Picnic Area Reservations: Ph: (408) 355-2201	Stevens Creek: No Power Boats Allowed Launch Ramp - Fee	Picnicking No Swimming Allowed at Stevens Creek or Lake Merced	Lake Merced: San Francisco Parks Ph: (415) 831-2773 Call for current info. on water level and conditions
	Lake Merced: Small Sail & Rowboats to 18 Feet Rentals: Row Boats	Hiking, Bicycle & Equestrian Trails Nature Study Birdwatching Golf Courses	

VASONA, LEXINGTON and LOS GATOS CREEK PARK

Located off Highway 17, these three Lakes are in the southwest corner of Santa Clara County and are under the jurisdiction of the Parks and Recreation Department. Lexington, the largest of the three, is popular with sailors, rowers, windsurfers and anglers. Electric trolling motors only are allowed. Vasona is a 57-acre Lake surrounded by 94 acres of lawn areas, picnic sites, playgrounds and paved paths. This family park offers good sailing and support facilities. Los Gatos Creek Park permits fishing and non-power boating in the northermost pond. Remote control model boating is allowed in the middle pond. There is also a flycasting pond for practice only (no hooks). It is equipped with circular targets. Picnic facilities are available as well as walking and bicycle paths.

INFORMATION: Santa Clara County Parks & Rec., 298 Garden Hill Dr., Los Gatos 95032—Ph: (408) 355-2200

CAMPING	BOATING	RECREATION	OTHER
Day Use Only *No Camping* Vasona & Los Gatos Creek Park: Entrance Fee: $4 per Vehicle Reservations for Group Picnics or Special Events Ph: (408) 355-2201	Lexington: Sail, Canoe, Row, Windsurfer, Paddleboats Electric Motors Only Launch Ramp - $3 *Check for Current Water* *Level Conditions* Vasona: Same as Lexington *except No Motors* Launch Ramp - $3 Docks, Dry Storage Rental Boats	Fishing: Trout, Bass, Bluegill, Catfish & Crappie Picnicking Group Sites Hiking & Bicycle Trails Playground at Vasona Oak Meadow Park: Ph: (408) 354-6809 (Next to Vasona) Billy Jones Wildcat Railroad & Carousel	Los Gatos Creek Park: North Pond: Non-Power Boating Model Boat Area Fly Casting Pond Trail - 14 Miles Leading to Lexington Reservoir for Hiking & Bicycling Pets on Leash Allowed Full Facilities in Los Gatos & San Jose

ALMADEN LAKE, CALERO, CHESBRO and UVAS RESERVOIRS

Almaden Lake Regional Park is administered by the City of San Jose and includes a 36 surface acre Lake for sailing and fishing along with a swim beach, lagoon and picnic sites. Guadalupe and Almaden Reservoirs are 60 surface acres each. They are under the jurisdiction of Santa Clara County and are adjacent to Almaden Quicksilver Park. This is a popular hiking and equestrian facility. Chesbro and Uvas, under the jurisdiction of Santa Clara Parks and Recreation Department, are primarily small fishing Lakes with picnic sites. Calero Reservoir, 349 surface acres, is a popular power boating and waterskiing Lake with a sandy beach and picnic facilities. At low water levels, from approximately October through January, the ramp may be closed.

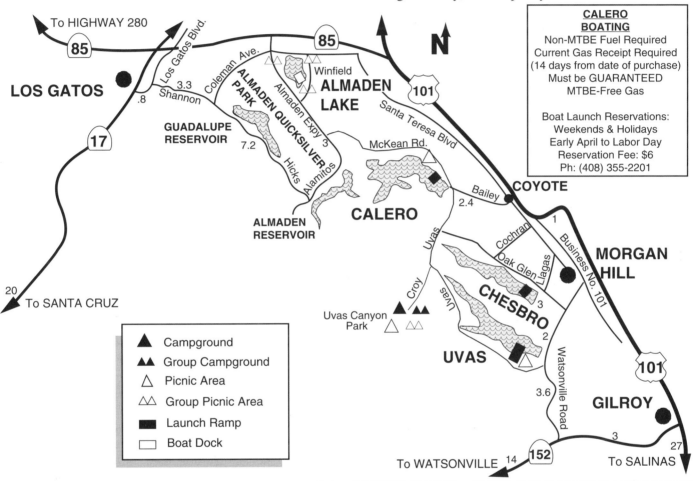

CALERO BOATING
Non-MTBE Fuel Required
Current Gas Receipt Required
(14 days from date of purchase)
Must be GUARANTEED
MTBE-Free Gas

Boat Launch Reservations:
Weekends & Holidays
Early April to Labor Day
Reservation Fee: $6
Ph: (408) 355-2201

Legend:
▲ Campground
▲▲ Group Campground
△ Picnic Area
△△ Group Picnic Area
■ Launch Ramp
☐ Boat Dock

INFORMATION: Santa Clara County Parks & Rec., 298 Garden Hill Dr., Los Gatos 95032—Ph: (408) 355-2200

CAMPING	BOATING	RECREATION	OTHER

Uvas Canyon Park:
  Youth Group Camp
  to 40 People Max. $30
  Plus 25 Campsites
  by Reservation
Fee for Reservations: $6
Ph: (408) 355-2201
No Camping at Other
  Lakes & Reservoirs
 	
Calero:
  Entrance Fee: $4
  Lake Use Fee: $5
	Almaden Lake: Sail & Row
	Boats up to 16 ft.,Windsurfing
	  No Power Boats
	  Launch Ramp - Fee: $2
	  Rentals: Windsurf &
	    Paddleboats
	Chesbro & Uvas: Sail,
	  Row & Electric Motors
	  Lake Use Fee: $3
	Calero: Power & Sailboats,
	  Waterskiing-Launch Ramp
	Guadalupe & Almaden
	  No Boating Allowed
		Fishing: Bass, Catfish,
		  Bluegill, Crappie, Carp
		Warning: Mercury
		  Contaminated Fish at
		  Calero, Guadalupe &
		  Almaden Reservoirs
		  Do Not Eat Fish
		  Catch & Release Only
		Swimming - Beach:
		  Almaden Lake Only
		Picnicking
		Group Picnic Sites
			Almaden Lake:
			  City of San Jose
			  408 S. Almaden Ave.
			  San Jose 95110
			  Ph: (408) 277-5130
			
			Almaden Quicksilver Park:
			  3,977 Acres
			  29 Miles Hiking Trails
			  23 Miles Equestrian Trails
			  10 Miles Bicycle Trails
			  Pets on Leash Allowed
			  Spring Wildflowers Display

The County of Santa Clara operates the Ed R. Levin ,Coyote-Hellyer and Joseph D. Grant Parks. Cottonwood Lake is located in the Coyote-Hellyer Park which also has a velodrome. Coyote Creek Parkway includes an 8-foot wide, 15-mile long bicycle trail that runs from Coyote Hellyer Park in South San Jose to Anderson Lake Park in Morgan Hill. The rugged 9,497 acres of Joseph D. Grant Park offers hikers and equestrians a 40-mile trail system. Mountain bikes are allowed on nearly half of the Park's trails. Camping and picnic areas are included in this well-maintained, remote County Park. Lake Cunningham Regional Park is under the jurisdiction of the City of San Jose. This 200-acre Park includes numerous picnic sites, walking and jogging paths and a 50 surface acre Lake for boating and fishing. Raging Waters has a variety of waterslides, activity pools, swim lagoon with beach, river rides and many other activities.

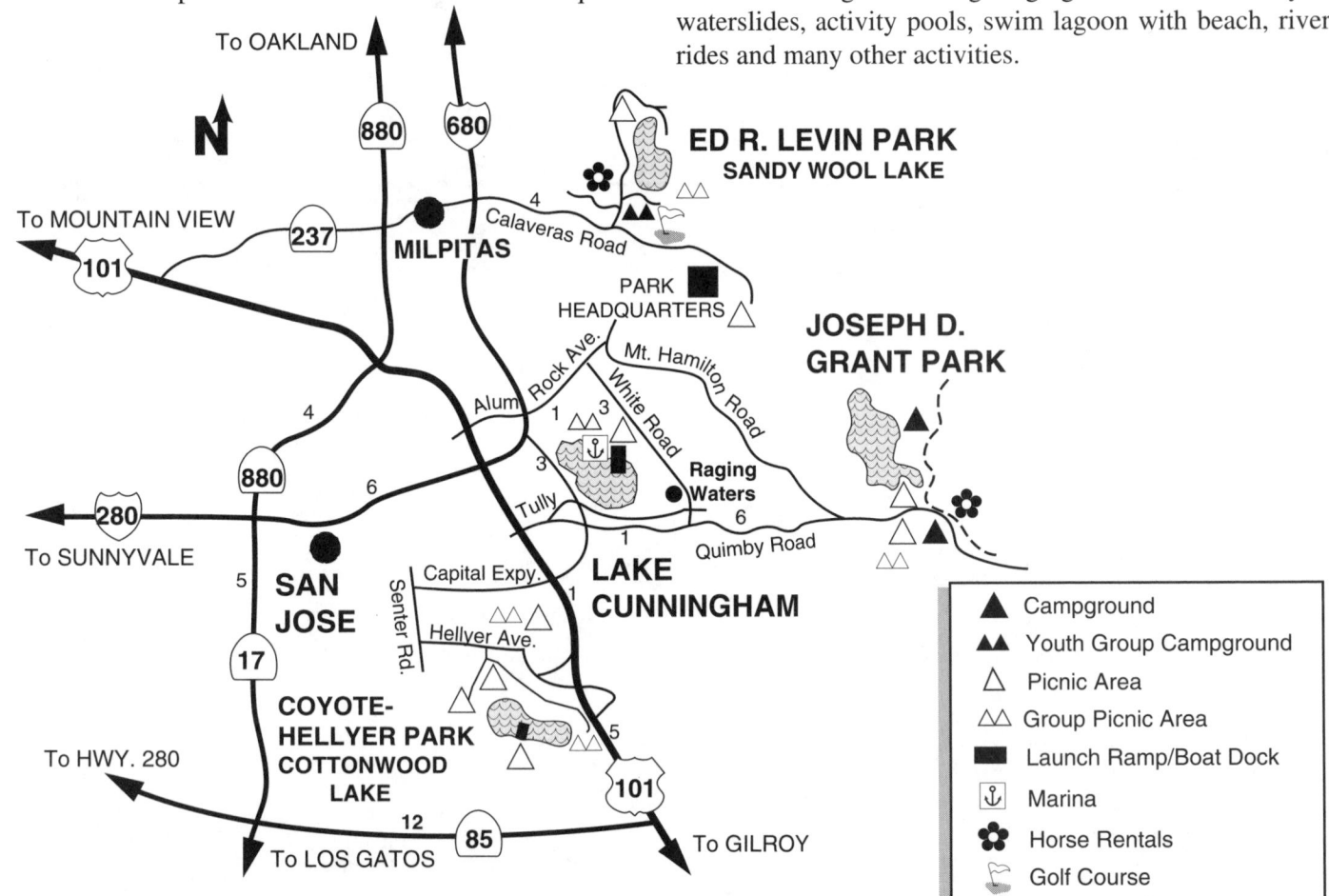

INFORMATION: Santa Clara County Parks, 298 Garden Hill Dr., San Jose 95032—Ph: (408) 355-2200

CAMPING	BOATING	RECREATION	OTHER
Youth Group Camping: Joseph D. Grant Park: Groups to 200+ Max. $30 Ed R. Levin: Groups to 200 Max. $30 Above Youth Group Sites Fee for Reservations-$6 Ph: (408) 355-2201 Joseph D. Grant Park: 22 Family Campsites Info Ph: (408) 274-6121 Coyote-Hellyer & Lake Cunningham: Day Use Only	Ed R. Levin & Cottonwood: Row & Sail Boats, Electric Motors Only Lake Cunningham: Row & Sail Boats, Electric Motors Only Launch Ramp: $2 Marina Rentals: Rowboats, Sailboats & Pedal Boats Boat Dock *Joseph D. Grant: No Boating Allowed*	Fishing: Catfish, Trout Picnicking - Group Sites Walking & Jogging Paths Hiking & Equestrian Trails Mountain Biking Trails Bicycling - Velodrome at Coyote-Hellyer Hang Gliding Golf Course & Horse Rentals Near Ed R. Levin Park Raging Waters Theme Park	Lake Cunningham 2305 S. White Rd. San Jose 95148 Ph: (408) 277-4319

Raging Waters: 2333 S. White Rd. San Jose 95148 Ph: (408) 238-9900 |

The largest body of fresh water in Santa Clara County, Anderson Lake is 7 miles long with a surface area of 1,245 acres. This is a popular boating and waterskiing facility and afternoon winds make for good sailing and windsurfing. There is a launch ramp and the angler will find a warm water fishery. The County of Santa Clara has picnic sites near the dam as well as a boat-in picnic area on the northwestern shore.

Anderson Park, a total of 2,149 acres, includes a multiple use 15-mile trail which follows Coyote Creek north to Coyote Hellyer County Park. An equestrian staging area leads to an 8-mile horseback riding trail. Parkway is a 35-acre privately operated fishing Lake. Planted year around with large trout, channel catfish and sturgeon, the Lake usually rewards the angler with a good catch.

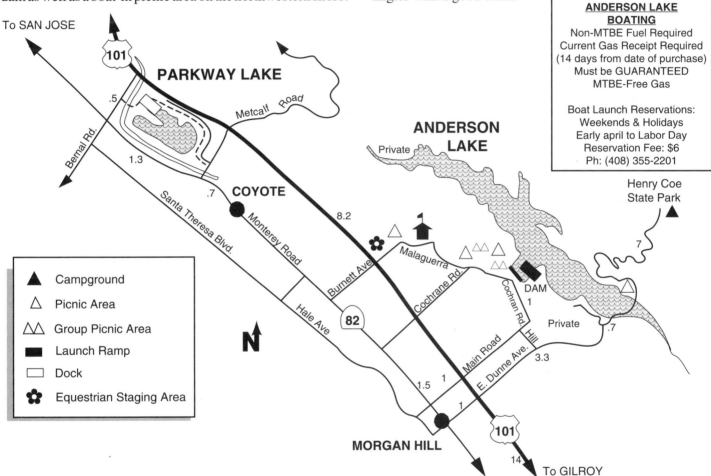

ANDERSON LAKE BOATING
Non-MTBE Fuel Required
Current Gas Receipt Required
(14 days from date of purchase)
Must be GUARANTEED
MTBE-Free Gas

Boat Launch Reservations:
Weekends & Holidays
Early april to Labor Day
Reservation Fee: $6
Ph: (408) 355-2201

Legend:
▲ Campground
△ Picnic Area
△△ Group Picnic Area
■ Launch Ramp
☐ Dock
✿ Equestrian Staging Area

INFORMATION: Santa Clara County Parks & Rec., 298 Garden Hill Dr., Los Gatos 95032—Ph: (408) 355-2200

CAMPING	BOATING	RECREATION	OTHER

Day Use Only
 	
Anderson Lake :
  Entrance Fee: $4
  Group Picnic Areas
  For Reservations:
  Ph: (408) 355-2201
 	
Nearby:
Henry Coe State Park:
  20 Tent & R.V. Sites
  Fee: $7
  Ph: (408) 779-2728
	Anderson: Open to All
	  Boating & Waterskiing
	  except *No PWCs*
	  35 MPH Speed Limit
	  Launch Ramp, Dock
	  Boat Use Fee: $5
	  Check for Current
	  Water Level Conditions
	Parkway:
	  No Private Boats
	  Rentals: Fishing Boats
	    with Trolling Motors
		Fishing: Rainbow
		  Trout, Largemouth
		  Bass, Catfish,
		  Crappie & Bluegill Plus
		  Sturgeon in Parkway
		Picnicking
		  Group Sites at Anderson
		Hiking, Skating, Bicycle &
		  Equestrian Trails
		Parkway Lake Fishing Fee:
		  $15 - Adults
		  $13 - Children to 12 yrs.
		  $ 3 - Spectator
			Parkway Lake:
			  Metcalf Road
			  Coyote 95013
			  Ph: (408) 629-9111
			  Bait & Tackle
			  Snacks
			  No Pets Allowed

LOCH LOMOND

Loch Lomond is located at an elevation of 577 feet in the Santa Cruz Mountains. This scenic 3-1/2 mile long Reservoir is under the jurisdiction of the City of Santa Cruz and is open to boats with electric motors only. Although there is a launch ramp, water level fluctuation can limit its use, so call for current status. Fishing is a prime attraction and often produc-

tive. As a watershed for Santa Cruz drinking water, an aeration system enhances the fishery. There are over 100 picnic sites around the shoreline. Several hiking trails extend along the water and into a forest of oak, madrone, pine and redwood trees. In addition to naturalist programs, there is a self-guided Big Trees Nature Trail.

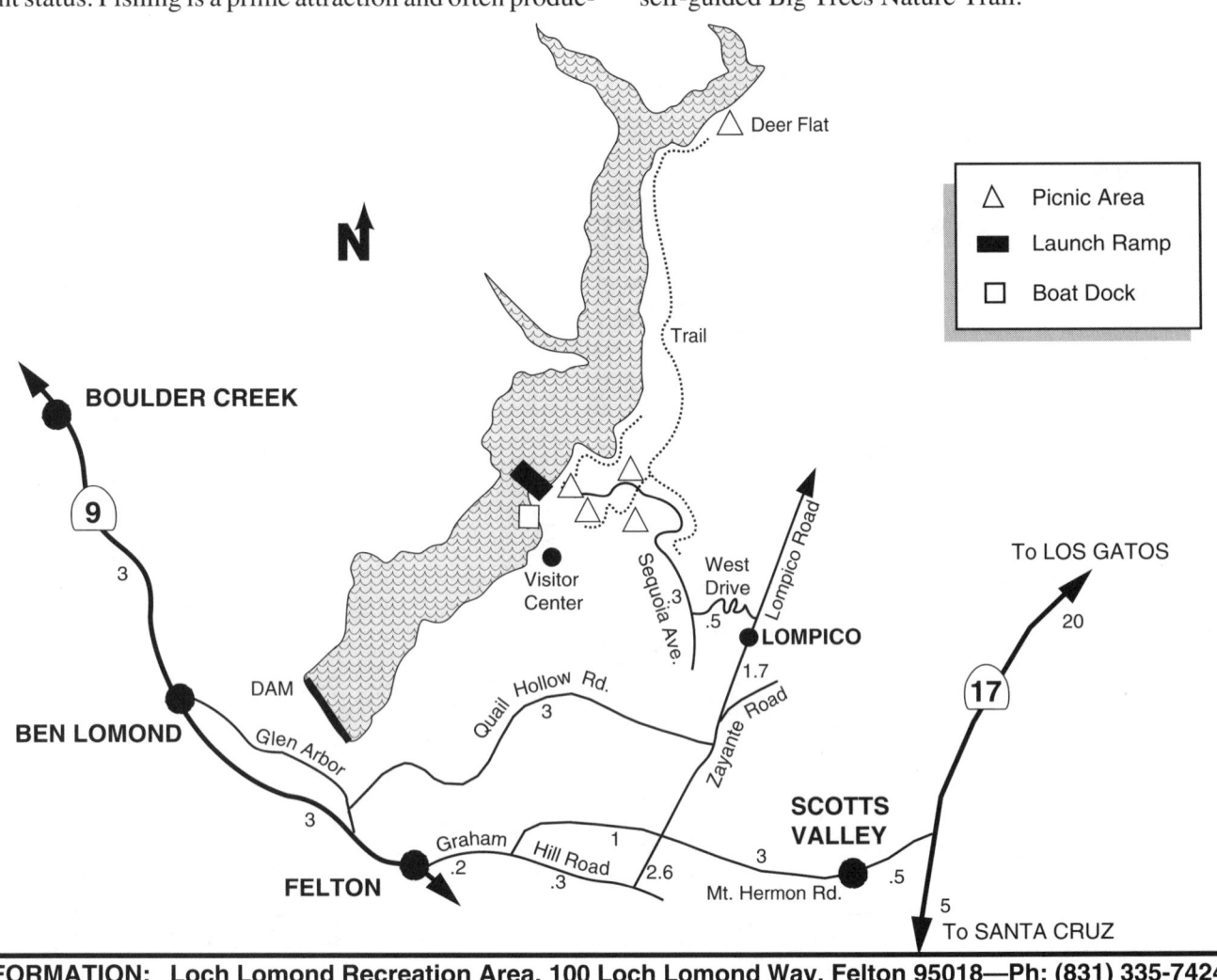

INFORMATION: Loch Lomond Recreation Area, 100 Loch Lomond Way, Felton 95018—Ph: (831) 335-7424

CAMPING	BOATING	RECREATION	OTHER

Day Use Only
   Fee: $4
 	
Open March 1 Through
   September 15
   6:00 a.m. to Sunset
	Row Boats
	   Electric Motors Only
	Rentals: Row &
	   Paddle Boats
	*No Sailboats or
	   or Float Tubes*
	
	Launch Ramp Fees:
	   Cartop: $2
	   On Trailer: $5
	Water Levels Fluctuate
		Fishing: Rainbow Trout,
		   Largemouth Bass,
		   Bluegill, Redear &
		   Green Sunfish,
		   Channel Catfish
		Fishing License
		   Required
		Picnicking
		Hiking & Nature Trails
		
		*No Swimming or Body
		   Contact with Water*
			Bait & Tackle
			Snack Shop

Under the jurisdiction of the City of Watsonville, Pinto Lake Park is privately leased and managed. This facility provides the visitor with R.V. sites, a picnic area, a group picnic site, large lawn areas and a baseball field. The 92 surface-acre Lake is popular with sailors and windsurfers who enjoy incoming Pacific breezes. There is a warm water fishery along with planted trout. Santa Cruz County maintains a 180-acre wildlife refuge along with a park on the north end of the Lake with over 130 species of birds, nature trails and group picnic facilities. For picnic reservations at the County Park, Ph: (831) 462-8333 between Noon and 4:00 pm.

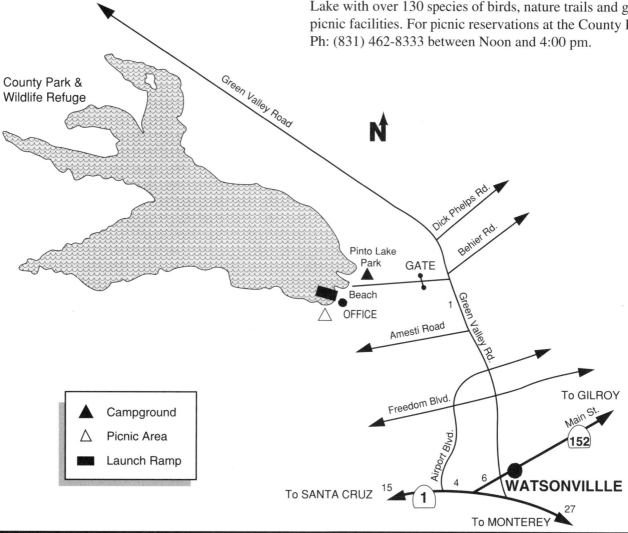

County Park & Wildlife Refuge

Green Valley Road

N

Dick Phelps Rd.

Behler Rd.

Pinto Lake Park

GATE

1

Green Valley Rd.

Beach

OFFICE

Amesti Road

▲ Campground

△ Picnic Area

■ Launch Ramp

Freedom Blvd.

To GILROY

Main St.

152

Airport Blvd.

4

6

WATSONVILLLE

To SANTA CRUZ 15

1

To MONTEREY 27

INFORMATION: Pinto Lake R.V. Campground, 451 Green Valley Rd., Watsonville 95076—Ph: (831) 722-8129

CAMPING	BOATING	RECREATION	OTHER

Pinto Lake Park:
    28 R.V. Sites with
       Full Hookups
Fee: $26
	Power, Row, Canoe,
	    Sail, Windsurf
	Speed Limit: 5 MPH
	
	Rentals: Row &
	    Pedal Boats
		Fishing: Rainbow Trout,
		    Largemouth Bass,
		    Bluegill,Crappie &
		    Catfish
		Picnicking
		Group Picnic Site
		    Can be Reserved
		No Swimming Allowed
		
		Hiking & Nature Trails
		Bird Watching
			Snack Bar
			Bait & Tackle

133

COYOTE RESERVOIR

At an elevation of 777 feet, Coyote Reservoir is located in the scenic, oak-covered hills near Gilroy. Santa Clara County Parks and Recreation provides facilities for lakeside camping, picnicking, hiking, fishing and all types of boating. With 796 acres, the County Park is nestled in the Mount Hamilton Range. The Lake with 635-surface acres is open at the northwest end so the winds come down the length of the Lake allowing good sailing and windsurfing. The Reservoir is open year around from 8:00 a.m. to 1/2 hour before sunset for boaters and sunset for day users. Campers can fish from shore during the night but there is no night boating permitted.

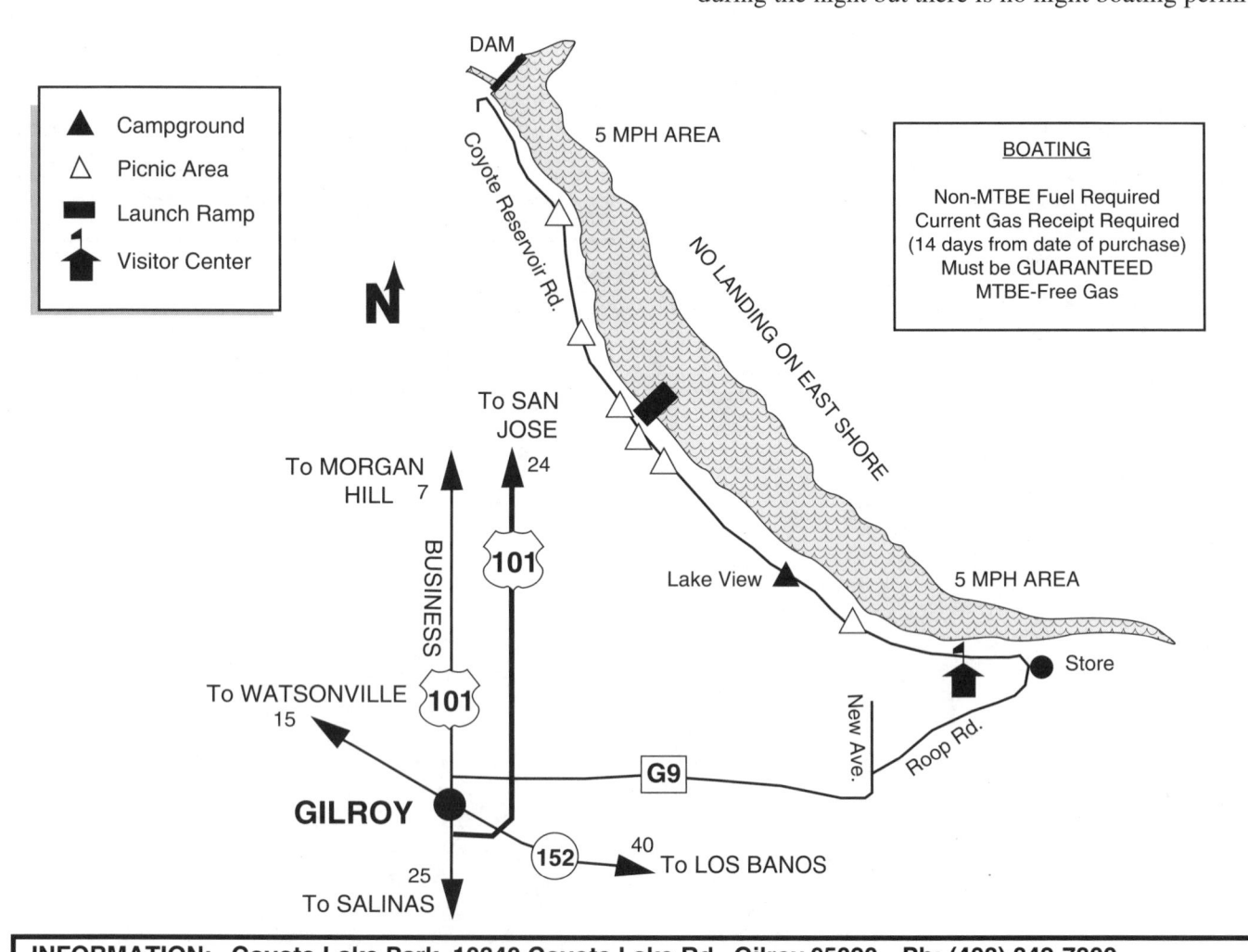

BOATING

Non-MTBE Fuel Required
Current Gas Receipt Required
(14 days from date of purchase)
Must be GUARANTEED
MTBE-Free Gas

INFORMATION: Coyote Lake Park, 10840 Coyote Lake Rd., Gilroy 95020—Ph: (408) 842-7800

CAMPING	BOATING	RECREATION	OTHER
64 Dev. Sites for Tents & R.V.s No Hookups Fees: $15 Reservations: Ph: (408) 355-2201 Day Use Fee: $4 Dog: $1	Power, Row, Canoe, Sail, Waterski & PWC's Speed Limit - 35 MPH *Counter Clockwise Traffic Pattern* 5 MPH Environmental Areas Launch Ramp Fee: $3 to $10	Fishing: Trout, Bluegill, Crappie & Bass Picnicking Hiking Trails *No Swimming*	Santa Clara County Parks & Recreation 298 Garden Hill Dr. Los Gatos 95032 Ph: (408) 355-2200 Visitor Center Full Facilities at Gilroy

EL ESTERO, LAGUNA SECA, LOWER and UPPER ABBOTT LAKES

These three Recreation Parks in Monterey County range from a day-use City Park in Monterey to a Forest Service Campground at Arroyo Seco. The Laguna Seca Recreational Area includes a campground and a small 10 acre Lake (no fishing). Campsites overlook the famous race car track. El Estero is a scenic Lake in downtown Monterey with a children's play area, picnic facilities and athletic fields. The Abbott Lakes are in the Los Padres National Forest and include family and group campgrounds and a warm water fishery. Trout fishing and swimming are popular in the Arroyo Seco River.

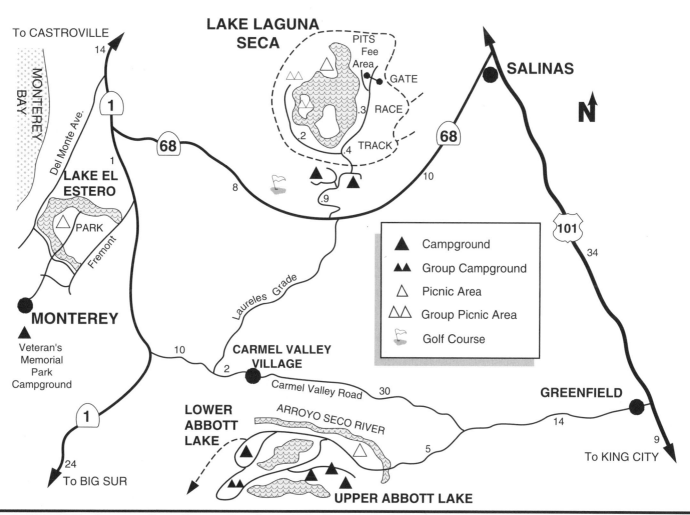

INFORMATION: Laguna Seca Recreation Area, P.O. Box 5279, Salinas 93915—Ph: (831) 755-4899

CAMPING	BOATING	RECREATION	OTHER
Laguna Seca: 　77 Tent & R.V. Sites: $18 　96 R.V. Sites - Electric & 　　Water Hookups: $22 　Reserve Ph:(831)755-4899 U.S.F.S. Arroyo Seco 　Abbott Lakes: 　46 Sites & Group Site 　King City Ranger Station 　Ph: (831) 385-5434 Veteran's Memorial Park: 　40 Sites - Tents & R.V.s 　Info Ph: (831) 646-3865	El Estero: 　Paddle Boat Rentals Abbott Lakes: 　Canoes Laguna Seco: 　No Boating	Fishing: Trout, 　Bass & Catfish *No Fishing at Laguna Seca* Picnicking - Group Sites Hiking & Bicycle Trails Playgrounds Laguna Seca: 　Race Track Events 　Rifle & Pistol Range 　Motorcross Track 　Festivals, Concerts 　Race School	El Estero Lake & Veterans Memorial Park: 　City of Monterey 　Recreation & Community 　Services Department 　546 Dutra St. 　Monterey 93940 　Ph: (831) 646-3860 Full Facilities & Golf 　Courses in Monterey Monterey Jazz Festival Salinas Rodeo

SAN JUSTO RESERVOIR

San Justo Reservoir, under the jurisdiction of San Benito County, rests in the low rolling hills west of Hollister. The Park has a 200 surface-acre Lake plus a total of 587 acres, including challenging trails for mountain bikers. Boating is restricted to non-powered craft except for those with electric motors. The prevailing winds make this a good Lake for sailing and windsurfing. The California Department of Fish and Game stock rainbow trout from January until late June. Black bass and catfish populations have also been established and are enhanced by anchored trees at the bottom of the Lake for fish habitat. Facilities include a launch ramp, sheltered picnic areas, a handicap-accessible floating fishing dock and a snack bar. The Lake is open to the public Wednesday through Sunday from sunrise to sunset except in winter when the Park can be closed.

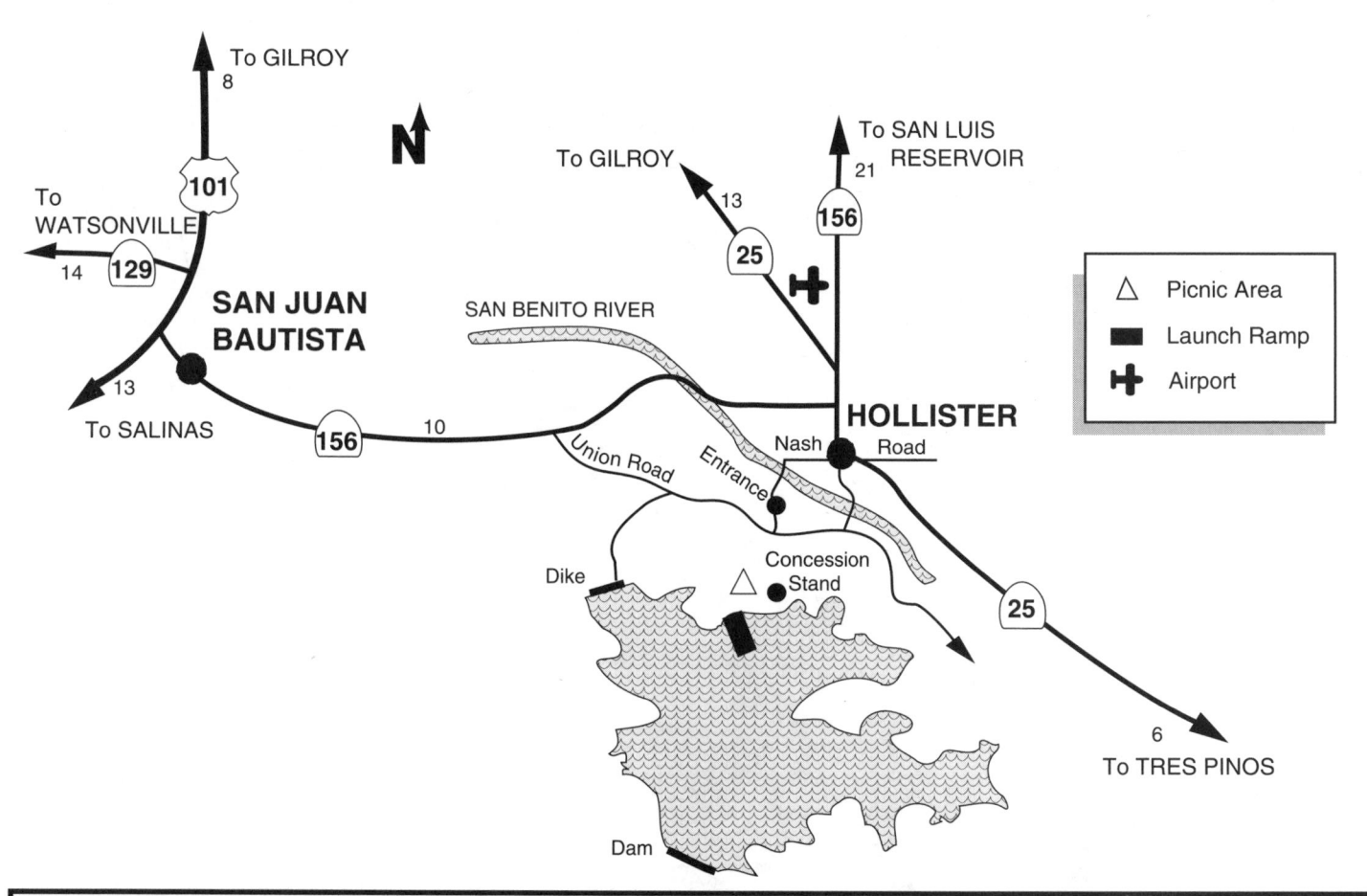

INFORMATION: San Justo Reservoir, 2265 Union Rd., Hollister 95023—Ph: (831) 638-3300

CAMPING	BOATING	RECREATION	OTHER
No Camping at Lake	Row, Sail & Windsurfing	Fishing: Rainbow Trout, Black Bass, Catfish, Blue Gill & Crappie	Bait & Tackle Snack Bar
Open for Day Use Wednesday - Sunday	Boats up to 18 feet Electric Motors Permitted Paved Launch Ramp	Fishing Derbies in Spring Picnicking	San Benito County Public Works
Entrance Fee: $5 Per Vehicle $2 for Walk-Ins & Bike-Ins	User Fees: $2 - Watercraft up to 13 Feet or Floating Device $3 - Watercraft over 13 Feet	Mountain Bike Trails *No Swimming*	3220 Southside Rd. Hollister 95023 Ph: (831) 636-4170
			Full Facilities in Hollister

SAN LUIS RESERVOIR and O'NEILL FOREBAY

San Luis Reservoir State Recreation Area is at an elevation of 544 feet in the eastern foothills of the Diablo Mountain Range west of Los Banos. This huge Reservoir has 13,800 surface acres and 65 miles of grassy shoreline. In addition to good fishing, San Luis Reservoir is popular for boating, swimming and windsurfing but sudden strong winds can be a hazard. Warning lights are located at the Romero Overlook, Basalt campground and Quien Sabe Point at the Reservoir as well as the Medeiros launch ramp and San Luis Creek area at the Forebay. The O'Neill Forebay has a surface area of 2,000 acres with 14 miles of brush-covered shoreline. The 67-mile San Joaquin Section of the California Aqueduct Bikeway ends at the Forebay. Boating and fishing are popular. Waterfowl hunting is allowed at these Lakes in season.

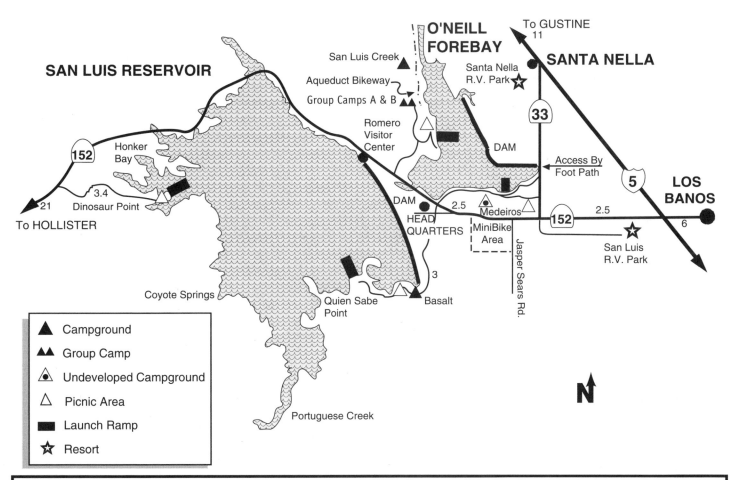

INFORMATION: San Luis Reservoir State Rec. Area, 31426 Gonzaga Rd., Gustine 95322—Ph: (209) 826-1196

CAMPING	BOATING	RECREATION	OTHER
Basalt: 79 Dev. Sites for Tents & R.V.s - $12 Disposal Station Reserve:Ph:(800) 444-7275 Medeiros: 350 Undev. Sites for Tents & R.V.s - $7 San Luis Creek: 53 Dev. Sites for Tents & R.V.s With Hookups - $14 Group Camps: A: 60 Pers. 15 Veh. $45 & B: 30 Pers. 10 Veh. $22.50 Day Use Only Fee: $2	Power, Row, Canoe, Sail, Waterski, Jets, Windsurf & Inflatable Launch Ramps *Beware of Sudden Winds* 24 Hour Weather Conditions Updated Every 20 Min. Ph: (800) 805-4805 *Water May Fluctuate up to 200 Feet Annually*	Fishing: Catfish, Bluegill, Crappie, Striped & Black Bass, Sturgeon, Shad Swimming - Beaches Picnicking Hunting: Waterfowl Only in Season 157 Acre Minibike Trail Area California Aqueduct Bikeway	Visitor's Center at Romero Overlook Santa Nella R.V. Park Full Hookups Ph: (209) 826-3105 San Luis R.V. Park Full Hookups Ph: (209) 826-5542 Full Facilities in Los Banos and Santa Nella

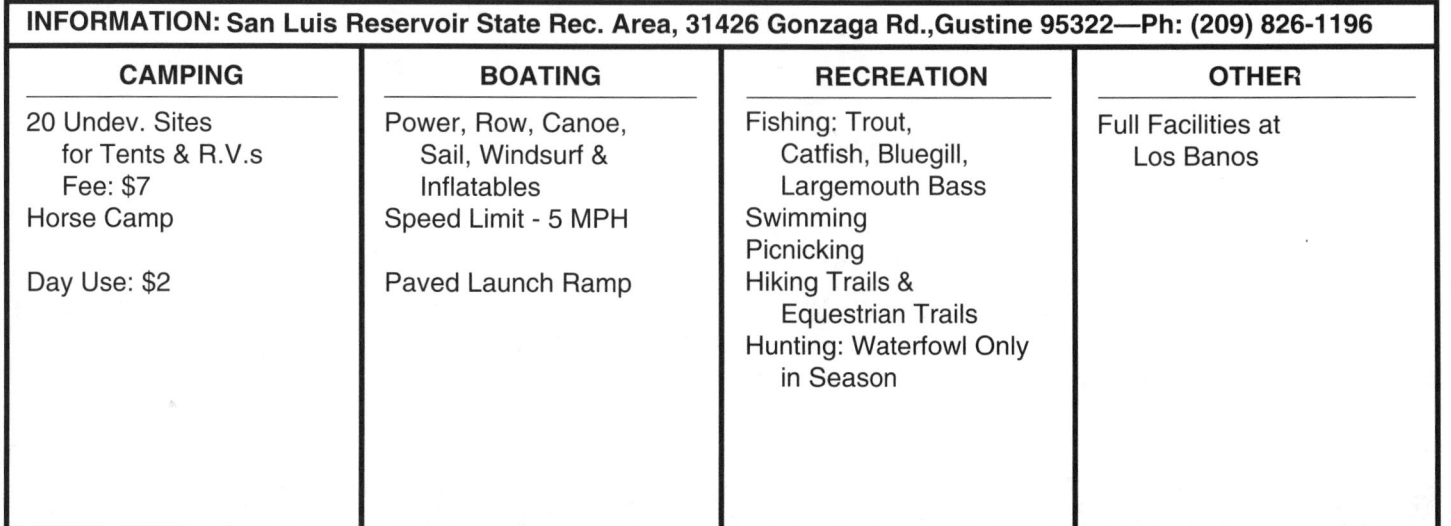

LOS BANOS RESERVOIR

At an elevation of 328 feet, Los Banos Reservoir is located in the hilly grasslands west of Los Banos. This Lake has 620 surface acres and 12 miles of shoreline. Los Banos is under the jurisdiction of the California State Parks system. There is a small undeveloped campground along with a horse camp and a paved launch ramp. There are several trees around the campgrounds along with shade ramadas. This facility is primarily used as a warm water fishery. Swimming is popular along with hunting for waterfowl in season. There are usually good winds for sailing and windsurfing.

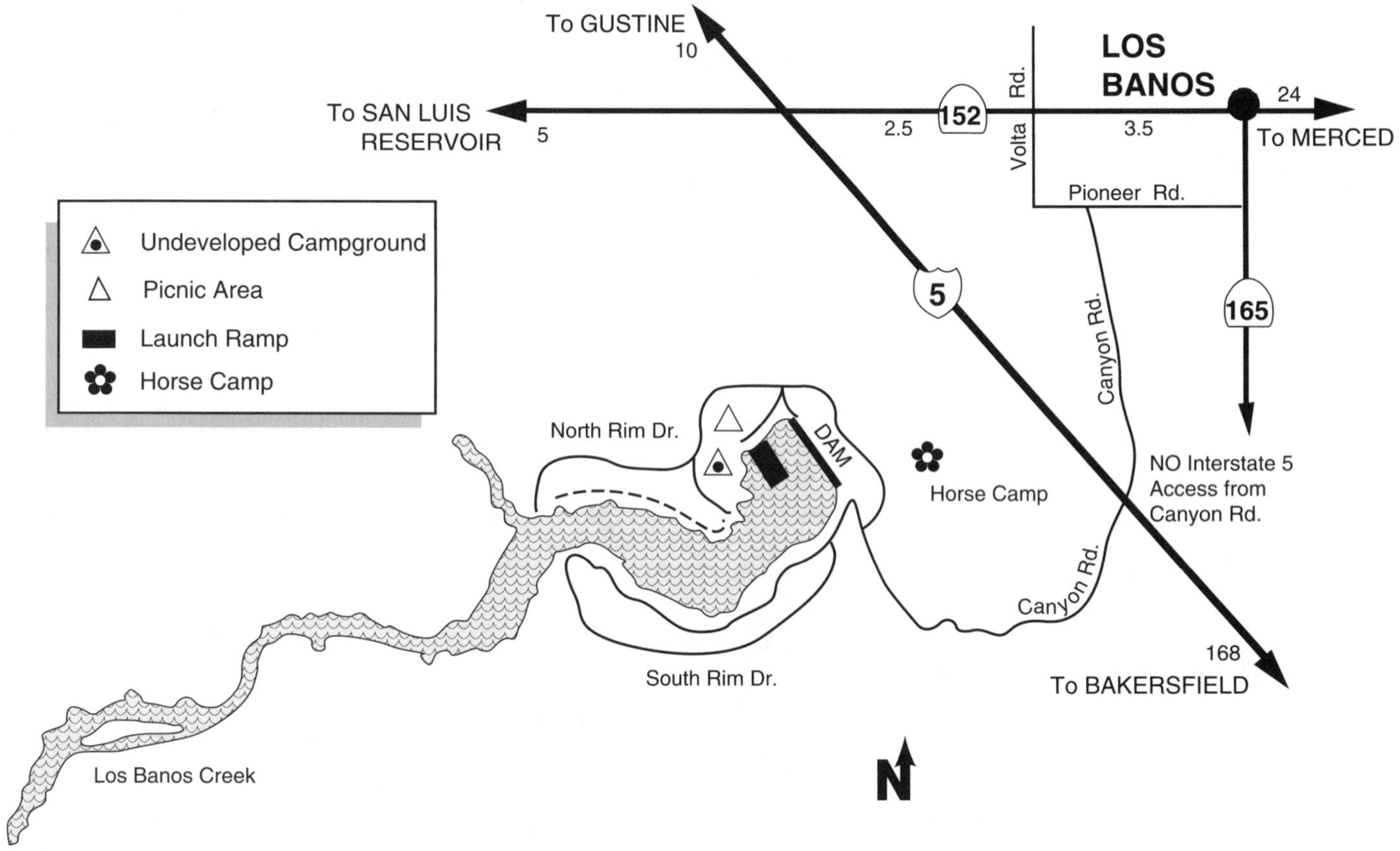

▲	Undeveloped Campground
△	Picnic Area
◼	Launch Ramp
✿	Horse Camp

To GUSTINE 10
To SAN LUIS RESERVOIR 5
LOS BANOS
152
Volta Rd.
2.5
3.5
24
To MERCED
Pioneer Rd.
5
165
Canyon Rd.
North Rim Dr.
DAM
Horse Camp
NO Interstate 5 Access from Canyon Rd.
South Rim Dr.
Canyon Rd.
168
To BAKERSFIELD
Los Banos Creek
N

INFORMATION: San Luis Reservoir State Rec. Area, 31426 Gonzaga Rd., Gustine 95322—Ph: (209) 826-1196

CAMPING	BOATING	RECREATION	OTHER
20 Undev. Sites for Tents & R.V.s Fee: $7 Horse Camp Day Use: $2	Power, Row, Canoe, Sail, Windsurf & Inflatables Speed Limit - 5 MPH Paved Launch Ramp	Fishing: Trout, Catfish, Bluegill, Largemouth Bass Swimming Picnicking Hiking Trails & Equestrian Trails Hunting: Waterfowl Only in Season	Full Facilities at Los Banos

HENSLEY LAKE

Hensley Lake lies at an elevation of 540 feet in the rolling foothills northeast of Madera. The surrounding area is covered with majestic oaks and granite outcroppings. The Lake has a surface area of 1,570 acres with 24 miles of shoreline. The U.S. Army Corps of Engineers provides campgrounds, picnic areas and boating facilities. The expanse of open water and many secluded coves are good for all types of boating. The angler will find an abundant warm water fishery. Hiking trails lead into the Wildlife Area where many birds, animals and native wildflowers can be observed.

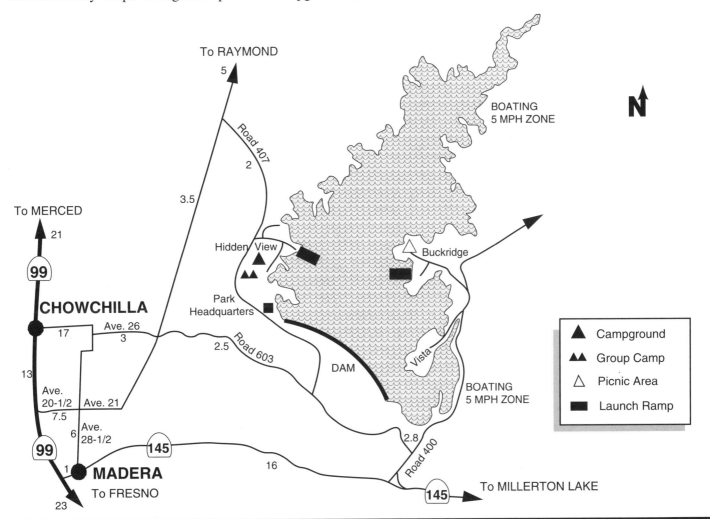

INFORMATION:U.S. Army Corps of Engineers, Hensley Lake, P.O. Box 85, Raymond 93653—Ph: (559) 673-5151

CAMPING	BOATING	RECREATION	OTHER
55 Dev. Sites for Tents & R.V.s Fees: $14 with Electric Hookups: $20 Disposal Station 2 Group Camp Areas to 100 People Fee: $50 Reservations: Ph: (877) 444-6777 Undev. Group Camp Area Reserve Ph: (559) 673-5151	Power, Row, Sail, Waterski, Jets, Windsurf & Inflatable 2 Paved Launch Ramps Fees: $2 per Day $25 Annual Pass Courtesy Docks *Low Water Levels Submerged Hazards*	Fishing: Largemouth Bass, Bluegill, Catfish & Crappie, Trout in Winter, Night Fishing Swimming - Beaches Picnicking Group Picnic Sites Reserve: (877) 444-6777 Hiking & Nature Trails Mountain Bike & Equestrian Trails	Full Facilities in Madera & Chowchilla

EASTMAN LAKE

Located in the oak-covered foothills 25 miles northeast of Chowchilla, Eastman Lake has 1,780 surface acres and is at 680 feet elevation. Winters are mild, although summer temperatures can be in the 100's. Eastman is a designated trophy bass fishery with a limit of one bass per day, 22 inch minimum size. The upper Lake, including the Chowchilla River, is closed to boating and fishing to protect nesting eagles. The Upper Chowchilla River is closed due to the invasive water weed Hydrilla. Be well aware of the "keep out" buoys as this area is closed to all water recreation. Berenda Reservoir to the west is a small day-use Lake with boating and fishing from shore during the summer only.

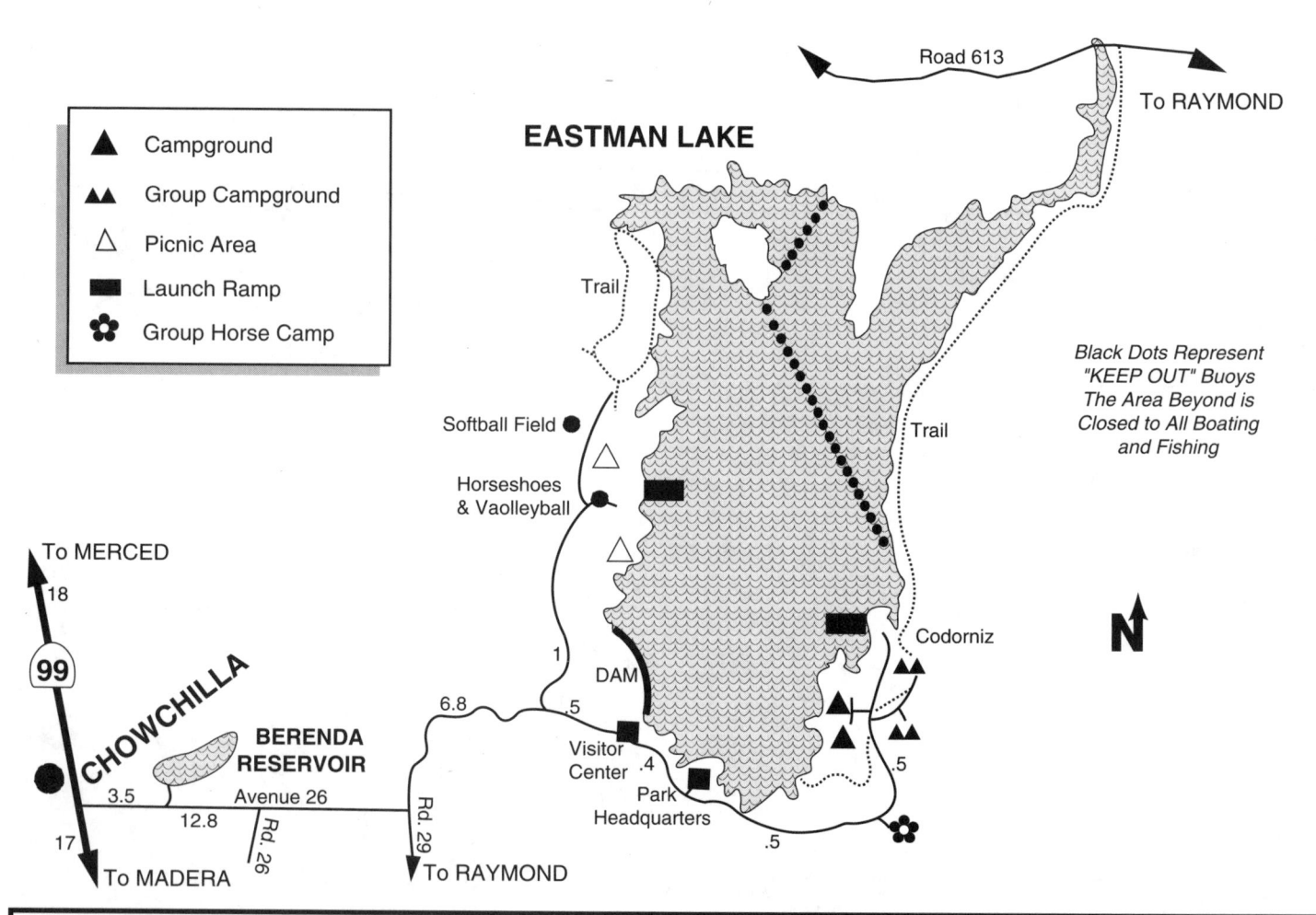

Legend

- ▲ Campground
- ▲▲ Group Campground
- △ Picnic Area
- ■ Launch Ramp
- ❁ Group Horse Camp

EASTMAN LAKE

Road 613
To RAYMOND

Black Dots Represent
"KEEP OUT" Buoys
The Area Beyond is
Closed to All Boating
and Fishing

Trail
Softball Field ●
Horseshoes & Vaolleyball
Trail
Codorniz
To MERCED
18
99
CHOWCHILLA
BERENDA RESERVOIR
1
DAM
6.8   .5
Visitor Center   .4
3.5   Avenue 26
12.8   Rd. 26
17   Rd. 29
Park Headquarters   .5
To MADERA   To RAYMOND
.5

INFORMATION: U.S. Army Corps of Engineers, Eastman Lake, Box 67, Raymond 93653—Ph: (559) 689-3255

CAMPING	BOATING	RECREATION	OTHER
66 Dev. Sites for Tents & R.V.s Fees: $14 with Electric Hookups Fees: $20 Disposal Station 3 Group Areas to 100 People Fee: $35 - $75 Per Night Equestrian Group Camp Fee: $25 Reservations: Ph: (877) 444-6777	Power, Row, Sail, Windsurf, Waterski & Inflatables Launch Ramps Day Use Fee: $3 Berenda Reservoir: Summers Only Drag Boat Racing For Information: Chowchilla Parks & Recreation Ph: (559) 665-4808	Fishing: Largemouth Bass, Catfish, Bluegill, Crappie, Trout in Winter Designated Trophy Bass Fishery - Limit: 1 per Day - 22 Inch Max. Size Swimming Picnicking - Shelter Hiking & Equestrian Trails Mountain Bike Trails Nature Study Horseshoes, Softball Shotgun & Bow Hunting	Day Use Fee: $3 Spring Wild Flowers Full Facilities in Chowchilla & Madera

Millerton State Recreation Area, 8,000 acres, is located along the San Joaquin River and is a part of the California State Park System. The popular 5,000 surface-acre Lake has over 40 miles of shoreline and offers excellent boating facilities. The angler will find a good warm water fishery. Sandy swim areas and picnic sites are located around the Lake.

Lost Lake Recreation Area is a separate facility under the jurisdiction of Fresno County. This 220-acre park on the San Joaquin River, below Millerton, includes a small 40-acre Lake, a campground, picnic areas, including group sites, and ball fields.

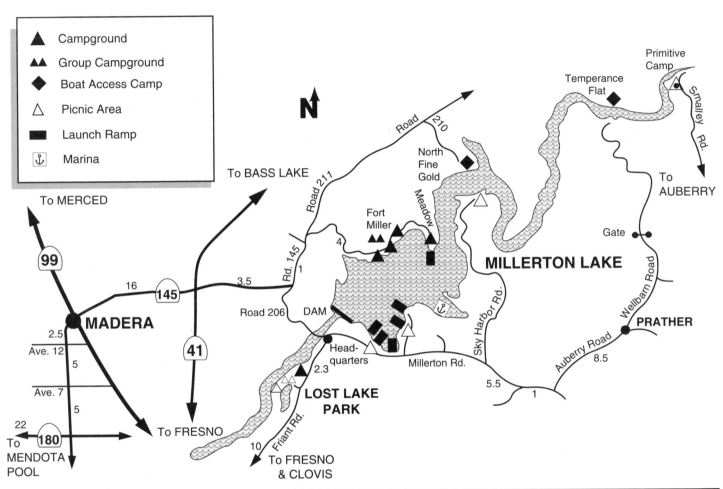

INFORMATION:	Millerton Lake State Recreation Area, P.O. Box 205, Friant 93626—Ph: (559) 822-2332		
CAMPING	**BOATING**	**RECREATION**	**OTHER**
Millerton Lake: 137 Dev. Sites for Tents & R.V.s to 36 Feet Fee: $12-$18 - No Hookups Group Sites for 40 to 75 People - Fees: $60 - $112 Disposal Stations Reserve: Ph: (800) 444-7275 Also Boat Camp Sites Day Use Fee: $3 Lost Lake-First Come Basis: 42 R.V. Sites - Fee: $9	Millerton: Open to All Boats Full Service Marina Launch Ramps: $5 Rentals: Fishing Boats & Motors, Party Barge Lost Lake: Small Boats Electric Motors Only Hand Launch Only	Fishing: Striped, Alabama Spotted, Large & Smallmouth Bass, Catfish & Panfish Picnicking Hiking & Equestrian Trails Swimming: Millerton Lake Birdwatching Nature Study Area Wild Life Refuge Playground Softball Field Volleyball Court	Bait & Tackle Store Lost Lake Rec. Area Fresno County Parks 2220 Tulare St. Fresno 93721 Ph: (559) 488-3004

BASS LAKE

At 3,500 feet elevation, Bass Lake is within the Sierra National Forest. This beautiful forested recreation area provides an abundance of recreational opportunities. Fishing and boating on this 1,165 surface-acre Lake is extremely popular. Water levels are generally maintained through Labor Day. Facilities on the South Shore are administered by the U. S. Forest Service and managed by California Land Management. There are numerous group sites for camping and picnicking at Crane Valley and Recreation Point. Several cabins and R.V. parks are available at privately owned areas around the Lake. This is a great place for old-fashioned family vacations. For full information, contact the Bass Lake Chamber of Commerce - Ph. (559) 642-3676.

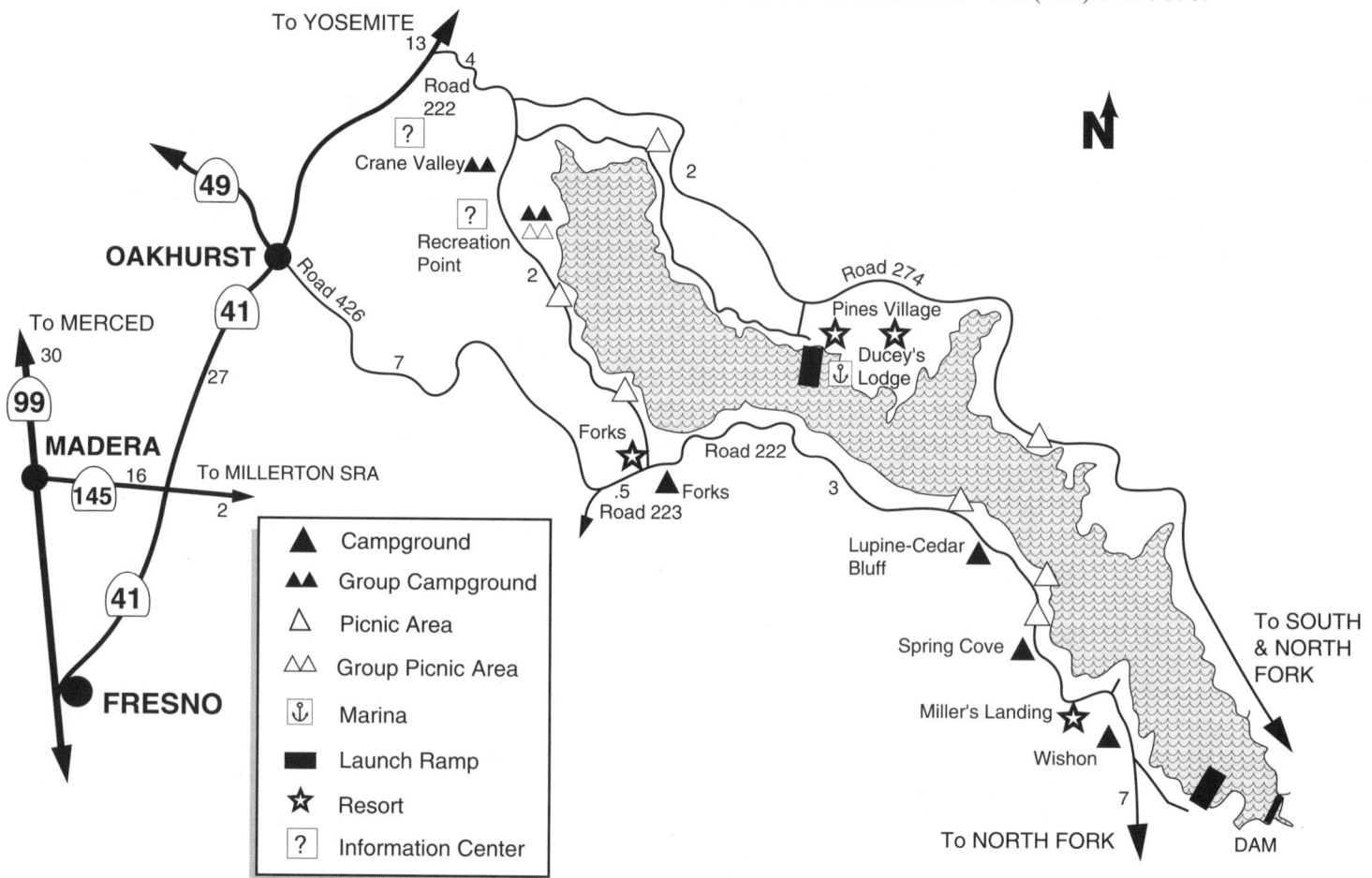

INFORMATION: Bass Lake Ranger District, 57003 Road 225, North Fork 93643—Ph: (559) 877-2218

CAMPING	BOATING	RECREATION	OTHER
Dev. Sites for Tents & R.V.s Fees: $16 - $30 Forks: 31 Sites Lupine-Cedar: 113 Sites Spring Cove: 63 Sites Wishon: 47 Sites Numerous Group & Youth Campgrounds & Picnic Areas Reserve: Ph: (800) 280-CAMP Disposal Stations	Power, Row, Canoe, Sail, Waterski, PWCs, Windsurfing & Inflatables Seasonal Boat Registration Fee: $32 - $63 Full Service Marina Launch Ramps Moorings & Gas Summer Cruises Rentals: Fishing, Canoe, Waterski, & Party Barges	Fishing: Rainbow Trout, Catfish, Bluegill, Perch, Crappie, Black Bass & Kokanee Salmon Swimming - Beaches Hiking & Equestrian Trails Visitor Programs Nature Study Chamber of Commerce Ph: (559) 642-3676	Ducey's Lodge Ph: (559) 642-3131 Forks Resort Ph: (559) 642-3737 Miller's Landing Ph: (559) 642-3633 The Pines Resort Ph: (800) 350-7463 Rustic Cabins to Deluxe Resorts Snack Bars & Restaurants Groceries, Bait & Tackle Gas Station

REDINGER LAKE and KERCKHOFF RESERVOIR

Redinger Lake, in the Sierra National Forest, is at an elevation of 1,400 feet. Located in a narrow valley, the surrounding mountains rise more than 1,000 feet above the Lake. The Lake is 3 miles long and 1/4 mile wide. This area of digger pine and chaparral is intermingled with live and valley oak. Redinger is primarily a boating Lake with limited fishing.

Kerckhoff Reservoir is located 6 miles to the west. Fishing for striped bass is the main activity and boating is limited to hand launched boats. Campgrounds are available at both Lakes. Redinger has numerous sandy beaches. The town of North Fork is an interesting place to visit and is the geographical center of California.

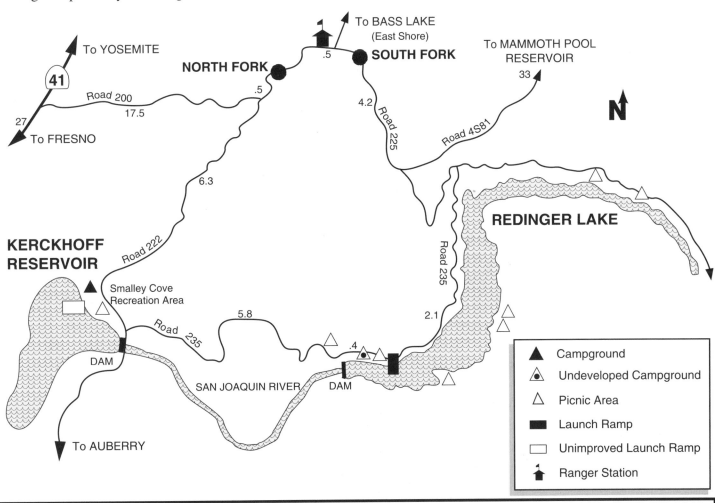

INFORMATION: Minarets Ranger District, 57003 Road 226, P.O. Box 10, North Fork 93643—Ph: (559) 877-2218

CAMPING	BOATING	RECREATION	OTHER
Redinger Lake: Primitive Camp Sites - Designated Areas Only Kerckhoff : Smalley Cove Recreation Area: 5 Campsites (1 for Handicapped) 5 Picnic Sites P.G.&E. Ph: (916) 386-5164 *Extreme Fire Danger* <u>*No Campfires*</u>	Power, Row, Canoe, Sail & Inflatables Speed Limit - 35 MPH Launch Ramp at Redinger Lake Car Top Boats Only at Kerckhoff	Fishing: Striped Bass Swimming Picnicking Hiking Nature Study White Water Rafting from Redinger Lake to Kerckhoff Reservoir Hunting: Valley Quail, Rabbit & Deer	North Fork Chamber of Commerce Ph: (559) 877-2410 Nearest Facilities at North Fork

MAMMOTH POOL RESERVOIR

Mammoth Pool Reservoir is located on the San Joaquin River at an elevation of 3,330 feet. The surface area is 1,050 acres when full although water levels drop 90 feet in the fall, closing the launch ramp. Southern California Edison Company completed the dam in 1959 to produce hydroelectric power. The Lake is nestled in a narrow valley of ponderosa pine, incense cedar, black and live oak with mountains rising 2,000 feet above the shoreline. The access road climbs to 5,300 feet making it impassable when winter snow arrives. Mile High Vista Point offers a 180 degree view of Mount Ritter and Mammoth Mountain.

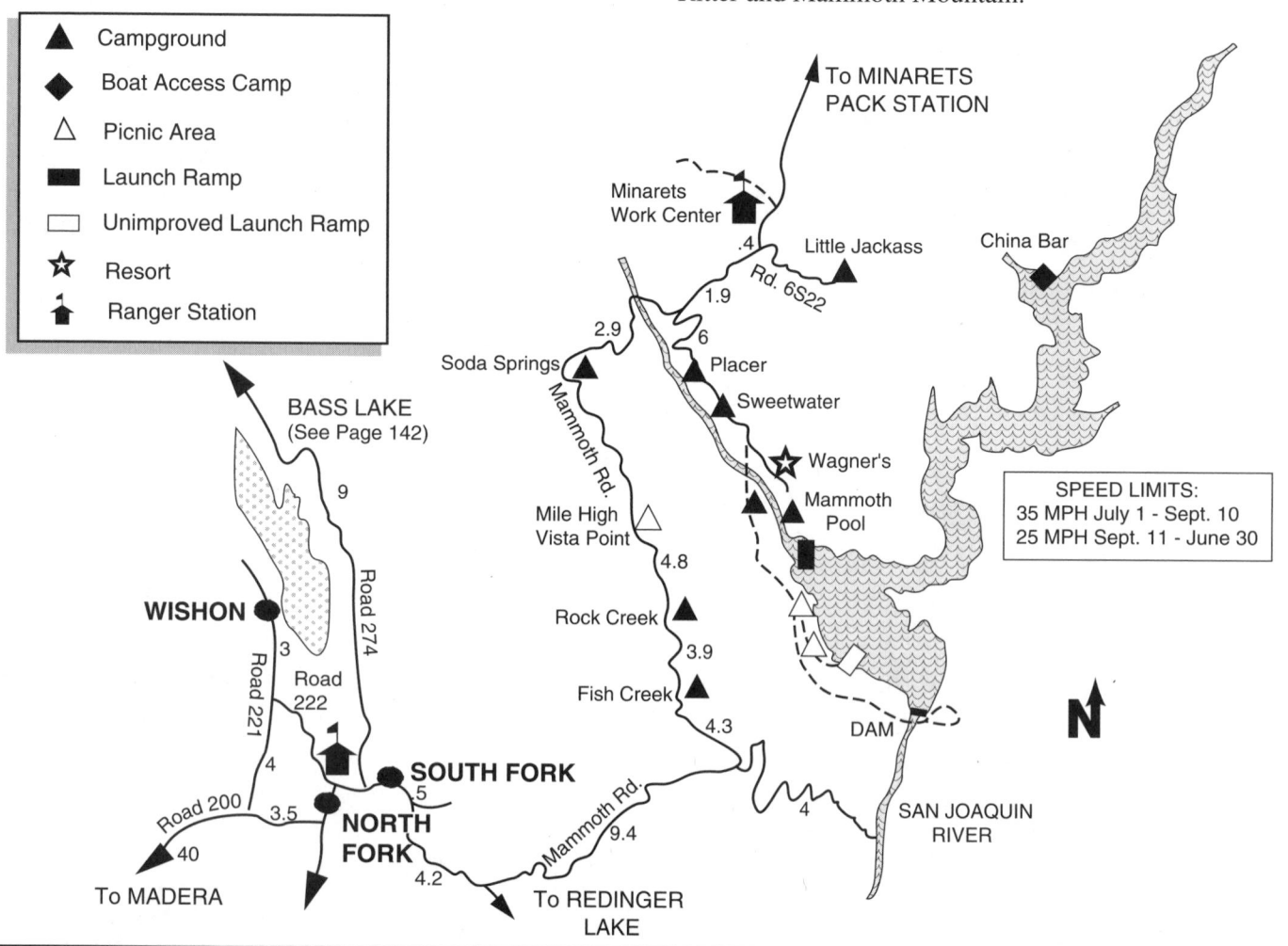

▲	Campground
◆	Boat Access Camp
△	Picnic Area
■	Launch Ramp
▭	Unimproved Launch Ramp
☆	Resort
⌂	Ranger Station

SPEED LIMITS:
35 MPH July 1 - Sept. 10
25 MPH Sept. 11 - June 30

INFORMATION: Minarets Ranger District, 57003 Road 226, P.O. Box 10, North Fork 93643—Ph: (559) 877-2218

CAMPING	BOATING	RECREATION	OTHER
30 Dev. Sites for Tents Only 35 Dev. Sites for 　Tents & R.V.s Fees: Mammoth Pool: $13 Placer & Sweetwater: $12 Reserve: 　Ph: (877) 444-6777 No Fees at Other USFS 　Campgrounds 6 Boat-In Sites at 　China Bar	Power, Sail, Row, 　Canoe, Windsurf & 　Inflatables Waterskiing Subject 　to 35 MPH Speed Limit Launch Ramps *Call for Current Lake Level Information*	Fishing: Rainbow, 　Eastern Brook & 　German Brown Trout Closed to 　Fishing & Boating 　May 1 to June 16 Swimming Picnicking Hiking - Nature Trail Pack Station Hunting: Deer, Turkey & 　Quail	Wagner's Resort 21101 Rte. 209 Madera 93638 35 Dev. Sites for 　Tents & R.V.s - Fee: $10 Ph: (559) 841-3736 Sandwiches Grocery Store Bait & Tackle Gas Station Open: 　End of May to Sept.15

COURTRIGHT, WISHON and BLACK ROCK RESERVOIRS

These Lakes range in elevation from 8,200 feet at Courtright, 6,600 feet at Wishon to 4,200 feet at Black Rock. They are all part of the Kings River System. Located in the Sierra National Forest, these Lakes offer good fishing for native trout. In addition, the angler can enjoy the Upper King's River. Wishon Village offers resort facilities in this remote area. The Forest Service operates numerous campgrounds as shown on the map. Hikers and equestrians will find trailheads leading into the John Muir and Dinkey Lakes Wilderness Areas. The Helms Creek Hydroelectric Project affects water levels daily at Wishon, Courtright and Black Rock.

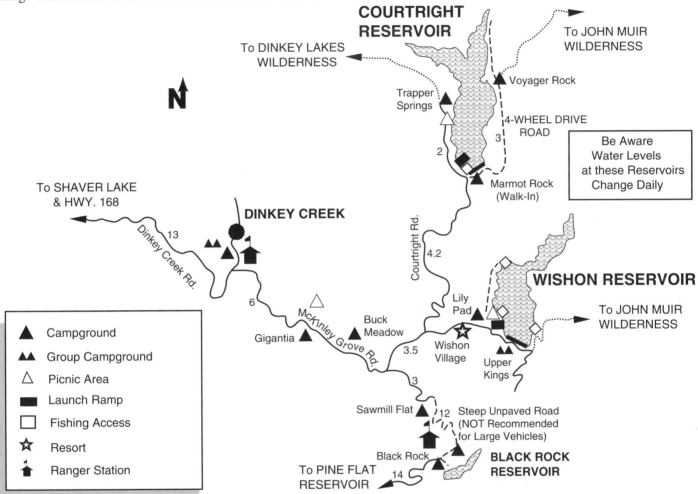

INFORMATION: Kings River Ranger District, 34849 Maxon Rd., Sanger 93657—Ph: (559) 855-8321			
CAMPING	**BOATING**	**RECREATION**	**OTHER**
P.G.&E. Dev. Sites:	Courtright & Wishon:	Fishing: Rainbow,	Wishon Village:
TrapperSprings-75 Sites:$15	Open to All Boating	Brown & Brook Trout	Mail: 66500 McKinley Grove
Marmot Rock-35 Sites: $16	*Except Waterskiing*	Swimming at Courtright &	Shaver Lake 93664
Lily Pad-15 Sites: $16	*& PWC's*	Wishon	Ph: (559) 865-5361
Black Rock-10 Sites: $10	15 MPH Speed Limit	No Swimming at Black Rock	25 Tent Sites &
Upper Kings Group: $125 -	No Boating at Black Rock	Picnicking	97 R.V. Sites - Full Hookups
up to 50 People		Hiking & Equestrian Trails	Store, Gas Station
Reserve Ph:(916) 386-5164	Rentals: Fishing	Horse Rentals & Pack	Laundromat, Hot Showers
	Boats at Wishon	Services	Propane, Ice, Bait & Tackle
USFS Dev. Sites		Hunting: Deer,	Dinkey Creek Inn - Cabins
Dinkey Creek: $16		Mountain Quail	Ph: (559) 841-3435
Dinkey Group Camp: $75		ORV Areas	Full Facilities at
Reserve Ph: (877) 444-6777		Rock Climbing	Shaver Lake

SHAVER LAKE

Shaver Lake is at an elevation of 5,370 feet in the Sierra National Forest. The Lake has a surface area of 2,000 acres with a shoreline of 13 miles surrounded by tall pine trees and granite boulders. This is a popular boating Lake with good marine facilities. In addition to excellent fishing at Shaver, there are numerous trout streams nearby for the angler. The John Muir and Dinkey Lakes Wilderness Areas are available for the backpacker and equestrian. Both the U. S. Forest Service and Southern California Edison maintain campgrounds in this beautiful setting.

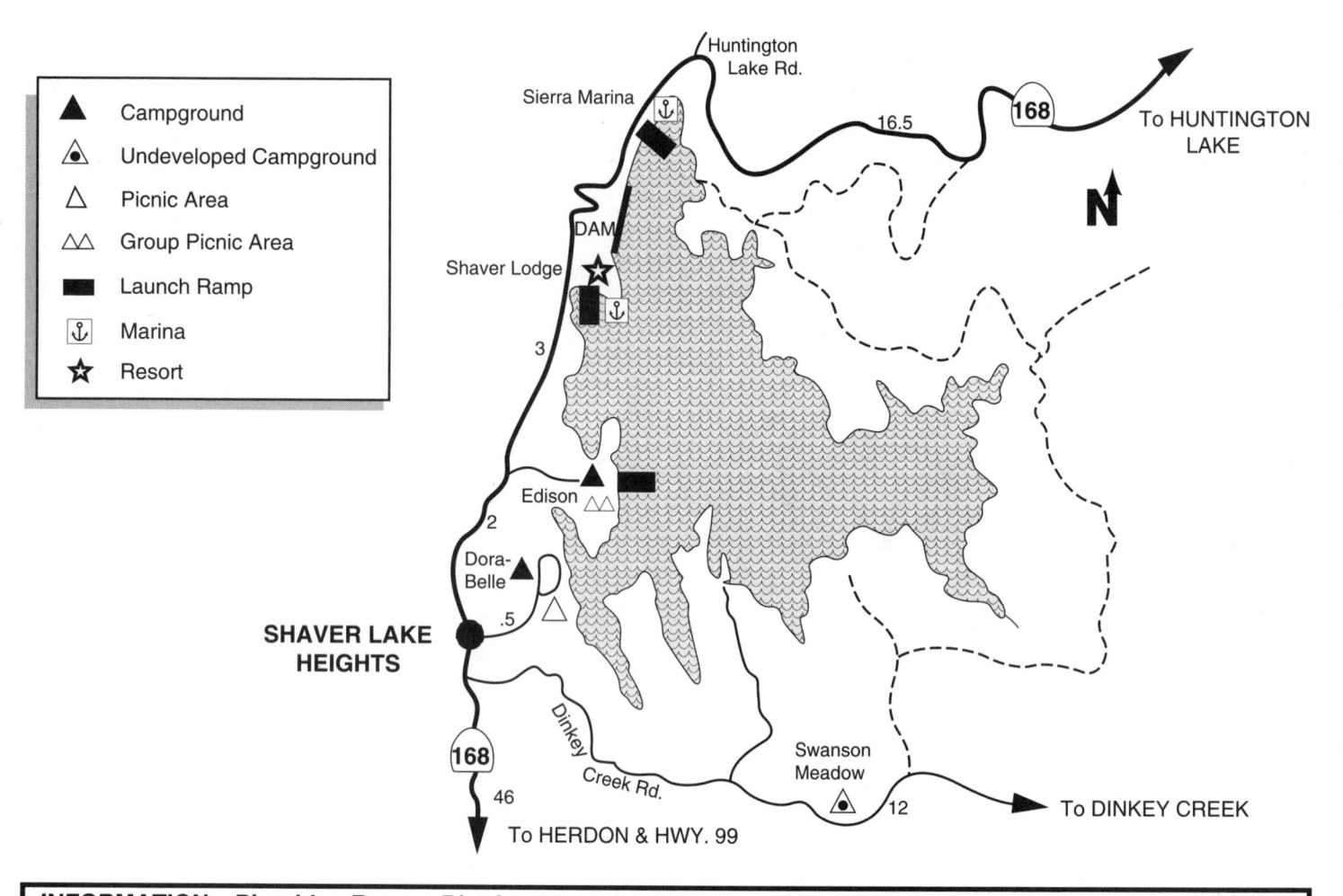

▲	Campground
⦿	Undeveloped Campground
△	Picnic Area
△△	Group Picnic Area
▬	Launch Ramp
⚓	Marina
☆	Resort

INFORMATION: Pineridge Ranger District, 29688 Auberry Rd., P.O.Box 559, Prather 93651—Ph: (559) 855-5360

CAMPING	BOATING	RECREATION	OTHER
U.S.F.S.: 69 Dev. Sites for Tents & R.V.s, Fee: $14 Reserve: (877) 444-6777 Plus 9 Primitive Sites So. Cal. Edison: 150 Dev. Sites for Tents & R.V.s, Fee: $18 Additional Vehicle: $5 Electric Hookups Disposal Station Ph: (559) 841-3134	Power, Row, Canoe, Sail, Waterski, Jets, Windsurf & Inflatable Full Service Marinas Rental: Fishing Boats & Motors, Pontoons Berths Gas	Fishing: Rainbow, Brown & Brook Trout, Kokanee, Large & Smallmouth Bass, Catfish & Sunfish Picnicking Swimming - Beaches Hiking & Equestrisan Trails	Motels & Cabins Restaurants Cocktail Lounges Grocery Stores Bait & Tackle Gas Station

HUNTINGTON LAKE

Huntington Lake is at an elevation of 7,000 feet in the Sierra National Forest. Resting in a forested natural basin, this man-made Lake is 6 miles long and 1/2 mile wide with 14 miles of shoreline. The Forest Service Campgrounds are operated by California Land Management. Many private resorts offer R.V. sites, cabins and restaurants. This is a good Lake for sailing and regattas are held in the summer to take advantage of the westerly winds. Hiking and equestrian trails surround Huntington Lake and Kaiser Wilderness Area, 22,750 acres, is nearby. Permits are required for entry. Fishing from shore or boat is usually productive and other nearby Lakes and streams offer the angler some good opportunities.

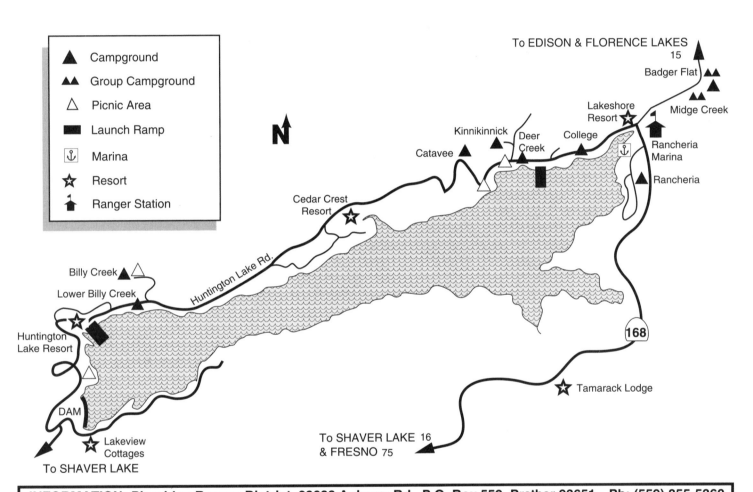

INFORMATION: Pineridge Ranger District, 29688 Auberry Rd. P.O. Box 559, Prather 93651—Ph: (559) 855-5360

CAMPING	BOATING	RECREATION	OTHER

297 Dev. Sites for Tents & R.V.s
Fees: $16 - $36
Group Camps
  Each to 100 People
  Maximum
Reserve:
  Ph: (877) 444-6777
	Power, Row, Canoe, Sail, Waterski
	Full Service Marinas
	Launch Ramp
	Rentals: Fishing & Sail Boats, Canoes, Paddleboats & Patio Boats
	
	Rancheria Marina:
	  Ph: (559) 893-3234
		Fishing: Rainbow, Brown & Brook Trout, Kokanee
		Swimming
		Picnicking
		Hiking & Equestrian Trails
		Backpacking [Parking]
		Horse Rentals
		Nature Study
		
		Visitor Center
		  Ph: (559) 893-6611
			Motels, Cabins & Condos
			Restaurants, Grocery Stores
			Bait & Tackle, Gas Station
			Cedar Crest Resort:
			  Ph: (559) 893-3233
			Huntington Lake Resort:
			  Ph: (559) 893-6750
			Lakeshore Resort:
			  Ph: (559) 893-3193
			Lakeview Cottages:
			  Ph: (559) 893-2330
			Tamarack Lodge:
			  Ph: (559) 893-3244

147

EDISON and FLORENCE LAKES

Edison Lake, at 7,700 feet and Florence Lake, at 7,400 feet are both located in the scenic high Sierras bordering the John Muir and Ansel Adams Wilderness Areas. Granite boulders and sandy beaches are located around the timbered shore-lines. Vermilion Valley Resort at Edison Lake offers cabins, restaurant, store, boat rentals and launch facilities. Florence Lake has a small store with supplies and a pack station. Mono Hot Springs Resort offers campgrounds, cabins and hot mineral baths. A water ferry service is available at both Lakes for backpackers going into the Wilderness Areas. Trout fishing can be excellent in these Lakes and many nearby streams.

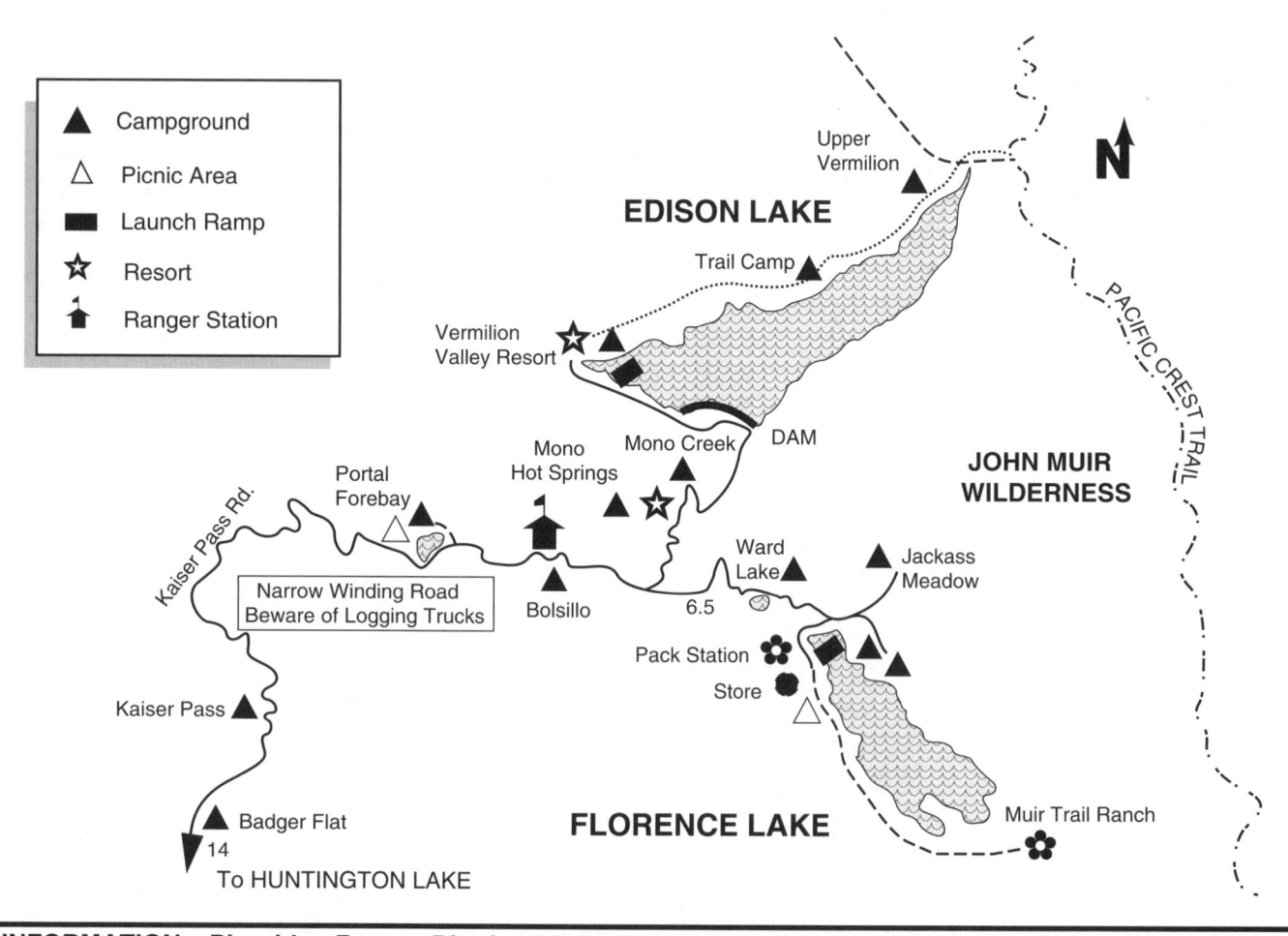

INFORMATION: Pineridge Ranger District, 29688 Auberry Rd., P.O. Box 559, Prather 93651—Ph: (559) 855-5360

CAMPING	BOATING	RECREATION	OTHER
162 Sites for Tents in This Area Fees: $14 - $28 Reserve: (877) 444-6777 R.V.s and Trailers *Use Caution - Narrow One Lane Winding Roads & Logging Trucks* Primitive Camping Allowed Anywhere Campfire Permit Required	Power, Row, Canoe & Inflatable Speed Limit - 15 MPH Launch Ramps Rentals: Fishing Boats & Canoes	Fishing: Rainbow, Brown & Brook Trout Picnicking Hiking & Equestrian Trails Lost Valley Pack Station Ph: (559) 855-3960 Water Ferry Service for Backpackers Entry Point to John Muir & Ansel Adams Wilderness Permit Required	High Sierra Visitor Center Ph: (559) 877-7173 Mono Hot Springs: Campground & Cabins Hot Baths Cafe & Store Ph: (559) 325-1710 Muir Trail Ranch: Cabins & Horse Trips Ph: (559) 966-3195 Vermilion Valley Resort: Cabins Ph: (559) 259-4000

PINE FLAT LAKE and AVOCADO LAKE PARK

Pine Flat Lake is at an elevation of 952 feet in the Sierra foothills east of Fresno. The Lake is 20 miles long with 67 miles of shoreline and up to 4,300 surface acres in the spring and summer. A moderate growth of pine and oak trees exists throughout the area. The U. S. Army Corps of Engineers has jurisdiction over this very popular Lake. In addition to the public campgrounds, there are privately owned resorts which offer overnight lodging and R.V. accommodations.

Waterskiers and swimmers will enjoy the warm water and the angler will find a variety of fish. Avocado Lake Park is on the Kings River below Pine Flat Dam. This small 83 surface-acre Lake offers non-powered boating and a warm water fishery. There is no camping permitted in the Park but there are picnic areas and a swim beach. *Call Lakes for current information as there can be extreme water fluctuation.*

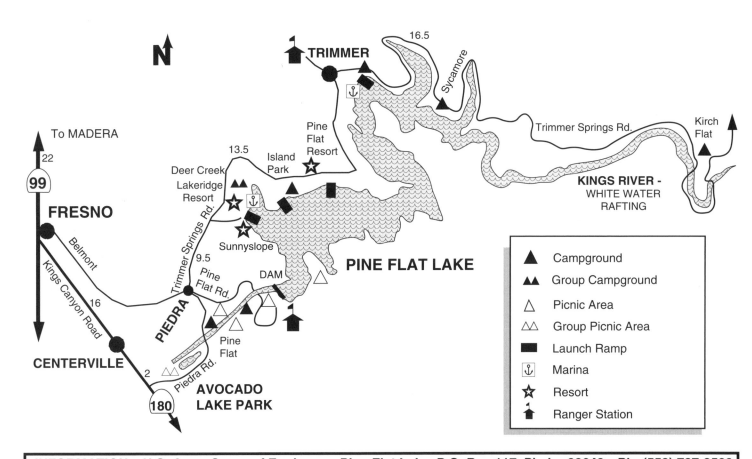

INFORMATION: U.S. Army Corps of Engineers, Pine Flat Lake, P.O. Box 117, Piedra 93649—Ph: (559) 787-2589

CAMPING	BOATING	RECREATION	OTHER
Island Park: 97 Dev. Sites for Tents & R.V.s Plus Overflow - Fee: $16 2 Group Sites - Fee: $60 Reserve: (877) 444-6777 Pine Flat R.V. Resort-Motel Ph: (559) 787-2207 Lakeridge Resort Ph: (559) 787-2260 Sunnyslope Campground: Ph: (559) 787-2730	Pine Flat: Open to All Boats Including Houseboats Full Service Marinas Launch Ramps - Fee: $3 Overnight Mooring Rentals: Fishing Boats, Pontoons, Jets, Houseboats Avocado Lake Park: No Gas-Powered Boats Hand Launch Only	Fishing: Rainbow Trout, Large & Smallmouth Bass, Catfish, Crappie, Bluegill Swimming Picnicking Hiking - Nature Trails Campfire Program River Raft Trips Hunting: Deer, Quail, Dove, Rabbit & Squirrel In Designated Areas Shotguns Only	Motels & Cabins Restaurants - Lounges Snack Bars - Stores Bait, Tackle & Gas Disposal Station USFS - Kirch Flat Camp Sites - No Water Ph: (559) 855-8321 Avocado Lake Fresno Co. Parks 2220 Tulare St. Fresno 93721 Ph: (559) 488-3004

149

HUME and SEQUOIA LAKES

Hume Lake, at 5,200 feet elevation, and Sequoia, at 5,300 feet, are in the scenic Sequoia National Forest. Hume Lake has 85 surface acres and Sequoia has 88 surface acres. The angler will find trout and the boater can hand launch small craft with electric motors at Hume. Sequoia Lake is operated by the YMCA and is open only to members. Early reservations are advised at this popular camp. Be sure to bring your camera to this beautiful country of the Giant Sequoia trees, survivors of the Ice Age, and the majestic Kings Canyon National Park.

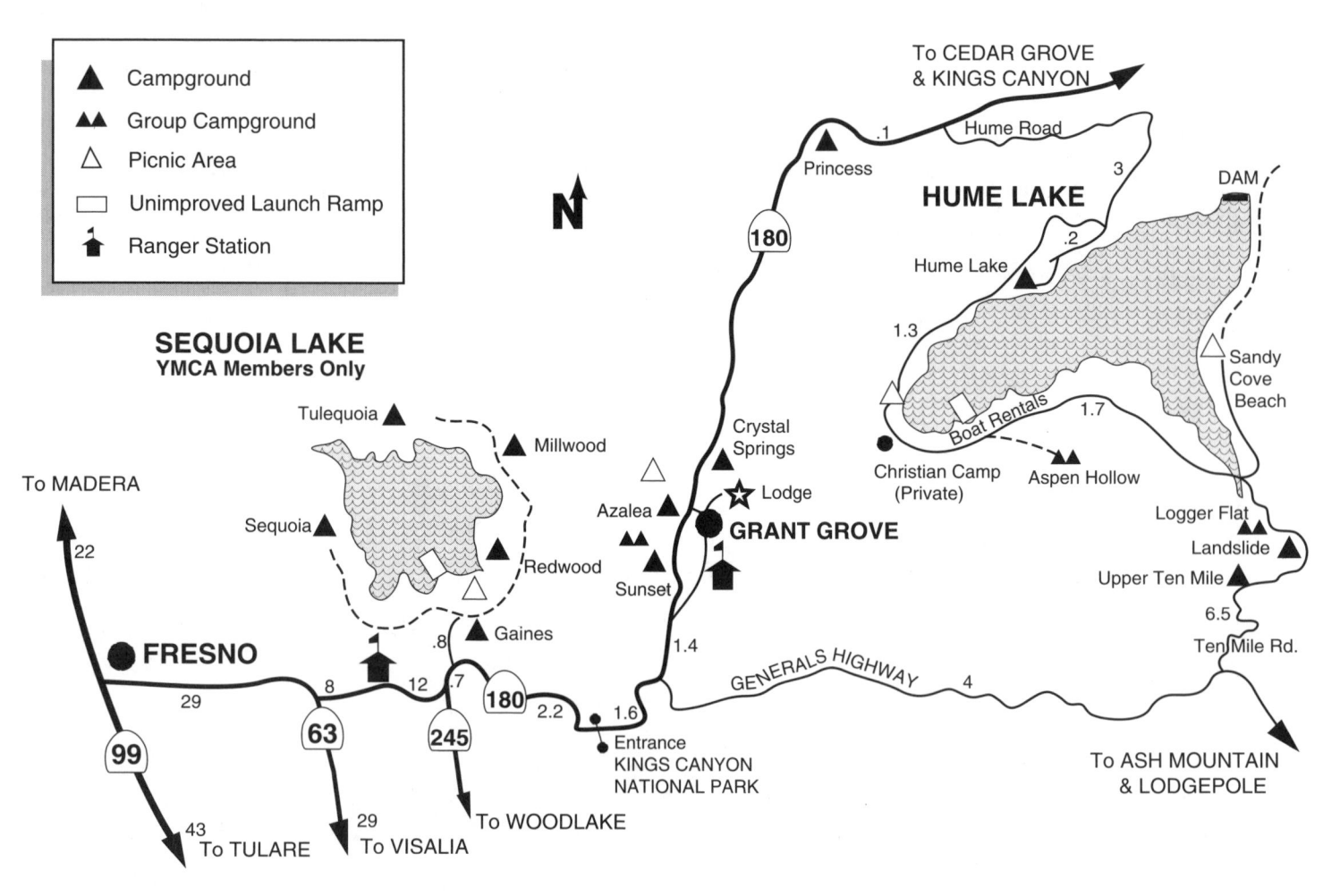

INFORMATION: Hume Lake Ranger District, 35860 E. Kings Canyon Rd., Dunlap 93621—Ph: (559) 338-2251			
CAMPING	**BOATING**	**RECREATION**	**OTHER**

Hume Lake:
   75 Dev. Sites for
      Tents & R.V.s
Fee: $16
No Hookups
Group Camps - To $113
Reservations:
   Ph: (877) 444-6777
Grant Grove:
   376 Dev. Sites for
      Tents & R.V.s
Fee: $14
Group Sites: $40
	Hume Lake:
	   Fishing Boats with
	      Electric Motors
	   5 MPH Speed Limit
	   Hand Launch
	
	Sequoia Lake:
	   YMCA Members Only
		Fishing at Hume Lake:
		   Rainbow &
		   Brown Trout
		Picnicking
		Swimming - Beaches
		Hiking & Backpacking
		Nature Study
		Hunting: Deer
		
		Giant Sequoia National
		   Monument
		   Ph: (559) 539-2607
			Grant Grove Lodge:
			   Ph: (559) 335-5500
			
			Hume Lake Christian Camp:
			   Gas, Store, Restaurant
			   Ph: (559) 335-2881
			
			Sequoia Family Camp:
			   Before July 1
			      Ph: (209) 233-5737
			   After July 1
			      Ph: (559) 335-2382

Inyo County operates several campgrounds along Highway 395. At 4,200 feet elevation, Pleasant Valley Reservoir does not allow boating but the angler can fish from shore. The campground is located along the Owens River. Tinnemaha Reservoir, open for fishing year around, is located about two miles from the campground. Diaz Lake is at an elevation of 3,700 feet on the eastern side of the Sierras, 15 miles from the Mt. Whitney Trailhead. This 86-surface acre Lake offers varied boating and is popular with waterskiers. There is both a trout and warm water fishery. Numerous ORV trails are throughout this entire area.

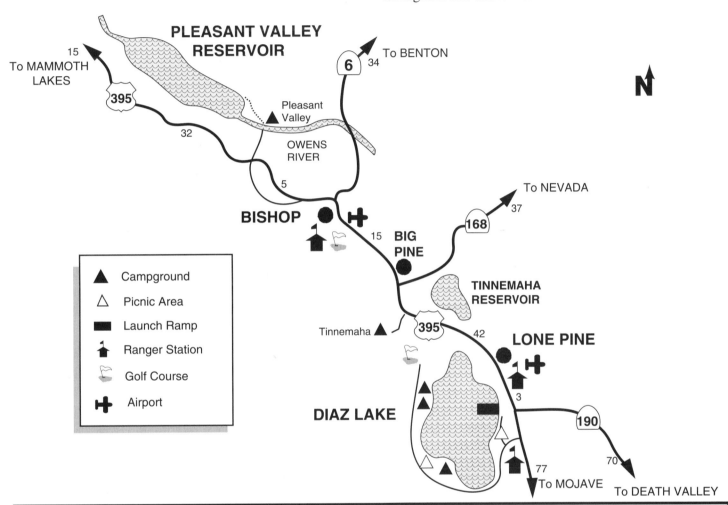

INFORMATION: Inyo County Parks & Recreation, 785 N. Main St. Suite 6, Bishop 93514—Ph: (760) 873-5577

CAMPING	BOATING	RECREATION	OTHER

Pleasant Valley:
    200 Tent & R.V. Sites
    No Hookups - Fee: $10
Tinnemaha:
    55 Tent & R.V. Sites
    Fee: $15
Diaz Lake:
    200 Tent & R.V. Sites
    No Hookups - Fee: $10
    Plus Group Sites
Reserve Ph:(760) 876-5656
	Diaz Lake: Power,
	    Row, Canoe, Sail,
	    Waterski, Jets &
	    Inflatables,
	Launch Ramp - $9
	May 15 through Oct. 31
	    Speed Limit - 35 MPH
	Nov. 1 through May 14
	    Speed Limit - 15 MPH
	Maximum Boat Size: 22 Ft.
	Noise Level Laws Enforced
	
	No Boats at Pleasant Valley
		Fishing: Rainbow &
		    Brown Trout,
		    Smallmouth Bass,
		    Bluegill & Catfish
		Swimming - Beaches
		Picnicking
		Hiking & Equestrian Trails
		Hang Gliding
		Hunting: Waterfowl
		ORV Trails
			Information for:
			    Diaz Lake
			    P.O. Box 503
			    Lone Pine 93545
			    Ph: (760) 876-5656
			        or (760) 873-5577
			
			Full Facilities at
			    Bishop & Lone Pine

South Section

Lakes 152 - 199

Numbers around highways represent lakes in numerical order
in this book. *See Index for complete listing.*

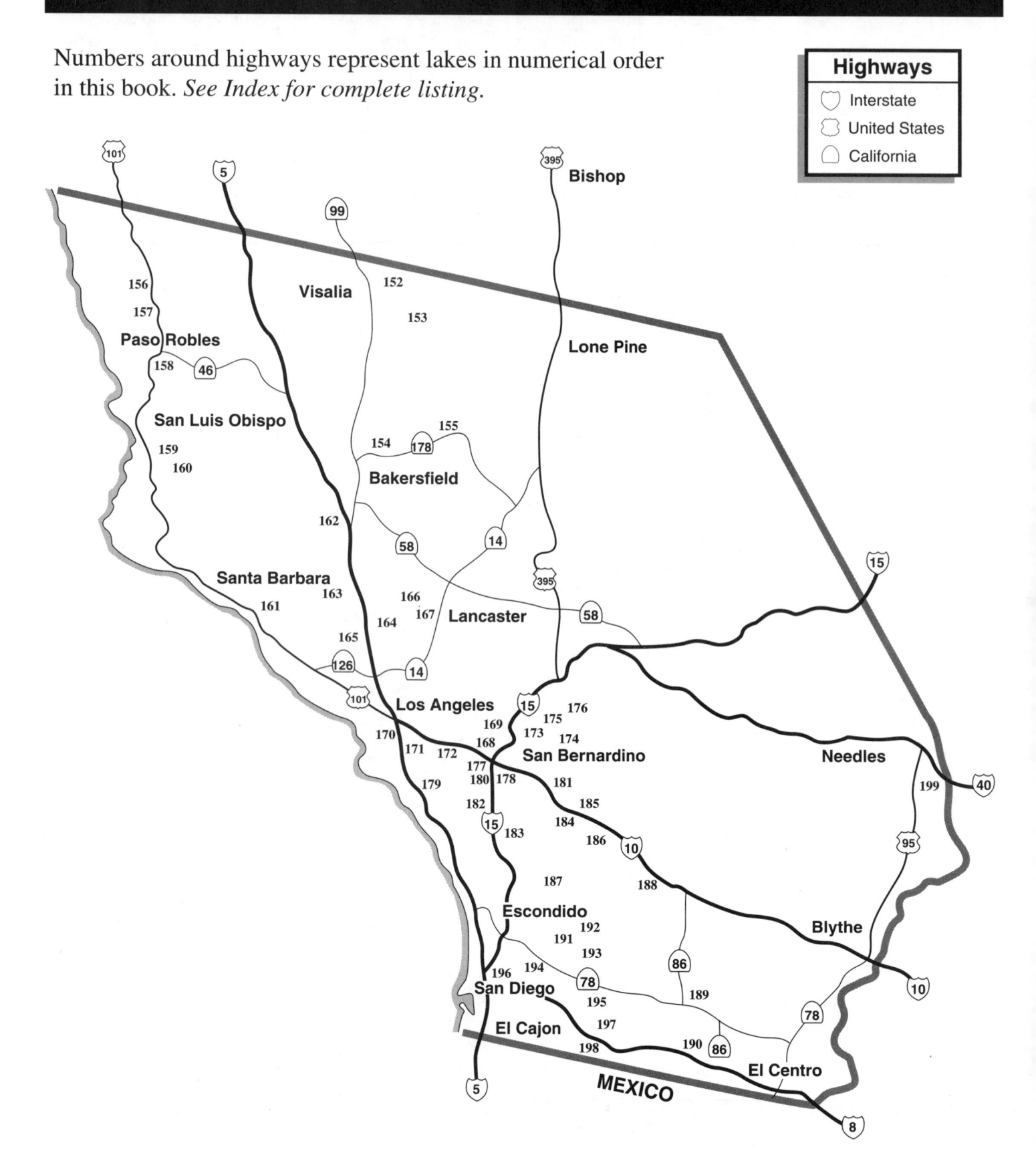

Highways

- Interstate
- United States
- California

Bishop

101

5

99

156
157

Visalia

152

153

Paso Robles

158 46

Lone Pine

San Luis Obispo

159
160

154 178 155

Bakersfield

162

58 14

Santa Barbara

163
161

58

395

166
167 **Lancaster** 58

164

165

126 14

101 **Los Angeles** 15 176

170

169 175 173 174
168

171 172

San Bernardino **Needles**

177
180 178 181 199 40

179

182 185

15 183 184

186 10 95

187 188

Escondido

192
191

193

196 194

San Diego 78 86 **Blythe**

195

El Cajon 197

189

198 190 86 78

MEXICO **El Centro**

5

8

At an elevation of 694 feet, Lake Kaweah is in the rolling foothills below Sequoia National Park. The Lake is 6 miles long with 22 miles of shoreline surrounded by oak-studded hills. There is a total surface area of 1,945 acres when full but there can be a 100-foot water level drop late in the season.

The U. S. Army Corps of Engineers maintain Terminus Dam, 250 feet high and 2,375 feet long, along with a campground, picnic areas and marina. Houseboating is popular with all the coves and inlets and the angler will find a broad variety of fish. *Submerged rocks are a hazard during low water.*

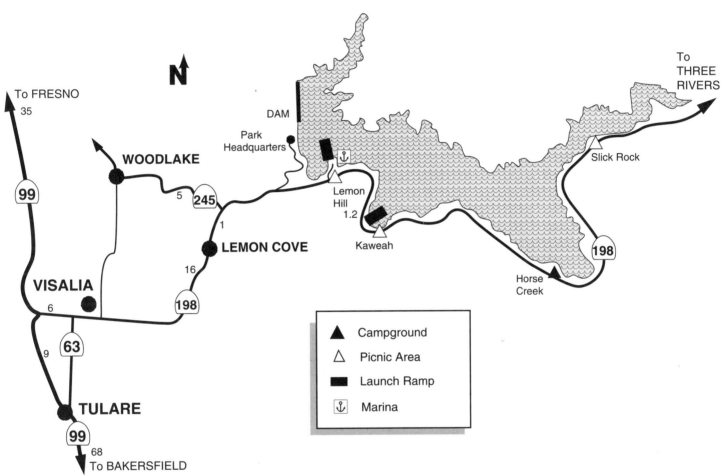

INFORMATION: U.S. Army Corps of Engineers, P.O. Box 44270, Lemon Cove 93244—Ph: (559) 597-2301

CAMPING	BOATING	RECREATION	OTHER
80 Dev. Sites for Tents & R.V.s (Handicap Site) Fees: $16 Disposal Station Reserve: Ph: (877) 444-6777 Boat Camping Permitted Anywhere Away From Shore	Power, Row, Canoe, Sail, Waterski & Jets Full Service Marina Ph: (559) 597-2526 Launch Ramps Fee: $2 Rentals: Fishing Boats, Houseboats & Pontoons Docks, Berths Moorings, Gas *Low Water Late in Season* *Submerged Rock Hazards*	Fishing: Largemouth Bass, Bluegill, Channel Catfish, Black & White Crappie, Rainbow Trout in Season Swimming Picnicking Hiking Trails Birdwatching Campfire Program Saturday Nights in Season	Snack Bar Bait & Tackle Full Facilities at Woodlake and Three Rivers

SUCCESS LAKE

Success Lake is at an elevation of 640 feet in the southern Sierra foothills. The Lake has 2,450 surface acres with 30 miles of shoreline. The U.S. Army Corps of Engineers has jurisdiction over the camping, marine and recreation facilities. There is a Wildlife Area open for public use where hunting is allowed, shotguns only, during appropriate seasons. There is good fishing year around and all types of boating are permitted from houseboats to waterskiing at this complete facility. The birdwatcher may find several rare or endangered species, such as the Bald Eagle.

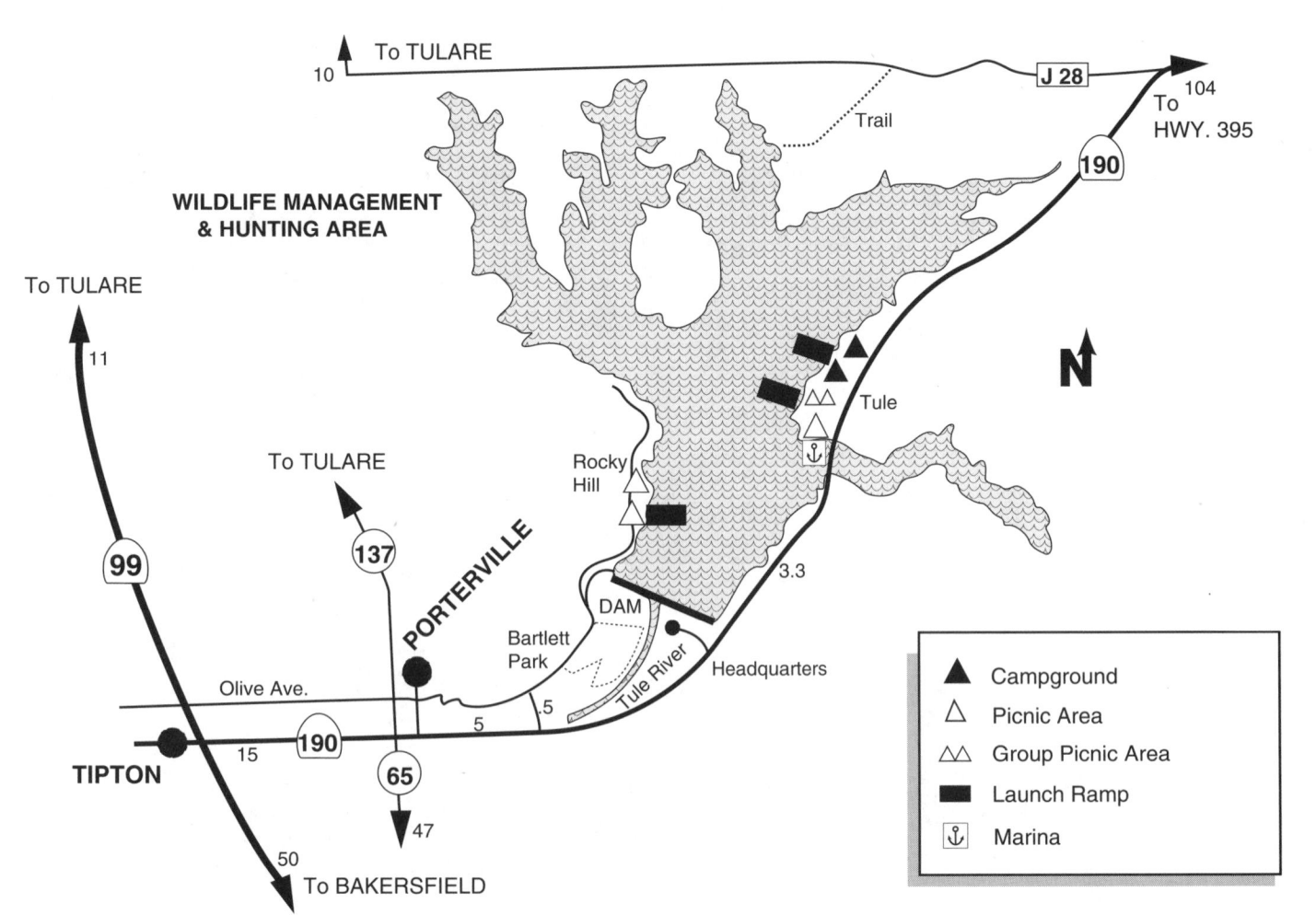

INFORMATION: U.S. Army Corps of Engineers, P.O. Box 1072, Porterville 93258—Ph: (559) 784-0215

CAMPING	BOATING	RECREATION	OTHER
104 Dev. Sites for Tents & R.V.s Fees: $14 Extra Vehicle: $7 Disposal Station Boat Camping Permitted	Power, Row, Canoe, Sail, Waterski, Jets, Windsurf & Inflatable Full Service Marina Ph: (559) 781-2078 Launch Ramps Rentals: Fishing, Houseboats & Pontoons Berths - Boats to 30 Feet Docks, Moorings, Gas	Fishing: Largemouth Bass, Catfish, Bluegill, Crappie, Rainbow Trout Swimming Playgrounds Hiking & Equestrian Trails Bird Watching Hunting: Pheasant, Dove & Rabbit, Shotgun Only in Wildlife Management Area Campfire Program Saturday Nights in Season	Grocery Store Bait & Tackle 24 Hour Information: Ph: (559) 783-9200 Full Facilities 5 Miles at Porterville

The facilities at Hart, Woollomes and Ming Lakes are under the jurisdiction of Kern County. The Kern River County Park has campsites and picnic areas within 28 landscaped acres. Lake Woollomes with 300 surface acres, and Hart Lake with 18 surface acres, offer non-powered boating and fishing. Lake Ming, 104 surface acres, is primarily a waterskiing and power boating Lake but sailing and fishing are scheduled as shown below. Brite Valley is under the jurisdiction of the Tehachapi Valley Recreation and Parks District. The 90-surface acre Lake rests at an elevation of 4,000 feet. It is open during the warmer months for non-powered boating and fishing but closed from November through April.

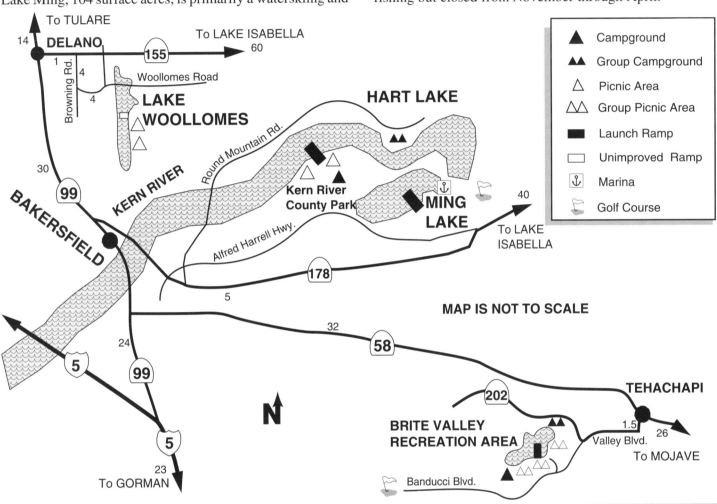

Campground	▲
Group Campground	▲▲
Picnic Area	△
Group Picnic Area	△△
Launch Ramp	■
Unimproved Ramp	▭
Marina	⚓
Golf Course	🏴

MAP IS NOT TO SCALE

INFORMATION: Kern County Parks, 1110 Golden State Ave., Bakersfield 93301—Ph: (661) 868-7000

CAMPING	BOATING	RECREATION	OTHER

Kern River County Park:
    50 Dev. Sites for Tents
    & R.V.s - No Hookups
    Fees: March 15-Oct. 15:
    $18 Per Vehicle
    Oct. 16-March 14: $10
    No Reservations
    Disposal Station
Brite Valley:
    Unlimited Open Camping
    No Water: $10
    12 Water & Electric
    Hookups: $15
	Woollomes & Hart:
	    Sail, Canoe, Row &
	    Pedal Boats Only
	Woollomes - Day Use: $3
	Ming:
	Designated Waterski Area
	Power Boats & Drag Races
	    Sailing Only - Allowed
	    Tuesdays & Thursdays
	    After 1:30 pm & the
	2nd Full Weekend of Month
	Brite Valley:
	    Electric Motors Only
		Fishing: Largemouth
		    Bass, Bluegill,
		    Crappie & Catfish
		Hart & Ming: Trout in
		    Winter
		Brite Valley: Trout, Catfish
		    & Bass
		Picnicking - Group Sites
		Hiking Trails
		Swimming at
		    Woollomes Only
		Golf Courses
			Brite Valley Aquatic
			    Recreation Area
			Tehachapi Valley
			    Recreation & Parks
			P.O. Box 373
			Tehachapi 93581
			Information:
			Ph: (661) 822-3228

ISABELLA LAKE

Isabella Lake lies at an elevation of 2,578 feet in the foothills east of Bakersfield. The surface area of the Lake is over 11,200 acres with a shoreline of 38 miles. The U. S. Forest Service maintains the numerous campgrounds. The main attractions at Isabella are boating, waterskiing, windsurfing and fishing. Activities range from white water rafting to bird watching. A target shooting range is available and hunting is allowed only in designated areas. Annual Boat Permits are required and can be obtained at any one of the Marinas.

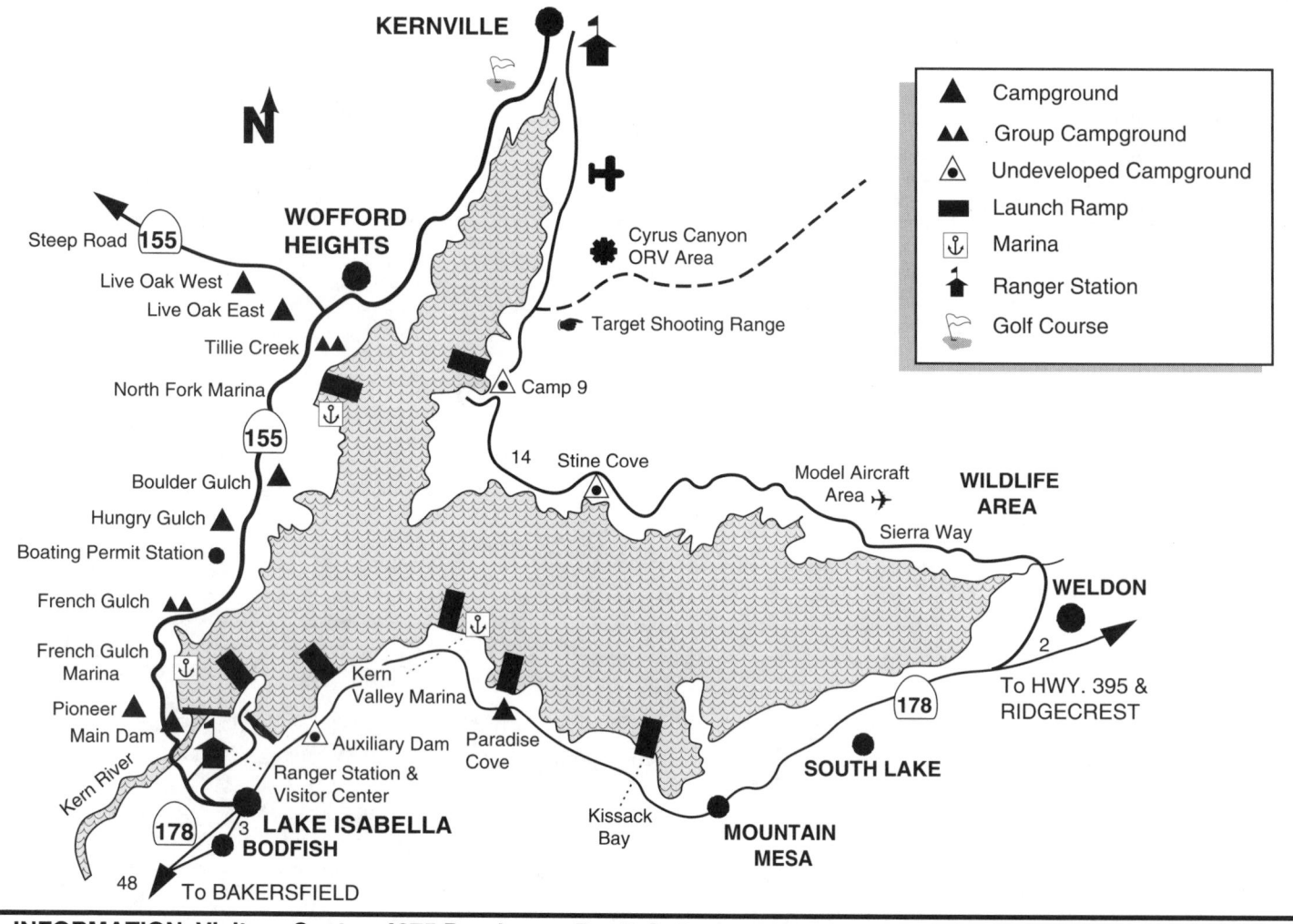

▲	Campground
▲▲	Group Campground
◬	Undeveloped Campground
▬	Launch Ramp
⚓	Marina
⛪	Ranger Station
⚑	Golf Course

INFORMATION: Visitors Center, 4875 Ponderosa Dr., P.O. Box 3810, Lake Isabella 93240—Ph: (760) 379-5646

CAMPING	BOATING	RECREATION	OTHER
800 Dev. Sites for Tents & R.V.s Fee: $14 Group Camps: $90-$185 Disposal Stations Reservations: Ph: (877) 444-6777 Plus Primitive Campsites No Fee	Power, Row, Canoe, Sail, Waterski, Jets, Windsurf & Inflatables Check for Restrictions *Annual Boating Permit Fees:* *Boat: $30 Sailboard: $20* Launch Ramps Full Service Marinas Rentals: Fishing & Waterski Boats Docks, Berths Moorings, Gas	Fishing: Trout, Catfish, Bluegill, Crappie & Largemouth Bass Fish Cleaning Station Swimming Picnicking Playgrounds Hiking & Bicycle Trails Campfire Programs Birdwatching Hunting: Quail & Waterfowl in Designated Areas	White Water Rafting: Kern River Trailer Rentals & Storage ORV Use Area Target Shooting Range Golf Course Airport - Auto Rentals Call for Current Water Levels Full Facilities at Towns Near Lake

SAN ANTONIO LAKE

San Antonio Lake is at an elevation of 900 feet in the rolling oak-covered hills of southern Monterey County. The Lake has a surface area of 5,500 acres with 60 miles of shoreline. There is an abundance of campsites, many with full hookups.

With mild water temperatures and a length of 16 miles, this is an ideal Lake for waterskiing. The warm water fishery makes San Antonio a good year around angler's Lake. The facilities are open all year with complete services for vacation activities. *Call for current water level conditions.*

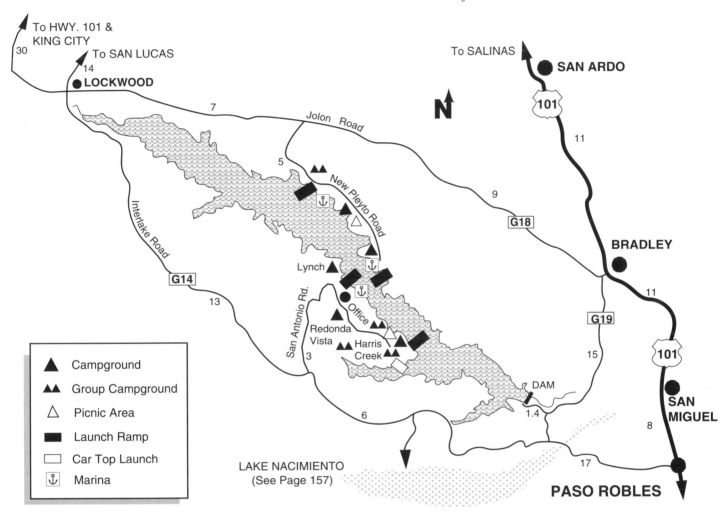

Legend:
- ▲ Campground
- ▲▲ Group Campground
- △ Picnic Area
- ■ Launch Ramp
- ☐ Car Top Launch
- ⚓ Marina

LAKE NACIMIENTO (See Page 157)

INFORMATION: Monterey County Parks Dept., 2610 San Antonio Rd., Bradley 93426—Ph: (805) 472-2311

CAMPING	BOATING	RECREATION	OTHER
767 Dev. Sites for Tents & R.V.s Many Full Hookups Fees: Winter - $16 - $20 Summer - $18 - $22 Group Camp Sites Overflow Camping Area Disposal Stations Day Use Fee: $6	Power, Row, Canoe, Sail, Waterski, Jets, Windsurf & Inflatable Full Service Marinas Launch Ramps - $5 Rentals: Fishing Boats, Pontoons & Ski Boats Docks, Mooring, Gas, Dry Storage Summer Boat Rides	Fishing: Catfish, Bluegill, Large & Smallmouth Bass, Striped Bass, Redear Perch & Crappie Swimming - Beach Picnicking Hiking, Bicyling & Equestrian Trails Nature Study Birdwatching Exercise Course Weekend Movies in Summer	19 Mobile Home Rentals Ph: (800) 310-2313 Cafe Grocery Store Bait & Tackle Laundromat Gas Station Game Room Visitor Center

LAKE NACIMIENTO

Nestled in a valley of pine and oak trees, Lake Nacimiento is at an elevation of 800 feet and has 5,370 surface acres with 165 miles of shoreline. Boaters can enjoy the many coves and warm, gentle winds. Fishing from shore or boat will usually produce largemouth, smallmouth or white bass. Waterskiing is excellent on this 16-mile long Lake with water temperature about 68 degrees. There are lakeside lodge accommodations and a good restaurant. Lake Nacimiento Resort offers an abundance of campsites, complete marina facilities and vacation activities. This is a great family recreation area.

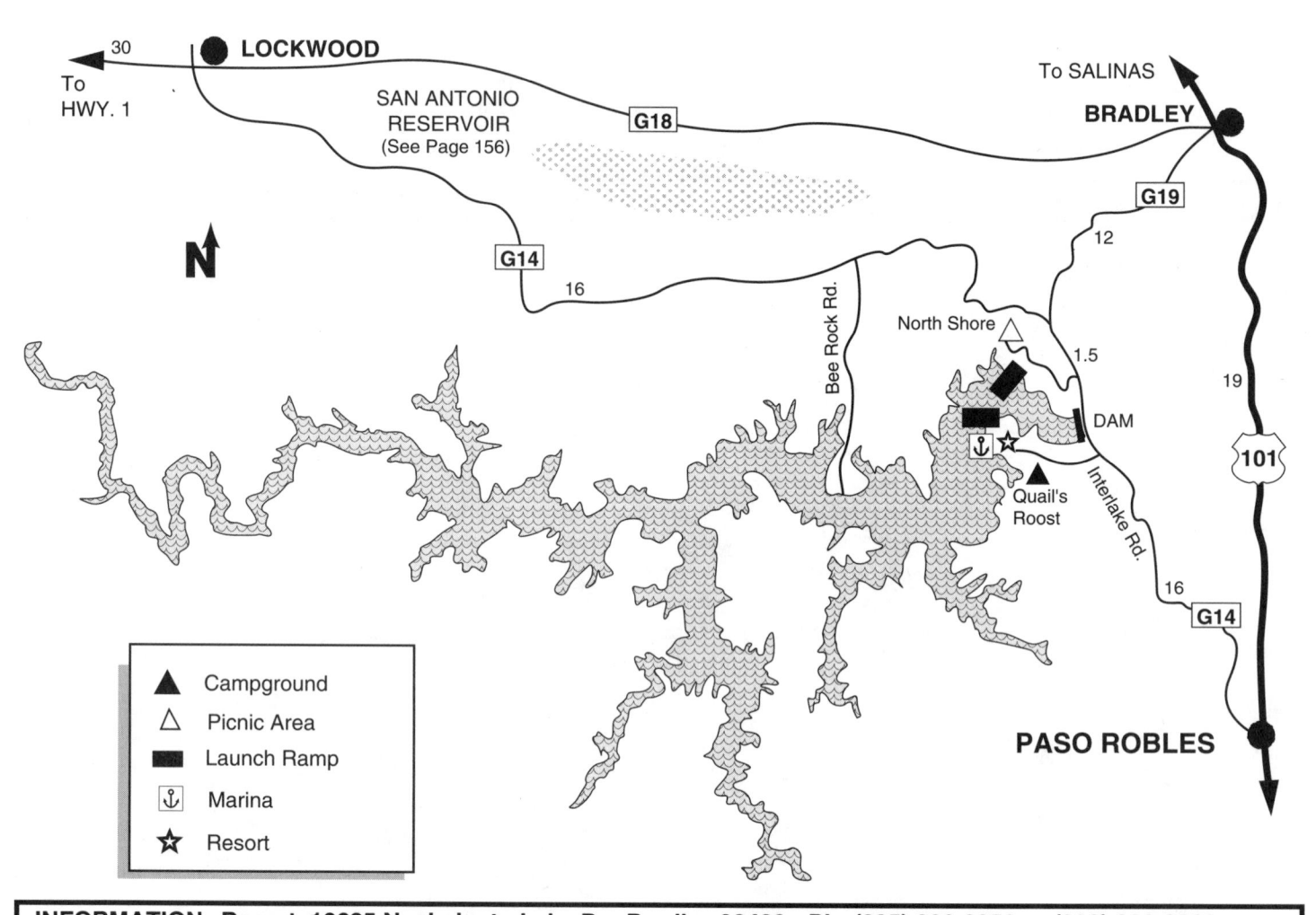

INFORMATION: Resort, 10625 Nacimiento Lake Dr., Bradley 93426—Ph: (805) 238-3256 or (800) 323-3839

CAMPING	BOATING	RECREATION	OTHER
350 Dev. Sites for Tents & R.V.s Fees: $25 a Night $140 a Week 40 R.V. Sites With Full Hookups Fees: $35 a Night $180 a Week Senior Discounts Group Sites Available Oct. 1 - March 1 Winter Rates: Oct. 1 to April 1	Power, Row, Canoe, Sail, Waterski, Jets, Windsurf & Inflatable Full Service Marina Launch Ramps Slalom Course Rentals: Fishing Boats, Pontoons Boating Use Fee: $5 a Day - $75 Year	Fishing: Catfish, Bluegill, Crappie, White Bass, Large & Smallmouth Bass Swimming Picnicking Hiking Trails *No Motorcycles* Day Use Fee: $10 - 2 People with Vehicle $3 Each Add'l. Person Under 12 - Free	Lodge Accommodations Restaurant Grocery Store Bait & Tackle Hot Showers & Laundry Disposal Station Gas & Propane Camp Trailer Rental Playgrounds Volleyball & Horseshoes Swimming Pool in Summer

SANTA MARGARITA LAKE, WHALE ROCK RESERVOIR and ATASCADERO LAKE

Located amid Central California's coastal range, Santa Margarita Lake has 1,070 surface acres and is a good warm water fishery with camping facilities and equestrian staging areas. Boats over 10 feet are allowed but waterskiing and windsurfing are not permitted. Whale Rock Reservoir is under the jurisdiction of the City of San Luis Obispo. Trout fishing is limited to 3 per day and boating or water contact are not permitted. Atascadero is a small city Lake with picnic sites and rental boats. Power boats are not allowed. The angler will find trout and bass.

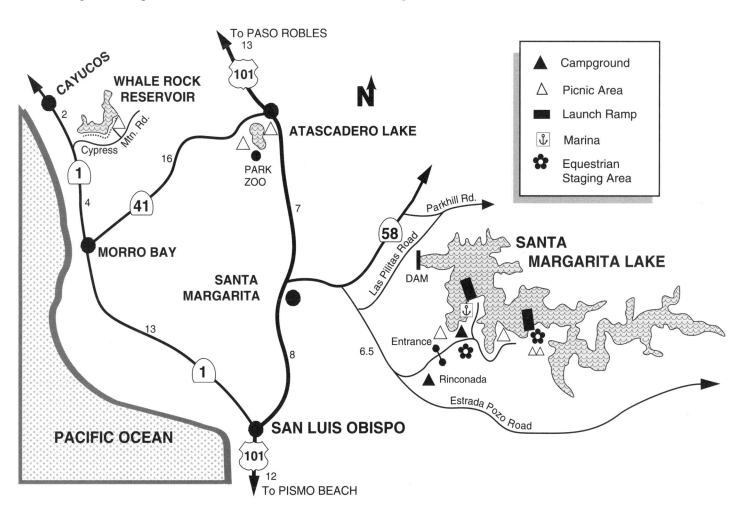

INFORMATION:San Luis Obispo County Parks, 1087 Santa Rosa St., San Luis Obispo 93408—Ph:(805) 781-5930

CAMPING	BOATING	RECREATION	OTHER

Santa Margarita:
  120 Dev. Sites for
    Tents & R.V.s
  Fees: $14
  No Hookups
  Reservations:
    Ph: (805) 788-2397
  Primitive Boat-In Sites
Rinconada Camp:
  Ph: (805) 438-5479
  60 Tent/R.V. Sites
  17 With Full Hookups
  Fee: $12 - $18
	Santa Margarita:
	  Boats Over 10 Feet Only
	  No Waterskiing or
	  Windsurfing
	  Approved Inflatables
	  Full Service Marina
	  Rentals: Fishing Boats &
	    Pontoons
	  Launch Ramp
	Whale Rock Reservoir:
	  No Boating
	Atascadero Lake:
	  Rental Boats
		Fishing: Black Bass &
		  Striped Bass, Rainbow
		  Trout, Bluegill & Catfish
		Swimming :
		  St. Margarita - Pool Only
		  Atascadero - Kiddie
		    Pool Only
		  Whale Rock - None
		Picnicking - Group Site at
		  Santa Margarita:
		  Ph: (805) 781-5930
		Hiking & Equestrian
		  Trails at Santa Margarita
			Santa Margarita:
			  Snacks & Drinks
			  Bait & Tackle
			Atascadero:
			  Information
			  Ph: (805) 461-5003

LOPEZ LAKE

Lopez Lake, with 22 miles of shoreline, is administered by the San Luis Obispo County Parks Department. The 950 surface acres are favored by westerly breezes coming off the Pacific making it a popular Lake for sailing and windsurfing. There are good marine facilities and special areas are set aside for sailing, windsurfing, jet skis and waterskiing. The angler will find a variety of game fish. In addition to the oak-shaded campsites listed below, there are overflow sites. This is a complete recreation facility offering a naturalist program which can be enjoyed on trails, by boat or around the campfire. The Mustang Waterslides are popular with the youngsters.

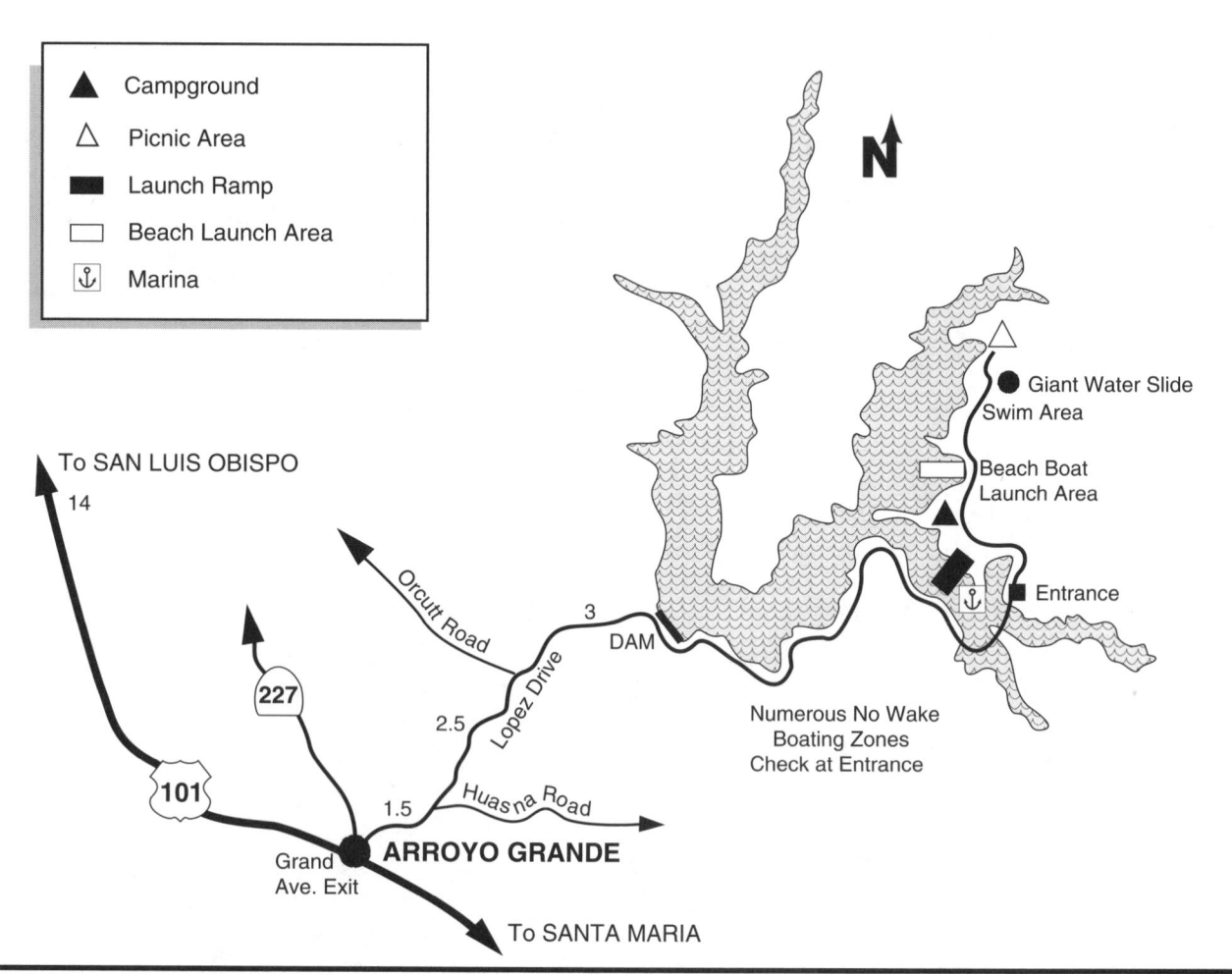

Map Legend:
- ▲ Campground
- △ Picnic Area
- ■ Launch Ramp
- ▢ Beach Launch Area
- ⚓ Marina

To SAN LUIS OBISPO
14

Orcutt Road

Lopez Drive

227

101

Grand Ave. Exit

ARROYO GRANDE

Huasna Road

1.5

2.5

3

DAM

To SANTA MARIA

N

Giant Water Slide
Swim Area

Beach Boat
Launch Area

Entrance

Numerous No Wake
Boating Zones
Check at Entrance

INFORMATION: Lopez Lake, 6800 Lopez Dr., Arroyo Grande 93420—Ph: (805) 788-2381

CAMPING	BOATING	RECREATION	OTHER
152 Dev. Sites for Tents & R.V.s Fee: $14	Open to All Boating Speed Limit: 40 MPH No Wake Zones	Fishing: Rainbow Trout, Catfish, Bluegill, Crappie, Redear	Marina & Store Ph: (805) 489-1006 Snack Bar
135 Dev. Sites with Full Hookups Fee: $18 - $23	Full Service Marina Paved Launch: Non-Motor $2.50	Sunfish, Large & Smallmouth Bass Swimming:	Bait & Tackle Laundromat Gas Station
Summer Only: 67 Sites with Electric Hookups - Fee: $16	With Motor $5 Beach Launch Area Moorings, Boat Docks	In Designated Areas Picnicking - Group Sites Hiking & Nature Trails	Mustang Water Slides & Hot Spas Ph: (805) 489-8898
Group Sites Disposal Station Reservations: Ph: (805) 788-2381	Boat & Trailer Storage Rentals: Fishing, Ski, Patio, Canoe, Paddle Boats & Waverunners	Boat Tours Campfire Programs Day Use Fee: $5	Dog: $2 a Day Proof of Dog Ownership & Leash Required

Lake Cachuma is at an elevation of 800 feet amid the oak-shaded hills of Santa Ynez Valley. This is one of the most complete recreation parks in the State with camping, marine, recreation and other support facilities. In addition to the campgrounds at the Lake, the Cachuma Recreation Area includes Live Oak Camp which will accommodate very large groups. This 3,200 surface acre Lake is open to most boating but waterskiing, kayaks, rafts and canoes are not allowed. The angler will find a large variety of fish. There are hiking, bicyling and equestrian trails. Rental bikes and swimming pools can be enjoyed from June through Labor Day. Park naturalists conduct a variety of programs. Through the City of Santa Barbara, Gibraltar Reservoir is open for trout fishing on a limited permit basis.

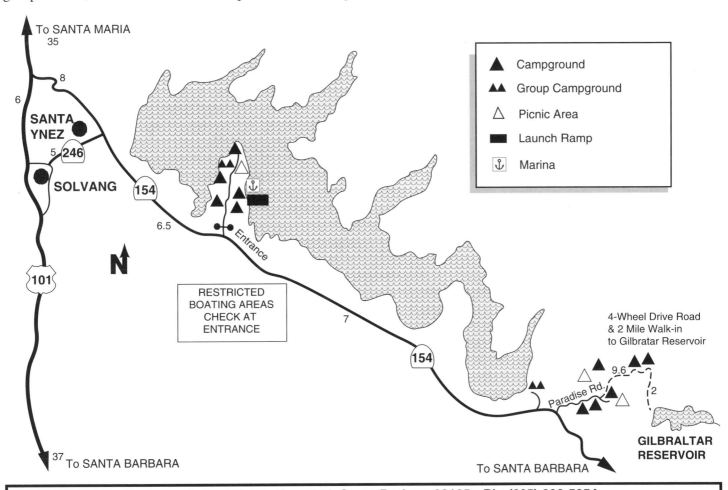

INFORMATION: Cachuma Lake, HC 58 - Hwy. 154, Santa Barbara 93105—Ph: (805) 686-5054

CAMPING	BOATING	RECREATION	OTHER
500 Dev. Sites for Tents & R.V.s 90 R.V. Sites with Full & Partial Hookups Fees: $16 - $22 Group Camps Disposal Stations Yurt Tents: Heat, Light & Lockable Door Fee: $35 - $55 Reservations: Ph: (805) 686-5050 Vehicle Entry Fee: $5	Most Boating Allowed Except No Canoes, Kayaks or Rafts No Waterskiing Launch Ramp - Fee: $5 Full Service Marina Docks, Berths & Moorings Boat & Trailer Storage Rentals: Row Boats & Motors, Paddle & Patio Boats Rates: $14 - $250	Fishing: Channel Catfish, Bluegill, Crappie, Large & Smallmouth Bass, Sunfish, Redear, & Rainbow Trout Swimming: Pools Only Picnicking Hiking & Equestrian Trails Bicycle Rentals Birdwatching Nature Tours & Boat Tours	General Store Bait & Tackle Snack Bar Laundromat Gas Station Recreation Center Nature Center Handicap Facilities

CASITAS LAKE

Lake Casitas is at an elevation of 600 feet in the oak-covered rolling hills west of the Los Padres National Forest. Under the jurisdiction of the Casitas Municipal Water District, this very popular 2,500 surface-acre Lake has 32 miles of shoreline. No swimming or body contact with the water is allowed.

Except for the main recreation area, the remainder of the shoreline is closed. Casitas is famous for big fish and holds State records for largemouth bass, catfish and redear sunfish. Night fishing is allowed one three-day weekend a month. The 6,200 acre tree-shaded recreation area offers extensive camping, boating and picnicking facilities.

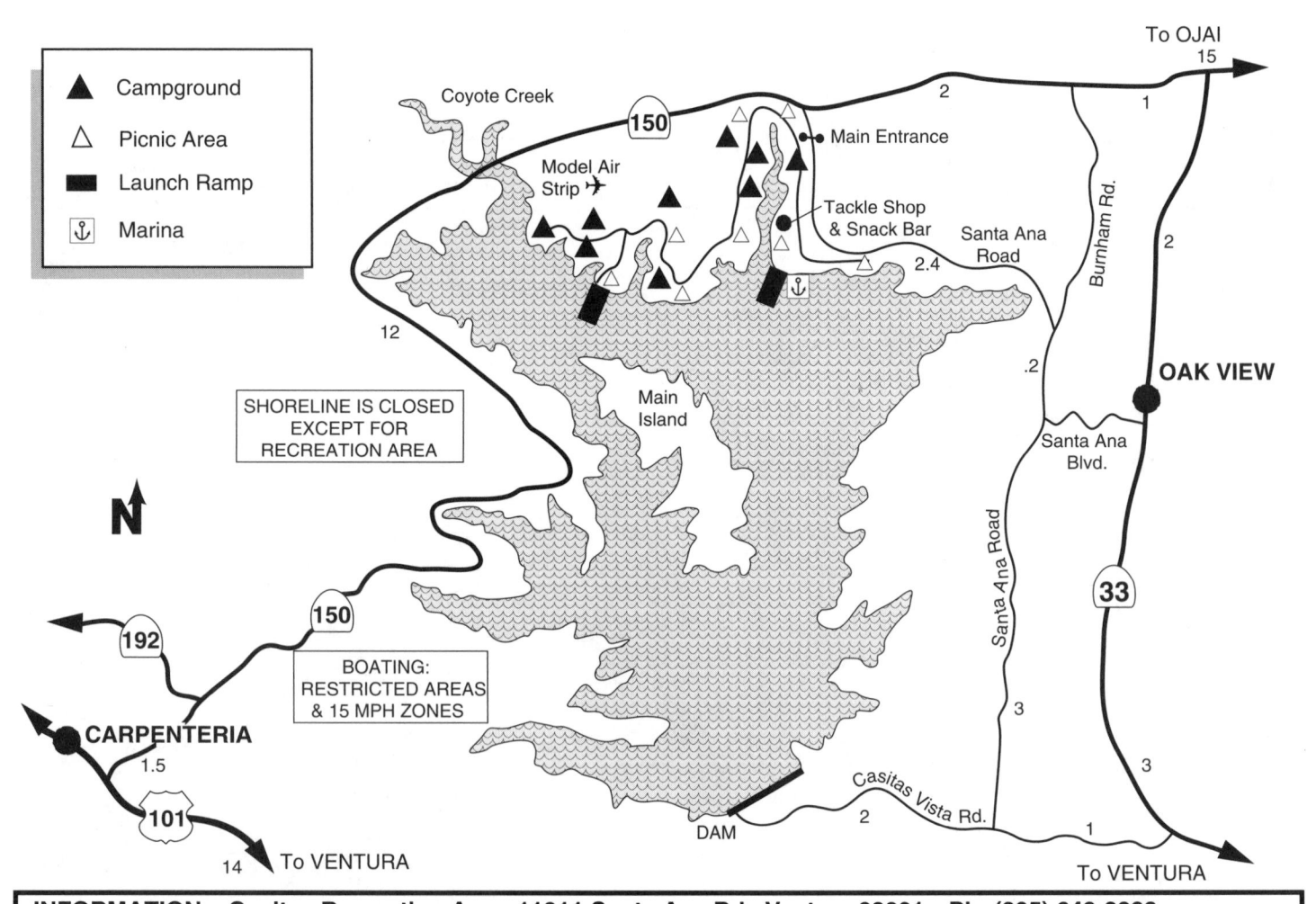

INFORMATION: Casitas Recreation Area, 11311 Santa Ana Rd., Ventura 93001—Ph: (805) 649-2233

CAMPING	BOATING	RECREATION	OTHER
Over 400 Dev. Sites for Tents & R.V.s Fee: $16-$18	Power, Row, Sail *Only* 11 feet Minimum Size to 26 feet Maximum	Fishing: Catfish, Trout, Bluegill, Largemouth & Florida Bass,	Snack Bar Restaurant Grocery Store
Hookups: $24-$42 Extra Vehicle: $10 Boat: $7.50 Reservation Fee: $6.50	*Strict Regulations Call for Information* Speed Limit - 35 MPH Boat Permit: $6 a Day	Redear Sunfish, Perch & Crappie Picnicking Hiking	Bait & Tackle Trailer Rentals Boat & Trailer Storage Frequent Visitor
Group Sites: $320 $65 Reservation Fee *Reservations Advised* Ph: (805) 649-1122	Full Service Marina Launch Ramps Rentals: Row Boats & Pontoons	Playgrounds Model Airplane Strip Bicycle Rentals Water Playground	Discount Cards Handicap Camping Facilities
Disposal Stations Day Use: $6.50 per Vehicle With Boat: $12.50	Docks, Moorings, Berths, Gas, Storage	*No Swimming in Lake*	

LAKE EVANS and LAKE WEBB— BUENA VISTA AQUATIC RECREATION AREA

Buena Vista Recreation Area is located at an elevation of 293 feet in the south San Joaquin Valley. This is Kern County's finest recreation area consisting of 1,586 acres and two Lakes with complete facilities for camping, picnicking, swimming and boating. Lake Evans has a surface area of 86 acres and Lake Webb has 873 acres. Both Lakes are stocked continu-ally with warm water game fish. Trophy trout are stocked in the winter months at Lake Evans. Boating is allowed at both Lakes but Lake Evans is restricted to a 5 MPH speed limit. Waterskiing is permitted at Lake Webb in a counter-clock-wise pattern. There are designated areas for sailboats, power boats and waterskiing.

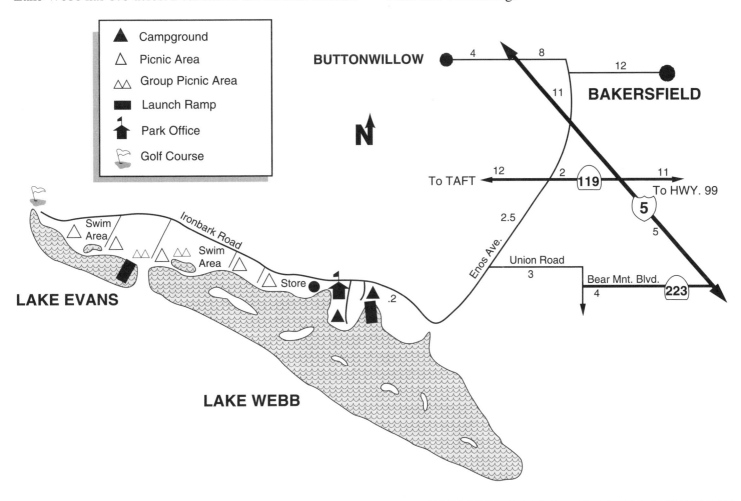

▲	Campground
△	Picnic Area
△△	Group Picnic Area
■	Launch Ramp
⬆	Park Office
🏁	Golf Course

INFORMATION: Kern County Parks, 1110 Golden State Ave., Bakersfield 93301—Ph: (661) 868-7000			
CAMPING	**BOATING**	**RECREATION**	**OTHER**
112 Dev. Sites for Tents & R.V.s	Power, Row, Canoe, Sail, Windsurf,	Fishing: Largemouth & Striped Bass,	Grocery Store Bait & Tackle
Fees: $21 - $25 Full Hookups	Jets & Inflatable With Restrictions	Catfish & Bluegill Lake Evans: Trout in Winter	Gas Station Propane
$27 - $32 Plus Overflow Area	Speed Limits: Lake Evans - 5 MPH	Lake Evans: Fishing $6 Swimming: Lagoons Only	Full Facilities
Fee: $10 Disposal Station	Lake Webb - 45 MPH Launch Ramps: $5	Picnicking - Group Sites to 400 People	14 Miles at Taft
Reserve Ph:(661) 868-7050 Reservation Fee: $7	Docks, Moorings, Gas Rental Boats:	Playgrounds Bicycle Trails	
Dog: $3 Day Use: $5	Evans Ph: (661)763-1268 Webb Ph: (661) 763-1770		

PYRAMID LAKE

Pyramid Lake is at an elevation of 2,606 feet in the Angeles National Forest in Northwestern Los Angeles County. This popular Lake has a surface area of 1,297 acres. Most of the 21 miles of rugged shoreline are accessible only by boat. There are boat-in picnic sites and restrooms scattered around the Lake. Spanish Point is a favorite spot with picnic sites and a beach. While there is also a good trout and warm water fishery, Pyramid is known as one of Southern California's prime striped bass waters. There are good marine and campground facilities under concession from the U.S. Forest Service. Quail Lake, the beginning of the southern portion of the California Aqueduct, offers no facilities. Anglers can fish for striped bass from the banks.

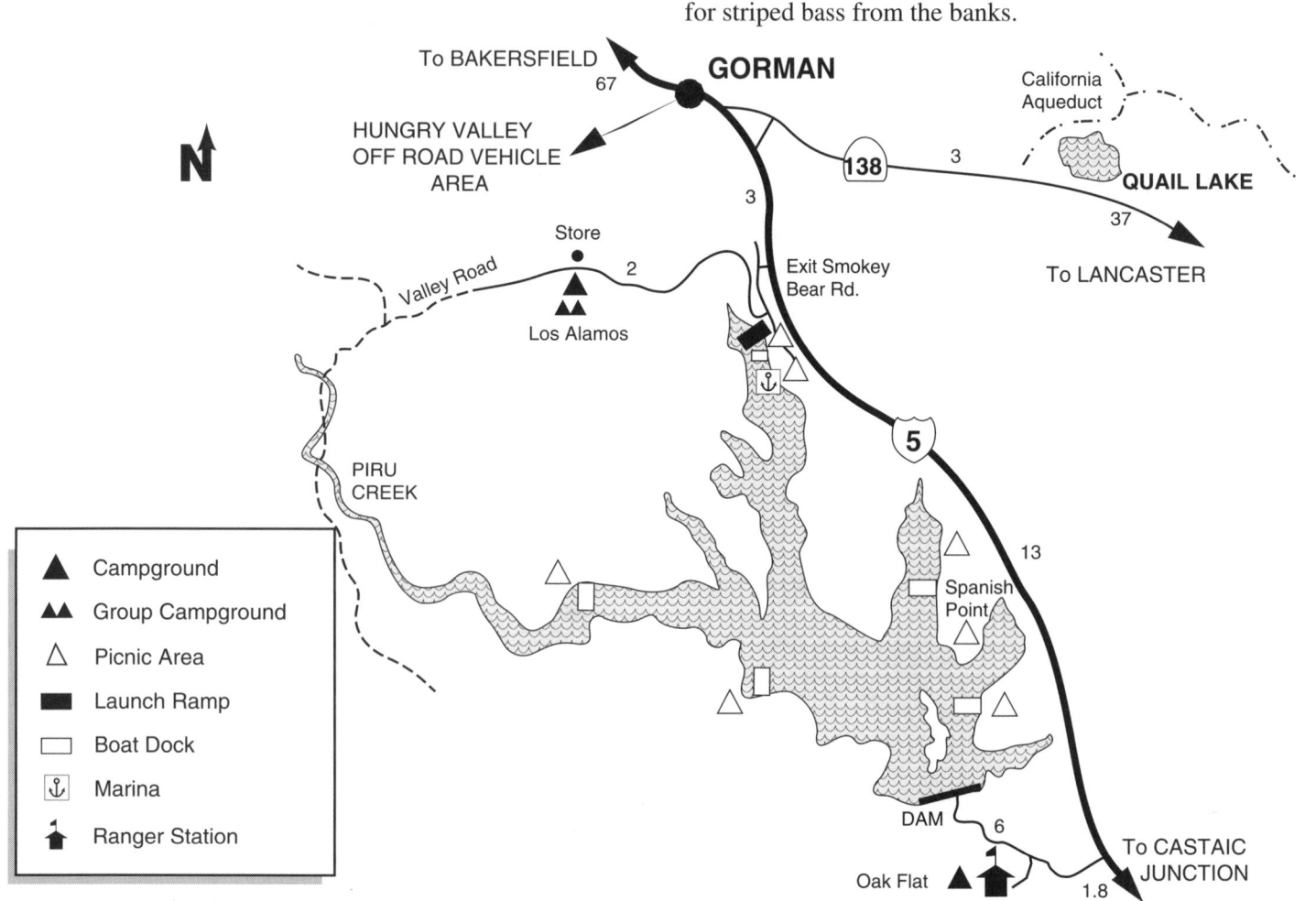

INFORMATION: Pyramid Lake, c/o Pyramid Enterprises, P.O. Box 249, Piru 93040—Ph: (661) 295-1245

CAMPING	BOATING	RECREATION	OTHER
Los Alamos: 93 Dev. Sites for Tents & R.V.s Fee: $12 48 First Come Basis 45 Sites Can be Reserved 3 Group Sites to 30 People Each Reservations Only Ph: (800) 416-6992	Open to All Boating, Waterskiing & Windsurfing Speed Limit 35 MPH Full Service Marina Ph: (661) 257-2892 Docks & Slip Rentals Launch Ramp Rentals: Fishing Boats	Fishing: Striped Bass, Largemouth & Smallmouth Bass, Rainbow Trout, Channel Catfish, Bluegill, Crappie & Sunfish Swimming Beaches Picnicking Boat-In Picnic Sites Off Road Vehicles: Only at Hungry Valley Designated Area	Snack Bar Bait & Tackle Fish Cleaning Station

Castaic Lake and the Afterbay Lagoon are at an elevation of 1,500 feet and operated by the County of Los Angeles. The large recreation area covers 8,800 acres. The Main Reservoir has 29 shoreline miles and the Afterbay Lagoon has 3 shoreline miles. The east arm of the Main Reservoir is open to slower boating while the west arm is for waterskiing and faster boating. The Lagoon is open to non-power boating and swimming from mid-June through September. Fishing at the Main Reservoir is from sunrise to sunset, but the Lagoon offers 24-hour fishing on the east shoreline. There is a good warm water fishery and trout are stocked in the winter months.

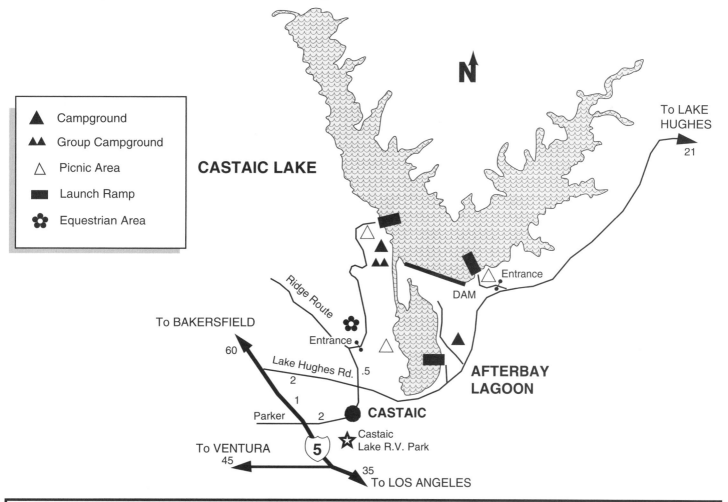

Legend:
- ▲ Campground
- ▲▲ Group Campground
- △ Picnic Area
- ■ Launch Ramp
- ✿ Equestrian Area

INFORMATION: Castaic Lake, 32132 Castaic Lake Dr., Castaic 91384—Ph: (661) 257-4050

CAMPING	BOATING	RECREATION	OTHER
60 Dev. Sites for Tent & R.V. Sites to 35 feet No Hookups Fee: $12 Tent Sites are Limited Disposal Station Reservations: Ph: (661) 257-4050 Day Use Fee: $6	Main Reservoir: All Boating Allowed 35 MPH Speed Limit Launch Ramps: $6 Rentals: Fishing Boats with Motors Afterbay: Non-Power Boats Launch Ramp: $6	Fishing: Trout, Catfish, Large & Smallmouth Bass Afterbay Lagoon: 24-Hour Fishing Area Afterbay Lagoon: Swim Beach Open Mid-May to Mid-Sept. Picnicking - Group Areas Hiking, Bicycle & Equestrian Trails Playgrounds	Snack Bar Bait & Tackle Marine Supplies Castaic Lake R.V. Park 103 R.V. Sites Full Hookups Fees to $37 Ph: (661) 257-3340 *No Launching After 500 Boats & 125 PWCs*

LAKE PIRU

Lake Piru is at an elevation of 1,055 feet in the Los Padres National Forest near Los Angeles. It is owned and operated by the United Water Conservation District. The surface area of the Lake ranges from 750 surface acres to 1,200 surface acres depending on the season. The water is deep and clear.

This is a good warm water fishery and also trout are planted twice a week in season. Piru Lake has complete marina facilities. Be aware that special boating restrictions apply. The campgrounds are located amid oak and olive trees above the launch ramp.

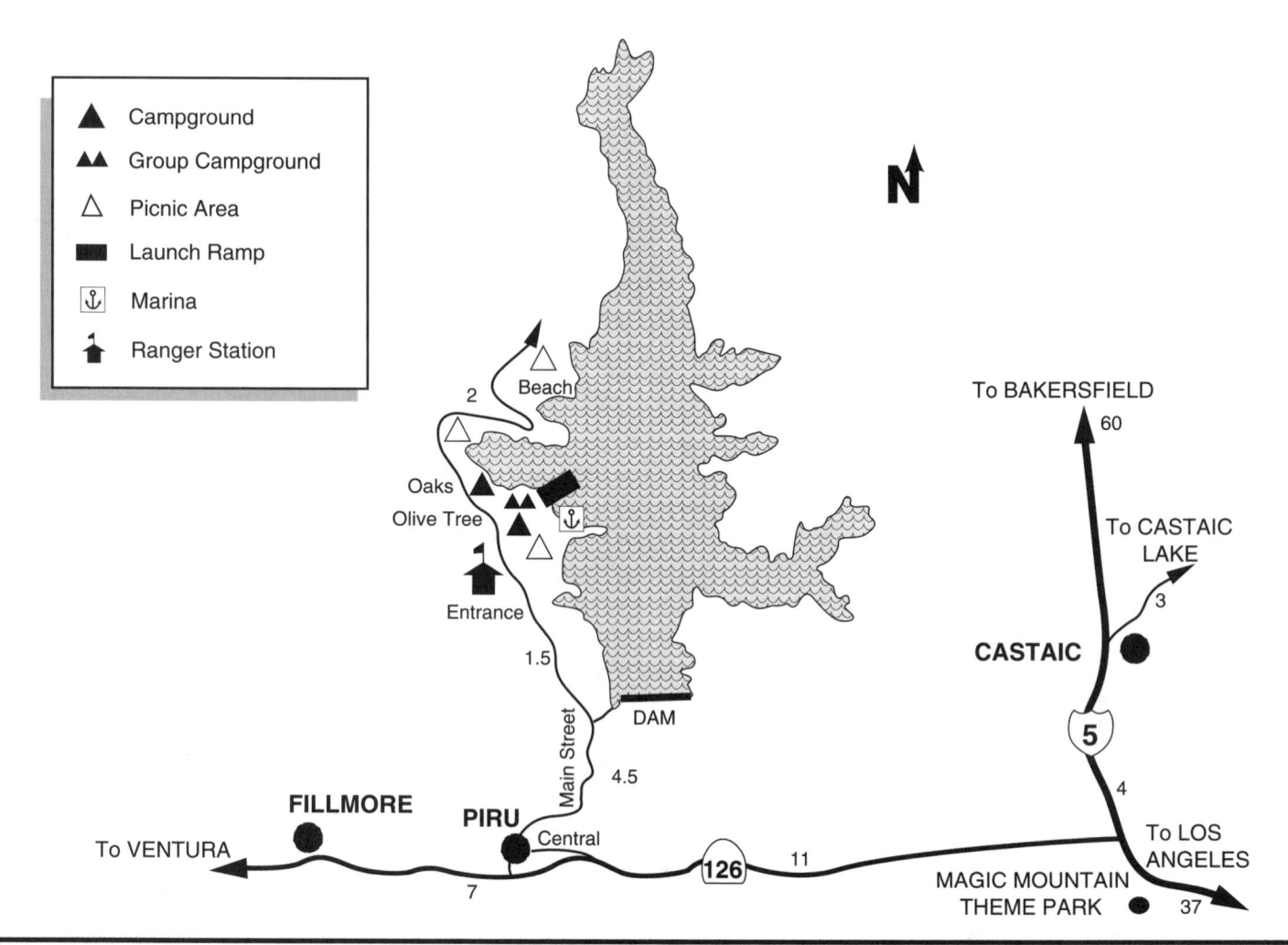

▲	Campground
▲▲	Group Campground
△	Picnic Area
■	Launch Ramp
⚓	Marina
♟	Ranger Station

INFORMATION: Park Manager, P.O. Box 202, 4780 Piru Canyon Rd., Piru 93040—Ph: (805) 521-1500

CAMPING	BOATING	RECREATION	OTHER
132 Dev. Sites for Tents & R.V.s - Fee: $21-$23	Power, Waterskiing, Sail & Inflatables	Fishing: Rainbow Trout, Largemouth Bass,	Snack Bar Restaurant
101 R.V. Sites with Electric Hookups Fee: $24-$28	*Call for Specific Regulations* Speed Limit: 35 MPH	Catfish, Crappie, Bluegill Swim Beach Picnicking	Bait & Tackle Grocery Store Marine Supplies
5 R.V. Sites with Full Hookups - Fee: $28-$32	*No Windsurfing or PWCs* Designated Boating Areas	Groups to 120 People Hiking & Equestrian	Dock, Moorings R.V. & Boat Storage
Group Camps Overflow Camping Area	Full Service Marina Ph: (805) 521-1231	Trails in Los Padres National Forest	Gas
Disposal Stations Reservations - Fee $5: Ph: (805) 521-1500	Launch Ramp Rentals: Fishing Boats & Pontoons	Day Use: Vehicle Fee: $7.50 Boat Fee: $7.50	Dogs on Leash: $2 Full Facilities in Piru

Elizabeth Lake and Lake Hughes are at an elevation of 3,300 feet in the Angeles National Forest north of Los Angeles. These Lakes are within 5 miles of each other and are separated by a small private Lake. Lake Hughes has a 35 surface acres. Access is through the resort which is open to the public all year and offers camping, fishing and boating. The western half of Elizabeth Lake is owned and operated by the U.S. Forest Service which maintains picnic sites and allows swimming. The eastern half of the Lake is private. There are warm water fisheries at both Lakes and trout fishing can be good in season at Elizabeth Lake.

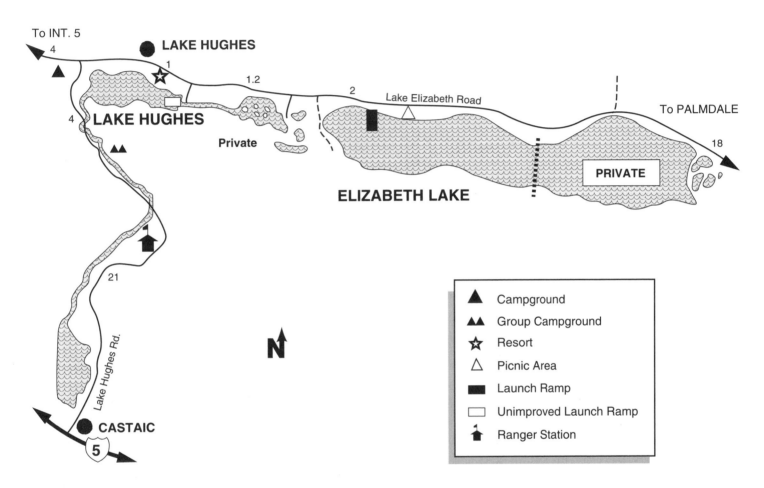

▲	Campground
▲▲	Group Campground
☆	Resort
△	Picnic Area
■	Launch Ramp
▢	Unimproved Launch Ramp
⚑	Ranger Station

INFORMATION: Saugus Ranger District, 30800 Bouquet Canyon Rd., Saugus 91350—Ph: (661) 296-9710

CAMPING	BOATING	RECREATION	OTHER

Hughes Lakeshore Park
  43677 Trail K
  Lake Hughes
  Ph: (661) 724-1845
  44 Dev. Sites for
    Tents & R.V.s
  Fees: $14 Vehicle plus
    $2 per Person
  Dogs on Leash: $1
Day Use:
  Fees: $10 Vehicle plus
    $1 per Person
	Sail Boats &
	  Power Boats
	  10 HP Motors Max.
	Launch Ramps
	Rentals: Row Boats at
	  Lake Hughes
	
	Check for Current
	  Water Level
	  Conditions
		Fishing: Catfish, Bass,
		  Bluegill & Crappie
		  Plus Trout at Lake
		    Elizabeth in Season
		Picnicking
		Hiking Trails
			Lake Hughes:
			  Snack Bar
			  Arcade
			  Pool Tables
			  Horseshoes
			  General Store
			  Restaurant
			  Playground

LITTLEROCK RESERVOIR, APOLLO PARK and FRAZIER PARK

Littlerock Reservoir, 150 surface acres, is located at 3,400 feet elevation in the Angeles National Forest. Fishing can be good for rainbow and brown trout, stocked every other week in season. Apollo County Park is a part of the Los Angeles County Regional Park System. The three Lakes, totaling 26 surface acres, are named for the astronauts of the Apollo flight that landed on the moon in 1969. There is a well-stocked catfish and trout fishery. Frazier Park has picnic sites and a very small fishing lake for trout, bass and catfish.

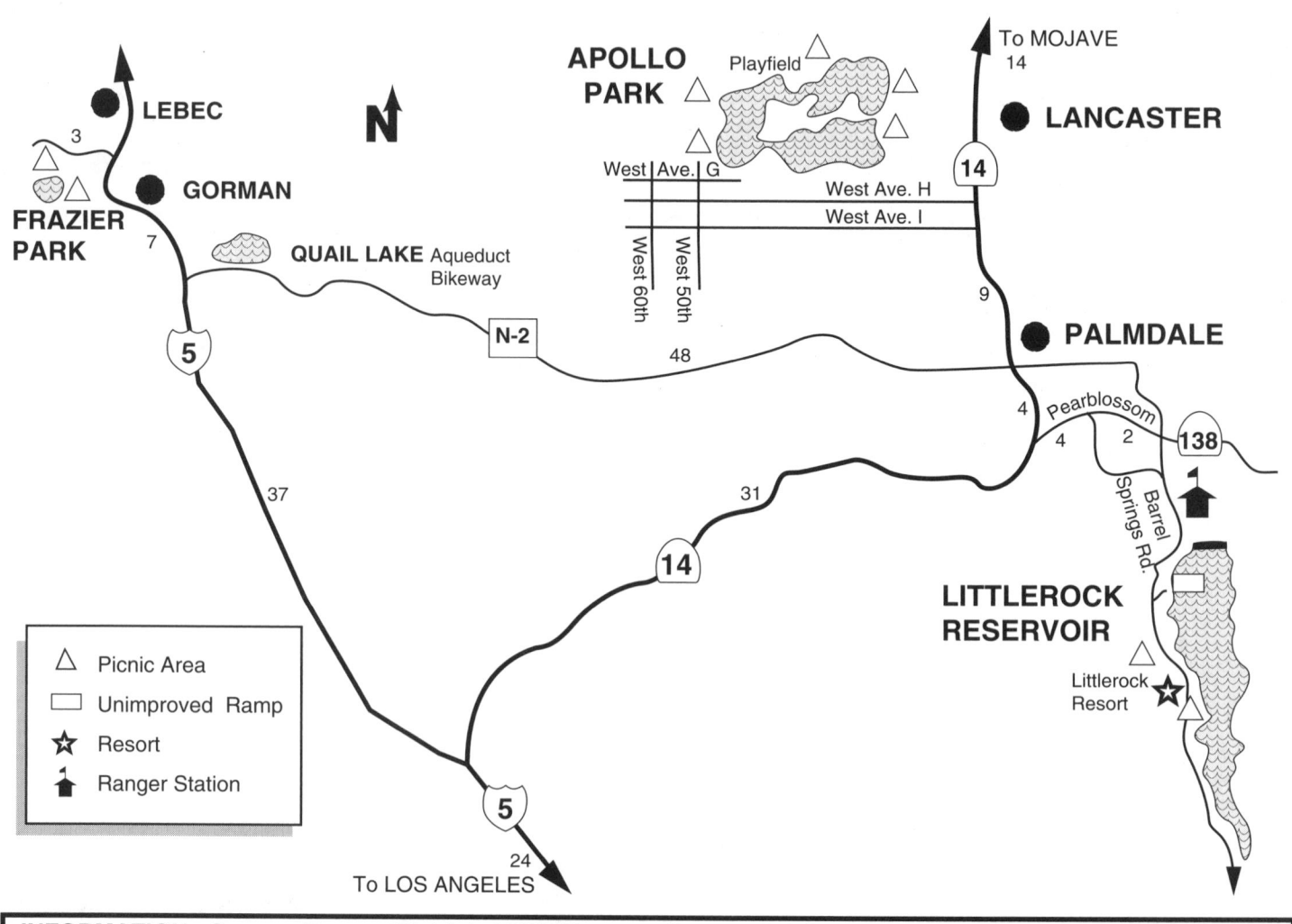

Legend:
- △ Picnic Area
- ▢ Unimproved Ramp
- ★ Resort
- ⬆ Ranger Station

INFORMATION: Saugus Ranger District, 30800 Bouquet Canyon Rd. Saugus 91390—Ph: (661) 296-9710

CAMPING	BOATING	RECREATION	OTHER
At this time there is No Camping at Littlerock Recreation Area as the Sites are Closed for Habitat Protection Call for Current Information Little Rock Canyon Day Use: $5 Apollo Park: Open 6 am to 10 pm	Littlerock Reservoir: Fishing Boats Only Speed Limit: 5 MPH Launch Area Row Boat Rentals at Resort Apollo Park: No Boating Frazier Park: No Boating	Fishing: Rainbow, German Brown and Kamloop Trout, Catfish Picnicking Hiking Hunting: Deer Children's Play Area Apollo Park: Fishing Derbies Littlerock Reservoir: Open Area for ORV Use When Water is Low	Littlerock Lake Resort 32700 Cheseboro Rd. Palmdale 93550 Ph: (661) 533-1923 No Camping at This Time - Day Use Only Grocery Store Cafe, Bait & Tackle Apollo County Park 4555 W. Ave. G Lancaster 93534 Ph: (661) 259-1750

MOJAVE NARROWS PARK, GLEN HELEN PARK and JACKSON LAKE

Mojave Narrows Regional Park is at an elevation of 2,700 feet in a high desert. Glen Helen Regional Park is at 1,000 feet, just 15 minutes from downtown San Bernardino. Campgrounds and many recreational facilities are located at these two Parks. Boating is limited but the angler will find trout stocked in winter, bass and channel catfish at Glen Helen and Mojave Narrows. Jackson Lake, at an elevation of 6,500 feet, is in the Big Pines Recreation Area. Trout can be found in spring, summer and fall at Jackson Lake along with campgrounds, picnic areas, hiking and equestrian trails.

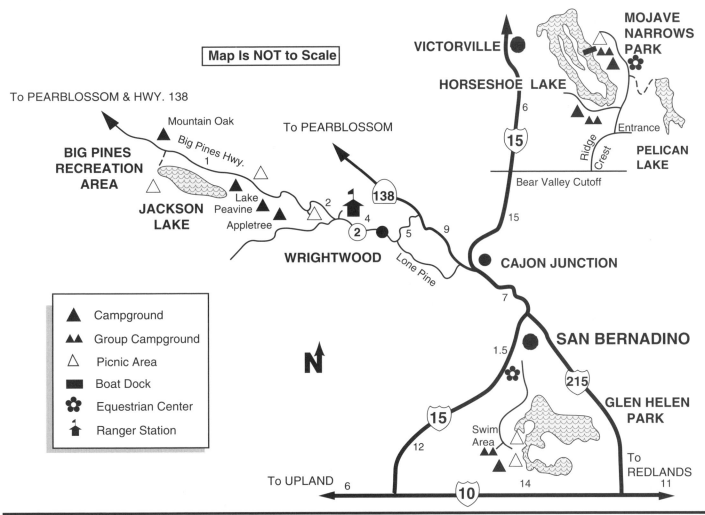

INFORMATION: San Bernadino County Reg. Parks, 777 E. Rialto, San Bernardino 92415—Ph: (909) 387-2594

CAMPING	BOATING	RECREATION	OTHER
Mojave Narrows: 　Ph: (760) 245-2226 　85 Dev. Sites for 　Tents & R.V.s 　　38 with Full Hookups Glen Helen Regional Park: 　Ph: (909) 887-7540 　45 Dev. Sites for 　Tents & R.V.s Fees: $10 to $15 Group Camp Areas Disposal Stations Day Use Fee: $5	Mojave Narrows & Glen Helen: 　Rentals: Row Boats & 　Paddle Boats Jackson Lake: 　Hand Launch Only 　No Motor Boats	Fishing: Trout, Bass, 　Catfish Picnicking Glen Helen: 　Swim Lagoon, 　Waterslides 　Playgrounds 　ORV Park 　Nature Trails Mojave Narrows: 　Group Picnic Areas 　Hiking & Equestrian Trails 　Horse Rentals	Big Pines Recreation Area Jackson Lake: 　Saugus Ranger District 　30800 Bouquet Cyn. Rd. 　Saugus 91390 　Ph: (661) 296-9710 Numerous Campgrounds in Area for Tents & R.V.s Reservations: 　Ph: (877) 444-6777

CRYSTAL LAKE

At an elevation of 5,700 feet, Crystal Lake Recreation Area is located in the Angeles National Forest. The small 5 acre Lake can have good fishing and limited small craft boating but *be certain to check water levels.* There are many miles of hiking trails ranging from self-guided nature trails to moderately strenuous hikes along the Pacific Crest Trail. The angler can fish along the North, East and West Forks of the San Gabriel River. Check with the Ranger District Office for hunting restrictions in this area. The San Dimas and San Gabriel Reservoirs are open to shoreline fishing only. There are no boating facilities.

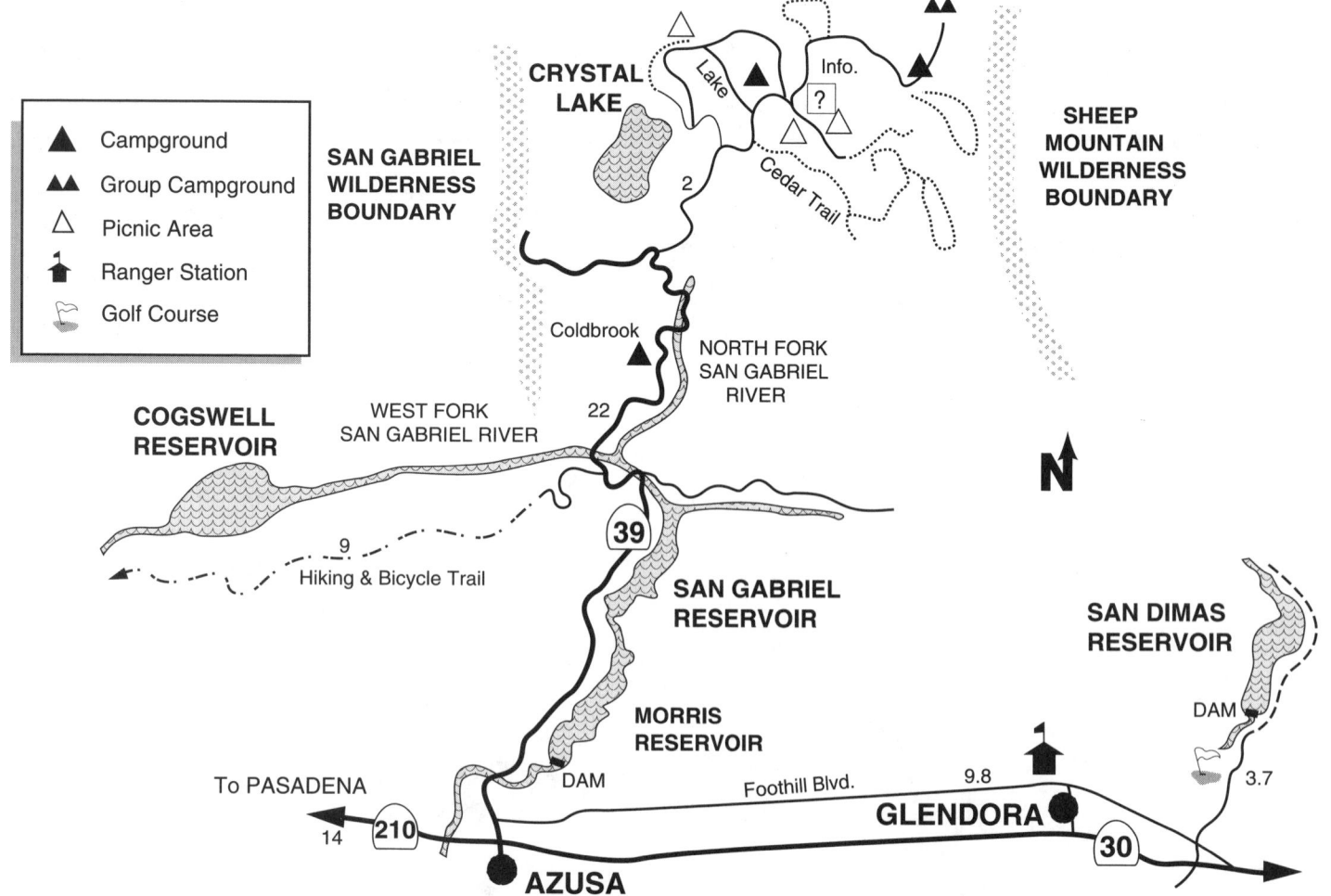

INFORMATION: Mt. Baldy Ranger District, 110 N. Wabash Ave., Glendora 91740—Ph: (626) 335-1251

CAMPING	BOATING	RECREATION	OTHER
Crystal Lake: 176 Dev. Sites for Tents & R.V.s Fee: $8 9 Group Sites Reservations: Ph: (877) 444-6777 Coldbrook: 24 Dev. Sites for Tents & R.V.s No Water - No Fee	Crystal Lake: Small Craft Only No Motors Hand Launch: 200 Yards Down Steps	Fishing: Rainbow Trout Hiking & Nature Trails Backpacking Nature Programs Golf Course at San Dimas No Swimming No Hunting Within The Crystal Lake Recreation Area	General Store Snack Bar Visitor's Center Ph: (626) 910-1149 Full Facilities In Azusa

ALONDRA PARK and HARBOR LAKE

Alondra Park, under the jurisdiction of Los Angeles County, is an 84-acre urban park with a small 8-acre Lake for fishing. Boating is not allowed. There are picnic sites, a swim area, community gardens and a playground. Harbor Lake Park is under the jurisdiction of the City of Los Angeles. There is no boating at this small lake although canoe groups can arrange to use it. The angler can find largemouth bass, bluegill, perch and catfish. There are youth group campgrounds, picnic areas and a playground. Harbor Lake Park is a wildlife sanctuary where a variety of plants, birds and animals can be observed in their natural habitats.

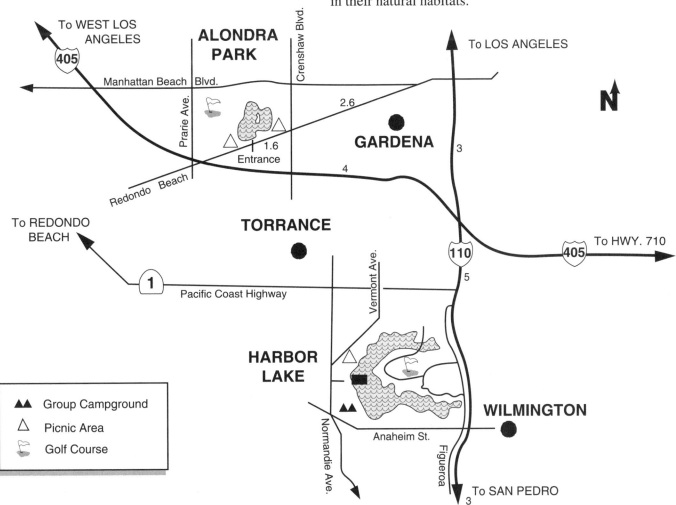

INFORMATION: Harbor Lake Park, 25820 S. Vermont, Wilmington 90744—Ph: (310) 548-7515

CAMPING	BOATING	RECREATION	OTHER
Harbor Lake: Youth Group Camping Only	Harbor Lake: No Private Boats Only Open to Group Canoes by Request No Swimming or Body Contact with the Water	Fishing: Largemouth Bass, Bluegill, Catfish & Perch Picnic Areas Playgrounds Athletic Fields Nature Study Golf Courses	Full Facilities Nearby
Alondra County Park 3850 W. Manhattan Beach Blvd. Lawndale 90260 Ph: (310) 217-8366 Day Use Only	Alondra Park: No Boating	Alondra Park: Swim Area Harbor Lake: Swimming in Pool Only - Open in Summer	

EL DORADO EAST REGIONAL PARK

El Dorado East is an urban park under the administration of the City of Long Beach with 802 acres of recreation facilities. Nestled amid the rolling green hills of the park are 4 small Lakes totaling approximately 40 surface acres. There are no boats allowed except for rental boats and model boats. Fishing from the shore for trout and warm water species is often good. Individual and group picnic areas are available along with a network of paved trails for the bicycler and rollerskater. There is a fitness course for the casual jogger or serious runner. An 85-acre nature center with 2 miles of trails can also be enjoyed. The Olympic Archery Range is the finest in Southern California.

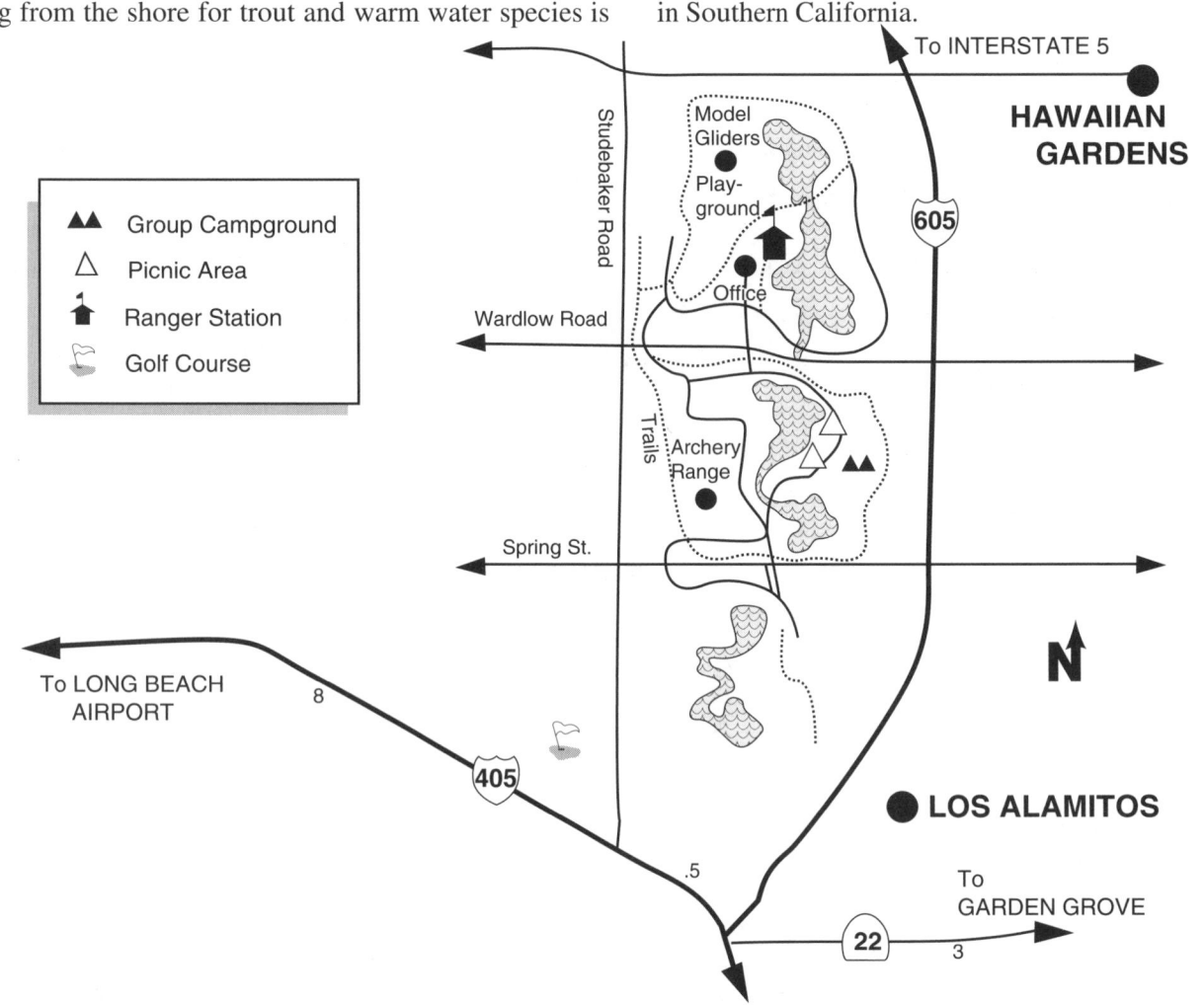

▲▲	Group Campground
△	Picnic Area
⌂	Ranger Station
⛵	Golf Course

INFORMATION: El Dorado East Regional Park, 7550 E. Spring St., Long Beach 90815—Ph: (562) 570-1771

CAMPING	BOATING	RECREATION	OTHER
No Camping Except for Youth Groups Under 18 Years Old 15 Children Minimum	No Private Boats Allowed	Fishing: Trout in Winter, Bluegill, Channel Catfish, Largemouth Bass,	Snack Bar Train Rides Pony Rides
	Rentals: Fishing Boats & Pedal Boats	Picnicking - Group Sites Jogging, Skating & Bicycling Trails	Full Facilities Nearby
Day Use Fees: $3 - $5	Model Boats	Olympic Archery Range Fitness Course Playgrounds Nature Center & Trails	
		No Swimming	

PECK ROAD, SANTA FE and WHITTIER NARROWS

These three Los Angeles County Parks include fishing Lakes, picnic areas, hiking and bicycle trails. The 80-acre Lake at Peck Road Water Conservation Park is open from Wednesday through Sunday but does not allow boating or swimming. Santa Fe Dam Park has a 70-acre Lake open to swimming and boats with no motors. There are also beaches, an equestrian staging area, a nature center and group picnic areas. Legg Lake, actually three small Lakes totaling 76.5 acres, is within Whittier Narrows Recreation Area. This 1,400-acre multi-purpose Park has a nature center, skeet and trap shooting range, archery range, model hobby areas, athletic fields, equestrian area, golf course, lighted tennis courts and group picnic areas. There is no private boating or swimming at Legg Lake but you can rent paddleboats. Youth group camping is available at Whittier Narrows and Santa Fe Dam.

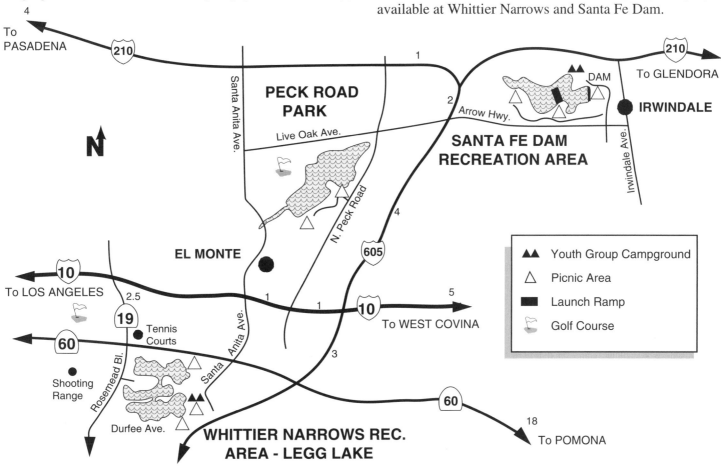

INFORMATION: County Parks & Recreation, 433 S. Vermont, Los Angeles 90020—Ph: (213) 738-2961

CAMPING	BOATING	RECREATION	OTHER
Whittier Narrows 750 S. Santa Anita Ave. S. El Monte 91733 Ph: (626) 575-5526 Day Use: $3 Picnic Reservations: Ph: (626) 575-5600 Youth Group Camping: Santa Fe and Whittier Narrows	Peck Road: No Boating Santa Fe: Small Boats No Motors Launch Ramp Rental Boats Whittier Narrows: No Private Boats Rentals: Paddleboats	Fishing: Trout in Winter, Largemouth Bass, Bluegill, Crappie & Catfish Picnicking Whittier Narrows: Group Picnic Area Hiking, Bicycle & Equestrian Trails Athletic Fields Skeet & Trap, Archery Golf Courses, Tennis Courts Model Hobby Areas	Nature Center at Whittier Narrows Santa Fe Dam Park 15501 E. Arrow Hwy. Irwindale 91706 Ph: (626) 334-1065 Day Use: $6 Boat Launch: $6 Water Play Area Fishing Licenses Required at All Facilities

SILVERWOOD LAKE

Silverwood State Recreation Area is located in the San Bernardino Mountains at an elevation of 3,350 feet. This is a popular recreation Lake with a surface area of 1,000 acres and 13 miles of shoreline. The Lake is open to all types of boating. Several brushy areas were left uncleared when filling the Lake which has provided a natural fish habitat. The angler will find a varied fishery with trophy size largemouth and striped bass. 10 miles of paved trails are available for the hiker and bicyclist and the Pacific Crest Trail passes through this area. Reservations are highly recommended at this scenic area. In addition to the oak-shaded campsites at Silverwood, the camper will find sites at nearby Mojave River Forks.

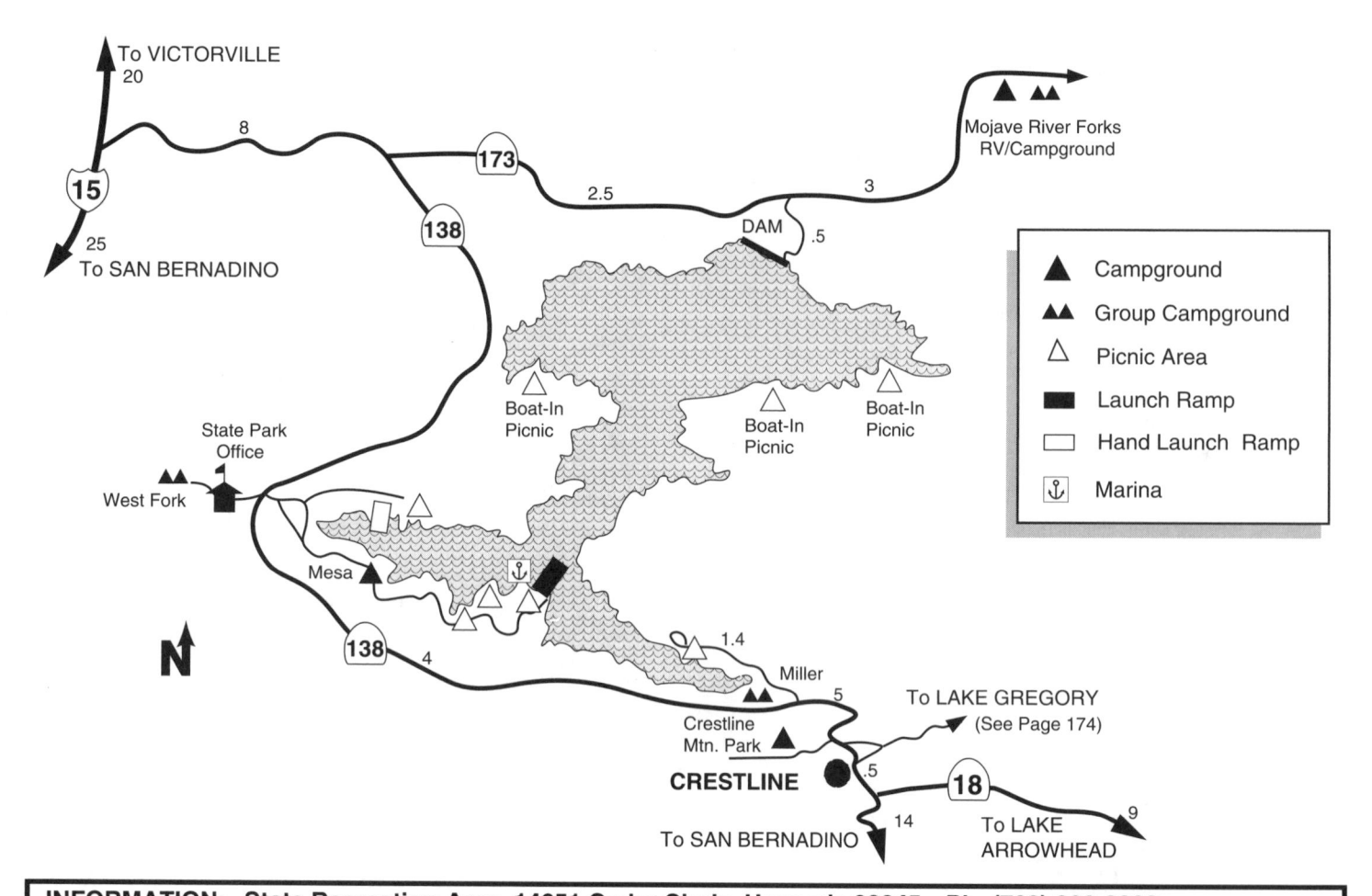

To VICTORVILLE
20
8
15
25
To SAN BERNADINO
173
138
2.5
DAM
.5
3
Mojave River Forks
RV/Campground

△ Campground
△△ Group Campground
△ Picnic Area
■ Launch Ramp
□ Hand Launch Ramp
⚓ Marina

State Park Office
West Fork
Boat-In Picnic
Boat-In Picnic
Boat-In Picnic
Mesa
N
138
4
1.4
Miller
5
To LAKE GREGORY
(See Page 174)
Crestline Mtn. Park
CRESTLINE
.5
18
To SAN BERNADINO
14
To LAKE ARROWHEAD
9

INFORMATION: State Recreation Area, 14651 Cedar Circle, Hesperia 92345—Ph: (760) 389-2303

CAMPING	BOATING	RECREATION	OTHER
131 Dev. Sites for Tents & R.V.s to 34 Feet Fee: $8 - No Hookups Group Sites: $40 to $75 100 People Maximum Disposal Station 7 Bike-In or Hike-In Sites Fee: $1 per person Reserve: Ph: (800) 444-7275 Reservations Recommended Summer Weekends No Campfires/Boat-In Areas	Power, Row, Canoe, Sail, Waterski, Jets & Windsurf Speed Limit - 35 MPH Designated Boating Zones Launch Ramps: $3 Rentals: Fishing Boats & Jets Docks, Berths	Fishing: Rainbow Trout, Catfish, Bluegill, Crappie, Trophy Largemouth & Striped Bass, Swimming Picnicking Hiking Trails Visitor Center Campfire Program Bald Eagle Boat Tours: Contact Park for Reservations	Snack Bar Grocery Store Bait & Tackle Disposal Station Mojave River Forks R.V. Campground 18107 Highway 173 Hesperia 92345 Ph: (760) 389-2322 90 Dev. Sites for Tents & R.V.s Group Campground

LAKE GREGORY

Lake Gregory is part of the San Bernardino County Regional Park System. Located at an elevation of 4,520 feet in the San Bernardino Mountains near Crestline, this popular day-use area offers a variety of water-related activities. There are sandy swim beaches, picnic facilities, snack bars, a 300-foot waterslide and a boat house. Boating is limited to rentals. The fish habitat is enhanced by an aeration system. In addition to the warm water species and rainbow trout, Lake Gregory is stocked with brown trout. This is a nice family park with full facilities in the village and nearby Crestline.

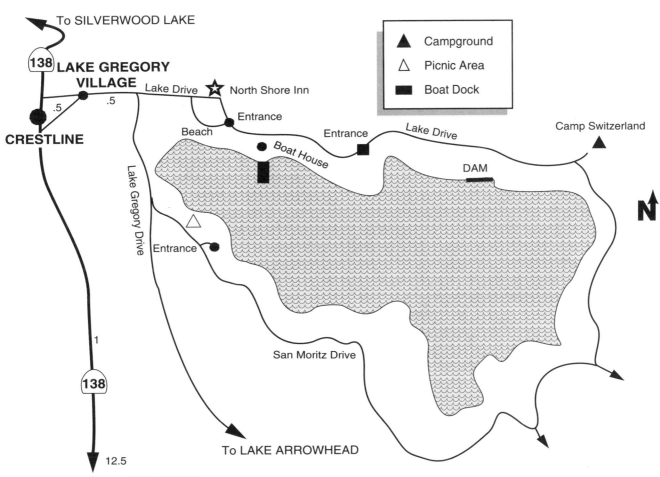

INFORMATION: Lake Gregory, P.O. Box 656, 24171 Lake Dr., Crestline 92325—Ph: (909) 338-2233

CAMPING	BOATING	RECREATION	OTHER

Camp Switzerland
    P.O. Box 967
    Crestline 92325
    Ph: (909) 338-2731
    10 Tent Sites
    30 R.V. Sites
        Full Hookups
    Cabins
Call for Current Fees
Reservations Advised
	No Private Boats
	Rentals Only:
	    Row Boats, Pedal Boats
	    Water Bikes & Sailboards
	You Can Bring
	    Your Own Electric Motor
	    For Use on Rental Boat
		Fishing: Rainbow &
		    Brown Trout,
		    Largemouth Bass,
		    Crappie, Bullhead &
		    Channel Catfish
		Picnicking
		Swim Beaches
		    (Memorial Day to
		    Labor Day)
		    Fee: $ 3 - Day
		          $35 - Season
		Volleyball Court
		Waterslide Fee: $6 All Day
			Snack Bars
			Bait & Tackle
			Horseshoe Pits
			Horse & Pony Rentals
			Hiking Trails
			Special Events
			Conference Facilities
			
			North Shore Inn:
			    Ph: (909) 338-5230
			
			Full Facilities
			    Nearby

ARROWHEAD, GREEN VALLEY, SNOW VALLEY, ARROWBEAR and JENKS LAKES

These Lakes are nestled high in the San Bernardino National Forest with elevations ranging from 5,100 feet at Lake Arrowhead to 7,200 feet at Green Valley Lake. The town of Lake Arrowhead is located in an alpine setting but the Lake is privately owned and not open to the public. The Forest Service has a number of campgrounds throughout this scenic area. There are many hiking and equestrian trails, especially near Jenks Lake and the San Gorgonio Wilderness Area. Green Valley is a small family oriented lake offering fishing, swimming and rental boats. Arrowbear is primarily a small fishing Lake. Snow Valley Ski Area has a scenic fishing lake on National Forest Land. You can take a chairlift up to it, fish and then bicycle or hike down.

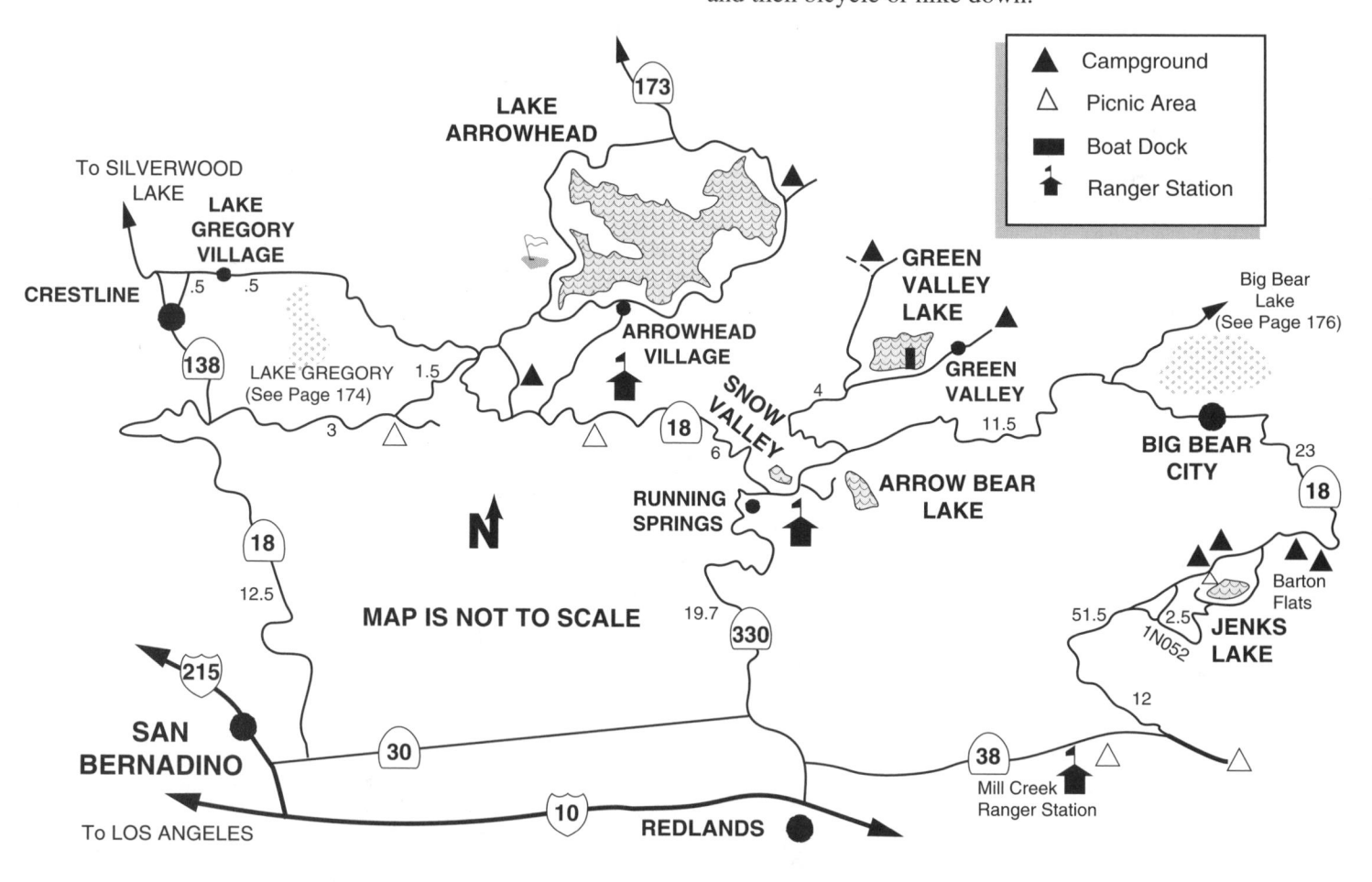

INFORMATION: Arrowhead Ranger Station, P.O. Box 350, Skyforest 92385—Ph: (909) 337-2444

CAMPING	BOATING	RECREATION	OTHER
Numerous Campgrounds through this Area Contact Arrowhead Ranger Station or Lake Arrowhead Chamber of Commerce & Visitors Center Ph: (909) 337-3715 Jenks Lake: Barton Flats & Green Valley Reservations: Ph: (877) 444-6777	Arrowhead: Closed to the Public Green Valley: Non-Power Rentals Arrowbear & Snow Valley: No Boating Jenks: Non-Power Hand Launch No Rentals	Fishing: Rainbow & Brown Trout, Smallmouth Bass, Kokanee Salmon, Catfish & Bluegill Picnicking Hiking & Equestrian Trails Horse Rentals Swimming Beaches	Lake Arrowhead Resort Ph: (800) 800-6792 Luxury Rooms, Restaurants, Pool, Private Beach Snow Valley Mtn. Resort: Ph: (909) 867-2751 Dev. Sites for Tents & R.V.s - Hookups Resorts & Other Facilities Nearby

BIG BEAR LAKE

Big Bear Lake is one of California's most popular recreation Lakes. Located in the San Bernardino National Forest at an elevation of 6,743 feet, this beautiful mountain Lake is just two hours from downtown Los Angeles. Originally created in 1884 by a single arch dam and enlarged by the 1911 multiple arch dam, Big Bear Lake now covers 3,000 surface acres. The Lake is over 7 miles long has a shoreline of 22 miles. Lake management is maintained by the Big Bear Municipal Water District. All types of boating are permitted, subject to size restrictions and a valid Lake Use permit which can be obtained at most marinas. In addition to the many Forest Service campsites, there are extensive private facilities at this complete destination resort.

....Continued....

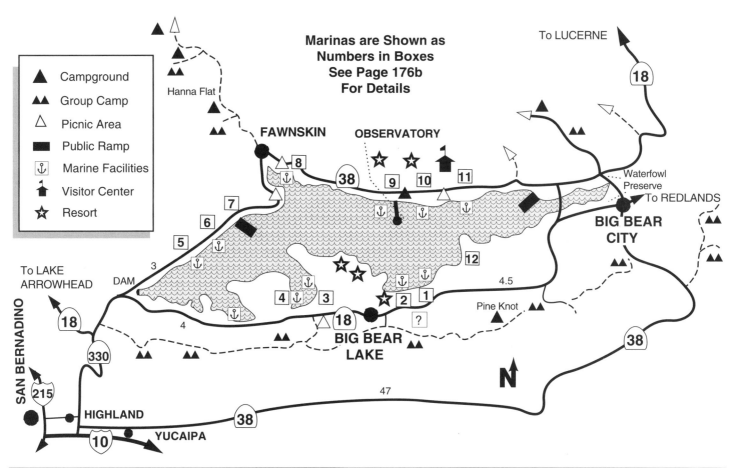

Legend:
- ▲ Campground
- ▲▲ Group Camp
- △ Picnic Area
- ▬ Public Ramp
- ⚓ Marine Facilities
- 🏠 Visitor Center
- ☆ Resort

Marinas are Shown as Numbers in Boxes See Page 176b For Details

INFORMATION: Visitor Information, 630 Bartlett Rd., Big Bear Lake 92315—Ph: (800) 4-BIG BEAR

CAMPING	BOATING	RECREATION	OTHER
U.S. Forest Service: 6 Campgrounds with 321 Dev. Sites for Tents & R.V.s Fee: $10 - $30 Full Hook-ups at Serrano Remote Area Camping: Adventure Pass Req'd. Group Sites $50 - $75 *See Following Pages*	Open to All Boating Subject to Length Maximum 26 Feet Valid Lake Permit Required - $15 Day $65 Year 35 MPH Speed Limit Full Service Marinas Launch Ramps Berths, Docks, Storage Rentals: Power, Sail, Fishing, Sailboard & Jets	Fishing: Trout, Bass, Channel Catfish, Bluegill, Carp & Crappie Swimming Hiking & Backpacking Equestrian Trails Horse Rentals Golf & Tennis Picnicking	Complete Resort Facilities *See Following Pages for Information*

BIG BEAR LAKE.............Continued

VISITOR & LODGING INFORMATION:
Big Bear Lake Resort Association
630 Bartlett - P.O. Box 1936
Big Bear Lake 92315
Ph: (800) 4-BIGBEAR

LAKE INFORMATION
Big Bear Municipal Water District
P. O. Box 2863
Big Bear Lake 92315
Ph: (909) 866-5796

CAMPING/HIKING INFORMATION:
Big Bear Discovery Center
Box 66
Fawnskin 92333
Ph: (909) 866-3437

U.S. FOREST SERVICE CAMPGROUNDS

The following sites - RESERVE: - Ph: (877) 444-6777

CAMPSITES:

BIG PINE FLAT - 7 Miles NW of Fawnskin on Forest Service Rd. 3N14 - 20 Tent & R.V. Sites, Trailers to 22 ft., Pack-In, Pack-Out - *Fee: $12.*

HANNA FLAT - 2-1/2 Miles NW of Fawnskin on Forest Service Rd. 3N14 - 88 Tent & R.V. Sites - *Fee: $17.*

HOLCOMB VALLEY - 4 Miles North on 2N09 to 3N16 East on 3N16 3/4 Mile - 19 Tent & R.V. Sites, Trailers to 15 ft., Pack-In, Pack-Out, No Water - *Fee: $10*

PINEKNOT - South on Summit Blvd., off Big Bear Blvd. - 48 Tent & R.V. Sites - *Fee: $18.*

SERRANO - North Shore Lane off Highway 38 - 2 Miles East of Fawnskin - 132 Tent & R.V. Sites - *Fees: $20 - $30.*

GROUP CAMPGROUNDS
(Dirt Roads)

BIG PINE HORSE CAMP - Near Fawnskin - 60 People, 5 Vehicles Max., Water, Horse Groups Only - *Fee: $65.*
BLUFF MESA - Off 2N10 - 40 People, 8 Vehicles Max., Tents & R.V.s, No Water - *Fee: $50.*
BOULDER - Off 2N10 - 40 People, 8 Vehicles Max., Tents & R.V.s, No Water - *Fee: $50.*
BUTTERCUP - Near Pine Knot - 40 People, 8 Vehicles Max., Tents & R.V.s - *Fee: $75.*
DEER - Off 2N10 - 40 People, 8 Vehicles Max., Tents & R.V.s, No Water - *Fee: $50.*
GREEN SPOT - Off 2N93 - 25 People, 10 Vehicles Max., Tents & R.V.s, No Water - *Fee: $50.*
GRAY'S PEAK - Off 3N14 - 40 People, 10 Vehicles Max., Tents & R.V.s, No Water - *Fee: $65.*
IRONWOOD - Off 3N97 - 25 People, 5 Vehicles Max., Tents & R.V.s, No Water, *Fee: $65.*
JUNIPER SPRINGS - Off 2N01 - 40 People, 8 Vehicles Max., Tents & R.V.s - *Fee: $50.*
ROUND VALLEY - Off 2NO1 - 15 People, 3 Vehicles Max., Tents & R.V.s - *Fee: Free.*
TANGLEWOOD - Off 3N15 - 40 People, 8 Vehicles Max., Tents & R.V.s, No Water - *Fee: $65.*
SIBERIA CREEK - 3,000 Feet Elevation Change - 3.6 Mile Hike-In, To 40 People, Tent Sites, No Water - *No Fee.*
Siberia Creek Only: Reservations at Big Bear Discovery Center - Ph: (909) 866-3437

....Continued....

PRIVATE CAMPGROUNDS:
Phone for Fees

LIGHTHOUSE TRAILER RESORT AND MARINA - Adjacent to the Observatory Access
10 - 15 R.V. Sites, Full Hookups, Store - *Ph: (909) 866-9464*

BIG BEAR SHORES R.V. RESORT & YACHT CLUB - East of Lighthouse Marina -
170 Deluxe R.V. Sites, Full Hookups - *Ph: (800) 222-5708 or (909) 866-4151*

HOLLOWAY'S MARINA AND R.V. PARK - South Shore on Edgemoor Road in Metcalf Bay
66 Sites for Tents & R.V.s, Full Hookups, Store - *Ph: (800) 448-5335 or (909) 878-4386*

MWD R.V. PARK - West of "The Village" on Lakeview Dr.
25 R.V. Sites, Full Hookups, Walking Distance to Shops - *Ph: (909) 866-5796*

MARINE FACILITIES - Boxed Numbers Shown on Map

1.   **PINE KNOT LANDING MARINA** - *Ph: (909) 866-2628 or 866-9512*
Docks, Moorings, Ramp, Storage, Bait & Tackle, Store, Tours. Rentals: Fishing Boats, Sail Boats, Pontoons, Canoes.

2.   **BIG BEAR MARINA** - *Ph: (909) 866-3218*
Docks, Moorings, Ramp, Gas, Storage, Bait & Tackle, Boat Permits. Rentals: Fishing Boats, Sail Boats, Pontoons, Jets.

3.   **HOLLOWAY'S MARINA & R.V. PARK**- *Ph: (800) 448-5335 or (909) 866-5706*
Docks, Moorings, Ramp, Gas, Bait & Tackle, Groceries, Boat Permits. Rentals: Fishing & Paddle Boats, Pontoons, Jets.

4.   **PLEASURE POINT LANDING** - *Ph: (909) 866-2455*
Docks, Moorings, Ramp, Gas, Bait & Tackle, Boat Permits, Snack Bar, Pirate Ship Boat Tours.
Rentals: Fishing Boats, Pontoons, Canoes.

5.   **GRAY'S LANDING** - *Ph: (909) 866-2443*
Bait & Tackle, Fishing Pier (Nights Also), Slips, Moorings. Rentals: Fishing Boats, Pontoons.

6.   **NORTH SHORE LANDING** - *Ph: (909) 878-4386*
Moorings, Dock, Snacks, Bait & Tackle. Rentals: Fishing Boats, Sail Boats, Jets.

7.   **MWD EAST & WEST LAUNCH** - *West Ph: (909) 866-2917 and East Ph: (909) 866-5200*
Boat Permits, FREE Launch Ramp, Day Use Area.

8.   **CAPTAIN JOHN'S FAWN HARBOR** - *Ph: (909) 866-6478*
Moorings, Snacks, Bait & Tackle, Lake Tours. Rentals: Fishing Boats, Sail Boats, Kayaks, Canoes, Pontoons.

9.   **LIGHTHOUSE TRAILER RESORT & MARINA**- *Ph: (909) 866-9464*
Docks, Moorings, Snacks, Bait & Tackle, Propane. Rentals: Fishing Boats, Pontoons.

10.   **BIG BEAR SHORES & R.V. RESORT**- *Ph: (909) 878-4386*
Launch Ramp, Moorings, Docks, Rentals: Fishing Boats, Pontoon Boats.

11.   **JUNIPER POINT MARINA**- *Ph: (909) 866-9464*
Boat Slips.

12.   **MEADOW PARK SWIM BEACH** - *Ph: (909) 866-9700*
Park Avenue Near Knight Ave., Public Swimming Area with Raft, Snack Bar, Picnic Tables, BBQ's.

PUDDINGSTONE LAKE

Puddingstone Lake is at an elevation of 940 feet within the 2,000 acre Frank G. Bonelli Regional Park. This complete recreation facility is administered by the Department of Parks and Recreation of Los Angeles County. The 250 surface acre Lake has good marina facilities and is open to all boating. The angler will find trout and a warm water fishery. This well landscaped park has picnic areas, a swim beach, multi-purpose trails along with the full facility East Shore R.V. Park and Campground. There is an Equestrian Center and riding trails throughout the park. Raging Waters is a large water theme park near the dam at Puddingstone Lake.

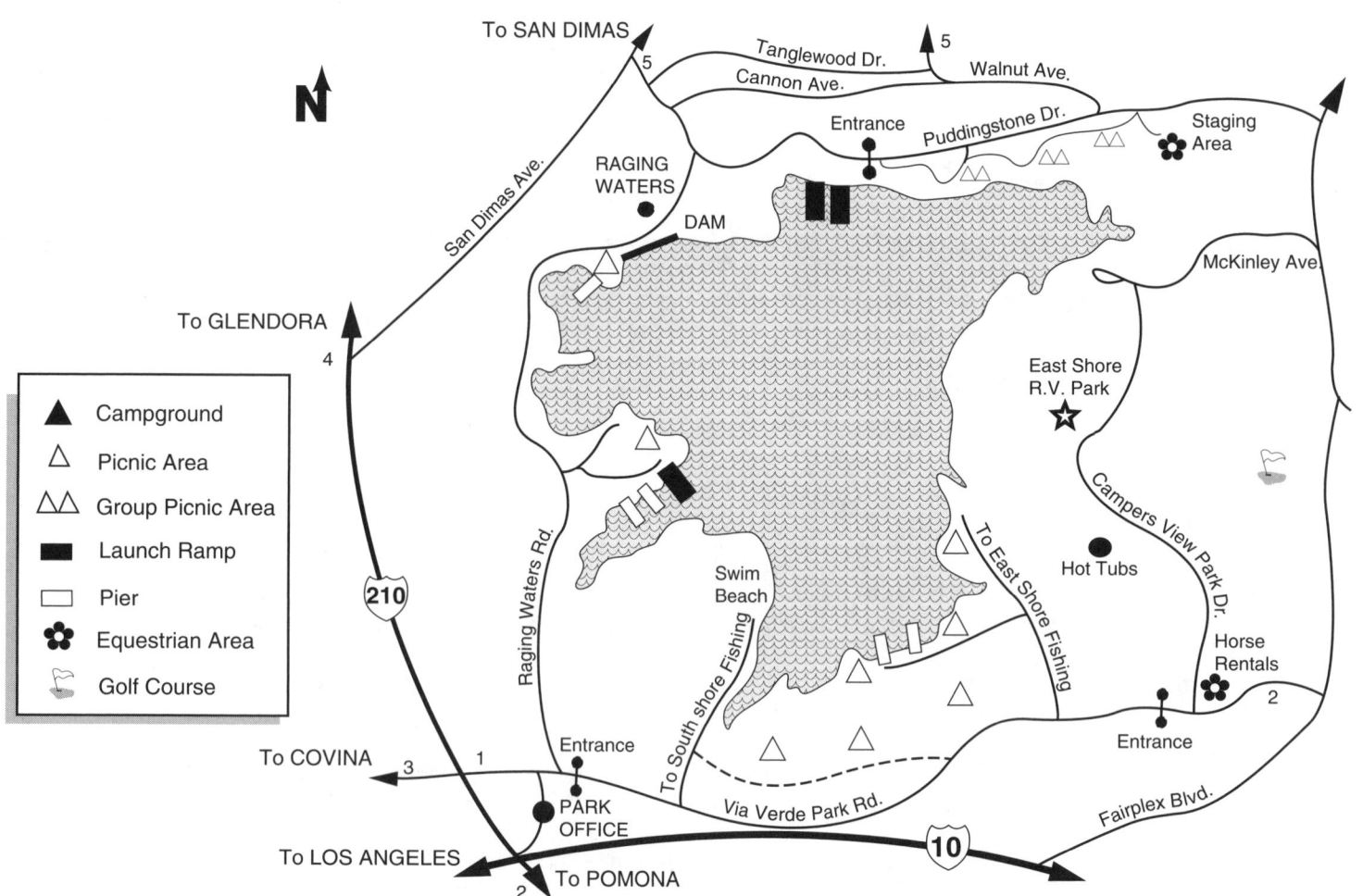

▲	Campground
△	Picnic Area
△△	Group Picnic Area
■	Launch Ramp
▢	Pier
✿	Equestrian Area
⚑	Golf Course

INFORMATION: Frank R. Bonelli Regional County Park, 120 E. Via Verde, San Dimas 91773—Ph: (909) 599-8411

CAMPING	BOATING	RECREATION	OTHER
East Shore R.V. Park 1440 Camper View Rd. San Dimas 91773 Ph: (800) 809-3778 25 Dev. Sites for Tents $8 Per Person 520 Dev. Sites for R.V.s with Full Hookups $30 to $32 (2 People) Disposal Station Swimming Pool, Rec. Room Store, Bait & Tackle Reservations Accepted	Open to All Boating All Boats Must be 8 Feet Minimum to 26 Feet Maximum Power Boats Must be 12 Feet Minimum Call for Designated Boat Use Days Launch Ramps - $6 Rentals: Fishing Boats	Fishing: Trout, Bass, Bluegill, Crappie, Perch & Caffish Picnicking Day Use - $6 Group Picnic Areas by Reservation Hiking & Equestrian Trails Equestrian Center: Ph: (909) 599-8830 Horse Boarding Roping Arena Golf Course Nearby	Snack Bar Hot Tubs: 1 - 100 People Ph: (909) 592-2222 Gazebo Area for Private Parties Raging Waters: Ph: (909) 802-2200 Water Slides, Wave Pool, Rapids, Kiddy Pool

LAKE PERRIS

Lake Perris State Recreation Area is the southern terminus of the California Water Project. The Lake's 2,200 surface acres are surrounded by rocky mountains towering to more than a thousand feet above the water's surface. Alessandro Island, rising to 230 feet, is a favorite boat-in picnic area. The complete recreation park provides an enormous number of activities and facilities. Fishing is good from boat or shore. This is a popular Lake for waterskiing, windsurfing, sailing and fishing. There are specific hunting areas for waterfowl and upland game. The hiker, bicycler and equestrian will find extensive trails. There are also designated rock climbing scuba diving areas. Camping reservations are a must.

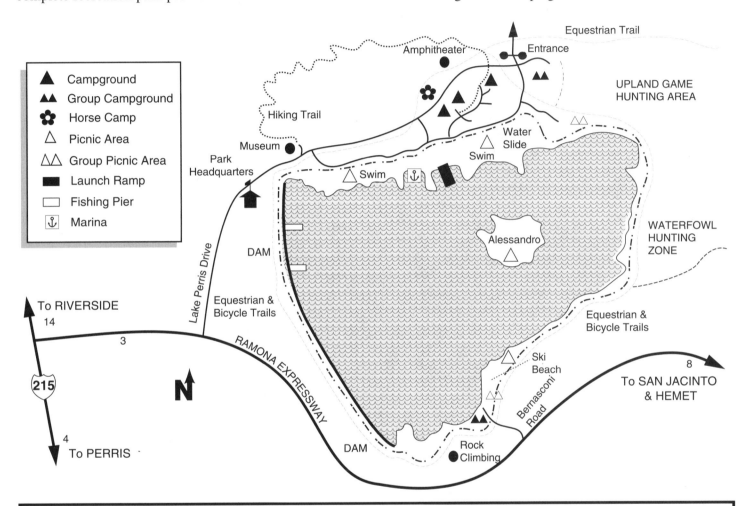

Legend

- ▲ Campground
- ▲▲ Group Campground
- ✿ Horse Camp
- △ Picnic Area
- △△ Group Picnic Area
- ■ Launch Ramp
- ▭ Fishing Pier
- ⚓ Marina

INFORMATION: State Recreation Area, 17801 Lake Perris Dr., Perris 92371—Ph: (909) 940-5603

CAMPING	BOATING	RECREATION	OTHER
167 Dev. Tent Sites Fee: $8	Open to All Boating Designated Zones	Fishing: Trout, Alabama Spotted & Largemouth	Horse Camp: Corrals,
254 R.V. Sites to 31 Feet with Hookups Fee: $14	35 MPH Speed Limit 5 MPH Areas Full Service Marina	Bass, Bluegill, Channel Catfish, Sunfish Picnicking	Picnic Tables to 50 People Snack Bar
6 Group Campgrounds Disposal Station Reserve: (800) 444-7275	Launch Ramps: Storage, Slips Gas, Docks	3 Group Sites Swimming, Scuba Diving Beaches & Waterslide	Restaurant Bait & Tackle
Boat Camping in Slips Only With Prior Approval	Rentals: Fishing & Patio Boats, Knee Boards, Life Jackets, Waterskis Marine Supplies Boat Repairs	Hiking, Bicycle & Equestrian Trails Rock Climbing Area Hunting: Waterfowl & Upland Game	

ORANGE COUNTY REGIONAL PARKS: CARBON CANYON, CRAIG, RALPH B. CLARK, YORBA, IRVINE, MILE SQUARE, WILLIAM R. MASON AND LAGUNA NIGUEL

The millions of residents and visitors to Orange County will find an abundance of regional parks, harbors and beaches. We have included only those regional parks that include a Lake. For those who are interested in the many other facilities, contact Orange County as listed on the following page. Laguna Niguel Regional Park Lake is run by a private concession so no State fishing license is required. Rental boats are available but private boats are not allowed at this Lake.

....Continued....

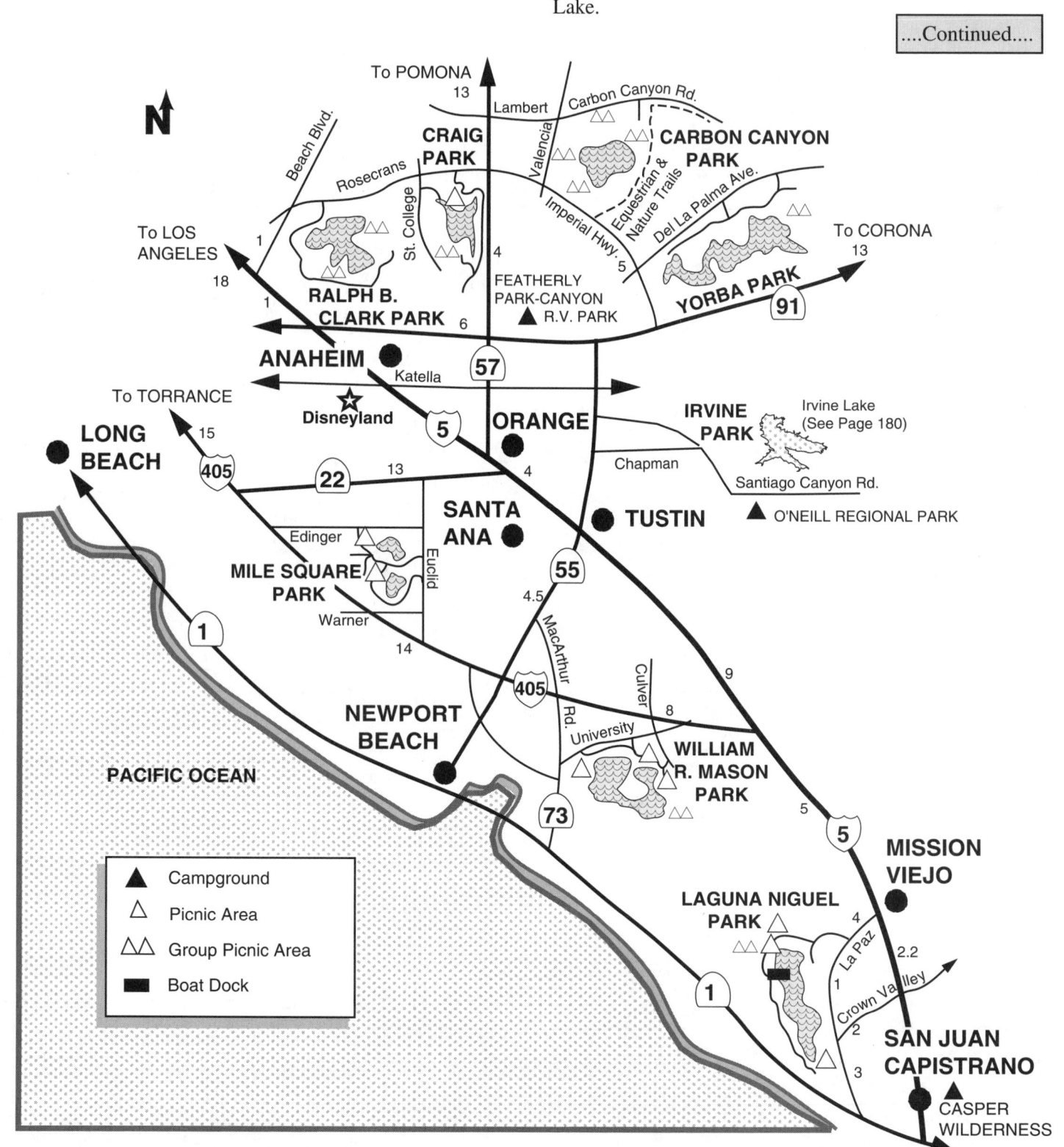

CARBON CANYON, 4442 Carbon Canyon Rd., Brea 92823—Ph: (714) 996-5252

This 124-acre park is in the foothills upstream from Carbon Canyon Dam. The park features a 10-acre grove of coastal redwoods amid sycamore, pepper, eucalyptus and pine trees. There is a fishing Lake with 4 surface acres and 2 piers along with hiking, bicycle and equestrian trails, group picnic areas, playgrounds, tennis, volleyball, softball and athletic fields.

CRAIG, 3300 N. State College Blvd., Fullerton 92635 Ph: (714) 990-0271

This 124-acre park includes picnic shelters, softball and baseball fields, horseshoe pits and a sports complex housing volleyball, racquetball, handball and a basketball court. Along with hiking, bicycling and equestrian trails, there is a 3 surface acre Lake open for fishing and model sailboats.

RALPH B. CLARK, 8800 Rosecrans Ave., Buena Park 90621—Ph: (714) 670-8045

Orginally acquired by the County of Orange in 1974 to preserve its rich fossil beds, this park features picnic areas, playgrounds, athletic fields, tennis and volleyball courts. The Lake offers fishing for largemouth bass, channel catfish and bluegill.

IRVINE, 1 Irvine Park Rd., Orange 92862 Ph: (714) 633-8074

This park lies amid oaks and sycamores on the hillside of Santiago Canyon. This is California's oldest regional park. The 447 acres include two small lagoons, group picnic areas, BBQs, snack shop, stage, playgrounds, athletic fields and train and pony rides. A paved trail for walkers and bicyclists is available. Horses, bicycles and aquacycles can be rented. The Park Ranger conducts interpretive programs. The Orange County Zoo, barnyard, historic boathouse and train rides are also popular. See Page 180 for details on Irvine Lake.

MILE SQUARE, 16801 Euclid St., Fountain Valley 92708—Ph: (714) 962-5549

This 640-acre park provides 3 golf courses, driving range, restaurants, soccer, baseball, softball, basketball, archery, tennis and sheltered picnic areas. The snack shop rents bikes and paddleboats. There are four miles of bicyling and jogging trails along with several playgrounds. There is a community center building and the park hosts all kinds of sporting tournaments. Swimming is not allowed in the 2 Lakes. The angler will find stocked catfish.

WILLIAM R. MASON, 18712 University Dr., Irvine 92612—Ph: (949) 854-2491

Throughout this 345-acre park, there are picnic shelters, playgrounds, a golf course and areas for softball and volley-ball. Hiking, jogging and bicycling trails are enjoyed by numerous visitors along with the amphitheater and a physical fitness course. The park includes a 123-acre wilderness area A large shelter for groups up to 500 people can be reserved. A 9 surface acre Lake is open to fishing.

YORBA, 7600 E. La Palma Ave., Anaheim 92807 Ph: (714) 970-1460

This 175-acre park has a series of 4 Lakes with connecting streams that are great for fishing or sailing model boats. There are group picnic shelters and BBQs provided. 20 miles of hiking, bicycling and equestrian trails lead to the Pacific Ocean. Playgrounds, volleyball, horseshoe pits, ball diamonds and a physical fitness course are all available.

Campgrounds in Area

Caspers Wilderness Park, 33401 Ortega Hwy., San Juan Capistrano—Ph: (949) 728-0235
Featherly Regional Park - Canyon R.V. Park, 24001 Santa Ana Cyn. Rd., Anaheim—Ph: (714) 637-0210
O'Neill Regional Park, 30992 Trabuco Canyon, Trabuco Canyon—Ph: (949) 858-9365

INFORMATION: Orange County Parks, 1 Irvine Park Rd., Orange 92669—Ph: (866) OC-PARKS			
CAMPING	**BOATING**	**RECREATION**	**OTHER**
Caspers Wilderness Park Campsites Plus Equestrian Sites Featherly Regional Park - Canyon R.V. Park 90 Dev. Sites for Tents & R.V.s - Plus 32 Sites with Hookups O'Neill Regional Park Dev. Sites for Tents & R.V.s Plus Group Sites	As Shown Above	Fishing: Largemouth Bass, Bluegill, Channel Catfish, Trout Picnic Areas Playgrounds Lighted Athletic Fields Hiking & Equestrian Trails Bicycle Paths Interpretive Programs Group Facilities: Permits at Least 15 Days in Advance	Laguna Niguel Park: 28241 La Paz Rd. Laguna Niguel 92677 Ph: (949) 831-2791 236 acre Park 44 surface acre Lake: Bluegill, Bass & Catfish Trout - Fishing Permit: $12 Rental Boats Only Picnic Areas and Shelters Equestrian, Bicycling & Jogging Trails, Horseshoes Golf, Volleyball & Tennis

These Lakes in Southern California are grouped together because they are all what anglers dream about. Irvine Lake, 725 surface acres with 10 miles of shoreline, is located near the city of Orange and offers some of the best bass fishing in California. Limits for trophy-sized trout and catfish are often caught also. Santa Ana River Lakes consists of three Lakes which include a Kids Lake and a Catfish Pond. This is an ideal spot for children to learn how to fish. Corona Lake, just off Highway 15 south of Riverside, has good spots for bass fishing along the east shore and around the flooded timber hideaway at the south end of the Lake. Float tube fishing is permitted at all these very popular fishing Lakes. Major trout, bass and catfish tournaments are held throughout the year.

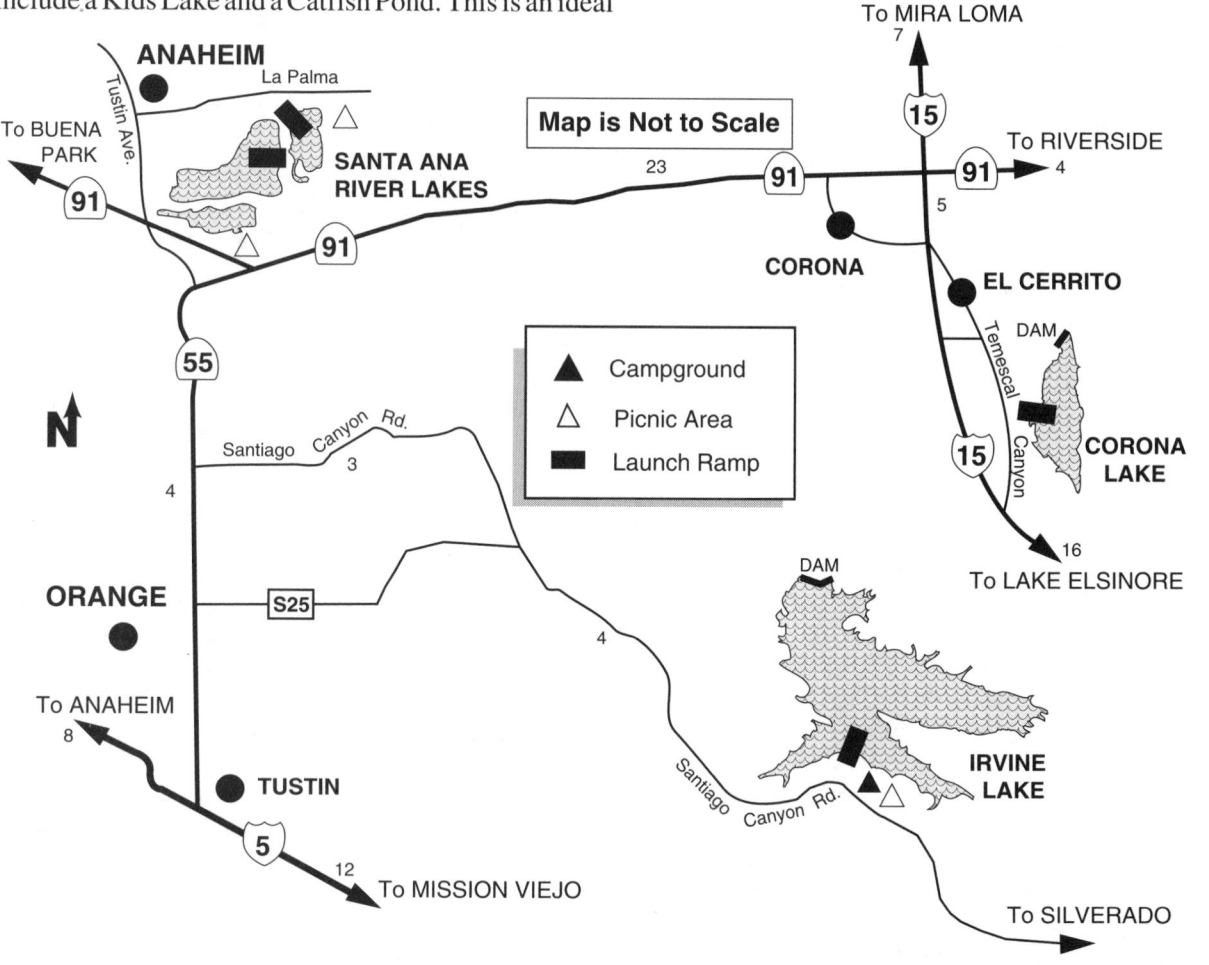

INFORMATION: *Only* Irvine Lake: 4621 Santiago Canyon Rd., Silverado 92676—Ph: (714) 649-9111

CAMPING	BOATING	RECREATION	OTHER
Irvine Lake: Tent & R.V. Sites Fees: $16 Fishing Fees: $9 - $16 Ph. (714) 649-9111 Santa Ana River Lakes & Corona Lake No Camping Fishing Fees: $5 - $16 No License Required	Irvine Lake: Launch Fee: $8 5 MPH Limit Rentals: Row, Motor & Bass Boats, Pontoons, & Electric Party Cruisers Santa Ana Rivers Lakes & Corona Lake Electric Motors Only Launch Fee: $8 Float Tubes: $5 Rentals: Row & Motor Boats	Fishing: Trout, Catfish, Striped Bass, Crappie, Bluegill, Sunfish, Sturgeon Irvine Lake: Group Facilities for Picnicking Kid's Fish'n Hole Volleyball, Horseshoes, Hiking Trails Santa Ana & Corona: Night Fishing Available	Irvine Lake Fish Report: Ph: (714) 649-2168 Santa Ana River Lakes Fish Report: Ph: (714) 632-7830 Corona Lake Fish Report: Ph: (909) 277-4489

CUCAMONGA-GUASTI, YUCAIPA PARK, PRADO PARK and FAIRMOUNT PARK

These small Lakes offer limited boating although the surrounding parks offer an abundance of recreational activities. Cucamonga-Guasti, Yucaipa Park and Prado Park are a part of the San Bernardino County Regional Park System. Fairmount Park is administered by the City of Riverside.

Fishing is popular year around for bass and channel catfish and in winter months, the angler will find planted trout. In addition to campgrounds, Prado has equestrian trails and staging areas. There is a variety of activities unique to each park from trap shooting to waterslides.

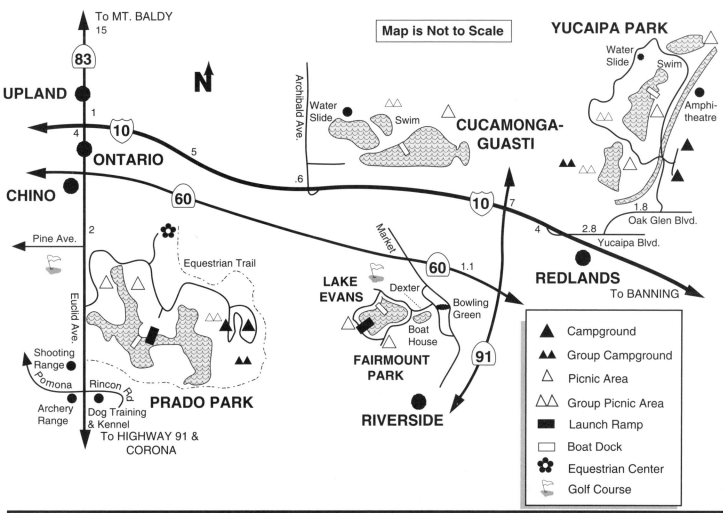

INFORMATION:San Bernadino County Regional Parks, 777 E. Rialto, San Bernardino 92415—Ph: (909) 387-2594

CAMPING	BOATING	RECREATION	OTHER

Yucaipa Park:
    Dev. Sites for Tents &
    R.V.s - 13 Hookups
    Fees: $11 - $18
    Group Sites
Prado Park:
    Dev. Sites for Tents &
    R.V.s - 50 Hookups
Disposal Stations
 	
Day Use Only:
Cucamonga-Guasti &
    Fairmount Park
	Yucaipa Park:
	    Rentals Only:
	    Pedal Boats
	Prado: Non-Power Boats
	    Launch Ramp
	Cucamonga-Guasti:
	    Rentals: Pedal Boats
	    & Aqua Cycles
	Fairmount Park:
	    Launch Ramp for
	    Rowboats Only
	    With Permit
	    Fishing Dock
		Fishing: Trout - Winter,
		    Bass & Catfish
		Swimming & Picnicking
		    Group Picnic Areas
		Yucaipa & Guasti:
		    Waterslides
		Hiking & Equestrian Trails
		Prado Park: Athletic Fields
		    Equestrian Center &
		    Horse Rentals
		Shooting-Archery Ranges
		Golf Courses
			Cucamonga-Guasti
			    Ph: (909) 481-4205
			Yucaipa Park
			    Ph: (909) 790-3127
			Prado Park:
			    Ph: (909) 597-4260
			
			Fairmount Park:
			    City of Riverside
			    Park & Rec. Dept.
			    3900 Main St.
			    Riverside 92522
			    Ph: (909) 826-2000

LAKE ELSINORE

Lake Elsinore is the largest natural freshwater lake in Southern California with over 3,300 surface acres. The Lake is popular for a variety of watersports including fishing and waterskiing. The Lake Elsinore Recreation Area, owned by the City of Lake Elsinore, offers quiet, shaded campsites close to the water. The city's boat launch facility provides an easy way to launch your watercraft. Numerous private campgrounds and resorts are available.

....Continued....

Legend:

- ▲ Campground
- △ Picnic Area
- ■ Launch Ramp
- ⚓ Marina
- ★ Resort

N

To CORONA
25

To PERRIS
10

15

74

Riverside Dr.

Lake Park Resort
Lake Elsinore Rec. Area
The Outhouse
Roadrunner
Elsinore West

Central Ave.
Turnoff

2.5

Main St. Turnoff
1

LAKE ELSINORE

2

Crane
Lakeside Park

Lakeshore Dr.

To SAN JUAN
CAPISTRANO & INT. 5

Weekend
Paradise

30

74

Playland
R.V. Park

Stadium

AIR FIELD

15

Grand Ave.

Corydon St.

68

To SAN DIEGO

INFORMATION: Lake Elsinore Recreation Area, 32040 Riverside Dr., Lake Elsinore 92530—Ph: (909) 471-1212

CAMPING	BOATING	RECREATION	OTHER

175 Dev. Sites for Tents & R.V.s
Fees: Tents - $15
R.V.s - Electric Hookups - $20
Disposal Station
Group Sites Available
Reservations:
  Ph: (800) 416-6992
 	
Day Use:
  Fees: $5 - Vehicle
  $2 - Walk-in
	Power, Row, Canoe, Sail, Windsurf Waterski & Jets
	35 MPH Speed Limit
	Lake Use Fee: $7
	Launch Ramps
	Rentals: PWCs
		Fishing: Bass, Crappie, Carp, Bluegill & Catfish
		Picnicking
		Hiking, Bicycling & Equestrian Trails
		Hang Gliding
		Parachuting
		Golf Nearby
			Full Facilities in Lake Elsinore
			
			See Following Page for Resorts & Marine Facilities

LAKE PARK RESORT
32000 Riverside Dr., Lake Elsinore 92530
Ph: (909) 674-7911
121 R.V. Sites, Full Hookups - *Fee: $24*, Cable T.V., Hot Showers, 26 Motel Rooms, Olympic Sized Pool, Picnic Area.

THE OUTHOUSE
32310 Riverside Dr., Lake Elsinore 92530
Ph: (909) 674-2766
Tent/R.V. Sites, Hookups - *Fee: $13 and up*
Permanent R.V. Sites, Full Hookups, Cable TV, Disposal Station, Laundry, Hot Showers, General Store, Swimming Beach, Launch Ramp, Picnic Area.

ROADRUNNER R.V. PARK
32500 Riverside Dr., Lake Elsinore 92530
Ph: (909) 674-4900
Tent Camping & R.V. Sites with Full Hookups - *Fee: $20*

ELSINORE WEST MARINA
32700 Riverside Dr.
Lake Elsinore 92530
Ph: (909) 678-1300 or (800) 328-6844
197 R.V. Sites, Full Hookups - *Fee: $35*, Tents - *Fee: $20*, Open Tent & R.V. Camp Area, Hot Showers, Cable T.V.

CRANE LAKESIDE PARK and RESORT
15980 Grand Ave., Lake Elsinore 92530
Ph: (909) 678-2112
18 Tent & R.V. Sites on the Waterfront, Water & Electric Hookups - *Fee: $27*
Weekly & Monthly Rates Available, 100 Permanent Sites,
Disposal Station, Hot Showers, Laundry Room, Sports Bar & Restaurant, Meeting Room, Launch Ramp.

WEEKEND PARADISE R.V. PARK
16006 Grand Ave., Lake Elsinore 92530
Ph: (909) 678-3715
R.V. Sites, Water & Electric Hookups - *Fee: $21*, Hot Showers, Disposal Station, Launch Ramp.

PLAYLAND R.V. PARK
16730 Grand Ave., Lake Elsinore 92530
Ph: (909) 678-4663
Tent Camping - *Fee: $10*, R.V. Sites with Full Hookups - *Fee: $25,* Launch Ramp

FOR OTHER FACILITIES AND ACCOMMODATIONS CONTACT:
City of Lake Elsinore
130 S. Main St., Lake Elsinore 92530
Ph: (909) 674-3124, Ext. 265

LAKE SKINNER and VAIL LAKE

Located at an elevation of 1,500 feet, Lake Skinner is amid rolling hills of wildflowers and oak trees. The Lake has a surface area of 1,200 acres with 14 miles of shoreline within the 6,040-acre Lake Skinner Park. This facility is operated by Riverside County Parks Department. In addition to the campsites, there is a half-acre swimming pool, ecology ponds, marine facilities, camp store and fishing beaches. There are a number of riding trails and an equestrian campground.

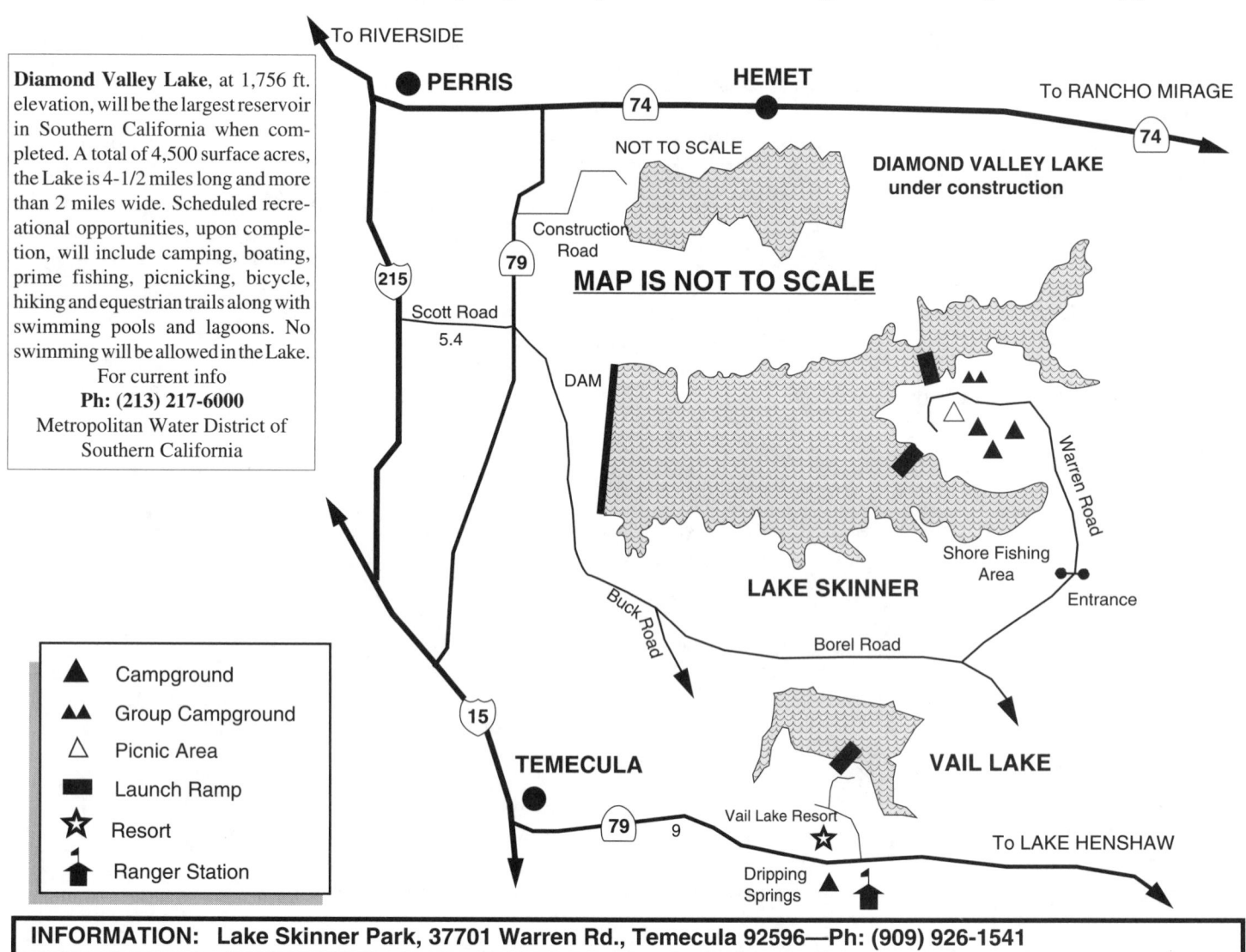

Diamond Valley Lake, at 1,756 ft. elevation, will be the largest reservoir in Southern California when completed. A total of 4,500 surface acres, the Lake is 4-1/2 miles long and more than 2 miles wide. Scheduled recreational opportunities, upon completion, will include camping, boating, prime fishing, picnicking, bicycle, hiking and equestrian trails along with swimming pools and lagoons. No swimming will be allowed in the Lake.
For current info
Ph: (213) 217-6000
Metropolitan Water District of Southern California

Legend:
▲ Campground
▲▲ Group Campground
△ Picnic Area
■ Launch Ramp
☆ Resort
🛑 Ranger Station

INFORMATION: Lake Skinner Park, 37701 Warren Rd., Temecula 92596—Ph: (909) 926-1541

CAMPING	BOATING	RECREATION	OTHER
Lake Skinner:	All Boats Must Be	Fishing: Trout,	Snack Bar & Store
41 Dev. Sites for	a Minimum of 10 Feet	Catfish, Bluegill,	
Tents - Fee: $15	Long, 42 Inches Wide	Crappie, Perch,	Vail Lake Resort
Dev. Sites for R.V.s	Sailboats Must Be	Bass, Carp	38000 Highway 79 South
18 Partial Hookups	12 Feet Long &	Fishing Permit: $5	Temecula 92589
Fee: $16	12 Inches of Freeboard	Swimming in Pool Only	Ph: (909) 303-0173
178 Full Hookups Fee: $18	*Canoes, Kayaks*	Memorial Day through	Tent & RV Sites
Disposal Station	*or Multihulled Boats*	Labor Day	Full Hookups
Primitive Overflow Sites	*MUST have Solid and*	Picnicking	Fees: $20 - $35
Fee: $12	*Fixed Decking*	Hiking & Equestrian Trails	
Group Camp Reservations:	Speed Limit - 10 MPH	Nature Study	Full Facilities:
Ph: (800) 234-7275	Launch Ramp, Marina		10 Miles at
Day Use: $2	Rentals: Row & Motor Boats		Temecula

REFLECTION LAKE, ANGLER'S LAKE and LAKE FULMOR

Reflection and Angler's Lakes, at 1,600 feet elevation, are privately owned fishing facilities. Angler's Lake has no limit for the number of fish you can catch. Reflection Lake offers a developed campground for tents and R.V.s. Boating is limited to rowboats, canoes and inflatables. Electric motors are allowed. Trout and channel catfish are planted weekly in season at both Angler's and Reflection Lakes. State fishing licenses are not required at these private facilities. Lake Fulmor is at an elevation of 5,300 feet near the scenic mountain resort community of Idyllwild. Although facilities are limited to Day Use at this small trout Lake, the visitor will find many campsites within the Mt. San Jacinto State Park along with U.S. Forest Service campgrounds in this area.

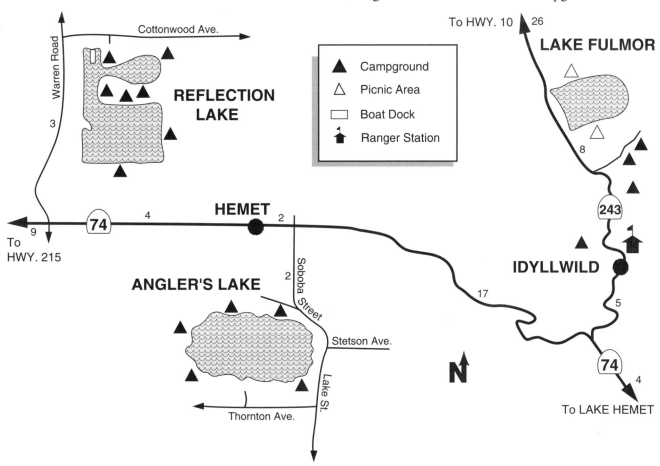

CAMPING	BOATING	RECREATION	OTHER
Reflection Lake: 121 Dev. Sites for Tents & R.V.s Water and Electric Hookups Fee: $17.25 With Hookups: $20.25 Disposal Station Angler's Lake: Open Campsites to 300 People Fee: $10	Reflection Lake: Row, Canoe & Inflatables, Electric Motors Only Angler's & Fulmor: No Boating *Check for Current Water Levels*	Fishing: Trout, Bass, Bluegill & Catfish Fishing Fees: Angler's Lake: $10 Stocked Twice a Week Every Week Reflection Lake: Campers: $7 Day Use: $9 No Limit Picnicking Hiking Trails No Swimming	Angler's Lake 42660 Thornton Ave. Hemet 92544 Ph: (909) 927-2614 Lake Fulmor: Idyllwild Ranger Station Ph: (909) 659-2117 Mt. San Jacinto State Park Ph: (909) 659-2607

INFORMATION: Reflection Lake, 3440 Cottonwood Ave., San Jacinto 92582—Ph: (909) 654-7906

LAKE HEMET

Lake Hemet is at an elevation of 4,340 feet in a mountain meadow within the San Bernardino National Forest. Surrounded by chaparral-covered hills, the 420 surface acre Lake has over 4 miles of shoreline and is under the jurisdiction of the Lake Hemet Municipal Water District. Only fishing boats with motors are allowed. Large trout are caught throughout the year. In addition, the angler will find a good bass and catfish population. There is a large developed campground at the Lake. Nearby Hurkey Creek has a campground operated by Riverside County.

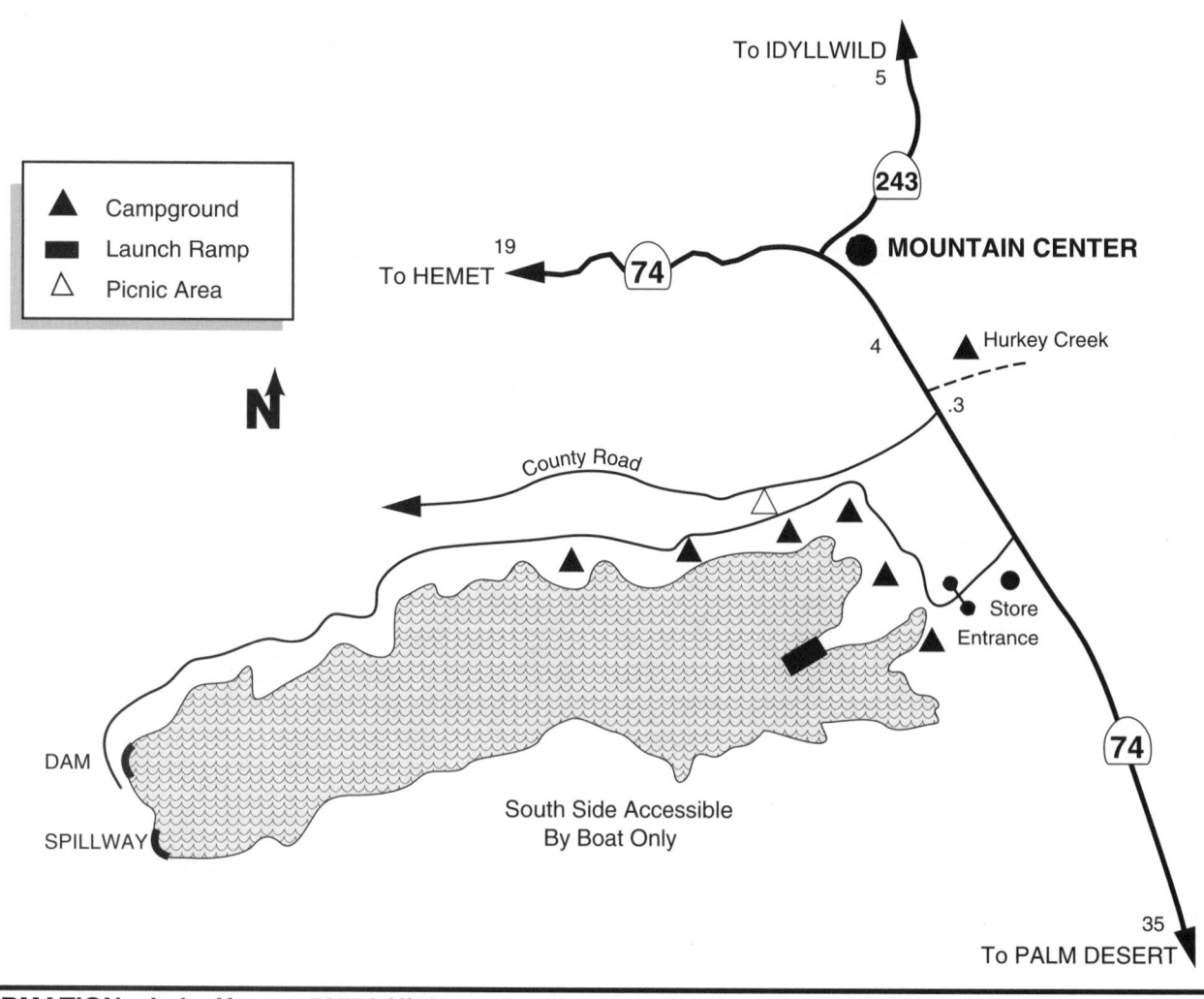

▲	Campground
■	Launch Ramp
△	Picnic Area

To IDYLLWILD
5
243
MOUNTAIN CENTER
19
74
To HEMET
4
Hurkey Creek
.3
County Road
Store
Entrance
DAM
SPILLWAY
South Side Accessible
By Boat Only
74
35
To PALM DESERT

INFORMATION: Lake Hemet, 56570 Highway 74, Mountain Center 92561—Ph: (909) 659-2680

CAMPING	BOATING	RECREATION	OTHER
Lake Hemet:	Fishing Boats with Motors	Fishing: Largemouth Bass,	General Store:
Dev. Sites for	Boats Must Be At	Trout, Bluegill & Catfish	Ph: (909) 659-2350
Tents & R.V.s	Least 10 Feet Long	Picnicking	Food, Camping Supplies
Some Hookups	No Canoes, Kayaks,	Hiking	Bait & Tackle
Fee: $15 - $18	Sailboats or Inflatables	No Swimming	Propane
Disposal Station	Rentals: Boats & Motors	Playgrounds	Operated by Riverside
No Reservations	10 MPH Speed Limit	Horseshoe Pits	County of Reg. Parks
	Launch Ramp	Basketball Court	Hurkey Creek:
Day Use: $8	Fee: $4	No Motorcycles	100 Sites for Tents &
			R.V.s to 40 ft.
			No Hookups
			Fee: $15
			Group Sites

LAKE CAHUILLA

Lake Cahuilla is at an elevation of 44 feet, southwest of Indio. This 135-surface acre Lake is owned by the Coachella Valley Water District. The palm-shaded park is operated by Riverside County. Located in the desert, temperatures can climb up to 100 degrees in summer but in winter months are often about 75 degrees attracting campers and anglers to this facility. There are campsites along with a secluded group campground and a shaded picnic area. A swimming pool with sandy beach is open from April to October. Trails and corrals are available for the equestrian.

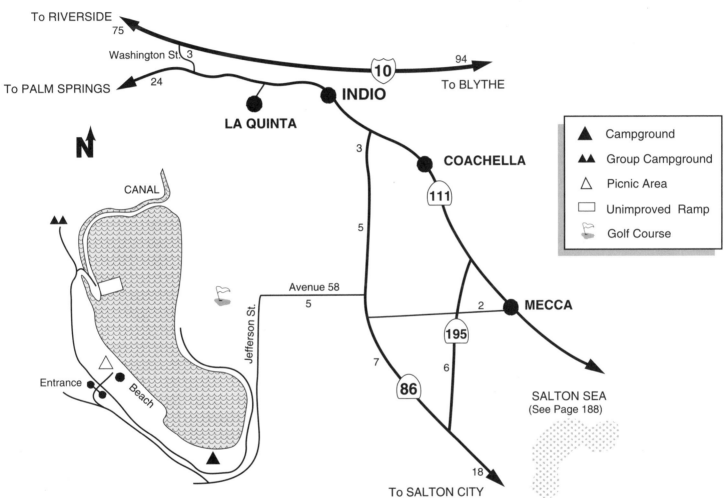

INFORMATION: Lake Cahuilla, 58075 Jefferson St., La Quinta 92253—Ph: (760) 564-4712

CAMPING	BOATING	RECREATION	OTHER
150 Dev. Sites for Tents & R.V.s 75 with Hookups Fees: $12 - $16 Group Sites Disposal Station Reservations: Riverside County Park District Ph: (800) 234-7275	Sail & Row Boats Electric Motors Only Speed Limit - 10 MPH Hand Launch Only	Fishing: Rainbow Trout in Winter, Channel Catfish, Striped Bass Fishing Pier Accessible to Handicapped Swimming Pool Open April - October Picnicking Group Area Hiking & Bicycling Trails Equestrian Trails & Horse Corrals	Full Facilities at Indio

WISTER UNIT, FINNEY - RAMER UNIT - IMPERIAL WILDLIFE AREA

The 6,127 acres of the Imperial Wildlife Area is one of Southern California's most abundant wildlife habitats. The Wister Unit consists of a series of deep and shallow water ponds, good for sightseeing and nature study. This is the home of a variety of birds, fish, amphibians, reptiles and mammals. With prime waterfowl hunting available, there are restrictions which apply to the number of hunters along other regulations; contact the Wildlife Headquarters for details. Located below sea level in the hot desert climate of the Imperial Valley, the temperature is often over 100 degrees in the summer months. A more temperate climate of 70 degrees prevails in fall, winter and spring.

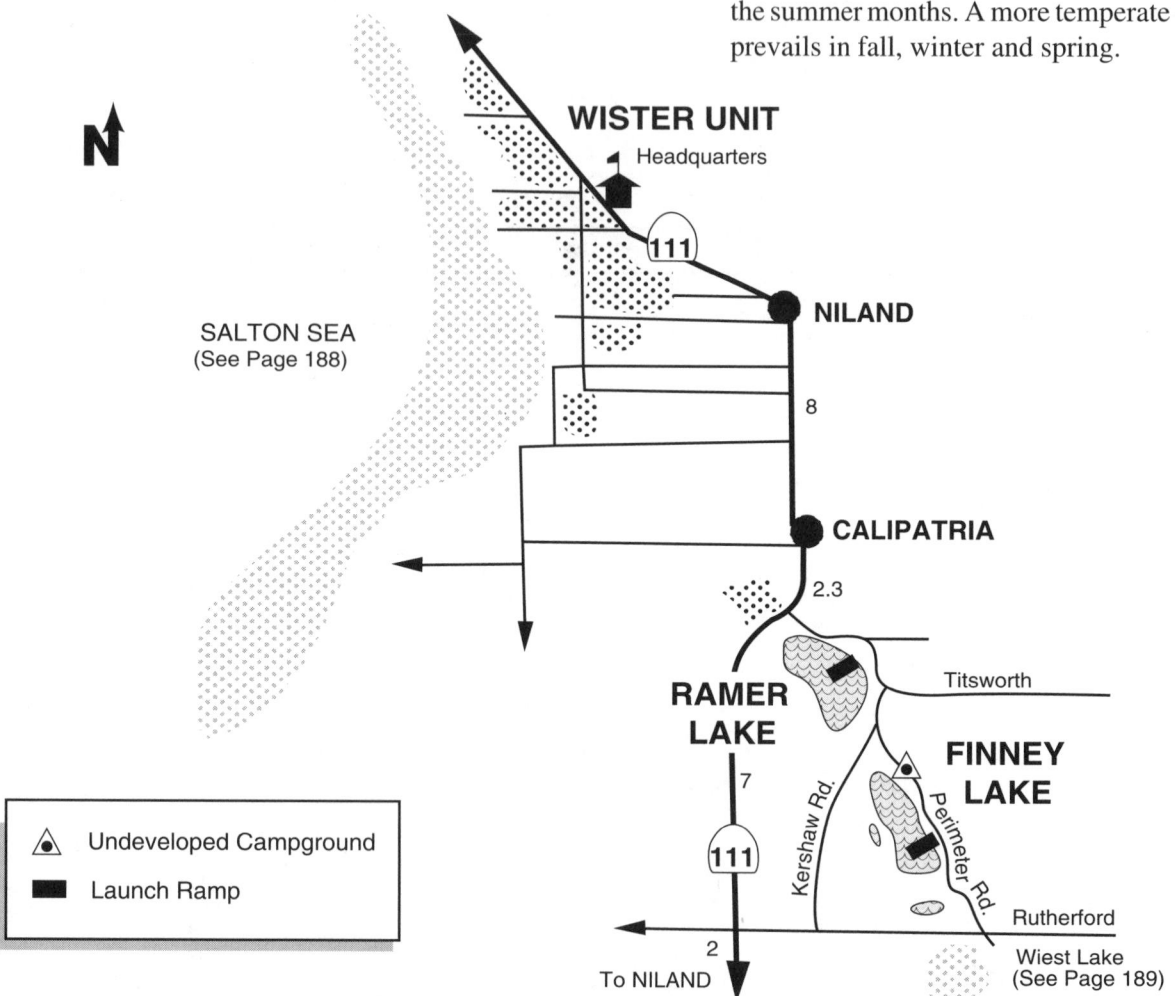

INFORMATION: Imperial Wildlife Area, 8700 Davis Rd., Niland 92257—Ph: (760) 359-0577

CAMPING	BOATING	RECREATION	OTHER
Primitive Open Camping with Fire Rings Day Use Permit Required Wister Unit Entrance Fee: $2.50	Finney-Ramer: Electric Motors Only Wister Ponds: No Boating *Call for Current Water Level Conditions*	Fishing: Largemouth Bass, Bluegill Crappie, Catfish & Carp Picnicking Hiking Nature Study Hunting - Shotguns Only Duck, Geese, Dove Quail, Pheasant & Rabbit *Check Restrictions*	Nearest Facilities in Niland

The Salton Sea, located in a desert valley 228 feet below sea level, is surrounded by mountains reaching to 10,000 feet. It is one of the world's largest inland bodies of salt water with a surface area of 360 square miles. Summer temperatures range to over 100 degrees. Fall, winter and spring temperatures are in the 70's. Orangemouth Corvina, Croaker (Bairdiella) and Sargo were introduced from the Gulf of California and the Tilapia was imported from Africa. The fish have flourished here at California's richest inland fishery and anglers enjoy the rewards. Numerous marinas, campgrounds and resorts support the recreational abundance of this desert oasis. *Very strong winds can come up at times causing dangerous boating conditions so caution is advised.*

....Continued..

INFORMATION: See Following Page

CAMPING	BOATING	RECREATION	OTHER

See Following Page for Campgrounds Resort and Marinas	Open to All Boating
	Full Service Marinas
	Launch Ramps
	Docks
	Dry Storage
	Gas
	
	Caution: Sudden Strong Winds Many Unmarked Underwater Hazards Especially at North & South Ends
		Fishing: Corvina,
		  Gulf Croaker, Tilapia
		Swim Beaches
		Picnicking - Shade
		  Ramadas
		Nature Trails
		Birdwatching
		9-Hole Golf Course
		Hunting: Waterfowl,
		  Pheasant, Dove &
		  Rabbit
			Full Facilities Around
			  the Lake
			Restaurants
			Mineral Spas
			
			For Additional Information
			Contact Westshores
			  Chamber of Commerce
			  P.O. Box 5185
			  Salton City 92275
			  Ph: (760) 394-4112

SALTON SEA.............Continued

SALTON SEA STATE RECREATION AREA - 100-225 State Park Rd., North Shore 92254—Ph: (760) 393-3052

Headquarters Campground:
25 Tent & R.V. Sites to 40 Feet, Wheelchair Accessible, 15 Full Hookups, Disposal Station, Hot Showers, Shade Ramadas, Shaded Picnic Area, Fish Cleaning Station, Campfire Programs, Nature Trail to Mecca Beach, Launch Ramp, Mooring, Boat Wash Rack. *Fee: $8- $16 - $2 Senior (62 plus) Discount - Reserve: Ph: (800) 444-7275*

Mecca Beach Campground:
108 Tent & R.V. Sites, Wheelchair Accessible, Solar Showers, Shaded Picnic Area, Fish Cleaning Station, Campfire Programs. *Fees: June 1 to Sept. 30:- $8 & Oct. 1 to May 31 - $12 - $2 Senior Discount*

Corvina Beach, Salt Creek & Bombay Beach Campgrounds:
1000 Primitive Sites on Water's Edge, Piped Water, Beach Launch. *Fee: $7 - $2 Senior Discount*

PRIVATELY OPERATED CAMPGROUNDS & MARINAS

BOMBAY MARINA & CAMPGROUND - 9518 Avenue B, Niland 92257, Ph: (760) 354-1694
50 Tent & R.V. Sites, 16 Full Hookups, Trailer Rentals, 18 Shaded Sites, Open Tent Camping, Hot Showers, Snacks, Bait & Tackle, Ice, Drinks, Boat Slips, Launch Ramp, Rental Boats.

RED HILL MARINA & CAMPGROUND - Imperial County, 7581 Garst Rd., Calipatria 92233 - Ph: (760) 348-2310
240 Acre Primitive Tent & R.V. Dry Camp plus 80 R.V. Sites, Electric & Water Hookups, 12 Sites Include Sewer Hookups, Hot Showers, Shade Ramadas, Disposal Station, Picnic Tables, Launch Ramp, Docks, Dry Storage, Fish Cleaning Station, Boat Wash Rack, Bait & Tackle, Ice, Day Use: $2.

SALTON CITY SPA & R.V. PARK - P.O. Box 5375, Salton City 92275, Ph: (760) 394-4333
315 R.V. Sites, Full Hookups, Hot Showers, Hot Spa, Swimming Pool, Pool Tables, Poker Room, Horseshoes, Picnic Tables, Dances, Potlucks, Large Recreation Hall, Dry Storage.

JOHNSON'S LANDING - North End of Sea Garden - P.O. Box 5312, Salton City 92275, Ph: (760) 394-4755
108 R.V. Sites - Fee: $15, Full Hookups, Hot Showers, Disposal Station, Weekly and Monthly Rates, Launch Ramp, Dock, Fish Cleaning Station, Boat Wash, Restaurant & Bar.

SALTON SEA BEACH MARINA - 288 Coachella, Salton Sea Beach 92274-9517, Ph: (760) 395-5212
R.V. Sites, Full Hookups, Monthly and Weekly Rates, Overflow Site for Tents & R.V.s, Water & Electric Hookups, 17 Shaded Cabanas, Hot Showers, Gas, Groceries, Bait & Tackle, Fish Cleaning Station, Disposal Station, Launch Ramp, Boat Wash Rack, Playground, Fire Pits & BBQs, Picnic Tables, .

DESERT SHORES TRAILER PARK & MARINA - Desert Shores 92274, Ph: (760) 395-5280
R.V. Sites with Full Hookups, Laundry, Hot Showers, Launch Ramp.

RANCHO MARINA - 301 N. Palm Dr., Desert Shores 92274, Ph: (760) 395-5410
75 Tent & R.V. Sites, 47 Full Hookups, Hot Showers.

WIEST LAKE

Wiest Lake is located 4 miles north of Brawley off Highway 111. The Lake is 110 feet below sea level in the rich agriculture area of Imperial Valley. Imperial County operates the recreation facilities. The Lake has 50 surface acres and is open to all types of boating from fishing boats to waterskiing. There is a good warm water fishery. The visitor will find picnic sites, a swim beach and hiking trails. Although there is no shooting within the park, the hunter will find waterfowl, dove and rabbit in the nearby Imperial Wildlife Area. Hot summer temperatures are very high but a more moderate climate prevails in the fall, winter and spring.

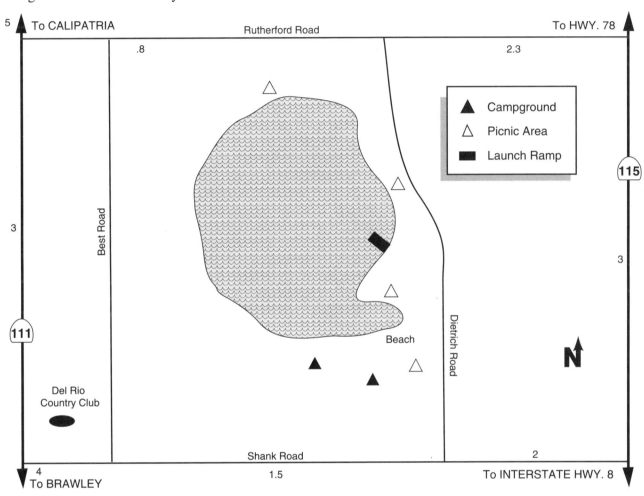

INFORMATION: Wiest Lake, 5351 Dietrich Rd., Brawley 92227—Ph: (760) 344-3712

CAMPING	BOATING	RECREATION	OTHER

20 Tent Sites
   Fee: $7
23 R.V. Sites
   Electric & Water
   Hookups
   Fee: $12
Handicapped Facilities
Disposal Station
	Open to All Boating
	Paved Launch Ramp
	Docks
		Fishing: Largemouth
		   Bass, Bluegill,
		   Catfish & Carp
		Picnicking
		Hiking
		Nature Study
		Swimming - Beach
		Nearby:
		   Hunting: Duck,
		   Geese, Dove,
		   Quail, Rabbit
			Full Facilities in
			   Brawley

189

SUNBEAM LAKE

Sunbeam Lake has a surface area of 22 acres and the Lagoon has 12 surface acres. Owned and operated by Imperial County, the park offers a variety of recreational opportunities. Boating is allowed on both the Lake and the Lagoon but no motors are permitted at the Lagoon. The angler will find a variety of warm water fish in the cool spring-fed Lagoon. These Lakes are 43 feet below sea level where summer temperatures average over 100 degrees. Fall, winter and spring are more moderate. Surrounded by palm trees, this Lake is a refreshing oasis located near Highway 8.

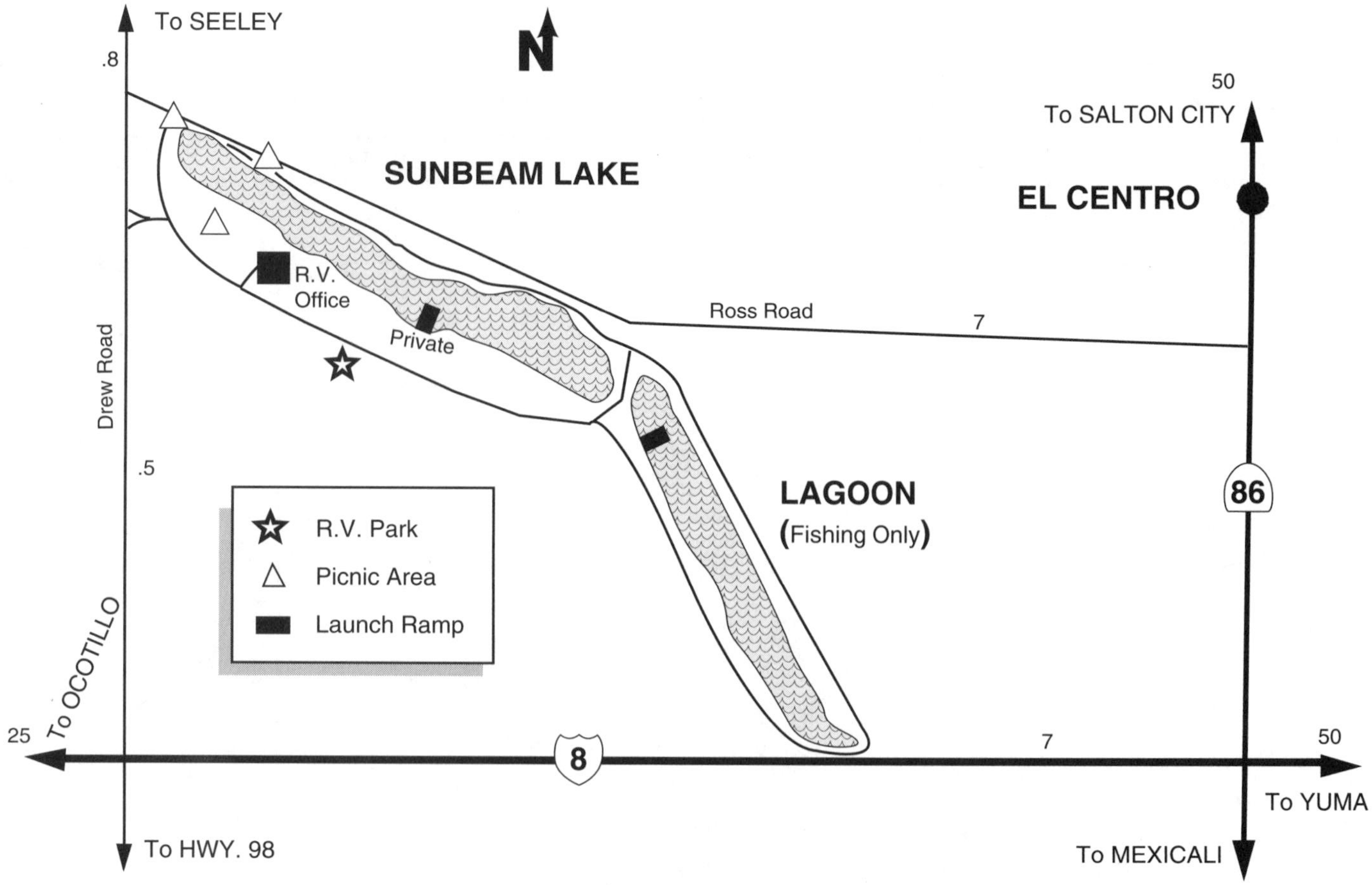

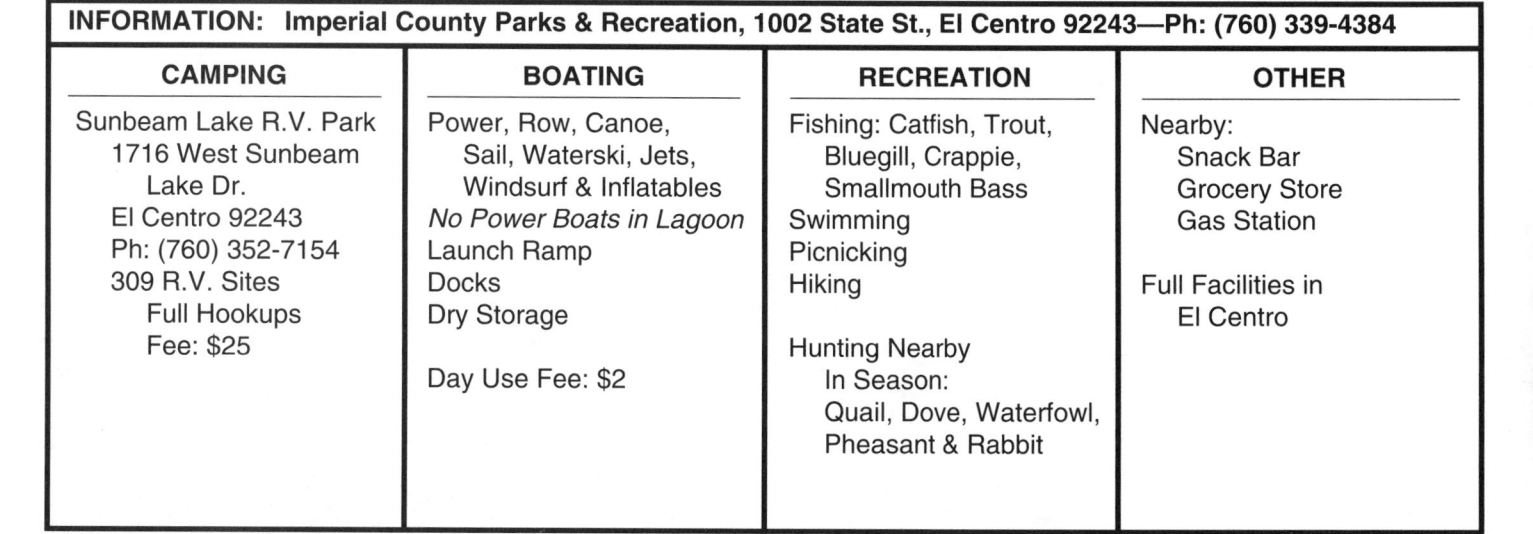

INFORMATION: Imperial County Parks & Recreation, 1002 State St., El Centro 92243—Ph: (760) 339-4384

CAMPING	BOATING	RECREATION	OTHER

Sunbeam Lake R.V. Park
   1716 West Sunbeam
     Lake Dr.
   El Centro 92243
   Ph: (760) 352-7154
   309 R.V. Sites
     Full Hookups
     Fee: $25
	Power, Row, Canoe,
	   Sail, Waterski, Jets,
	   Windsurf & Inflatables
	No Power Boats in Lagoon
	Launch Ramp
	Docks
	Dry Storage
	
	Day Use Fee: $2
		Fishing: Catfish, Trout,
		   Bluegill, Crappie,
		   Smallmouth Bass
		Swimming
		Picnicking
		Hiking
		
		Hunting Nearby
		   In Season:
		     Quail, Dove, Waterfowl,
		     Pheasant & Rabbit
			Nearby:
			   Snack Bar
			   Grocery Store
			   Gas Station
			
			Full Facilities in
			   El Centro

DIXON LAKE

Nestled in chaparral and avocado-covered foothills, Dixon Lake is at an elevation of 1,045 feet. It has a surface area of 70 acres with 2 miles of shoreline within the 527 acre park. The Dixon Lake Recreation Area is operated by the City of Escondido Parks and Recreation Department. The facilities include camping, fishing and picnicking. Private boats are not allowed but rental boats are available. Many large bass and catfish await the angler. Trout are stocked at Dixon Lake from November through May and catfish from June through August.

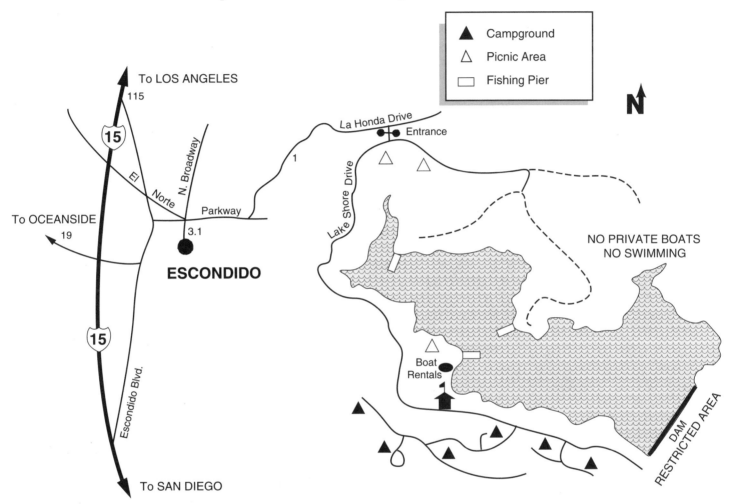

INFORMATION: Public Works Dept. - Lakes, 201 N. Broadway, Escondido 92025—Ranger Ph: (760) 839-4680

CAMPING	BOATING	RECREATION	OTHER

45 Tent & R.V. Sites
   Fee: $12
   2nd Vehicle: $2
10 with Full Hookups
   Fee: $16
   2nd Vehicle: $2
Disposal Station
Reservations Accepted
   for Camping &
    Picnicking
Reservation Fee: $5
Ph: (760) 741-3328
7 a.m. - 4 p.m.
	No Private Boats
	Rentals: Rowboats
	   with Electric Motors,
	   Paddleboats
		Fishing: Trout,
		   Catfish, Bluegill,
		   Redear Sunfish,
		   Florida Bass
		Fishing Pier with
		   Handicapped Facilities
		No Swimming or
		   Wading
		Picnicking
		Nature Trails
		Campfire Programs
			Snack Bar
			Bait & Tackle
			
			Full Facilities in Escondido

LAKE HENSHAW

Lake Henshaw is at an elevation of 2,740 feet nestled in a valley on the southern slopes of Mt. Palomar. With up to 25 miles of shoreline, water levels vary depending on the season. Large oak trees around the resort create a pleasant contrast to semi-arid mountains surrounding the area. The resort has a campground with excellent support facilities. Housekeeping cabins are also available. No swimming is permitted in the Lake but there is a pool. Lake Henshaw is known for good fishing for bass, crappie, bluegill and channel catfish.

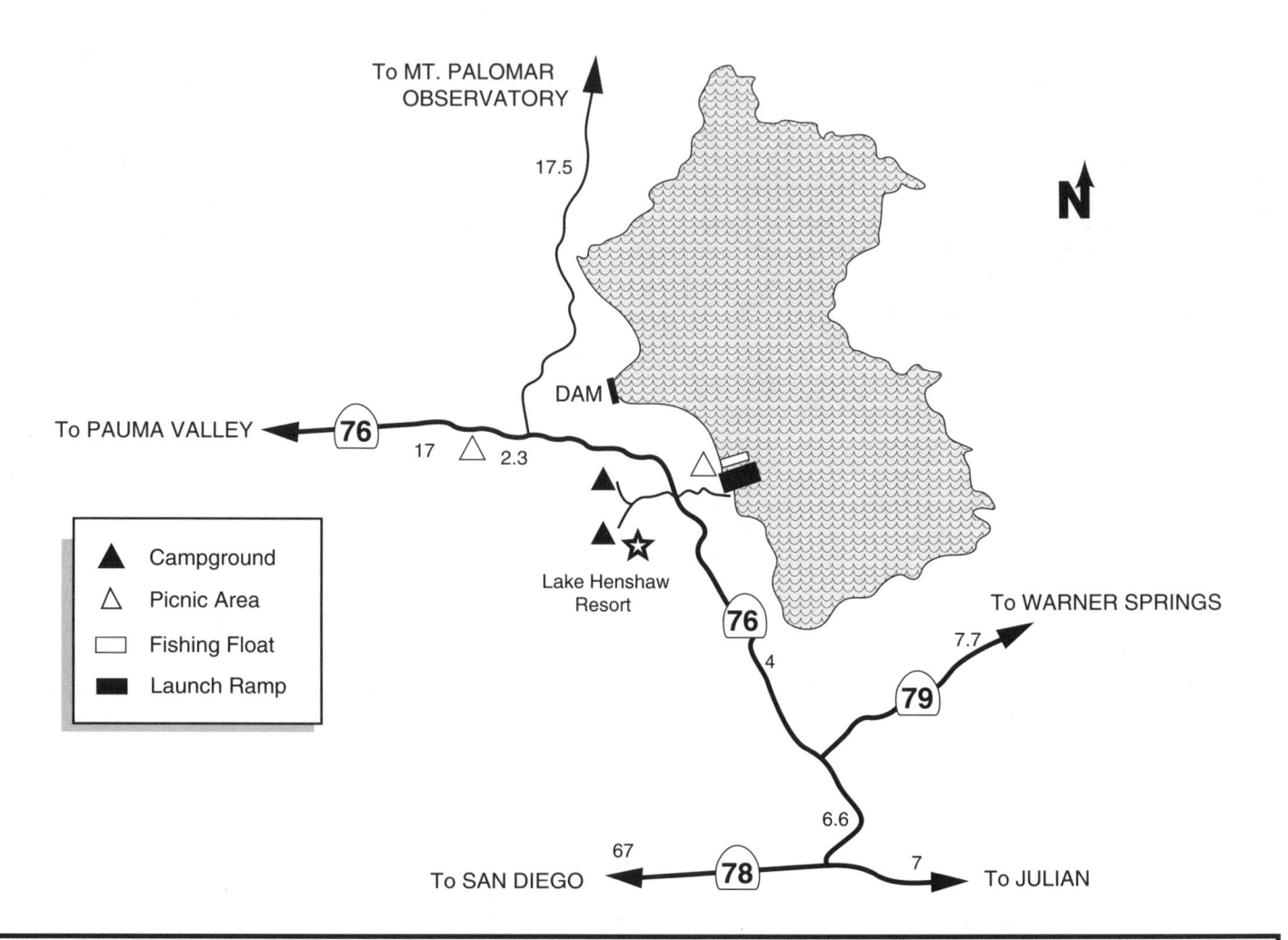

To MT. PALOMAR OBSERVATORY

17.5

N

To PAUMA VALLEY ◄ 76

17 △ 2.3

DAM

Lake Henshaw Resort

▲ Campground
△ Picnic Area
☐ Fishing Float
■ Launch Ramp

76

4

79

7.7

To WARNER SPRINGS

6.6

To SAN DIEGO ◄ 67 78 7 ► To JULIAN

INFORMATION: Lake Henshaw Resort, 26439 Hwy. 76, Santa Ysabel 92070—Ph: (760) 782-3501

CAMPING	BOATING	RECREATION	OTHER

84 Dev. Sites for Tents
    Fee: $14
20 Dev. Sites for R.V.s
    Full Hookups
    Fee: $16
    (Available at Times -
    Several Permanent
    Residents - Call for
    Details)
Disposal Station
    Fee: $5
	Power & Row
	    10 Feet Minimum
	    Length
	    NO Canoes or Rafts
	10 MPH Speed Limit
	Launch Ramp
	Rentals: Fishing Boats
		Fishing : Catfish, Bluegill,
		    Crappie & Bass
		Fishing Float
		Swimming - *Pool Only*
		Picnicking
		Hiking
		Playgrounds
			17 Housekeeping Cabins
			    Reservations:
			    Ph: (760) 782-3487
			Restaurant
			Club House
			Grocery Store
			Bait & Tackle
			Hot Showers
			Laundromat
			Propane
			Jacuzzi

AGUA HEDIONDA LAGOON, LAKE WOHLFORD, and PALOMAR PARK (DOANE POND)

From a saltwater lagoon to a coniferous mountain meadow pond at 5,500 feet, the Lakes on this page offer a striking contrast. Agua Hedionda Lagoon is a large saltwater lagoon off Interstate Highway 5 which offers all types of boating. This is a popular waterskiing and kayaking facility. There is a water ski school along with personal water craft rentals, a pro shop, 3-1ane paved launch ramp, dry storage and a concession.

Lake Wohlford, at 1,500 feet elevation, is a good fishing Lake for trout in season. Wohlford is famous for trophy-size largemouth bass. Channel catfish are also available. Sailboats and rafts are not permitted. Doane Pond, a separate facility, is in the Palomar State Park with hiking trails, picnic sites and campgrounds. Anglers can catch trout with the best months being November through June.

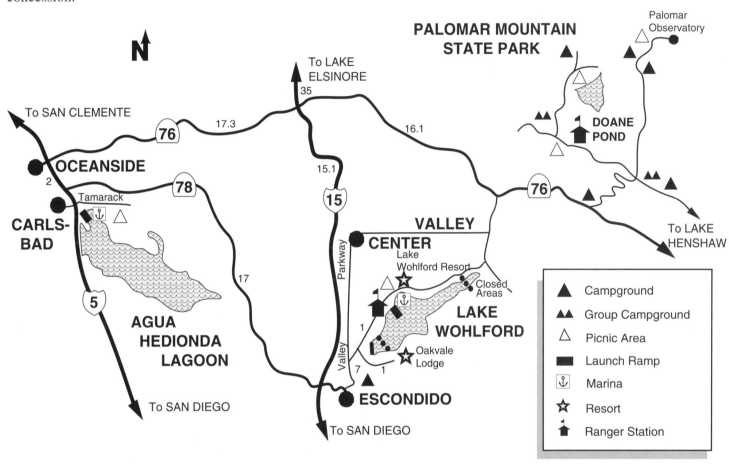

INFORMATION: Agua Hedionda - Snug Harbor Marina, 4215 Harrison St., Carlsbad 92008—Ph: (760) 434-3089

CAMPING	BOATING	RECREATION	OTHER
Agua Hedionda Lagoon: Summer Youth Camp	Agua Hedionda: Open to All Boats *Call for Regulations* Launch Fee Speed Limit: 45 MPH	Fishing: Trout, Bass, Catfish, Crappie & Bluegill Picnicking Hiking Trails	Lake Wohlford Ranger Station: Ph: (760) 839-4346 Lake Wohlford Resort:
Doane Valley Campground: 31 Dev. Sites - Fee: $12 Groups Camps - 15 to 25 People - Fee: $72 Reservations: Ph: (800) 444-7275	Rentals: Jetskis, Canoes & Kayaks Lake Wohlford:No Sailboats 20 Feet Max. Length Speed Limit: 5 MPH Rentals: Fishing Boats Private Launch: $4 Doane Pond: No Boating	Agua Hedionda: Waterski & Wakeboard School Lake Wohlford: No Swimming Doane Pond: No Swimming	25484 Lake Wohlford Rd. Escondido 92027 Ph: (760) 749-2755 6 R.V. Sites to 35 feet Full Hookups 5 Cabins with Kitchens Swimming Pool, Cafe

193

SANTEE LAKES and LAKE POWAY

These Lakes in the San Diego area provide a popular warm water fishery. In addition, the angler will find trout planted during the winter months. The Santee Lakes Recreational Area offers campsites plus a swimming pool, picnic facilities, playgrounds, volleyball courts and horseshoe pits.

The Lake Poway Recreation Area provides 8 primitive camp sites in an oak grove located via a one-mile hike from the Lake. Picnic sites, nature and equestrian trails and an archery range are also available. The 60 surface acre Lake is open to row and electric motor boat rentals. Night fishing is allowed June to mid-September on Friday and Saturday only. Both Poway and Santee Lakes are closed to private boating but rentals are available.

LAKE POWAY

SANTEE LAKES

Rancho Bernardo Rd — DAM — Play Field — Espola Road — To RAMONA — POWAY — Mission Gorge Road — SAN DIEGO — EL CAJON — To TIJUANA, MEXICO

Swimming Pool — Play Field — Lake Canyon — Mast Blvd. — Carlton Oaks — Entrance

▲ Campground
◉ Undeveloped Campground
△ Picnic Area

INFORMATION: Santee Lakes, P.O. Box 719003, Santee 92072—Ph: (619) 596-3141

CAMPING	BOATING	RECREATION	OTHER
Santee Lakes: 172 R.V. Sites, Full Hookups Fees: $29 - $35, 60 Primitive Sites Fee: $20, Disposal Station, Laundry & Groceries, Swimming Pool. Lake Poway: 8 Walk-in Only Sites With Water	Lake Poway: *No Private Boats*, Rentals: Sail, Row & Motor Boats, Paddleboats & Canoes. Santee Lakes: *No Private Boats*, Rentals: Rowboats, Paddleboats, Kayaks & Canoes	Fishing: Trout (Winter), Florida Bass, Bluegill & Channel Catfish. Picnicking Group Sites. Hiking, Equestrian & Nature Trails - Poway. Santee Lakes: Playgrounds, Volleyball Courts, Horseshoe Pits, Store	Lake Poway P.O. Box 789, Poway 92074, Ph: (858) 679-5465. Snack Bar, Bait & Tackle, Playgrounds, Tournament Volleyball Courts, Horseshoes, Softball - Night Lights, 15 Acre Grass Picnic Area Group Reservations, Ph: (858) 679-4342

Lake Cuyamaca is at an elevation of 4,650 feet in a mountain setting of oak, pine and cedar trees. The dam was originally built in 1887. Thanks to a dedicated group of residents and sportsmen, the minimum pool is 110 surface acres. Normally this is the only Lake in San Diego County that has trout all year. Cuyamaca stocks 44,000 pounds of rainbow trout each year and also offers excellent fishing for warm water fish. Cuyamaca Rancho State Park covering 25,000 acres has over 100 miles of scenic equestrian and hiking trails. Los Caballos campground offers developed sites including corrals for families with horses. In addition, Los Vaqueros campground is for equestrian groups with facilities for 45 horses.

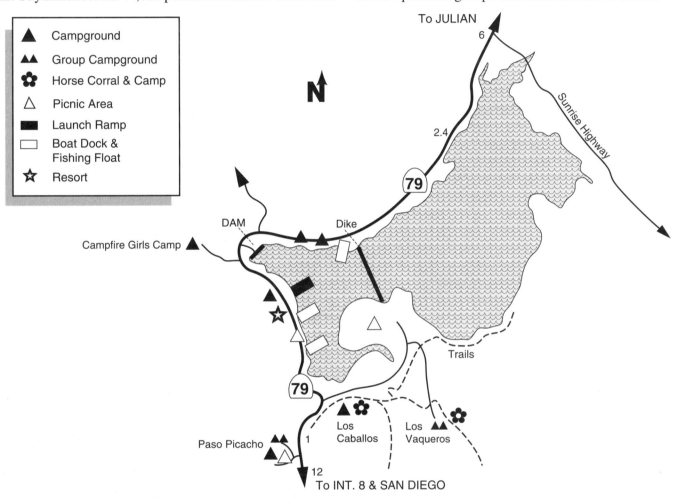

INFORMATION: Manager-Lake Cuyamaca, 15027 Highway 79, Julian 92036—Ph: (760)765-0515 or (877)581-9904

CAMPING	BOATING	RECREATION	OTHER
54 Dev. Sites for Tents & R.V.s - Some w/Hookups Plus Self-Contained Parking Fees: $13 - $18	Power & Row Boats Between 10 Feet & 26 Feet Only Inflatables Must Have Bow & Stern,	Fishing: Trout, Crappie, Catfish, Bluegill & Smallmouth Bass Fishing Fees:	Snack Bar Restaurant Grocery Store Bait & Tackle
Cuyamaca Rancho State Pk: 160 Dev. Sites For Tents & R.V.s To 30 Feet No Hookups - Fee: $12	9-18 Feet Wood Bottom and Multiple Inflatable Compartments	Adults - $5 & Children Over 8 Yrs. - $2.50 Under 8 Yrs. - Free Free Fishing Class	Disposal Station Gas Station Hunting: Duck Wed. & Sun. a.m. in
2 Group Sites - 60 People ea. 16 Equestrian Sites Plus Group Site to 80 People & 45 Horses in Corrals Reserve:Ph: (800) 444-7275	Speed Limit - 10 MPH Launch Ramp Rentals: Boats & Motors, Canoes, Paddle Boats	Sat. @ 10 am No Swimming or Body Contact with Water Picnicking Hiking & Equestrian Trails	Season Rustic Cabins for up to 8 People - Fee: $15

SAN DIEGO CITY LAKES: HODGES, SUTHERLAND, MIRAMAR, SAN VICENTE, EL CAPITAN, MURRAY, UPPER and LOWER OTAY and BARRETT

These popular Lakes provide some of the best bass fishing in America. They are operated by the City of San Diego.

See the following page for full details on each Lake.

....Continued....

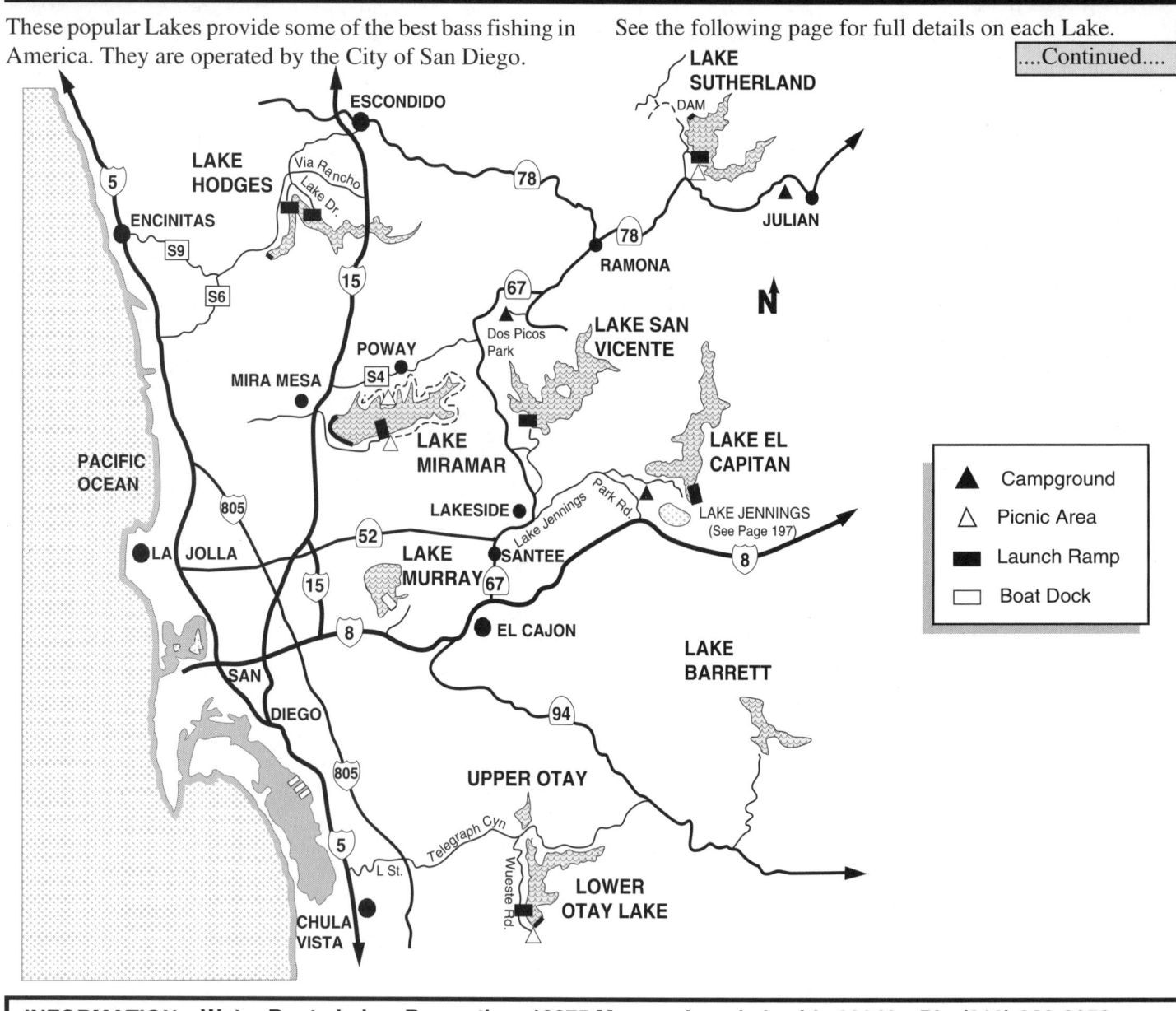

▲	Campground
△	Picnic Area
■	Launch Ramp
▭	Boat Dock

INFORMATION: Water Dept., Lakes Recreation, 12375 Moreno Ave., Lakeside 92040—Ph: (619) 668-2050

CAMPING	BOATING	RECREATION	OTHER
There is No Camping at Any of These San Diego City Lakes	Power, Row, Sail & Inflatables	Fishing Hot Line: Ph: (619) 465-3474	Information: Hodges (760) 272-3275
	Subject to Inspection	Fishing Permits:	Sutherland (619) 698-3474
	Speed Limits Vary	Adults: Fee $5	All Others (619) 390-0222
See Following Page for Nearest Camping	Fee: $5 Any Private Boat Use Including Canoes & Kayaks	Children 8-15 years: Fee $2.50	
		Water Contact Activities:	Privately Operated Concessions at each Lake Except Barrett:
	Rentals: Rowboats, Motorboats, Canoes, Paddleboats	Adults: Fee $5	Offer Sale of Permits, Licenses, Bait & Tackle, Food & Beverages
		Children 8-15 years: Fee $2.50	
		Slalom Course: $10	

The following Lakes are open from Sunrise to Sunset.

LAKE HODGES at an elevation of 330 feet, is located approximately 31 miles north of San Diego and 5 miles south of Escondido. This Lake has a maximum surface area of 1,234 acres with 27 miles of chaparral-covered shoreline. The Lake is open from mid-March through October on Fridays, Saturdays and Sundays for picnicking, hiking, boating and fishing for bass, crappie, bluegill, channel catfish and carp. A sailboarding program is also offered from mid-April to mid-October. For wind conditions call (858) 756-8221. In addition to rowboat and motorboat rentals, the concession rents canoes, kayaks and sailboards and provides sailboard lessons.

LAKE SUTHERLAND at an elevation of 2,074 feet, is located 45 miles northeast of San Diego between Ramona and Julian. This Lake has a maximum surface area of 557 acres with 11 miles of oak and chaparral-covered shoreline. The Lake is open from March through September on Fridays, Saturdays, and Sundays for picnicking, hiking, boating and fishing for bass, bluegill, sunfish, crappie, channel catfish and blue catfish. During the season (October through January) this Lake also offers waterfowl hunting on Wednesdays and Saturdays. The nearest camping is at William Heise County Park or Dos Picos County Park.

LAKE MIRAMAR at an elevation of 714 feet, is located about 18 miles north of San Diego. This small Lake has a maximum surface area of 162 acres and 4 miles of shoreline. The Lake is open from early November through September on Saturdays, Sundays, Mondays and Tuesdays for boating and fishing for bass, bluegill, sunfish, channel catfish, and trout (stocked November through early April). The Lake is open 7 days a week for picnicking, walking, jogging, bicycling or skating. Rentals include rowboats, motorboats rentals, canoes and pedal boats.

LAKE SAN VICENTE at elevation of 659 feet, is located in Lakeside, approximately 25 miles northeast of San Diego. The Lake has a maximum surface area of 1,069 acres with 14 miles of shoreline. The Lake's winter schedule (mid-October to mid-May) is Thursdays and Fridays, for both water contact activities (water-skiing, wakeboarding, tubing, etc.) and fishing for bass, bluegill, crappie, sunfish, channel, blue and white catfish and trout (planted from November to February). Saturdays and Sundays, the lake is open for fishing only. The Lake's summer schedule (mid-May to mid-October) is Wednesdays for fishing only, Thursdays for both fishing and water contact activities, and Fridays, Saturdays and Sundays for water contact activities only. A slalom course is available on a first-come basis. Nearest camping is at Lake Jennings County Park.

LAKE EL CAPITAN at an elevation of 750 feet, is located in the foothills of Lakeside approximately 30 miles northeast of San Diego. There is a maximum surface area of 1,562 acres with 22 miles of bushy shoreline. The Lake is open on Fridays, Saturdays and Sundays for picnicking, hiking, boating, use of personal watercraft (jet skis, waverunners, etc.), and fishing for bass, bluegill, blue and channel catfish, crappie and sunfish. Nearest camping is at Lake Jennings County Park.

LAKE MURRAY is the "in town" reservoir located between San Diego and La Mesa at the base of Cowles Mountain. The Lake has a maximum surface area of 172 acres with four miles of shoreline. The Lake is open from early November through Labor Day on Wednesdays, Saturdays, and Sundays for boating and fishing for bass, crappie, bluegill, channel catfish and trout (stocked November to early April). The Lake is open year raound, seven days a week, for picnicking, walking, jogging, bicyling and skating. Rentals include rowboats, motorboats, canoes and pedal boats.

LOWER OTAY LAKE is in the rolling chaparral-covered hills east of Chula Vista, approximately 20 miles southeast of San Diego. The maximum surface area is 1,100 acres with 25 miles of shoreline. The Lake is open from February through September on Wednesdays, Saturdays and Sundays for picnicking, hiking, boating and fishing for bass, crappie, bluegill and channel, blue and white catfish. Nearest camping is at Sweetwater Summit County Park.

UPPER OTAY LAKE is located just north of Lower Otay. The maximum surface area is 20 acres with 5 miles of shoreline. The Lake is open from February through September on Wednesdays, Saturdays and Sundays for fishing for bass, bluegill, bullhead and trout (stocked prior to opening in February). This is a Catch and Release fishery with use of barbless hooks on artificial lures only. No boats are allowed, fishing is from shore, waders or float tubes only. Permits can be purchased at the concession at Lower Otay.

LAKE BARRETT is located in a remote area 35 miles east of San Diego. The maximum surface area is 861 acres with 12 miles of shoreline. The Lake is open from mid-March through November. The schedule is Wednesdays, Saturdays and Sundays through May, with patron participation determining how many days it will be open after that, generally weekends only. There are no concession services available at this Lake. This is a catch and release fishery with use of barbless hooks on artificial lures only. Reservations can be obtained from Ticketmaster by calling (619) 220-TIXS. During the season (October through January), this Lake also offers waterfowl hunting on Wednesdays and Saturdays.

In addition to the days listed above, the Lakes (with the exception of Barrett) are open on certain holidays. All Lakes are closed Thanksgiving, Christmas and New Year's Day.

Fluctuating water levels may cause closure of launch ramps and boat docks. All schedules are subject to change. Please call 24-hour recording (619) 465-3474 to verify status before going to any San Diego City Lake.

LAKE JENNINGS

Lake Jennings County Park is east of El Cajon at an elevation of 690 feet. It is owned by the Helix Water District which administers this domestic water supply reservoir with 180 surface acres and 2,500 feet of shoreline. The fairly steep shoreline is semi-arid and dotted with sumac trees and a few pines. Lake Jennings County Park, a total of 100 acres, is

open year around. The Park is open 7 days a week for campers and Fridays, Saturdays and Sundays only for day use. Trout season runs from October through May. Catfish season runs from June through September. The Lake remains open until midnight on Fridays and Saturdays during catfish season only. This is the Lake for big channel or blue catfish. There is also a 190-foot handicapped accessible fishing float.

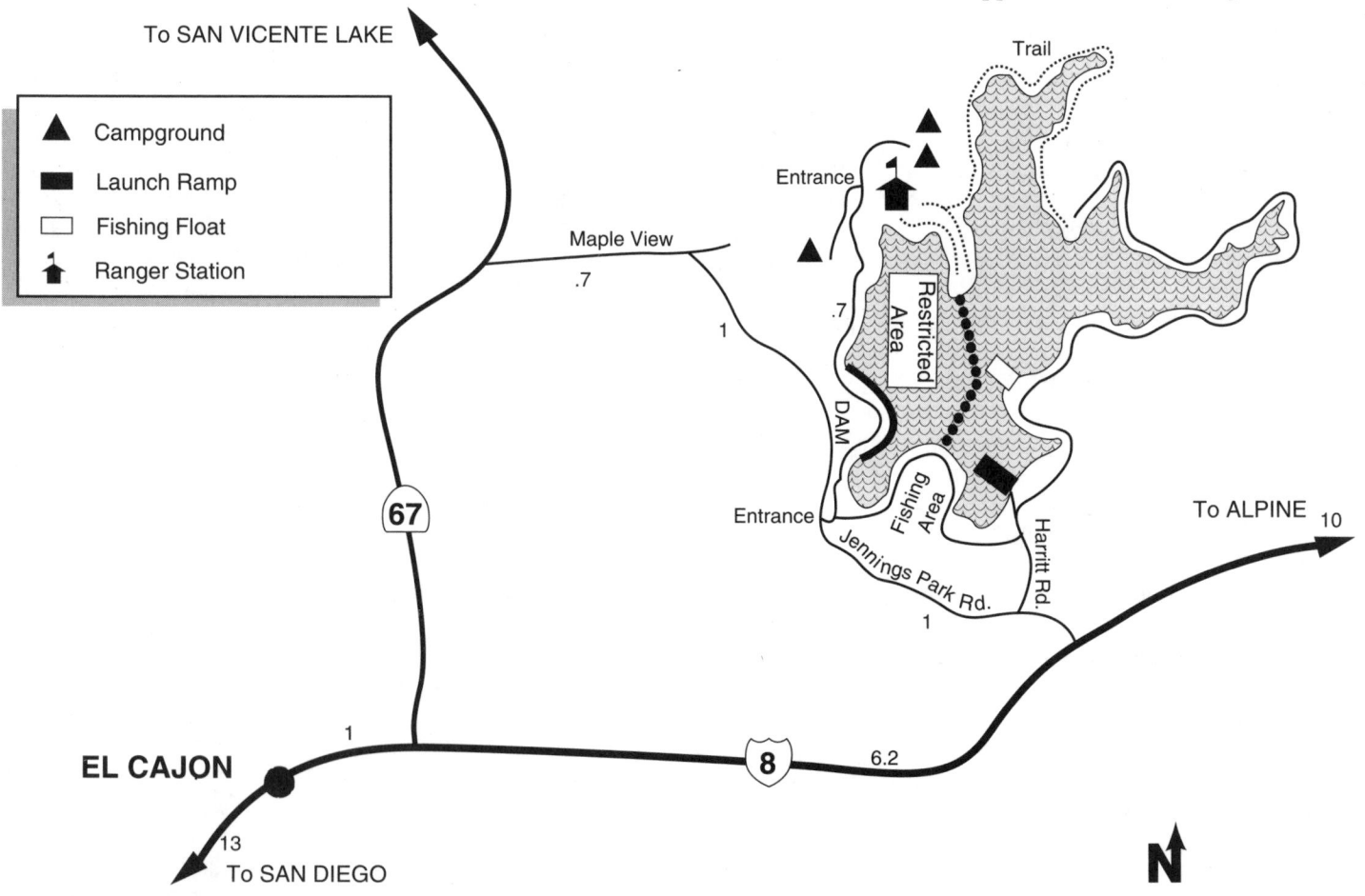

INFORMATION: Department of Parks & Recreation, 5201 Ruffin Road, San Diego 92123—Ph: (619) 694-3049

CAMPING	BOATING	RECREATION	OTHER

96 Dev. Sites for Tents & R.V.s - Full & Partial Hookups
Group Campground
Youth Group Camp
Walk-in Camp Sites
Fees: From $10
Disposal Station
Reservations Advised:
  Ph: (619) 565-3600
	Fishing Boats Only
	  Friday, Saturday &
	  Sunday
	10 MPH Speed Limit
	Launch Ramp
	Rentals: Fishing
	  Boats & Motors
		Fishing: Trout,
		  Catfish, Bluegill, Bass
		  Permit Required
		  From Shore: Daily
		  From Boat: Friday,
		  Saturday & Sunday
		  Only
		Fish Plants Weekly
		Fishing Float
		No Swimming
		Hiking Trails
		Playground
		Horseshoes
			Snack Bar - Open
			  In Season
			Bait & Tackle
			
			Full Facilities in
			  El Cajon
			
			*Only Campers Can
			Fish From Shore
			Year Around*

LAKE MORENA

Lake Morena, at an elevation of 3,000 feet, is in the Cleveland National Forest east of San Diego. Surrounded by chaparral, oaks and grassland, the Lake is in the middle of 3,250 acres of parkland maintained by San Diego County. Lake Morena has a surface area of over 1,500 acres at capacity. There is an abundant population of warm water fish including the Florida strain of largemouth bass. Trout are planted during the winter months and fishing is the primary activity. Boating is limited to 10 MPH and inflatables are subject to strict standards. Hikers, backpackers and equestrians can enjoy the nearby Pacific Crest Trail. In Campo, you can take a train ride through the backcountry or visit the local museum.

INFORMATION: Department of Parks & Recreation, 5201 Ruffin Rd., San Diego 92123—Ph: (619) 694-3049

CAMPING	BOATING	RECREATION	OTHER
86 Dev. Sites for Tents & R.V.s - 58 With Water & Electric Hookups Group Campground Youth Group Camp Primitive Camp Sites Wilderness Cabins Fees: From $10 　For Information: 　Ph: (619) 694-3049 Disposal Station Reservations Advised: 　Ph: (619) 565-3600	Power, Row & Inflatables (Strict Regulations) 10 MPH Speed Limit Launch Ramp Rentals: Fishing, Motor & Row Boats *Check for Current Water Levels*	Fishing: Florida Bass, Bluegill, Catfish & Crappie - Trout in Winter Picnicking Hiking Trails Equestrian Trails Pacific Crest Trail Interpretive Programs	Lake Morena R.V. Park 2330 Lake Morena Dr. Campo 91906 Ph: (619) 478-5677 42 R.V. Sites - Full Hookups Fee: $20 Disposal Station Morena Village: 　Gas, Restaurant, Store Campo: 　Railroad Museum 　Train Ride

LAKE HAVASU

Lake Havasu is at an elevation of 482 feet in the desert between Arizona and California. Flowing out of Topock Gorge, the Colorado River becomes Lake Havasu. This 19,300 acre Lake of secluded coves, quiet inlets and open water backs up 45 miles behind Parker Dam. Famed for its outstanding fishery and excellent boating waters, Lake Havasu attracts thousands of visitors. Major fishing, powerboating and waterskiing tournaments are held each year. Numerous campgrounds, resorts and marinas are located around the Lake. The hub of the area is Lake Havasu City and Pittsburg Point which offer complete facilities.

....Continued....

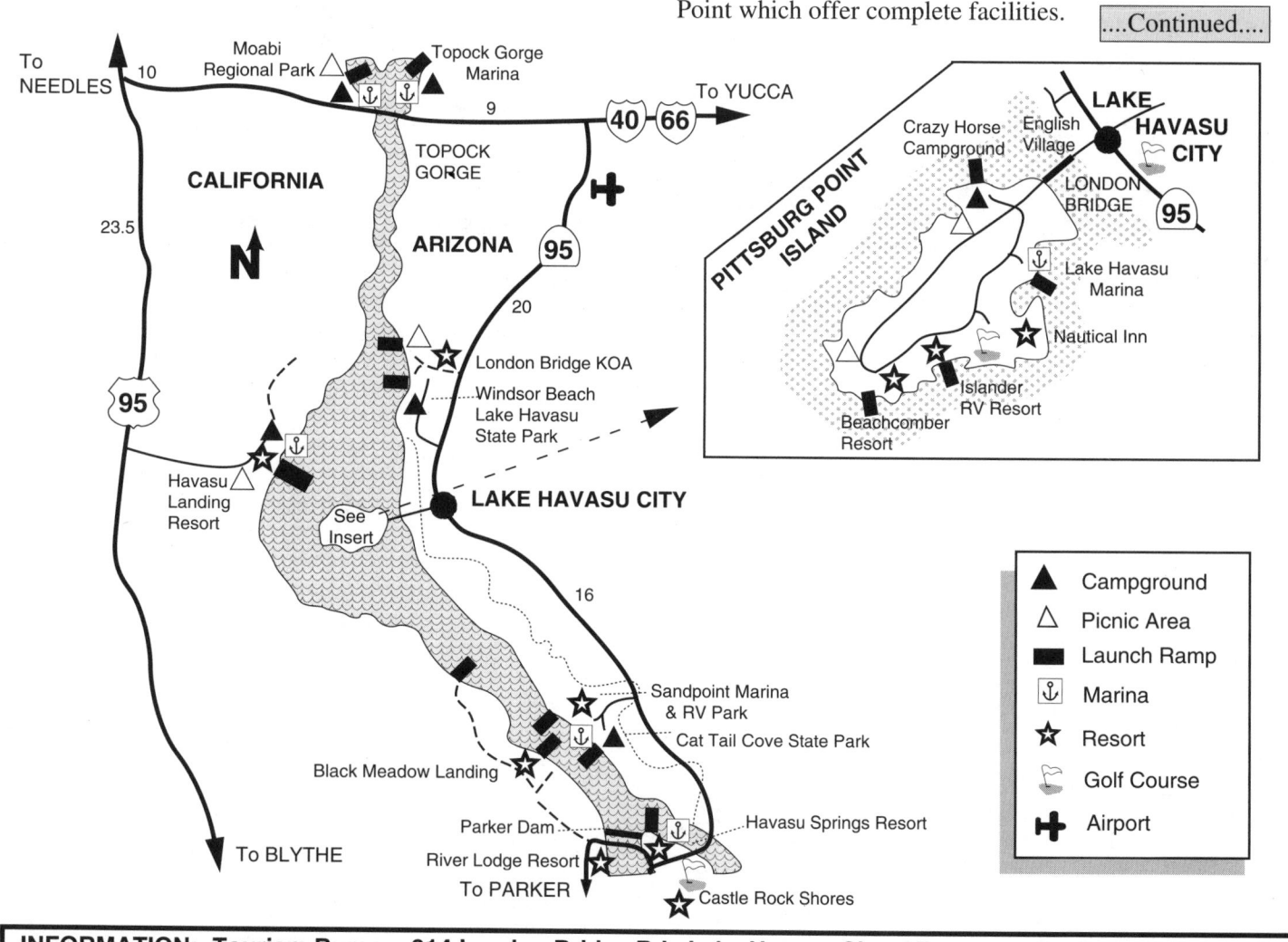

INFORMATION: Tourism Bureau, 314 London Bridge Rd., Lake Havasu City, AZ 86403—Ph: (928) 453-3444

CAMPING	BOATING	RECREATION	OTHER
Numerous Campgrounds Around Lake See Following Pages	Power, Row, Canoe, Sail, Waterski, Jets, Windsurf & Inflatable — Full Service Marinas — Rentals: Fishing, Power, Pontoons & Houseboats — *High Winds can be a Hazard in Fall & Spring*	Fishing: Catfish, Bluegill, Crappie, Largemouth & Striped Bass — Swimming — Picnicking — Hiking Trails — Nature Study — Hunting: Waterfowl, Quail & Dove	Full Resort Facilites — Airport — Golf Courses — Tennis Courts — Boat Excursions — Casino Trips — Home of the London Bridge

CAMPGROUNDS & RESORTS AS SHOWN ON MAP - *Call for Fees*

MOABI REGIONAL PARK
Park Moabi Rd., Needles 92363, Ph: (760) 326-3831
Group and Individual Campsites in Main Section of Park and Along 2-1/2 Miles of Shoreline, Unlimited Tent Sites,
25 Group Camp Areas, 35 Full & 35 Partial Hookups, Showers, Laundromat, Picnic Sites with Tables & BBQs,
Disposal Station, Beach, 5-Lane Launch Ramp, Waterfront Cabanas, Dry Storage, Recreation Hall, General Store, Ice,
Full Service Marina, Gas Docks, Rentals: Pontoon Boats, Ski & Fishing Boats, Kayaks, Courtesy Dock, Bait & Tackle.

TOPOCK GORGE MARINA
HC-12, Box 502, Topock, AZ 86436, Ph: (928) 768-2325
R.V. Sites, Full Hookups,
General Store, Restaurant, Bar, Gas, Fuel Dock & Launch Ramp, Courtesy Dock,
Rentals: 50 Boat Slips, Mobile Homes & Rental Spaces.

DESERT HILLS R.V. PARK
3825 N. London Bridge Rd., Lake Havasu City, AZ 86403, Ph: (928) 764-3113
39 R.V. Sites with Full Hookups,
Swimming Pool, Showers, Groceries, Propane, Mobile Home Rentals.

LONDON BRIDGE KOA
3405 London Bridge Rd., Lake Havasu City, AZ 86403, Ph: (928) 764-3500
58 R.V. Sites with Full Hookups, Tent Area, Showers, Swimming Pool, Store, Cafe, Rec. Hall.

WINDSOR BEACH - LAKE HAVASU STATE PARK
2 Miles North of London Bridge on London Beach Rd., Ph: (928) 855-2784
Tent & R.V. Sites, Boat-In Camps, Disposal Station, 3 Launch Ramps, Walking Trail.

HAVASU LANDING RESORT & CASINO
P.O. Box 1707, Havasu Lake 92363, Ph: (760) 858-4593 or (800) 307-3610
Owned by the Chemehuevi Tribe. Over 1,500 Tent & R.V. Sites, Full Hookups,
Unlimited Boat Access Camping Along the Shoreline of the Community, Showers, Laundromat, Snack Bars,
Market & Deli, Full Service Restaurant & Lounge, Casino, Full Service Marina, 3 Launch Ramps, Slips,
Courtesy Dock, Houseboat Rentals, Tour Boat with Hourly Trips to Lake Havasu City, Mobile Home Park.

BLACK MEADOW LANDING
P.O. Box 98, 156100 Black Meadow Rd., Parker Dam 92267, Ph: (760) 663-4901 or (800) 742-8278
375 R.V. Sites with Full Hookups, Disposal Station,
Showers, Laundromat, Ice, Restaurant, Launch Ramp, Grocery Store, Tackle Shop,
75 Motel Units, 5-Hole Golf Course.

RIVER LODGE RESORT
P.O. Box 159, Parker Dam 92267, Ph: (760) 663-4934 or (800) 577-4837
290 R.V. Sites with Full Hookups, Tent Sites,
Showers, Groceries, Launch Ramp.

SANDPOINT MARINA AND R.V. PARK
P.O.Box 1469, Lake Havasu City, AZ 86403, Ph: (928) 855-0549.
173 Sites for Tents & R.V.s with Full Hookups, Disposal Station,
Showers, Laundromat, Ice, Cafe, Game Room, Grocery Store & Tackle Shop, Gas Dock,
Playground, Swim Beach, Launch Ramp, Boat Slips with Electrical Hookups, Cable T.V.,
Rentals: Fishing Boats, Houseboats, Pontoons and Travel Trailers.

....Continued....

LAKE HAVASU.............Continued

CAT TAIL COVE STATE PARK
Route 95, Mile Post 168, P. O. Box 1990, Lake Havasu City, AZ 86405, Ph: (928) 855-1223.
61 Tent & R.V. Sites, Electric & Water Hookups, 28 Boat-In Camps,
Disposal Station, Showers, Boat Ramp, Boat Rentals.

HAVASU SPRINGS RESORT
2581 Highway 95, Parker, AZ 85344, Ph: (928) 667-3361.
136 R.V. Sites, Full Hookups,
Cable T.V., Showers, Laundromat, Restaurant & Lounge, 44 Motel Units, Grocery Store, Swimming Pool & Beach,
Boat Ramp, 310 Slips, Boat Rentals, Houseboats, Dry Storage, Gas, Ski Beach, Video Game Room, Golf Course.

CASTLE ROCK SHORES
Route 2, Box 655, Parker, AZ 85344, Ph: (928) 667-2344
200 Tent & R.V. Sites, Full Hookups,
Motel Units, Groceries, Propane, Showers, Launch Ramp, Golf Course.

PITTSBURG POINT ISLAND

CRAZY HORSE CAMPGROUND
1534 Beachcomber Blvd., Lake Havasu City, AZ 86403, Ph: (928) 855-4033.
600 Tent & R.V. Sites, Full & Partial Hookups, Disposal Station, R.V. Storage,
Showers, Laundromat, Grocery Store, Ice, Propane, Boat Ramp, Beach, Swimming Pool, Spa, Rec. Hall.

LAKE HAVASU MARINA
1100 McCulloch Blvd., Lake Havasu City, AZ 86403, Ph: (928) 855-2159.
6-Lane Launch Ramp, Permanent Docks, Gas Dock, Slips, Pumpouts & Repairs for Boats, Boat Cleaning,
Grocery Store, Ice, Bait & Tackle, Waterski Equipment, Dry Storage.

NAUTICAL INN RESORT
1000 McCulloch Blvd. Lake Havasu City, AZ 86403, Ph: (928) 855-2141.
150 Rooms - Suites and Condos Overlooking the Lake, Private Beach, Dock, Swimming Pool,
18-Hole Golf Course, Conference Center, 2 Restaurants, Cocktail Lounge, Gift Shop, Store.

ISLANDER R.V. RESORT
751 Beachcomber Blvd., Lake Havasu City, AZ 86403, Ph: (928) 680-2000
500 R.V. Sites with Full Hookups, Some Beachfront Sites.
1-1/2 Miles of Shoreline, Swim Beach, Concrete Patios, Picnic Tables, 2 Swimming Pools,
Pet Exercise Area, Grocery Store, Trailer Rentals, Gated Storage, Launch Ramp, Boat Slips, Courtesy Dock,
Full Resort Facilities, Adjacent to 18-Hole Golf Course.

BEACHCOMBER RESORT
601 Beachcomber Blvd., Lake Havasu City, AZ 86403, Ph: (928) 855-2322.
500 R.V. Sites with Full Hookups.
Showers, Laundromat, Ice, Launch Ramp, Swimming Pool, Recreation Hall, Courtesy Docks.

FOR ADDITIONAL ACCOMMODATIONS AND FACILITIES CONTACT:
Lake Havasu Tourism Bureau
314 London Bridge Road
Lake Havasu City, AZ 86403
Ph: (800) 242-8278 or
(928) 453-3444

Here is a list of frequently used camping gear. This is a good basic start, but your own personal needs will largely influence your equipment selection. The available space in your vehicle should also be a factor in your preparation.

Air Mattress
Batteries
Camera and Film
Radiant Heater (in cold weather)
Coffee Pot
Compass
Cooking Utensils
Cooler
Cups and Dishes
Dishpan and Pot Scrubbers
Eating Utensils
First Aid Kit
Flares/Mirror-Other Emerg. Devices
Flashlights
Folding Chair or Camp Stool
Fuel
Ground Cloth
Hammer
Hand Axe
Ice or Ice Substitutes
Insect Repellent
Jug of Water
Knife
Lantern & Mantle
Lighter-Disposable Butane
Maps
Matches in Waterproof Container
Pen & Paper
Prescription Medicine
Ropes
Shovel-Small Folding Type
Sleeping Bag or Blankets
Snakebite Kit
Soap-Biodegradable
Stove & Propane
Sunglasses
Sun Block
Tablecloth
Tent, Poles & Stakes
Toilet Paper
Toiletries - Toothbrush & Paste
Towels-Paper & Bath
Trash Bags
Water Purification Tablets
Whistle

You may want to keep track of those pieces of equipment which you had and didn't need or needed and didn't have. This would help you on your future trips. Happy Camping!

Courtesy of The Coleman Company

Pack out all trash and tread lightly.

Be sure to bring along
RECREATION LAKES OF CALIFORNIA

A

Is the water safe?
Unless it is piped, it usually is not.

A microscopic organism, Giardia Lambia, is polluting most of our lakes and streams. By drinking this contaminated water, a severe intestinal disease is passed on to you. Giardiasis can cause extreme discomfort and must be treated by a doctor. Medication is the only way to get rid of this problem.

Unless you are certain there is clean drinking water, it is best to bring your own. There are several methods for purifying water. Although water purification tablets kill bacteria, they are not reliable when it comes to Giardiasis. Portable filtration systems are fast and effective. A sure protection is to boil the water for at least ten minutes or longer at higher altitudes.

Giardia is very easily transmitted between animals and humans. All feces, human and animal, must be buried at least eight inches deep and one hundred feet away from natural water. *Protect against Giardiasis by keeping our lakes, rivers and streams free of contamination.*

Dogs are welcome at most recreation facilities. A nominal fee is charged and there are some specific requirements. The dog must have a valid license and proof of a current rabies vaccination. There is usually a leash rule - the dog must be restrained by a leash no longer than ten feet. Be certain to call the campground or facility for full information before you take your pet with you.

Dogs must not be allowed to contaminate the water. As a rule, they are not permitted in public areas such as beaches and hiking trails. They are permitted in Wilderness Areas only when they are under your direct control. Keep your dog next to you and be sure to pick up after it.

USE LOW-IMPACT CAMPING TECHNIQUES TO PROTECT OUR NATURAL RESOURCES.

BOATING and SWIMMING

Boating is a popular activity at our California Lakes. Many of these Lakes permit boating of all types from sailboats to jet skis. All are subject to specific rules and regulations which vary from Lake to Lake. *Particular restrictions often apply to inflatable boats or boats that you assemble yourself.*

The type of boating permitted varies at each Lake. *Although RECREATION LAKES OF CALIFORNIA lists what type of boats are allowed, it is always wise to check for regulations by calling the information number to confirm your particular boat can be launched. Don't be disappointed by arriving at your destination only to find you cannot enjoy your boat.*

Before launching a boat, check the local laws. The speed limit is specific at each Lake. *There are always 5 MPH speed limits in certain areas such as near swimmers, docks or congested areas.* There are often restricted areas or specific areas for waterskiing, sailing or fishing. The local ranger or manager will usually give you a copy of the rules and regulations.

For California State Boating Regulations, see "ABC's of California Boating Laws." This booklet may be obtained at your DMV Office.

Swimming in our California Lakes is popular but there are potential hazards that can be minimized by using common sense and following some basic rules. *Never swim alone;* always have a partner. Never venture beyond your swimming and physical ability. Always *swim in designated areas and obey the local regulations.* Know the water conditions and environment prior to taking unnecessary risks such as diving. *In high mountain Lakes were the water is very cold, hypothermia takes over quickly.*

WATER SKIER HAND SIGNALS

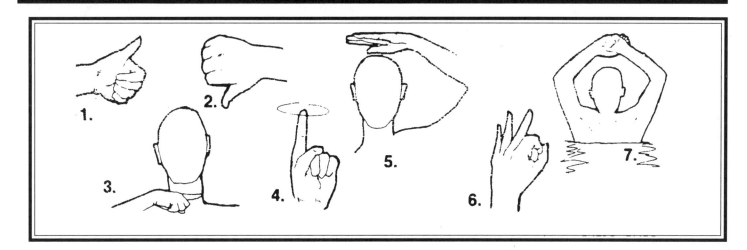

1. **Thumb Up:** Speed up the boat.
2. **Thumb Down:** Slow down the boat.
3. **Cut Motor/Stop:** Immediately stop boat. Slashing motion over neck (also used by driver or observer).
4. **Turn:** Turn the boat (also used by driver). Circle motion— arms overhead. Then point in desired direction.

5. **Return to Dock:** Pat on the head.
6. **OK:** Speed and boat path OK. Or, signals understood.
7. **I'm OK**: Skier OK after falling.

Courtesy of the American Water Ski Association

C

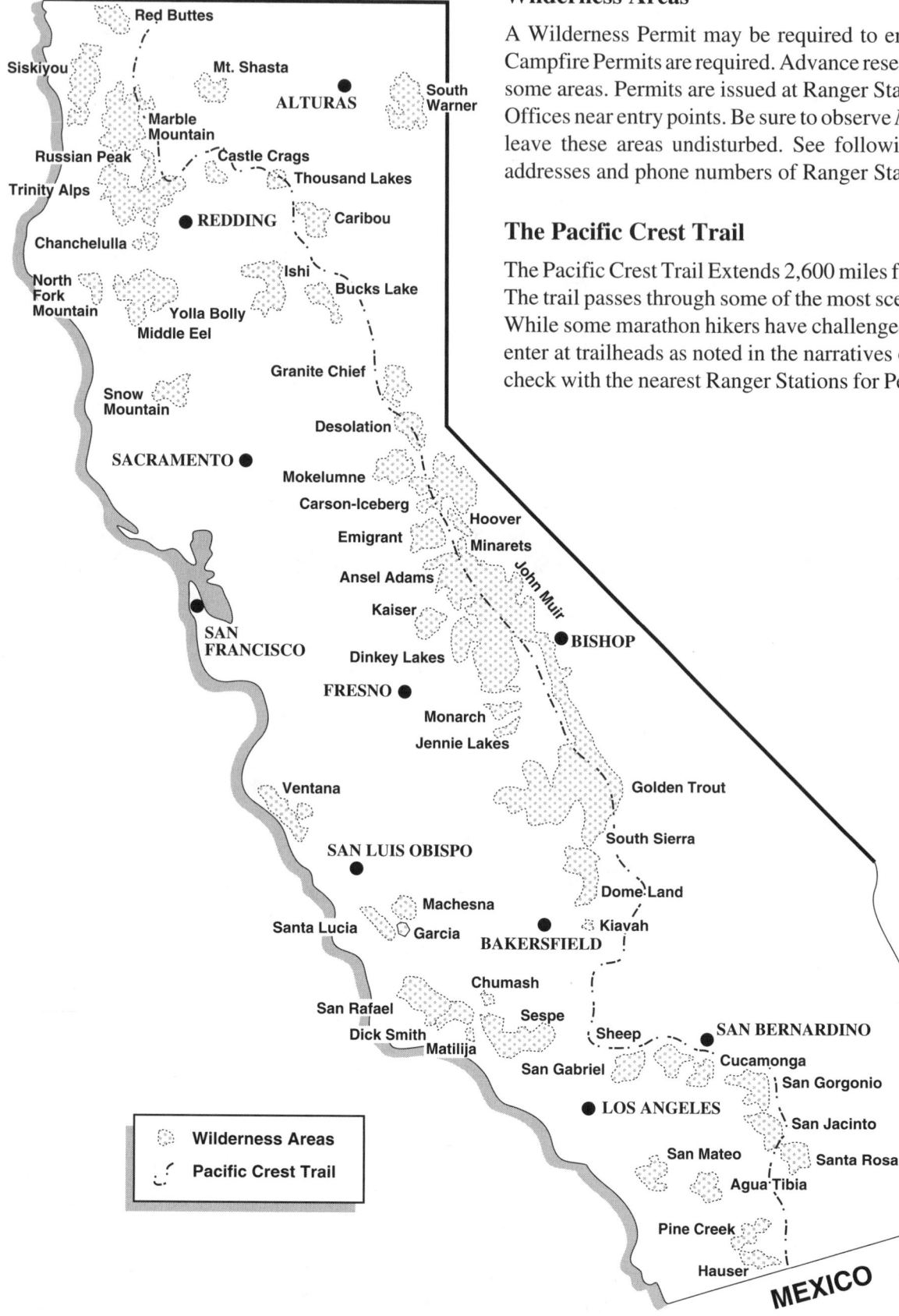

Wilderness Areas

A Wilderness Permit may be required to enter Wilderness Areas. Campfire Permits are required. Advance reservations are advised for some areas. Permits are issued at Ranger Stations or Forest Service Offices near entry points. Be sure to observe *No-Trace Camping* and leave these areas undisturbed. See following section for current addresses and phone numbers of Ranger Stations.

The Pacific Crest Trail

The Pacific Crest Trail Extends 2,600 miles from Canada to Mexico. The trail passes through some of the most scenic areas of California. While some marathon hikers have challenged its entire length, most enter at trailheads as noted in the narratives of this book. Be sure to check with the nearest Ranger Stations for Permits and information.

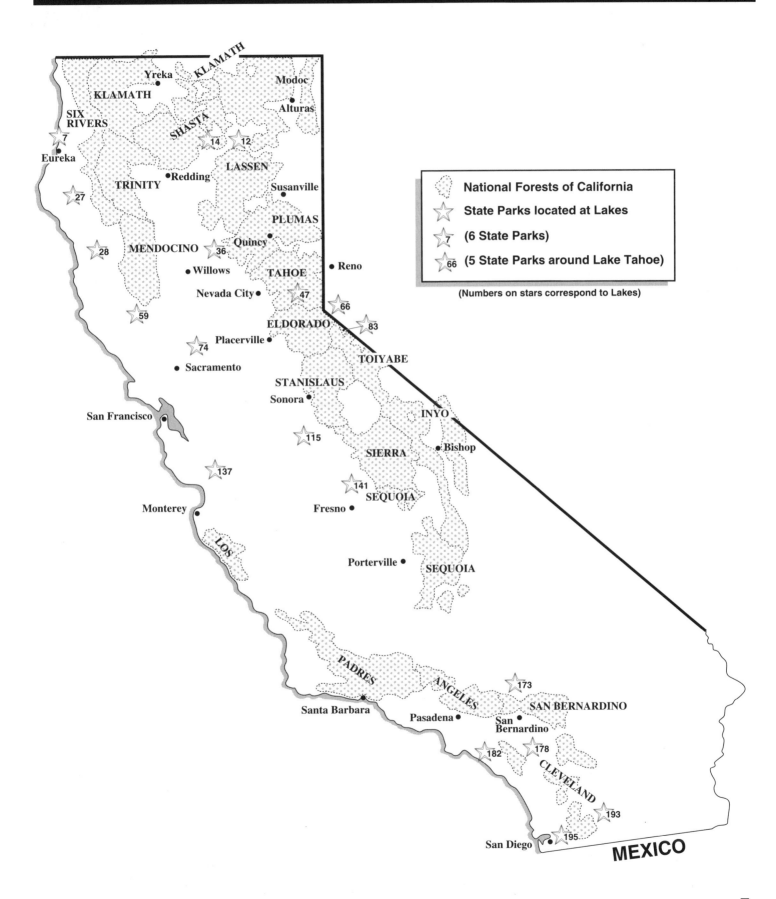

NATIONAL FORESTS and STATE PARKS of CALIFORNIA

KLAMATH

Yreka

Modoc

KLAMATH

SIX
RIVERS

Alturas

SHASTA

14   12

7

Eureka

LASSEN

TRINITY

Redding

Susanville

27

PLUMAS

28

MENDOCINO

Quincy

36

Willows

TAHOE

Reno

59

Nevada City

47

66

ELDORADO

83

74

Placerville

TOIYABE

Sacramento

STANISLAUS

Sonora

San Francisco

INYO

115

SIERRA

Bishop

137

141

Monterey

SEQUOIA

Fresno

LOS

Porterville

SEQUOIA

PADRES

ANGELES

173

SAN BERNARDINO

Santa Barbara

Pasadena

San
Bernardino

182

178

CLEVELAND

193

San Diego

195

MEXICO

Legend:

National Forests of California

State Parks located at Lakes

7   (6 State Parks)

66   (5 State Parks around Lake Tahoe)

(Numbers on stars correspond to Lakes)

E

FEDERAL RECREATION PASSPORT PROGRAM & CAMPGROUND RESERVATIONS

GOLDEN EAGLE PASSPORT - Persons Age 17 to 61 - $65
This is an annual entrance pass to Federally operated *National Parks, monuments, historic sites, recreation areas and national wildlife refuges* that charge ENTRANCE FEES.

NATIONAL PARK PASSPORT - Persons Age 17 to 61 - $50
This is an annual entrance pass to Federally operated *National Parks* that charge ENTRANCE FEES.

The Permit Holder and any passengers in a single, private, noncommercial vehicle are admitted. These passports do NOT cover use fees such as camping, parking and tours.

1 Calendar Year January 1 through December 31
Non-refundable - Non-transferable
Purchase at any National Park Service Entrance or by mail at:
National Park Service
1100 Ohio Dr. SW - Room 138
Washington DC 20242
Attn: Passports
or Ph: 1 (888) GO-PARKS

GOLDEN ACCESS PASSPORT - Blind and Disabled Persons with proof of being medically determined to be blind or permanently disabled and eligible for receiving benefits under federal law - at any National Park Service Entrance.

GOLDEN AGE PASSPORT - Persons 62 and older with proof of age - a State driver's license, birth certificate or passport plus a one-time fee of $10 - at any National Park Service Entrance.

These two above passports are lifetime entrance passes to federally operated National Parks, monuments, historic sites, recreation areas and national wildlife refuges that charge ENTRANCE FEES. Plus a 50% discount on federal use fees charged for facilities and services such as camping, boat launching and parking. It does NOT cover fees charged by private concessionaires or special recreation permit fees. The Forest Service, however, requires private concessionaire operators of federally owned campgrounds or national forest lands to honor the 50% discount for the recreation use fee. Admits Permit Holder and any accompanying passengers in a single, private, noncommercial vehicle.

CAMPGROUND RESERVATIONS

While reservations are not required at some campgrounds, they are often advised. Group campsites require reservations. For those requiring specific information on the many public and private facitities listed in this guide, there is an information phone number and address on each page. Most U. S. Forest Service campsites are on a first-come, first-served basis. Selected National Forest campgrounds may now be reserved. Reservations are advised from Memorial Day to Labor Day. Senior citizen and disabled discounts are available.

FOR U.S. FOREST SERVICE RESERVATIONS:
Ph: 1-877-444-6777
FOR CALIFORNA STATE PARK SYSTEM
RESERVATIONS: Ph: 1-800-444-7275 (PARK)
FOR NATIONAL PARK SERVICE CAMPGROUNDS:
Ph: 1-800-365-CAMP (2267)
Non-Refundable Reservation Fee and a Cancellation Fee is charged for each Campsite.
ALL FEES ARE SUBJECT TO CHANGE*
RESERVATION PHONE NUMBERS LISTED ABOVE ARE ALSO SUBJECT TO CHANGE.

CALIFORNIA STATE PARKS SYSTEM
P. O. Box 94296
Sacramento, CA 94296
Information Ph: 916-653-6995

Publications Office
1416 Ninth Street - Room 118
Sacramento, CA 95814
Information Ph: 916-653-4000

CALIFORNIA OFFICE OF TOURISM
801 "K" Street
Sacramento, CA 95814
Information Ph: 916-322-1396 or
916-322-2881
For Information Packet
Ph: 1-800-862-2543

DEPARTMENT OF FISH & GAME OFFICES
HEADQUARTERS
1416 Ninth Street - 12th Floor
Saramento 95814
Ph: 916-455-0411

REGIONAL OFFICES:
Northern California & North Coast Region
601 Locust Street
Redding 96001
Ph: (530) 225-2300
Sacramento Valley & Central Sierra Region
1701 Nimbus Rd.
Rancho Cordova 95670
Ph: (916) 358-2900
Central Coast Region
7329 Silverado Trail
Yountville 94558
Ph: (707) 944-5500
San Joaquin Valley & Southern Sierra Region
1234 E. Shaw Ave.
Fresno 93710
Ph: (559) 222-3761
South Coast Region
4949 Viewridge Ave.
San Diego 92123
Ph: (858) 467-4201
Eastern Sierra & Inland Deserts Region
4775 Bird Farm Rd.
Chino Hills 91709
Ph: (909) 597-9823
Marine Region
20 Lower Ragsdale Dr. #100
Monterey 93940
Ph: (831) 649-2870

RANGER STATIONS and FOREST SERVICE OFFICES

CALIFORNIA REGION OF THE U.S. FOREST SERVICE

General Information, Maps and Wilderness Permits may be obtained at the following locations:

Pacific Southwest Region
USDA Forest Service
630 Sansome Street
San Francisco 94111
(415) 705-2874

ANGELES NATIONAL FOREST

Forest Supervisor's Office
701 N. Santa Anita Avenue
Arcadia 91006
Ph: (626) 574-1613

Arroyo-Seco Ranger District
Oak Grove Park
Flintridge 91011
Ph: (626) 790-1151

Mt. Baldy Ranger District
110 N. Wabash Avenue
Glendora 91740
Ph: (626) 335-1251

Saugus Ranger District
30800 Bouquet Canyon Rd.
Saugus 91350
Ph: (661) 296-9710

LA River Ranger District
12371 N. Little Tujunga Cyn. Rd.
San Fernando 91341
Ph: (818) 899-1900

Valyermo Ranger District
29835 Valyermo Road
Post Office Box 15
Valyermo 93563
Ph: (661) 944-2187

CLEVELAND NATIONAL FOREST

Forest Supervisor's Office
10845 Rancho Bernardo Rd.
San Diego 92127
Ph: (619) 673-6180

Decanso Ranger District
3348 Alpine Boulevard
Alpine 91901
Ph: (619) 445-6235

Palomar Ranger District
1634 Black Canyon Road
Ramona 92065
Ph: (760) 788-0250

Trabuco Ranger District
1147 E. Sixth Street
Corona 91719
Ph: (909) 736-1811

ELDORADO NATIONAL FOREST

Forest Supervisor's Office
100 Forni Road
Placerville 95667
Ph: (530) 622-5061

Amador Ranger District
26820 Silver Drive & Hwy. 88
Pioneer 95666
Ph: (209) 295-4251

Georgetown Ranger District
7600 Wentworth Springs Rd.
Georgetown 95634
Ph: (530) 333-4312

Information Center
3070 Camino Heights Drive
Camino 95709
Ph: (530) 644-6048

Pacific Ranger District
7887 Highway 50
Pollock Pines 95726
Ph: (530) 644-2349

Placerville Ranger District
4260 Eight Mile Road
Camino 95709
Ph: (9530) 644-2324

Placerville Nursery
2375 Fruitridge Road
Camino 95709
Ph: (530) 622 9600

Continued...

INYO NATIONAL FOREST

Forest Supervisor's Office
873 North Main Street
Bishop 93514
Ph: (760) 873-2400

White Mountain Ranger District
798 North Main Street
Bishop 93514
Ph: (760) 873-2500

Lee Vining Ranger District
Mono Basin Scenic Area
Post Office Box 429
Lee Vining 93546
Ph: (760) 647-3044

Mammoth Ranger District
Post Office Box 148
Mammoth Lakes 93546
Ph: (760) 924-5500

Mt. Whitney Ranger District
Post Office Box 8
Lone Pine 93545
Ph: (6760) 876-6200

KLAMATH NATIONAL FOREST

Forest Supervisor's Office
1312 Fairlane Road
Yreka 96097
Ph: (530) 842-6131

Goosenest Ranger District
37805 Highway 97
Macdoel 96058
Ph: (530) 398-4391

Scott River Ranger District
11263 N. Highway 3
Fort Jones 96032
Ph: (530) 468-5351

Ukonom Ranger District
Post Office Drawer 410
Orleans 95556
Ph: (530) 627-3291

Happy Camp Ranger District
Post Office Box 377
Happy Camp 96039
Ph: (530) 493-2243

LAKE TAHOE BASIN MANAGEMENT UNIT

(This Unit covers parts of Eldorado, Tahoe and Toiyabe National Forests)

Forest Supervisor's Office
870 Emerald Bay Rd., Suite 1
South Lake Tahoe 96150
Ph: (530) 573-2600

Tahoe Visitor Center
1/2 Mile from Camp Richardson
Ph: (530) 573-2674
Open Summer Only

William Kent Information Station
William Kent Camground
Ph: (530) 583-3642
Open Summer Only

LASSEN NATIONAL FOREST

Forest Supervisor's Office
55 South Sacramento Street
Susanville 96130
Ph: (530) 257-2151

Almanor Ranger District
Post Office Box 767
Chester 96020
Ph: (530) 258-2141

Eagle Lake Ranger District
477-050 Eagle Lake Rd.
Susanville 96130
Ph: (530) 257-4188

Hat Creek Ranger District
Post Office Box 220
Fall River Mills 96028
Ph: (530) 336-5521

Continued...

⛭ LOS PADRES NATIONAL FOREST ⛭

Forest Supervisor's Office
6144 Calle Real
Goleta 93117
Ph: (805) 683-6711

Monterey Ranger District
406 S. Mildred
King City 93930
Ph: (831) 385-5434

Mt. Pinos Ranger District
HC1 Box 400
Frazier Park 93225
Ph: (661) 245-3731

Ojai Ranger District
1190 E. Ojai Avenue
Ojai 93023
Ph: (805) 646-4348

Santa Barbara Ranger District
Star Route, Los Prietos
Santa Barbara 93105
Ph: (805) 967-3481

Santa Lucia Ranger District
1616 N. Carlotti Drive
Santa Maria 93454
Ph: (805) 925-9538

⛭ MENDOCINO NATIONAL FOREST ⛭

Forest Supervisor's Office
875 N. Humboldt Avenue
Willows 95988
Ph: (530) 934-3316

Corning Ranger District
22000 Corning Road
Post Office Box 1019
Corning 96021
Ph: (530) 824-5196

Covelo Ranger District
78150 Covelo Road
Covelo 95428
Ph: (707) 983-6118

Stonyford Ranger District
Post Office Box 160
Stonyford 95979
Ph: (530) 963-3128

Upper Lake Ranger District
10025 Elk Mountain Road
Upper Lake 95485
Ph: (707) 275-2361

Genic Resource Center
2741 Cramer Lane
Chico, CA 95928
Ph: (530) 895-1176

⛭ MODOC NATIONAL FOREST ⛭

Forest Supervisor's Office
800 West 12th Street
Alturas 96101
Ph: (530) 233-5811

Big Valley Ranger District
Post Office Box 159
Adin 96006
Ph: (530) 299-3215

Devil's Garden Ranger District
800 West 12th Street
Alturas 96101
Ph: (530) 233-5811

Doublehead Ranger District
Post Office Box 369
Tulelake 96134
Ph: (530) 667-2246

Warner Mountain Ranger District
Post Office Box 220
Cedarville 96104
Ph: (530) 279-6116

⛭ PLUMAS NATIONAL FOREST ⛭

Forest Supervisor's Office
159 Lawrence Street
Post Office Box 11500
Quincy 95971
Ph: (530) 283-2050

Beckworth Ranger District
23 Mohawk Hwy. Road
Post Office Box 7
Blairsden 96103
Ph: (530) 836-2575

Challenge Visitor's Center
18050 Mulock Road
Challenge 95925
Ph: (530) 675-1146

Feather River Ranger District
875 Mitchell Avenue
Oroville 95965
Ph: (530) 534-6500

Greenville Work Center
128 Hot Springs Road
Greenville 95947
Ph: (530) 284-7126

Mt. Hough Ranger District
39696 Highway 70
Quincy 95971
Ph: (530) 283-0555

Continued...

SAN BERNARDINO NATIONAL FOREST

(909 Area Codes are Due to Change-Check Info.)

Forest Supervisor's Office
1824 S. Commercenter Circle
San Bernardino 92408
Ph: (909) 383-5588

San Gorgonio Ranger District
Mill Creek Station
34701 Mill Creek Road
Mentone 92359
Ph: (909) 794-1123

Arrowhead Ranger District
28104 Highway 18
Post Office Box 350
Skyforest 92385
Ph: (909) 337-2444

Big Bear Ranger District
Post Office Box 290
Fawnskin 92333
Ph: (909) 866-3437

San Jacinto Ranger District
Idyllwild Ranger Station
54270 Pinecrest Ave.
Idyllwild 92549
Ph: (909) 659-2117

Cajon Ranger District
Lytle Creek Ranger Station
1209 Lytle Creek Road
Lytle Creek 92358
Ph: (909) 887-2576

SEQUOIA NATIONAL FOREST

Forest Supervisor's Office
900 W. Grand Avenue
Porterville 93257
Ph: (559) 784-1500

Hume Lake Ranger District
35860 E. Kings Canyon Rd.
Dunlap 93621
Ph: (559) 338-2251

Cannell Meadow Ranger District
Post Office Box 6
Kernville 93238
Ph: (760) 376-3781

Lake Isabella Station
4875 Ponderosa Dr.
Post Office Box 3810
Lake Isabella 93240
Ph: (760) 379-5646

Greenhorn Ranger District
15701 Highway 178
Bakersfield 93306
Ph: (805) 871-2223

Tule River Ranger District
32588 Highway 190
Springville 93265
Ph: (559) 539-2607

Hot Springs Ranger District
Route 4, Box 548
Calif. Hot Springs 93207
Ph: (805) 548-6503

BLM Visitor's Center
(Manned by USFS)
Post Office Box 6129
Bakersfield 93386
Ph: (661) 391-6088

SHASTA-TRINITY NATIONAL FOREST

Forest Supervisor's Office
2400 Washington Avenue
Redding 96001
Ph: (530) 246-5222

Mt. Shasta Ranger District
204 West Alma
Mt. Shasta 96067
Ph: (530) 926-4511

Big Bar Ranger District
Star Route 1, Box 10
Big Bar 96010
Ph: (530) 623-6106

Shasta Lake Ranger District
14225 Holiday Road
Redding 96003
Ph: (530) 275-1587

Hayfork Ranger District
Post Office Box 159
Hayfork 96041
Ph: (530) 628-5227

Weaverville Ranger District
Post Office Box 1190
Weaverville 96093
Ph: (530) 623-2121

McCloud Ranger District
Post Office Box 1620
McCloud 96057
Ph: (530) 964-2184

Yolla Bolla Ranger District,
HC 10, Box 400,
Platina 96076
Ph: (530) 352-4211

SIERRA NATIONAL FOREST

Forest Supervisor's Office
1600 Tollhouse Road
Clovis 93611
Ph: (559) 297-0706

Minarets Ranger District
57003 Road 226
Post Office Box 10
North Fork 93643
Ph: (559) 877-2218

Mariposa Ranger District
43060 Highway 41
Oakhurst 93644
Ph: (559) 683-4665

Kings River Ranger District
34849 Maxon Road
Sanger 93657
Ph: (559) 855-8321

Pineridge Ranger District
Shaver-Huntington
29688 Auberry Road
Post Office Box 559
Prather 93651
Ph: (559) 855-5360

Kings River Ranger District
Dinkey Ranger Station
Dinkey Route
Shaver Lake 93664
Ph: (559) 841-3404 (Summer Only)

Continued...

SIX RIVERS NATIONAL FOREST

Forest Supervisor's Office
1330 Bayshore Way
Eureka 95501
Ph: (707) 442-1721

Lower Trinity Ranger District
Post Office Box 68
Willow Creek 95573
Ph: (530) 629-2118

Mad River Ranger District
Star Route, Box 300
Bridgeville 95526
Ph: (707) 574-6233

Orleans Ranger District
Drawer B
Orleans 95556
Ph: (530) 627-3291

Smith River NRA
Post Office Box 228
Gasquet 95543
Ph: (707) 457-3131

Salyer Fire Station
Lower Trinity Road
Post Office Box 551
Willow Creek 95573
Ph: (530) 6290-2114

Zenia Fire Station
General Delivery
Zenia 95495
Ph: (707) 923-9669

STANISLAUS NATIONAL FOREST

Forest Supervisor's Office
19777 Greenley Road
Sonora 95370
Ph: (209) 532-3671

Calaveras Ranger District
Highway 4
Post Office Box 500
Hathaway Pines 95233
Ph: (209) 795-1381

Groveland Ranger District
24545 Highway 120
Groveland 95321
Ph: (209) 962-7825

Mi-Wok Ranger District
Highway 108 East
Post Office Box 100
Mi-Wok Village 95346
Ph: (209) 586-3234

Summit Ranger District
#1 Pinecrest Lake Road
Pinecrest 95364
Ph: (209) 965-3434

TAHOE NATIONAL FOREST

Forest Supervisor's Office
631 Coyote Street
Post Office Box 6003
Nevada City 95959
Ph: (530) 265-4531

Downieville Ranger District
N. Yuba Ranger Station
15924 Highway 49
Camptonville 95922
Ph: (530) 478-6253

Foresthill Ranger District
22830 Foresthill Road
Foresthill 95631
Ph: (530) 478-6254

Sierraville Ranger District
Post Office Box 95
Highway 895
Sierraville 96126
Ph: (530) 994-3401

Truckee Ranger District
10342 Highway 89
Truckee 96161
Ph: (530) 478-6257

NATIONAL PARKS

Lassen Volcanic National Park
Mineral 96063
Ph: (530) 595-4444

Sequoia-Kings Canyon National Park
Three Rivers 93271
Ph: (209) 565-3341

Yosemite National Park
Post Office Box 577
Yosemite National Park 95389
Ph: (209) 372-0265

A Abbott 135
Agua Hedionda 193
Almaden Lake Park 129
Almanor 24
Alondra 170
Alpine (Marin County) 118
Alpine (Stanislaus National Forest) 85
Amador 89
Anderson 131
Angler's 184
Antelope 26
Anza 119
Apollo Park 167
Arrowbear 175
Arrowhead 175
Atascadero 158
Avocado 149
B Barrett (Mammoth Lakes) 104
Barrett (San Diego) 196
Bass 142
Bathtub 19
Baum 12
Bayley 4
Bear River 78
Beardsley 95
Beauty 69
Benbow 27
Berenda 140
Berkeley Aquatic Park 119
Berryessa 88
Bethany 124
Bidwell 23
Big (Fall River Valley) 12
Big (Tahoe National Forest) 61
Big Bear (Gold Lakes Basin) 38
Big Bear (San Bernardino National Forest) ... 176
Big Lagoon 7
Big Sage 4
Bishop Creek Canyon 108
Black Butte 34
Black Rock 145
Blue (Alpine County) 82
Blue (Lake County) 58
Blue (Modoc National Forest) 11
Boca 45
Bon Tempe 118
Bowman 40
Bridgeport 97
Briones Regional Park 120
Brite Valley 154
Britton 14
Buena Vista Aquatic Area 162
Bucks 30
Bullards Bar 39
Bullseye 6
Butt Valley 25
Butte 19

C C Reservoir 4
Cachuma 160
Cahuilla 186
Calero 129
Camanche 91
Camp Far West 62
Cape 30
Caples 80
Carbon Canyon 179
Caribou 20
Carmen 95
Carr 40
Cascade 41
Casitas 161
Castaic 164
Castle 8
Cave 2
Chabot 123
Cherry 96
Chesbro 129
Clark 179
Clear (Klamath Basin) 3
Clear (Lake County) 59
Clear (Modoc National Forest) 11
Clementine 61
Cleone 28
Cogswell 169
Collins 50
Contra Loma 122
Convict 105
Copco 1
Corona 180
Cottonwood 130
Courtright 145
Coyote 134
Coyote-Hellyer Park 130
Craig 179
Crater 20
Crowley 106
Crystal (Angeles National Forest) 169
Crystal (Fall River Valley) 12
Crystal (Mammoth Lakes) 104
Cucamonga-Guasti 181
Cull Canyon 123
Cunningham 130
Curtz 83
Cuyamaca 195
D Dark 69
Davis 31
Delta 4
Del Valle 125
De Sabla 29
Diamond Valley 183
Diaz 151
Dixon 191
Doane Pond 193
Don Castro 123

Don Pedro 112
Donnells 95
Donner 47
Dorris 4
Duncan 4

E Eagle (Lassen National Forest) 21
Eagle (Tahoe National Forest) 41
Earl 7
East Park 33
Eastman (Fall River Valley) 12
Eastman (Madera County) 140
Echo 68
Ed R. Levin 130
Edison 148
El Capitan 196
El Dorado East 171
El Estero 135
Elizabeth (Angeles National Forest) 166
Elizabeth (Fremont) 124
Elk Grove 76
Ellery 102
Elsinore 182
Englebright 52
Evans (Buena Vista Aquatic Recreation Area) 162
Evans (City of Riverside) 181
Evergreen 82

F F Reservoir 4
Fairmount 181
Fall River 12
Fallen Leaf 67
Faucherie 40
Fee 2
Feeley 40
Finney 187
Finnon 65
Fish 7
Florence 148
Folsom 74
Fordyce 41
Francis 51
Frazier Park 167
French Meadows 63
Frenchman 32
Freshwater Lagoon 7
Fuller 40
Fulmor 184

G Gardisky 101
George 104
Gerle Creek 70
Gibraltar 160
Gibson Ranch 76
Glen Helen 168
Gold Lakes Basin 38
Goose (Gold Lakes Basin) 38
Goose (Modoc National Forest) 2
Granite 82
Grant (June Lake Loop) 103
Grant Park 130
Grassy 38
Graven 4
Green Valley 175

Greenstone 101
Gregory 174
Grover Hot Springs 83
Gull 103

H Harbor 170
Hart 154
Hartley 95
Havasu 199
Haven 38
Heenan 83
Hell Hole 64
Hemet 185
Hennessy 88
Henshaw 192
Hensley 139
Highland 93
Highland Springs 59
Hobart 49
Hodges 196
Horseshoe (Mammoth) 104
Horseshoe (Mojave Narrows) 168
Horseshoe (Fremont) 124
Hughes 166
Hume 150
Hummingbird 101
Huntington 147

I Ice House 71
Independence 42
Indian Creek 83
Indian Tom 5
Indian Valley 60
Iron Canyon 13
Iron Gate 1
Irvine 180
Isabella 155

J Jackson 168
Jackson Meadow 42
Jenkinson 73
Jenks 175
Jennings 197
Jordan Pond 123
Joseph D. Grant 130
Juanita 5
Junction 72
June 103
Juniper 19

K Kaweah 152
Kelly 55
Kent 118
Kerckhoff 143
Keswick 17
Kidd 41
Kirkwood 80
Kirman 95
Klamath Basin 3

L Lafayette 121
Laguna Niguel 179
Laguna Seca 135
Lagunitas 118
Lake Valley 55
Lakes Basin Recreation Area 38

Leavitt 95
Legg 172
Letts 33
Levin 130
Lewiston 16
Lexington 128
Lily 2
Lily Pond 33
Lindsey 40
Little Grass Valley 37
Little Medicine 6
Littlerock 167
Little Tule 20
Loch Lomond 132
Long (Gold Lakes Basin) 38
Long (Tahoe National Forest) 41
Loon 70
Lopez 159
Los Banos 138
Los Gatos Creek Park 128
Los Vaqueros 126
Lost 141
Lost Creek 37
Lower Bear River 78
Lower Blue 82
Lower Bucks 30
Lower Klamath 3
Lower Letts Valley 33
Lower Otay 196
Lundy 100
Lyons 94
M   Mamie 104
     Mammoth 104
Mammoth Pool 144
Manzanita 19
Marlette 49
Martis Creek 48
Mary 104
Mason Regional Park 179
Mc Cloud (Mammoth Lakes) 104
Mc Cloud (Shasta-Trinity) 9
Mc Clure 116
Mc Coy Flat 21
McCumber. 19
Mc Murray 40
Mc Swain 116
Meadow 82
Medicine 6
Meiss 5
Mendocino 57
Merced 127
Merritt 119
Mile Square 179
Millerton 141
Milton 42
Ming 154
Miramar 196
Modesto 113
Mojave Narrows Park 168
Mono 100
Morena 198

Morning Star 61
Morris 169
Mosquito 93
Mountain Meadow. 24
Mud (Modoc County) 10
Mud (Gold Lakes Basin) 38
Murray 196
N   Nacimiento 157
     Natoma 75
New Hogan. 92
New Melones 109
Nicasio 118
North 108
O   Oakwood 114
     O'Neill Forebay. 137
Oroville 36
Orr 5
Otay 196
P   Packer 38
     Palomar Park 193
Paradise 29
Pardee 90
Parkway 131
Peck Road 172
Pelican 168
Perris 178
Philbrook 29
Phoenix 118
Pillsbury 56
Pine 20
Pine Flat 149
Pinecrest 94
Pinto 133
Piru 165
Plaskett 33
Pleasant Valley 151
Poway 194
Prado Park 181
Prosser Creek 44
Puddingstone 177
Pyramid 163
Q   Quail 163
Quarry 124

R   Ralph B. Clark 179
     Ralphine 87
Ralston Afterbay 64
Ramer 187
Rancho Seco 76
Red 81
Redinger 143
Reflection 184
Rice 82
Rock 2
Rock Creek 107
Rollins 54
Round 38
Round Valley 23
Rucker 40
Ruth 22

O

S

Sabrina 108
Saddlebag 101
Salmon 38
Salt Springs 77
Salton Sea 188
San Antonio 156
San Diego City Lakes 196
San Dimas 169
San Gabriel 169
San Justo 136
San Luis 137
San Pablo 120
San Vicente 196
Santa Ana River 180
Santa Fe 172
Santa Margarita 158
Santee 194
Sardine 38
Sawmill 40
Scotts Flat 53
Sequoia 150
Serene 41
Shadow Cliffs 124
Shasta 18
Shastina 5
Shaver 146
Shoreline 127
Silver (Eldorado National Forest) 79
Silver (Gold Lakes Basin) 38
Silver (June Loop) 103
Silver (Lassen National Forest) 20
Silver (Plumas National Forest) 30
Silverwood 173
Siskiyou 8
Skinner 183
Sly Creek 37
Sly Park 73
Smith 30
Snag (Gold Lakes Basin) 38
Snag (Lassen National Forest). 29
Snag (Modoc National Forest) 2
Snake 30
Snow Valley 175
Solano 88
Sonoma 86
Sotcher 104
Soulajule 118
South 108
Spaulding 46
Spicer Meadow 93
Spooner 49
Spring 87
Stafford 118
Stampede 43
Starkweather 104
Sterling 41
Stevens 83
Stevens Creek 127
Stone Lagoon 7
Stony Gorge 35
Strawberry 94

Stumpy Meadows 65
Success 153
Sugar Pine 61
Summit (Alpine County) 83
Summit (Lassen National Park) 19
Summit (Shasta-Trinity National Forest) 14
Sunbeam 190
Sutherland 196

T

T.J. 104
Tahoe 66
Talawa 7
Tamarack 82
Temescal 119
Tenaya 102
Thermalitos Forebay-Afterbay. 36
Tinnemaha 151
Tioga 102
Topaz 84
Trinity 15
Trumbull 99
Tule (Fall River Valley) 12
Tule (Klamath Basin) 3
Tulloch 110
Turlock 115
Twin (Alpine County) 82
Twin (Mammoth Lakes) 104
Twin (Toiyabe National Forest) 99

U

Union. 93
Union Valley 72
Upper Blue 82
Utica. 93
Uvas 129

V

Vail 183
Vasona 128
Virginia 99

W

Ward 148
Weaver 40
Webb 162
Webber 42
West Valley 10
Whale Rock 158
Whiskeytown 17
Whittier Narrows 172
Wiest 189
William R. Mason 179
Wishon 145
Wister Unit 187
Wohlford 193
Woods 81
Woodward 111
Woollomes 154
Wrights 69

Y

Yorba Park 179
Yosemite 117
Yucaipa 181